P9-DFB-062

BOOKS BY LARRY J. DANIEL

Shiloh: The Battle That Changed the Civil War

Island No. 10

Soldiering in the Army of Tennessee

Cannoneers in Gray

The Battle That Changed
the Civil War

SIMON & SCHUSTER

SHILOH

LARRY J. DANIEL

SIMON & SCHUSTER
Rockefeller Center
1230 Avenue of the Americas
New York, NY 10020

Copyright © 1997 by Larry J. Daniel
All rights reserved,
including the right of reproduction
in whole or in part in any form.
SIMON & SCHUSTER and colophon are
registered trademarks of Simon & Schuster Inc.
Designed by EDITH FOWLER
Manufactured in the United States of America

10 9 8 7 6 5 4 3 2 1

Library of Congress Cataloging-in-Publication Data
Daniel, Larry J., date.
Shiloh : the battle that changed the Civil War /
Larry J. Daniel
p.   cm.
Includes bibliographic references and index.
1. Shiloh, Battle of, 1862.   I. Title.
E473.54.D36   1997
973.7'31—dc21   96-51539 CIP
ISBN 0-684-80375-5

Acknowledgments

I AM DEEPLY INDEBTED to my friend Dr. Richard McMurry of Americus, Georgia, for his encouragement to write this book and his critique of the early chapters. Others who assisted in providing material or information that might otherwise have been missed include Gregg and Karel Lea Griggs of Celina, Ohio; Dr. Lawrence Hewitt, Hammond, Louisiana; Art Bergeron, Baton Rouge, Louisiana; Dr. Michael Parrish, Austin, Texas; and Bill Wagoner, Adamsville, Tennessee.

The staff of the Shiloh National Military Park was superb. Park Superintendent Woody Harrell, Chief of Interpretation Paul Hawke, and Park Rangers Brian K. McCutchen, Joe E. Davis, Floyd Rickman, and Don Todd deserve special mention. Park Historian Stacy Allen is mentioned several times in footnotes, but I would be remiss if I did not single him out for his patience, knowledge, and graciousness. Stacy probably knows more about the details of the Battle of Shiloh than any person living. He enthusiastically shared his vast knowledge, even when I called him at his home on several occasions. As partial repayment to the kindness of the staff, I have presented all of my research material (four feet of file folders) to the park.

My appreciation is extended to *Civil War History* for permission to expand upon a theme I first presented in their journal in December 1991.

Dedicated to
GEORGE A. REAVES III
Chief of Interpretation, Shiloh National Military Park
1975–1994

HIS HEART WILL ALWAYS BE AT SHILOH

Contents

List of Maps

Preface

THREE MODERN MONOGRAPHS have appeared on the Battle of Shiloh: Wiley Sword's *Shiloh: Bloody April*, James Lee McDonough's *Shiloh: In Hell Before Night*, and O. E. Cunningham's "Shiloh and the Western Campaign of 1862," the last being an unpublished dissertation available to the public through University Microfilms of Ann Arbor, Michigan. Although not the first book on the subject, the present volume tells the story with a different twist. More attention is paid to the entire campaign, especially the role of politics. It is my contention that the battle cannot be viewed apart from the dynamics that occurred in the White House in Washington, D.C., and the Executive Mansion in Richmond, Virginia. The involvement of certain politicians, such as Elihu Washburne of Illinois and Henry Foote of Tennessee, is also explored.

Additional sources have been uncovered, and previously used material has been re-examined. I have also paid as much attention to maps as I have to the text. Measurably assisting in this task was a previously unpublished regimental-level map in the Albert Sidney Johnston Papers at Tulane University, as well as countless trips to the Shiloh National Military Park, where plaques and terrain were studied. The plaques were invaluable in establishing a standardized time for certain actions, and in supplying information not given in official reports. A close examination will reveal differences between the battle maps of this volume and those in previous works. In an effort to demythologize the events that occurred, contemporary drawings have been discounted in favor of photographs.

There are some new interpretations: the number of attacks upon the Hornet's Nest, the effect of Daniel Ruggles's artillery barrage, and Lew Wallace's march to the battlefield. Also examined are the larger imperatives: war aims, policies, diplomacy, the will to win, strategic planning and execution, and ultimate defeat and victory. By the time this volume appears, some twenty years will have lapsed since the last full-length book on this subject. New assessments by authors such as Steven Woodworth, Benjamin Cooling, and Archer Jones have been considered.

Leadership decisions are evaluated according to the information at hand. Commanders do not know outcomes—only options. Thus, Don Carlos Buell is defended for his slow advance upon Nashville, but criticized for his subsequent lethargy south of the city.

The heroes who emerge in the story are, by and large, uncommon names—Allen Waterhouse, Henry Allen, David Stuart—small-unit commanders. The principal leaders receive mixed reviews. The campaign was Henry Halleck's to lose, and lose it he almost did. There is no question that the Federal army was surprised at Shiloh, and for that Ulysses S. Grant and William T. Sherman cannot escape substantial blame. Responsibility for the dismal performance of the Confederates during the first day of battle is placed upon the shoulders of Albert Sidney Johnston and P. G. T. Beauregard. Yet all of these men at various times revealed a remarkable grasp of the issues—a far simpler task for those of us 135 years later.

The story is told in the format of different scenarios. This literary technique is to show that events did not occur in well-ordered sequence, as though one mind controlled the outcome. The reader is also given a sense of the geographic breadth of the events taking place. I have attempted to avoid lengthy biographical vignettes. The reader learns about the principal characters throughout the text. This, after all, is how we meet people in life; everything is not learned at first acquaintance.

The Battle of Shiloh has become very real to me. Being from Memphis, only two hours' driving time away, I have often frequented the park. Bloody Pond, the Hornet's Nest, Grant's Last Line have all become memorized sights. I must constantly remind myself, however, that none of the events that were acted out in the wilderness around Pittsburg Landing, Tennessee, in April 1862 was inevitable. They were the end results of policies, personalities, and the individual actions of men. All must be seen in their intertwining totality for the epic struggle to be told.

LARRY J. DANIEL
Murray, Kentucky

ONE

The Capitals

Richmond, Virginia

To ALL OUTWARD APPEARANCES, Southerners had reason to celebrate New Year's Day in 1862. During the previous eight months, the Confederacy had won most of the major land battles: Manassas; Wilson's Creek; Lexington, Missouri; Belmont; and Ball's Bluff. Confederate forces defiantly stood their ground from northern Virginia, through southern Kentucky, to the southwest corner of Missouri. The war had not yet turned vicious; Southern casualties totaled fewer than 5,000. Nor had the Richmond government felt the crushing weight of Northern industry and manpower. Hoped-for British intervention seemed closer than ever with the Federal seizure of two Confederate diplomats, James Mason and John Slidell, aboard the British steamer *Trent*. "King Cotton" diplomacy appeared to be working. More than 80 percent of England's cotton came from the American South, and the mills of England were already reduced to half-time. Although no official dialogue had occurred with Confederate commissioners, informal meetings had been conducted.[1]

Bright sunshine and a springlike breeze warmed the streets of Richmond that New Year's Day. At 11 A.M., President Jefferson Davis hosted the first of what would become annual receptions at the Executive Mansion, the old three-story Brockenbrough house at East Clay and Twelfth Streets. The fifty-three-year-old president was frequently short-tempered, rarely compromising, and often impatient with disagreement. Although he had never fought in a duel, he had come dangerously close to it on no fewer than ten occasions. Davis's military as well as political background caused him to view himself as the emerg-

15

ing nation's war manager, a responsibility he probably could not have avoided even if he so desired. He was commonly seen as cold and aloof, and today proved no exception; several guests considered his cordiality forced and insincere. The wife of Colonel Joseph Davis, the president's nephew, stood in for the First Lady, Mrs. Varina Davis, who was indisposed. For four hours the chief executive, standing at the door of the main drawing room, greeted an uninterrupted line of visitors.[2]

The sanguine veneer soon disintegrated. Even as Davis greeted guests that morning, information had reached the capital that the "Trent Affair" had been defused. The United States had offered a face-saving compromise that proved acceptable to the British. Confederate newspapers continued to carry articles for several days claiming that the British were preparing for war, but the peaceful resolution had dashed all immediate hope for intervention. This fact was not immediately evident to Davis and his Cabinet. John B. Jones, a perceptive clerk in the War Department, saw the situation clearly. He wrote in his diary that evening: "Now we must depend upon our own strong arms and stout hearts for defense."[3]

Both the North and the South mistakenly believed that Great Britain desired to go to war with the United States. In truth, England had much more to lose in a war with the Union than she had to gain by diplomatic recognition of the Confederacy. The reason for the mill slowdown was not a cotton shortage (inventories were at an all-time high in December 1861), but, rather, that the market was already saturated with cloth. The British needed Northern grain far more than raw cotton, which could be purchased in Egypt and India. They were not going to risk their merchant shipping in a prolonged war that could not be won with the United States. For now, however, Davis continued to cling to the illusion of foreign intervention, a naïveté that would have far-reaching implications for the Confederacy.[4]

The administration had adopted a policy of territorial defense that called for protecting as much territory as possible. Troops were kept widely scattered rather than concentrated on a few strategic points. This policy was, to a degree, political appeasement, but it went deeper than that. The proverbial tail wagging the dog was foreign intervention. Davis considered it vital that the fledgling nation prove its viability by protecting its territory. To relinquish large chunks of land would send the wrong signal. Even after the flaws of the policy became blatantly apparent, Davis asserted that the gamble had been worth it.[5]

Politicians, the Southern press, and the Davis administration had focused largely on the Virginia front. Popular sentiment dictated that it was there that the war would be won or lost. Ominous clouds soon began to loom, however, over the vast expanse west of the Appalachian Mountains known as the western theater.

A BLAST OF ARCTIC COLD soon replaced the unseasonably mild temperatures. Snow blanketed the streets of Richmond on January 14 as Colonel St. John Liddell trudged to the door of the Executive Mansion. A black boy answered and showed him into a room where a lamp hung suspended over a center table. The setting offered Liddell a comfortable respite from his exhausting railroad journey from Bowling Green, Kentucky. Davis shortly entered the room. The two men had been formally introduced six months earlier, although Liddell vaguely remembered Davis from his childhood; they had lived in the same county in Mississippi, and their families were well associated. The colonel handed him a letter from General Albert Sidney Johnston.[6]

Liddell's mission was an attempt by a frustrated Johnston to bypass the War Department and capitalize upon his long friendship with Davis. Their mutual admiration dated back to Transylvania College days in Lexington, Kentucky (Johnston was five years his senior), and to West Point. They subsequently fought Sioux together in the Northwest and Mexicans at Monterey. As secretary of war, Davis had appointed Johnston to the coveted position of commander of the 2nd United States Cavalry Regiment. Believing him to be the South's premier general, Davis wrote ecstatically when Johnston later tendered his services to the Confederacy: "I hoped and expected that I had others who would prove generals; but I knew I had one, and that was Sidney Johnston." Johnston's assignment in September 1861 to command the vast Department No. 2, which stretched from the Appalachians to the Ozarks, did not result from mere cronyism. Their prior association was probably not even necessary, the Johnston lobby being formidable. The general's appointment received support from a broad consensus.[7]

The press coverage that preceded Johnston's odyssey from California would ultimately prove to his detriment; it produced exaggerated expectations on the part of both government officials and the populace. Historians' claims that he was overrated, though arguably true, have been influenced by subsequent events; the character flaws that marked his Civil War career were not apparent in the fall of 1861.[8] The issue of whether he was the best selection for Department No. 2

must be seen in the context of "compared with whom." His prewar accomplishments exceeded those of Joseph E. Johnston, P. G. T. Beauregard, and Braxton Bragg.[9]

Among his peers, only Robert E. Lee proved the exception. Although Lee graduated from West Point three years after Johnston and was subordinate to him in the 2nd Cavalry, he was offered top command of the United States Army at the beginning of the war, second only to Winfield Scott. When he declined, the position was offered to Johnston, who similarly refused. Davis subsequently made Lee commander of all the Confederate armies, where he functioned as a presidential chief-of-staff, while Johnston received the actual field command. How different the war might have been had the roles been reversed.[10]

Friendship had not generated favoritism, however, and Johnston's frequent calls for additional troops even encountered occasional resistance. On September 30, 1861, Davis had labeled one of the general's early requests unwarranted. In December, Secretary of War Judah Benjamin insisted that Johnston had underestimated his Bowling Green force by one-half. Such looseness with the figures "made me very uneasy," Benjamin wrote, and the president was "equally at a loss to make out how matters stand." When Johnston attempted to raise troops himself, he was instructed by the War Department to cease.[11]

Davis had not deserted his friend, however. After the early months of the war, few western regiments had been sent to Virginia, and some units en route to that state were diverted to Johnston. During the winter of 1861–62, the administration had even made a minimal effort to send troops from Virginia to the west. In December, Brigadier General John Floyd's brigade of Virginians was ordered to Bowling Green. The reinforcements proved insufficient.[12]

During the fall and winter of 1861, Johnston watched nervously as Federal troop strength in the west far outpaced his forces. His impracticable four-hundred-mile line (east of the Mississippi River), with 57,500 troops, now faced twice that many Federals. Johnston's forces were concentrated in four key locations: 22,000 men under Major General Leonidas Polk at Columbus, Kentucky; 5,000 troops at the Tennessee and Cumberland River forts of Henry and Donelson; 24,500 troops at Bowling Green under Major General William J. Hardee; and 6,000 troops in eastern Kentucky commanded by Major General George Crittenden. Shortly after Liddell's departure from Richmond, Johnston had written Benjamin that he had 19,000 men (though his own reports revealed 4,000 more) to oppose a 75,000-man army under General Don Carlos Buell. The estimate of enemy troop strength was based upon a document stolen from Federal headquarters in Louisville, Kentucky. Indeed, an article had appeared in the *Richmond Examiner*, taken from the *New York Tribune*, that listed regiments and numbers in Kentucky.[13]

Contrary to some modern assertions, Confederate administration officials fully understood Johnston's numerical weakness. Diarist John Jones noted this on January 23, 1862: "Again the Northern papers gave the most extravagant numbers to our army in Kentucky. Some estimates are as high as 150,000. I know, and Mr. Benjamin knows, that Gen. Johnston has not exceeded twenty-nine thousand effective men." Benjamin later conceded that the Bowling Green force had no more than twenty-four thousand effectives. What Davis may not have fully appreciated was the disproportionate numbers that Johnston faced. In a January 6 Cabinet meeting, the president had said that he did not accept the captured Louisville document, and that Buell's strength "could not exceed 45,000 effectives." He thought that the additional troops on the way to Bowling Green, although not giving Johnston parity, would close the numerical gap.[14]

As Davis sat quietly reading Johnston's letter, his features grew pained, even angry. "My God," he erupted to Liddell. "Why did General Johnston send you to me for arms and reinforcements when he must know I have neither? He has plenty of men in Tennessee, and they must have arms of some kind." The brusque and opinionated Liddell, an unlikely emissary, retorted that the troops could come from the army at Manassas, Virginia, which was then not occupied. Davis insisted that Virginians were already angered about the loss of Floyd's brigade to Kentucky. Obstinately persisting, the colonel inquired whether troops could be spared from Charleston, Savannah, Pensacola, or even New Orleans. The president interrupted: "Do you think these places of so little importance that I should strip them of the troops necessary for their defense?" Liddell proved unrelenting, arguing that these locations were not as significant as the heartland of the Confederacy. Unless Johnston held his position, the Mississippi River would be lost and communications severed with the trans-Mississippi. "My God! Why repeat?" Davis again exclaimed, annoyed with Liddell's persistence. The colonel countered that he was simply attempting to make the facts of Kentucky and Tennessee known. The president quieted as Liddell explained Johnston's desire that all available troops be concentrated in Kentucky and Virginia to take the offensive. Davis did not disagree, but he claimed that the time was not right. The conversation was cut short, but Davis invited the colonel to have dinner with him the next night.[15]

The president's claim of inadequate troops was not true. There were armed units, but, in keeping with the administration policy of territorial defense, they were widely scattered. At the time of Liddell's visit, 25,000 Confederates (6,800 troops at Pensacola, 9,300 at Mobile, and 8,900 at New Orleans) sat idly on the Gulf Coast, not to mention 4,000 troops in eastern Florida. If Davis had taken advantage of interior lines and acted decisively at this moment (as he would three weeks later), events in the west might have taken a different turn. The subsequent chain of events must be viewed in the light of this mistaken administration policy.[16]

The evening after his first confrontation with Davis, January 15, Liddell found the president more genial. He spoke of his earlier days and carefully avoided the subject of Johnston's dilemma. Liddell attempted to broach the issue, but the expression on the president's face made it apparent that he did not consider the subject appropriate table talk. Showing Liddell to the door at the conclusion of the evening, Davis said: "Tell my friend, General Johnston, that I can do nothing for him. He must rely upon his own resources." The colonel, rapidly coming down with a bronchial infection and a painful cough, found it cold on the streets of Richmond that night.[17]

"WE HAVE HEARD bad news today from Kentucky." Thus began the January 23 diary entry of Thomas Bragg, Confederate attorney general. A dispatch had been received at the War Department via Johnston's headquarters at Bowling Green. Initial information was sketchy and came only from a Northern newspaper—the *Louisville Democrat* of January 21. A Confederate division under Major General George Crittenden had been routed near Somerset, Kentucky, and Brigadier General Felix Zollicoffer was counted among the slain. Davis immediately canceled his Cabinet meeting for the day. "The President and Sec'y of War keep military matters to themselves—they have been in conference today. I hope they have been able to devise some means to repair the disaster in Kentucky," Bragg concluded.[18]

A second dispatch arrived at the War Department that evening from Johnston's headquarters. A Crittenden staff officer confirmed the repulse of the division "by superior numbers." The Southerners lost five hundred men, including all of their baggage and artillery, and the division was "in full retreat" southwest toward Nashville.[19]

A stunned populace read the story the next day in the Richmond press. Although there had been other Confederate reversals earlier in the war, at Rich Mountain in western Virginia and at Port Royal, South Carolina, the eastern-Kentucky loss was serious and had far-reaching implications. Johnston's right flank was now uncovered, exposing Cumberland Gap and the east-west rail link connecting Richmond, Virginia, and Memphis, Tennessee. Several poorly armed and widely scattered Confederate regiments protected Cumberland Gap, Knoxville, and Chattanooga, but for all intents and purposes, eastern Tennessee, already crawling with Union partisans, was open to invasion. Indeed, an unconfirmed report (false, as it turned out) stated that 22,000 Federals were advancing on Cumberland Gap against a Southern garrison of 1,500. The road to Nashville also lay exposed to the east.[20]

Johnston clearly understood his difficulty and proposed plugging the breach around Burkesville, Kentucky, about a hundred miles from Nashville. Crittenden's troops would be of no assistance, however, for they were retreating along the south bank of the Cumberland River to Gainesville, Tennessee, eighty miles from Nashville, and the column would not stop until it reached Chesnut Mound, only fifty miles from the state capital. Widespread desertions marred the withdrawal. Johnston urgently warned the War Department that he was about to be overwhelmed: "All of the resources of the Confederacy are now needed for the defense of Tennessee."[21]

" 'Old Jeff's' blood is up, and he intends to repair the disaster in Kentucky at any cost whatsoever." That is what George Bagby's confidential sources related to him, as he gathered information in Richmond for his "News & Gossip" column in the Charleston *Mercury*. In a Cabinet meeting on January 31, Davis expressed concern about the situation and declared that "the place where troops were most needed now was East Tennessee." Nevertheless, by the end of the first week in February, two weeks after Johnston's urgent appeal, no decision had been made regarding reinforcements, and no additional arms had been sent.[22]

Crittenden did not file his report on the Battle of Somerset until mid-February, but increasingly rumors were afoot in the capital. By the end of January, the western press had turned nasty, and the target was Crittenden. Serious allegations concerning the general's state of sobriety during the battle had cropped up. Thomas Bragg confidentially recorded his own concerns: "It is already circulated here that he [Crittenden] is very intemperate and that it was known when he was appointed. I fear it is too true." Bagby conducted his own personal investigation by mixing with the Tennessee congressional delegation. He discovered that fugitives in Knoxville were writing their congressmen that Zollicoffer had protested the attack at Somerset but Crittenden had refused to listen. Charges of treachery also surfaced, since Crittenden's brother Thomas commanded a division in the Federal army. The War Department directed Johnston to initiate an investigation.[23]

Davis's role in the eastern-Kentucky front had been twofold. First, his faulty political/foreign policy had not allowed for timely reinforcements. Second, he failed to recognize the serious leadership gap that existed in the west. Both Zollicoffer and Crittenden were totally unfit for high rank, the former being a political general, and the latter being a known alcoholic who had close family ties to Davis. Additional troops would only be wasted if placed under the same incompetent commanders. Crittenden's later claim that his 4,000 men had engaged 12,000 Federals was untrue. At the actual point of contact in the battle, the two sides had been evenly matched. Somerset had been lost not because of inferior numbers, but because of inferior leadership. This would become a theme often repeated in the west throughout the war.[24]

Zollicoffer was now dead, and as only the third Southern general to be killed in the war, he was a hero. As for Crittenden, the press quickly linked the president to this dishonored general. The anti-administration *Mercury* condemned Davis for "selecting a known drunkard for a Major General." Tennessee Senator Landon Haynes and Representative J. D. C. Adkins, a member of the powerful Military Affairs Committee, soon demanded Crittenden's ouster. A court of inquiry was ordered, but for now Davis continued to support his friend.[25]

WHILE DAVIS FRETTED over the western theater, certain politicians took more definite action. Shortly after the news of the Somerset defeat, Mississippi Valley congressmen met in conference with the Military Affairs Committee. In their view, the next crisis would be on Johnston's left flank, along the Mississippi River. Somerset had demonstrated that, even though Johnston had unified command in the west, his line was too extended to provide adequate supervision. The general needed help—a second-in-command. The man they had in mind was the hero of Fort Sumter and Manassas—General P. G. T. Beauregard.

From Davis's perspective, the flamboyant forty-four-year-old

Louisiana general was scheming, contentious, and highly overrated. Although their feud may have had some prewar genesis, it did not grow serious until the months following Manassas. In October 1861, a synopsis of Beauregard's battle report found its way to the antiadministration *Richmond Whig*. The report claimed that he had a plan to capture Washington after the victory at Manassas, but that the president had prevented its execution. This was not true, and Davis angrily chastised the general. Instead of responding directly, Beauregard submitted his acid response in the *Whig* for publication. Even if the incident alienated some of his political friends, Beauregard maintained powerful contacts, including his father-in-law, Louisiana Senator John Slidell.[26]

In approving the transfer to the west, Davis apparently had mixed motives. He had deep concerns about the Mississippi Valley, and the Louisiana general's name clearly had propaganda value. In a January 31 Cabinet meeting, he spoke of the general's engineering talent, although he left the distinct impression, according to Thomas Bragg, that he did not hold a high opinion of the general. Davis clearly detested the letter-writing Creole and was relieved at the prospect of moving him away from the capital. Some of Beauregard's friends believed that Davis initiated the scheme to exile him to the west. John Jones apparently believed such, for on January 24 he wrote: "Beauregard had been ordered to the West. I knew that doom was upon him."[27]

Virginia Representative Roger Pryor, a Beauregard supporter, approached the general about the prospect of transferring to the west. Pryor related that he had been told by the War Department that Johnston had 40,000 troops in and around Bowling Green and Polk had 30,000 at Columbus. If such a figure was given, either Pryor misunderstood or Benjamin lied. The War Department knew that Johnston had no such force at his disposal. Beauregard eventually accepted the transfer, flattered by the attention and perceiving himself as the savior of the west. Since he was already serving as Joseph E. Johnston's second-in-command in Virginia, the offer (on paper at least) was not a demotion. On February 24, the general boarded a train at Centreville, Virginia, and departed amidst the shouts of his men: "Goodbye, General, God bless you, General."[28]

DAVIS'S ONE-MAN REINFORCEMENT did nothing to forestall the next Federal move. The congressmen had also been wrong in their projection; the target was not the Mississippi Valley, but the Tennessee Valley. On February 6, a joint Federal land-naval expedition captured Fort Henry, on the Tennessee River. That artery now lay open all the way to Florence, Alabama, where the shoals prevented further ascent. The War Department received the first news of the surrender at noon on February 7. A dispatch via Memphis stated that the fort had fallen after a two-hour struggle, the upriver railroad bridge was in enemy possession, and communications between Bowling Green and Columbus were now severed. Fearful that nearby Fort Donelson was in danger and that his forces would be caught north of the Cumberland River, Johnston withdrew his Bowling Green corps to Nashville.[29]

Reaction throughout the War Department was of shock and dismay as Federal gunboats raided upriver. Jones feared the enemy would get a footing in northern Mississippi and Alabama; Robert G. H. Kean heard of the destruction of government stores at Florence. On February 11, Thomas Bragg wrote: "No news from Tennessee and [to] the South. The enemy have already I think cut off all communications South, crossing the Tennessee below Florence. Well—it [is] a long road that has no turning."[30]

Faced with twin disasters, Davis belatedly abandoned his policy of dispersed defense and ordered additional troops to Johnston. Despite Benjamin's assurances that heavy reinforcements would be sent to the west, even this move, undertaken on February 8, proved limited in scope. Major General Mansfield Lovell, commanding at New Orleans, was directed to send 5,000 troops to Polk at Columbus. To shore up Johnston's battered right wing, four regiments were ordered from Virginia to eastern Tennessee, and a like number from Major General Braxton Bragg's Gulf Coast department, between Pensacola and Mobile. Johnston's forces at Bowling Green also received 3,600 arms, including 1,200 imported Enfield rifles.[31]

The troops would arrive too late to affect Fort Donelson, the fate of which was now very much in question. Johnston pieced together a force of 21,000 troops under Generals John Floyd, Gideon Pillow, and Simon Buckner for its defense. War Department officials believed the garrison (thought to be 15,000 strong) was being enveloped by 75,000 Federals. "Was ever such [mis]management known before?" John Jones disgustedly wrote. "Who is responsible for it? If Donelson falls, what becomes of the ten or twelve thousand men at Bowling Green?" Administration officials nervously awaited news from Tennessee.[32]

A LIGHT RAIN and sleet fell in Richmond the greater part of February 17, covering the trees with ice. Despite the gloomy weather, initial re-

MAP 1: THEATER OF OPERATIONS

Mississippi River

Ohio River

ILLINOIS

KENTUCKY

Ohio River

Tennessee River

Bowling Green ○

MISSOURI

Columbus

Island No.10

POLK

Fort Donelson

Union City

Fort Henry

Nashville ○

C. F. SMITH

TENNESSEE

Duck River

BUELL

Murfreesboro

Jackson

Columbia

Mississippi River

ARKANSAS

Crump's
Landing

JOHNSTON

VAN DORN

Savannah

Waynesboro

Fayetteville

Memphis ○

Memphis &
Charleston R.R.

Bethel
Station

Pittsburg Landing

Corinth

Iuka

Bear Cr.

Tennessee River

Huntsville

Tuscumbia

Decatur

MISSISSIPPI

RUGGLES

Mobile &
Ohio R.R.

ALABAMA

Grenada

BRAGG

☐ UNION TROOPS

▨ CONFEDERATE TROOPS

0   50   100

Scale in Miles

ports from the west had been uplifting. Confederate forces at Fort Donelson had more than held their own. A Federal gunboat attack on the 14th had been repulsed. The next day, according to one dispatch, Southern forces had succeeded in driving the enemy from its position, inflicting over 1,500 casualties.[33]

At 11:30 that night, officials at the War Department were shocked when a telegraph clicked over the wire from Johnston announcing the fall of Fort Donelson on February 16. Floyd and Pillow had escaped to Nashville with a thousand troops, leaving Buckner to surrender the fort. The Bowling Green corps had safely crossed the Cumberland River.[34]

Depression spread throughout Richmond as the news was read in the morning papers. Few details were known, and Bragg conceded that he had "heard nothing but a thousand rumors." Northern press accounts claimed 15,000 prisoners. War Department insiders remained at a loss as to particulars; the *Examiner* even denounced the story as a false rumor. Confederate administrative officials obtained a February 17 issue of the *New York Herald* that confirmed earlier accounts of a mass surrender.[35]

In his weekly column, George Bagby admitted that facts were "very obscure," but, even making allowance for exaggeration, it seemed clear that something of serious proportions had happened. The offices of the War Department, telegraph, and newspapers were so choked with citizens seeking information that Benjamin issued a public circular. In it he claimed that no news had been received other than on Saturday night, February 15, when a telegraph operator had sent a baseless rumor over the wires. No additional information had been received from Nashville, simply because of ice on the wires. The circular was a lie. It did not take long for the truth to emerge, for exhausted refugees from Nashville began arriving in Richmond on the 18th. Bagby's private sleuthing soon uncovered information that government officials had known the truth "as early as Sunday night [February 17]."[36]

Davis received a telegram from Hardee on February 21 (dated the 19th) stating that his corps had withdrawn from Nashville to Murfreesboro, Tennessee. The message came via Atlanta, not Nashville, raising further speculation as to the status of the Tennessee capital. No additional information had been received by the evening of February 21, and Thomas Bragg and others were beginning to believe that initial reports were false, or at least exaggerated. Benjamin claimed that he had no concrete information.[37]

The administration became increasingly concerned about the fate of Nashville. By February 21, the government acknowledged that the Nashville telegraph office had been closed and that the public must draw its own inference. Thomas Bragg feared that the city had probably fallen, a suspicion that was confirmed on February 24. "That the loss of Nashville is mortifying no one can deny but its fate was inevitable after the fall of Fort Donelson," the *Richmond Dispatch* concluded.[38]

IT BEGAN DRIZZLING early in Richmond on February 22, and by mid-morning a steady rain fell, attended by a cold wind. Indeed, Davis's inauguration on George Washington's Birthday—his previous swearing in had been only provisional—had more the quality of a wake than of a celebration. Just before he left the capital, Davis received confirmation of the extent of the Donelson loss; his worst fears were realized. Confederate forces in Tennessee were reeling back in confusion. Arriving in Washington Square at noon, Davis, who had been ill for weeks, delivered his address on a temporary platform before a statue of George Washington. About five hundred spectators milled about, and the pattering of rain on umbrellas drowned out his voice. A veiled statement in his address noted that the "tide for the moment is against us," but no specifics concerning Donelson were given. The president, according to Jones, appeared "self-poised in the midst of disasters."[39]

Despite outward appearances, the executive branch was privately mortified at the turn of events. A melancholy Davis wrote a friend in New Orleans for solace, although he apparently had second thoughts and never mailed the letter. Vice-President Alexander Stephens, having just recovered from a severe attack of facial neuralgia, plunged into depression. "The Confederacy is lost," he confided to a friend one night as they left Congress.[40]

On February 15, Major General Braxton Bragg, a Davis associate, had written him concerning a change in military strategy. Bragg believed that the policy of dispersal should be abandoned in favor of concentration for a few strategic points. "Kentucky is now the point," he judged. Davis discussed the proposal, virtually identical to the one that Colonel Liddell had presented a month earlier, during a Sunday, February 16, Cabinet meeting. On February 18, Bragg again suggested giving up the seaboard for "the vital point."[41]

Bragg was not being totally selfless, as some historians have suggested. He did not volunteer his entire Gulf Coast corps for this concentration, as popularly believed. Indeed, he suggested that the needed forces not come from his department, but from an abandonment of the Florida interior, Texas, and possibly Missouri and portions of the Atlantic Seaboard. In response to an earlier request to send only four regiments to eastern Tennessee, Bragg had written: "I am not decided to send them." He subsequently did send the troops, but he was not beyond the parochialism that blinded other commanders.[42]

Obviously a drastic policy change was in order, regardless of the political ramifications. Davis had slowly conceded that his policy of territorial defense had failed and, even before Bragg's letter, had contemplated abandoning the seaboard in favor of reinforcing Tennessee. Although still lacking information from Johnston, Benjamin notified Bragg on February 18 that he was to withdraw his forces from Pensacola and Mobile and proceed to Tennessee. On February 21, Davis informed his brother that he was determined to "assemble a sufficient force to beat the enemy in Tennessee, and retrieve our waning fortunes in the West."[43]

The move may have been unprecedented, but its scope was not as great as some historians have suggested. Bragg, the advocate of concentration, decided to retain Mobile and 40 percent of his department's strength, and he sent only 10,000 troops, 7,700 of whom were "present for duty." No troops were ordered from the Atlantic Coast, Texas (where 11,000 men idled away), or Major General Earl Van Dorn's army in Arkansas. Even considering the 5,000 troops previously ordered to Tennessee, Davis still retained 14,000 men along the Gulf Coast and in eastern Florida.[44]

AN ANXIOUS DAVIS, his hand ever on the international pulse, was especially concerned about Britain. On February 27, the steamer *Nashville* came through the blockade at Beaufort, North Carolina, bringing encouraging news of popular sentiment in Europe. A single London mercantile house had advanced the captain £400,000 sterling—$2 million. It was widely rumored abroad that Britain would soon recognize the Confederacy, to be followed shortly by Belgium.[45]

Bad reports from the west now had serious repercussions. The pro-Southern *London Times* stated: "There are symptoms that the Civil War cannot be very long protracted." James Mason conceded that the lost forts "have had an unfortunate effect upon the minds of our friends here." Popular British sentiment held that the war might soon be over. John Slidell encountered a similar reaction on the Continent. Confederate officials attempted to mitigate the damage by assuring the British that the actual number of prisoners taken at Donelson was between 6,000 and 7,000.[46]

FORT DONELSON was not just a defeat; it was a catastrophe. The loss of the Tennessee and Cumberland Rivers meant that the Federals had penetrated deep into the Southern interior. In two weeks, Johnston had fallen back a hundred miles, Nashville had been abandoned, and the forts along the Mississippi River appeared doomed. A Union army and a formidable river separated the corps of Polk and Hardee. Most significantly, at least 15,000 prisoners had been taken, about one-third of Johnston's forces east of the Mississippi River. Because of the policy of prisoner exchange, most of these regiments would be back in service again within seven months.[47] The troops were not available when they were needed most, however—the first day at Shiloh. Whether an additional corps would have made a decisive difference in the first day's battle can only be left to speculation, but it undoubtedly would have had a considerable effect.

As at Somerset, Davis had played a significant role in the defeat. He had ordered reinforcements to Tennessee too late and in piecemeal fashion. In failing to concentrate and take advantage of interior lines, the president had gone against the pleadings of Johnston. It took the shock of Henry-Donelson to give him a clear perspective.[48]

Also as at Somerset, inadequate numbers cannot explain the loss at Fort Donelson. Despite the claim of overwhelming numbers, Floyd's 21,000 Confederates never faced more than 27,000 Federals. Indeed, for the first two days of the battle, the Southerners outnumbered the Yankees, even by their own estimates. The blunders at Donelson were the direct result of the inept leadership offered by Floyd and Pillow, two Davis political generals. It was Pillow's stupidity in ordering Confederate troops back into the fort after they had broken out that spelled the doom of three divisions. To complete the comedy of errors, both men had cowardly passed command and escaped before the surrender had been consummated.[49]

Johnston's decision to abdicate command at Donelson has long been questioned. Since Johnston had chosen to play the role of corps commander rather than a department chief, he should have at least placed the experienced Hardee in charge of the Cumberland River defenses. Interestingly, Floyd had been a prewar ally of Johnston. As secretary of war he had strongly, but unsuccessfully, argued that Albert Sidney Johnston, not Joseph E. Johnston, should be quartermaster general. Whether or not the Fort Donelson command was a conscious reciprocation cannot now be determined.[50]

Confusion and chaos continued to dominate Richmond throughout the latter half of February. Anger soon replaced shock, however, as politicians and the public demanded answers. The focus of their attention would be Albert Sidney Johnston.

Washington, D.C.

THERE WAS A FLURRY of activity in the headquarters of Union General-in-Chief George B. McClellan on February 17, 1862. A telegraph had just arrived from Major General Henry W. Halleck, commanding the Department of Missouri, announcing the capture of Fort Donelson by combined land and naval forces under Brigadier General Ulysses S. Grant and Flag Officer Andrew Foote. For half an hour, McClellan basked in the congratulations of his staff officers. The news arrived at noon in the office of Edwin M. Stanton, the newly appointed secretary of war. The morning assembly greeted the dispatch with loud cheering and a congratulatory telegram returned to Halleck.[51]

Congress reacted to the news with elation. When the dispatch was read from the Senate floor, grave old men threw up their hats and canes. A similar reaction occurred in the House, where representatives and spectators in the gallery responded with deafening cheers. Although the House did not adjourn, further business proved impossible—"The news is too good," proclaimed a congressman.[52]

Press accounts from across the country told of the electrifying response. In Chicago, business suspended on the Board of Trade, and on the streets complete strangers embraced one another. A national salute was fired on Bunker Hill in Boston, where the celebration was described as unequaled in the memory of living men. Shrieking newsboys made the announcement known in New York City, where Horace Greeley's *Tribune* printed an extra: "Freedom! Fort Donelson Taken!" Business ceased on the Merchant's Exchange, and "The Star-Spangled Banner" echoed throughout the building. Despite a drenching rain in Baltimore, the streets quickly filled with cheering people.[53]

The enthusiasm continued on February 18. Congress directed that, immediately following the reading of George Washington's Farewell Address on February 22, a citywide celebration would be held in Washington. Several captured Rebel flags, trophies from Mill Springs (the Northern name for Somerset) and Fort Henry, had been rushed to the War Department by Adams & Company Express. A public viewing of the flags would take place in the House of Representatives. That night all government buildings would be illuminated.[54]

Throughout the next few days, midwesterners caught a glimpse of the Fort Donelson captives on their way to prison camps. New York and Chicago correspondents snobbishly observed that the privates appeared to be "ignorant and ordinary men," the type of common laborers seen working along the roadside. With disdain they noted that the privates' uniforms were "just no uniforms at all." Thousands of citizens showed up at the Camp Douglas rail station to see the famished prisoners file out. Midwesterners quickly acquired an attitude of superiority.[55]

Such unrestrained euphoria inevitably led to overexpectation. Many people rushed to the conclusion that the war would be over by year's end—perhaps by the Fourth of July. The *Chicago Tribune* described Fort Donelson as the turning point of the war. The *New York Tribune* concluded, "The monster is already clutched in his death struggle," and a correspondent of that paper proclaimed, "The end is at hand."[56]

A few weeks earlier, such a joyful spree would have been considered a sacrilege. The war had not been going well for the North. The Army of the Potomac, in winter quarters along the Potomac River, appeared more like a beached whale than a caged tiger. Halleck and Brigadier General Don Carlos Buell, commanding the Missouri and Kentucky departments respectively, remained at loggerheads and in virtual competition for top command in the west. As late as February 20, Charles Francis Adams, the United States minister to London, had written that a war with England over the *Trent* incident was imminent and that it might even spread to the Continent. Although the incident was peacefully resolved, many believed British recognition of the South still possible.[57]

A White House ball announced for early February brought an angry response, including eighty declined invitations. Unable to cancel the ball, President and Mrs. Abraham Lincoln announced there would be no dancing. The affair proved ghastly. Lincoln's eleven-year-old child, Willie, idolized by his parents, was deathly ill with fever, incurred while riding his pony on a chilly day. Dorothea Dix noted that the Marine band played at the foot of the steps while the child lay dying upstairs. The president and the First Lady sadly greeted guests at the large door of the East Room. Dix expressed hope for the lad's recovery.[58]

It was not to be. On the afternoon of February 20, at 5 P.M., Lincoln slowly walked into the office of his secretary, John J. Nicolay. With a choked voice he said: "Well, Nicolay, my boy is gone—he is actually gone!" He then broke down and wept. With funeral services planned for February 22, Congress, out of respect, canceled the planned celebration. The Lincolns' personal loss in the midst of national celebration served as a sobering note. Certain senators began to caution that the war had not yet ended. That night of February 22, some children in the capital city, feeling cheated of the festivities, set off Chinese firecrackers and ran through the streets with torches.[59]

LINCOLN HOPED that the Fort Donelson victory would stir new volunteers. By the winter of 1861–62, interest had waned even in the west, where recruiting had been successful. The apathy in Iowa, noted Illinois Governor Richard Yates, had spread into his state. Increasingly there was talk of a draft. The cries of Northern generals to the contrary, the problem had never been a shortage of raw manpower. By January 1862, more than 700,000 men filled the Union ranks, twice the number of Confederates. Sufficient troop strength existed to crush the rebellion, but McClellan (in his role as commander of the Army of the Potomac), Halleck, and Buell insisted that their forces were each too weak for a forward movement. As in the South, the problem was not lack of numbers but lack of leadership.[60]

This fact was easily demonstrated in Buell's Department of the Ohio. Throughout the winter of 1861–62, Buell placed Rebel troop strength at Bowling Green at 40,000—an overestimate of 15,000. In February he stated that his forces contained 61,000 present for duty, with an aggregate of nearly 80,000. McClellan desired Buell to send 50,000 troops against Bowling Green and 15,000 to liberate eastern Tennessee, a pet project of Lincoln's. This arrangement would have given Buell superiority of numbers against Johnston even by his own inflated estimates and, in actuality, an army twice that of the Rebels. He nonetheless refused to move against Johnston and instead argued strategy with Halleck and McClellan.[61]

Fort Donelson not only gave the North its greatest tactical win in the war to date but also marked the emergence of Ulysses S. Grant. Overnight, he became a national hero. His initials earned him the sobriquets "Unconditional Surrender," "United States," and "Uncle

Sam." Lincoln and Grant had never met, and the administration, pre-occupied with the Virginia front, was frankly taken aback that such an unknown as Grant had gained such a significant victory.[62]

From the outset of the war, Grant had proved inept in cultivating political ties. He wrote his father that he was "perfectly sickened at the political wire pulling for all these commissions," yet he was not beyond intra-army politics himself. His awkward attempts to get a commission through old army connections were all rebuffed; McClellan, once his junior, refused even to see him. Despite his disdain for political pull, Grant would finally emerge from the shadows through a Washington connection—Illinois Representative Elihu Washburne.[63]

Forty-six years old and a Harvard law graduate, Washburne had won the Galena seat in the House of Representatives as a Republican in 1852. Grant, clerking at his father's leather store at the time, became a street acquaintance of the congressman. It was thus a curiosity that Washburne would sponsor Grant (a nominal Democrat) for his colonelcy and later for a brigadier's commission. The general would later recall that he believed Washburne never liked him well. Washburne, of course, cared nothing for personal relationships. If this local West Pointer did well, then the congressman, as his patron, would have his own career enhanced.[64]

The thirty-nine-year-old Grant had little to recommend him. His father had arranged his appointment to West Point without his knowledge or approval. He later resigned from the Regular Army under a cloud, the rumors being that he could not leave the bottle alone. Grant went to New York City in a futile attempt to collect an old debt and in the process ran up a hotel bill. He was on the verge of being ejected when his old army friend Simon Buckner came to his rescue and guaranteed his debt. The next time the two would meet would be in a hotel at Dover, Tennessee, at the surrender of Fort Donelson.[65]

Grant moved to St. Louis, where he lived in a log house and worked cutting firewood. A reputation for intemperance continued to dog him. After failing at farming and real estate, he moved to his father's home at Galena. His shabby appearance and his penchant for drinking and smoking (he switched from a pipe to cigars after 10,000 congratulatory cigars were sent him following Donelson) made him thoroughly western, although he did not swear; indeed, he was soft-spoken. His background showed little promise.[66]

There was, nonetheless, more to Grant than a simple talent for being at the right place at the right time. If he did not excel in a peacetime army or civilian pursuits, he did in battle. It was precisely this, his love of battle, that separated Grant from McClellan. Schooled in the art of European tactics, McClellan was a maneuverer. Grant, who cared little for Napoleon, was a fighter.[67]

Grant insisted that he had never asked anyone to intercede in his behalf. He nevertheless acknowledged his congressman's role in securing a brigadier's commission. "That's some of Washburne's work," he related to a chaplain upon hearing the news of his promotion. By October 1861, the congressman was promoting his protégé for major general.[68]

Grant first came to national attention when, in November 1861, he led an expeditionary force of 3,000 troops against the Confederate outpost at Belmont, Missouri, across the river from Columbus, Kentucky. Although initially driven back, the Rebels received reinforcements and counterattacked; Grant's force narrowly escaped. The engagement was severely criticized in the North as having been unnecessary and barren of results. The word spread that Brigadier General John McClernand, a Grant rival, had saved the day, and Lincoln even sent him congratulations. The engagement did, nonetheless, reap some benefits. It served to turn Confederate attention away from the twin rivers. The Battle of Belmont established the significance of joint land-naval operations, which proved to be the key to success at Fort Donelson. Also, Grant's name had emerged from the pack.[69]

The Grant-Washburne relationship proved significant not only for jump-starting the general's career but also because the congressman assumed the role of Grant's Washington defender. In mid-December, Washburne received the disturbing news that Grant had resumed his hard drinking. The congressman wrote Grant's chief-of-staff, John Rawlins, a former Galena lawyer, who denied the charge. He insisted that Grant adhered to strict abstinence and that, according to those who knew him well, such had been his habit for five or six years. The rumors did not die, but time and again the Illinois congressman would provide defensive cover for the general on the Washington scene. Because of this role, Washburne would become a significant player in the Shiloh campaign.[70]

When the Fort Donelson victory was announced in the House of Representatives on February 17, Congressman Washburne boasted to his peers: "I want . . . to state that General U.S. Grant, who commanded the land forces that captured the fort, is from Illinois, and from Galena, in my district." The next day the Chicago press confidently predicted that the Senate would quickly confirm Grant as major general. On February 21, Grant wrote Washburne expressing thanks for placing him in a position to command and voicing his hope that he would not disappoint him. Washburne's protégé was performing well.[71]

A POWER STRUGGLE that developed among Stanton, McClellan, and Halleck added another dimension to the Fort Donelson story. Differing strategies were at stake, but personalities also lay at the root of the problem. Although all three proved highly competent organizers, they were also intense, scheming individuals who sought complete autonomy for themselves. Not surprisingly, each detested the others.[72]

The feud between Stanton and Halleck started before the war. Sporting a long beard streaked with gray, the cantankerous Stanton developed a national reputation as a lawyer and served as attorney general under President James Buchanan. In 1858, the Ohio Democrat became a special counsel to the United States government in prosecuting fraudulent land claims in California. Stanton first encountered Halleck during the Almaden Quicksilver Case and became convinced that Halleck had perjured himself in court. As secretary of war, Stanton publicly stated that he harbored no grudges against Halleck and that his feelings remained "neutral." In private, however, he passionately berated him. He warned McClellan that Halleck was "the greatest scoundrel and the most barefaced villain in America," a person "totally destitute of principle." When Halleck later met McClellan in Washington, he reciprocated the warning about Stanton. On January 15, 1862, Halleck wrote his wife: "Mr. Stanton does not like me, and of course will take the first opportunity to injure me."[73]

McClellan and Halleck also held each other in mutual contempt. Halleck became increasingly resentful of his superior (who was eleven years his junior), who differed in strategy, refused to send reinforcements, remained preoccupied with matters in his own theater of operations, and had denied Halleck's request for overall command in the west. For his part, McClellan was convinced that former General-in-Chief Winfield Scott had favored Halleck as his successor and had even outstayed his usefulness in the hopes that Halleck would come east and replace him. McClellan later characterized Halleck as "hopelessly stupid" and never having "a complete military idea from beginning to end."[74]

Stanton disliked McClellan from the outset, and their relationship quickly deteriorated. The arrogant general had opposed Lincoln's policies, held professional disdain for civilian leadership, and was not above being personally rude to the commander-in-chief. Stanton became irritated at McClellan's inaction. Also, the cold and dictatorial secretary of war liked subordinates to defer to him; McClellan crawled to no one. Stanton undoubtedly influenced the president's unusual decision of January 27, 1862, ordering a simultaneous move by all Federal armies to begin on February 22.[75]

When the capture of Fort Donelson was announced, McClellan's friends absurdly claimed that he had personally directed the operation from his headquarters on the Potomac. Stanton facetiously commented to correspondent Charles Dana: "Was it not a funny sight to see a certain military hero [McClellan] in the telegraph office organizing victory, and by sublime combinations capturing Fort Donelson *six hours after* Grant and [C. F.] Smith had taken it. . . . It would be a picture worthy of Punch."[76]

The Northern press increasingly credited Stanton with the Donelson victory. The fort had surrendered one month to the day after his assumption of office, a fact widely noted by journalists. The *Chicago Tribune* flatly stated that McClellan had contributed nothing to the campaign, and that in fact his plan had greatly differed from that of Stanton and Halleck. The Fort Donelson victory was "due to Stanton, in large measure, and in part to the President himself." Greeley's *New York Tribune* echoed a similar theme. Attorney General Edward Bates believed that Fort Donelson had greatly enhanced Stanton's reputation.[77]

As for McClellan, the western successes placed greater pressure upon him to act. Presidential secretary John Hay concluded that Forts Henry and Donelson "showed that Halleck was doing his share," an obvious comparison to McClellan. Despite this pressure, Washington's Birthday came and went with no movement by the Army of the Potomac. Stanton subsequently wrote a letter that appeared in Greeley's paper in which he extolled Grant and the Donelson victory. He obviously intended the words to point at McClellan's inaction. The *Washington Star* attempted to downplay the schism, stating that Stanton and McClellan were friends and the entire affair had been an Abolitionist attempt to create discord.[78]

On February 17, Halleck proposed a western reorganization that would combine the departments of Missouri and Kentucky with him at the head. Some 50,000 troops of the Army of the Potomac would be sent to the west to reinforce him, followed by a concerted effort up the Cumberland and Tennessee Rivers. Despite his dislike for Halleck, Stanton took the proposal seriously, believing that the war might be won in the west. McClellan, not unexpectedly, rejected the plan. The secretary of war (unknown to Halleck) had previously attempted to lure McClellan to top command in the west, a move to get a more active general over the Army of the Potomac without causing a political eruption.[79]

The power struggle intensified. Halleck, claiming that he had fathered the Henry-Donelson operation (although pushing on to Donelson had been Grant's idea), attempted to ride the victory to top western command. "I ask this in return for Forts Henry and Donelson," he boldly wrote. Receiving no reply from McClellan, he wired again the next day. "May I assume command? Answer quickly." The general-in-chief tersely refused. McClellan had not sought a unified command in the west because he thought departmentally. He believed the mission of Buell's army to be the capture of Nashville (equal, he thought, in political prestige to Fort Donelson) and the liberation of eastern Tennessee, while Halleck concentrated on Memphis and the Mississippi River. If Halleck had his way, Buell would be drawn away from Chattanooga.[80]

Unswayed by McClellan, Halleck ignored chain of command and wrote directly to Stanton. The secretary approved the idea of western reorganization, but felt constrained to present the idea to Lincoln, "so much depressed by anxiety" over his son Willie. The otherwise heartless Stanton may have genuinely sympathized with the president, for his own youngest son, James, was dangerously ill at the time. Not similarly moved, Halleck wired back the same day (February 21) urgently requesting that Stanton break in on Lincoln—"there is not a moment to be lost. Give me authority and I will be responsible for results." Stanton replied the next day, stating that Lincoln had rejected any departmental changes. Historians have generally denounced the decision, but the Federals had won their greatest victory in the west with a divided command, against a Confederate general who had unified command.[81]

Further attempts by Halleck to get Buell's cooperation proved fruitless. Halleck, hardly able to control himself, bitterly wrote McClellan: "You will regret your decision against me on this point [unified western command]. Your friendship for individuals [Buell] has influenced your judgement. Be it so." The tide was beginning to turn, however: Lincoln, disgusted with McClellan's inactivity, began to take a second look at western reorganization.[82]

PRIOR TO FORT DONELSON, the administration had been fixated on the war in the east. Bates, a prowestern advocate, proved to be the exception on the Cabinet. Westerners were aware of their stepchild status. An Indianapolis paper questioned whether the eastern press would ever give as much value to a western victory as they would to an eastern defeat. The same paper questioned the perceived administration policy of "stripping the West to protect the East, and the capital."[83]

Lincoln remained mindful of certain problems in the west. Sectionalism was strong there, and the people looked with distrust upon the east. A soured economy fueled the disenchantment. Midwestern Democrats also harbored intense racism. Critics of change and peace Democrats (Copperheads) flourished. The Democratic antiwar leaning had, nonetheless, cost the party heavily. The Republicans had scored big in the 1860–61 elections, nearly sweeping the midwestern governorships. The Democrats did remain strong in Congress. In an attempt to tie down the war cause in southern Illinois, the president had appointed John McClernand, a popular prowar Democrat congressman, as brigadier.[84]

The Fort Donelson victory was thus particularly well timed, for it helped consolidate the war movement in the west. Westerners gloated that they, not the east, were successfully prosecuting the war. The success on the Cumberland was specifically seen as an "Illinois victory," especially pleasing to the native Lincoln. The *Chicago Tribune* boasted, "Every school district in the State had its representative there [Fort Donelson]." Illinois had, in fact, provided the life's blood for Grant's command, with twenty-one regiments present. Governor Richard Yates promptly left for Fort Donelson, ostensibly to supervise the care of the state's wounded but probably also to gain favor with voters and an identification with the victory.[85]

The political ramifications went beyond the emergence of western recognition. Many of the top generals at Donelson had been Democrats, which broadened Lincoln's war coalition. The Democratic *Cincinnati Commercial* crowed that Grant "certainly had never shown a symptom of anti-slaveryism" and that C. F. Smith was "rather proslavery than otherwise." McClernand of Illinois and Brigadier General Lew Wallace of Indiana were both widely known Democrats. Indeed, all Grant's division commanders save one were "anti-Republican," according to the paper.[86]

The news of Fort Donelson also temporarily stimulated the western economy. "The fate of Fort Donelson has caused a corresponding rise in pork," proclaimed the Chicago press. In Dubuque, Iowa, buyers began paying more for pork and wheat. On February 25, the Legal Tender Act became law over Democratic opposition, and greenbacks were successfully floated—in part because of the buoyant national mood over the recent western victories.[87]

Geopolitical ramifications aside, the primary benefit of the campaign had been military. The Confederate defensive line in the west had been pierced. The Federals had exploited the cordon defense of the Southerners by concentrating on a single point. Grant desired to push forward and, on February 24, wrote his wife, Julia, "Gen. Halleck is clearly of the same way of thinking."[88]

TWO

A Crisis of Faith

Nashville

IN POPULATION and prominence, Nashville, with 30,000 inhabitants, was second only to New Orleans in the western Confederacy. The state capitol, completed in 1858, dominated the skyline. (Civil War photographs, seemingly showing construction on the building, actually depict landscaping work.) Settled in 1779 as a river town, the city, during the seven or eight years prior to the war, had evolved as a major railroad terminus, with five roads radiating from the center city. Nashville boasted its own water system and gaslight company, two theaters, five daily newspapers, and a paid fire department with two steam fire engines. There were three regional educational facilities— the University of Nashville, Shelby Medical College, and the Nashville Female Institute. Travelers could be housed at several hotels, including the huge and ornate Maxwell House, a portion of which was still under construction. The citizenry annually imported 3,500 tons of ice for mint juleps and food preservation. Less benign indulgences also existed: a flourishing prostitution business counted sixty-nine brothels. The prosperity spread into the suburbs, where immense mansions such as Belle Meade, Belmont, and Roxeby dotted the hillsides.[1]

Nashville also represented Sidney Johnston's industrial and logistical base. Located in or near the city were the T. M. Brennan cannon foundry, a percussion-cap manufactory, the state penitentiary (housing four hundred men at work on military items), and numerous private contractors supplying saddles, cartridge boxes, bridles, horseshoes, sabers, and knapsacks. The Sycamore Stamping Mill had furnished

Johnston's army with 100,000 pounds of powder, besides sending a considerable amount to New Orleans and other places. Thirteen hospitals and numerous private homes provided accommodations for fifty-four hundred sick and wounded soldiers. The Wilson & Armstrong meat-packing plant had slaughtered and prepared thirty thousand hogs for the army by February 1862. The deplorable condition of the Louisville & Nashville Railroad meant that only one thirteen-car train had been able to roll north from Nashville to Bowling Green daily, a fraction of what was needed, but a thin lifeline that kept Hardee's corps supplied. Johnston has been criticized for establishing his base too far north, but he inherited a logistical network previously founded by the state of Tennessee, and his options were limited.[2]

Nashvillians, many of them in church on Sunday morning, February 16, soon learned that Fort Donelson had fallen and that, despite public assurances, Johnston's army would not make a stand. Wild rumors prevailed that Buell's army was at Springfield, Tennessee, only twenty-five miles distant, and that the Federal ironclads would be at the city by afternoon. Panic-stricken civilians soon filled the streets. The railroad depots quickly became jammed, with Governor Isham G. Harris, state legislators, and the city elite—the so-called Nashville gods—among the passengers. Four hundred terrified boarding students at the Female Institute hurriedly packed. A stampede ensued at the Gordon Hospital as sick soldiers needlessly abandoned their beds and went streaming down the clogged roads leading south. A news correspondent found the Franklin Pike choked with refugees.[3]

Before noon on Sunday, and continuing throughout Monday, Johnston's troops, exhausted from their grueling winter march of Saturday, began to cross the Cumberland River suspension bridge. As they filed through the streets of Nashville and out the Murfreesboro Pike, stragglers by the droves broke ranks and mingled with citizens. Johnston, accompanied by an aide, Major Edward Munford, ignominiously departed the city in a buggy on Tuesday, February 18, in the midst of a driving rain.[4]

The army had not cleared the city before riffraff, drunken soldiers, and a lawless element took control of the streets. The doors of the quartermaster and commissary warehouses were thrown open for destitute women, but when the word got out on the street, a near riot developed. Thousands of poor women showed up with wagons, wheelbarrows, even baskets, anything with which to carry a piece or two of meat. Mounted deserters rode into their midst brandishing swords and cocked revolvers and nearly trampling numbers of women and children. Crowds stood in Court House Square, beneath the windows of four- and five-story buildings, as huge bundles were tossed out. Four shopkeepers were shot as they attempted to close their stores to the angry throng.[5]

Floyd, who arrived in the city on Monday from Fort Donelson, was placed in charge of the evacuation. By Tuesday, the efforts of police and two army units, the 1st Missouri and John Hunt Morgan's Kentucky Cavalry Squadron, had proved unavailing, and a serious riot appeared imminent. That morning, Colonel Nathan Bedford Forrest's Tennessee Cavalry Regiment, last of the Donelson refugees, arrived in the city. The forty-one-year-old former Memphis slave-trader and plantation owner was a man of contrasts. He neither smoked nor drank, and loved children; yet he attracted violence. In his earlier years, he and his uncle had been ambushed in Hernando, Mississippi, by a feuding family. Although his uncle was murdered, Forrest killed or wounded all four of the bushwhackers in the gunfight that ensued. Twice his troopers formed ranks and charged the rioters with drawn sabers. When a stout Irishman grabbed Forrest by the collar, the colonel struck him over the head with the butt of his revolver, sending him howling in pain.[6]

Having restored order, Floyd now turned his attention to the burning of two seven-hundred-foot-span Cumberland River bridges. The demolition occurred on the night of February 19, despite futile pleas from civilians to spare the bridges for trade purposes. Dr. John Lindsley, working late in the hospital that night, noted that the "wire bridge was a flooring of fire; the whole lit up brilliantly the quiet sleeping city and suburbs." By 3 A.M., both bridges lay smoldering.[7]

Throughout February 20–22, the Confederate rear guard made efforts to remove the immense stores of the city. Johnston recalled thirty-five railroad cars from Chattanooga; Floyd swept Nashville for all available wagons and carts, eventually gathering ninety vehicles with teams. This transportation enabled troops and volunteer citizens to haul to the railroad and remove seven hundred boxes of clothing, several hundred bales of cloth, seven to eight hundred wagonloads of meat (amounting to 250,000 pounds of bacon), and thirty wagonloads of small-arms ammunition and fixed-artillery rounds. Crates of rifling and percussion-cap machinery were taken away, as well as an unspecified number of field guns, caissons, and battery wagons. Trains were loaded as fast as they arrived. Twelve hundred sick soldiers jammed aboard boxcars for the trip to Chattanooga. Transportation ceased on late Saturday, February 22, when two small bridges of the Nashville &

Chattanooga Railroad south of the city were washed away by heavy rains, leaving only the railroad to Decatur, Alabama, operational. Fortunately, 30,000 butchered hogs at Shelbyville, Tennessee, were safely removed to Atlanta, Georgia.[8]

Despite these Herculean efforts, the losses incurred by the withdrawal from Nashville proved incalculable. About 75,000 pounds of pork remained at the wharf, and several warehouses were never even opened. Another 400,000 to 500,000 pounds of pork were reportedly left at the insane asylum. Five hundred barrels of government whiskey were smashed at the railroad depot. An enormous amount of quartermaster stores, including 10,000 pairs of shoes and boots and 500 new tents, was lost to the Yankees, not counting what was stolen by looters or simply given away. Over forty cannon were spiked and a dozen left lying at the Brennan foundry. Forrest, still embittered over the loss of Fort Donelson, blamed Floyd for the debacle. More to the point, Johnston exhibited a complete lack of leadership throughout the crisis. Even though his staff had had five months to formulate an evacuation plan, at a time when he fully expected Buell's army to advance in overwhelming numbers, no such contingency had been devised. If Fort Donelson had demonstrated Johnston's inability as a strategist, Nashville revealed his deficiency as a logistician.[9]

Murfreesboro

JOHNSTON WITHDREW his five brigades to Murfreesboro, Tennessee, a prosperous town of 2,000 inhabitants thirty-five miles southeast of Nashville. A journalist who viewed the troops noted their varied dress. Martial law was declared, and army headquarters were established in the Rutherford County Courthouse.[10]

In deportment and appearance, Johnston seemed well suited for his present assignment. Although fifty-nine years old, he was vigorous and, according to a correspondent, the "picture of good health." Standing slightly over six feet in height, he weighed just under two hundred pounds, making him somewhat "heavy set," according to the reporter. The streaks of gray in his wavy dark-brown hair and his rapidly receding hairline revealed his age. He had a thick mustache, blue-green eyes, and a square jaw. Two scars marked his right side, at the pelvis and the hip, the result of a ball that had struck him in an 1838 duel. Although possessing a serious nature, Johnston was not without a dry wit and could be sarcastic. His demeanor was quiet and modest. He smoked a pipe, possessed a contemplative nature, and was on occasion subject to depression. Modern characterizations of a floundering, frustrated, and disappointed man, with a weak personality, an overly gentle nature, and a childlike faith leave much unsaid. All those who knew Johnston at West Point, and subsequently became his peers in the Regular Army, saw him as impressive and formidable.[11]

Although perhaps initially dazed and paralyzed following the loss of Fort Donelson, Johnston quickly regained his composure. Chief Engineer Jeremy Gilmer wrote his wife: "The General wears a very anxious face. Still he expressed confidence that better fortunes await us." W. C. Whitthorne, a Tennessee state official, visited the general at Murfreesboro, and recalled how he smiled, talked confidently, and promised to recapture Nashville by the end of May. Before a Mobile reporter, Johnston stoically accepted the public censure and talked optimistically of the future.[12]

The Confederate forces at Murfreesboro increased when Crittenden's two brigades, fresh from their defeat at Somerset, made a juncture. Including the remnants of the Fort Donelson garrison, 17,000 men were now concentrated. Johnston consolidated his separate commands into three divisions under Hardee, Crittenden, and Pillow, with a reserve brigade under Brigadier General John C. Breckinridge. Forrest's Cavalry Regiment and John Wharton's Texas Rangers remained unassigned. The structure was unwieldy, showed little effort, and lacked creativity.[13]

Johnston began the task of rebuilding his army. On the afternoon of February 27, Hardee conducted a review of Patrick Cleburne's brigade on the Shelbyville Pike two miles south of Murfreesboro. Local citizens congregated as the troops marched to martial music and flags snapped in the February wind. Many of the Tennessee troops deserted after Fort Donelson, a fact conceded by Johnston. Support within the officer corps remained feeble. Writing to his wife from Murfreesboro, Colonel Liddell confided: "Here the conclusion is almost universal that he [Johnston] is totally unfit for the position he holds in the Confederate army, and if he does nothing to retrieve his character soon, he will be regarded as hopelessly embicile [sic]." Although Hardee quieted one of his staff officers who openly denounced the general, in private he agreed with Liddell's assessment.[14]

Opinion was mixed even on Johnston's personal staff. Assistant Adjutant General A. P. Brewster and aides George Baylor, Edward Munford, and Thomas Jack all solidly supported him. Another assistant adjutant general, Yale law graduate William Preston, was Johnston's brother-in-law. Colonel William Mackall, the army chief of staff, considered Johnston overrated. Another staff officer, Chief Engineer Gilmer, later expressed his opinion of Johnston and his generals: "Among them all, I fear there is not a Napoleon."[15]

More crucial than the army's dissatisfaction was its degenerating strategic position. Buell's army in Nashville was estimated at no fewer than 40,000 men and possibly as many as 65,000. Grant's force, believed to be 50,000 strong, maintained its position at Fort Donelson and Clarksville. Faced with overwhelming numbers, Johnston feared he would be caught in a pincer movement.[16]

Although the public, North and South alike, expected a major battle at Murfreesboro, Johnston never intended to make a stand. He had decided on February 7, at the Covington House conference at Bowling Green, that if Nashville fell the army would withdraw to Stevenson, Alabama, in order to protect Chattanooga. In a meeting with Beauregard (who had arrived days earlier) in Nashville on February 14, Johnston repeated his plan to fall back along the line of the Nashville, Stevenson, and Chattanooga rail line.[17]

Once at Murfreesboro, however, Johnston began to reconsider his options and looked to Decatur, Alabama, midway between Chattanooga and Corinth, Mississippi. The shift was significant, because it drew the "army" increasingly away from the Tennessee Valley toward the Mississippi Valley. Some historians have questioned the decision, asserting that the Tennessee Valley held far greater logistical and strategic value. It has been suggested that Beauregard's alarmist telegrams from western Tennessee and his dominant personality served as a magnet in drawing Johnston west rather than east.[18]

There is no evidence that Beauregard suggested a shift to Decatur prior to February 22. On that date, Colonel Gilmer wrote to his wife: "We expect to leave here [Murfreesboro] in a few days to some point south of this—maybe Decatur—maybe Chattanooga—maybe some other point." Also on that date, Johnston ordered Hardee to send Brigadier General Thomas Hindman's brigade to Huntsville, Alabama. Hindman was to examine and protect the roads and ferries by which the Tennessee River could be crossed to reach Decatur. Governor Harris conferred with Johnston in Murfreesboro, probably on February 23. Having previously met with Beauregard in Jackson, Tennessee, the governor expressed the Creole's desire that both wings of the army concentrate at Corinth. Johnston, according to Harris, promptly replied that he was in the process of making just such a move. On February 24, Johnston informed Davis that he was moving via Decatur "to the valley of the Mississippi."[19]

In postwar years, Johnston and Beauregard supporters fought bitterly over who should be credited with selecting Corinth. Most historians have concluded that the town was an obvious choice and that both generals probably decided independently upon the location. Johnston's February 22 dispatch to Hardee confirms that the general had shifted his destination from Stevenson to Decatur prior to Harris's visit. Whether or not Johnston planned to move to Corinth, as Harris expressed, or was influenced by Beauregard, cannot now be determined.[20]

Assuming that Johnston independently chose the Mississippi Valley, several factors may have influenced his decision. For six months, the army commander had chosen to fight a two-front war. The selection of Stevenson, made before the surrender of Fort Donelson, continued that strategy. Following the loss of the garrison, Johnston probably considered this strategy no longer feasible. Desperation dictated that a choice be made. "I am compelled to elect whether he [enemy] shall be permitted to occupy Middle Tennessee, or turn Columbus, take Memphis and open the valley of the Mississippi," he wrote Davis on February 27. The general stated his preference for the Mississippi Valley. The issue was still being debated a year later, this time by Joseph E. Johnston. Interestingly, he chose Tennessee over Mississippi for concentration. Davis refused to take a stand either way, believing that both areas could be held.[21]

Johnston may also have been operating under the false assumption that the Richmond government had secured Chattanooga. Following the Somerset defeat, the War Department rushed reinforcements to eastern Tennessee—six regiments from Virginia, four from the Gulf Coast, and scattered units from North Carolina. In addition, Johnston had dispatched Floyd's 2,500-man brigade (which had escaped at Fort Donelson) to Chattanooga. These forces, it was believed, made good the loss of Crittenden's division. The new "army" turned out to be a paper force. Major General E. Kirby Smith, commanding the District of East Tennessee, reported that three of the regiments from Virginia had been mustered out before they arrived and two others had been redirected to Huntsville. Measles had decimated two of the Gulf Coast regiments. No sooner had Floyd's Virginians arrived in Chattanooga than the inept general furloughed them. As a result, eastern Tennessee lay open to invasion.[22]

Johnston continued to act as a corps commander, choosing to direct the eastern wing of the army personally. Even more significant, he increasingly viewed the two wings not as corps of the same army but as separate armies. Some historians have noted that Johnston sat passively while Beauregard named his wing the "Army of the Mississippi Valley." Some weeks before that, however, Johnston himself had labeled the eastern wing the "Central Army," and he even spoke of the force as "my command." In his February 27 letter to Benjamin, Johnston spoke of moving to Decatur in order to "cooperate or unite" with the Louisiana general, a virtual admission that he considered Beauregard an equal.[23]

Jackson, Tennessee

BEAUREGARD'S REPUTATION had preceded him. The Confederate press claimed that he had come to the west to replace George Crittenden in eastern Tennessee. Halleck heard via McClellan that the Louisiana general was bringing fifteen regiments from the Virginia army with him. Both rumors proved false, but Halleck acted upon his information and hurriedly moved on the twin rivers. Beauregard thus arrived in the west just as Johnston's position in central Kentucky disintegrated. As the Bowling Green column withdrew to Murfreesboro, Beauregard was given virtual independent command of the troops between the Tennessee and Mississippi Rivers.[24]

On February 17, 1862, while he was on the way to inspect the Columbus fortifications, Beauregard's declining health forced him to stop at Jackson, Tennessee, a railroad town of six hundred inhabitants. He had undergone throat surgery before leaving Virginia that resulted in laryngitis, a condition made worse by a bronchial infection and fever. So depressed was he over the state of affairs that he initially considered returning to Virginia. His correspondence croaked with pessimism. He bitterly complained to Representative Pryor: "I am taking the helm when the ship of state is already on the breakers." Exactly what he meant by "taking the helm" has led to some interesting speculation. It has been argued that from the outset it was Beauregard's intent to wrestle de-facto, if not formal, command from Johnston, whose reputation lay shattered on the heels of Fort Donelson. Others insist that the Louisiana general simply rushed in to fill the leadership void that existed.[25]

Two very different portraits of Beauregard have emerged. Some historians speculate that a dazed, shaken, and floundering Sidney Johnston gradually began to hand more power over to the grasping and calculating Creole. Others have characterized Beauregard as hysterical over the deteriorating military situation in western Tennessee, panicking, unable to handle the responsibility laid upon him. There is little doubt that the gaunt and emaciated general approached physical collapse. On February 22, he admitted that he was unable to take command. Four days later, his health was "not much improving." From his arrival at Jackson to the end of February, however, he engaged in numerous conferences, dictated correspondence, and formulated strategy. Even in sickness, Beauregard was a factor with which to contend.[26]

The most telling evidence of his capabilities during this time was his dealings with Leonidas Polk. Summoned to Jackson, the former Episcopalian bishop and personal friend of Jefferson Davis and Johnston arrived on February 19. Besides his questionable military credentials, Polk's main problem was that he had been a bishop too long to take orders. He also bristled at being superseded in command. Polk initially submitted his resignation, but Davis talked him into staying. Hearing that Beauregard planned a withdrawal from Columbus, the bishop loudly protested. Six months he had labored to build up the defenses of that place, and he remained mentally unprepared to evacuate. "I felt in leaving it as if I were leaving home," he confided to his daughter. Polk attempted to compromise, suggesting that a reduced garrison of 6,000 to 7,000 troops would suffice, but Beauregard proved unrelenting.[27]

The ailing general's firmness with the uncooperative Polk, someone whom Johnston had been unable to master, proved to be one of his finest moments in the Shiloh Campaign. The Creole saw Columbus for what it was—a trap. Had Polk been left to his own devices, it is likely that his corps would have gotten bottled up in the town and ultimately captured. Such a scenario, coming on the heels of Fort Donelson, would have broken the backbone of Confederate resistance in the west. Beauregard correctly warned the War Department that Columbus "must meet the fate of Fort Donelson, with the loss of [Polk's] entire army."[28]

Richmond

As DETAILS of the Fort Donelson fiasco became known, Johnston became the subject of severe criticism. The populace, which had strongly supported his appointment five months earlier, now clamored for his removal. The Richmond press was loud in its denunciation, labeling Johnston as "mechanical and unimaginative." Because of his close friendship with Davis, the press quickly linked the bungled affair to the administration. "Shall the Cause fail because Mr. Davis is incompetent? . . . Tennessee under Sidney Johnston is likely to fall. Mr. Davis retains him," wrote Bagby of the *Mercury*. Nor was the general spared in the western press. The *Memphis Appeal, New Orleans Crescent, New Orleans Delta*, and the Atlanta *Southern Confederacy* all denounced Johnston.[29]

Colonel Josiah Gorgas, at the Ordnance Bureau, looked past Johnston and placed culpability at the door of the Executive Mansion: "Ten thousand men would have converted Donelson from an overwhelming disaster to a victory—and 18,000 men were literally doing nothing under Gen. Bragg at Pensacola and Mobile. Our President is unfortunately no military genius and could not see the relative value of position. Pensacola was nothing compared to Donelson."[30]

During the second week in March, the political crisis became more focused. On March 8, senators and representatives of the Tennessee congressional delegation, with the exception of Judge G. W. Swan of Knoxville, called upon the president. The delegation was headed by Gustavus H. Henry, who, ironically, had earlier petitioned for Johnston's appointment. The petition pleaded for Johnston's removal from command. No suggestion was made as to a successor, the delegation believing that choice to be Davis's prerogative. The president strongly defended his friend, however, concluding: "If Sidney Johnston is not a General, the Confederacy has none to give you."[31]

Obviously not appreciative of Davis's loyalty to his appointee, the Tennesseans took their case to the halls of Congress. On March 10, a heated debate ensued in the lower house pertaining to the conduct of the Quartermaster Department in the Fort Donelson surrender. Representative John Adkins, usually a Davis supporter, declared that Johnston had lost the public's confidence in Tennessee. He moved, therefore, that the investigation be expanded to include the general's conduct in the losses of Forts Henry and Donelson and Nashville.[32]

Some congressmen from Kentucky, Johnston's home state, and

from Texas, his adoptive state, came to the general's defense. The fist-pounding Henry Foote of Nashville, archenemy of the Davis administration, remained adamant in his denunciation. The vote on congressional investigation was finally called, with the yeas prevailing fifty-two to twenty-three. A select committee of five western congressmen, with Foote as chairman, was appointed to investigate the western department concerning the recent losses.[33]

Davis faced a serious problem. If he relieved Johnston, the obvious replacement would be his second-in-command—Beauregard. Elevating him to top command in the west, although it would have been a popular decision, proved unacceptable to Davis. Yet there is no evidence that this factor blocked Johnston's removal. Nor is there any evidence that alternatives were considered—Polk, Bragg, or Hardee. Davis's inordinate loyalty to Johnston never wavered.[34]

The issue was far from resolved. On March 11, the congressional committee found the reports of Pillow and Floyd unsatisfactory regarding their conduct at Fort Donelson. Davis ordered Johnston to relieve them. Political pressure remained intense. On March 12, Thomas Bragg noted in his diary that Tennessee congressmen bitterly complained of Johnston's "abandonment of Ten. as they term it." On March 17, the bellicose Foote once again took to the floor of the House. He charged that Secretary of War Benjamin, who had not cooperated with the committee, should be held in contempt of Congress, which would mean actual censure of the Davis administration.[35]

Some did come to the support of the Davis-Johnston team. A number of congressmen, including Judge Swan, a member of the Military Affairs Committee, continued to express their confidence in the general. Additionally, some western newspapers began to express a different view. The *Memphis Avalanche, Mobile Daily Advertiser & Register,* and *New Orleans Picayune* all proclaimed that Johnston was being wrongly singled out. The last flatly blamed congressmen who were afraid to risk unpopularity and who threatened Davis with opposition if he did not retain troops in their districts.[36]

St. Louis

HEAVYSET FORTY-SEVEN-YEAR-OLD Henry W. Halleck, "Old Brains" to his men, had a well-deserved reputation as an intellectual. Phi Beta Kappa, bilingual, third in his class at West Point, prolific military au-

thor, offered a Harvard engineering professorship, head of a successful law firm—the profile was impressive. Even Grant, who would one
day grow to detest him, conceded his brilliance. He was also distant,
lacking in charm, devious, and possessed of a schoolmasterly demeanor, given to conversing with a bug-eyed stare and picking his
teeth after dinner. Essentially a bureaucrat and a theorist, he lacked the
charisma and temperament of a bold and inspiring field commander.
Rarely did he venture beyond his headquarters at the Planter's House
Hotel.[37]

Halleck and Grant had no West Point or Mexican War connections and had met only once, while in California, yet the department
commander disliked Grant from the outset. Although "Old Brains"
could be unnecessarily contemptuous, he had reason for suspicion. He
probably had heard of Grant's reputation for drinking in the old army
and very clearly knew of, and believed, recent rumors of alcoholism at
Belmont and Cairo, Illinois. Upon hearing of the victory at Fort
Donelson, he reportedly expressed his amazement that "a drunkard"
could win such a prize. Halleck was also aware of, and most likely re-
sented, the fact that Grant had obtained his position through political
ties. He considered the brigadier's performance at Belmont to be reckless.[38]

Back in January 1862, Grant, at his own request, had gone to St.
Louis to confer with Halleck on strategy. The meeting proved a disaster. The department commander represented everything Grant was
not—institutional army, successful civilian, intellectual. Grant confessed that he was intimidated and stammered. When he took out a
map and proposed a strike at the twin rivers, Halleck cut him short
and, according to the story told by an officer present, curtly said, in effect, that when Grant's opinion was wanted it would be asked for.
Within ten minutes the conference had concluded. What Grant did
not know, nor was he told, was that Halleck had previously endorsed
just such a plan.[39]

Subsequent press accounts did not help Grant's case. Correspondents learned that the Illinois general had not entrenched at Fort
Donelson and was not present on the battlefield when the Confederate
attack began (failings that would recur at Shiloh). Several journalists
omitted Grant's name from press accounts and credited C. F. Smith
with the Donelson victory. One reporter, probably Frank Chapman of
the *New York Herald*, spread a false rumor that Grant was so drunk before the battle that he had to be helped onto his horse.[40]

Halleck's continued animosity may have been twofold in cause.

The St. Louis commander was embarrassed that the man whom he had planned to replace had become a national hero. As late as February 8, following the victory at Fort Henry, Halleck had requested the assignment of old Brigadier General Ethan Allen Hitchcock, a personal friend living in retirement in St. Louis, to command Grant's forces. Hitchcock, in poor health, had recently shown more inclination toward spiritualism than toward military affairs. He declined the offer, writing in his diary: "As soon as Donelson surrendered to Grant I felt it a positive duty to decline the commission & did so." The victory on the Cumberland also brought on more pressure for action, for which Halleck was neither logistically nor mentally prepared. Although instructed to be cautious, Grant moved swiftly to Clarksville, Tennessee. From his perspective, Halleck was "one of the greatest men of the age," a feeling not reciprocated.[41]

The crux of the matter came down to simple jealousy: Halleck had been eclipsed by a subordinate. The department commander barely acknowledged Grant's role in the Fort Donelson victory (a personal congratulatory note was never sent him) and instead recommended C. F. Smith for promotion—a veiled insult to Grant. Sensing the mood of the nation, Halleck later bowed to the inevitable and recommended Grant for promotion. The Senate quickly confirmed Grant as major general. Despite all his efforts to the contrary, a chagrined Halleck viewed Grant as the only one whose career had materially benefited from Donelson.[42]

By early March, it appeared to Halleck that the army commander was flaunting his self-imposed independence. "I have had no communication with General Grant for more than a week," he wrote McClellan on March 3, adding that Grant had taken an unauthorized trip to Nashville (in Buell's jurisdiction) and failed to send in returns, and that his army, according to accusations that had reached St. Louis, appeared demoralized by victory. "It is hard to censure a successful general immediately after a battle, but I think he richly deserves it." The general-in-chief quickly replied: "Do not hesitate to arrest Grant if the good of the service requires it, and place C. F. Smith in command." McClellan, perhaps also jealous of Grant's recent notoriety, may have taken some satisfaction in making this response.[43]

Brigadier General William T. Sherman, a friend of Halleck's, later wrote that the department commander had worked himself "into a passion" and should have been more patient. The tension created by being ignored during so crucial a period, however, must have been intense. Not until March 9 did Halleck finally hear from Grant. A trip to

Grant's headquarters in early March would have been in order. Halleck instead remained glued to his desk and vented his frustration to Washington. Precisely what he was seeking—the destruction of Grant's career, or merely solace for himself and censure for the general—is not clear. His irritation at having been turned down for theater command a week and a half earlier may have been a contributing factor. Whatever the case, McClellan's response may have served to up the ante. Halleck now had to make certain that a true leadership crisis had indeed existed. Thus, on March 4, he told McClellan that Grant had "resumed his former habit"—an obvious reference to drinking. He did not, however, "deem it advisable to arrest" the popular general "at present." Halleck immediately ordered Grant to remain at Fort Henry and he placed C. F. Smith in command. Thus, precisely sixteen days after the greatest victory in the war to date, Grant was without a command.[44]

Fort Henry

BY EARLY MARCH, Grant and his army were back at Fort Henry on the Tennessee River, where a major expedition was taking shape. Unaware that any problem existed with department headquarters, the Illinois general, suffering from a severe chest cold and a prolonged headache, was stunned to read Halleck's telegram of March 4. Tears welling up in his eyes, he passed the dispatch around for his staff to read. The general later wrote that he considered himself virtually under arrest. On March 5, he wrote of the circumstances to Julia, concluding, "It may well be all right but I don't now see it." Chief Surgeon John Brinton remembered how Halleck's order "cut him [Grant] bitterly." To a friend the surgeon wrote, "Halleck did not arrest Grant, but ordered him to remain here [at Fort Henry], as bad if not worse."[45]

On March 6, Halleck continued his attack by firing off another letter. He called Grant's trip to Nashville after its surrender "a serious complaint at Washington." Grant calmly insisted that he had not disobeyed orders. Returns of troop strength had been regularly forwarded to the department chief-of-staff, Brigadier General George W. Cullum, at Cairo, Illinois. As for the trip to Nashville, it had been solely to consult with Buell and not for any personal reasons. He concluded that he would remain aboard *Tigress* rather than at Fort Henry as ordered, since the fort was six feet under water. Halleck could not miss the caustic implication that he was so out of touch with matters at the front that he was unaware of the flooding on the Tennessee River.[46]

Grant began to question whether there were "enemies between you [Halleck] and myself," referring to Cullum and the possibility that vital information had not been forwarded to St. Louis. "You are mistaken," Halleck emphatically replied. "There is no enemy between you and me." He insisted that no information had been received concerning numbers and positions and that McClellan was "out of all patience waiting for it."[47]

Meanwhile, command of the upcoming Tennessee River expedition fell to Major General Charles F. Smith, recently promoted for his conduct at Fort Donelson. It was not the first time his name had surfaced. The fifty-five-year-old Smith had been commandant at West Point when Grant was a cadet. Many in the old army, Halleck among them, believed an injustice had been committed by placing Smith under Grant. Politics had made the difference, and Grant as much as admitted the unfairness of the situation. He maintained an awe for the old soldier and even found it difficult to give him orders—"He dislikes to give me an order and says I ought to be in his place," Smith wrote. Grant turned his command over to him and graciously extended his congratulations. On the last evening before the expedition, the two walked together, and their relationship, according to Brinton, was "stronger than ever."[48]

Smith proved a popular choice. He looked like a general—over six feet tall, slender, with a long twisted white mustache. He was highly revered by Regular Army officers, many of whom had been cadets at West Point while he was commandant. There were some questions concerning his age and health: he had become very ill from exposure at Fort Donelson, where he lay all night in the snow.[49]

As the army bustled with activity, Grant sat idled and disheartened. Surprisingly, considering his newfound fame, an organized public outcry never developed. A story leaked to the Washington press corps stated that Grant had been relieved because of his conduct at Fort Donelson, specifically his absence on the battlefield at the moment of the Confederate attack. Even the Democratically controlled *Chicago Times* gave a muted response. Though hoping that the issue would soon be resolved, the paper conceded that Grant's absence at the critical moment "was avoidable." The troops in Grant's army at first gathered sympathetically in front of *Tigress*, but quickly embraced Smith as their new commander.[50]

During this time, a small but significant ceremony was held aboard *Tigress*. An ivory-handled presentation sword was given to Grant to honor the victory at Fort Donelson. The assembled audience included brigadiers, colonels, and staff officers, who used the occasion to renew their confidence in the general. Colonel C. C. Marsh of the 20th Illinois condemned "the jealousy caused by your brilliant success." Grant hurried onto the deck, where his friend Chief Surgeon Brinton found him crying. "Doctor, send it to my wife. I will never wear a sword again," he said.[51]

Even at that moment, the power struggle was turning in Grant's favor. Standing by his innocence, the general requested to be relieved—not from duty, but pointedly "from the Dept." In Washington, Stanton and Washburne belatedly entered the fray. Rawlins had earlier written the latter declaring, "We are lying at Fort Henry, I believe, to the petty jealousies of some interested parties." Nine of Grant's senior officers (including McClernand) also came to his defense, signing a letter that deplored his removal. C. F. Smith openly denounced Grant's treatment. Eventually Lincoln himself concluded the affair by demanding that facts, not rumors, be forthcoming. Halleck blinked. The issue of his own making was turning on him. More than ready to drop the matter, he feebly explained to Washington that all issues had been satisfactorily resolved.[52]

Once Grant was restored to command, the western press belatedly came to his support. The *Cincinnati Gazette* claimed that the entire episode had been "frivolous." Even the Republican-dominated *Chicago Tribune*, though admitting "no love" for Grant, concluded that the charges had been "the product of red tape spirit and policy." The paper stated that the general's alleged intemperance, which was well known on the streets of Chicago, was untrue.[53]

The mystery of the miscommunication was finally resolved. The telegram line ended at Cairo, Illinois, but an advancing line had been extended to Paducah and Smithland, at the mouths of the Tennessee and Cumberland Rivers. Grant's dispatches went by boat to Cairo, but many of Halleck's messages went to the end of the advancing line. The telegraph officer at Fort Henry turned out to be a Rebel sympathizer who, for over a week, had withheld some of Halleck's dispatches, thus creating the crisis. In this campaign, big doors would swing on small hinges.[54]

Occupied Nashville

OHIO-BORN FORTY-FOUR-YEAR-OLD Don Carlos Buell had fought in the
Mexican War, but most of his recent military service had been in the
adjutant general's office. Unlike Grant, Buell had no hint of moral
scandal in his background, although he did harbor a skeleton in the
closet. Two years after graduating from West Point, he faced a court-
martial for using the flat of his sword to punish a soldier. Although he
was acquitted, certain politicians demanded a new trial. President John
Tyler ended the matter, but Buell had gained a reputation as a harsh
disciplinarian.[55]

Buell owed his present position largely to his friend McClellan—
"It was McClellan's own work," claimed a New York journalist. His
letters to McClellan began "Dear Friend." He had worked tirelessly
during his three-month tenure, rarely going to bed before 2 or 3 A.M.
As a proslavery Democrat married to a Southerner, he came under Republican suspicion. His policy of not brigading regiments by states
brought him into early conflict with Governors Oliver P. Morton and
Richard Yates—both Republicans. The lenient rule he was to impose
upon Nashville (he strongly, but vainly, opposed Lincoln's policy of a
military governor over Tennessee) also angered the Radicals. Aloof,
stern, and rarely confiding in others, Buell was competent but not brilliant.[56]

A Cincinnati correspondent criticized Buell for moving too
slowly to Nashville, thus allowing Johnston's army to escape. He con-
tended that the march could have been completed in two or three days
rather than the actual nine. The *New York Tribune* added its condem-
nation. The picture at Army of the Ohio headquarters was somewhat
murkier. By February 18, "reliable information" indicated that the
Confederates were concentrating a heavy force at Nashville. As late as
February 23, intelligence reports stated that Johnston had assembled
40,000 men in middle Tennessee—an army the size of Buell's. Rumors
were also afoot that large detachments had left the Southern army at
Manassas, Virginia, bound for Tennessee.[57]

What were Buell's options under the circumstances?

He could have ignored his own scout reports (all faulty, as it
turned out) and hastened to Nashville. In hindsight, such a gamble
might have paid off, and Johnston's rear guard might have been
mauled. Yet the stakes were high and the results unknown. A year and a
half later, General William Rosecrans attempted something similar in

northern Georgia and almost got the Army of the Cumberland destroyed in the process.[58]

Buell could have adopted Halleck's plan and moved the Army of the Ohio to Clarksville and thence upriver by transports to Nashville, jointly with his forces. Although there was a turnpike from Bowling Green to Nashville, there was only an ordinary road to Clarksville. Buell insisted on February 19 that the road was virtually impassable because of recent rains and that he would require eight to ten days to reach Clarksville.[59]

The third option was to take the reports seriously and move on Nashville in force. Buell rightly chose this option, but it meant repairing the railroad and all bridges en route. The general promised to move on the Tennessee capital "with all the speed I can," but explained that he could make no formal advance until repairs had been completed. On February 22, he did place a thousand men on railroad cars that the Rebels had failed to destroy at Bowling Green. He anticipated that they could come within nine miles of Nashville that evening. Heavy rains further damaged the track, however, and the troops did not arrive at the city outskirts until the evening of February 24, about the same time as the brigades marching by the turnpike. Lincoln was nonetheless highly pleased with Buell's "cautious vigor."[60]

The ironclads could have taken Nashville on February 22, a full three days before Buell arrived. Halleck had received information that Johnston had evacuated the city, panic had erupted, and no resistance would be made. Despite the pleadings of Grant and Flag Officer Andrew H. Foote, Halleck denied the gunboats passage beyond Clarksville. Since Nashville was in Buell's jurisdiction, he waited to receive word "from Kentucky and Washington." Foote thus sat and fumed as the Rebels were allowed an additional seventy-two hours to remove tons of valuable supplies. "It [the decision to wait] was jealousy on the part of McClellan and Halleck," Foote disgustedly related to his wife.[61]

When the Ohio general finally arrived with Ormsby Mitchel's division at the Cumberland River, opposite Nashville, he discovered, much to his surprise and embarrassment, that William "Bull" Nelson's division of his army had already secured the city and raised the Stars and Stripes over the capital. Buell, at Lincoln's suggestion, had previously sent the division to reinforce Grant at Fort Donelson. By the time it arrived, the battle had been won, so Grant, ignoring department lines, sent the division upriver on transports to Nashville. Finding the city evacuated, Nelson landed on the south bank. Having struggled with mud, burned bridges, and damaged tracks for a week and a half, Buell had been beaten to the prize by Grant—in his own department and with his own troops![62]

Humiliated and furious, Buell immediately returned the transports to Clarksville with orders for C. F. Smith's division of Grant's army to rush to Nashville. Since Nelson's division (6,000 troops) was on the south bank "contrary to my [Buell's] orders" (meaning that Grant had interfered), the division was in immediate danger of a Confederate attack. Smith contemptuously commented to Grant, who had arrived at Clarksville, that the order "was nonsense," but "of course I must obey."[63]

The incident bordered on the ludicrous. Johnston, hanging on for dear life at Murfreesboro, had no intention of attacking. Even if there had been a danger, Buell could have used the transports to cross Mitchel's division (10,000 strong) to the south bank, or to withdraw Nelson's men to the north bank. Also, George Thomas's division (15,000 men) was moving up fast in the rear. Indeed, Smith's division returned to Clarksville the same day it arrived at Nashville.[64]

Nor had Buell's discomfiture ended. Grant decided once again to ignore jurisdictional lines and go to Nashville to confer with him. He arrived on February 27, only to discover that the department commander—for security reasons, according to a journalist—was still in Edgefield, on the north bank. Grant had no such qualms and freely went about the city, visiting the hospitals and even paying respects to Mrs. James K. Polk, widow of the late president. The incident, widely reported in the Northern press, left Buell in a most foolish light. Grant sent him a rather terse note which said, among other things, that Johnston was now not far from the Tennessee line, the implication being that Buell could relax. He signed the note: "U. S. Grant, major general," as though he were writing to a junior, not a department head.[65]

On his way to the wharf at the end of the day, Grant finally met with Buell; the exchange was formal and cool. The Ohio department commander insisted that the Rebels were still in the area and that fighting was occurring only ten to twelve miles away. Grant dismissed this as fighting with the Confederate rear guard. Buell adamantly claimed that "he knew" his information was correct. "Well, I do not know," retorted Grant. He later wrote innocently of the trip in his memoirs, but Grant, enamored with his good press, had acted cockily and interfered in Buell's affairs. The trip accomplished nothing, other than alienating Buell and further straining relations with Halleck.[66]

The bickering between Buell and Halleck continued unabated.

The two vaguely agreed to meet and confer, although, unknown to Halleck, the Ohio general planned to have McClellan present. Halleck continued his ineffectual efforts to get Buell to move his army up the Tennessee River in a joint operation with Grant's forces. "If Johnston has destroyed the railroad and bridge in his rear he cannot return and attack you. Why not come to Tennessee and operate with me?" he queried. Buell countered with a proposal to meet in Louisville (his ground), but Halleck insisted that he could not possibly leave St. Louis for the present.[67]

By the first week in March Buell had amassed four divisions, 3,000 wagons, and 15,000 to 18,000 horses and mules at the Nashville wharf. By mid-March, six divisions with 55,000 men had assembled. Two army telegraph operators accompanied Buell's army and took over the Confederate telegraph office, which had been left conveniently intact. By March 26, the Louisville & Nashville Railroad bridge had been repaired.[68]

Many of the Federals held a decidedly low opinion of the city. Writing to his wife on March 5, Hoosier Thomas Harrison noted: "Nashville is not so pretty a town as Indianapolis. The grounds are very uneven and the streets look like alleys. They are narrow." Artilleryman James Mohr noted to his brother that every shop in town had been shut up. Michigan cannoneer Harold Bartlett related to his wife: "I tell you, Nashville is a desolate looking city. All is to be seen is soldiers by the thousands coming in all the time."[69]

Although Federal picket posts extended ten miles south of the city, minor skirmishing kept Buell's army huddled within the Nashville perimeter. Audacious raids by Captain John Hunt Morgan magnified Rebel intentions. Northern press accounts generally gave Johnston's strength at 12,000; the *Chicago Times* insisted that the number could not exceed 20,000. Buell, however, continued to believe that the number was closer to 30,000. If Buell had moved rapidly, he perhaps could have moved down the Murfreesboro Pike and annihilated the Southern army. It would have been a running fight, however, for Johnston would have hastily withdrawn.[70]

THREE

Golden Opportunities

New Orleans

NEW ORLEANS, with its 160,000 inhabitants, was the largest city in the Confederacy. Many of the old customs held firm, but the blockade and increasing fear of a naval attack had dulled much of the festive atmosphere. Unemployment ran high, food had become scarce, and the number of destitute poor was increasing. A public outcry was thus heard when, in February 1862, the War Department ordered 5,000 troops from the city to reinforce Johnston in Tennessee. Lovell replied on February 12 that he would start a brigade of five regiments and a battery within two days, but was convinced that the departure would create a panic in the city. Commanding the troops would be Massachusetts-born Brigadier General Daniel Ruggles, a grousing old man in poor health who was generally detested by those around him.[1]

A transportation shortage caused the brigade to be strung out for days. The 19th Louisiana boarded boxcars at the New Orleans, Jackson & Great Northern Railroad on February 16 and, after switching to tracks of the Mississippi Central at Jackson, arrived at Grand Junction, Tennessee, the next afternoon. The 18th Louisiana could not get a train out and had to be housed in a cotton shed until February 25. By March 9, seven regiments and two batteries, the Miles (Louisiana) Light Artillery and the Vaiden (Mississippi) Light Artillery, had departed. The 20th Louisiana left the Crescent City on March 11.[2]

Some outfits were drawn in from coastal duty. Colonel Henry Allen's 4th Louisiana, scattered along the Louisiana-Mississippi coast, reassembled in New Orleans. After conducting a dress parade in Annunciation Square on February 24, the troops boarded two trains for the journey north. The 7th Mississippi and 3rd Mississippi Battalion also departed, the former on February 27. An accident occurred at Amite, Louisiana, when the "down" train collided with the troop train, smashing two passenger cars and leaving twenty-one dead and forty-five injured. "I counted twenty dead bodies lying side by side and I don't know how many wounded there were. It was an awful affair," recorded a witness.[3]

On February 21, Beauregard prepared a confidential circular to the governors of Tennessee, Alabama, Mississippi, and Louisiana calling for ninety-day troops. The response from the first three proved negligible; Alabama and Mississippi sent only a few cavalry companies. Demonstrating the general's powerful Louisiana connections, however, results from that state proved more substantive. Governor Thomas Moore released perhaps 1,500 militia—all New Orleans men. The War Department balked at the ninety-day aspect of the call-up, but eventually relented.[4]

Moore's troops included the Washington Artillery (5th Company), Orleans Guard Artillery, Orleans Guard Battalion, Crescent Regiment, and Confederate Guards Response Battalion. Joseph Lyman, a member of the last, complained that he and twenty-eight others were herded aboard a boxcar that had been previously loaded with molasses. The Crescent Regiment, also known as the "Kid Glove Regiment," included some of the elite of the city, who reported to duty in elegant carriages. There were eleven companies, including one of New Orleans firemen. The Orleans Guard Battalion left the city on March 18 "packed like sardines in a can." The Washington Artillery, with its own share of city bluebloods, boarded a train amid the cheers of hundreds of spectators. The troops proceeded to Grand Junction, a town they found as disagreeable as the bitterly cold weather.[5]

Mobile and Pensacola

THE GRASSY-PATCHED sandy beaches of Alabama and western Florida seemed far removed from Sidney Johnston's Department No. 2. Soon, however, troops under forty-five-year-old Major General Braxton Bragg would be streaming from that sector into Tennessee. Although Bragg seethed over not having been given command at New Orleans, he had done good work at Mobile and Pensacola. Already there were hints of the contentiousness that would characterize his Civil War career. Brigadier General Jones Withers found him "self-willed, arrogant, and dictatorial." He nonetheless retained the confidence of Davis and Benjamin.[6]

The logistics involved in transporting entire brigades from the coast proved formidable. So badly had the railroads been damaged by recent rains that Bragg wrote on February 22 that prompt movement would be impossible. By the 28th, however, five regiments, four cavalry companies, and a battery were loading at Mobile. The first train to leave Pensacola for that city did not depart until March 4. On March 7, a train carrying the 5th Mississippi rattled out of Mobile, to be followed the next day by the 17th Alabama and the Washington (Georgia) Artillery. Lieutenant James Williams of the 21st Alabama was frankly relieved that his wife chose not to appear at the railroad depot when his regiment pulled out; the scene "would have given you the blues for a week," he wrote. The 1st Florida Battalion trailed in the rear, not leaving Pensacola until March 17.[7]

Numerous difficulties were encountered. The 26th Alabama crossed Mobile Bay on the steamer *Dorrance*; when a large pine log slammed against the side of the boat, seventy to eighty men jumped overboard, fearing a capsize. The trains ran only during the day to prevent accidents; just one slight wreck occurred, outside Corinth. Wagons, baggage, and ordnance supplies brought up the rear. On March 15, an express train, with 88,000 cartridges and 165,000 percussion caps, left Mobile for Corinth. Sixty-one wagons and teams and several ambulances were sent from Pensacola.[8]

Secretary of War Benjamin ordered a near abandonment of the department. No troops were to remain at Pensacola, and only a slight garrison for the forts at Mobile. The last would keep the Federal navy at bay for the present, he believed, but the risk had to be taken. Despite these clear instructions, both cities remained occupied. The War Department relented and allowed two regiments, the 8th and 27th Mississippi (770 troops), to remain at Pensacola. Bragg also retained a division-sized force at Mobile, a move that was never challenged by Benjamin. Though some of the troops remaining at Mobile had not yet been properly organized and armed and others were required to man the heavy guns, a 1,600-man brigade could have been released. Indeed, some of that number, the 680 troops of the 24th Alabama and Waters's Alabama Battery, were sent to Corinth immediately after the Battle of Shiloh. Had Benjamin rigidly enforced his own orders, an additional 2,500 troops could have been on the battlefield.[9]

The term "corps" is frequently used in referring to Bragg's reinforcements. In truth, only ten regiments, a battalion, four cavalry companies, and three batteries ever went to Corinth. The actual number of troops was not significantly higher than the total received from Lovell's department. What Bragg's regiments offered Johnston, however, went beyond numbers. Although lacking combat experience, they were proficiently drilled and highly disciplined. Even the Northern press had heard of their vaunted superiority. Brigadier General Arthur M. Manigault, who arrived in Corinth after Shiloh, found the former Pensacola-Mobile troops a cut above the rest of the army in appearance and discipline.[10]

Jackson, Tennessee

THE NEWSPAPER ACCOUNTS were wrong: Beauregard did not have diphtheria. He nonetheless remained nearly incapacitated by his month-old throat surgery. On February 28, he informed Richmond that he was "in deep despair about my health—nervous affection of the throat." His physician advised him to stop all talking. He also bordered on a nervous breakdown and was instructed by doctors to "avoid undue excitement." On March 16, he admitted to Virginia Representative W. P. Miles, "The least excitement throws me back." His desperate mental state was captured in the self-analogy of a drowning man attempting to "catch a straw."[11]

A certain paranoia also prevailed at headquarters. Around February 23, Colonel Thomas Jordan, West Point roommate of William T. Sherman, veteran of the Seminole War, and assistant quartermaster general in the Regular Army for thirteen years, arrived in Jackson. As Beauregard's friend and adjutant general, he had temporarily remained in Richmond to confer with Benjamin concerning "certain matters." The results, he reported, were "in the main unfruitful." This report, coupled with Beauregard's disillusionment at what he found in Tennessee, resulted in a belief that the War Department, according to an aide, was "very unfriendly to you [Beauregard]." When Beauregard's subsequent requests to have assigned to him certain officers in the Virginia army were denied, the Louisiana general became convinced of this hostility. That no evidence exists to suggest the administration was working either overtly or surreptitiously to undercut the general is irrelevant; he *believed* it to be otherwise.[12]

Bragg arrived in Jackson on March 4 and was shocked to discover the general's condition. Beauregard remained "distressed and worried," and the alarmist Polk was not helping the situation. "Every interview with Genl Polk turns [Beauregard's recovery] . . . back a week," Bragg informed his wife, Elise. "But for my arrival here to aid him I do not believe he would now be living." Although assigned to command the sector south of Jackson, Bragg remained in town nearly a week, apparently fearful of leaving the general's side.[13]

Beauregard has been praised for bringing structural cohesion to the Mississippi Valley forces. Though he did bring a semblance of order, his accomplishments have been overrated. After detaching one of Polk's divisions to Island No. 10, he merged the remaining two divisions into a single "Grand Division." The organization of the Gulf Coast troops he left to Bragg, who turned the details over to Ruggles. The result was an unwieldy and nonsensical structure called the 1st Corps, 2nd Grand Division (four brigades under Ruggles), and the 2nd Corps, 2nd Grand Division (two brigades under Brigadier General A. H. Gladden). Beauregard grandly styled his command the "Army of the Mississippi," revealing that his ego, unlike his health, had not failed.[14]

AFTER THE FALL of Fort Donelson, Beauregard desperately hoped that the enemy would "give us time to withdraw." The Federal command did not disappoint him; a precious two and a half weeks elapsed before the next offensive. The Creole general sensed that he had a window of opportunity, but he did not know exactly how to use it. On February 21, he exceeded his authority and proposed an offensive in conjunction with Earl Van Dorn's army in Arkansas. This so-called army actually consisted of an Arkansas-Texas division of 8,700 troops and a Missouri division of 6,800, thus making it more appropriately a corps. At that time Beauregard counted 12,000 troops at Columbus, 4,000 at New Madrid–Island No. 10, and 5,000 under Ruggles and Brigadier General James Chalmers at Corinth and Iuka, making a total of 21,000, of which 15,000 would be available for field operations. Coupled with 10,000 from Van Dorn and 15,000 new levies, the Louisiana general figured, a 40,000-man army could advance up the Mississippi River and threaten Paducah and Cairo. The movement would be a joint operation with a gunboat flotilla that was then organizing in New Orleans.[15]

This "brilliant programme," as he vainly termed it, was totally impracticable. Besides Samuel Curtis's 11,000-man Federal army in Missouri, a new 18,000-man army under John Pope was organizing at

Commerce, Missouri. Perhaps Halleck might have held back Sherman's division, then staging at Paducah, but Grant's army would have been free to attack Beauregard's exposed right, or even Corinth or Memphis. The Confederate gunboat squadron turned out to be a flimsy group of converted New Orleans river steamers, which could have been blasted out of the water by the powerful Federal ironclad flotilla. There would thus be no secure line of communications. Nor was there sufficient manpower: the 15,000 levies were not forthcoming.[16]

Van Dorn, for strategic reasons, or perhaps through vanity, in which the diminutive general was Beauregard's match, thought little of the plan. He had previously received permission from the War Department for an offensive against Curtis's army in Missouri, a move condoned by Johnston. By defeating Curtis and threatening St. Louis, he could possibly divert troops from Grant. The opposing armies joined battle at Pea Ridge, in northwestern Arkansas, on March 7–8, 1862. Van Dorn, despite superiority of strength, was defeated. Once again leadership, not numbers, proved decisive.[17]

By at least March 15, probably sooner, Johnston had been notified of the battle. At that point, some historians contend, he should have ordered Van Dorn east of the Mississippi River to join the Corinth concentration. The message that Johnston received, however, did not admit to defeat. Although conceding that the field was left in enemy possession, Van Dorn's dispatch could have been construed to mean the battle had been a tactical draw. He spoke boldly of remaining on the offensive. Johnston apparently still hoped for a trans-Mississippi diversion. He failed to understand that the Federals possessed sufficient manpower west of the Mississippi River to contain Van Dorn's "army." On March 19, Beauregard vainly appealed a second time for Van Dorn to cross the river. Johnston failed to press the issue and thus lost an opportunity to make good the losses at Fort Donelson.[18]

INCREASINGLY, BEAUREGARD's attention focused on Island No. 10. Following the evacuation of Columbus, the island, located in a river bend opposite New Madrid, Missouri, represented the northernmost fort on the Mississippi River. In early March 1862, Pope's army invested the town; it fell on March 14, but not before the garrison escaped by river transports. By mid-March, Beauregard had bolstered the Island No. 10 garrison to 8,000 troops and fifty-one heavy guns. The makeshift gunboat flotilla protected the downriver approach at Tiptonville, Tennessee, in case the Yankees attempted a crossing on rafts from the west bank. The eastern or Tennessee approach to the island was blocked by Reelfoot Lake. The same swampy, cypress-entangled waters that kept the Federals out, however, also kept the Confederates in. If the escape route at Tiptonville was ever blocked, the garrison would be caught in a cul-de-sac.[19]

Commanding the Confederate forces was Major General John P. McCown, "an old dilapidated fellow with very little energy," according to an unimpressed colonel. Beauregard had no confidence in the man. McCown's near-hysterical messages placed Pope's strength at 30,000 (even higher than exaggerated press reports), whereas Beauregard believed it to be 15,000 to 20,000. The Mississippi Valley commander was also furious about what he perceived to be a feeble stand at New Madrid. He soon began looking for a replacement. The officer he had in mind was Brigadier General Mackall, who happened to be a part of the anti-Davis faction.[20]

Beauregard frankly did not know what to do with Island No. 10. He had long felt that the position would be untenable if New Madrid fell. At first he considered sending reinforcements, but quickly abandoned the idea. When a Federal ironclad flotilla made an appearance on March 15, 1862, Beauregard ordered a reduction in the garrison. Eventually, 3,500 troops were withdrawn and sent to Corinth. Although encouraging McCown to "be of good cheer and hold out," Beauregard was actually prepared to sacrifice the division, as he virtually admitted in postwar years. The decision was a correct one. The fight for control of the upper Mississippi Valley would be at Corinth, not Island No. 10. If McCown's 4,500 troops could hold in check an entire Federal corps (which eventually peaked at 22,000 troops) during the crucial period of Confederate concentration, a major victory might be scored along the Tennessee River. Beauregard clung to the hope that the garrison might hold out long enough so that "we can relieve you by a victory here [Corinth]."[21]

Johnston had originally proposed a Mississippi Valley defensive line that extended from Columbus, Kentucky, to Jackson and Grand Junction, Tennessee, with Memphis, Grenada, and Jackson, Mississippi, as points of retreat. Beauregard's new line stretched diagonally from Island No. 10 to Humboldt, Tennessee; Jackson; and Corinth, thus throwing his forces forward of the Louisville & Nashville and Memphis & Charleston Railroads. Using the Mobile & Ohio, he could concentrate quickly if Grant advanced overland from Fort Henry or attempted to establish a beachhead along the Tennessee River between Coffee Landing, Tennessee, and Eastport, Mississippi.[22]

In early March, Polk's reorganized division of 7,000 troops arrived at Humboldt, at the intersection of the Memphis, Clarksville & Louisville and the Mobile & Ohio Railroads. A line of infantry outposts extended from Union City to Lexington, by way of Dresden and Huntington. The cavalry, still in its infancy and without competent leadership, was dispersed along the northern perimeter: 500 at Paris, 200 at Jackson, and 500 at Union City. Mounted parties kept the Tennessee River under close observation.[23]

Grant's army could advance directly on Humboldt by way of the Memphis, Clarksville & Louisville Railroad, or, more likely, strike the Confederate rear by a rapid move up the Tennessee River. The latter Beauregard considered "the more dreaded movement." Bragg, mindful of the potential for raids, kept his units scattered. Perhaps 10,000 troops were in Corinth, with detachments at Pittsburg Landing and Bethel Station. Chalmers's 2,500-man brigade was positioned at Iuka, and about 1,000 Tennessee state troops organized at a camp of instruction at Henderson, north of Bethel Station. All of the New Orleans militia outfits remained at Grand Junction until late March. Two regiments, the 4th Louisiana and 7th Mississippi, were held in reserve at Jackson. Beauregard, too sick to move, retained his headquarters at the city hotel in Jackson, much to the displeasure of citizens, according to one soldier. "Gen. B[eauregard] has made quite a stir in this important place by making it his HQtrs. The good people wish him out of it lest it might be an inducement for the Yankees to visit it."[24]

Beauregard has been criticized for bombarding Johnston with alarming notes about a possible Federal offensive, ostensibly to bring Hardee's corps under his control. Already he had assimilated Bragg's corps into his command. It is true that on March 2 Beauregard telegraphed Johnston that he should hurry to Corinth for an anticipated battle, even though at that time there was no such indication. It must be remembered, however, that Johnston had only agreed to change his destination from Stevenson to Decatur to "cooperate or unite" with Beauregard's forces. A March 5 telegram from Johnston, mentioned by Beauregard in postwar years but not found in extant records, stated that once at Decatur he would decide upon the fastest route to Corinth.

There remained some question, however, about exactly what Johnston intended to do at Decatur. This was confirmed by Johnston's own chief engineer, Jeremy Gilmer, who as late as March 6 had not mentioned Corinth in his letters to his wife, but only Decatur as "the point of concentration for [the] army." Beauregard dispatched aides to Decatur in an attempt to persuade Johnston to come west. In a March 10 letter to his daughter, Polk wrote, "We are hoping to have Johnston's [army] from Middle Tennessee to join us," implying uncertainty. As late as March 16, Bragg expressed relief that Johnston had decided upon a juncture. There is insufficient evidence to conclude that Beauregard was doing a right thing for a wrong reason. The more significant point is that Johnston still had to be coaxed into doing what was obviously needed. The opposing forces would soon be engaged in a race for concentration. The winner of that race might well determine the victor of the fight for control of the Mississippi Valley.[25]

Corinth, Mississippi

INTERSECTING RAILROADS, the Memphis & Charleston and the Mobile & Ohio, coming together at a sixty-degree angle, gave Corinth its strategic value and sobriquet—"the Crossroads of the Confederacy." Settled in 1854, the town had a prewar population of 1,200. The business district consisted primarily of one- and two-story gabled woodframe structures. Most of the stores were whitewashed, with the notable exception of the post office, which was pink. Businesses included the usual drygoods stores, blacksmith shops, livery stables, saloons, and restaurants, along with a drugstore, bakery, tailor shop, picture gallery, the local office of the Aetna Insurance Company, and three hotels, the most renowned of which was the Tishimingo, located next to the Memphis & Charleston depot. There was a square brick courthouse, five churches (only one of which was bricked), a sawmill, and a long farmer's market with cupola. A number of quaint French-style cottages graced the western section of town, along with the three-story Corona Female College. Many trees on the residential side offered a pleasant shade. Ruggles arrived in town on February 17 and, by order of Polk, assumed command of northern Mississippi and Alabama.[26]

The vulnerability of the region had already been demonstrated. Shortly after the fall of Fort Henry, a squadron of three Federal gunboats had ascended the Tennessee River to Florence, Alabama, where they docked on February 8. More hysteria than damage was created, although nine of the thirteen steamboats below Muscle Shoals were destroyed. The gunboats then returned casually downriver, burning an abandoned Confederate camp at Savannah, Tennessee.[27]

The immediate supervision of northern Alabama fell to Brigadier General Leroy P. Walker, with headquarters in Tuscumbia. Only four and a half months earlier, this Huntsville, Alabama, native had served as secretary of war in the Davis administration, but a dispute with the president and poor health had forced his resignation. The paltry force at his disposal included James Clanton's 1st Alabama Cavalry, scouting the north bank of the Tennessee River, and a poorly armed Arkansas battalion at Tuscumbia. Ruggles forwarded two twenty-four-pounder siege guns to Walker, who made plans to construct a battery at Chickasaw, about ten miles above Eastport, Mississippi. The work would not be completed until March 10.[28]

Eastport concerned Ruggles. An enemy force landing at that place could take the fourteen-mile road to Iuka and destroy the vital eighty-yard-long Bear Creek bridge of the Memphis & Charleston Railroad, four miles east of town. To guard against such a possibility, Brigadier General Chalmers had been sent to Iuka to command a makeshift brigade composed of units recently arrived from eastern Tennessee.[29]

On the night of February 20, Ruggles received news of yet another naval incursion. That morning a lone gunboat (U.S.S. *Tyler*) had landed at Hamburg, Tennessee. Residents were told (falsely) by sailors that transports would follow the next day. Actually, the Federals had planned a bold dash upon the Bear Creek bridge. After moving on to Eastport that day, the Yankees were informed by excited locals that the bridge was protected by 3,000 to 4,000 Confederates (in truth about 1,500). Having only fifty sharpshooters aboard, Lieutenant William Gwin canceled the operation and leisurely returned to Cairo.[30]

Leaving Eastport and Tuscumbia to Chalmers and Walker, Ruggles concentrated on the landings north of Corinth. On February 18, only two regiments were in town, the 16th and 19th Louisiana, the last having no cartridges. The 17th and 18th Louisiana and a battery were on the way, however, and would thus secure the town. He dispatched two companies of the 2nd Mississippi Cavalry Battalion to Purdy, Tennessee, to observe east, toward the river. In late February, the 18th Louisiana, the Miles Light Artillery, and a cavalry detachment were dispatched to watch river activity at a place twenty-three miles north of Corinth by the name of Pittsburg Landing.[31]

• • •

THIRTY-THREE-YEAR-OLD Colonel Alfred Mouton, a West Point graduate, civil engineer, and son of a former Louisiana governor and United States senator, was a man with a mission. He had been ordered to monitor activity at Pittsburg Landing, a site nine miles upriver from Savannah and on a direct approach to Corinth. His 18th Louisiana arrived on February 28, following a grueling two-day march, with the battery coming up the next morning.[32]

The Louisianians found their destination rather bleak—"three log cabins and a pigsty," described one. The Pittsburg-Corinth Road cut through the bluff down to the river. Near the edge of the bluff, north of the road, sat a log dwelling, and about a hundred yards back was a second cabin, a ravine separating the two. The third cabin was positioned two hundred yards south of the road. A cultivated field, two hundred yards wide and a half-mile long, ran along the back of the bluff; behind the field was a heavily wooded area. The landing had originally been settled back in 1848 by the family of Pittser Miller Tucker, called "Pitt" Tucker. He established a frontier trading post that dealt largely in hard liquor. When other families settled nearby, Pitts Landing became Pittsburg Landing.[33]

About noon on March 1, two Federal gunboats rounded Diamond Island and steamed into view. Shots were exchanged with Claude Gibson's battery for ten to fifteen minutes. Mouton ordered his eight companies to safety in a deep ravine behind the bluff, but two or three shots passed so close they "could feel the wind raising the hair on our heads," wrote a member. Gibson's gunners were "compelled to travel." The eight-inch navy guns continued to pound the landing for an hour, after which a hundred armed sailors and infantry sharpshooters boarded skiffs and put ashore. After burning one of the cabins, they formed a line and advanced toward the woods. The Louisianians suddenly burst forth from ambush. "As we rose the brow of the bluff, Corporal Huggins C. Ensign, of the Orleans Cadets, fell, torn and mutilated by a [navy] shell, his left arm broken and left side torn out," noted a horror-stricken comrade. The Yankees quickly fell back to the safety of their boats. Mouton counted twenty-one casualties in the sharp engagement, the enemy about thirteen. Although claiming victory, the colonel thereafter kept only a light picket in observation. He withdrew his regiment inland about three miles to a log Methodist church by the name of Shiloh.[34]

"IT IS POSSIBLE," Bragg tersely wrote Ruggles on March 6, 1862, that "we shall soon have a heavy column of the enemy upon your flank by way of the Tennessee River." Ammunition was immediately issued to the troops, the sick and extra baggage were sent south, and arrangements were made to gather in commissary supplies from both sides of the Tennessee River in northern Alabama. Additional and foreboding intelligence came in the next day from Major H. C. King, commanding the Kentucky Cavalry Battalion on an outpost east of Paris, Tennessee. Fourteen troop transports had passed that place, with many more downriver, at the mouth of the Sandy River and at Fort Henry; rumor placed the number at sixty. The invasion was at last under way.[35]

Tension increased throughout the 8th and 9th as Beauregard notified Johnston that a major offensive was unquestionably under way. Ruggles began entrenching at Corinth. Fearful of a raid on the Mobile & Ohio Railroad, Bragg ordered Brigadier General A. H. Gladden and a detachment of two regiments, a battery, and three companies of the 2nd Mississippi Cavalry Battalion to Bethel Station. At Paris, King's battalion was unexpectedly attacked by a battalion of the 5th Iowa Cavalry and a battery raiding from Fort Henry. The Federals sustained ten casualties, the Confederates fifteen.[36]

By the night of March 11, fifty-seven transports, with an estimated 25,000–30,000 troops, had arrived at Savannah, Tennessee, but most remained aboard their ships. Exactly where the Federals would ultimately debark would depend upon their target. If the mission was to cut the M & O Railroad, they would likely land at Savannah, or four miles upriver at Crump's Landing, and strike out for Bethel Station. If a direct move upon Corinth was the intention, the expedition would pull in at Pittsburg Landing or Hamburg, both of which had ridge roads leading directly to town.[37]

There were several possible beachheads for a raid on the Memphis & Charleston Railroad. If the Federals landed at Chambers Creek, they could march to the village of Farmington, which would both outflank Ruggles at Corinth and place them within striking distance of the railroad. Tyler's Landing, at the mouth of Yellow Creek, offered a twenty-mile road running to Burnsville, Mississippi, located on the railroad. A regiment could perhaps detain a raiding party long enough for reinforcements to come from Iuka, about three hours' marching time away. Strangely, Ruggles left Burnsville unprotected. Cook's Landing, at Indian Creek, and Eastport both had roads to Iuka and to the Bear Creek bridge. By March 12, Beauregard had determined that the target was the Memphis & Charleston. Because of low water, however, he believed that the Yankees would debark at Pittsburg Landing.

An action that took place that day seemed to support Beauregard's suspicions. Two Federal gunboats, *Tyler* and *Lexington*, steamed ahead to Chickasaw and engaged the heavy battery at that place. The two twenty-four-pounders atop the bluff were manned by two infantry companies trained on the big guns at Pensacola. The gunboats fired more than a hundred rounds but inflicted no casualties or damage and soon retired. Rebel gunners suspected (wrongly) that they had crippled one of the boats.[38]

Chalmers, who had moved his brigade up from Iuka to Eastport, reported the situation under control. With the addition of three Mississippi regiments—the 5th, 7th, and 10th, recently arrived from Pensacola—and another new arrival, the 9th Texas, his command had swelled to 2,500 troops. The countryside was well adapted to keeping an enemy force in check until reinforcements arrived. Besides, Chalmers suspected that the demonstration had been merely to test the range of the Chickasaw guns and that the real target was Corinth, not the railroad. "I am inclined to believe the landing will be at Hamburg," he concluded.[39]

If Beauregard and Chalmers had differing views, so did Gladden. His scouts, thrown out on the Purdy-Adamsville Road toward the river, had also detected the massive Federal presence at Savannah. If the destination was the Mobile & Ohio, which he suspected, the Yankees would soon be marching toward his detachment at Bethel Station. He had neither a sufficient force to contest such an advance nor train transportation to escape. Reinforcements from Humboldt would be twenty-four hours in coming.[40]

Until the Federals debarked and revealed their intention, their exact objective remained uncertain. Ruggles, at Corinth, had to be prepared to reinforce Gladden on the left, to support Chalmers on the right, or to parry a direct thrust. On the morning of March 12, Captain Charles G. Field, observing enemy activity across the river from Savannah, sent a message that would echo throughout the Confederate chain of command: "The enemy are landing in force."[41]

St. Louis

FOLLOWING THE FALL of Fort Donelson, Halleck realized that he faced a "golden opportunity." If the Federals moved quickly, they could destroy either half of the divided Confederate command before they concentrated. Grant likewise believed that the army must push forward vigorously.[42]

Halleck's first, and perhaps best, option was to use the Tennessee River as a shield against Johnston and march Grant's army about seventy miles west from Fort Henry to Hickman, Kentucky, or to Union City, Tennessee, and invest Columbus from the rear. With John Pope's army advancing from the north and Grant's army from the west, Polk could have been caught in a pincer movement and perhaps another Fort Donelson–type capture could have been achieved. Even if Polk's corps had escaped by river transports and railroad, Grant would have been in a position to strike his flank and rear as he withdrew. The most obvious advantage to such a strategy was that it would be entirely within the confines of his own department, thus eliminating the maddening lack of cooperation from Buell that had occurred in the previous campaign. Halleck squandered his golden opportunity, however, by immersing himself in the politics of command—namely, by replacing Grant and obtaining top western command for himself.[43]

By early March, the strategic situation had changed. The Rebels had escaped from Columbus and dug in at Island No. 10. Halleck received "reliable information" that Polk's corps, 8,000 to 10,000 strong, had fallen back to Henderson (the bishop was actually thirty-five miles north, at Humboldt), that some 15,000–20,000 enemy troops had concentrated at Corinth and another 8,000 to 10,000 (actually 2,500) at the Bear Creek bridge. Halleck had the option of marching Grant's army along the line of the Memphis, Clarksville & Louisville Railroad, from Paris, through McKenzie, to Humboldt. The drawback was that Beauregard's army was not truly vulnerable from an overland approach. He would certainly withdraw south to Jackson and ultimately to Corinth, all the while growing stronger as reinforcements arrived from the Gulf Coast.[44]

Eager to repeat success, Halleck chose a turning movement by use of the waterways. Only the Tennessee River offered the rapid mobility and secure communication lines needed to exploit the Confederate center, where Johnston was weakest. Once the Memphis & Charleston had been secured at Corinth, Grant could move west and capture Memphis. The surrender of that city would mean that the string of Mississippi River fortifications to the north—Island No. 10, Fort Pillow, Fort Randolph—would fall like dominoes.[45]

On February 20, Halleck had decided to move, with or without Buell. Since Grant's army might not be supported, the St. Louis commander's plan called for merely a raid, the object being the Memphis

& Charleston and the Mobile & Ohio Railroads. Although Grant's entire army would be embarking, the mission would essentially be a swift cavalry dash before the enemy could mount serious opposition. A general engagement was to be avoided at all costs. If successful, the army would return to Savannah.[46]

The plan, though bold, was not well developed. If Buell failed to cooperate, as there seemed to be every indication he would, Grant's 27,000-man army would be deep in enemy territory facing, by his own estimates, more than 38,000 Rebels. True, they were widely scattered, but Beauregard had both north-south and east-west rail communications, thus allowing rapid concentration. The prospect of cavalry raids' inflicting serious damage was also dubious. All in all, it was too big a gamble for too small a return.[47]

It is difficult not to conclude that Halleck, understanding that time was of the essence, moved ahead with only a vague plan in the hope that Buell would not leave Grant out on a limb. If so, his plan backfired. The Ohio department commander remained aloof, despite Halleck's pleas for assistance. Even his request for a single division went unheeded. Underlying the Missouri department commander's frustration was also fear, as the weakness of his own plan became increasingly self-evident. "What a mistake that Buell did not send forces to move with us up the Tennessee, so as to seize that point," Halleck bitterly noted to a War Department official. "Smith has gone to do it, but I fear it will be too late and that he is too weak."[48]

Halleck began a frantic search for reinforcements. Sherman's newly organized division, nearly 8,000 strong, was sent from Paducah to Fort Henry to join the expedition. Instead of continuing to carp at Buell's lack of cooperation, however, the St. Louis commander could actually have done much more. He maintained Pope's army of 18,000 on the west bank of the Mississippi River, investing an estimated 5,000 Rebels (actually only 3,500) at New Madrid. By March 7, he had become increasingly jittery about Grant's army, now under Smith, and ordered Pope to disengage for service up the Tennessee River. Fearful of losing his independent command, Pope convinced him that progress was being made. Halleck relented, hoping that the lethargic Foote would attack Island No. 10 with his ironclads in an effort to draw away the Southern vessels that were keeping Pope's divisions at bay.[49]

Halleck attempted to convince Buell that Beauregard had 50,000 troops poised along the Mississippi River, but the Ohio commander remained unconvinced. Buell quickly replied that he had reliable information that only 5,000 Confederates were at New Madrid and none in Memphis. Halleck skirted the issue and continued his fixation on concentrating Smith's and Buell's forces. As the bickering continued, the expedition steamed ahead.[50]

U.S. Expeditionary Forces, Tennessee River

GRANT, AT FORT HENRY and temporarily without a command, had been about the task of outfitting the mammoth expedition taking shape on the Tennessee River. By March 2, he had collected twenty steamers capable of carrying 15,000 troops and 3,000 horses. Some fifty-eight transports, escorted by *Tyler* and *Lexington*, were eventually assembled. Two badly needed coal barges had been detained at Paducah for want of boats to tow them—"Have not a single one [steamer]. Everything up Tennessee," Department Chief of Staff Cullum reported.[51]

Spearheading the expedition would be Sherman's new 5th Division, of mostly Ohio troops. The men boarded seventeen transports on March 6–8, 1862, and steamed upriver from Paducah to Fort Henry. Upon arrival, 1st Brigade Commander Colonel Stephen G. Hicks continued on with his two regiments, unescorted. *Golden State*, with one-half of the 40th Illinois, docked at Savannah on the 8th, followed the next day by the 46th Illinois. Hicks, an old militia officer whose disdain for Regular Army officers dated back to the Mexican War, had been under arrest for weeks while at Paducah for his failure to instill rigid discipline among his troops. An angry Sherman reprimanded him for jeopardizing his brigade.[52]

The balance of the division followed with only one minor incident. On March 10, while they were passing a shore lined with waving women and children, a shot rang out from the bank above, wounding a man of the 48th Ohio. Hicks's soldiers greeted the boats as they neared Savannah. "The weather was soft and fine, and one or more flags floated over every boat. Nearly every regiment had a band of music," recalled one officer.[53]

By March 9, some 25,206 infantry, 1,900 cavalry, and all the artillery save one battery had embarked. Still awaiting transportation were 5,740 troops at Fort Henry and another 1,216 at Fort Donelson. Grant vainly scoured the Tennessee River for additional steamers. He then ordered that all boats passing Fort Donelson be stopped and redirected for service up the Tennessee, thus interrupting Buell's supply line.[54]

The sheer grandeur of the expedition captivated many of the men. A party atmosphere prevailed aboard *Meteor*, transport of the 81st Ohio, with Governor Yates of Illinois and a bevy of women aboard. Frolicking soldiers of the 21st Missouri practiced shots from the deck of their boat, sometimes aiming at civilians on shore. Fourteenth Illinois Lieutenant Colonel William Camm described the "dense volume of smoke" and decks "dark with blue-coated soldiers." The men of the 25th Missouri sang gaily, although occasional sparks from the boat's funnels singed their clothing and blankets. Timothy Blaisdell summarized to his wife: "I wish you could see our fleet as we move up the river these splendid moonlight nights. It is the grandest sight I ever saw." The men were not informed of their destination, but most speculated it was Memphis by way of Savannah, or that they would steam directly to Florence.[55]

The river, out of its banks in many places, forced residents inland. The few who remained "cheered us and made great profession of union," declared an Iowa soldier. Third Iowa member Saul Sylvester cautiously concluded that the Union sentiment appeared strong. An Illinois artilleryman was encouraged by the waving of handkerchiefs and cheering and was certain that "the people of this region are generally 'sound in the goose.' " There were few sights along the way, beyond the destroyed 1,200-foot-long Memphis, Clarksville & Louisville Railroad trestle, near Danville, Tennessee. The bridge had been knocked out by the Federal navy shortly after the fall of Fort Henry, leaving only the piers and a 250-foot span. One transport slammed broadside against a pier in the choppy water, causing great alarm that the boat might break apart.[56]

The adventure soon dulled, and the men began grumbling over their miserable conditions, especially the overcrowding. Some 970 men of the 12th Michigan, along with camp equipment, baggage, and officers' horses, jammed aboard a transport, slowing the boat to a tedious five miles per hour. A cavalry trooper revealed that his transport did not have sufficient berths for half the men, leaving hundreds to sleep up and down the social-hall floor. An Iowan aboard the "shaky old tub" *Minnehaha* noted that every available space was taken, and "around the boilers the men are packed like swine." It rained almost daily, adding to the misery. Franklin Bailey, stricken with fever, had little choice but to lie down with his head on his knapsack and "sweat like a hog."[57]

Several casualties occurred along the way. At least seven men drowned, including three members of the 46th Ohio who fell overboard when their transport tossed about in choppy waters. On March 9, shouts of "Man overboard!" rang out from *Champion No. 4.* A soldier had fallen off the hurricane deck; his body was never recovered. Combat casualties, mostly from sniping, resulted in at least six killed, ten wounded, and four missing. At Clifton, Tennessee, a transport was fired on by bushwhackers, wounding two men. In hastily loading his musket to return fire, a Federal shot his nearby comrade in the head, killing him instantly. The boats temporarily docked at Paris Landing, where four men of the 58th Illinois wandered off to shoot hogs. They were never heard from again, presumed captured by lurking cavalry. A sniper fired into the transport of the 8th Iowa near Savannah, killing one man and wounding another.[58]

The expedition made good time, despite some delays: frequent stops had to be made for wood, and dense fog curtailed passage on several nights; debris occasionally clogged the paddlewheels. Most of the vessels had docked at Savannah by March 12. The transports were crowded four and five deep on both sides of the river.[59]

Sitting atop the bluff at Savannah was the prominent white brick mansion of William H. Cherry, soon to become the headquarters of Major General Smith. The house had been built in 1830 by Cherry's father-in-law, David Robinson. A staunch Unionist, Cherry owned several thousand acres of farmland, a store, a ferryboat and, ironically, a number of slaves. A short distance back from the bluff sat the town, with about eight hundred inhabitants. There was the square brick Hardin County Courthouse and a single business street, described by one Federal as "lined with dilapidated, weatherworn, wooden buildings." The locals, strongly pro-Union, welcomed the Federal presence, and about three hundred men from the surrounding countryside came in for protection. More than a hundred joined the ranks, nearly half of them enlisting in the 46th Ohio.[60]

Halleck explained his choice of Savannah by writing that it was near a railroad and between Corinth and Henderson. The strong Union sentiment may also have been a factor. The town's most valuable strategic asset, its location on the east bank, seems not to have been a factor. Indeed, Halleck also considered Florence, on the opposite bank.[61]

Hardin County, bisected nearly in half by the Tennessee River, had been settled only forty years earlier and remained largely wilderness in areas. The strong Union sentiment, especially on the east bank, was well known. Corn, not cotton, was the primary crop, which affected the county's racial makeup—only 15 percent of the 11,000 inhabitants were black. Although a few mansions dotted the riverbank, this was not plantation country. The whites were relatively poor, lived in log cabins, and scratched out a living on small farms. William Skinner of the 71st Ohio was blunt in his assessment: "The country here is not worth fighting for, as it is a very desolate looking place, I assure you."[62]

THIRTY-FOUR-YEAR-OLD Lewis "Lew" Wallace, who would later write *Ben Hur*, had gained his brigadier's commission through political ties—he was a member of the Indiana state legislature and son of a former governor. He began the war as the Indiana state adjutant general, an appointment received through Governor Morton. His major general's grade, however, had been earned by an outstanding performance at Fort Donelson. He received national attention when *Leslie's* ran a full-page engraving of him leading the charge of the 8th Missouri and 11th Indiana on February 15, 1862.[63]

On the evening of March 12, Wallace was aboard the transport *John J. Roe* at Savannah when Major General Smith unexpectedly entered his cabin. Although he had kind words for him in his memoirs, Wallace believed that Smith, feeling jealous, had slighted him in his Fort Donelson report. The new army commander explained that he was to proceed with his division to Crump's Landing, where his infantry would support the cavalry in a raid on the Mobile & Ohio Railroad. Smith sounded a note of caution. Frank Cheatham's Rebel division was allegedly at Pittsburg Landing. Since Snake Creek was flooded, however, the Confederates could cross to the north bank only by use of a single bridge. Coincidentally, a man by the name of Wallace lived nearby, but the locals referred to the crossing simply as Snake Creek Bridge.[64]

As Smith was returning to his transport, he lost his balance while stepping into the skiff. His shin was badly injured from ankle to knee, the wound cutting all the way to the bone. He clenched his teeth in pain as one of the boatsmen raised him up, then returned to his boat, where a surgeon attended to him. For the next few days, he got about by limping from chair to chair. The wound would soon become fatally infected; Smith had only weeks to live.[65]

During the early-morning hours of March 13, Wallace's veterans embarked upon transports and steamed four miles upriver to Crump's Landing, where they filed off in a pelting rain. Enemy vedettes offered only slight resistance. The landing derived its name from Dr. Richard W. Crump, a local physician and landowner, who died in 1857. His widow, Elizabeth, still lived in the four-room log-and-clapboard cabin. A local resident greeted the Federals by promptly raising the Stars and Stripes.[66]

After detaining some fifteen or twenty citizens, Wallace sent Major Charles S. Haynes's battalion of the 5th Ohio Cavalry, guided by a Union man from the area, out the Purdy Road nineteen miles toward Bethel Station. He then advanced Colonel John M. Thayer's brigade to Adamsville, while Colonel Morgan L. Smith's brigade encamped at the Linton farm, at the intersection of the Pittsburg Landing and Purdy Roads. Fearing a large enemy force in the vicinity, Wallace kept up a ruse by changing lines during the day and lighting multiple fires by night.[67]

Confederate forces in the area were actually minimal. Gladden had thrown forward the seven hundred infantry of the 1st Louisiana Regulars and 22nd Alabama, along with 130 cavalry and two guns of Ketchum's Alabama Battery, to within five miles of Crump's Landing, holding an Alabama battalion of three hundred men and the balance of Ketchum's guns at Bethel Station. As for troops in Wallace's rear, there was but a single regiment, the 18th Louisiana, at Monterey.[68]

The drenching rain continued through noon of March 13. When Haynes had not returned by 4:30 P.M., Wallace began to feel uneasy. Four captured Confederate pickets revealed (although extant records cannot verify) that heavy Southern reinforcements had already arrived in the area. Taking a circuitous route, the Ohio horsemen had managed to avoid Gladden's detachments and at 10 A.M. on March 13 struck the Beach Creek bridge, between Bethel Station and Brown's Station, pulling down the trestle and tossing the rails into the creek. A detachment of Rebel cavalry, perhaps fifteen to twenty men, happened across the Buckeyes but were easily driven back; two were captured. The Federals narrowly missed seizing an approaching train, but citizens gave warning. The linkup with Wallace was made later that evening, and by 11 P.M. the entire division was once again aboard the transports and headed downriver for Savannah.[69]

Half of Halleck's grand raid had been completed. Wallace, pleased with the results, praised Haynes for his energy. The conclusion proved premature. At 11:30 P.M. on March 14, not thirty-six hours after the reported destruction of the trestle, Bragg matter-of-factly telegraphed Beauregard: "The damaged bridge is repaired."[70]

• • •

"WHEN I FIRST SAW HIM in Missouri," a correspondent wrote of William Tecumseh Sherman, "his eyes had a half-wild expression, probably the result of excessive smoking. . . . Sherman was never without a cigar. . . . Sometimes he works for twenty consecutive hours. He sleeps little; nor do the most powerful opiates relieve his terrible cerebral excitement."[71]

Sherman seemed to attract the attention of everyone—especially journalists. The forty-one-year-old, red-bearded, six-foot-tall division commander spoke incessantly and in a rather sarcastic tone. He moved constantly and spoke erratically, causing a general to comment later that he was "a splendid piece of machinery with all of the screws a little loose." His problem ran deeper than a few idiosyncrasies. While commanding Federal forces in Kentucky in 1861, he had suffered a nervous breakdown and even considered suicide. Ellen, his stepsister and wife of eleven years, knew of insanity in his family and feared for his "unhealthy state."[72]

It was his comment that he needed 200,000 men to squelch the rebellion in Kentucky that landed him in the deepest trouble. A headline in the December 1861 *Cincinnati Times* declared him "insane," a charge too readily repeated by other papers. Sherman was relieved of command. Fortunately, Halleck, who knew him before the war, continued to express confidence. He brought him to St. Louis to recuperate, slowly drew him into strategy sessions, and eventually gave him command of the District of Cairo, where he forwarded troops to Grant during the Henry-Donelson campaign. In late February 1862, he was given command of the newest division in Grant's army.[73]

Grant and Sherman undoubtedly knew one another before the war, but their much-written-about partnership had not bloomed by March 1862. Physically and emotionally they were opposites, but their backgrounds had similarities. Grant had struggled with alcohol and Sherman with emotional instability. Both had unspectacular Regular Army careers and had failed in business pursuits. Sherman, like Grant, had political backing at the commencement of the war—his foster father, Senator Thomas Ewing, Jr., and brother, Senator John Sherman.[74]

Sherman had been in a bit of a mood at Savannah. As previously stated, he had had a row with Colonel Hicks, his 1st Brigade commander. He was also outraged that some sick soldiers of the 46th Ohio had been placed in a house in town with "a parcel of women." He promptly ordered the patients to vacate the premises. When they failed to move quickly enough, he repeated the order "very violently, and in the most silly and brutal manner," according to an officer in the 46th.[75]

On the morning of March 14, Smith summoned Sherman to his boat. The suffering general, his leg wound barely thirty-six hours old, directed that Sherman proceed with his division upriver to the vicinity of Eastport to break the Memphis & Charleston Railroad. It was a raid similar to and nearly simultaneous with Wallace's. Exactly why Smith entrusted this potentially dangerous assignment to his rawest division is not known. Perhaps he desired to give the troops experience. For whatever reason, Sherman, "Cump" to his friends, had a chance to prove himself. Since Frank Cheatham's Rebel division was reportedly lurking at Pittsburg Landing, he did request that a backup division be sent to secure that location.[76]

By noon, the division had embarked upon nineteen transports and, under escort of *Tyler,* proceeded past Pittsburg Landing, where a couple of shells were dropped, but with no response. The boats continued to the mouth of Yellow Creek, thirty-two miles from Savannah, and pulled in at Tyler's Landing, Mississippi, at 7 P.M. Major Elbridge G. Ricker's battalion of the 5th Ohio Cavalry, four hundred strong, began disembarking in the midst of a deluge. Ricker, with the assistance of a local guide, was to move his men three miles to Red Sulphur Springs and then turn southwest to Burnsville, seventeen miles distant. The rain temporarily let up as the column galloped off at 11 P.M., but by 1 A.M. on the 15th it was pouring again. Sherman was still hopeful that Ricker could reach his destination in five hours. Time was of the essence; the area was thought to be crawling with Rebels. The enemy concentration at Iuka was the primary concern, but the main encampment, at Corinth, was only twenty-two miles from Tyler's Landing. In advancing his infantry to support Ricker, Sherman might get cut off from the rear.[77]

Exactly how much danger Sherman actually faced is debatable. Chalmers had foolishly moved his entire brigade from Iuka to Eastport to protect the Chickasaw heavy guns. Since the Red Sulphur Springs Road forked and went to Iuka, as well as Burnsville, the vital Bear Creek bridge lay exposed. When Chalmers mistakenly received orders to join the Bethel Station concentration, he returned his brigade, minus his artillery and a company of cavalry, to Iuka, to await transportation. By happenstance, the town was thus protected, but Burnsville had no garrison. As for the Confederates' moving out of Corinth, the possibility was remote. Even if scouts had immediately detected the landing (which, in fact, they did), by the time this was related to Corinth and Ruggles's division moved out, so that battle could be offered, it would have been late afternoon of the 15th. By that time, Sherman was gone. After leaving a garrison, Ruggles might have had 7,000 or 8,000 troops to oppose an equal number of Federals, backed by *Tyler*. The Yankees, of course, lacked such information, and the situation remained tense.[78]

The river was rising so rapidly that the infantry did not debark until 3 A.M. on March 15. Retaining two brigades at the landing, the division commander planned to march his other two brigades six miles into the interior, to the intersection of the Burnsville and Iuka Roads. The column trudged forward at 5 A.M. "The road was pretty muddy at first awhile, but after we got away from the river, the road was much better," Christian Zook of the 46th Ohio wrote his friends. Only four and a half miles into the march, the column encountered an impassable bayou, nearly a half-mile wide and deep enough to swim a horse through at places. While pondering this dilemma, Sherman received a message from Ricker. So treacherous was the terrain in the icy downpour (three of his men nearly drowned in the process of wading a swollen stream) that it proved impossible to continue. The only alternative was to return to the transports. Retracing their steps proved tricky: a creek that had been easily waded by the infantry at 5 A.M. was nearly six feet deep four hours later; the troops crossed a makeshift bridge, but the field guns had to be dragged across and almost mired in the creek bottom. Nevertheless, the cavalry had returned to the landing by 11:30 A.M.[79]

Sherman was not yet beaten. He reboarded *Tyler* and proceeded to scout the upriver landings. He found Cook's Landing, at the mouth of Indian Creek, totally under water. The gunboat steamed to within range of the Confederate battery at Chickasaw, Alabama, but there appeared to be no activity. As for a landing site, the entire river from Chickasaw back to Pittsburg Landing was flooded. Sherman's transports steamed back to the first high ground—Pittsburg Landing. In response to Sherman's earlier request, Stephen A. Hurlbut's division was awaiting him in transports. That evening an Ohio officer disgustedly summarized the entire affair by jotting in his diary: "A very silly expedition under the circumstances and adding hundreds of weakly men to the sick list."[80]

Washington, D.C.

IN EARLY MARCH 1862, there were indications that the Confederate Army at Manassas Junction, Virginia, under Joseph E. Johnston, had fallen back. Lincoln notified Buell that enemy detachments were moving off and that they "may be destined to meet you." McClellan hurried off to the front to verify the news. His subsequent advance to Manassas proved a fiasco.[81]

On the afternoon of March 9, the president met with his Cabinet, openly discussing the bleak state of affairs in Virginia. Stanton demanded that the nation be freed from the "Potomac incubus," and Edward Bates pleaded with Lincoln to "command the commanders." Later that afternoon, the president drafted General Order No. 3, relieving McClellan as general-in-chief. A new Department of the Mississippi was created, essentially merging the departments of Missouri and Ohio. Only Halleck was considered for top command; he had seniority, and no one could claim his accomplishments. Clearly he wanted it; he had openly courted the appointment.[82]

That evening Lincoln requested John Hay to summon Stanton, Secretary of State William H. Seward, and Chase. Seward arrived first. The president read him the order, which received his full endorsement. Indeed, Seward believed that a great kindness had been extended to McClellan by allowing him to remain commander of the Army of the Potomac. He urged that the order go out under Stanton's name, in order to strengthen the secretary of war's hand.

By this time Stanton had arrived. Although agreeing with the decision, he believed that his name on the document would allow McClellan's friends to accuse him of retaliation for a recent row with the general. "The President decided to take the responsibility," noted Secretary Hay. That evening, without notifying McClellan, the White House released the order to the press. Brigadier General Randolph B. Macy read the article in the morning edition of the *National Intelligencer* and immediately telegraphed the army commander at his Fairfax Courthouse, Virginia headquarters. McClellan was stunned and his staff mortified. Although the general responded gracefully at the time, he bitterly insisted in postwar years that the order had been intended to ensure the failure of the upcoming Peninsula Campaign. *The New York Times* hailed the order, claiming that it would bring unity to the west.[83]

The west had never had a single controlling hand. It was Lincoln who had encouraged cooperation between Halleck and Buell; McClellan held different objectives for both. The order was also significant because it proved to be the genesis of a strategy shift for the administration. Even at this early stage of the war, Lincoln and Stanton had inclinations that, contrary to popular view, the war could be won in the west rather than the east. As for Halleck, he had finally achieved western command. The Tennessee River expedition would now shift from a raid to an invasion.[84]

FOUR

The Armies

Bethel Station

ALARMED BY exaggerated reports of 18,000 Yankees (rather than the actual 5,000) at Crump's Landing, Beauregard feared a major enemy incursion. Sensing an imminent battle, he directed Polk's corps to hasten south from Humboldt to Bethel Station, two of Jones Withers's Alabama regiments at Fort Pillow to proceed by river via Memphis, and Ruggles to rush troops north from Corinth. Bragg hurried from Jackson to command the concentrated force. In his near-panic state, Beauregard made no allowance for the possibility of a Federal diversion or of a simultaneous raid upriver.[1]

Throughout March 14, a constant flow of troop trains rumbled south from Humboldt. That morning a soldier in Henderson noted that he had been "aroused by the cars; they were carrying soldiers from one point to another in great haste; seven regiments passed here today before dinner [noon]. General Bragg landed here today." J. G. Law of the 154th Tennessee, a regiment that maintained its old militia number, was among the reinforcements. "The rain poured down in torrents all day and night," he noted in his diary, "and the cars were so densely packed, that I was compelled to stand on top of a boxcar, with no protection from the rain."[2]

By Saturday morning, March 15, Bragg was convinced that the danger had passed. The Federals at Crump's Landing had reembarked, and the country people had assured Bragg that no sizable force could now move on the road from Pittsburg Landing. The next day, however, intelligence indicated a Federal landing at Pittsburg Landing. Exaggerated estimates placed the total at 30,000; Sherman's and Hurlbut's divisions were actually half that number. Eager for battle, Bragg planned for Polk's troops to unite with Ruggles's division at Adamsville for an advance upon the enemy.[3]

One historian has argued that, had Bragg's plan been implemented on March 16, a combined Confederate force of approximately 11,000 would have attacked Sherman's division at Pittsburg Landing. Given odds of 11,000 to 8,000, it "might well have been enough, if they had been well managed, to drive the Federals into the river." The dynamics of such a tactic would actually have been more complex than suggested. Ruggles's 7,000 troops would have encountered Sherman's 8,000 around Monterey, before the juncture of Bragg's forces took place. Bragg, with about 3,000 or 4,000 of Polk's troops, could have moved on Pittsburg Landing, but he would not have found it vacant. Even though Hurlbut's 7,000-man division did not disembark until March 18, the troops were present aboard transports on March 16. If the Confederates had moved faster, the Federals would have also.[4]

No action occurred on March 16, however, other than a small fray on the Pittsburg-Purdy Road, in which three companies of the 4th Illinois Cavalry easily chased off about sixty Rebel horsemen. Beauregard and Bragg now began to have second thoughts. The Louisiana general, believing that Adamsville was too close to the enemy for a juncture point, preferred Purdy. He had also lost his appetite for the offensive, preferring now a "defensive-offensive" stance—that is, to go on the defensive and then, when the Federals were within striking distance, "take the offensive and crush him." Bragg also backed down, claiming that Polk's troops were arriving too slowly and were too poorly organized and ill-disciplined.[5]

Beauregard bungled at Bethel Station. The entire affair had been premature. Confederate forces would have been forming a juncture in the face of a supposedly superior force—a most risky venture. He was also committing too much of his "army" to the left flank, thus leaving the right exposed. C. F. Smith could easily have held Savannah with a division, while his other two divisions moved upriver, past Pittsburg Landing, for an attack on a site like Farmington. Beauregard had little choice but to take delaying actions and remain on the defensive until Johnston's wing arrived at Corinth. The Creole anxiously awaited his arrival.

With Johnston's Column

AT SUNRISE on February 28, 1862, Johnston's wing of the army trudged south from Murfreesboro—two days behind schedule because of a washed-out bridge. The general initially considered falling back to Stevenson and taking the railroad to Decatur. Such a move would theoretically have been rapid and might have misled the Federals into thinking that the corps was retiring to Chattanooga. Since there was an immense amount of commissary stores that could only be moved by rail, however, he decided to march the troops and transport the supplies. Gilmer advised that, by taking the wagon road due south through Shelbyville, Fayetteville, and Huntsville, Alabama, the infantry and artillery could move as expeditiously as by rail. The route was also midway between Chattanooga and the direct turnpike from Nashville to Decatur, meaning that Johnston could offer battle if Buell advanced by either route. Rumors were spread that the corps was falling back to Chattanooga; all mail went to that place, and Floyd's brigade marched toward the town. The ruse worked, but only for a few days.[6]

Johnston's cavalry swept the roads radiating from Nashville. McNairy's Tennessee Battalion escorted the wagons and artillery, while Wirt Adams's Mississippi regiment and John Wharton's Texas Rangers served as rear guard. John Hunt Morgan, already the darling of the Southern press, boldly probed toward Nashville with small raiding parties, capturing forty-three men. When not harassing the Yankees, the major courted the flirtatious twenty-one-year-old Martha Ready of Murfreesboro, whom he would wed by year's end. Biffle's Tennessee Battalion (seven companies) scouted east toward Columbia, and Colonel J. S. Scott's 1st Louisiana Cavalry guarded the vital Duck Creek bridges at Columbia. Reports sent to Johnston indicated that Buell was not moving, either to intercept the retreat or to unite with Grant's forces.[7]

The march proved uneventful but difficult, thanks to two weeks of unremitting rain and bitterly cold weather. The troops filed into Shelbyville under a light snow on March 2. After resting two days in their tents, they resumed on March 4, and arrived the next day at Fayetteville—"quite a pretty little village," as one Mississippi soldier described it. Johnston and his staff pushed ahead to Huntsville on March 5, staying in the home of J. J. Fackler. The command divided at Fayetteville, part going southwest to Athens, Alabama, and part due south to Huntsville. At the last, soldiers were greeted with Confederate banners flying from every house. A steady rain slowed the Athens column to a crawl.[8]

Johnston arrived at Decatur on March 10 and established his headquarters in an out-office of the McCarty House Hotel. Troops continued to trickle in for the next three days. A. H. Mecklin of the 15th Mississippi thought the community of eight hundred inhabitants "an old looking place." The Tennessee River was out of its banks, but the approach to the railroad trestle had been constructed for just such weather. A two-and-a-half-mile fifty-foot-high embankment shouldered both sides of the track above the flood plain. Planks were placed along the sides of the track for horses and men. Because of varying axle lengths, wagons and artillery pieces had to be loaded aboard flatcars on the north bank and transported over—a time-consuming process.[9]

Johnston remained concerned about the immense pork supplies at Shelbyville—upward of 30,000 butchered hogs. Hardee was sent to that place, along with Patrick Cleburne's brigade and two regiments and a battalion of cavalry, to bring the meat out. Scott also sent a detail to Patriot, Tennessee, to secure the pork and beef under contract with Bruce & Company. Most of the reserve commissary supplies were shipped to Chattanooga and south to Atlanta.[10]

The march from Decatur to Corinth was fraught with danger. Johnston's column would be strung out for ninety-three miles with either Grant or Buell able to pounce upon his flank. Mackall and Gilmer, the general's top staff officers, openly advised against such a risk. In a letter to Davis, Johnston admitted that he was involved "in a most hazardous movement." The most crucial matter was the Florence bridge. The two-story structure, with the track above the wagon road, had been left standing by the Union gunboats during the raid of early March. Smith's army could retake the bridge by marching forty-five miles overland from Savannah. Fortunately, the Tennessee River was now too shallow for the gunboats and transports to pass Colbert Shoals.[11]

Buell could threaten Florence, Alabama, by an overland march via Columbia and Waynesboro, Tennessee. In early March, a Texas doctor arrived from Nashville at Bragg's headquarters and reported that the Yankees intended such a move. The man was interrogated, and the information sounded reliable. On March 15, Chalmers, at Iuka, learned from scouts that Buell intended to move upon Florence. It was not until March 18, however, that Johnston made "silent arrangements" to destroy the Florence bridge if the enemy approached.[12]

By March 14, a crisis loomed. During the early-morning hours, Beauregard urgently telegraphed Johnston for reinforcements for an anticipated battle at Iuka—actually Sherman's Burnsville raid. The two lead brigades of Johnston's column, T. C. Hindman's and S. A. M. Wood's, were at Courtland, Alabama, fifty-two miles distant. Over thirty-six hours passed before a hundred rail cars could be collected at Courtland, which allowed the passage of Hindman's troops and two of Wood's regiments, without wagons, heavy baggage, or artillery. By the time they arrived at Iuka, the crisis had concluded, so the troops proceeded to Corinth.[13]

Johnston failed to deal quickly with significant details. Not until March did he assign a scout to map out northern Alabama and Mississippi between the railroad and the river. Even more significant were his rolling-stock needs. On March 17, Johnston belatedly directed Beauregard at Jackson to collect four hundred cars with locomotives and send them to Decatur. By that time, much of the stock of the Memphis & Charleston had been directed by Ruggles to bring in Bragg's troops and equipment from the Gulf Coast, leaving only a hundred cars. Some thirteen engines and two hundred cars of the Mobile & Ohio had been committed to transport Polk's troops from Humboldt. The best Beauregard could do was to piece together 160 cars of the Mississippi Central Railroad for Johnston's use.[14]

The incessant rains seriously hampered Johnston's movements. On March 13, Brigadier General John S. Bowen telegraphed from Huntsville that his brigade would be unable to get to Decatur unless boxcars were made available. Floyd was directed to send cars from Chattanooga. Two days later, Hindman reported that the creeks at Courtland and Tuscumbia were impassable. He estimated that it would be ten days to two weeks before artillery and wagons could use the dirt road. On the same day, Gilmer described their plight to his wife: "We live in mud and water and the roads have come to such a pass that we can't move much longer." Johnston informed Davis that troop movements were "for the present impossible." Of course, the same rains, muddy roads, and swollen creeks that delayed Johnston also prevented Sherman from severing the railroad on March 15.[15]

By March 20, Johnston's column stretched throughout northern Alabama and Mississippi. Wood's and Hindman's brigades had arrived at Corinth. William Statham's brigade halted at Iuka, and the 15th Arkansas at Burnsville. Bowen's brigade was at Courtland, and Cleburne's and W. H. Carroll's brigades were at Tuscumbia. John Breckinridge's brigade brought up the rear at Decatur. The cavalry was also thinly deployed: Adams's and Wharton's regiments on the north bank of the Tennessee at Decatur, Biffle's battalion en route to that place, the 1st Louisiana and Morgan's Kentucky Squadron observing the enemy and collecting supplies at Pulaski and Shelbyville, respectively. Colonel Ben Helm's Kentucky Regiment guarded Tuscumbia, and McNairy's battalion escorted wagons at Jacinto, Mississippi.[16]

The Federals were clearly in a position to interdict Johnston's march, a fact well appreciated by Johnston and his staff. On March 12, Gilmer predicted that the Yankees might be successful in preventing the juncture. Upon arriving at Corinth, Johnston acknowledged Bragg's role in the concentration, proclaiming that his decisive move to Corinth had "saved the country."[17]

Some historians, pointing to the lapse of an entire month before the two-hundred-mile journey was completed, have concluded that Johnston dawdled. Although a case could be made in his defense, it would seem that Johnston lacked Beauregard's sense of urgency. Clearly the army commander understood the importance of the juncture: he admitted to Davis that it was the only thing that would save his tarnished career. Yet he stayed much too long at Decatur, seemingly more focused on saving pork supplies than on the concentration of troops.[18]

Major H. M. Dillard gave a postwar account in which he and Colonel Jordan went to Johnston at Decatur and expressed Beauregard's sense of urgency regarding the concentration. Johnston allegedly made a final commitment to the juncture at that time, but claimed that he had been ordered by the government to stop at Decatur and reorganize. Jordan never mentioned the incident and remained of the opinion that Johnston did not fully commit himself to the juncture until Beauregard telegraphed for emergency reinforcements. Jordan's understanding appears more creditable. Johnston did not request large numbers of rail cars until after Sherman's raid.[19]

Corinth

JOHNSTON ARRIVED at Corinth on the night of March 22. William M. Inge, a local attorney on furlough in the Confederate Army, offered his home as headquarters. Known locally as the Rose Cottage because of its pink color, it was located at the corner of Filmore and Bunch

Streets. The next day, Johnston held a conference with Beauregard, Polk, and Hardee.[20]

It was during the meeting the day after that, on March 24, Beauregard later claimed, that Johnston committed himself to preemptively striking Grant's army before Buell could make a juncture. William Preston Johnston, Johnston's biographer-son, insisted that this had been his father's desire from the outset. Beauregard's version may well be true, however, for only a week and a half earlier Johnston had argued that the base of operations should be moved from Corinth thirty-eight miles northwest to Bolivar, Tennessee, on the south bank of the Hatchie River. Far from moving away from the enemy, Beauregard advocated advancing eleven miles north to Monterey, placing the army closer to Pittsburg Landing. They settled the difference by remaining at Corinth, but Johnston was obviously thinking defensively and Beauregard offensively.[21]

Beauregard later suggested that between March 19 and 22 an excellent opportunity was missed to strike Grant's scattered army—one division at Crump's Landing, two at Pittsburg Landing, and one at Savannah. (A fifth division would later be added.) Had the Confederates advanced to Monterey, insisted Alfred Roman, they would have been in a position to crush the force at Pittsburg Landing. It is true that perhaps 28,000 Southerners could have been mustered to attack 15,000 Federals—an inviting prospect. There is no evidence, however, that Beauregard so clearly understood Federal dispositions at the time, or even proposed such a move.[22]

By March 24, Grant's army, estimated at 50,000 strong, was known to be concentrated primarily at Pittsburg Landing, with a division at Crump's Landing. Buell's army, also with 50,000, was reported at Columbia. Buell probably intended to link up with Grant, but there was no consensus on the subject. Some believed that Buell would continue due south, strike the railroad between Decatur and Stevenson, and threaten Chattanooga. According to Gilmer's wishful thinking, Grant and Buell would make a juncture, but only to steam back downriver to reinforce Pope on the Mississippi River. If Buell did intend to reinforce Grant, it was crucial that Johnston strike before he faced an army twice the size of his own.[23]

Johnston kept his army huddled within the Corinth defenses and prepared for an offensive. Hardee's 13,000 men continued to arrive by rail through March 27, with Breckinridge's brigade halting at Burnsville. During a two-day period, no fewer than fifteen troop trains pulled in at Corinth. Bragg's corps swelled to 13,500 with the arrival of the New Orleans troops from Grand Junction. Polk's corps, bolstered by some newly arrived regiments from Island No. 10, numbered 9,000. The 4,400 cavalry brought the total strength of the army present for duty to over 40,000.[24]

Beauregard remained particularly watchful of his left flank. Cavalry vedettes were advanced from Purdy and Monterey, and a line of pickets was established from Bethel Station to Corinth, with relays five miles apart. Parties of five to fifteen infantrymen protected local bridges—there were twenty-three such parties between Bethel Station and Corinth alone. Bennett's Tennessee Cavalry Battalion watched the river below Savannah at Coffee, and J. H. Miller's battalion picketed east of Jackson at Lexington, Tennessee.[25]

Bushrod Johnson's brigade guarded Bethel Station, with Colonel Preston Smith's 154th Tennessee advanced to Purdy. The regiment arrived on the afternoon of March 17 and the next day made quarters in the abandoned Purdy University building. No sooner had the troops set aside their gear than a courier galloped into the village and reported the enemy nearby. The regiment quickly formed a line of battle. Soon a body of Yankee cavalry appeared on a nearby hill, their sabers glistening in the sun. "We charged with a cheer, when the enemy turned their faces toward the Tennessee River and fled without a single exchange of compliment," noted one of Smith's men.[26]

A troubled Beauregard decided to bolster the Bethel Station force. On March 27, he dispatched to that place Major General Frank Cheatham, a popular Tennessee Democrat with an affinity for liquor, with his remaining brigade (W. H. Stephens's), making a total division strength of about 4,000. The troops marched overland and did not arrive for several days. Meanwhile, the 2nd Tennessee and two guns of Polk's Tennessee Battery reinforced Smith's regiment at Purdy. A cavalry foray toward Adamsville succeeded in capturing three Yankees, who claimed that they were a part of Lew Wallace's division at Crump's Landing.[27]

The Confederates also probed toward Monterey and Lick Creek. On March 19, a scouting party, led by McNairy County surveyor Benjamin Saunders, crossed Lick Creek and found the Federals in force. On March 23, the Crescent Regiment, accompanied by a cavalry company, scouted north of Corinth, toward Lick Creek. So swollen were the creeks that an ax party had to be sent ahead to fell trees as makeshift bridges. At places the entire regiment had to cross single-file. At one deep stream three men fell in, and one of them nearly drowned. The regiment came to within three miles of Lick Creek, and the advance "could plainly hear their [enemy] drums." Despite such probes, information remained sketchy and numbers imprecise.[28]

"THIS POINT [Corinth] is the 'Grand Point' at which troops are collected from all parts of the Confederacy for some great move," 11th Louisiana member Charles Johnson explained to his wife on March 23. From across the western Confederacy, thousands of troops arrived aboard stifling and overcrowded boxcars. A Louisiana soldier grumbled about the crowded conditions and "a suffocating odor of cattle bile."[29]

Reaction to the massive encampment was generally unfavorable. So rain-soaked was the countryside that Corinth struck one Louisiana soldier as a "slough . . . full of mud and surrounded by water." The white tents appeared to "be floating about through the mist and rain." A Tennessee private wrote in a similar vein: "The place where we are camped now is heavily timbered with oak and hickory with swamps around us in every direction and altogether I think this just about the poorest country I ever saw." A member of the Orleans Guard Battalion, expecting to see a huge expanse of camps, could hardly discern the tents in the woods.[30]

Despite Johnston's assertion that morale had been restored after previous setbacks, many of the men remained pessimistic. John Cato did not think a single man in the 7th Mississippi would re-enlist unless the present situation changed. A. H. Tarlske gloomily predicted that Tennessee was gone.[31]

The army that assembled at Corinth was thoroughly western in origin, the overwhelming majority coming from Tennessee, Kentucky, Alabama, Mississippi, Arkansas, and Louisiana. A sprinkling of troops hailed from Texas and Florida, and Georgia furnished a battery and an infantry company, the latter attached to the 38th Tennessee. Though the army contained relatively few foreigners, some ethnic outfits came from the larger cities. The 2nd Tennessee of Memphis claimed the sobriquet the "Irish Regiment." The 21st Alabama, largely from Mobile, had a company of French and another of Spaniards. The 20th Louisiana comprised six companies of Irish and four of Germans. The most colorful outfit was the Avengo Zouaves—six companies of the 13th Louisiana from New Orleans. One soldier thought them to be "a hard-looking set composed of Irish, Dutch, Negroes, Spaniards, Mexicans and Italians with few or nor Americans." Their bright-red caps, baggy trousers of the same color, and blue shirts with gold braid that glistened in the sun set them apart in the army.[32]

The uniforms worn by most of the men were nondescript. "Some wore uniforms, some half uniforms, some no uniforms at all," observed a Louisianian. Artilleryman Richard Pugh from New Orleans found that the troops were not as poorly clothed as he had expected and all seemed to have good shoes. Many of the men wore a cotton uniform with a butternut hue called "Kentucky jeans." Several of the Gulf Coast outfits, such as the Washington Artillery and Crescent Regiment, donned dark-blue coats and trousers. Just prior to the battle, the 2nd Texas received undyed cotton uniforms, prompting one ungrateful member to comment: "Do these generals expect us to be killed, and want us to wear our shrouds?"[33]

Sickness among the men, compounded by the swampy surroundings and bad water, brought down thousands. A correspondent noted that the 19th Louisiana could not turn out two hundred sound men in the event of a movement. A 17th Louisiana member informed his wife that half the regiment was sick, principally with pneumonia resulting from exposure. Lieutenant Jobe Foxworth estimated that half the 7th Mississippi was stricken with sickness. The statistics told the grim story. Of the 49,745 troops present on April 3, some 7,956, or 16 percent, were on the sick list. Another 2,709 patients were recuperating in general hospitals or at home.[34]

Many of Johnston's regiments were woefully under strength; Hardee's regiments averaged fewer than four hundred men. Most of the troops lacked combat experience. Some batteries went into battle never having fired their pieces. Bragg referred to the army as a "mob," and contemptuously wrote that few of them had ever performed a day's labor.[35]

Most of the small arms consisted of a motley collection of squirrel rifles, percussion muskets, flintlocks, and shotguns. Only a third of the cavalry possessed any weapons. Fortunately, Johnston had received a few shipments of the highly accurate English-made Enfield rifles, which had an effective range of three hundred yards and could kill at up to five hundred yards. Some one thousand Enfields had been received from the cargo of *Bermuda* in September 1861, and another 3,760 the next month from *Fingal* at Savannah, Georgia. The War Department shipped Johnston 3,600 arms in February 1862, including 2,000 Enfields from *Kate*. Some of these rifles were being issued to the troops as late as April 3.[36]

Most of Johnston's cannon were homemade. T. M. Brennan & Company of Nashville supplied the pieces for Rutledge's Tennessee Battery; Quinby & Robinson of Memphis those for Byrne's Mississippi Battery and Bankhead's Tennessee Battery; and Leeds & Company of New Orleans those for the Washington Artillery, Gage's Alabama Battery, and Robertson's Florida Battery. Polk's Tennessee Battery had guns cast at both Quinby & Robinson and the John Clark & Company foundry of New Orleans.[37]

Visually underscoring the lack of army cohesion were the different styles of battle flags in use. Beauregard attempted to standardize the flags of the Mississippi Valley forces by adopting the same design that he had initiated in the eastern theater. It consisted of twelve white stars on a blue St. Andrews cross on a field of red. In February 1862, he ordered a set of such flags made in New Orleans and issued them to Bragg's corps. Polk designed his own flag, consisting of eleven stars on a red "Christian" cross on a field of blue. A set of these banners was ordered from New Orleans in March 1862. When Johnston's "army" arrived at Corinth, the troops carried two different styles of flags. Crittenden's division from eastern Tennessee bore the "Stars and Bars," and Hardee's brigades carried a blue flag, bordered in white and bearing a white "silver moon."[38]

SOMETIME ON OR AROUND March 26, Johnston considered offering overall command to Beauregard. In conferring with Colonel Munford, he remarked that Beauregard had chosen the position and collected additional men. When Munford argued that the upcoming battle might offer the general the opportunity to redeem his reputation, Johnston merely smiled and answered: "I think it but right to make the offer." And make the offer he did, much to the dismay of Kentucky Governor George W. Johnson, who pleaded with him not to do it.[39]

According to Beauregard's version of the story, Johnston admitted that he had lost the confidence of both the army and the people. He agreed to confine himself to department administration, with headquarters at either Memphis or Holly Springs, Mississippi. The Louisiana general politely declined the offer and pledged his full support. Munford recalled the scene somewhat differently. Beauregard thanked Johnston and said that he would consider the offer. The next day he declined, primarily for health reasons, but also graciously added: "I could not think of commanding on a field where Sidney Johnston was present."[40]

William Preston Johnston argued that the offer was a chivalrous gesture and that his father never intended to abdicate supreme command. Although he was technically correct, Johnston would have been little more than a figurehead. The general could not have missed the fact that he had been eclipsed in the popular mind. He may also have been under the impression that he was about to be replaced anyway, not by Beauregard but by Davis. Newspaper rumors circulated that the President was on his way to the west to assume personal command. In a communication to Johnston, Davis told him that he was coming to the west. Johnston pre-emptively replied on March 20: "Were you to assume command, it would afford me the most unfeigned pleasure." The president chose to remain in Richmond, but the thought of relinquishing command must have been on the general's mind before he arrived at Corinth.[41]

Beauregard thus retained his position as second-in-command. Some historians have insisted that the Creole became the de-facto army commander, issuing orders, reorganizing the army, and even devising the battle plan. It is difficult to conclude otherwise, although it must be remembered that Beauregard, too, had earlier lost self-confidence. In desperately attempting to reinforce the Mississippi Valley only weeks earlier, he had offered Bragg his command.[42]

The responsibility for organizing the army fell to Beauregard, although the final plan was most likely discussed with Johnston prior to submission.[43] The resulting structure represented little more than the assignment of a corps number to each pre-existing army component. The 1st Corps, under Polk, consisted of two divisions of two brigades each, totaling 9,136 men. Bragg's 2nd Corps had two divisions, each with three brigades, and numbered 13,589 troops. Hardee's Army of Central Kentucky was divided, with three brigades (6,789 men) forming the 3rd Corps under Hardee and three brigades (6,439 troops), a Reserve Corps, under Crittenden. The rationale of dividing the army into four small corps was partly to deceive the enemy. Since a corps in the Regular Army comprised about 20,000 men, such an organization might give the appearance of an 80,000-man army. Although Grant did subsequently place Southern strength at 80,000, there is no evidence that he did so based on such a connection.[44]

Beauregard's organization of the Army of the Mississippi, as the army was styled, has been variously evaluated by historians.[45] In light of subsequent performance, it is clear that the structure was unwieldy and lacked imagination. Its basic flaw rested in the unequal distribution of troops: Bragg's corps constituted one-third of the army. A more viable (and rather obvious) distribution would have been to limit Bragg's corps to the troops from Pensacola, Mobile, and New Orleans, giving the balance (five regiments) to Polk. Ruggles could then command his own New Orleans troops (two brigades), and Withers those of the Gulf Coast (three brigades). Hardee's 3rd Corps could have comprised two divisions of three brigades each, eliminating the Reserve under the incompetent and highly suspect Crittenden. Such an organization would have more equally distributed the troops and resulted in a more compact structure.[46]

Some shifting of regiments between brigades occurred. Charles Johnson of the 11th Louisiana claimed that petitions were circulated within his outfit asking that it not be brigaded with Tennesseans. When subsequently assigned to Robert Russell's brigade with three Tennessee regiments, Johnson concluded that the men would have to "be content with being lashed to the tail of a Tennessee rabble." Bragg wrote Elise that he intended to scatter his Tennessee regiments "among better men" in his corps.[47]

The army was in need of a new adjutant general. Mackall, Johnston's adjutant, had been promoted to brigadier upon his arrival at Corinth and sent to relieve John P. McCown as commander at Island No. 10. He was told that the garrison would likely fall, but that he must hold out at least twelve days—that is, through April 8. When Mackall subsequently arrived in Memphis, he grumbled to a Johnston staff officer that he had been ordered into "that infernal trap." Jordan became the new army adjutant.[48]

Bragg was tapped as army chief-of-staff, a position known in European armies but for which the Confederate Congress had made no provision. Since the general did not relinquish command of his own corps, it is unclear exactly what role he played. The position may have been largely nominal and was meant to give him authority over Polk, his senior in rank. Jordan later claimed that the title was given so that Bragg could give orders in the name of Johnston in the event of an emergency.[49]

Bragg expressed to Elise his disdain for Polk and even for Johnston. He considered his corps "far superior to Polk's and Johnston's." Plundering was widespread throughout the army, and, he wrote, "Polk and Johnston do nothing to correct this. Indeed the good Bishop sets the example, by taking whatever he wishes." As chief-of-staff, Bragg did address a potentially scandalous situation. Rumor had it that Crittenden, still under a cloud from Somerset, had continued his drinking habits. Hardee was sent to Burnsville to investigate. In a shocking development, both Crittenden and one of his brigadiers, William H. Carroll, were arrested for drunkenness and relieved of command.[50]

Naming a replacement proved somewhat of a predicament. The senior brigadier in the division was John C. Breckinridge, former vice-president of the United States and an officer lacking in military training. His commission antedated by a few months that of Brigadier General John S. Bowen, a West Point graduate. Johnston opted for prestige over experience and appointed Breckinridge as corps commander. As it turned out, Breckinridge's friends had been quietly working for several weeks in Congress to get him promoted to major general.[51]

Van Buren, Arkansas

"SOME OF THE REGIMENTS are ordered in the direction of the Miss. river and every indication is that we will soon be under marching orders in the same direction," Texas Battery Commander John J. Good wrote his wife on March 21, 1862, from Van Buren, Arkansas. Unknown to Good, the troops were marching toward Jacksonport, Arkansas, on the White River, the next point of concentration for the straggling and demoralized Army of the West.[52]

Following his defeat at Pea Ridge, Van Dorn had withdrawn his brigades to Van Buren, a village on the Arkansas River not far from Fort Smith and the border of Indian Territory. Morale had been shattered, and confidence in the general, never high from the outset, plummeted. The original purpose of this eastward movement was to relieve the garrison at New Madrid, Missouri, but Van Dorn subsequently learned that the town had been evacuated. He now sought Beauregard's advice. The Louisiana general, still at Jackson, Tennessee, on March 23, again urged him to join the forces concentrating in the Mississippi Valley.[53]

The next day, March 24, at the general's conference at Corinth, the topic of the Army of the West came under discussion. Bragg, who boasted to Elise that his opinion had "some weight with Johnston and Beauregard," joined the Creole in urging that Van Dorn's army come east of the Mississippi River. Johnston ordered the trans-Mississippi army to Memphis, explaining to Davis that Van Dorn was not being menaced by the enemy and that northwestern Arkansas could not sustain his army.[54]

Van Dorn, who did not receive the order until March 27, determined to move his troops to Des Arc, Arkansas, a town on the White River, about fifty miles south of Jacksonport. From there boats would be made available for the trek to Memphis. The dapper forty-one-year-old West Point graduate, a member of the Mississippi aristocracy and a close friend to the president, then hurried to Corinth to confer with Johnston and Beauregard. "He looked to me more like a dandy than a general of the army," observed a disgusted soldier. Van Dorn's indiscretions with women, a poorly kept secret, would ultimately lead to his death in May 1863 at the hands of a jealous husband. He arrived in Corinth late one evening in March 1862 (the precise day is unknown) and departed three and a half hours later. In a letter to the president on March 30, the general urged Davis to "be with us in the great Battle of Corinth." As fate would have it, Van Dorn himself would not be present.[55]

Meanwhile, his troops continued their grueling two-hundred-mile march from Van Buren. So wretched were road conditions that Van Dorn estimated three weeks would be required for his 20,000 troops and seventy field guns to reach Jacksonport. Exactly how long Johnston could wait for the trans-Mississippians was problematic. On March 27, Captain Good again took pen in hand: "The whole army are on the moove [sic] eastward. But our destination is a mystery to all."[56]

Richmond

IN EARLY MARCH 1862, Colonel Liddell was again in Richmond. Recalling his failed mission of the previous January, he had begged Johnston to be excused, but to no avail. In addition to hand-delivering the Fort Donelson reports of Floyd and Pillow, he was to convey Johnston's commitment to concentrate his forces below the Tennessee River for a decisive blow. The meeting with the president occurred on March 7. The colonel found him again to be in a sour mood. Davis confined his remarks to Floyd and Pillow, who he believed were entirely responsible for the Fort Donelson surrender. "I was very careful to say nothing," Liddell noted.[57]

The chief executive was not pleased with Johnston's lack of responsiveness concerning the losses of Fort Donelson and Nashville. A congressional investigation was now under way, and answers had to be forthcoming. On March 12, he gently reminded Johnston that, although he respected the general's decision to suffer in silence, the question of culpability was "public in its nature."[58]

Johnston responded in a letter dated March 18, a dispatch delivered to Richmond personally by Captain T. M. Jack on March 26. The president was in a gracious mood on that day and inquired about "my friend General Johnston." As Davis read Johnston's letter, Jack engaged in a conversation with General Robert E. Lee, who happened to be present. While listening to Lee, the captain occasionally glanced at the president, hoping to catch the expression on his face. Johnston's letter presented a lengthy defense of his actions in the late campaign. He was now engaged in "a hazardous experiment" to join Beauregard at Corinth, the successful conclusion of which would silence his critics. Jack later recalled that Davis bordered on tears.[59]

Davis replied by assuring Johnston that his confidence in him had never wavered. Although the general had performed "wonderfully well," Davis admitted that he would "breathe easier" once the juncture had been completed. Upon Jack's return to Corinth, Johnston immediately asked the captain how he had been received. "As the aide-de-camp of his friend," came the reply.[60]

Pittsburg Landing

THE SO-CALLED Yellow Creek expedition having failed, Sherman withdrew his troops to Pittsburg Landing, where they made a juncture with Hurlbut's division, awaiting them in transports. Sherman continued on to Savannah aboard *Continental* to confer with the ailing Smith. Determined to redeem his reputation, the Ohio general proposed another venture. Union sympathizers had indicated that the Confederates expected an attack on Corinth. Using this to his advantage, he would debark his division at Pittsburg Landing and feint toward Corinth while a cavalry raid was being made on the Memphis & Charleston Railroad, toward Farmington. Smith approved the plan, commenting that he would soon come in person and move out in force toward the railroad. Sherman was to encamp back from the landing and leave sufficient room for the entire army.[61]

The brigadier general rejoined his division at Pittsburg Landing, accompanied by Lieutenant Colonel James B. McPherson, an engineer temporarily attached from Halleck's staff who two years later would command the Army of the Tennessee. Still concerned about the alleged presence of Cheatham's division, Sherman rode out three miles toward Bethel Station and made a personal reconnaissance. Convinced that the landing was clear, he put his plan into action. Lieutenant Colonel Thomas Heath's ad-hoc battalion of companies from the 5th Ohio Cavalry (350 men) and 4th Illinois Cavalry (eighty-five troopers) was brought ashore on the evening of March 16. Heath was to proceed with his column down the Pittsburg-Corinth Road toward Monterey. Once there, he would consult with Major W. D. Sanger, a Sherman staff officer who would accompany the troopers, to ascertain whether a dash could be made on the railroad. Sherman encouraged Heath to make the attempt if at all possible.[62]

As the cavalry departed, Sherman began disembarking his infantry. The 1st Brigade, under Colonel John A. McDowell, filed off at midnight, followed an hour later by Colonel David Stuart's 2nd Brigade. "It was a clear and frosty night" as the troops passed up the bluff, remembered an Illinois soldier. When McDowell's infantry had marched a mile out the Pittsburg-Corinth Road, they suddenly encountered Heath's returning troopers, who had butted against an estimated five enemy cavalry companies just beyond Shiloh Church. Two Rebels were taken prisoner and four Federals wounded in the fifty-minute skirmish that ensued. More significantly, the Southerners were alerted to Sherman's raid.[63]

At sunrise on Monday, March 17, the balance of Sherman's division disembarked. That morning the division moved out, three brigades proceeding down the Pittsburg-Corinth Road, and the fourth (Stuart's) south along the Hamburg-Savannah Road to guard the Lick Creek ford. The 6th Iowa marched out the Purdy Road to protect the Owl Creek approach. Past Shiloh Church, Sherman found the debris of the previous night's encampment—horses straying about and mired in the swampy bottoms, and discarded saddles, swords, and shotguns. Spotty intelligence claimed that two enemy regiments were at Monterey and five at Purdy. Confederate strength at Corinth and its vicinity was estimated at 30,000.[64]

Sherman remained feisty, despite his two unsuccessful attempts on the railroad. He now proposed a third option that combined aspects of the first two plans. A direct approach toward Corinth from Pittsburg Landing was not feasible: "The ground is well watched," he conceded. He therefore proposed a diversion toward Monterey with the infantry, while a cavalry raid was made far to the left, on Burnsville. About two hundred troopers, supported by an infantry regiment, would be transported by steamboat to Tyler's Landing under the protection of a gunboat, in a scaled-down version of the Yellow Creek expedition.[65]

Meanwhile, Sherman maintained his troops in the Shiloh Church vicinity. Hurlbut's division disembarked on March 17 and moved a mile inland. As the troops explored their new surroundings, one particular sight attracted their morbid curiosity. In a field atop the bluff (where the national cemetery would one day be located), two or three Confederates had been buried in shallow graves—casualties of the March 1 engagement. Some of the men got sticks and exposed the dead soldiers' faces. "He keeps pretty well," joked one wag; another remarked, "What a red moustache this fellow had!" John S. Wilcox of the 55th Illinois informed his wife that he had visited one such grave— "the sight was not pleasant."[66]

Sherman had his eye on more significant matters. On March 17, he and McPherson had made a reconnaissance of the rolling plateau back from the landing. He was greatly impressed with the nine-square-mile flat surface, bounded by Snake Creek and its tributary, Owl Creek, on the north, and Lick Creek on the south. The last, so named for the deer licks in its bottoms, was bordered on the north by a range of sloping hills two hundred feet high. Any attack made by the Rebels would have to come through the three-mile opening between the creeks.

The terrain remained wilderness in places—uneven, thickly wooded, dense undergrowth—and cut by sloughs, ridges, and deep ravines. Some five to seven hundred years earlier, an unknown Indian tribe had left a cluster of seven mounds, five to fifteen feet in height, three-fourths of a mile south of the landing. Three dozen farms dotted the area, mostly log cabins with adjoining forty-to-eighty-acre fields of cotton and corn and some orchards. Sherman believed there was ample campground for 100,000 men.[67]

About a mile from the landing, the Pittsburg-Corinth Road connected with three roads. The first led to Crump's Landing and was called the Hamburg-Purdy Road, or River Road, as it became more popularly known. The second, a half-mile farther, was the Eastern Corinth Road, which swung inland and connected with the Bark Road. The Pittsburg-Corinth Road ran west of and parallel to the Eastern Corinth Road and was sometimes referred to as the Western Corinth Road. The eastern and western roads were connected by the Hamburg-Purdy Road. Numerous other paths crisscrossed the terrain.

Sherman reported his findings, but not to Smith. Word had

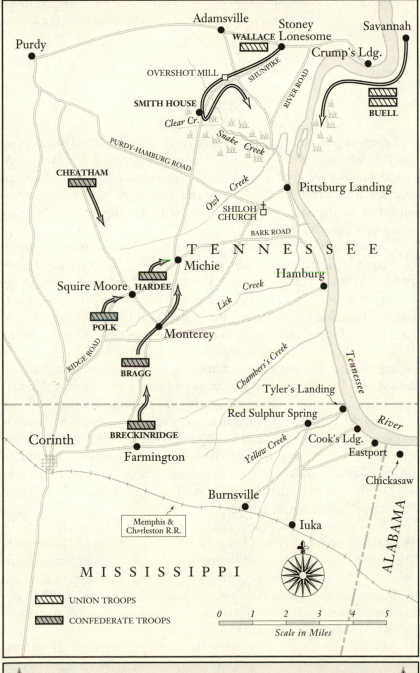

MAP 2: THE SHILOH CAMPAIGN

Purdy

Adamsville

Stoney
Lonesome

Savannah

WALLACE

Crump's Ldg.

OVERSHOT MILL

SHUNPIKE

RIVER ROAD

BUELL

SMITH HOUSE

Clear Cr.

Snake Creek

PURDY-HAMBURG ROAD

CHEATHAM

Owl Creek

Pittsburg Landing

SHILOH
CHURCH

BARK ROAD

T E N N E S S E E

Michie

Hamburg

Squire Moore

HARDEE

Lick Creek

POLK

Monterey

RIDGE ROAD

Chambers's Creek

Tennessee

BRAGG

Tyler's Landing

Red Sulphur Spring

River

BRECKINRIDGE

Yellow Creek

Cook's Ldg.

Corinth

Eastport

Farmington

Chickasaw

Burnsville

A L A B A M A

Memphis &
Charleston R.R.

Iuka

M I S S I S S I P P I

UNION TROOPS

CONFEDERATE TROOPS

0   1   2   3   4   5

Scale in Miles

reached him of a change of command: Grant had arrived at Savannah. Cump's observations would have a significant influence on the events that followed.

Savannah

"THE POWER is in your hands; use it & you will be sustained by all above you." With these words, Halleck grudgingly restored Grant to command. Having received overall western command, the St. Louis commander also changed the nature of the campaign. No longer was it a raid, but an invasion, in conjunction with a move by Buell's army southwest from Nashville.[68]

Grant, still suffering from a bout of diarrhea and fever, departed on March 16, 1862, aboard *Tigress*, a speedy Ohio River packet. He arrived at Savannah the next day and established his headquarters in the Cherry mansion. By his side was the thirty-one-year-old, cantankerous, profane, but highly loyal John A. Rawlins. The captain continued to serve as Grant's guardian against drink, an obsession driven by Rawlins's own father's alcoholism, which had driven his family to poverty. Other assistants in the adjutant general's office offered a similar loyalty. Captain W. S. Hillyer was a former St. Louis real-estate agent who had known Grant before the war. Captain William R. Rowley, a neighbor of Grant's in Galena, was appointed to his position by Congressman Washburne. The thirty-eight-year-old captain, a former tax assessor, circuit-court clerk, and sheriff, served as a link to Grant's Republican supporters in Galena. An unimpressed Sherman wrote after the war that Grant's "staff at Shiloh was very inferior, Rawlins, [Clark] Lagow, Hillyer, etc."[69]

Serving as chief-of-staff was fifty-one-year-old Colonel Joseph D. Webster. A native of New Hampshire and a graduate of Dartmouth, Webster had served with distinction in the U.S. Topographical Engineers. He eventually returned to private life and was living in Chicago at the start of the war. Grant had confidence in "the old soldier" and had recommended him for a brigadier's commission. As chief-of-staff, he served as both adviser and troubleshooter.[70]

Grant was dismayed by what he found at Savannah. Discipline was lax, and a shortage of coal and forage existed. More significantly, he realized that his army was dangerously divided—two divisions at

Pittsburg Landing, each composed of new levies; one at Crump's Landing; and two on the east bank at Savannah, both veteran. Influenced by Sherman's report, he immediately ordered the troops at Savannah to concentrate at Pittsburg Landing. It would be his first major decision of the campaign, and clearly his most devastating.[71]

Hindsight dictated that Savannah, on the east bank, would have been the more prudent choice. The possibility of the Confederates' crossing the river in force was virtually nil. The Florence bridge remained intact, but a major crossing so far upriver would have left Corinth vulnerable. It would be the spring of 1864 before the Southerners built a train of 120 pontoons to bridge the river. There were several steamboats at Florence that had escaped the earlier Federal raid. Ferrying troops across would be risky with Federal gunboats on the prowl. More important, there is no evidence that the Confederates even considered such a move. Grant could have used the security of Savannah until Buell's army made a juncture. Then, under the shield of the gunboats and two hundred field guns, the combined armies could cross to Pittsburg Landing with maximum security.

By choosing Pittsburg Landing, Grant (who never directly addressed the issue in his memoirs) apparently had several factors in mind. Smith, in face of whom Grant was overly awed, had already contemplated such a move. Grant also remained eager for a forward movement before the Confederates concentrated. Toward that end, he dispatched Captain Hillyer to St. Louis to plead for a quick strike at the railroad, which still remained the primary objective.[72]

On the evening of March 19, before Hillyer's arrival at department headquarters, it appeared as though Halleck sanctioned such a move. Information had been received at St. Louis that 26,000 Confederates were moving out of Corinth to cut off river transportation to the Federals north of Savannah. Halleck advised a strike at Corinth. Although Grant realized that the flooded riverbanks would keep the Rebel artillery out of range of the transports, he made immediate preparations for a move on Corinth. Notified of this development on March 20, Halleck was taken aback by Grant's promptness. He telegraphed the next day, cautioning him not to be drawn into an engagement. Grant was to wait for Buell's army—and, he might have parenthetically added, for himself.[73]

In the rush of telegrams, the issue of the west-bank encampment got lost. If the objective was the railroad, or Corinth, then Grant's view of a quick strike had merit. The proper objective, however, which neither Grant nor Halleck seemed to grasp, should have been not geography but the Rebel army. As for the Confederate attack north of Savannah, it proved to be more faulty information.[74]

Pittsburg Landing

THROUGHOUT THE LAST two weeks of March and into early April 1862, Pittsburg Landing mushroomed into an enormous army camp. Transports docked at the landing five deep. Sherman's raw 5th Division of 8,500 mostly Ohio troops were encamped in the Shiloh Church vicinity. Hurlbut's 4th Division, 6,500 primarily midwestern and prairie-state men, contained a mix of veterans and new levies and was encamped near the Eastern Corinth and Hamburg-Savannah Roads. Smith's veteran 2nd Division, 8,500 mainly Illinois and Iowa troops, arrived on March 19 and was placed in reserve, about a mile north of the landing. McClernand's predominately Illinois 1st Division, nearly 7,000 veterans strong, was ordered up on March 20 and was encamped in the rear of Sherman's division. The nonhistoric 6th Division, organized on March 26 from 4,000 levies, was led by Brigadier General Benjamin M. Prentiss. Its two brigades camped at the only remaining vacancy—on the outer rim, to the left of Sherman, at right angles across the Eastern Corinth Road.[75]

Grant's army at Pittsburg Landing totaled 34,500 men present for duty on March 31, with another 7,500 noncombatants—cooks, hospital staff, teamsters, and the like. Additional outfits continued to arrive throughout early April, swelling army strength (exclusive of Lew Wallace's division) to 45,000. The 16th Iowa arrived on the evening of the 4th, and the next day the 15th Michigan, 18th Wisconsin, and B, 2nd Illinois Light Artillery debarked. The latter, commanded by Captain Reilly Madison, was a siege battery with five huge twenty-four-pounder siege guns, meant to be used against the Corinth fortifications. Four of the weapons bore personal names: "Old Abe," "Dick Yates," "Sec. Hatch," and "J. K. Dubois." On the morning of April 6, the 15th Iowa and 23rd Missouri arrived, both fresh from camps of instruction. Supporting Grant's army were twenty-one batteries with 102 guns and three cavalry regiments and eight companies spread out among the divisions, sometimes with little rhyme or reason.[76]

Contrary to popular notion, the Federals did not possess a significant edge in firepower. The majority of the infantry shouldered smooth-

MAP 3: PITTSBURG LANDING AND VICINITY

Tennessee River

Pittsburg Landing

Lick Creek

Pond

McCULLER FIELD

Orchard

HAGY FIELD

Dill Branch

INDIAN MOUNDS

CLOUD FIELD

Orchard

CHAMBERS'S FIELD

ROAD

WICKER FIELD

Peach Orchard

SARAH BELL FIELD

Orchard

LARKIN FIELD

Locust Grove

SAVANNAH

HAMBURG

Pond

SPAIN FIELD

MULBERRY FIELD

DUNCAN FIELD

DAVIS WHEAT FIELD

CAVALRY FIELD

Branch

EASTERN CORINTH ROAD

Tilghman

PERRY FIELD

JONES FIELD

WOOLF FIELD

REVIEW FIELD

PURDY-HAMBURG ROAD

BARNES FIELD

LOST FIELD

SOWELL FIELD

Water Oaks Pond

REA FIELD

SEAY FIELD

Owl Creek

CRESCENT FIELD

FIELD

HOWELL FIELD

SHILOH CHURCH

CORINTH ROAD

FRALEY FIELD

PITTSBURG

WOOD'S FIELD

MILL

FIELD

Shiloh Branch

WIDOW HOWELL FIELD

To Purdy

Owl Creek

Scale in Miles

0   .5   1

bore muskets altered to percussion. A few entire regiments claimed Enfield rifles or cumbersome old Austrian rifles, but typically these arms
were issued to a company or two within certain regiments. After the battle, a Rebel reported that the Yankee arms were not superior—the barrels were like gas pipes and the hammers difficult to cock. Though the
artillery boasted a number of fine James and Parrott rifles, nearly half the
field guns were smoothbore six-pounders and twelve-pounder howitzers.[77]

Sickness in the Union Army continued unabated, diarrhea being
the chief complaint. Chief Surgeon Henry C. Hewitt remained under
a cloud from alcoholism and the alleged mistreatment of Federal
wounded at Fort Donelson. Since there was only a single hospital boat,
City of Memphis, Grant sent Surgeon Brinton to St. Louis to request
additional transports. In the meantime, the sick continued to accumu-
late at Savannah and in camp. On March 24, the chief surgeon issued
an order that all those unable to withstand the rigors of a campaign be
discharged. It was estimated that one-sixth of each regiment could le-
gitimately be sent home. On March 28, Grant complained that his
army had been out of some medicines for a week.[78]

Halleck, forever sour, fired off an angry letter charging "gross ir-
regularities" in Grant's medical department. His sick were supposed to
be sent to Cincinnati, yet "large numbers" continued to arrive at St.
Louis, where the hospitals were already filled to overflowing. Lew
Wallace had sent two hundred sick patients to New Albany, Indiana,
where there were no hospital accommodations. Surgeons also freely
dispensed furloughs to those merely wishing to go home. Grant, who
had been at Savannah only a few days, conceded the problem with the
furloughs, but denied that he had ever been notified to send his sick to
Cincinnati.[79]

Grant's attention soon focused on his top officers. Pompous and
overbearing, 1st Division Commander John A. McClernand was again
causing problems. Relations between him and Grant, strained even before Fort Henry, deteriorated after Fort Donelson. The Illinois political general, besides writing to his fiancée, Minerva Dunlap, twenty-four
years his junior and the sister of his deceased wife, still found time to become embroiled with Smith (who detested him) over seniority. Lieutenant Colonel Adolph Englemann, with a regiment in McClernand's
division, advised his wife not even to place a division number on her
mail, for McClernand insisted that his should be "First Division" and
"outrank the other [Smith]." Grant, who had little patience with the

matter, temporarily retained McClernand at Savannah so he could place Sherman (McClernand's junior) in charge at Pittsburg Landing.[80]

The Union command was plagued by other political generals. Leading the 4th Division was forty-seven-year-old Stephen A. Hurlbut, an Illinois Republican known for his embarrassing drunken binges and shady land-deals. Colonel Isaac C. Pugh, commanding a regiment in the division, confided to his wife on March 22: "Genl Hurlbut is a drunkard & is drunk all the time when he can get anything to drink on." A petition circulated throughout the division to request his resignation was ignored.[81]

Smith's condition continued to decline, forcing Grant to face the possibility that he might have to replace his most experienced division commander. On March 22, he approached Brigadier General William H. L. Wallace and intimated that a change would be forthcoming in the 2nd Division. The forty-one-year-old former Illinois lawyer had received his brigadier's commission only the previous day. Although a nonprofessional, he had fought in several engagements in the Mexican War. He clearly lacked the credentials to fill Smith's shoes, which he acknowledged when he formally received the command in late March.[82]

Directing the new 6th Division was forty-one-year-old Brigadier General Benjamin M. Prentiss, another Illinois lawyer, who had dabbled in Republican politics and reportedly had ties to President Lincoln. He, too, had fought in the Mexican War and, quite coincidentally, had served in the same company as W. H. L. Wallace. A year earlier, at Cairo, Illinois, he had feuded with Grant over seniority, and the two were not particularly cordial. Prentiss had previously mentioned to a journalist that he would not serve "under a drunkard [Grant]."[83]

Thus, the only West Point professional commanding a division at Pittsburg Landing was Sherman, still suspect because of earlier press charges of insanity. His wife, Ellen, insisted that McClellan had plotted to discredit him. For his part, the humiliated brigadier general desired to put the past unpleasantness behind him. He discouraged family efforts to obtain retractions and expressed that he wished only "to be left alone."[84]

THE SHEER MAGNITUDE of the Pittsburg Landing encampment awed recruits and veterans alike. "There is no end to the tents. We can see them scattered in all directions as far as we can see," described Private

Franklin Bailey. The scene "reminds one of a camp meeting, only on a rather large scale," observed a member of the 52nd Illinois. Everywhere were the sounds of pounding axes, beating drums, and braying mules. Concluded an Illinois infantryman: "No doubt a 'looker-on' would be led to think war 'a glorious thing.' "[85]

The enlisted men slept in large white teepee-shaped Sibley tents, each capable of accommodating sixteen, and officers stayed in wall tents. Franklin Bailey explained to his parents that each company had five tents for enlisted men, and at the head of the row was a wall tent for the officers. Some ten to fifteen feet separated the companies to allow room for washing and cooking. The quartermaster and hospital tents were located somewhat to the side.[86]

Most of Grant's troops hailed from rural areas, but a heavy infusion also came from towns and cities. The 8th Missouri was composed of St. Louis steamboat men, and its officers had been former passenger agents of the packet lines. Hundreds of men in several outfits came from Chicago. The 20th Illinois was a Joliet regiment, and the 21st Illinois, Grant's old "Lead Mine Regiment," drew from Galena and Rockford.[87]

Ethnic outfits, though not plentiful, were sprinkled throughout the army. The 43rd Illinois, a downstate regiment, had two companies of Swedes and eight of Germans, although the latter were mostly sons of immigrants. The 45th and 58th Illinois were half German, as were the 24th Indiana and 18th Wisconsin. The 57th Illinois had a Swedish company. Captain Charles Mann's Missouri Battery was of Dutchmen, and H, 1st Illinois Light Artillery had Scandinavians. The 6th Indiana Light Artillery consisted of Germans, as did a large percentage of the 7th Iowa.[88]

The days remained uncomfortably wet and chilly through March 22; at night the ground was blanketed with frost. Gentle spring temperatures soon came to the Mississippi Valley, bringing new life to the countryside. A light foliage covered the trees, and peach orchards turned pink with blossoms. "We have a most lovely spot here to camp. This is nice country, heavily timbered with oak, ash, maple, beach, poplar, etc. just like Indiana," commented one soldier.[89]

The mild weather lasted but a few days, after which temperatures surged uncomfortably upward. An Illinois artilleryman wrote his father: "It has got to be real warm weather here, so warm that we go in our shirt sleeves." "During the last two or three weeks," Timothy Blaisdell indicated to his wife, "we have been having not warm, but hot weather, hotter than I ever saw in June in Chicago. The fruit trees were two weeks ago all in blossom, and no one thinks of wearing a coat."[90]

The days typically passed in drills and inspections. Bela T. St. John informed his parents that his regiment drilled in the middle of a peach orchard. According to another Illinois infantryman, colonels would frequently get up a competition between their regiments. On March 31, a Hoosier in the 4th Division was in a parade with twelve regiments. He wrote: "To a civilian the scene would have been quite imposing, but to us it was only a 'little grand.' " When in camp, the men lulled themselves by writing letters, reading week-old Chicago newspapers, playing horseshoes, and browsing about sutlers' wagons, which arrived "in great numbers." Numerous poker and dice games commenced on payday.[91]

The Federals, fresh from their victory at Fort Donelson, remained confident—too confident. Cannoneer Enoch Colby informed his parents: "We shall not have more than one fight, and that will probably be at Corinth, Mississippi." In like mind, William Skinner wrote his brother and sister: "I think the rebellion is getting nearly played out, and I expect we will be home soon." Many men feared taking a leave, according to Elijah Shepard, lest the war end in their absence. General officers shared in the confidence. Lew Wallace expressed to his wife, " 'Sesesch' is . . . about on its last legs in Tennessee." One final battle, he predicted, would "be the last in the west." Grant concurred, and wrote Julia on March 18: "With one more success I do not see how the rebellion is to be sustained."[92]

St. Louis

HALLECK SAT STOICALLY as he listened to Captain Hillyer explain at length Grant's desire to attack the Confederates before they concentrated. Indeed, the scene was strangely reminiscent of Grant's visit with Halleck back in January. As the captain concluded, he was brusquely dismissed. The dispatches handed to him only repeated earlier orders to avoid a general engagement.[93]

"Old Brains," initially at least, was more sensitive in his dealings with Buell. He assured the Ohio general on March 13 that the "new arrangements of departments" would not interfere with his command; he even proposed a consultation. Buell disingenuously expressed that cooperation between the armies was necessary and Halleck's appointment "eminently proper." Responding on March 14 as though he intended to operate independently, however, Buell proposed a strike on the Memphis & Charleston at Florence. Halleck did not receive the message until March 26, but by the 16th he had already abandoned his forced cordiality. Buell was to march toward Savannah "so that the enemy cannot get between us." The next day, he was even more typically himself, as he directed Buell to begin immediately for Savannah. "Don't fail to carry out my instructions. I know I am right."[94]

In the third week in March, Halleck wrote the secretary of war an update on western operations. Pope, with an army of 25,000, was working his way through the swamps south of New Madrid. Buell would make a juncture with Grant by March 24, placing 70,000 men at the Confederate center. Halleck's plan to send additional reinforcements to Savannah from Missouri had been sidetracked by War Department orders to dispatch 5,000 troops to New Mexico. As the St. Louis commander pondered his positions, he entertained "no chance of failure."[95]

Columbia, Tennessee

BY MID-MARCH 1862, Buell was finally prepared to advance. A garrison force of 18,000 remained in Nashville and middle Tennessee. Major General Ormsby Mitchel's 8,000-man division protected the flank by marching toward Murfreesboro and south to Fayetteville. The former was entered without incident on March 20. If the Confederates did not attempt an offensive, Mitchel was to proceed into northern Alabama and strike the Memphis & Charleston Railroad. Hearing rumors of twenty-five or thirty enemy regiments fronting Cumberland Gap, Buell also dispatched Brigadier General George Morgan's division to that place.[96]

On March 16–17, the balance of the Army of the Ohio, five divisions of 37,000 troops, filed southwest from Nashville along the Central Alabama Railroad toward Columbia, a town of 3,500 residents on the south bank of the Duck River forty-two miles from the state capital. Spearheading the column was Brigadier General Alexander McCook's 2nd Division. "The country we passed through is splendid," explained Corporal Alexander Varian of the 1st Ohio. "We passed plenty of cotton plantations and some of the finest wheat I ever saw." Gangs of slaves watched along the roadside as the soldiers passed.

There was talk in the ranks that the Rebels might attempt one last stand, but A. S. Bloomfield noted to his sister, "I guess they will conclude that the old way of fighting is the best, that is running and burning all they leave behind."[97]

During the early-morning hours of Sunday, March 16, troopers of the 1st Ohio Cavalry galloped across the Harpeth River bridge and down the main street of Franklin, Tennessee. Frightened women came running into the streets in nightgowns to view the raiders. The cavalrymen stopped only briefly outside of town before riding off again.[98]

The plan was to make a quick dash with cavalry in order to secure the sixty-foot-long Rutherford Creek bridge, four miles north of Columbia, and the two 180-foot-long Duck River bridges. Although the former had already been damaged, the troopers successfully came within view of Columbia, only to find the bridges there in flames. Nearly all of the houses in town had tin roofs that glistened in the sun. Unfortunately, dark clouds had dominated for days, and the rain-swollen Duck River was now forty feet deep. As at the Barron River bridge at Bowling Green, Kentucky, Buell had been stopped again.[99]

McCook's men, who arrived on March 19, had little choice but to stop. A battalion of inexperienced engineers went to work on bridge repair, assisted by the 32nd Indiana, a German regiment boasting a large number of mechanics. Some of the Ohio cavalrymen swam their horses across and claimed the town, which was largely deserted. From his headquarters in Nashville, Buell informed Halleck that he would be delayed by four or five days.[100]

Buell has been castigated for not having prepared a pontoon train during his three-week stay in Nashville. Strangely, several days after reaching Columbia, Buell notified Halleck that pontoons were being fitted out and would be transported by steamer to Savannah. Thus, pontoons were being sent to Grant, whose army had already crossed the river, while Buell's divisions sat idle for lack of pontoons![101]

Between March 21 and 24, a late snow dusted the ground around Columbia, hampering the work of engineers. Buell arrived late on Wednesday, March 26, expecting to find the bridge completed. He conceded, in a message to Halleck the next morning, that the project was far more involved than he had anticipated. His revised completion date was March 31.[102]

Precisely what Buell knew and when he knew it has long been debated. In 1866, he insisted he casually learned that Grant's army was on the west bank only a few days before arriving at Savannah. This was incorrect. On March 19, Grant had sent him a message (received

March 23) stating that troops were massing at Pittsburg Landing. In the press of matters, however, this fact apparently did not register with the Ohio general. On March 27, when he finally arrived in Columbia, Buell was taken aback to learn from scouts that the Army of the Tennessee had crossed the river. Staff officer T. J. Bush distinctly recalled the surprised expression on Buell's face when he learned that Grant was on the west bank.[103]

Fourth Division Commander William "Bull" Nelson also heard the news that day. The rotund brigadier general, who, oddly, had been a twenty-one-year navy veteran before the war, was viewed by many as an obnoxious tyrant, "a cruel and foul-mouthed man." Immediately perceiving the danger, Nelson reportedly exclaimed: "By God, we must cross the river [Duck] at once, or Grant will be whipped!" Late that afternoon, he received Buell's permission to attempt a fording on March 29.[104]

Later that evening, Nelson explained to Colonel Jacob Ammen, one of his brigade commanders, that the division would be crossing. Ammen inquired whether the bridge had been completed. "No," Nelson answered. "Are there any boats?" Ammen asked. "No," replied Nelson, "but the river is falling, and damn you, get over, for we must have the advance and get the glory." McCook, who had seniority, would traditionally lead the march with his division; Ammen jotted in his journal that evening, "He [Nelson] enjoined secrecy, lest we should be prevented from taking the advance." On March 28, Ammen made preliminary moves for the crossing without arousing the suspicion of McCook. The river remained two hundred yards wide with a swift current. Some cavalry troopers waded in, and a few wagons actually forded; the water just touched the beds.[105]

March 29 dawned cold and disagreeable as Nelson's men, stripped to their drawers, plunged into the frigid, waist-deep water. "It was fun to see the men jump into the water. All of them would take off the greater part of their clothing. Some all of them," wrote an amused spectator. The infantry crossed without incident, but the wagons encountered difficulty. To keep supplies dry, some wagon bodies were flipped over and placed on top of other wagons. Boxes were stacked on the upside-down vehicles. By sunset, the entire division had crossed. The next day, Crittenden's division forded. After a ten-day delay, Buell's army was finally on the move.[106]

ONCE THEY LEFT the turnpike south of Columbia, the Army of the Ohio followed a narrow and tortuous eighty-two-mile country road through Waynesboro to Savannah. Nelson's division had a good twelve-to-fifteen-hour lead. Crittenden's division came second in line, followed by McCook's, Thomas Wood's, and then George H. Thomas's. The enormous wagon train (the 20th Brigade alone counted 85 wagons and 510 mules) traveled between Wood's and Thomas's divisions, placing the latter so far in the rear that it was still forty miles away when the battle began. Despite the mud-churned road and swollen creeks, the column set a moderate pace of about twelve miles a day.[107]

Unlike the lush plantation country of Maury County, the poor people and the sandy soil of the "Tennessee Barrens" left the troops unimpressed. The locals, nonetheless, were predominately Union, and small Federal flags on several houses greeted the troops as they entered Waynesboro. "Women ask to let the band play some old tunes—Yankee Doodle, etc. The music makes them weep for joy," commented one officer.[108]

Grant's army had been doing all the fighting and was stealing the headlines thus far. Buell's troops had wearied of tedious and seemingly unproductive marches. Michigan artilleryman Harold Bartlett was "afraid they [Southerners] will keep us chasing them around all summer, but we will corner them by & by." First Ohio Corporal Alexander Varian was of a like mind: "They say there are some Rebels [at Decatur]. I am sure I'd like to see them. I hope they won't run for I am tired running after them."[109]

FIVE

Storm Clouds

Corinth

JOHNSTON BADLY NEEDED INFORMATION. He knew that the bulk of the Yankee army was at Pittsburg Landing and a division at Crump's Landing, but he remained uncertain as to the extent of their lines. On March 26, he ordered that at least twenty reliable citizens be recruited as guides. Such men as Benjamin Saunders and Lafayette Veal, both of McNairy County, Tennessee, offered valuable assistance. Scouts such as Joseph H. Fussell made rough sketches of the terrain north of Corinth, but professional engineering maps remained scarce. Johnston counted only five engineer officers, among them Lieutenant S. M. Steel, a former Nashville civil engineer and surveyor, who conducted a number of dangerous missions to obtain topographical information.[1]

On March 31, Bragg ordered Randal Gibson's brigade to outpost duty at Monterey, replacing Joe Wheeler's 19th Alabama. Screening the movement would be Colonel James H. Clanton's 1st Alabama Cavalry. James Chalmers's brigade, accompanied by a hundred of Clanton's troopers, forded Lick Creek and reconnoitered the Federal flank. On April 1, Gibson's troops arrived at Monterey, where they remained for two days on short rations. One of their number noted: "We expect to see the elephant now."[2]

Army headquarters soon buzzed with activity. On April 1, the 1st and 3rd Corps were placed on standby and ordered to be prepared to move out within twenty-four hours.[3] That same day, scouts reported that a few Federal transports and gunboats had passed Yellow Creek, probing the Confederate right once again. A later dispatch indicated that the Yankees landed at Eastport and Chickasaw, spiked the two heavy guns in position (almost under water at the time), and marched toward Iuka before breaking off the expedition and returning to their transports. Breckinridge rushed seven hundred infantry by railroad from Burnsville to Iuka, and by sunrise of April 2 two full brigades (Statham's and Bowen's) had arrived. Intelligence reports received on April 2 indicated that Buell's army, 30,000 strong, had finally crossed the Duck River and was moving rapidly toward Savannah. A linkup of the Federal armies appeared imminent.[4]

A seemingly insignificant incident on the night of March 31, but not learned about in Corinth until late on April 2, had serious implications. On April 1, Beauregard ordered that Cheatham, whose division remained detached at Bethel Station, make a secret reconnaissance from Purdy toward the Tennessee River. He gave careful instructions not to arouse the suspicions of the enemy. Unknown to Beauregard, Robinson's Tennessee Cavalry Company had already probed toward Adamsville. On the evening of March 31, Robinson's troopers attacked pickets of the 5th Ohio Cavalry, who happened to be even more poorly armed than the shotgun-toting Southerners. Three Yankee prisoners were taken, including one who was mortally wounded.[5]

Precisely what Beauregard feared now occurred. When Lew Wallace heard of the incident, he suspected that his 3rd Brigade at Adamsville was being menaced by Cheatham's division. He promptly rushed his remaining two brigades to Adamsville; both arrived by midnight. At sunrise on April 1, startled Confederate scouts found an entire Yankee division in line of battle. This information was related to Cheatham at Bethel Station, who in turn telegraphed Polk that his front was seriously threatened by Wallace's division. Both sides thus mistakenly feared an attack.[6]

Polk, who received the telegram about 10 P.M. on April 2, forwarded it to Beauregard. There were several possible interpretations. Wallace might be moving to cut Cheatham's division off from the main army. The incursion could also be a reconnaissance-in-force, a diversion, or another raid on the Mobile & Ohio Railroad. Wallace's march could possibly be the prelude to a larger Federal offensive, or, as was actually the case, it could be another false alarm. Beauregard, as he had done two weeks earlier, jumped to a single conclusion—the Federals had divided their forces for another raid on the Mobile & Ohio. Since this information was now thirty-six hours old, time was of the essence. He promptly endorsed the telegram: "Now is the moment to advance and strike the enemy at Pittsburg Landing."[7]

Jordan carried the dispatch to Johnston at the Rose Cottage. Upon reading it, the general proceeded to the Curlee house on Jackson Street, where he roused Bragg. The corps commander, remaining in bed throughout the conversation, concurred with Beauregard's endorsement, but Johnston (according to Jordan) protested that the army was not prepared for an offensive. Only after the colonel had allayed his fears did the army commander allow the appropriate order to be drafted. Historians have questioned the account, citing inconsistencies in Jordan's own writings. It is possible that, in the context of dialogue, Johnston raised legitimate concerns that Jordan later exaggerated. It is hardly conceivable that Johnston opposed an offensive, since only twenty-four hours earlier he had issued an order to put the army on standby. Johnston really had no choice but to advance; only boldness could redeem western misfortunes—and his career.[8]

Turning to a table in Bragg's bedchamber, Jordan wrote a circular order to Polk, Bragg, and Hardee, directing that the corps commanders be prepared to move out by 6 A.M. on April 3. The rough draft was approved by Johnston, and copies were made by one of Bragg's aides. Polk and Hardee received the order at 1:40 A.M. on April 3, and Breckinridge was wired at Burnsville. Captain A. R. Chisolm awakened Beauregard at 5 A.M. and informed him of Johnston's order to advance. The Creole began making detailed notes on the backs of envelopes and old telegrams. These notes became the basis for the order of march and battle that were later drafted.[9]

After breakfast, Jordan returned to Beauregard's headquarters at the Fish Pond House on Kilpatrick Street. There he found the Creole briefing Johnston on the plan of operations. Bragg, Hardee, and Polk later joined the conference. Since the only engineering map they had was at Jordan's office, Beauregard made a rough sketch on his camp table. Time would be required to formulate the order and make copies, so the first day's march was explained orally. President Davis was also notified that the army was advancing to give battle at Pittsburg Landing before Buell could make a juncture.[10]

Jordan composed what would become known as Special Order No. 8, which was not completed until the morning of April 4. He kept before him as a model Napoleon's battle plan for Waterloo. The completed document, generally condemned by historians, proved a blueprint for disaster. Its primary flaw was its lack of simplicity.[11]

Only two narrow roads led toward Pittsburg Landing—the Ridge Road, which ran north and then turned northeast, and the Monterey Road, which initially snaked northeast but turned north at the village of Monterey, where it became the Savannah Road. The Savannah Road and the Ridge Road intersected at the James Michie (often misspelled Mickey) farmhouse, about four miles from the Federal line. Previous reconnaissance patrols had revealed the wretched condition of both roads.

The march order directed that Hardee's corps advance on the Ridge Road, followed by Charles Clark's division of Polk's corps. Cheatham's division, at Bethel Station, would unite with Polk on the march at the intersection of Ridge and Purdy Roads. Bragg's corps was to file out the Monterey Road. Once past the village of Monterey, Withers's division would proceed to Michie's via the Savannah Road, to arrive by sunset. Ruggles's division was to take the Purdy Road from Monterey until it intersected with the Ridge Road. Polk was to halt his troops at the intersection and allow Ruggles's division to pass. The Reserve Corps, marching from Burnsville, would travel the most convenient route to Monterey, and thence to Michie's. The plan put more than half the army on the longest route. A more practicable approach, as suggested by one writer, would have been for Bragg and Hardee to take the Ridge Road, and Polk and Breckinridge the Monterey Road.[12]

There is no evidence that the Confederates ever considered a flank attack. James Chalmers, in his reconnaissance of April 2, scouted Lick Creek via the Hamburg-Savannah Road but found it unfeasible. The creek became fordable by April 5—a fact that was probably not known to Johnston but would have made little difference. Johnston and Beauregard proposed to turn the enemy's left away from the river and the landing and into the Owl Creek bottoms, thus forcing a surrender. Such a tactic would necessarily expose the Confederate right flank to the fire of the gunboats. Beauregard apparently never saw the destruction of Grant's army as the objective. He intended to drive the Federals away from the landing in order to remove stores and munitions before Buell arrived. Remaining in possession of the landing, in Beauregard's own words, "was never contemplated."[13]

The most serious blunder of Special Order No. 8 was unquestionably the alignment of corps in successive waves. If the purpose of the attack was to turn the Yankee left, more strength should have been placed on the Confederate right. The troops instead were evenly distributed along a three-mile front, the rationale being that the Federals could never withstand three parallel lines. Such a plan virtually assured confusion, however, as the lines intermingled. After the war, Jordan weakly explained that he placed Hardee's corps first in line because it was the best one—a dubious assertion. The linear formation was adopted because of the terrain, he wrote, although no amplification was offered.[14]

Exactly what alignment Johnston originally had in mind became fodder for yet another postwar dispute. In an April 3 telegram to Davis, Johnston explained that his corps would attack in a three-wing formation: Polk on the left, Hardee in the center, Bragg on the right, with Breckinridge in reserve. Beauregard's plan called for tandem lines, not abreast, prompting William Preston Johnston, Bragg, and Davis later to charge that the Creole deliberately altered Johnston's formation. In 1874, Bragg wrote William Preston Johnston: "To be candid with you, I believe Beauregard, or his man Jordan, is entitled to all the blundering of those details." Davis even claimed that he received a telegram from Johnston on April 4 that gave his plan of battle, but that it was later lost. There is no extant evidence to confirm or refute the allegation, and historians have split on the issue.[15]

On April 6, 1885, exactly twenty-three years to the day after the Battle of Shiloh, a statue of Johnston was unveiled in Lemarie Cemetery in New Orleans. More than 10,000 persons were present, with Mrs. Johnston, William Preston Johnston, Beauregard, Davis, and Senator Randal L. Gibson all on the platform. Davis, in his speech, continued to claim that an additional telegram had been sent from Johnston. "The mistake he [Johnston] made," Davis bitterly continued, with Beauregard only feet away, "was in allowing somebody else [Beauregard] to direct the order of march."[16]

That Beauregard's plan was horrid is without dispute. The more significant point is that Johnston, through either self-doubt or lack of forcefulness, allowed Beauregard to run the show. The army commander had twelve days to devise his own plan, yet on the morning of April 3 he acted as little more than Beauregard's rubber stamp. Johnston did not even see the order until after the march had commenced, prompting some writers to conclude that it was too late to make changes. Such was not the case. If he had strongly objected to the proposed alignment, then it would have been his duty to make a change, either by amending the written order or by giving orders orally. Once again he acquiesced to his junior.[17]

Logistical arrangements had to be completed hurriedly. For more than two weeks, Johnston had been stockpiling ammunition—a million rounds from the Memphis Arsenal, and 800,000 cartridges from the Richmond Arsenal, in addition to 4,000 artillery rounds and 3,000 friction primers. On April 3, the men were ordered to strip down for action—one hundred rounds per man (forty in the cartridge boxes and sixty in the wagons), two hundred rounds per field gun, five days' rations (three in the haversacks and two in the wagons), two tents per company, and one wagon per two companies. A train appeared at the depot with a load of "knocked-down" wagons—wheels in one car; axles, bodies, and covers in another. Fifty wheelwrights and mechanics assembled the vehicles; seventy men arranged the harnesses and gathered the 130 mules that had come by the ordinary dirt road. The men worked with lanterns throughout the night, and by sunrise all of the wagons were operational and each was harnessed with four mules.[18]

Arrangements also had to be made for the defense of Corinth. The 51st Tennessee, 9th Alabama Battalion (Blount's), 7th Arkansas Battalion (Deshea's), and two regiments of Carroll's brigade en route to Corinth would remain as a garrison. The Vaiden (Mississippi) Light Artillery and Carnes's Tennessee Battery were also retained. A chagrined Lieutenant W. W. Carnes learned that his seventy-five men were two dozen short for his six guns. Long after the army had departed, he turned over two of his guns to the local ordnance officer and sped with his company to the field of battle. He met the army as it was returning.[19]

Johnston vainly attempted to bolster the ranks by placing blacks as cooks and teamsters. He sent officers into the countryside, but the appeal netted only fifty slaves. "I regret this disappointment—a single brigade may determine the fate of a battle," he told Colonel Munford. The dearth of arms actually remained the far more serious problem. The newly recruited 25th Louisiana arrived in Memphis via steamboat on April 2. Rather than rushing to Corinth, the troops idled away at the local fairgrounds awaiting small arms. Several Mississippi regiments awaiting arms in camps of instruction could actually hear the sounds of the Battle of Shiloh.[20]

"WELL, ON THURSDAY MORNING [April 3] I was awakened by the long roll that was sounded throughout the camp," related a Louisiana soldier. "Everybody was in motion. . . . Drums were beating, trumpets sounded, fifes blowing, brass bands playing and men hurrying." Tennessean Albert Fielder noted that he was roused at 4 A.M. and told that the regiment would march in two hours. Joseph Lyman hurriedly wrote a letter to his wife: "Good-bye. If I do not write it will be because I am working or fighting or wounded or sick or dead."[21]

The first day's march proved a fiasco. The finalizing of administrative matters, which should have been tended to days earlier, consumed hours. The 6 A.M. march order had to be canceled. At the generals' briefing at Beauregard's headquarters at 8 A.M., the new start time was set for noon. By that hour, the streets of Corinth were clogged with troops, wagons, and field guns. Still the army did not move.[22]

Beauregard pointed a finger at Polk, because Clark's division blocked the Ridge Road. An aide rode out to investigate and allegedly found the bishop awaiting a written order. Beauregard, through an aide, immediately ordered the road cleared. William Polk, the bishop's son, convincingly rebutted the charge. Charles Clark's 4,500 men were encamped two miles outside of town, in fields and woods. William Polk, who happened to be present, attested that neither troops nor wagons came onto the road until after Hardee's corps had passed.[23]

As best as can be pieced together, the delay was primarily the result of administrative confusion. Lacking written orders, Bragg, as chief-of-staff, directed Hardee to begin the march "as soon as practicable." Hardee probably did not receive written instructions until 3 P.M., when his corps finally moved out. Bragg's late start on the Monterey Road was also partly due to staff bungling. Assistant Adjutant General George Gardner sent an order to Ruggles to begin the march "early tomorrow morning, 6 A.M." The note was written before midnight of April 2, so Gardner had April 3 in mind. Ruggles did not actually receive the directive until 2:30 A.M. of the 3rd, however, and thus interpreted "tomorrow morning" to be April 4.[24]

Vague orders to Cheatham almost kept his division out of the battle. The Tennessean was directed to defend Purdy and Bethel Station if attacked, but if not pressured he was to rejoin the parent corps. There were no precise instructions on how long he should wait, or what road to take in a rendezvous with Polk. Rather than linking up on April 4, as Beauregard had projected, Cheatham's division did not leave Bethel Station until the morning of April 5.[25]

At 3 P.M. on April 3, Hardee's corps at long last filed north on Filmore Street, past the Rose Cottage, to the strains of regimental bands playing "Lorena," "The Mocking Bird," and the popular "The Girl I Left Behind Me." Those units that did not have flags were presented with new banners as they departed, some given personally by Johnston. Bragg's corps marched out the Monterey Road about 4:30, preceded by Wirt Adams's and John Wharton's cavalry regiments. The day had turned out pretty, although one soldier complained that the sun was "burning hot as August." Another of Bragg's men noted the confusion: "I could see thousands of soldiers moving in different directions marching and countermarching. . . . Sometimes we marched very slow and sometimes double quick."[26]

Once on the road, Hardee's men made good time. Staff officers were placed at the state line to inform the troops when they crossed into Tennessee; the announcement was greeted with loud cheers. In the pitch-darkness a serious problem occurred. Desiring to make camp by water, Hardee moved his command onto a blind road to the right of the Ridge Road that led to a spring. Clark's division, following after a half-hour interval, found the Ridge Road clear and continued on. The division eventually encountered Hardee's pickets, posted a mile in advance of the corps. Since it was by now midnight, Clark's weary troops dropped on the road for the night. At 2 A.M., a torrential downpour with hail came. A light rain continued the next morning as Hardee's troops resumed the march, only to find the road blocked by Clark's men. It became necessary for teamsters and soldiers literally to lift Clark's wagons to one side of the road so that Hardee's troops could pass.[27]

Johnston left the Rose Cottage on the morning of April 4. Turning to Mrs. Inge, he said, "Madame, I am going out to fight for the protection of your home." Unknown to him, she had placed two sandwiches and a piece of cake in his coat pocket. As Johnston paused at the doorstep, Munford heard him mutter, "Yes, I believe I have overlooked nothing."[28]

Monterey, Tennessee

MONTEREY WAS an unimpressive hamlet of a dozen log cabins and a single good dwelling. A New York journalist accompanying the Federal army as it later advanced to Corinth contemptuously wrote of the ignorant, dirty people, who were no better than "a fifth-rate Indian tribe." On the afternoon of April 4, a cabin in the village became the headquarters of Albert Sidney Johnston.[29]

The army commander rode into the village sometime after noon. Beauregard's rigid timetable had fallen apart. At 8:30 A.M., Withers's division had passed through the hamlet and proceeded up the Savannah Road to Michie's farmhouse. Ruggles's division, which lagged far behind, was supposed to take the Purdy Road past Monterey. Citizens reported the road to be in such a wretched condition, however, that at

10 A.M. Bragg directed Ruggles to follow in the rear of Withers. Realizing that Clark's division was waiting at the intersection of the Ridge Road and Purdy Road for Ruggles's troops to pass, Bragg sent a messenger to inform Polk of the change. Clark's division had been waiting three hours by the time the message arrived. Ruggles's troops continued to trudge along the horrid Monterey Road. A journalist, traveling in an ambulance of the 4th Louisiana, described the road as "very rough and hilly, with numerous mud holes, and occasional swamps." The division did not arrive at Monterey until late afternoon of April 4, nearly twenty-four hours behind schedule.[30]

Yet a third road ran from Monterey south of the Savannah Road, past the Chamberses' farm (not to be confused with Jack Chambers's farm on the Ridge Road). The Southerners must have known about the road, for pickets had been thrown forward and even skirmished with Yankee cavalry on April 3. Had Bragg's corps taken this route (present Highway 22) rather than marching to Michie's farm, it might well have been in position on the morning of April 5. The road was apparently avoided because of flooding at Adkin's Ford on Lick Creek and the Tan Yard Branch of Lick Creek.[31]

Nothing had been heard from Breckinridge by 10 A.M. of April 4. Spearheaded by Nathan Bedford Forrest's regiment, the division had left Burnsville at 5 A.M. that day and marched through Farmington. The lead elements reached Monterey before sunset, but the column was strung out for miles. When a Breckinridge aide informed Johnston that the artillery was mired in the mud, he inquired about axes to cut a new road. When told that they had no axes, Johnston impatiently snapped: "What! Start on a battlefield with no axes?" It would be long after midnight before the mud-clogged wagons and field guns rolled in.[32]

At 5 P.M., Johnston held a conference with Beauregard and Bragg; staffs were excluded. The army commander conceded the inevitable and postponed the attack until 8 A.M. the next day, April 5. Before the meeting had concluded, nearly a score of Yankee prisoners, captured a few hours earlier in a skirmish with Hardee's men, were escorted into the village. Among their number was Major LeRoy Crockett of the 72nd Ohio. He smiled pleasantly, saluted officers, and openly exclaimed: "This means a battle. . . . They don't expect anything of this kind back yonder." To Colonel Marshall Smith of the Crescent Regiment he said: "A fine set of soldiers you have, Colonel; if they were in blue I would have taken them for my own boys." A Louisiana soldier nonetheless noted that he "looked upon us [enlisted men] with insolent regard."[33]

Johnston was quite anxious to know whether breastworks had been thrown up; spy and scout reports had differed. The sound of axes and trees being felled raised the fear that earthen works were being erected. Colonel Preston casually interrogated the talkative Major Crockett. The Yankee officer openly told of his adventure. Preston remarked that he did not quite understand why cavalry had been deployed to protect Grant's entrenched artillery. Crockett let it be known that there were no earthworks and that they had only been sent to reconnoiter. As he was taken away, he offered his last comment: "Why, you seem to have an army here; we know nothing of it."[34]

At 7:30 P.M., Breckinridge arrived in Monterey and conferred with Johnston and Beauregard. At that moment he was notified of the time change for the battle and his place in the deployment. Colonel Jordan, apparently because of his conversation with Crockett, grossly underestimated enemy strength at 21,000 to 25,000, organized into four divisions—Smith's, McClernand's, Wallace's, and Sherman's.[35]

That evening, the rain once again came down in torrents. During a slack period, Johnston summoned Lieutenant George W. Baylor: "Lieutenant, I wish you to go to General Beauregard and ask him if we had better not postpone the attack until Sunday, on account of the rain." Baylor slushed over to the Creole's tent, into which he was escorted by a lieutenant who spoke almost no English. Although it was then past midnight, the general was awake and hard at work. In response to Johnston's question, he replied that time was of such importance that "we had better commence the attack at daylight." This incident, related by one of Johnston's own aides, suggests not so much that one general dominated the other, but that each needed the other in decision-making. It was a partnership of sorts, but a partnership built upon mutual weakness.[36]

The troops were formed in ranks by 3 A.M. of April 5, but were detained by the drenching rain. According to James Rosser, "One of the hardest rains fell I ever saw in life and wound up in considerable hail." A Tennessean noted, "We were drawn up on the edge [of the road]. As we stood there, troops tramped by in the mud and rain and darkness. . . . To us who were simply standing in line in the rain it was bad enough, but those men who were going by were wading, stumbling and plunging through water a foot deep." Taylor Beatty scrawled in his diary: "So dark we can't see to move, so we had to stand under arms in a pelting rain until daylight."[37]

Michie's Farm

THE PRESENT-DAY SITE of the Michie farm is an unassuming and iso-lated place, crossed by two county roads. On the morning of April 5, 1862, it proved to be the focal point of Confederate operations. Old man Michie had moved away, and the house had been fitted up as a hospital by Dr. George W. Lawrence, Hardee's medical director. A yellow hospital flag with a white star snapped in the spring wind.[38]

Hardee's corps, which had camped at the farm on the night of April 4, advanced two abreast at dawn on the 5th. Only three miles from the Federal line, the Confederates received their first challenge of the march. An unidentified mounted man, partly hidden in the brush, shouted, "Who are you?" Startled officers replied, "This is Hardee's corps." "Well, advance and give the word," the picket de-manded. Not knowing any password and seeing that the man was wearing butternut breeches, the officers asked if he would meet them halfway. Confronting the lone vedette face to face, the officers ex-plained that he was holding up the advance of an entire corps. He re-luctantly relented: "I suppose you can go on; but its agin' orders."[39]

Both Clark's division (on the Ridge Road) and Withers's division (on the Savannah Road) had encamped near Michie's on the night of April 4. About dawn on the 5th, Clark's troops arrived at the intersec-tion and waited for Bragg's corps to pass in front. Johnston arrived at Michie's at perhaps 7 A.M. and, after conferring with Polk, rode on with his staff to the Y-shaped intersection of the Pittsburg-Corinth and Bark Roads. Just ahead he found Hardee's corps deployed in line of battle.[40]

Back at Michie's, a massive traffic snarl began to occur as Polk's and Bragg's commands converged, with troops, wagons, and artillery churning up the rain-soaked intersection. Once Withers's division had passed, some of Polk's leading units, not realizing that Ruggles's divi-sion had not yet arrived, marched forward, thus dividing Bragg's corps. In the midst of the confusion, the 4th Louisiana band struck up a lively tune. Colonel Randal Gibson rode up and demanded, "Stop that mu-sic." He then politely added: "Wait, boys, until this fight is over, and then you may play either the Dead March or the Bonnie Blue Flag."[41]

Withers's division continued up the Ridge Road and filed off to the right on the Bark Road. There it deployed on the right half of the second battle line. A. H. Gladden's brigade advanced to the first line and extended Hardee's right. The left of Brigadier General John K.

Jackson's brigade anchored on the Pittsburg-Corinth Road, with Chalmers's brigade to his right, en echelon behind Gladden. Clanton's 1st Alabama Cavalry formed in the rear of Chalmers's troops.[42]

The army was to strike the Yankee line at 8 A.M., but by 9:30 Ruggles's division had still not come up. An increasingly nervous Johnston sent Colonel Munford to ask Bragg why Ruggles was not in position. Bragg explained that he, too, was in the dark, but that he would investigate and report. Ten o'clock came, 11:00, 11:30—still no sign of Ruggles. Again Munford was sent to see why the division was not yet in line. The same answer was given. At 12:30 P.M., Johnston looked at his watch, glanced up at the sun, and exploded in anger: "This is perfectly puerile! This is not war! Let us have our horses." Together with three staff officers, Johnston rode to the rear. He finally found the head of Ruggles's division idling in a field some distance off the road. The Ridge Road past Michie's, as it turned out, was jammed by Polk's wagons and artillery. Johnston barked orders to clear the road immediately. Two of Ruggles's brigade commanders, Preston Pond and Patton Anderson, became so impatient that they marched their commands through the woods parallel to the road. It was 2:00 before the road was cleared. Ruggles's division finally came in line to the left of the Pittsburg-Corinth Road: Gibson on the right, Anderson in the center, and Pond on the left, with four independent cavalry companies protecting the flank.[43]

Clark's division, most of which was still back at Michie's, marched forward, but still more maddening delays occurred. Polk was misinformed by an aide that if he continued down the Ridge Road he would interfere with the formation of Bragg's line. The march was thus halted to ascertain the direction of Bragg's corps. It was 4:00 before Clark's division finally deployed as the third line. Polk was then handed a message that Beauregard desired to see him.[44]

Intersection of the Pittsburg-Corinth and Bark Roads

WITH BATTLE only hours away, tempers began to flare. About 4:00 P.M., Beauregard arrived at Bragg's temporary headquarters at the intersection of the Pittsburg-Corinth and Bark Roads. The two generals pondered the bleak state of affairs. It was obviously too late to attack on April 5; Cheatham's division was still not in position, and Breckinridge's weary troops were far to the rear. Many of the men had no rations remaining. The generals agreed that the offensive should be canceled, and the army returned to Corinth.

Polk arrived shortly and became entangled in a heated exchange with Beauregard. The two men, never on friendly terms, now detested one another. Unfairly blaming Polk (as he would after the war) for all the mounting problems, Beauregard spoke with great passion. "I am very much disappointed at the delay which has occurred in getting troops into position," he snapped. The bishop blamed Bragg for not forming his line promptly. An unconvinced Beauregard made the surly reply that the attack would have to be postponed. Johnston happened by and stopped to ask what was going on. The Creole argued that the attack must be canceled. Food was in short supply, valuable hours had been squandered, and, because of Hardee's sharp skirmish the day before, the element of surprise had obviously been lost. "Now they will be entrenched up to their eyes," he cried. At 5:00, a staff officer noted in his journal that Beauregard and Bragg "think provisions short, and the delay of 36 hours will cause failure."

Johnston, somewhat taken aback, directed Preston to check on the state of Breckinridge's division. By chance, Breckinridge shortly joined the impromptu council. The army commander insisted that a retreat "will never do." Polk, asked for his opinion, concurred: "We ought to attack." Johnston abruptly broke off the conversation with the words: "Gentlemen, we shall attack at daylight tomorrow." As he walked off, he said to Preston: "I would fight them if they were a million. They can present no greater front between these two creeks than we can; and the more men they crowd in there, the worse we can make it for them. . . . Polk is a true soldier and friend."[45]

Although Johnston's rare moment of resolve has been touted by historians, he actually remained pathetically insecure. Following the conference, he quietly continued the discussion with at least three staff officers, attempting to win their assurance. Although the conversation was punctuated with determination ("I intend to hammer 'em!" he told Munford), he clearly remained anxious.[46]

Though he did not witness the Beauregard-Polk exchange, one New Orleans journalist did see Johnston and Bragg in solemn, low-voiced conversation. Each stooped and made drawings in the dirt. The correspondent believed that the dramatic moment should have been captured on canvas.[47]

The drama heightened at 8 P.M., when the generals again gathered about a fire. Polk sat on a stool outside the circle, his head in his hands, as though in deep thought. Breckinridge lay stretched out on a blanket near the fire. Beauregard paced about and spoke rapidly; Bragg also made frequent comments. Johnston stood apart from the rest. Bragg had by now changed his opinion, leaving Beauregard unsupported in his views. Thirty-five years later, Lieutenant George Baylor recalled that the Creole spoke of fighting western men, who understood the use of firearms. He feared a repulse and a "victory turned into defeat." A Beauregard aide believed that the Creole dominated the group and Johnston was "lost in attention." The meeting broke off about 10 P.M.[48]

Some of Beauregard's objections had merit. The march on April 5 had been a frolicking affair. As the rain ceased, soldiers began firing their muskets to see if they worked. One entire regiment, the Texas Rangers, let loose a volley. Drums beat and bugles blasted. When Johnston appeared before the 2nd Texas, the troops gave a loud cheer, although the general waved his hand to silence them. Hardee's men gave a thunderous cheer that could be heard for miles when a deer was shot in front of the battle line. Was it reasonable to assume that the Federals, only one and a half miles away, could not have heard the racket?[49]

The shortage of rations also remained a serious concern, although canceling the offensive would not have immediately resolved the problem; commissary wagons remained far in the rear. Some of the men complained of receiving only a few pieces of meat and a biscuit since the march began. Others wrote of living on a single biscuit a day. On the evening of April 5, Bragg boasted that his well-supplied commissary could provide additional rations, but none were forthcoming.[50]

Considering the stakes, however, it is difficult to understand Beauregard's hesitancy. If the Federals were indeed entrenched and the attack failed, the army could then withdraw to Corinth. To retreat after so torturous a march without even an attempt would have devastated the morale of the troops and possibly caused desertions. Besides, there had been an encouraging bit of news. Just before the generals' evening conference, a Federal surgeon and his orderly, out on a night excursion, had ridden into a Confederate picket post. The men were taken to headquarters and interrogated by both Johnston and Beauregard. Although practically "speechless with astonishment," the prisoners did state that Grant had returned to Savannah for the evening, Sherman was in command, and none suspected an attack.[51]

Years later, Beauregard would claim that he had not proposed a retreat, but a reconnaissance-in-force to lure the enemy out. Given that a retreat was out of the question, perhaps he did offer such a compromise. At best, however, it would have caught only a fraction of the Yankee army in a trap. On the other hand, the scheme might well have backfired. Grant, once warned of the Southern presence, could simply have dug in and waited for Buell. He would then have advanced with overwhelming numbers and caught the Confederates out in the open, far from their Corinth fortifications.[52]

If Johnston had listened to Beauregard, postwar and modern writers would doubtless have envisioned a hypothetical Battle of Shiloh in which Grant's army was crushed. For once, however, Johnston found his individuality. He related to Dr. D. W. Yandell that Beauregard's three-month illness had clouded his thinking. Preston, closer to Johnston than anyone, perhaps expressed the general's thoughts when he wrote after the battle: "Strong reasons demanded an immediate attack, as delay increased the danger of discovery." Yet there was undoubtedly more to Johnston's character change than that. Perhaps, as has been suggested, he had grown weary of Beauregard's dictatorial nature. Maybe he reflected upon the bitter public and political criticism that had dogged him since Fort Donelson. Possibly he thought of the trust that his friend Davis had placed in him to deliver a victory. More likely, he realized that there simply had been too much hype to back down; his career had come down to this single moment; the weight of a nation was upon his shoulders and there could be no retreat. For good or for ill, a battle would be fought on April 6, 1862.[53]

THE NIGHT was clear and cold. Strict orders had been given that no fires could be started—not even a cigar lit. Many of the men, not realizing the horror that awaited them in the morning, remained quietly jovial. A captain in the 4th Kentucky wondered why there was not a more serious atmosphere. Others were more reflective. "The Great Battle of the Mississippi Valley has come to issue at last I reckon," Charles Johnson wrote his wife. Somewhere in the third battle line, a young cannoneer by the name of George Jones of Stanford's Mississippi Battery made an entry in his diary: "I have the shakes badly. . . . I do hope our Heavenly Father will shield and protect every one of us."[54]

In the stillness of the night, drums were distinctly heard beating a tattoo. An angry Beauregard dispatched a staff officer to investigate. He returned to report that the sound had come from the enemy's camps. Writing thirty-nine years later, a member of the 16th Louisiana vividly remembered shivering that night as he listened to a Yankee band in the distance play "Home Sweet Home."[55]

Camps of the 5th Division, Army of the Tennessee

As the first Federal division to be deployed at Pittsburg Landing, Sherman's brigades had been deployed to cover the three main approaches. Colonel David Stuart's 2nd Brigade marched a mile and a half south of the landing along the Hamburg-Savannah Road. Pickets were thrown out a mile from camp to guard the Lick Creek ford. The lion's share of the division camped a mile and a half west, around Shiloh Church, to cover the main road to Corinth and the Owl Creek bridge of the Hamburg-Purdy Road. The 7,300 troops around the church, only 6,000 of whom were "present for duty," stretched for a mile. So irregularly spaced were the camps (the left brigade was out of line with the other two) that a prolonged line could not be formed if the division was called out. Sherman had camping in mind—not fighting.[56]

Colonel Ralph P. Buckland's 4th Brigade was west of the church, nearly at a right angle with the Pittsburg-Corinth Road. Seventieth Ohio Colonel DeWitt Loudon noted: "The left of our regiment rests on a log church called Chilo Chapel." It was a "hard looking structure. From its appearance, I judge it to belong to the Baptists of the hard shell persuasion." The church, built in 1854, actually belonged to the Methodist Episcopal Church, South—Methodism, foreshadowing national division, had previously split along regional lines. The structure, twenty-five by thirty feet, was built of rough-hewn logs and a clapboard roof. Inside was a middle aisle, dividing two rows of wooden benches. The name "Shiloh" came from 1 Samuel and referred to a religious center to which the Hebrews annually made a pilgrimage. It roughly translated as "peace," although after the battle New York Jews interpreted it "deliverance."[57]

East of the church and the road was Colonel Hildebrand's 3rd Brigade. Sherman's directive to face all camps west and to have no more than twenty-two paces between regiments was largely ignored to achieve convenient access to water. The regiments all fronted different directions and were out of alignment even within the brigade. The 53rd Ohio camped four hundred yards in front of its nearest regiment, with a spring separating them.[58]

Colonel John A. McDowell's 1st Brigade formed on Sherman's right. A lateral ravine (still present today) separated McDowell's left and Buckland's right. Two of his regiments camped on the edge of Ben Howell Field, with two others on the Hamburg-Purdy Road. The 6th Iowa, armed with Springfield rifles, represented the extreme right of the Union Army. A detail of the regiment guarded the Owl Creek bridge.[59]

Prentiss's newly organized 6th Division was to the left of Sherman, but a gap of about 650 yards (not the half-mile to a mile critics later claimed) remained between the divisions. Sherman always denied its existence, and on his postwar battlefield map attempted to close the space artificially by placing the camps of Raith's brigade (McClernand's division) at a right angle to the Purdy-Hamburg Road, rather than parallel to the road, as they actually were. It has been suggested that one of Buell's divisions was to occupy the gap, but by the time of the battle Grant had determined to send Buell's army to Hamburg.[60]

Although the 5th was the most advanced division, and therefore closest to the enemy, it consisted entirely of raw recruits. Sherman disgustedly wrote that the men had "as much idea of war as children." His brigade commanders were hardly better. Buckland was a fifty-year-old Ohio political general. McDowell—younger brother of General Irvin McDowell, who had been defeated at First Bull Run—had some slight experience in a militia company but by profession had been a civil engineer. Sixty-two-year-old Jesse Hildebrand, former stage driver, businessman, and sheriff, served as the mail agent on the railroad between Marietta and Cincinnati before the war. Long connected with the Ohio militia, he had obtained the militia rank of major general, although he never mastered the intricacies of basic drill. He established his headquarters on the extreme right of the brigade—as far away as he could get and still remain within his brigade limits. He had no staff, not even an orderly.[61]

The most critical mistake was the lack of fortifications, for which neither Sherman nor Grant can escape culpability. C. F. Smith had counseled against the use of trenches, arguing that it would take away the men's fighting edge. He even suggested that the lack of entrenchments might serve as a lure: "I ask nothing better than to have the Rebels come out and attack us. We can whip them to hell!" Even after the battle, Sherman insisted that trenches would have shown weakness and invited an attack. Grant directed McPherson to lay out a fortified line, but the engineer reported that it would have to be placed in the rear of the line of encampments. The fact is, Grant simply did not anticipate that the enemy would be so audacious as to leave a fortified base. Underestimation of the enemy, neglect, fear of losing the aggressive touch, failure to learn from his Fort Donelson experience—all played a role in this grave blunder.[62]

• • •

THE WORD HAD COME down through the chain of command: Halleck needed more hard intelligence concerning enemy strength and positions. Accordingly, on the night of April 2, Sherman placed the 54th Ohio in ambush at Jack Greer's house on Lick Creek. Beginning at midnight, the 5th Ohio Cavalry, four hundred strong, made a sweep around the Monterey Road in an attempt to drive enemy cavalry toward the trap at Greer's. The troopers stumbled about in the darkness for a mile and a half before calling it quits. Early Thursday morning, April 3, they continued on to the Chamberses' house, where they dispersed a picket of the 1st Alabama Cavalry, capturing one man. Little was learned in the interrogation beyond the fact that the Rebels were in brigade strength at Monterey.[63]

Later that morning, Sherman ordered Buckland to take his brigade out the Ridge Road to scout around—"a kind of picnic excursion," thought one private. At the intersection of the Bark and Monterey Roads, two companies were sent out on each road. Both encountered enemy pickets within a half-mile. In accordance with instructions, Buckland withdrew to Shiloh Church. That day, pickets brought in three Rebel prisoners who claimed that Johnston had only 50,000 troops at Corinth (not the much-touted 100,000) and that three German regiments were so unreliable they could not be trusted on picket duty.[64]

On the morning of April 4, Captain William B. Mason commanded the picket post of the 77th Ohio—one of Hildebrand's outfits. Some of his men noted that rabbits and squirrels had been scampering into their lines. Mason sent two men to investigate the cause. These men reported that they had seen a sizable force of enemy infantry a quarter-mile away, apparently preparing a noon meal. Mason sent Sergeant C. J. Eagler to notify Hildebrand. When the news eventually made its way to division headquarters, Sherman became enraged and ordered that Sergeant Eagler be arrested for filing a false report. Mason refused to surrender him and pleaded with Hildebrand to come see for himself. The colonel rode out and, with the aid of a field glass, could clearly see a line of infantry with muskets stacked. Hildebrand related this information to Sherman, who dismissed the Rebels as nothing more than a reconnoitering party.[65]

That afternoon, Buckland's brigade again marched out the Ridge Road and drilled in the fields near Jack Chambers's house. Buckland watched as Major LeRoy Crockett shouted to the 72nd Ohio: "Now boys, I'll have you form a hollow square to resist a cavalry charge."

About 2:00, shots rang out near the house. Buckland rode ahead, ordering Crockett to bring up the 72nd. All eight pickets at Jack Chambers's house were missing, either lost in the woods or captured by marauding Southern cavalry. Buckland notified Sherman of this development. Meanwhile, Crockett foolishly sent Company B of the 72nd on a wide sweep to the right of the house. Fearing that the inexperienced troops might become lost in the thickets, Buckland compounded the error by sending Company H to retrieve them. Thus satisfied that the situation was under control, he retained the remaining eight companies of the 72nd Ohio at Jack Chambers's house and returned with the balance of the brigade to Shiloh Church.[66]

Back in camp, Buckland became increasingly concerned when the 72nd failed to report. He hastened back to the picket line, where he heard the steady crack of musketry. Worried that Crockett's two advanced companies had been intercepted, he double-quicked with a hundred men from the 72nd. A linkup was soon made with Company H, but Crockett had been captured and Company B cut off. Although temporarily detained by a near-blinding rainstorm—Buckland complained that his high-top boots overflowed with water—the relief column pushed ahead on the Ridge Road. Two miles beyond Jack Chambers's house, they found Company B, which had been holding off 150–200 cavalry for more than an hour. Seeing the gray horsemen forming for a charge, the advancing Buckeyes opened fire, dropping a number of horses and killing and wounding several men.

Ricker's battalion of the 5th Ohio Cavalry, sent by Sherman, arrived at Jack Chambers's house about 3:30. Hearing the shooting off to the right, the major sent two of his companies up the Ridge Road and moved against the enemy flank with the remaining two companies. When the Ohio troopers arrived at Buckland's position, they viewed the Southern cavalry slowly retiring in the distance. Although they had some difficulty in clearing a strip of fallen timber, the blue horsemen vigorously pursued for three or four hundred yards till the Rebels disappeared over the brow of a hill. Six of Ricker's men surged over the hill, only to rein up in shock. Ahead of them was a long line of gray infantry with three field guns. Each piece blasted forth a shot, stampeding the troopers' horses and causing one rider nearly to careen out of control directly into the enemy line. He brazenly drew his revolver and killed two Rebels before being riddled with bullets. The excited cavalrymen told Ricker that they had seen 2,000 infantry with one or two batteries.[67]

Both sides had been bloodied and appeared content to break off the contest. Buckland's infantry and Ricker's cavalry retired to the picket line, where they found a stern-faced Sherman, with two regiments of infantry and a battery drawn up in line of battle. Sherman had rushed forward with reinforcements at the sound of artillery. Buckland's salute was not returned, and the division commander asked sharply what the colonel had done. Buckland answered that he had accidentally become involved in a scrap and "there are the fruits of it," pointing to a dozen Rebel prisoners, all of the 1st Alabama Cavalry. Sherman rebuked him, stating that he might have drawn the entire army into a fight before it was ready. He ordered Buckland to "take your regiment back to camp; I will see you later."[68]

Back at Pittsburg Landing, the distant booms had created quite a stir. The long roll was sounded in many camps, and some divisions formed in line of battle. The 1st Brigade of Hurlbut's division quick-marched a mile to the front before being stopped. Sherman remained unruffled by the affair, and insisted that it was nothing more than a reconnaissance-in-force. Buckland had actually encountered the advance of Hardee's corps—two regiments of Pat Cleburne's brigade and Captain John T. Trigg's Arkansas Battery. When both Ricker and Buckland suggested the possibility of an enemy advance, Sherman merely gave a patronizing sneer: "Oh! tut; tut. You militia officers get scared too easily."[69]

The Rebel prisoners, held at Shiloh Church that evening, openly boasted of being part of a grand army that would drive the Federals into the river the next day. Two wounded prisoners were taken to the widow Howell's house, where one of them, a man by the name of King, died within hours. In his final words he related that there would "be many more killed." Even the widow Howell admitted that the Confederates had told her there would be a big battle fought on her farm. Sherman discounted all of these stories, and when W. H. L. Wallace and Colonel McPherson visited him that night he appeared "in fine spirits."[70]

The Buckland incident was not the only action that occurred on April 4. At 3 P.M., a company of the 6th Iowa, on picket duty at the Owl Creek bridge, was suddenly attacked by a body of Confederate cavalry. A drummer boy was struck in his hand, which later had to be amputated. A company of cavalry and two infantry companies went in pursuit and happened across a sizable enemy cavalry contingent about two miles from the bridge. Sherman concluded that it was the same group of cavalry that Buckland had come into contact with on April 3.[71]

At least one officer had a premonition of pending trouble.

Colonel Thomas Worthington of the 46th Ohio came from an affluent and politically well-connected Ohio family. His father had been both a United States senator and an Ohio governor. In 1827, at the age of twenty, Thomas graduated from West Point. He resigned his commission the next year to oversee, along with his brother, the family business outside Chillicothe. In 1839, he became a brigadier in the Ohio militia, and briefly served in the Mexican War. He devoted himself to literature and was an accomplished scholar, but was vain and stubborn.[72]

Worthington's persistent complaints became a source of irritation to Sherman. Being older than Halleck, Grant, or Sherman, the colonel "claimed to know more of war than all of us put together," wrote Sherman. While at Savannah, the division commander complained, Worthington went "flying about giving orders, as though he were commander-in-chief." The eccentric colonel made a habit of dressing in civilian clothes and wandering about in regimental camps far from his own. Even C. F. Smith knew of his obnoxious behavior.[73]

Days before the Southern army left Corinth, Worthington became convinced that the Federal army was in imminent danger. He kept a journal (portions of which were later altered, Sherman insisted) in which he frequently noted "indications of an attack." On March 27, he entered: "He [Sherman] snubs me, and has no time even to hear a suggestion." On March 29, he requested seventy-two axes to build an abatis around his camp, but Sherman reduced the number to twenty-two; even those were not forthcoming. On the 31st, he wrote: "Sherman is inviting an attack, which I hope may occur, but for which we are unprepared." By April 4, he was convinced that the attack would come "at every hour."[74]

It proved to be the right message but the wrong messenger. Sherman "became tired" of Worthington's constant carping. The only reason he predicted an attack, Sherman would later state, was that he always "predicted the worst." Sherman even reciprocated with stubbornness of his own. "What business was it of his whether his superior invited an attack or not," he later foolishly testified. The words of the annoying Worthington would nonetheless return to haunt Sherman.[75]

A series of troubling events occurred on Saturday, April 5. At 7 a.m., Union pickets at the widow Howell's house were suddenly driven in. Long after the battle, Sherman continued to insist (wrongly) that the widow-Howell picket post had never been abandoned. He also incorrectly believed that pickets extended a mile beyond the house.[76]

About 2 P.M., pickets at the Seay house were driven back two hundred yards. Concurrent with this spatter, Hildebrand, Buckland, and several regimental officers out on a reconnaissance encountered startled Union fatigue parties claiming to have spotted enemy cavalry. The officers rode forward and saw three to five hundred gray horsemen near James Wood's house. Sherman learned of these events about 3 P.M., but thought little of them.[77]

That afternoon, pickets of the 40th Illinois reported what they thought to be the glimmer of sun reflecting off three brass field guns, positioned southeast of the widow Howell's house. Buckland rode out to check but saw nothing. At 5 P.M., Captain A. G. Sharpe of the 46th Ohio confirmed the sighting of a single field gun, which he assumed to be Confederate, for it was pointed at Buckland's camps. The officer personally reported the incident to Sherman, who replied that he would have artillery in readiness.[78]

Sherman became increasingly irritated as other disturbing reports came in. Thirty-one-year-old Colonel Jesse J. Appler of the 53rd Ohio had been an auditor and a probate judge in Portsmouth, Ohio. He had earlier served in the Ohio militia and his presence was a good drawing card in recruitment. Sherman had been impressed with him in their first meeting. About 4 P.M. on April 5, enemy cavalry was seen at the end of Rea Field, south of the 53rd's camp. A jittery Appler sent a platoon to investigate, but continued to drill his troops. Suddenly shots rang out in the woods. An officer ran into camp and reported that he had been fired upon by a "line of men in butternut clothes." The colonel sprang into action: the long roll was sounded and a messenger sent to Sherman. The courier returned shortly and, within hearing distance of many of the men, reported: "Colonel Appler, General Sherman says: 'Take your damned regiment back to Ohio. There is no enemy closer than Corinth.'" Laughter erupted in the ranks, and the regiment broke formation almost before the order was given.[79]

Sherman was actually more concerned about Stuart's brigade, near Lick Creek, than about the Shiloh Church sector. On April 5, the creek dropped to three feet and was no more than eighty to a hundred feet across at the ford. Sherman, McPherson, and Stuart crossed over and scouted the east bank, but found no evidence of the enemy.[80]

That night, Captain I. P. Rumsey, an aide to W. H. L. Wallace, and his brother, Lieutenant John W. Rumsey, notified Sherman that they had been on the picket line and had seen squads of enemy cavalry both in front of Prentiss's division and farther to the right, in Sherman's front. "Yes," Sherman replied, "they have been up on the right three times and fired on McDowell, but I have positive orders from Grant to do nothing that will have a tendency to bring on a general engagement until Buell arrives." Then he nervously complained that the Army of the Ohio should have arrived ten days earlier.[81]

Adding to Sherman's woes was an ill-timed artillery-and-cavalry reorganization that had been ordered on April 2 but did not occur until the 5th. The result was that on Saturday, the day before the battle, the 5th Division lost Ricker's battalion of the 5th Ohio Cavalry and two batteries, all of which were reassigned. Thus, throughout the afternoon of crucial Saturday, Sherman, incredibly, had no cavalry! Eight companies of the 4th Illinois Cavalry, commanded by Colonel T. Lyle Dickey, arrived at dusk. Dickey asked permission to take his regiment out on a scout that night, but Sherman held them back.[82]

The evidence received by Sherman on April 4 and 5, though not overwhelming, warranted more attention than it received. Even if entrenching and abatis were considered unacceptable, other preventive measures could have been taken. The 53rd Ohio could have been drawn in from its exposed position in Rea Field. The division batteries could have been brought up and positioned. Infantry pickets could have been extended two miles. Beyond strengthening his picket line, however, Sherman did nothing. Attempts have been made to explain his negligence—his contempt for militia officers and the conviction that Johnston would never leave his base—but the root cause may run deeper. When he had fallen victim to exaggeration back in Kentucky, he had been labeled insane. To have appeared shaken and overly alarmed would have subjected him to a similar criticism—"they'd call me crazy again," he wrote Ellen. In presenting a posture of confidence, he overlooked legitimate causes of concern.[83]

On Saturday night, a free exchange of ideas took place among Buckland, Hildebrand, and several regimental officers concerning the possibility of an attack. Sherman made an appearance and was incredulous that such a thought was contemplated. Colonel Wills DeHaas of the 77th Ohio remembered: "General Sherman's positive manner of uttering his opinions had the effect to quiet the apprehensions of some of the officers present." Buckland, nonetheless, had a drummer boy sleep in his tent that night in the event the long roll had to be quickly sounded.[84]

That evening, Sergeant William Stephenson of the 53rd Ohio scrawled a letter to "Tillie." How much longer the war would last he did not know—many in camp guessed the Fourth of July. The thought briefly occurred to him that, "should they [enemy] whip us out [here], with the Tennessee river to our backs, escape would be impossible and would end in our destruction." Hours later, a Confederate soldier would find the unmailed letter in Stephenson's tent; it was then printed in the *New Orleans Picayune*.[85]

Headquarters, *Army of the Tennessee*

GRANT CONTINUED to maintain his headquarters at Savannah, where he daily expected Buell. Although McClernand was by this time at Pittsburg Landing, Grant continued to use Sherman as an informal commander. As the skirmishing increased in early April, Grant made daily trips to the army, sometimes staying until night.[86]

Estimates of enemy troop strength varied. The Northern press reported 60,000 to 80,000 Rebels at Corinth, a number confirmed by deserters. Although initially conservative in his estimates, Grant eventually accepted these figures. He remained remarkably placid under the circumstances, but he expected Buell's army shortly and maintained not "the slightest doubt about the result."[87]

Grant subsequently did become concerned, but not about Pittsburg Landing. His focus was on Crump's Landing, where Lew Wallace's isolated division guarded the army's supplies. He feared that Johnston might make a quick dash upon the base. On April 4, Wallace notified Grant that the Confederates at Purdy numbered eight infantry regiments and 1,200 cavalry, with an equal number at Bethel. It made little difference that Wallace had grossly exaggerated Cheatham's strength; Grant had to take the threat seriously. He ordered W. H. L. Wallace's division to be on standby to reinforce Crump's Landing.[88]

On the afternoon of April 4, Grant, while at Savannah, heard the distant thunder of artillery—Buckland's fray on the Ridge Road. He hastened to Pittsburg Landing, but it was dark and raining by the time he arrived. He rode out two miles and met with W. H. L. Wallace, who assured him the situation was under control. On the return trip, Grant's horse stumbled in the mud, pinning the general's ankle. He would painfully hobble about on crutches for the next two or three days and limp for several weeks.[89]

Nelson's division, the van of Buell's army, arrived in Savannah on the morning of April 5. Grant anticipated his arrival; advanced units had arrived two days earlier. Grant had actually notified Nelson not to hurry, since his troops could not be put across the river until Tuesday, April 8. The bombastic division commander nonetheless continued at the same pace.[90]

At 1 P.M., Nelson reported to Grant at the Cherry mansion, requesting permission to press on and pitch his tents at Pittsburg Landing. "Not immediately," Grant replied; "you will encamp for the present at Savannah." The impulsive Nelson asked whether he was not concerned about Beauregard attacking—"The wonder to me is that he has not done so before." Grant casually answered that he had more troops than he did at Fort Donelson and that he could hold his own. C. F. Smith was present and offered reassurance: "They're [enemy] all back at Corinth, and, when our transportation arrives, we have got to go there and draw them out, as you would draw a badger out of a hole."[91]

Nelson's 4,500 troops bivouacked near town, with Jacob Ammen's brigade a half-mile southwest of the village, and William B. Hazen's and Sanders D. Bruce's brigades a short distance back, on the Waynesboro Road. A surgeon noted in his journal: "Genl Grant called to see us. Did not give no orders to go on to Pitts[;] said he had plenty of men to relief [sic] them. Genl Nelson was anxious to be within sight of Pittsburg—Genl Grant seemed indifferent." At 3 P. M., Grant called on his old associate Colonel Ammen. When asked if the division should not press forward, the army commander commented that it would be impossible to march through the swamps of the east bank. "Make the troops comfortable; I will send boats for you Monday or Tuesday, or some time early in the week."[92]

Grant's sins of omission were mounting. If he was nervous about Crump's Landing, he should have at least crossed Nelson's division to that place. The truth was that very few boats were available. Most of the supplies had been kept loaded on the transports, in the event that a change of base to Hamburg or Eastport became necessary. Buell, minus his staff, arrived in Savannah about sunset on April 5, following a grueling day's ride. Grant was at Pittsburg Landing and would not be back until late evening. He notified Buell that he would meet with him on Sunday morning, April 6.[93]

While at Pittsburg Landing on the 5th, Grant received a message from Lew Wallace. Two of his civilian scouts had reported that the Rebel army was on the move and that the target was Pittsburg Landing. Even Wallace doubted the story. Both scouts were unsavory types, and one was suspected of being a Confederate spy. Indeed, after reporting to Wallace, the men had become embroiled in an argument that almost ended in a gunfight. Sherman assured Grant that, with the exception of enemy cavalry patrols and two infantry regiments and a battery about six miles out, his division front was clear.[94]

That evening, Grant returned to the Cherry mansion, unaware that Buell was in Savannah. He penned two notes to Halleck, informing him that the main enemy force was at Corinth. He then added words that would shadow him for the balance of his army career: "I have scarcely the faintest idea of an attack (general one) being made upon us."[95]

Federal Camp of the First Brigade, Sixth Division

ON THE AFTERNOON of April 4, Colonel Everett Peabody reviewed his 1st Brigade of Prentiss's division in Spain Field. A downpour came and canceled the drill, but before then a squad of enemy cavalry was seen moving leisurely about in the woods to the south. Many of the men found it curious that the Rebels were allowed to come so close to the main encampment.[96]

The next afternoon, Brigadier General Benjamin Prentiss reviewed his entire division in Spain Field. During the exercise, Major James E. Powell of the 25th Missouri noticed a party of mounted men in the woods keeping a close watch. He notified the division commander, who in turn ordered a 4 P.M. reconnaissance. The patrol would consist of two companies of the 25th Missouri and three companies of the 21st Missouri, with Colonel David Moore commanding. The troops cautiously marched a mile and a half toward Seay Field. There they encountered several blacks, who informed them that earlier in the day two hundred Rebels had been seen. Visibility was increasingly poor as dusk came on, but D. B. Baker of the 25th would vividly recall, "We could hear the enemy moving in every direction." Moore returned after sunset, reporting that he had not seen the enemy.[97]

Captain Gilbert D. Johnson of the 12th Michigan commanded one of the companies that had been ordered to strengthen the picket line. His men, somewhat extended beyond the line, could hear considerable movement in the darkened woods ahead. Prentiss ordered the company to draw back and told Colonel W. H. Graves of the 12th not to be alarmed.[98]

Johnson remained unconvinced. In company with Major Powell, he took his story to Colonel Peabody. A descendant of a prominent Massachusetts family and a Harvard graduate, the thirty-one-year-old Peabody had become a successful railroad engineer in the west. Back in September 1861, he had been seriously wounded and captured in the siege of Lexington, Missouri. He wrote his brother on March 31, 1862, that it seemed "funny to be called [acting] General; but the boys are all delighted, and I think I will do good service at the proper time."[99]

About midnight, the anxious colonel rousted Captain Simon S. Eveans and Acting Lieutenant James Newhard from their sleep. With or without the consent of his superior, Peabody intended to find out exactly what was going on in his front. On his own authority, he ordered Powell to take three companies of the 25th Missouri and two companies of the 12th Michigan and return to Seay Field. The stage had been set for one of the greatest battles in American history.[100]

Chicago, Illinois

CHICAGO SEEMED a world away from the events unfolding in the wilderness around Pittsburg Landing, Tennessee. Yet the city had more than a passing interest in the campaign; hundreds of her sons served in Grant's army. Companies A, K, and E of the 12th Illinois hailed from Chicago, as did Company D, 43rd Illinois; Company E, 58th Illinois; and scores of men in the 55th Illinois. Four batteries of the 1st Illinois Light Artillery (A, B, E, H) had been exclusively recruited in the midwestern city of 110,000 inhabitants. There was thus some apprehension when, in early April 1862, a *Chicago Tribune* correspondent with the Army of the Tennessee related a note of caution. Unless Halleck pushed forward Buell's army, Grant's position at Pittsburg Landing "may be overcome, and we might meet with a terrible reverse." The editor felt compelled to allay the fears of his readers by adding an addendum. No other journalist had expressed such comments, and Buell's army had undoubtedly already linked up with Grant. There was absolutely no expectation of trouble. Chicagoans slept soundly.[101]

SIX

The Opening Attack

Fraley Field

IT WAS A CLEAR NIGHT during the early hours of April 6 as Powell's patrol, four hundred strong according to later press accounts, filed from their encampment along the Seay Field Road between Rea and Seay Fields.[1] Bumping into a picket post of the 57th Ohio of Sherman's division, Powell boasted that he was "going to catch some Rebels for breakfast." As the Federals cautiously advanced, a near disaster was averted when two of the three squads almost opened fire into each other. Peabody had gone out on a limb for this patrol. What if he were wrong about the Rebels, and friendly-fire casualties resulted? The troops neared the Pittsburg-Corinth Road, where slightly to the north were two cabins owned by Wilse Wood. Beyond the road, enemy vedettes moving through the underbrush fired three quick shots, wheeled about, and rode off into the pitch-black.[2]

Powell formed his five companies into a skirmish line and advanced into Fraley Field, a forty-acre cotton field bisected by the west branch of Shiloh Creek. Twenty-two years to the day later, James J. Fraley would be giving guided tours of the battlefield at the first Federal veterans' reunion at Shiloh. On the day of battle, however, the thirty-six-year-old farmer, his wife, and two children had moved away on advice of Confederate officers. Surprisingly, his horse and cow survived the battle unscathed, the latter because no one could bridle her.[3]

Powell clearly did not realize the danger ahead. In the darkness, barely seven hundred yards away, was S. A. M. Wood's brigade of Hardee's corps; the Rebel army had at long last been discovered. The previous night, Wood had thrown forward a skirmish line consisting of Major Aaron B. Hardcastle's 3rd Mississippi Battalion, 280 muskets strong. The young Hardcastle had been a lieutenant in the Regular Army and was part of the escort that had accompanied Sidney Johnston from California to Tennessee early in the war. He deployed his men on a rise in the southeast corner of the field. Two picket posts extended from the main line.[4]

About 5 A.M., the outposts fired a single volley at the approaching Yankees and quickly retired to the main line. As the Federals closed to within two hundred yards, Hardcastle's Mississippians opened fire. In the darkness, only flashes could be seen coming from the timber and brush. For the next hour and fifteen minutes, as streaks of daylight flashed across the sky, the two sides doggedly traded blows, each refusing to give ground. Powell's casualties were never reported, although one officer stated that "many killed and wounded" were carried back to camp. Despite Hardcastle's claim that most of the enemy shots passed over his men, he later tallied four killed and twenty wounded, half of those seriously.[5]

During a brief lull, Powell noticed what appeared to be a body of cavalry attempting to work its way around his left flank. It was actually an escort company, the Jefferson Mounted Rifles, searching for a route through the underbrush to bring up artillery. Powell had his bugler sound retreat.[6]

Headquarters, Army of the Mississippi

BEFORE DAWN, JOHNSTON and his staff gathered around a small fire and had a breakfast of coffee and crackers. Several general officers soon assembled, with Bragg, Hardee, and Beauregard among them, and the discussion of the previous night continued. Johnston was "mainly a listener," according to Isaac Ulmer, a member of his escort company. A sudden crash of musketry was heard up the Pittsburg-Corinth Road— the skirmishing in Fraley Field—cutting the debate short. "There," said Preston, "the first gun of the battle!" Johnston replied, "The battle has opened gentlemen; it is too late to change our dispositions." He asked Munford and Preston to note the time. In postwar years, Munford recalled that it was precisely 5:14, but Preston's memorandum book read: "5:30 Sharp volleys of musketry from Hardee's front between the roads."[7]

A buoyant Johnston, wearing a soft black hat with sweeping

plume, tucked his sword under his arm and mounted his bay thoroughbred, Fire-eater. The magnificent animal, originally named Empire, was a product of the famous Woodstock Farm of Kentucky. Turning to his staff, Johnston said: "Tonight we will water our horses in the Tennessee River." As he confidently rode to the front, he paused long enough to speak to Randal Gibson, a friend of his son: "Randal, I never see you but I think of William [Johnston]. I hope you may get through safely this day, but we must win a victory." Early reports appeared to indicate that the Yankees had been caught napping, but Johnston could hardly believe it. "Can it be possible they are not aware of our presence?" he inquired of Beauregard. "It is scarcely possible they are laying a trap for us," the Creole cautiously replied.[8]

Johnston assigned Beauregard the task of forwarding men and supplies. In directing his army from the front rather than the rear, assert some historians, Johnston reversed roles with his second-in-command. Others insist that Johnston remained in control and made every major decision throughout the morning.[9]

At the last moment, Johnston had concerns for Greer's Ford on Lick Creek. If Buell's army landed at Hamburg and took the ridge road over Greer's Ford, it could get between the Confederate Army and Corinth. The 19th Tennessee of Breckinridge's division and Forrest's Cavalry Regiment protected the potential trouble spot, but Johnston decided to also send five companies of the 1st Tennessee (the other five companies still being in Chattanooga). He gave the Tennesseans a stirring speech and rhetorically asked if all the men had a full supply of ammunition. An innocent lad broke the solemn mood by shouting that he was short two rounds![10]

Headquarters, Peabody's Brigade

AT THE BRIGADE HEADQUARTERS of Colonel Peabody, faint shots could be heard to the southwest. A dispatch received from Powell indicated that his men were being driven back by an enemy force estimated at 3,000. Henry Bentley, journalist of the *Philadelphia Inquirer*, was present, and later indicated that the colonel believed the engagement to be only a sharp skirmish. The sound also attracted the attention of Brigadier General Prentiss, who rode "very leisurely" into the camp of the 21st Missouri that morning. He arrived at brigade headquarters and demanded to know what the shooting was about. The colonel an-

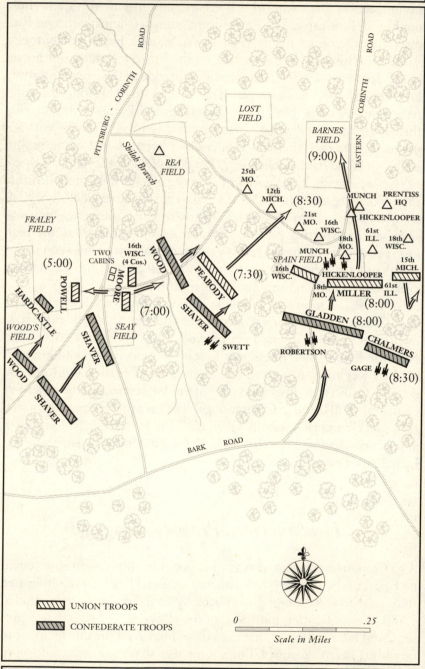

ROAD

PITTSBURG - CORINTH *ROAD*

Shiloh Branch

LOST FIELD

BARNES FIELD (9:00)

REA FIELD

25th MO.

12th MICH. (8:30)

FRALEY FIELD

(5:00)

MUNCH

PRENTISS HQ

HICKENLOOPER

21st MO.

16th WISC.

TWO CABINS

16th WISC. (4 Cos.)

WOOD

POWELL

MOORE

PEABODY

(7:30)

61st ILL.

18th WISC.

18th MO.

MUNCH

SPAIN FIELD

16th WISC.

15th MICH.

HARDCASTLE

(7:00)

SHAVER

SEAY FIELD

HICKENLOOPER

18th MO.

61st ILL.

WOOD'S FIELD

MILLER (8:00)

SHAVER

SWETT

GLADDEN (8:00)

WOOD

SHAVER

ROBERTSON

CHALMERS (8:30)

GAGE

BARK   ROAD

⬜ UNION TROOPS

⬛ CONFEDERATE TROOPS

0   .25

Scale in Miles

swered that he had sent out a reconnaissance. The infuriated general accused him of precipitating an attack, for which he would be held responsible. Peabody, although angered, kept silent. He sat down on a camp chest and began his breakfast.[11]

Prentiss ordered Colonel David Moore and five companies of the 21st Missouri to support Powell's patrol. He also directed an aide to bring in the brigade pickets. As Captain Edward Saxe's Company A, 16th Wisconsin, returned from the picket line, it encountered Moore's column moving forward. An ultraconservative Democrat who had even been accused of being a secessionist prior to the war, Saxe threw down his coat and shouted, "Boys, we will fall in on the right and lead them."[12]

Minutes later, the sound of skirmishing doubled in intensity. Peabody sprang to his feet and ordered the long roll sounded. There was "great excitement in camp, and I felt sure that I was going to see a sure enough battle," George Washburn of the 21st Missouri wrote his wife. As the troops scrambled into formation, an infuriated Prentiss rode up, jerked on the rein, and again accused the colonel of bringing on an attack. Peabody, mounted and positioned on the far right of the line, snappily saluted and said, "If I brought on the fight, I am to lead the van." The five companies remaining of the 25th Missouri and the 12th Michigan advanced a half-mile in linear formation and halted on a slightly inclined ridge north of the east branch of Shiloh Creek. There the troops waited as they listened to the din of battle to the south.[13]

Prentiss rode to alert his 2nd Brigade. As he passed through the camp of the 16th Wisconsin (the far-left regiment of Peabody's command), he found the men leisurely eating breakfast, obviously unaware that the brigade had been called to arms. Prentiss ordered Colonel Ben Allen to form his men immediately and advance. The regiment promptly marched in line about 440 yards in front of the camp to a thicket of small timber.[14]

Seay Field

ABOUT 6:30, AS POWELL'S MEN fell back from Fraley Field, they were met by Moore's advancing column. A forty-five-year-old pork packer and merchant from Wrightsville, Missouri, Moore could "get madder and swear longer than any man I ever saw," recalled an acquaintance.

As he viewed Powell's men withdrawing, Moore became characteristically livid. He berated them as cowards and insisted that they had encountered only a skirmishing party. Relieving Powell of command, Moore ordered all those not wounded to face about and return to the fight. He did send Lieutenant Henry Menn back to camp with a request to bring up the remaining five companies of the 21st.[15]

Menn related Moore's message that if he was given the balance of the regiment he could "lick them." Prentiss immediately ordered out the remaining companies of the 21st Missouri under Lieutenant Colonel Marshall Woodyard. There was bad blood between Moore and Woodyard. A prominent lawyer and real-estate developer who dabbled in state politics, Woodyard had attempted to raise his own regiment early in the war. When neither he nor Moore could complete his own complement, Halleck had the outfits merged and placed Moore in command. Woodyard remained irked about his rank. His troops united with those of Moore and Powell, and together the command of sixteen companies proceeded four men abreast down the Seay Field Road.[16]

About 7 A.M., after marching only three hundred yards, the Federal column, led by Saxe's company, arrived at the northwest corner of Lewis Seay's cotton field. A Union sympathizer, the sixty-four-year-old Seay was related to nearby Wilse Wood, who favored the Southerners. Seay's cabin, on the southern edge of the field, would be one of the few structures to survive the battle.[17]

A heavy fire suddenly erupted from the fence row on the southern edge of the field. Captain Saxe and a sergeant in his company fell dead on the first volley. "We could not see the rebels behind the fence, but we could see them across the field and down the road near an old house [Seay's]," recounted a Wisconsin soldier. Moore directed that the fence along the western edge of the field be torn down, but after only one or two rails had been removed he ordered a charge. It was an imprudent order that would have proved costly if carried out, but suddenly a loud scream was heard. Moore had been struck in the right leg below the knee, shattering the bone. Shortly thereafter, Lieutenant Menn was grazed in the head and knocked insensible. An officer ran up to Powell shouting, "For God's sake Major, take command quick, the Colonel is wounded." The firing soon died down, and Powell, believing the skirmish to be over, ordered his companies to retire. Saxe's men also withdrew, carrying with them the bodies of their sergeant and captain, the first officer to be killed in the battle.[18]

Woodyard's 21st Missouri, six hundred strong, remained alone. The Rebel line began a westward extension. Woodyard formed his regiment facing southwest on the brow of an incline in the middle of Seay Field. Four companies of the 16th Wisconsin, which had been on picket duty and eagerly rushed to the assistance of Company A, arrived on the scene. Woodyard placed them east of the field, on a slight ridge, out of enemy range. The 21st then withdrew to the woods north of the field, connecting with the Wisconsin troops. Whether the Federals understood the engagement to be a general attack or simply an extended skirmish is not certain. There would soon be little doubt.[19]

On Line with Hardee's Corps

PERHAPS TOO MUCH CREDIT has been given to Peabody's predawn patrol. True enough, the Federals had been alerted, and technically the surprise had been foiled. Had the Confederates attacked at sunrise (6 A.M.), however, the near advantage would have been maintained. Such was not the case. It took an hour for Johnston's advance order to trickle down, meaning that the attack did not commence until 6:30. Even then, the advance proved sluggish and uncoordinated, hardly the "Alpine avalanche" later boasted by Beauregard. Another hour was wasted in useless skirmishing before Seay Field was cleared. In losing an hour and a half of precious daylight, the Confederates squandered their own surprise.[20]

Hardee's first-in assault line totaled 9,000 infantry and artillery and covered a front of one and one-quarter miles. Sometime before the battle, Hardee awkwardly formed a provisional division. Although he maintained overall command, the two center brigades would be led by the hot-tempered and scheming Thomas C. Hindman. Hindman's command comprised the brigades of S. A. M. Wood and Hindman's own, now under Colonel R. G. Shaver.[21]

When the skirmishing began in Fraley Field, Wood's brigade was positioned west of the Pittsburg-Corinth Road, southwest of James Wood's cotton gin and field. At sunrise, Wood—lawyer, politician, and editor of his hometown newspaper in Florence, Alabama—called his 1,900 infantry into line. The sun had not yet burned off the morning mist when the advance finally began; "the men went eagerly," Wood reported. The brigade no sooner got under way when it ground to a halt, because some company commanders failed to observe their alignments. The broken ground caused a gap between Shaver and Wood, and the 55th Tennessee had to be shifted to extend the line.[22]

While these adjustments were being made, the 8th Arkansas and 9th Arkansas Battalion, 420 muskets, advanced as skirmishers, replacing Hardcastle's Mississippians. The Arkansans took position at the southwest corner of Seay Field, and it was these troops that had been sparring with Moore's Yankees. Leading the 9th was boyish-looking, twenty-two-year-old Major John H. Kelly, destined to become the youngest general in the Confederate Army, before he fell mortally wounded in a cavalry raid on Franklin, Tennessee, in November 1864.[23]

Wood's brigade stumbled ahead in the semidarkness in conjunction with Shaver's troops in the thickets to the right. Typical among Shaver's regiments was the 6th Arkansas, consisting primarily of rough and untaught knife-toting backwoodsmen. At the time of mustering, one company of ninety-nine men counted but one married man. Colonel Alexander T. Hawthorne was clearly a cut above most of his men. For two years he had studied law at Harvard, and became an attorney in Camden, Arkansas. His distinguished service this day would earn him a brigadier's star. Also in the ranks was an illegitimate twenty-one-year-old by the name of Henry Stanley. Still years ahead was the time when he would become a journalist and an African explorer, internationally known for his search for Dr. David Livingstone. A teenage friend next to him placed some violets in his hat. "Perhaps the Yankees won't shoot if they see me wearing such flowers, for they are a sign of peace." "Capital," replied Stanley, "I will do the same."[24]

Hindman's two brigades swept northward, Wood astride the Seay Field Road and Shaver clawing through the thickets to his right, both crossing the western branch of Shiloh Creek. Woodyard made his next stand on a slight ridge north of the creek, where he was joined by Peabody and the 25th Missouri. After briefly contesting the advance, the Federals withdrew.[25]

On Line with Peabody's Brigade

AT 7:30 A.M., PEABODY'S BRIGADE, the troops standing at rest, beheld a startling sight—dozens of terrified rabbits rushing toward their line. "We were soon dumbfounded by seeing an enormous force of Con-

federate troops marching directly toward us," described Private
Charles Morton of the 25th Missouri. To another Missourian the sight
presented a "sublime but awful scene, as they advanced slowly, steadily
and silently till within about 125 yards." The 25th Missouri, composed
largely of discharged soldiers from the Regular Army (recruited in
Kansas City and St. Joseph) and country boys familiar with hunting,
held firm as Lieutenant Colonel Robert Van Horn steadied them. Approaching their line were Shaver's brigade and the four right regiments of Wood's brigade (the others having veered off toward Rea
Field)—perhaps 2,200 men in tight line formation.[26]

Wood's two right-flank regiments, the 55th Tennessee and 3rd
Mississippi Battalion, arriving in advance of Hindman's other troops,
received the full brunt of the first Yankee volley. The unseasoned
Southerners staggered to a halt and then broke in utter confusion. As
they ran pell-mell to the rear, shouting, "Retreat! Retreat!," they collided with Shaver's right-wing regiment, Lieutenant Colonel James M.
Dean's 7th Arkansas, stampeding that unit. Only with great difficulty
did the officers, including General Johnston, rally the command.[27]

The Confederates closed to within seventy-five yards before
opening fire. Peabody's troops held steadily, as casualties mounted on
both sides. After the battle, Federal observers went to the Rebel position and found an appalling number of bodies. The Yankees jeered,
"Why don't you come on?" as the Southerners yelled in reply: "Bull
Run!" In order to extend Peabody's line, the 16th Wisconsin moved up
in right echelon, but after several volleys Prentiss withdrew it.
Peabody's flanks were soon enveloped, and his line drifted slowly back
toward the brigade encampment.[28]

Captain Charles Swett's Warren (Mississippi) Light Artillery
from Vicksburg galloped up and unlimbered their six field pieces to
the right of Shaver's men. Their destructive fire ripped through Sibley
tents, plowed up the ground, and tore large limbs from trees. Being
within rifle range, the gunners soon began to take casualties. Hardee
directed Hindman to save the battery.[29]

A furious assault was mounted on the encampment. Colonel
Peabody, who had been on a fruitless search for Prentiss, returned to
find his brigade on the verge of collapse. Although wounded four
times, he attempted to rally his men, gesturing them to make a stand.
Above the din of battle he was heard to shout: "The 25th Missouri is
disgraced." He suddenly threw up his arms, reeled back, and fell dead
from his horse, a ball having entered his upper lip and passed to the
back of his head. His riderless horse ran wildly across the line, the stir-

rups flapping in the air. Although justice and notoriety for his actions at Shiloh would largely escape him in life, history would make amends. Peabody was temporarily buried the next day, and within three weeks his body had been reinterred in the family cemetery in Springfield, Massachusetts.[30]

The badly scattered and broken Federal ranks streamed back through the tents, firing from behind trees and bales of hay. Powell briefly took command in one sector before he was killed. Colonel Allen had his horse shot from under him, and a second animal was shot as he remounted. The Chicago press later falsely reported that Allen had been struck in the lungs and killed. Prentiss ordered the colonel to fall back to the trees and attempt to hold until reinforcements came. By 8:30, Peabody's brigade had been rolled up, and his camps were in enemy possession.[31]

All was chaos at the brigade hospital. Ambulances raced to the rear as frantic soldiers jumped in, fighting off their comrades. Samuel Eels, surgeon of the 12th Michigan, tended the wounded as bullets zipped through his hospital tent. When it became evident that the Federal line would not hold, the medical staff resolved to remain with the wounded. "Though some [Confederates] leveled their guns at us and we rather expected them to shoot than otherwise," revealed Eels, Hindman rode up and guaranteed their safety. Two Rebel surgeons established tents nearby, making liberal use of the captured stores and medicine.[32]

Spain Field

PEABODY RODE TO ALERT Colonel Madison Miller, commanding the 1,700-man 2nd Brigade. The fifty-one-year-old Miller, besides being a Mexican War veteran, had been a successful railroad executive and the mayor of Carondelet, Missouri. The colonel was having his breakfast with his staff when the alarmed Prentiss rode up and shouted, "Colonel Miller, get out your brigade! They are fighting on the right!" The officers jumped to their feet, the long roll sounded, and within minutes the 18th Missouri had formed in line.[33]

The camp adjacent to the Missourians was that of old Colonel Jacob Fry's 61st Illinois. It had been unusually quiet that Sunday morning as the men completed breakfast and prepared for 9:00 inspection. Suddenly, off to the right, a dull "pum pum" was heard, followed by a muffled roar. As the men sprang to their feet and looked inquiringly into one another's faces, the long roll began to sound. In the midst of the ensuing confusion, a staff officer galloped into camp, took a hurried glance about him, and exclaimed: "My God! this regiment not in line yet! They have been fighting on the right over an hour!"[34]

The 18th Wisconsin, on the far left, had arrived the previous afternoon at Pittsburg Landing. Organized in Milwaukee in the winter of 1861–62, the men, numbering 862 present for duty that Sunday morning, were fairly proficient in drill, but their only experience with their Austrian rifles was in shooting at birds and logs on the river trip down from St. Louis.[35]

At 7:30, Miller deployed his troops on the northern edge of Peter Spain's field, behind a slight but ready-made protection of stumps, logs, and underbrush, which had been cleared to form a drill ground. Prentiss, dissatisfied with the position, ordered the brigade repositioned on the southern portion of the field. Miller reluctantly obeyed, forming an L-shaped line facing south and west, in the direction of the firing. Twenty-seven-year-old Captain Andrew Hickenlooper's 5th Ohio Battery, a Cincinnati outfit, unlimbered in the northwestern corner of the field, east of the Eastern Corinth Road. Also anchoring Miller's right flank was Captain Emil Munch's 1st Minnesota Battery, astride and to the west of the road.[36]

In the midst of the confusion came the farcical episode of the 15th Michigan. The regiment had arrived the previous afternoon and coincidentally reported for duty just as the Confederate attack formed. The men hurriedly came into line, to the left of the 18th Wisconsin, and watched in near shock as a long line of enemy troops advanced on the slope in their front. The 15th stood at order arms with their muskets. There was little else they could do; they had not yet been issued ammunition![37]

Miller's troops did not have to wait long—perhaps five minutes. "We were drawn up in line of battle. I was looking as anxious for the Secesh as I ever did a squirrel," attested Edgar Embly of the 61st, "but I did not look long before I seen their guns glittering in the brush."[38]

ADVANCING ON A NORTHWESTERN SLANT, parallel to and on either side of the Eastern Corinth Road, were the brigades of A. H. Gladden and James Chalmers, the latter having been moved up from the second line. Once again the Confederates had encountered early problems. As Hardee's troops advanced, they inclined to the left, leaving a space between their right and Lick Creek. Johnston filled the vacancy by moving up Chalmers's "Pensacola Brigade." What he did not realize, at least not at this time, was that Lick Creek turned sharply to the northeast, thus increasing the gap on the right as the troops advanced. For now, Clanton's 1st Alabama Cavalry swept toward the creek and guarded the flank.[39]

Gladden's troops, perhaps slightly in advance of Chalmers's, encountered great confusion as the men crossed a marsh and were thrown out of alignment. The 1st Louisiana Regulars, on the left, emerged from the morass first and veered to the right, squeezing out the regiment on its right, Lieutenant Colonel William D. Chadick's 26th Alabama. Chadick had no choice but to move his men across the rear of the brigade and form on the extreme right. About 8 A.M., Gladden's brigade struck Miller's line in front and obliquely to the right and left. The men had to cross a shallow branch of Locust Grove and then advance up a gentle slope, the summit of which was only 150–200 yards from the enemy line. As they rushed forward, the Southerners came under a galling infantry-and-artillery fire and recoiled along the line.[40]

The Confederates established counter-battery fire. Captain Felix Robertson positioned his four twelve-pounder Napoleon guns across the Eastern Corinth Road. Gage's Alabama Battery advanced up a small trail leading off the Bark Road and closed to within two hundred yards of the enemy. No sooner did the cannoneers come into action than one was killed and three wounded. One of the wounded, Daniel King, swallowed the bullet that passed through his mouth. "It was a wonder to me that our whole company was not cut up," a member scrawled to his mother. Robertson's battery similarly came under a hail of bullets.[41]

Brigadier General Adley H. Gladden urged his men forward. Although a prominent New Orleans merchant at the beginning of the war, the portly Gladden had notably commanded the Palmetto (South Carolina) Regiment during the Mexican War. At 8:45, a cannon projectile struck him, horribly mangling his left arm and shoulder. "Scott," he mumbled to his aide, "I am struck, but let's go on." After moving but a few steps, he uttered, "It is a serious hurt, help me down, Scott." An ambulance carried the mortally wounded brigadier to the rear, where a correspondent noted that he was "pale, faint, but still smiling."[42]

Command of the brigade fell to Colonel Daniel Adams, a politically well-connected lawyer in civil life. Nineteen years earlier, he had killed in a duel a Vicksburg newspaper editor who had questioned the political views of Adams's father, a federal judge. Seeing his men falter under the blistering fire, Adams seized the flag of the 1st Louisiana Regulars and called upon the brigade to follow. As the troops charged, Robertson's cannoneers dragged their guns by hand behind the infantry.[43]

By 8:30, Chalmers's brigade had become involved. Chalmers gave the order to charge, but the word was not heard down the line, and only the 10th Mississippi, about 360 men, dashed up the hill. The 7th and 9th Mississippi followed shortly, putting the 18th Wisconsin to flight. Taylor Beatty of the 1st Louisiana Regulars wrote that "after engaging them for about 20 minutes [we] drove them from their position." The cost had been high; the regimental medical staff counted twenty-eight killed and eighty-nine wounded in the assault.[44]

Hickenlooper's battery, in Spain Field, was caught in an exposed position. In the lull before the second assault, Prentiss had ordered a "change front to the right." In executing the maneuver, the charging Confederates caught the Ohio gunners in their exposed flank. Within minutes, fifty-nine horses fell dead in their harness, "all piled up in their struggles," observed a Southern officer. Hickenlooper glanced up to see a gray line that stretched as far as he could see. Although two of his guns were overrun, the Buckeyes furiously cut out the dead animals and managed to escape with four pieces.[45]

Even before Munch's Minnesota Battery got into position, the Rebels were barely a hundred yards distant. The six pieces formed a semicircle on either side of the Eastern Corinth Road. The left gun, a six-pounder, became disabled when the carriage trail snapped at the elevation screw. Another piece became unserviceable when a shot jammed halfway down the barrel. As Munch gave the order to retire, his horse tumbled to the ground with a bullet wound. The captain, in attempting to retrieve his saddle, caught a bullet in his thigh. All six guns were safely withdrawn, the two disabled pieces being taken to the landing.[46]

Within half an hour, Miller's brigade had been driven through their camp. The Rebels surged triumphantly ahead, shouting "Bull Run!" As Leander Stillwell of the 61st Illinois fled past his tent, he turned and saw his first Rebel flag—"a gaudy sort of thing with red bars." For a fleeting moment he thought about stopping for his knapsack, but quickly determined to run for his life. The 61st was unfairly singled out by the Chicago press as "the only Illinois boys that acted badly." Miller made no apologies for his brigade; he merely pointed to the number of bodies found after the battle "in that old [Spain] field."[47]

The Confederates pursued the enemy through their tents and slightly beyond before breaking off the chase and pausing to regroup. Walking in the streets of the encampment, a member of the 26th Alabama saw "the dead and wounded which lay thick over the camp ground. They were mangled in every conceivable form." Among the trophies collected were the battle flags of the 18th Missouri and 18th Wisconsin, caps, love letters, and a pistol belonging to Colonel Allen.[48]

Rea Field

IRISH IMMIGRANT JOHN CORNELIUS REA (commonly misspelled Rhea) settled in Hardin County sometime before 1830. He and his wife, Jincy, raised their two daughters and worked a cornfield and small orchard near their cabin. In 1848, at age fifty-four, John died of an apparent heart attack as he fetched water at a nearby spring that bore his name. Jincy died six years later, and both were buried in what became known as Shiloh Church Cemetery. At the time of the war, the land was probably being farmed by Levi J. Howell and John A. Campbell, both married to the Rea daughters.[49]

On the eastern portion of the field, the 53rd Ohio made its encampment. Like all the regiments in Sherman's 5th Division, it was green. The men, mostly foundrymen and miners, came from counties chiefly along the Ohio River in the southeastern portion of the state, and also included three companies of Kentuckians. Sickness had plagued the regiment; as many as 250 patients remained in camp.[50]

The sighting of enemy scouts had caused the 53rd's colonel, Jesse Appler, to become jittery. On Saturday night, April 5, he had taken an unauthorized action by sending out a sixteen-man detail beyond the picket line to the south end of Rea Field. As the camp sutler opened for business and the troops began their breakfast on Sunday morning, the detachment returned to camp with troubling news. An enemy scouting patrol had been sighted on the road at the end of the field, and heavy firing could be heard about a quarter-mile to the left (Fraley Field). The pickets were quite convinced that a large enemy force was in the regiment's front.[51]

Appler, doubtless remembering Sherman's mocking remark from the previous day, momentarily vacillated. As a wounded soldier of the 25th Missouri stumbled into camp shouting, "Get into line; the Rebels are coming," the colonel hesitated no longer. The long roll was sounded, and messengers were sent to brigade and division headquarters. Colonel Jesse Hildebrand ordered two companies of the 53rd to reinforce the picket line. The messenger sent to division headquarters returned shortly and, in a low voice, repeated Sherman's caustic reply: "General Sherman says you must be badly scared over there." These words would later be printed in the Northern press; one outraged journalist noted that Sherman had "made fun" of Appler's warning.[52]

Hildebrand's other regiments began to come to life, as firing could now be heard all along the brigade front. In the camp of the 77th Ohio, southeast of Shiloh Church, information was received (from Colonel Moore) that the Rebels were swarming in Fraley Field. The message was relayed to Hildebrand, who lay ill at the time. Colonel Wills DeHaas thus passed the information on to division headquarters. Sherman and DeHaas listened intently to the distant crack of musketry. Although Sherman remained doubtful of an attack, he ordered the brigade in readiness. The 57th Ohio formed, fronting nearly west, their right about three hundred yards south of the church. To their right was the 77th Ohio, facing south, which moved from their camp down a gentle slope leading to Shiloh Branch, about 150 yards away. The underbrush and small timber had been cleared from the tents to the creek, and only large trees remained. From that position, Appler's 53rd Ohio could be seen coming into line in Rea Field. Supporting the brigade was Captain Allen Waterhouse's Battery E, 1st Illinois Light Artillery, from Chicago, an outfit that had received its horses ten days earlier and drilled with them only three times. Four James rifles were unlimbered on a ridge north of Rea Springs, and the remaining section across the spring, near the old Rea cabin, to the right of the 53rd. The entire brigade line was clearly visible from Shiloh Church.[53]

As Appler's troops came to arms, First Sergeant Milton Bosworth admitted that he was "wholly unconscious of the reason for doing so." A half-dressed officer, just out of bed, came running into line shouting, "Colonel, the Rebels are crossing the field." Appler ordered the regiment to file left and face south. While executing this movement, one of the companies sent out to support the picket line came running back and took its place in line; the excited captain yelled, "The Rebels are out there thicker than fleas on a dog's back." Some enemy skirmishers suddenly emerged from the woods on the right flank. An astonished Appler ordered the regiment to wheel right and fall back through the camp: "This is no place for us," he was heard to mutter. All was chaos as the sick, camp cooks, teamsters, and scores of others fled to the rear. The regiment formed in the woods and faced west, the men lying down in the brush. On the far left, a temporary breastwork was fashioned of logs and bales of hay.[54]

At 7 A.M., Sherman and his staff rode into Rea Field, several hundred yards in front of the 53rd. The division commander still refused to believe what was happening. Looking through his binoculars, he remarked that there might be a sharp skirmish. An officer abruptly called his attention to the right, where a line of enemy skirmishers suddenly emerged from the brush-lined creek to the west. "We are attacked!" Sherman exclaimed, and threw up his hand as if to ward off a shot. Shots rang out, and the general's orderly fell dead; Sherman himself had been struck in the hand. After instructing Appler to hold his ground, he rode off with his staff to bring up reinforcements. Encountering Major Samuel M. Bowman of the 4th Illinois Cavalry near division headquarters, Sherman, his hand wrapped in a handkerchief, spoke in an excited tone. "Major, give me some extra men for orderlies, one of mine has been shot already." He then ordered the regiment up the road, stating: "The devil's to pay, sure enough!"[55]

BRIGADIER GENERAL PATRICK R. CLEBURNE had arrived in America from Ireland thirteen years earlier. Believing that he had humiliated his father by his failure to enter the apothecary trade, he escaped his guilt by entering the British Army. The move to the United States was an extension of his run from failure. In perhaps a subconscious attempt to please his father, Cleburne became part-owner of a drugstore in Helena, Arkansas. Eventually finding his own identity, he took up the study of law and became a prominent attorney. Although awkward and bashful around women, he feared no man. He was a friend of another Helena attorney, Thomas Hindman; the two were attacked one day by political enemies of Hindman. Both fell seriously wounded, but not before Cleburne killed one of the bushwhackers and chased off the other three.[56]

As the young Irishman's troops advanced to the left of Wood's brigade, they suddenly encountered the swampy thickets of Shiloh Branch. The brigade split into two parts, the 6th Mississippi and 23rd Tennessee pressing to the right, and the balance of the regiments slogging to the left. While extricating himself from the mire, the brigadier general was unceremoniously thrown from his horse. Clearing the steep ravine, the overly aggressive Cleburne (he had not yet learned his role as the "Stonewall Jackson of the West") directed an assault on the

53rd Ohio's position. The thousand men of the 6th Mississippi and 23rd Tennessee would advance unsupported; Bragg's second line was not yet in sight. Nor would there be artillery backing. Trigg's Arkansas Battery, after hurling a few shells into Appler's camp, repositioned for a better view.[57]

About 7:30, the two regiments pressed forward, "moving as quietly and steadily as on dress parade, a magnificent sight," thought one of Appler's men. Their formation quickly broke among the tents. Cleburne's men were savagely struck by a hail of bullets and artillery fire that inflicted serious loss and sent them reeling back down the ravine. "Boys, do not be discouraged," shouted Cleburne; "that was not the first charge that was ever repulsed." Again the regiments moved out, only to be driven back in confusion. "We fired 4 times and killed fifty [Rebels] within the limits of our camp, for we buried them ourselves on Tuesday," noted a Buckeye.[58]

The 6th Mississippi, mostly farmers from the piney central woodlands of the state, attempted two additional assaults. Their effort was as fruitless as it was suicidal: the troops were mowed down by a galling fire from Appler's men and Waterhouse's guns. "As the Mississippi Legion in the first column came into sight we fired a volley killing their colonel and 36 others (so say wounded prisoners) and wounded their lieutenant colonel and scores of others, driving them back. Their return fire wounded 2 or 3," Bosworth related. He was wrong about the colonel. Physician-turned-regimental-commander John J. Thornton fell severely wounded from a bullet in his thigh as he personally carried the regimental banner, but he lived. When the smoke cleared, some 300 of 425 men lay dead or wounded—a staggering 70.5 percent. Only sixty men remained to answer roll call.[59]

At the very moment Appler's troops were winning the engagement, the colonel cried: "Retreat, and save yourselves!" The regiment fell back in disorder behind Colonel Julius Raith's brigade of McClernand's division, which had come up in response to Sherman's call for help. "We should have held them there [Rea Field] but Colonel Appler simply 'travelled,' and cried 'retreat,' " Bosworth disgustedly related. The 53rd Ohio rallied and subsequently moved up a hill near Sherman's headquarters. Appler remained with his troops but walked about in a daze. When Lieutenant Ephraim Dawes, the regimental adjutant, cursed him and refused to execute one of his ludicrous orders, Appler jumped to his feet and literally ran away.[60]

For half an hour, Lieutenant Colonel A. V. Rice's 57th Ohio (Colonel William "Fiddling Bill" Mungen had been ill for several days) held on the color line and aided Appler's men in checking Cleburne's attacks. As the 53rd Ohio gave way, the 57th fell back north through their encampment toward the ridge and Waterhouse's guns. Sergeant Edward Gordon looked back toward the 53rd's camp and saw nothing but Rebels and a "confused mass of smoke." By the time the ridge was obtained, half of the 57th Ohio had melted away. "They poured in on us like blackbirds into a cornfield," described a member. Sherman later noted with contempt that the 53rd broke having lost no officers and only two men, and the 57th two officers and seven men.[61]

The 77th Ohio, commanded by Major B. D. Fearing (Lieutenant Colonel DeHaas assisted the brigade commander), comprised troops from Marietta and vicinity. Following Cleburne's repulse in Rea Field, some of Fearing's men naïvely believed the engagement to be over and broke ranks toward the creek to collect souvenirs. The Federals remained crouched on their knees when their pickets suddenly came rushing in, dodging from tree to tree as they ran. The 77th soon came under artillery fire from Major Francis Shoup's Arkansas batteries, positioned to the west of the Main Corinth Road, about eight hundred yards from the church. The shells cut off large tree limbs but otherwise inflicted no damage. Fearing's men, though shaken, continued to hold, their left connecting with the remnants of the 57th Ohio.[62]

Several companies of the 4th Illinois Cavalry had been encamped next to Waterhouse's battery in the vicinity of Sherman's headquarters. One of the troopers watched in horror as he witnessed the chaos in Hildebrand's rear. "The pickets were running in every direction but our camp was so close to the lines that wee had to leave evrything that wee had but our horses and sadels and our arms. The teams were running in every direction. Some of the drivers was scart so bad that they cut the horses loos from the wagons and mounted them and put spurs to them," explained S. F. Martin.[63]

The defense of Sherman's left now rested upon the performance of two young men from Chicago—twenty-eight-year-old former businessman Samuel Barrett and twenty-nine-year-old Allen Waterhouse. The cannoneers of Barrett's Battery B, 1st Illinois Light Artillery, posted their six guns across the road from Shiloh Church and became engaged in a duel with Shoup's artillery. "We could only see the smoke of their guns and could not get perfect range on that account," attested one of Barrett's men. The Confederate fire typically overshot, the shells landing in the camps to the rear. One projectile made a direct hit on a caisson, causing a huge explosion.[64]

Waterhouse's battery also held firm. The section near the Rea

THE POLITICIANS

U.S. Representative
Elihu Washburne of Illinois.

U.S. Representative
Henry S. Foote of Tennessee.

RIGHT TOP: Major General Don Carlos Buell.

RIGHT BOTTOM: Brigadier General Benjamin M. Prentiss.

BELOW: A laundry line stretches across the U.S.S. *Tyler*.

The Hornet's Nest in a postwar photograph.

RIGHT: The tangled thickets of the Hornet's Nest were still visible in this 1895 photograph.

The plowed area in front is the Sarah Bell Field. Traces of the Peach Orchard can be seen beyond the rail fence in this postwar photograph, taken perhaps in the 1880s.

LEFT: The Prentiss surrender site as seen in a postwar photograph.

General Albert Sidney Johnston in an 1860 photograph taken in Salt Lake City.

The corner of Filmore and Cruise Streets in Corinth. To the left rear of the photographer was the Memphis & Charleston depot.

TWO PHOTOS: CHICAGO HISTORICAL SOCIETY

Major General Ulysses S. Grant in an
1863 photograph.

Men of the 5th Company Louisiana Washington Artillery posed for a photographer only weeks before they fought at Shiloh.

RIGHT: A photographer captured Pittsburg Landing several days after the battle.

The Union's siege guns had still not been moved from their combat position when this photograph was taken shortly after the battle.

RIGHT: Crump's Landing maintains its Civil War appearance in this 1895 photograph.

SHILOH NATIONAL MILITARY PARK

TWO PHOTOS:
SHILOH NATIONAL MILITARY PARK

LEFT: This 1903 photograph of the Purdy-Hamburg Road is the earliest known to exist. The statue commemorating the 77th Pennsylvania is seen in Review Field to the left.

The Sunken Road as photographed in 1895. The Union forces faced to the right.

SHILOH NATIONAL MILITARY PARK

The Bloody Pond, circa 1907.

Pierre Gustave Toutant Beauregard,
General, C.S.A.

cabin, after firing a couple of rounds, withdrew 150 yards to the main position. Despite the hasty retreat of the 53rd Ohio, Cleburne was in no position to press the attack upon Waterhouse. The Chicago gunners now saw a large number of troops obliquely crossing the southern edge of Rea Field, about a thousand yards distant, moving northwest toward the woods that bordered the field. Major Ezra Taylor, Sherman's artillery chief, hesitated to open fire, since the men appeared to wear blue uniforms. Taylor was actually seeing the dark jackets of the 16th Alabama of Wood's brigade. As the Alabamians passed into the woods unmolested, they were followed by Tennesseans, who "wore a uniform not to be mistaken." A brisk fire was opened, inflicting several casualties. The 27th Tennessee and 16th Alabama wheeled right to attack, but suddenly encountered Peabody's skirmishers in the woods to their front.[65]

On Line with Buckland's Brigade

THE THREE OHIO REGIMENTS of Ralph Buckland's brigade, camped west of the Pittsburg-Corinth Road on Hildebrand's left, comprised raw troops recruited the previous fall. At sunrise on Sunday, the men had roll call and prepared breakfast. In Barrett's battery, the horses were unharnessed in preparation for 9:00 inspection. "We contemplated spending a pleasant day," an artilleryman related to his father.[66]

Like Appler and Prentiss, Buckland had been very uneasy throughout Saturday night. He was up before sunrise on Sunday and had his horse saddled. The colonel soon received information that his pickets were being driven in. After ordering the long roll sounded, Buckland rode to the front, where he discovered that his reserve pickets had been driven across a log bridge to the north side of Shiloh Branch. He instructed them to hold as long as possible and then galloped to division headquarters to apprise Sherman of the situation. Sherman ordered him to advance a regiment to reinforce the picket line.[67]

The task fell to Buckland's center regiment, the 48th Ohio, commanded by Irish-born Colonel Peter Sullivan, a Mexican War veteran who had recently paid for the organizational expenses of four regiments. Sullivan was an odd character, a decent man but in no way fitted to lead a regiment. He always addressed his men as "gentlemen" and requested them "please to present arms." The Buckeyes cautiously advanced in line five hundred yards toward the creek, with orders to cross the log bridge and take position in the woods to the front. The more logical stand would have been on the north bank, but it made no difference. By the time they arrived, the Rebels had already formed in the creek bed. "We . . . had been there but a short time until on came the secesh pell mell at us at a distance of 20 rods [110 yards]. They having crossed through a deep hollow with thick underbrush which was the reason of their getting so close to us before we saw them," Virgil Moats wrote shortly after the battle. Sullivan promptly counter-marched his men and deployed them to the left of the 72nd Ohio.[68]

Buckland advanced the entire brigade two hundred yards from the color line. It was now approaching 8 A.M., and the troops had been in formation for an hour. The Rebels suddenly exploded from the woods a hundred yards distant, their first volley killing and wounding a number of men. Lieutenant Colonel J. R. Parker of the 48th Ohio admitted that his troops wavered and the flag-bearer shamelessly ran. The 48th held, however, and drove the Confederates back to the creek.[69]

The attacking column constituted the left segment of Cleburne's divided brigade, four regiments of about 1,500 men, supported by Shoup's twelve guns. Although initially stunned, Buckland's 2,200 men not only held the numerical advantage, but also his right overlapped Cleburne's left. The terrain, likewise, strongly favored the Northerners. The 4th Brigade crowned a bushy slope with a bend in the ridge that gave the 70th Ohio an enfilading fire. The right of the 72nd Ohio was pushed forward toward a narrow ravine to form an obtuse angle. The Southerners also had to negotiate the swampy thickets of Shiloh Branch. "A worse place could not have been selected for men to go through, wading creeks, going through thick underbrush & swamp land in mud & water up to our waste [sic]," explained one of Cleburne's men.[70]

Martinet Colonel William "Old Grits" Bate led the 2nd Tennessee. Although he initially advanced en echelon, Bate moved his regiment up on Cleburne's left. His skirmishers unknowingly bounded into the angle of the 72nd Ohio, where the Yankees lay in the underbrush with cocked muskets. "Immediately a brigade of the enemy rose as one man about thirty yards in front of us from ambush and poured a most terrific fire upon us," noted Robert Smith of the 2nd. From atop his stallion Black Hawk, Bate charged his men three times into the "murderous cross-fire," each time being checked. Humphrey Bate, William's younger brother, fell mortally wounded as the colonel lit his cigar. For the remainder of his life, William would chew a cigar but thereafter never lit one. The 2nd Tennessee, originally 365 strong, retired to the creek, leaving thirteen officers and nearly one hundred men dead and wounded.[71]

In Cleburne's center, the 24th Tennessee and 15th Arkansas met a like fate. The 15th lost many men, including its major, J. T. Harris, who moved to within pistol range before being shot. Stocky, full-bearded Lieutenant Colonel Thomas H. Peeples of the 24th continued to ride his horse up and down the line. Although his clothes became riddled by bullets and his horse was killed, Peeples survived. He later came up to a friend, threw his arms around him, and wept that "Providence protected him."[72]

The Southerners came on with terrific yells, their bayonets glistening through the trees on the opposite side of the ravine. Colonel Benjamin Hill's 5th (later designated 35th) Tennessee moved across Rea Field west of the Main Corinth Road against Barrett's battery. "After a heavy volley (which wounded several of our horses) they dashed across the ravine and right up the hill at us," declared a Union gunner. The Tennesseans broke under the vicious blasts of canister and scrambled back to the creek. The cannoneers cheered, tossed their hats in the air, and "danced about like madmen."[73]

Evidence of both bravery and cowardice existed in the ranks of the 5th Tennessee. Fifteen-year-old Private John Roberts, although knocked down twice by spent bullets, remained far ahead of his company. Private Samuel Evans, who had a bullet pass through his cheeks, refused to leave the field and cheered on his comrades. Unfortunately, a private, a sergeant, and three officers were singled out for skulking in the rear, including a captain whom Colonel Hill threatened to shoot for hiding.[74]

Determined to silence Barrett's battery, Bates moved the 2nd Tennessee to the right of the line in order to resume the attack. In the process of performing a personal reconnaissance, the colonel received a ball in his lower left leg, penetrating to the horse. Several men caught him before he slipped from his animal. Surgeons insisted upon amputation, but Bate kept them at a distance with his revolvers. He survived but thereafter required a crutch.[75]

HARDEE'S DRIVE (6–9 A.M.) quickly degenerated into a frontal assault, rather than the projected right-wing wheeling motion. Cleburne's brigade was wrecked in utterly useless attacks upon the wrong flank. A wide gap also developed between his right and the balance of the corps brigades. Had a Union division been encamped between Prentiss and Sherman, as projected, Hardee's line might well have been hurled back. The Confederates nonetheless rolled up three front-line Federal brigades. The tactical surprise had more than offset the Northern advantages of near parity of strength (11,000 Confederates versus over 10,000 Federals) and operating on the tactical defensive. It appeared that Sidney Johnston was well on his way to winning a decisive victory along the banks of the Tennessee River.[76]

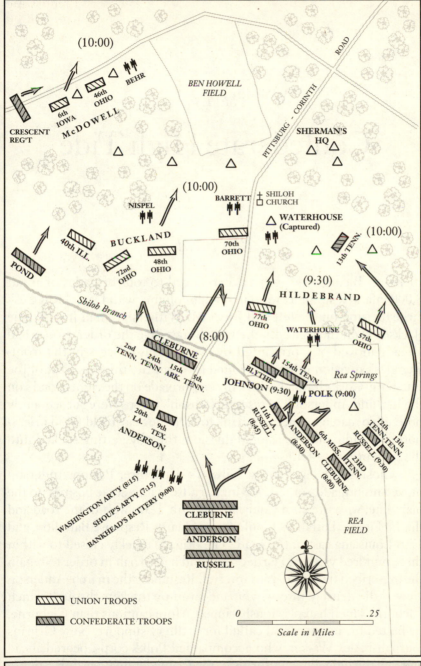

(10:00)

BEHR

CRESCENT
REG'T

6th
IOWA

46th
OHIO

McDOWELL

BEN HOWELL
FIELD

SHERMAN'S
HQ

(10:00)

NISPEL

BARRETT

SHILOH
CHURCH

WATERHOUSE
(Captured)

BUCKLAND

70th
OHIO

13th TENN.

(10:00)

40th ILL.

72nd
OHIO

48th
OHIO

POND

Shiloh Branch

77th
OHIO

HILDEBRAND

(9:30)

WATERHOUSE

57th
OHIO

CLEBURNE

(8:00)

2nd
TENN.

24th
TENN.

15th
ARK.

5th
TENN.

154th TENN.

BLYTHE

JOHNSON (9:30)

Rea Springs

POLK (9:00)

20th
LA.

9th
TEX.

ANDERSON

11th LA.
RUSSELL
(8:45)

ANDERSON
(8:30)

6th MISS.
TENN.

CLEBURNE
(8:00)

12th
TENN.-TENN.

23RD
TENN.

RUSSELL (9:30)

13th
TENN.-TENN.

WASHINGTON ART'Y (8:15)

SHOUP'S ART'Y (7:15)

BANKHEAD'S BATTERY (9:00)

CLEBURNE

ANDERSON

RUSSELL

REA
FIELD

 UNION TROOPS

CONFEDERATE TROOPS

0   .25

Scale in Miles

SEVEN

Confederate High Tide

Rea Field

BRAXTON BRAGG'S ASSAULT LINE, reduced to four brigades of about 8,000 infantry, swept forward in double column, with Daniel Ruggles's large division on the left and Jones M. Withers's remaining brigade (Jackson's) on the right. By the time Bragg gave the order, troops had already moved out, prompted by overzealous officers in the front. Ruggles's division initially trudged through the thickets west of the Pittsburg-Corinth Road, with Gibson's brigade on the right, Pond's on the left, and Anderson's in reserve. Gibson's troops were subsequently ordered to march by the right flank toward the Seay Field Road in support of Hindman's provisional division, thereby getting sucked into the fight in the center.[1]

Closing the gap left by Gibson's departure, Patton Anderson moved his brigade, some 1,478 infantry, from its reserve position to the main line, with the 20th Louisiana and 9th Texas west of the road and the 1st Florida Battalion, Confederate Guards Response Battalion, and 17th Louisiana east of the road. The brigade quickly closed to within three hundred yards of Hardee's line and had to halt in order to regain the prescribed thousand-yard interval. Resuming the march, Anderson viewed the densely interwoven and swampy thickets through which Cleburne's men had previously ripped. More cautious than Cleburne, he halted his infantry and called for artillery support. New Orleans journalist Alex Walker, who accompanied Polk's corps, peered ahead and saw the light-blue uniforms of the Confederate Guards Response Battalion; Anderson's men were lying down and resting.[2]

Artillery rounds soon exploded within their midst—the work of

Ezra Taylor's guns. Anderson's men jumped to their feet, and not a few of them fled to James Wood's cotton shed, far in the rear. "No wonder the simple-minded Floridians [1st Florida Battalion] were broken and many of them hurried to the rear," Walker noted. Anderson, former U.S. marshal and congressman, dashed along the line in an attempt to regain order.[3]

About eight hundred yards south of Shiloh Church, and east of the Pittsburg-Corinth Road, the Confederates assembled a powerful array of artillery. Shoup's twelve-gun Arkansas Battalion had been shelling Sherman's camps since 7:15. Shortly after 8:00, Captain Irving Hodgson's Louisiana Washington Artillery came into position next to Shoup's guns. Four of Hodgson's pieces and two of Shoup's concentrated on Lieutenant George L. Nispel's Battery E, 2nd Illinois Light Artillery, supporting the center of Buckland's line. The gray cannoneers found the range and quickly disabled one of Nispel's guns, besides inflicting four casualties and killing five horses.[4]

Anderson took advantage of the cover fire to work his infantry through the boggy thickets of Shiloh Branch. The mixed Irish-German 20th Louisiana, on the far left, passed through undergrowth so thick the men could not see five paces in front of them. In struggling through the morass, the 20th angled to the left and split from the brigade. Realizing his mistake, Prussian-born Colonel August Reichard had his men retrace their steps. While making the maneuver, the Louisianians were stunned suddenly to view Bate's 2nd Tennessee run pell-mell through their ranks, having been bloodily repulsed. Reichard regained order and led his men ahead under a hail of bullets. Though caught in a savage crossfire, the troops "had not yet fired a shot," noted a member.[5]

To the east of the road, the 1st Florida Battalion, Confederate Guards Response Battalion, and 17th Louisiana slowly clambered the creek bank and came into Rea Field. The three units, a meager 745 men, found themselves in a nasty spot. Under a severe blasting from Waterhouse's six guns, the troops recoiled to the creek embankment.[6]

Rea Field was no-man's-land. Half of Cleburne's brigade had been wrecked and half of Johnson's brigade stopped cold. With no forward movement, the successive Confederate waves began to stack. Colonel Robert M. Russell's 2,440-man brigade of Polk's corps, advancing up the Pittsburg-Corinth Road, arrived in that sector. Sidney Johnston, who appeared to be everywhere that morning, instructed Major General Charles Clark—the Mississippi planter-general, as the press referred to him—simply to hold the brigade in position.[7]

Shortly after Johnston's departure, Bragg rode up and ordered Clark to capture the battery dominating Rea Field—Waterhouse's. Colonel Sam Marks's 11th Louisiana went into action. In edging through the vines and undergrowth of Shiloh Branch, the 550 Louisianians became fragmented, and only four companies emerged onto the battle-scarred field. They made a pretty good showing, considering their numbers, but were staggered by infantry and artillery fire. Barrett's battery, opposite the church, also conducted a fierce enfilade fire. Although the flag-bearer held firm, Marks's men scurried back to the creek, with the colonel reporting "a considerable loss" in killed and wounded.[8]

Russell succeeded in rallying the bewildered 11th and prepared the brigade for another assault. Major General Clark directed him to lead the two left regiments, the 11th Louisiana and 22nd Tennessee, while he commanded the right, consisting of the 12th and 13th Tennessee. The wings became disjointed in the near-impenetrable thickets, and only seven of Russell's twenty companies actually made it into the camp of the 53rd Ohio. The mixed Tennessee-Louisiana troops stormed to the west of the Rea cabin, stepping over a carpet of dead and wounded comrades. The vicious fire caused them to flee in panic, creating confusion in Anderson's brigade, which followed obliquely in the rear. The 17th Louisiana, though torn in two by the stampeding 22nd Tennessee, got off several volleys before retiring.[9]

Clark's wing, slowed by tents and picket ropes, finally emerged into the enemy's camp, just in time to see the 11th Louisiana fleeing in wild disorder. Colonel Alfred J. Vaughn's 13th Tennessee poised with fixed bayonets to stop their flight, but, according to a private, "they brushed our guns aside and [ran] thru our ranks." The 12th and 13th Tennessee succeeded in driving back the 57th Ohio five hundred yards. A fifteen-minute firefight ensued, during which Clark received a severe shoulder wound. He recovered, only to be crippled four months later in the Battle of Baton Rouge. Feebled and on crutches, he nonetheless became wartime governor of Mississippi.[10]

As Bragg surveyed the field from the Pittsburg-Corinth Road, a Yankee sharpshooter's bullet struck the head of his horse; the animal fell on the general's right leg, bruising but not seriously injuring it. As Bragg remounted a second horse, he was dismayed to see the 11th Louisiana scrambling back in full retreat. "They belonged to Polk's mob," he disgustedly wrote Elise.[11]

At 8:30, Brigadier General Bushrod Johnson's brigade of Polk's corps approached Rea Field. Johnson, a former college professor and

Fort Donelson escapee, had years earlier resigned from the Regular Army rather than be cashiered for profiteering. Although initially marching toward Barrett's six guns, Bragg redirected the right two regiments, Colonel A. K. Blythe's Mississippi Regiment and the 154th Tennessee, against the 77th Ohio and Waterhouse's battery. A hillock placed a gap between the regiments.[12]

Colonel Preston Smith brought up his 650-man 154th Tennessee. The Tennesseans closed to within three hundred yards of the enemy; here they were met with a murderous fire. Private Samuel Shelton admitted that he could not see the enemy through the smoke and underbrush, "but [we] fired rapidly in the direction of the battery on the ridge." Lieutenant Colonel R. C. Tyler drew his revolver on some of his own men when they began to falter.[13]

At 9:00, Captain Marshall T. Polk's Tennessee Battery from Memphis unlimbered near the Rea cabin. A single gun was wheeled forward for close-in work, a favorite Napoleonic tactic, but the horses quickly became disabled and the piece had to be abandoned. Yankee sharpshooters picked off the cannoneers and horses in the parent battery with alarming rapidity. The company was wrecked, losing twenty-four of 102 men, thirty of eighty-one horses, and all six caissons. A Tennessean noted the actions of one artilleryman who boldly remained at his post, single-handedly loading and firing double canister three times. A Cincinnati reporter later viewed the battery remains; he counted the bodies of thirty men and thirty-two dead horses within the space of fifty square yards. The young Polk, badly wounded in the leg, was taken to the widow Howell's house, where he was later captured.[14]

The fight for control of Rea Field was now in its second hour. Parts or all of four Confederate brigades, at least 5,300 rookies, had been thrown into the struggle against Waterhouse's battery and fewer than a thousand supporting infantry. Seven Rebel assaults, all frontal and piecemeal, had been bloodily repulsed, and literally hundreds of men were wasted in the process. Sheer force would soon win out.

At 9:30, assaults were renewed from several directions. Bragg ordered the 154th Tennessee and Blythe's Mississippi Regiment, supported by Anderson's and Russell's brigades and perhaps 350 of Cleburne's survivors, back into the fray. Blythe fell dead from his horse, and within minutes Lieutenant Colonel D. L. Herron of the same regiment was mortally wounded. A shell fragment struck Brigadier General Johnson, leaving him, it was initially feared, mortally wounded. The 57th Ohio eventually collapsed under the onslaught. Captain Waterhouse, wounded in the thigh, retired his battery, leaving a single caisson. Believing that every inch of ground should be contested, Major Ezra Taylor incredibly ordered that the guns again be unlimbered only three hundred yards from the previous position; the battery was doomed.[15]

Through a confused—though fortunate, as it turned out—command mix-up, the 13th Tennessee divided. Six companies under Colonel Vaughn made a wide sweep around the camp of the 53rd Ohio. The troops then wheeled left into a ravine, which masked their movement, and approached the battery from the left flank. Suddenly, testified Samuel Hoover of Waterhouse's battery, a large body of Confederates came around a clump of trees to their left and approached to within 150 yards before they were seen. Three guns had to be abandoned, the horses being dead, and a fourth disabled piece was later ditched. A Tennessean gloated that one gun might have been saved, "had I not shot one of their artillery horses and tangled him up with the harness and wheels so that the piece could not be removed." From a distance, a Federal officer observed that the Southerners "swarmed around them [guns] like bees. They jumped upon the guns and on the hay bales in the battery camp, and yelled like crazy men." The troops of the 13th Tennessee then surged toward Shiloh Church, barely a hundred yards distant. The 4th Illinois Cavalry had sabers drawn and Sharps carbines at the ready to fall upon the Confederate flank, but, related a disgusted trooper, "our colonel kept us out of the action."[16]

Shiloh Church

BUCKLAND'S OHIO BRIGADE held firm and suffered lightly (fewer than 150 casualties) against odds not as overwhelming as at Rea Field—2,200 Federals versus perhaps 3,000 Confederates. Southern attacks had been uncoordinated, and a wall of fire had cut them down in windrows. After the battle, eighty-five Rebel bodies were counted at and along the ravine occupied by the 72nd Ohio, and another sixty-eight fronting the 48th Ohio. Although uncertain as to the progress of the battle to his left, Buckland suspected things were not going well when Sherman denied his request for reinforcements.[17]

As Hildebrand's brigade disintegrated east of the Pittsburg-Corinth Road, Buckland's outfits began to topple like dominoes. Barrett's battery now witnessed the 77th Ohio "run like sheep." Artilleryman T. M. Blaisdell disgustedly related: "The Col. of the 77th [Hildebrand] sat down on a log near me and cried like a child at the cowardice of his men, whom he was unable to rally. Some of our company drew revolvers on the cowards, but nothing could keep them to their posts." The blue cannoneers got their guns out just in time; one piece had to be hauled off by hand.[18]

Buckland's left regiment was the 70th Ohio, commanded by former Democratic politician Colonel Joseph Cockerill. He viewed the enemy about a half-mile away, bearing down at nearly right angles to his line. The colonel withdrew the regiment to the color line and refused his left-flank companies. Lieutenant George Nispel, who had gotten out of his sickbed that morning, shifted his battery toward the church. The crowded formation proved a tempting target for the Confederate artillery on the high ground south of Shiloh Church. Many of the shots went high and pounded the tents in the rear, but Cockerill admitted the loss of a few killed and wounded. Nispel, though he had to abandon one gun, was able to remove his three remaining pieces.[19]

Sherman, steady and cool, was magnificent that morning as he gave his personal attention to the Shiloh Church sector. Bullets whizzed about him, one cutting his bridle rein within two inches of his hand, and another deflecting off his metallic shoulder strap, leaving no mark but considerably more pain than his earlier hand wound. (Ellen was horrified to hear, wrongly, that his hand had been amputated.) The brigadier's horse was shot from under him, and within twenty minutes his remount lay dead. By 10 A.M., it was apparent that a change of line was necessary. Sherman sent a staff officer, Captain J. H. Hammond, to notify Buckland's regiments to fall back north of the Purdy Road, which would become the new line.[20]

Sherman has been unjustly criticized for making a stand at the church, rather than falling back on McClernand's division in his rear. Sherman's staunchness not only bought time for the Federals, but also caused the Southern command to overreact and commit troops to the wrong flank. For three hours, Hildebrand's and Buckland's troops held against four Rebel brigades. Upward of four hundred Southern dead were counted in their front—mute testimony to their desperate stand. The Confederates had paid a stiff price for their failure to remain focused on the master plan. The battle now rolled toward Sherman's far-right brigade—McDowell's.

• • •

McDowell's 2,000-man brigade, on Sherman's right, had barely fired a shot throughout the morning as the battle raged around Shiloh Church. Buckland had advanced his brigade to assume a better position, leaving a quarter-mile gap between his right and McDowell's left. He requested a support regiment to prevent the Rebels from getting in between the two brigades. Colonel Stephen Hicks's 40th Illinois moved up to the right rear of the 72nd Ohio. When the 72nd ran low on ammunition, Buckland directed Hicks to take its place in line. The colonel refused, claiming that he had been instructed not to become engaged unless attacked.[21]

The balance of McDowell's brigade, the 46th Ohio and 6th Iowa, moved only fifty yards forward of their camps along the Purdy Road. Captain Frederick Behr's all-German 6th Indiana Light Artillery unlimbered on a hill (still present today) in front of and to the left of the 46th. Rebel sharpshooters in a corncrib took sniping shots until chased off by a few well-placed shots. A section of Behr's guns and a company of the 6th Iowa were subsequently ordered to join the single company guarding the Owl Creek bridge, a half-mile from the brigade right. McDowell's troops held firm, even though thirty to forty of Hildebrand's refugees, fleeing west rather than north, spread panic.[22]

By 10 a.m., Sherman's entire division was in retreat. As Hicks withdrew the 40th Illinois, a body of troops in blue uniforms (a scouting party of the 18th Louisiana) was seen descending the opposite slope. Convinced that they were the enemy, Hicks's men anxiously cocked their muskets, but uncertain officers ordered them to withhold their fire. When Hicks naïvely shouted for them to identify themselves, they replied that they were an Indiana regiment. Thus falsely reassured, Hicks about-faced his troops, only to have them fired upon.[23]

McDowell's infantry assembled in Ben Howell Field and moved by the left flank, four hundred yards northeast of the Purdy Road, toward Crescent Field. Lieutenant Colonel Morkoe Cummings, commanding the 6th Iowa, unexplainably marched several of his companies back and placed them in line of battle, while retaining his other companies in the woods. The enraged McDowell rode back and demanded to know what was going on. An officer replied: "It means, sir, that the [Lieutenant] Colonel is drunk." Cummings was relieved and Captain John Williams placed in command. In sharp contrast, McDowell performed nobly throughout the day, always in the thick of the fight.[24]

• • •

ALTHOUGH MCDOWELL'S BRIGADE escaped almost unscathed, it was not due to the lack of a Confederate presence in the area. Colonel Preston Pond's brigade, on the extreme left of the Southern line, had been late in taking up the march that morning. At 8 A.M., the 38th Tennessee, Crescent Regiment, a section of Ketchum's battery, and Wharton's Texas Rangers were detailed to the left, toward the Owl Creek bridge. The remaining outfits—the 16th and 18th Louisiana, Orleans Guard Battalion, and the remaining guns of Ketchum's battery—moved toward Shiloh Branch, attempting to connect with Anderson's left. Difficulties were encountered while crossing the branch. The Orleans Guard Battalion came to an abrupt halt at a deep ravine ("It was a real precipice," commented a member) and was forced to fall back and make another approach. Major Leon Querouze's horse sank to its belly in mire.[25]

The Crescent Regiment paraded up the Purdy Road and into the camp of the 6th Iowa. A random artillery shot struck one of the drummers, "carrying his head off his shoulders," noted a horrified witness. Nothing remained of the decapitated head other than a chin with a bit of hair. A corporal salvaged a Union flag that had been tossed into a campfire. A captain entered a tent and quickly ran out with a sickened expression. He had seen a victim of one of Ketchum's shells: a dead Yankee's head leaned against his own hand, though the lower part of his torso had been blown away.[26]

Pond's pursuit now stalled as the troops squandered over half an hour in rifling the abandoned tents. Smoldering campfires and wet clothes in wash buckets told of the completeness of the surprise. The Southerners feasted on hot bread and butter, and a sutler's wagon yielded wine, sardines, and fruit.[27]

Headquarters, Army of the Tennessee

CAPTAIN JOHN A. RAWLINS arose at dawn on April 6, awakened in the middle of the night by the returning Captain Hillyer and having been unable to go back to sleep. He routinely began sorting mail at Grant's office in the Cherry mansion. Army headquarters was scheduled for a move to Pittsburg Landing later that day, a decision borne of necessity rather than choice. Two days earlier, Grant had been notified of Senate confirmation of Lew Wallace and McClernand as major generals. Mc-

Clernand would now be the ranking general at base camp, a situation unacceptable to the army commander.[28]

Grant hobbled downstairs at dawn, his sprained ankle still swollen and in pain. The general and his staff had just begun breakfast, about 7 A.M., when a distant but distinct boom was heard. Everyone sat frozen; Colonel Webster finally broke the silence by uttering: "That's firing." An orderly entered the room and announced that artillery fire could be heard upriver. All rushed to the door and listened to the muf-fled roar of cannon. "Where is it, at Crump's, or Pittsburg Landing?" Webster asked. "I think it's at Pittsburg," Grant answered. Staffs, clerks, and orderlies made hurried preparations to board *Tigress*, which already had steam up. Grant leaned on Webster as he attached his buff sash and sword.[29]

The general hurried aboard the sidewheeler and sat in a chair on the boiler deck, where he dictated two messages. Brigadier General Nelson was ordered to obtain the service of a local guide and march with his division along the east bank of the river to the shore opposite Pittsburg Landing. Squire Walker, a local resident, assured Grant that two scouts could be found. The scheduled meeting with Buell had to be canceled, but Grant did notify the Ohio general of the supposed conditions upriver and that he had given orders to Nelson. Buell, ap-parently still unknown to Grant, was already in Savannah and even then on his way to the Cherry mansion. By the time he arrived, *Tigress* had departed.[30]

About 8:30, the steamer approached Crump's Landing. The boat slowed and came alongside *Jesse K. Bell*, where Lew Wallace stood on the hurricane deck. All were silent as the generals talked over the rails. Wallace believed the firing was "undoubtedly a general engagement." Grant feared that Pittsburg Landing was perhaps a diversion and the main effort might still be made at Crump's Landing. He directed Wal-lace to hold his division in readiness and said that orders would be forthcoming. Wallace's staff, taken aback by Grant's order to remain on standby, broke into an undercurrent of talk. Wallace quickly raised his hand to silence them. He reiterated to Grant that his brigades had already been concentrated at Stoney Lonesome and that the men were "ready now." Grant merely directed him to await further orders. A bell sounded, and *Tigress* slowly steamed out of sight.[31]

The boat had not gone far when the steamer *John Warner* was seen racing downriver under a full head of steam. The boat hailed, a plank was pulled out, and a lieutenant boarded with a message from W. H. L. Wallace. The dispatch indicated that the army was under a general attack and that the right and center wings had been driven back. The lieutenant himself added that the enemy were in great force. Grant remained unshaken, did not rise from his chair, and only muttered that when he arrived he would surround the enemy.[32]

The din of battle steadily increased as the steamer neared the landing. By 9:00, when *Tigress* docked, the roar was so incredible that a deckhand believed the battle was raging just over the brow of the bluff. All was confusion at the landing as a swarm of wounded, teamsters, and stragglers huddled below the bluff. Eyewitnesses conservatively placed the number at 3,000; it would get much worse. Grant was assisted onto his horse with his crutch strapped to his saddle.[33]

Grant attempted to bring some order to the landing sector. Recalling his ammunition-supply problem at Fort Donelson, he immediately organized an ordnance train. Two regiments, the 23rd Missouri and 15th Iowa, had just gotten off the boat from St. Louis, the latter debarking to the tune of "The Girl I Left Behind Me." The 23rd Missouri was ordered to join Prentiss's division, while the 15th Iowa hastened atop the bluff to intercept stragglers. The 16th Iowa, which had been sitting at the landing since Friday night, was ordered, along with Edward Bouton's Battery I, 2nd Illinois Light Artillery, to extend the 15th Iowa's line. Colonel Hugh T. Reed related that even threats failed to stem the stampede to the rear. "Most of them had the Bull Run story," he reported, "that their regiments were all cut to pieces, and that they were the only survivors."[34]

Grant's paltry two-regiment reserve was not much, but he knew that he had two additional divisions, one of which (Nelson's) should already be on the march. A half-mile up the Corinth Road, Grant encountered W. H. L. Wallace, who briefed him on the particulars of the attack. For the first time, the army commander became convinced that the main attack was at Pittsburg Landing. He directed Captain Rawlins to send an officer to Crump's Landing with orders to bring up Lew Wallace's division. He also sent a message to Nelson to hurry up his division.[35]

About 10 A.M., Grant held a brief conference with Sherman at Jones Field.[36] He then rode on to McClernand's headquarters, where he found the situation so desperate that he ordered up his only reserve—the 15th and 16th Iowa. The army chief in turn visited all of his division commanders. His amazing poise in the midst of seeming disaster was partially based upon his belief that Lew Wallace's division would be arriving by early afternoon. "General, this thing looks pretty squally, doesn't it?" Captain Rowley asked. "Well, not so very bad,"

Grant replied. "We've got to fight against time now. Wallace must be here very soon." About noon, when the army chief saw some Federal troops approaching from the right, he mistook them for the 3rd Division and exclaimed with delight: "Now we are all right—there's Wallace."[37]

As Grant and his staff traversed the northern edge of Duncan Field, a Rebel battery spotted the party and got the range. A shell suddenly exploded in front of Grant's horse. The major general spurred up, saying: "We must ride fast here!" The officers dashed behind a cabin, but shells came crashing into the roof, showering them with shingles. As the party rode on, a shell fragment struck Grant's scabbard, throwing his sword onto the ground. It had been a close call for the army commander. McPherson's horse was heard panting and about to drop; a cannonball had completely passed through the back of the animal.[38]

Pittsburg-Corinth Road

FOR SEVERAL DAYS, Major General John McClernand had been suspicious. That in and of itself was not unusual, but this time his suspicion extended beyond some of his fellow officers to the enemy. The sauciness of the Rebels throughout early April had raised his eyebrows. On April 1, as he reviewed his division in Jones Field, three men dressed in butternut watched from the roofs of two small cabins at the southern end of the field. They claimed to be Union men, but quickly disappeared after the review. Buckland's incident on April 4 also caused some concern. Nonetheless, McClernand's warnings to both Sherman and Grant had gone unheeded.[39]

When the shooting started on Sunday morning, the 1st Division commander dispatched a rider to Sherman for information. The messenger returned shortly with Sherman's request for cavalry, to join his own, for a morning reconnaissance. Before Stewart's and Carmichael's companies arrived at 5th Division headquarters, Sherman hastened back with the news that he had been attacked and needed support. McClernand rushed to fill the gap between the 5th and 6th Divisions, but his camps were not positioned for a quick response. Although the 3rd Brigade encamped along the old Purdy-Hamburg Road, in the direct path of the enemy, the other two brigades stretched due north for over a mile, from Woolf Field to the northern portion of Jones Field. The disposition gave his division depth but not length.[40]

In Colonel Abraham C. Hare's brigade camp in Jones Field, the 18th Illinois had lined up for Sunday-morning inspection. A messenger rode into camp with the shocking news that Sherman's division was "all cut to pieces" and the "woods were full of Rebels." Word of the approaching enemy came more abruptly in Colonel Carroll Marsh's brigade: a random shell flew directly over the camp of the 20th Illinois, north of Woolf Field.[41]

The wife of 11th Iowa Colonel William Hall happened to be visiting her husband in camp that morning. The consorts lay in a sleepy embrace when the long roll suddenly sounded. Before Mrs. Hall could don her clothing, her garments had been perforated by several stray bullets. She escaped unharmed and later quipped to reporters that she had not been properly prepared to receive company.[42]

The confused state of affairs in the all-Illinois 3rd Brigade, the one closest to the fighting, resulted in a near debacle. Colonel Leonard F. Ross, the brigade commander, had lost his wife and had not yet returned from leave in Illinois. Command fell to Colonel J. S. Reardon, who, on the fateful morning of April 6, happened to be sick. Heavy firing had already begun when the only remaining colonel in the brigade, Julius Raith (pronounced "right"), was unexpectedly informed that he now commanded the brigade. Although a Mexican War veteran, the forty-three-year-old Raith had operated a large flour mill before the war and had limited military skills.[43]

Firing could be heard as early as 7 A.M., but was dismissed as a mere picket fray. The troops were not called to the color line until 7:30, as the shooting became louder and parties of wounded hobbled to the rear. Even then the 49th Illinois, near the southeast corner of Review Field, failed to respond. Lieutenant Colonel Adolph Englemann, now commanding the 43rd Illinois, frantically rode into the camp of the 49th and ordered it to turn out. His words went virtually ignored, for the men, just completing breakfast, insisted that the noise was nothing more than some companies in a nearby regiment clearing their muskets. "The infatuation that no enemy was about was so general, that I was to a great extent affected by it," Englemann admitted.[44]

It was 8 A.M. before the brigade finally moved up to support Sherman's hard-pressed left. The troops formed near the base of a hill in the rear of the 57th Ohio camp. Raith's right was some 350 yards behind Waterhouse's battery, and his left along Oak Creek. As scores of

Sherman's men fled north through the underbrush, they "came near getting shot by our boys," recalled a member of the 43rd Illinois. Although offering some support fire, which at times became sharp, the Illinois troops mainly watched as Sherman's left disintegrated before their eyes. The brigade had been misplaced, being too far removed to protect Sherman's left, and too far advanced from its own division to have its own flank protected. Observing a heavy Confederate force threatening his left, Raith refused his left-flank companies along a ravine. The brigade soon joined the tide of refugees toward the Purdy Road, having received orders to retire to the northwest and form McClernand's right. A lieutenant in the 17th Illinois seized a musket and took a parting shot, dropping the Rebel flag-bearer who had just planted his banner on Waterhouse's guns. The flag was soon raised again, as the enemy continued their northward drive.[45]

JUST NORTH OF the Purdy-Hamburg Road, the Pittsburg-Corinth Road took almost a right-angle turn. Although lacking the terrain advantages of Sherman's first position, the road, running nearly east-west, followed a slight ridge and provided a logical second defensive position for the Federal right. The new line stretched for three-quarters of a mile and could not have fallen short of 12,000 infantry and twenty-five guns, exclusive of McDowell's brigade. Over half of the men were veterans of Fort Donelson, and, on paper at least, the line should have been a strong one.[46]

McClernand's sector appeared formidable. The stern but highly popular Colonel Abraham C. Hare formed the division left. The brigade, of two Iowa and two Illinois regiments, came into line about a hundred yards south of the Pittsburg-Corinth Road and north of Review Field. Four twenty-four-pounder howitzers of Captain Edward McAllister's Battery D, 1st Illinois Light Artillery, unlimbered in the apex of Review Field, between the 1st and 2nd Brigades. The left of the 13th Iowa and right of the 13th Illinois initially overlapped, before Hare rectified the faulty formation. There would be "plenty of Rebels there to be shot at, without peppering one another!" he exclaimed. Colonel C. Carroll Marsh, a thirty-three-year-old New York native who had distinguished himself at Fort Donelson, deployed his 1,500 Illinois infantry in the dense timber between Review Field and the Pittsburg-Corinth Road. Colonel James C. Veach's brigade of Hurlbut's division arrived in response to Sherman's earlier plea for reinforcements and formed in line behind Marsh. McClernand, still suffering from exposure at Fort Donelson, spent most of his time with

Dresser's Battery D, 2nd Illinois Light Artillery, and the 11th Iowa at Water Oaks Pond.[47]

Sherman held the sector west of the intersection. The 13th Missouri, of W. H. L. Wallace's division, had earlier been ordered to the crucial intersection. Unfortunately, the Missourians had only sporting rifles with no bayonets. The remnant of Hildebrand's brigade, including the greater portion of the 77th Ohio and some companies of the 53rd and 57th Ohio, formed on the left of the 13th. So reduced was Hildebrand's command that the colonel, to the chagrin of his men, simply attached himself to McClernand's staff. Buckland's brigade, the enemy hot on their heels, extended along the Purdy Road toward Ben Howell Field. The 70th Ohio became separated, leaving only two regiments. Buckland's right was in the air, McDowell's troops having fallen back to Crescent Field.[48]

THROUGHOUT THE MORNING, Brigadier General Alexander P. Stewart's brigade had been groping about in the thickets in search of a fight. The brigade had sustained two casualties by artillery fire while crossing the southern end of Rea Field, but otherwise was fresh. At 10:00, the troops entered the abandoned camp of the 4th Illinois Cavalry in what later became known as Lost Field. A staff officer directed the Tennessee-Arkansas troops to angle to the left, but Colonel Rufus P. Neely's 4th Tennessee failed to receive the order and veered to the right. The brigade splashed across Shiloh Branch and rested, while Stewart went in search of the wayward 4th.[49]

About 10:30, a Bragg staff officer sighted Stewart with Neely's 4th Tennessee. He directed the brigadier general to capture the four-gun battery in the northwest corner of Review Field (McAllister's). Supported by Captain Thomas J. Stanford's Mississippi Battery in Lost Field and another separated regiment, the 12th Tennessee of Russell's brigade, Stewart and Brigadier General Hindman guided the Tennesseans into position. Hindman, in an oilcloth poncho, rode about "whooping like a Commanche, and with his horse on a dead run." A shot suddenly rang out from one of McAllister's howitzers. The shell struck the front quarters of Hindman's horse, splattering it to pieces, and hurling the brigadier general ten feet in the air. He struggled to his feet, shouted, "Tennesseans take that battery," and then collapsed and had to be carried from the field.[50]

The 4th Tennessee gallantly quick-stepped the eight hundred yards across Review Field, bearing toward the woods to the left to avoid a direct approach. They came under a galling fire from McAllister's guns and the 45th Illinois. Smoke so obscured the field that the Illinoisans were ordered to cease fire—"Those are our troops," shouted a Yankee officer. The mistake was realized too late. The Tennesseans marched to within thirty paces, fired a murderous volley ("Our men fell like autumn leaves," recalled a Federal), and rushed forward with a yell, driving off the blue-coats. McAllister, though slightly wounded four times, whisked away three of his guns; the fourth had to be abandoned. The 4th Tennessee paid a high price for its trophy: its approach was strewn with the bodies of thirty-one dead and 160 wounded. Along with the 12th Tennessee, the Southerners surged past the Pittsburg-Corinth Road, followed by Smith P. Bankhead's Tennessee Battery, which unlimbered slightly to the north of the captured gun.[51]

The left of Marsh's brigade was already in flight when Shaver's brigade crossed Review Field under a punishing fire. Marsh confessed that they approached "with a steadiness and precision which I had hardly anticipated." Shaver was quickly unhorsed. Before the brigade reached the edge of the field, Hare's brigade, seeing the line to their right dissolve, retreated in confusion. The 13th Iowa broke after firing a single volley.[52]

Nearly simultaneous with the departure of McAllister's battery, S. A. M. Wood's brigade passed through Raith's camp and inched north of the Purdy-Hamburg Road toward Marsh's brigade and Captain Jerome B. Burrow's battery. A bullet pierced the chest of 27th Tennessee Colonel Christopher Williams; his body was later removed to his home in Memphis. Lieutenant Colonel B. H. Brown, despite the pleadings of a captain, conspicuously mounted Williams's black mare. He was in turn shot, the ball penetrating his left thigh. Captain Isham G. Hearn shouted, "Charge the tigers!" as a bullet entered his brain just above the right eye. A nearby comrade sadly recalled that years earlier Hearn had been his Sunday-school teacher. Major Alexander H. Helvenson of the 16th Alabama was also struck in the thigh.[53]

A brief but brutal ten-minute exchange ensued between Wood's and Marsh's men, during which the Illinois veterans took more casualties than in all of their previous engagements combined. One colonel, two lieutenant colonels, and numerous line officers went down. The 48th Illinois was the first to break, followed by Marsh's entire brigade. The 27th Tennessee and 16th Alabama overran twenty-eight-year-old Captain Burrow's battery, capturing all six pieces. The Ohio cannoneers also lost twenty-nine men and seventy horses.[54]

Veach's brigade, in a prone position near the Pittsburg-Corinth Road, could not fire for fear of hitting Marsh's men, who were franti-

MAP 6: COLLAPSE OF THE FEDERAL RIGHT 10:30–11:30 A.M.

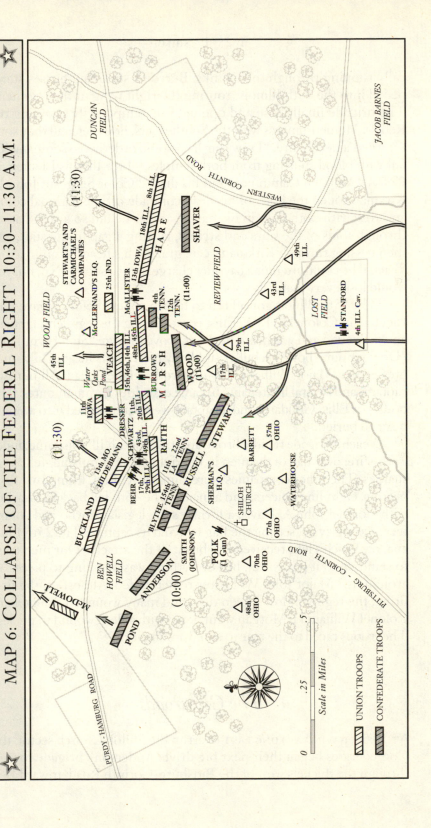

DUNCAN FIELD

JACOB BARNES FIELD

WESTERN CORINTH ROAD

STEWART'S AND CARMICHAEL'S COMPANIES (11:30)

WOOLF FIELD

McCLERNAND'S H.Q.

25th IND.

18th ILL. 8th ILL.

HARE

SHAVER

49th ILL.

13th IOWA

McALLISTER

13th IND.

4th TENN.

12th TENN.

45th ILL.

48th, 45th ILL.

15th, 46th, 14th ILL.

VEACH

BURROWS

MARSH

WOOD (11:00)

REVIEW FIELD (11:00)

43rd ILL.

29th ILL.

17th ILL.

LOST FIELD

STANFORD

4th ILL. Cav.

Water Oaks Pond

11th IOWA

DRESSER

(11:30)

13th MO.

HILDEBRAND

SCHWARTZ 11th, 20th ILL.

BEHR 17th, 43rd, 49th ILL. 29th ILL.

BLYTHE 154th TENN.

RAITH

11th LA. 22nd TENN.

RUSSELL

STEWART

BARRETT

57th OHIO

WATERHOUSE

SHERMAN'S H.Q.

SHILOH CHURCH

77th OHIO

BUCKLAND

BEN HOWELL FIELD

SMITH (JOHNSON)

ANDERSON (10:00)

POLK (1 Gun)

70th OHIO

48th OHIO

PITTSBURG - CORINTH ROAD

McDOWELL

POND

PURDY - HAMBURG ROAD

Scale in Miles

0   .25   .5

UNION TROOPS

CONFEDERATE TROOPS

cally running through their ranks. Burrow's surviving horses stampeded into the 14th Illinois, routing the right wing of the regiment. The brigade finally rose and opened fire, temporarily stunning the Rebels. Momentum was with the Southerners, however, and they soon returned a deadly fire. "I saw our handsome orderly of Company 'G' fall with blood spurting from both temples," 14th Illinois Lieutenant Colonel William Camm noted in his diary. "Color Sergeant John K. Kirkman rolled the body of his dead comrade off the national colors and rose with both flags in his hands; and as he did so a shot passed through folds of the stars and stripes, cutting a gap in the staff, and then passing through Kirkman's cap, grazing his head." Camm asked Veach if he could attempt a bayonet charge, but was told: "No, no, you would lose every man."[55]

The 15th Illinois got off ten to fifteen volleys before it gave way. Lieutenant Colonel E. F. W. Ellis, commanding the regiment, ignored an arm wound and was heard to shout above the din: "Stand firm!" and "Do your duty, boys!" A bullet suddenly pierced his heart. Only minutes earlier, Major William R. Goddard had fallen dead. All but two captains and several lieutenants became casualties within minutes. The bodies of Ellis, Goddard, and a captain were later stuffed into a single box and buried.[56]

Veach's brigade rapidly broke apart. The 46th Illinois came under a crossfire; over half of the men in the right-flank companies fell as casualties. The other companies were similarly cut up, losing two flag-bearers, eight line officers, and a major. The 46th fell back in disarray, with Colonel John A. Davis, a former state legislator who had volunteered as a private, seizing the flag to avoid its capture. The 25th Indiana, on Veach's left, received the brunt of the attack. "Our men tried to stand up to it [crossfire], but everything was breaking to pieces all around us," Major John W. Foster remembered. Almost on the first firing, the regiment lost fifteen dead and many wounded. Lieutenant Colonel William H. Morgan went down with a flesh wound to the leg. The troops raced to the rear to avoid annihilation.[57]

The Crossroads

AT 10:00, HAVING AT LONG LAST overrun the Shiloh Church sector, the Confederates began their next big drive. Anderson's brigade forged through the thickets west of the Pittsburg-Corinth Road, toward Ben

Howell Field, while Bushrod Johnson's brigade, now under Colonel Preston Smith, advanced between Anderson's right and the road. The brigades were badly fragmented, their numbers seriously reduced, and the men exhausted. Smith could only initially assemble two hundred men from Blythe's Mississippi Regiment, 150 from the 15th Tennessee, his own casualty-ridden 154th Tennessee (perhaps five hundred men), and the single remaining gun of Polk's Tennessee Battery under Sergeant J. J. Pritle.[58]

The 154th Tennessee and Blythe's regiment sallied toward the intersection of the Pittsburg-Corinth and Purdy-Hamburg Roads, crashing into Raith's brigade and Major Adolph Schwartz's three guns. Smith rode in search of reinforcements. About two hundred yards in the rear, he found Stewart's brigade, minus its commander and the 4th Tennessee. The brigade was ordered to continue cross-country toward the Pittsburg-Corinth Road. Smith, though reinforced, ordered all of his units back to regroup. Men of the 13th Arkansas assisted Sergeant Pritle in removing his gun. Russell's two regiments (the brigade was still divided) came up, but, seeing other units withdrawing, he, too, fell back. Witnessing the line to his right retiring, Anderson's brigade also began to falter.[59]

Having consolidated their position, the Confederates now plunged ahead, Smith's and Russell's troops west and east of the Pittsburg-Corinth Road respectively, and Stewart's brigade to the right of Russell. Anderson's brigade received artillery support (probably the Washington Artillery) and established counter-battery fire against Schwartz's guns. At 11:00, the final drive for possession of the crossroads began.[60]

BEHR'S INDIANA BATTERY, McDowell's teams, Buckland's brigade, the remains of Nispel's battery, and Hildebrand's fragments all made for the same point—the so-called crossroads, the intersection of the Pittsburg-Corinth and Purdy-Hamburg Roads. The area soon became jammed with wagons, teams, and fugitives. Buckland lamented that many of his men joined the exodus to the rear. Behr's 6th Indiana Light Artillery added to the chaos as it careened down the Purdy-Hamburg Road and came into position west of the crossroads. As the pieces were being wheeled about, Behr suddenly fell dead from his horse. Much to Sherman's ire, the stunned German cannoneers panicked and bolted to the rear, leaving five of six guns.[61]

The renewed Confederate attack smashed into Raith's brigade. Raith received a painful wound that totally shattered his right thigh.

Carried to the rear by four men, he was in such intense pain that he insisted on being left. He remained all night in the rain, and the next day was carried by the Confederates to a tent, where he was later found by a Union patrol. On April 9, an amputation was performed aboard *Hannibal*, but Raith died on April 11. Having lost their mother, Raith's wife, prior to the war, his two children, ages seven and ten, were left orphaned.[62]

Following Raith's wounding, the 29th and 49th Illinois fell back, having exhausted their ammunition, and the 17th Illinois soon followed. The 43rd Illinois, failing to receive orders, became surrounded and cut its way out, losing forty-three killed, all of whom were buried in a single trench. The wounded Major Schwartz limbered up his guns, but one sank in the mud and another capsized as the horses were shot. The 13th Missouri, its ammunition exhausted, also fell back from the crossroads.[63]

Colonel Smith's brigade rolled through the intersection, with the 154th Tennessee in the lead. S. A. M. Wood's victorious troops converged from the east. As Stewart's brigade ascended a ravine in the rear of Wood's troops, they saw through the smoke and haze what they thought to be Yankees and opened fire. Wood's brigade took a direct volley, killing five in the 9th Arkansas Battalion and a lieutenant in the 8th Arkansas, and wounding many more. Wood galloped back with several officers and shouted for the men to cease fire. Stewart's infantrymen ignored the command and unleashed another volley, throwing Wood from his horse and forcing him temporarily to leave the field in a dazed condition. Despite the momentary chaos, the Southerners continued to swarm toward "a pond of water and mud"—Water Oaks Pond—and then moved into "an open field"—Woolf. "Without a waver the long line of glittering steel moved steadily forward," an awed Iowan described to a friend, "while, overall, the silken folds of the Confederate flag floated gracefully on the morning air."[64]

Colonel William Hall of the 11th Iowa, deployed near Water Oaks Pond, later reported that his 750 troops had barely gotten into line before the enemy came on in force. Lieutenant James P. Timony, commanding Dresser's battery, explained that his men had been deceived by the flags and uniforms of the Rebels until they were within eighty yards in his front and fifty yards on his right. A devastating fire routed the 11th Iowa. As Timony gave the order to limber up, he was shot three times, stunned by the explosion of a shell, and carried senseless from the field. The Southern infantry literally engulfed the battery, capturing four guns, five caissons, and a limber. Fifty dead artillery horses lay in several heaps.[65]

Three regiments of Stewart's brigade, the 5th and 33rd Tennessee and 13th Arkansas, all under the temporary command of Colonel Alexander W. Campbell, crossed the Pittsburg-Corinth Road in the rear of Wood's brigade. Wood's men had stopped and were firing in a prone position, meaning that Campbell's troops would have to stand exposed in order to fire over them. When Wood's men refused to advance, Campbell ordered his troops to charge over them. Wood's brigade followed in their path.[66]

The carnage wrought in less than an hour was staggering. Eighteen of twenty-five Federal field guns had been captured and Raith's brigade camp overrun. In McClernand's division, nine field officers (two colonels, two lieutenant colonels, and five majors) lay wounded, one mortally. By 11:20, the Confederates had complete possession of the Pittsburg-Corinth Road. It is difficult to understand why the Federals were so thoroughly smashed at all points. Their lateness in forming the line, the lack of terrain advantages, the unrelenting momentum of the Rebel attack, and the sheer shock and terror of the event all played a part. To accomplish such a trouncing victory, however, the Confederates had overcommitted strength to their left flank. Time had thus been gained for the Union center and left.[67]

Jones and Sowell Fields

BY LATE MORNING of April 6, Sherman's and McClernand's Pittsburg-Corinth Road line had cracked. A new stand would have to be made to the north—in the Jones and Sowell Fields vicinity. Although Sherman's 3rd Brigade had been effectively destroyed, and his 4th Brigade damaged, McDowell's 1st Brigade remained intact. At 10:30, it passed along the western edge of Crescent Field, where the troops faced west and briefly exchanged shots with Pond's brigade. Major Sanger, a Sherman staff officer, ordered McDowell to move to the rear. The brigade marched northeast into Sowell Field and faced south, its left at the George Sowell house.[68]

Colonel Cockerill's 70th Ohio, which had become separated from Buckland's brigade, withdrew through the woods north of the Purdy-Hamburg Road. The Buckeyes spotted a large regiment, clothed in blue, moving through a field directly across their front—probably one of Pond's regiments traversing the northeast corner of Crescent Field. Cockerill could hardly believe the outfit to be friendly, but he dared not open fire. Just then the wind shifted, revealing the Louisiana state flag. Cockerill halted his men, brought them to a front, and unleashed a volley, easily scattering the regiment. The 70th then continued its march and arrived on Jones Field, where Barrett's six guns were already in position.[69]

About 10:00, the 15th and 16th Iowa, over 1,500 strong, arrived in the northern edge of Jones Field. The regiments were completely raw, the former having debarked only hours earlier. After hurriedly being issued ammunition at the landing, the Iowans rushed into battle, with Lieutenant Colonel William Dewey of the 15th Iowa loudly swearing between swigs of whiskey. The two regiments had orders to support McClernand's division, but the only infantry unit in Jones Field was Cockerill's 70th Ohio.[70]

About 11:00, as the 15th Iowa approached mid-field in column of fours, the regiment was ambushed from the east. Incredibly, some Confederates of Russell's brigade had already penetrated into Jones Field and lay in waiting in the ravines and tents of Marsh's brigade. Two Huskers fell dead, several were wounded, and the regiment was thrown into complete panic. The Iowans fumbled into formation and advanced in line of battle, the 16th along the eastern edge of the field and the 15th in the timber to their left. "The enemy lay in ambush at the farther side of the field. We at first could not see them only the puffs of white smoke came from the thickets and brush and every log and tree," described an Iowan.[71]

The two regiments advanced unsupported, one soldier noting with disgust that the 70th Ohio, initially to the right of the 16th Iowa, left the field. The 16th moved to the timber on the south end of Jones Field, and the 15th Iowa crossed a creek and trudged a few paces in front. They were hit by the full brunt of Russell's brigade backed by artillery. "It was every man for himself. We knew nothing about officers or orders. Indeed the companies now became all mixed up and without organization," appraised Thomas Boyd of the 15th. The Northerners lay flat, only half rising to shoot. Both colonels fell wounded, Hugh T. Reed of the 15th in the neck and Alexander Chambers of the 16th in the arm. The regiments withdrew to the north of Jones Field at 11:30, having sustained 316 killed and wounded.[72]

At 11:30, Major Ezra Taylor advanced nine guns to the slight ridge in southern Jones Field—one of Nispel's, two of Dresser's, and

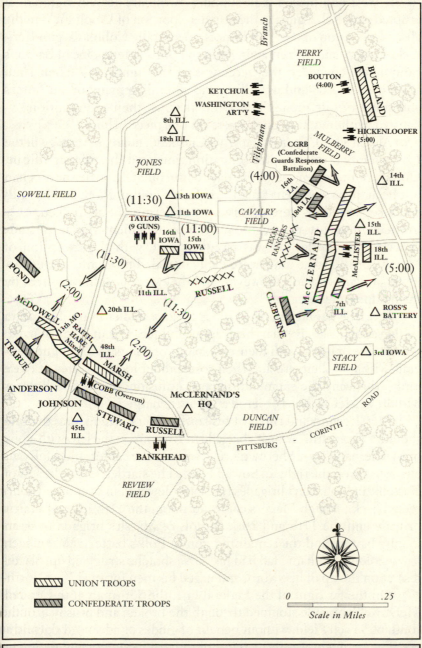

Branch

PERRY FIELD

BOUTON (4:00)

BUCKLAND

KETCHUM

WASHINGTON ART'Y

8th ILL.

18th ILL.

HICKENLOOPER (5:00)

MULBERRY FIELD

Tilghman

JONES FIELD

CGRB (Confederate Guards Response Battalion)

(4:00)

16th LA.

14th ILL.

SOWELL FIELD

(11:30)

13th IOWA

11th IOWA

18th LA.

TAYLOR (9 GUNS)

16th IOWA

15th IOWA

(11:00)

CAVALRY FIELD

TEXAS RANGERS

McCLERNAND

McALLISTER

15th ILL.

18th ILL.

(5:00)

POND

(11:30)

(2:00)

11th ILL.

RUSSELL

McDOWELL

13th MO.

RAITH-HARE Mixed

20th ILL.

(11:30)

(2:00)

CLEBURNE

7th ILL.

ROSS'S BATTERY

TRABUE

48th ILL.

MARSH

STACY FIELD

3rd IOWA

ANDERSON

COBB (Overrun)

McCLERNAND'S HQ

JOHNSON

45th ILL.

STEWART

RUSSELL

DUNCAN FIELD

CORINTH ROAD

BANKHEAD

PITTSBURG

REVIEW FIELD

UNION TROOPS

CONFEDERATE TROOPS

0   .25

Scale in Miles

Barrett's six. Sherman pulled the 40th Illinois out of McDowell's line to the west and placed it in support of the artillery. A fierce duel erupted with Rebel guns in the northern portion of Woolf Field in the abandoned camp of the 45th Illinois, specifically Cobb's six-gun Kentucky Battery and the remaining gun of Polk's battery. One of Barrett's cannoneers conceded the fierceness of the fighting—"Their shell burst over and around us, killing and wounding many of our horses and some of our men." The Federal guns, their ammunition exhausted, withdrew at noon; Barrett left one piece behind.[73]

Also at 11:30, Sherman and McClernand, taking advantage of the Confederate artillery's preoccupation, initiated the first significant Union counteroffensive of the day. Unfortunately, many outfits had not been given sufficient time to replenish ammunition, and had become separated or were otherwise wandering about. Indeed, only fourteen of twenty-two regiments can be documented as having advanced. The battle line was irregular and, with the exception of Marsh's brigade, the units were badly mixed. The Confederates suffered similar problems, however, and they were caught off-guard by the boldness of the move.[74]

From his vantage point in Jones Field, a soldier in the 11th Iowa could see the Rebels "marching right oblique, just in front of us, in double line of battle with their two stands of colors flying." The Federals withheld their fire and then rose and let loose a volley at close range, throwing the enemy into great confusion. As the Southerners withdrew, McClernand ordered a bayonet charge.[75]

McClernand and three of his staff officers raced along the line shouting "Forward!" Marsh's brigade moved out on the left, with a mix of McClernand's and Sherman's regiments in the center, and McDowell's brigade on the right, in Sowell Field. The startled Confederates of Russell's and Johnson's brigades (the latter fewer than a thousand men) reeled back through Marsh's camp. At noon, the 11th Iowa of Hare's brigade and the 11th and 20th Illinois of Marsh's brigade overran Cobb's battery and the remaining gun of Polk's battery. When 11th Iowa Colonel William Hall had his horse shot, he struggled up, placed his hat on the tip of his sword, and urged his men forward.[76]

On the far right of the Federal line, the 550-man 46th Ohio of McDowell's brigade stomped through the broken and brushy ground south of Sowell Field, without benefit of guides or advanced skirmishers. The regiment was thrown out of sight of its supporting regiment on the left, the 6th Iowa. A captain beckoned to Colonel Thomas Worthington as the 46th passed a small stream to its front. In an undertone he warned that the "grays" had been seen gathering "thick as bees" in a ravine to the right. Worthington, in open-mouthed amazement, suddenly viewed several enemy regiments advancing down the slope to his right, while not sixty yards to his rear an enemy line kneeled at the ready-fire. "Squat, boys! squat! —— you, squat for your lives as you get into line," the colonel cried. A terrible fire rained into the Buckeyes.[77]

As the 46th chaotically fell back, a gap of some four hundred yards developed to their left, leaving the regiment isolated. The 40th Illinois, which had been supporting the artillery in Jones Field, rushed in to rescue the beleaguered Ohioans. When the 40th finally arrived, they were greeted by loud cheers from Worthington's men.[78]

Colonel Stephen Hicks soon realized that he had merely inherited Worthington's predicament. The Confederates, having received timely reinforcements, were driving north in a fierce counterattack. Within half an hour, the 40th Illinois lost forty-six killed and as many wounded. Hicks had his horse shot, dumping both animal and rider. As the colonel hobbled up, a bullet struck him in the left shoulder. The Illinois troops had had enough and rushed back to their staging area in Jones Field. McDowell's brigade, which had come off so lightly in the initial attack around Shiloh Church, had now been shattered. The 6th Iowa alone lost fifty-two killed, all buried in a single trench near where they fell, and the brigade sustained losses of one-third.[79]

SURGING THROUGH the woods west of the 20th Illinois camp was Colonel Robert Trabue's brigade of Breckinridge's Reserve Corps. The thirty-eight-year-old colonel, "Old Trib" to his men, came from a prominent Kentucky family. He had lived and practiced law in Mississippi prior to the war, but returned to his native state to raise a regiment. Encountering Hardee, he inquired: "General, I have a Kentucky brigade here. What shall I do with it?" "Put it where the fight is thickest, sir," Hardee replied. Trabue deployed his troops between Anderson's and Pond's brigades, with the 4th Kentucky on the left, 6th Kentucky in the center, 5th Kentucky on the right, and the 31st Alabama in reserve, perhaps 1,600 men (a regiment and a battalion had previously been detached). When George W. Johnson, the Kentucky provisional governor, had his horse killed while crossing Crescent Field, he took up a musket and joined the ranks of the 4th Kentucky as a private. The reduced brigade smashed against the 46th Ohio, 6th Iowa, and 13th Missouri, nearly routing the former and taking prisoners in all three regiments.[80]

At 12:30, the Louisiana Washington Artillery galloped up and unlimbered in the camp avenues of the 20th Illinois, barely a hundred yards southwest of Cobb's battery wreckage. The New Orleans gunners opened with canister but were soon forced back by sniper fire. The "horses were [being] shot down, and we were ordered to Limber up and get away, as the place was to[o] hot for us," Richard Pugh described to his wife.[81]

The battery soon returned and went back into action, followed by a charge of the 4th Kentucky, about 150 yards to their left. The Kentuckians pushed ahead fifty yards before the attack sputtered out. By 1:00, the Federal line had slowly drifted back toward its origin in Jones Field. Cobb's battery was retaken in the seesaw fighting, although the outfit had sustained thirty-seven casualties and lost seventy-eight animals. Cobb removed four of his pieces with mules, but had to abandon two guns and all six caissons.[82]

During Trabue's attack, Pond's brigade, sweeping around on the Confederate far left, managed to get in front of the main Southern line. Glancing at the blue uniforms of the Orleans Guard and 18th Louisiana, the Kentuckians mistook them for the enemy and opened fire, killing and wounding several men. The Louisianians fell back to a ravine, where they frantically waved their flags. "Notwithstanding our cries and gestures, it was not until they had all fired that we succeeded in having them recognize us," noted one of Pond's men. The Orleans Guard again cautiously advanced, rounding up twenty-nine prisoners in Hare's camp.[83]

Meanwhile, about 2:30, Wharton's Texas Rangers swung far to the left in an attempt to get in the Federal rear. John Wharton, a former Texas attorney, would survive the war only to be shot to death during a quarrel in a Houston hotel in April 1865. The shooter was Colonel George W. Baylor, an aide to Albert Sidney Johnston. The hard-riding Texans galloped through Sowell Field and toward the northwest corner of Jones Field. The troopers had to cross single-file over a boggy ravine, which caused the regiment to be stretched for four hundred yards. A large body of Federals, hiding in ambush, suddenly rose and fired a savage volley into the advance company. The Yankees were positioned at a right angle to the troopers, and thus struck the column from end to end. Five of the cavalrymen were killed and twenty-six wounded, including Colonel Wharton, who was shot in the leg and had his horse hit three times. The Rangers staggered to a halt and then fell back in confusion.[84]

In conjunction with Wharton's attack, Captain John Hunt Morgan's Kentucky squadron of three companies struck near the northwest end of Jones Field. They encountered enemy skirmishers in the edge of the woods to the left of the field. Morgan drove them back to the main regiment—according to a prisoner from the 6th Iowa. Some of the Kentuckians charged in for close-in work with revolvers and sabers. Lieutenant Basil Duke, while slashing away, was wounded in both shoulders, one bullet narrowly missing the spine. Morgan's men retired, having lost four killed and several wounded. The Federals sustained a dozen killed and several captured.[85]

As McClernand's and Sherman's Federals withdrew, the Confederates used the time to replenish their ammunition and take a brief respite. Once this was completed, most of the Southern brigades on the left shifted southeast, toward the big fight shaping up in the center. Though victorious on the left, the Confederates had been badly mauled. Cleburne's brigade had been wrecked by 10:00. Bushrod Johnson's brigade had lost in the neighborhood of 62 percent of its battle strength. Such a costly investment of manpower now threatened victory on the right flank.[86]

Sarah Bell's Cotton Field

As SHERMAN AND McCLERNAND struggled to stabilize the Union right, fighting shifted to the center. Prentiss's division had been pulverized, leaving no organized Union presence for a mile and a half. The Confederates stalled for at least half an hour, partly to regroup and partly to pilfer the Yankee camps. By the time their sweep was renewed, the bluecoats were ready.

The division of Stephen A. Hurlbut camped on either side of the Hamburg-Savannah Road. Colonel N. G. Williams's 1st Brigade stretched along the southeast edge of Cloud Field and northwest toward Stacy Field; and Colonel James C. Veach's 2nd Brigade slightly over a mile and a half north, in and to the east of Mulberry Field.[87]

Lieutenant Belzar Grebe was with his regiment, the 14th Illinois, in Mulberry Field that Sunday morning. A German by birth, he had immigrated to America years earlier, and moved from Baltimore to Illinois while working odd jobs. This was his second hitch in the army; he had rejoined when he failed to find work. As he disassembled his musket for inspection, he suddenly lifted his head to hear "a rushing sound like a train rushing by." Others in the division heard the distant crack of musketry, followed by the boom of artillery. The long roll sounded, and the troops promptly formed on the color line. A detachment of the 5th Ohio Cavalry, sent out to investigate, shortly returned with the report that Peabody's brigade was smashed and the colonel dead.[88]

At 7:30, responding to an urgent plea from Sherman, Hurlbut dispatched Veach's 2,700-man brigade to the right. A courier galloped up to Colonel Veach, who was eating breakfast, and excitedly reported: "We are attacked by a heavy force. General Hurlbut directs that you move to support General Sherman's left!" Within ten minutes of formation, the troops were on the march. Shortly after, a pressing request for reinforcements came from Prentiss on the left. At 8:00, Hurlbut led the 1st and 3rd Brigades, 4,100 infantry and three batteries of sixteen guns, down the Hamburg-Savannah Road, past the Widow Wicker Field. Hurlbut's bluecoats represented the only organized resistance on the Federal left center to stem the gray tidal wave.[89]

Hurlbut's men advanced amidst a steady flow of panic-stricken refugees from Prentiss's division, some wounded but most of them simply scared. An Iowan remembered feeling shame at seeing so many men in flight, all having tossed away their muskets. One of Hurlbut's men, seeing a hatless young boy race to the rear, asked why he was in such a hurry. Came the reply: "You go a little further and you will find out what's the matter." Other horrified fugitives yelled: "You'll catch it—we are all cut to pieces—the Rebels are coming." A captain in the 32nd Illinois shouted to his men that anyone in the regiment seen running would be shot, words that were greeted with a resounding cheer from the troops. The Federals shortly caught their first glance of a Rebel, as a wagon passed by with several prisoners. The Southerners defiantly swore that they would give them enough of "Dixieland" before the day was over.[90]

Hurlbut's troops filed off to the right onto the Wheatfield Road, passing the Manse George cabin, and coming into line on the southern edge of Sarah Bell's cotton field. The brigades formed at nearly right angles, with N. G. Williams on the left extending to the Hamburg-Savannah Road, and Lauman on the right, his line stretching into the timber. Lieutenant Edward Brotzmann commanding Mann's Missouri Battery (four guns) came into battery near the intersection of the Hamburg-Purdy and Hamburg-Savannah Roads, but soon shifted to the connecting angle of the two brigades. Captain William H. Ross's Battery B, 2nd Michigan Artillery (six guns), initially unlimbered in front of Williams's line, but withdrew to the right rear of the brigade. "We could see the enemy advancing at a rapid rate," recounted one of the Michigan cannoneers.[91]

First Brigade commander Colonel Nelson G. Williams had been a classmate of Grant's at West Point but had quit because of poor math grades. His tyrannical methods spawned hatred among men and officers alike. Williams's midwesterners lay down in a slight ravine; this offered protection from the shells that soon began exploding around them, most of which burst harmlessly overhead. The Rebels could be seen passing through the woods south of the Purdy-Hamburg Road. For the first time, related 3rd Iowa Lieutenant Seymour D. Thompson, "we caught sight of the enemy, his regiments with their red banners flashing in the morning sun." About 9 A.M., Williams's infantry opened a dilatory fire. Hearing the shooting to their left, Lauman's jittery troops opened fire without orders, but their smoothbores proved useless at such ranges. The musketry elicited no response from the enemy, who stood in formation at a distance. An exploding projectile suddenly struck Colonel Williams's horse, entering the breast and exiting the saddle. The colonel was so badly injured by the fall that he had to be carried from the field. He remained paralyzed for weeks, and eventually resigned from the army. Colonel Isaac Pugh of the 41st Illinois, a white-haired Mexican War veteran, assumed command.[92]

About 9:30, Captain John Myers's 13th Ohio Battery rumbled down the Wheatfield Road. Hurlbut complained that the outfit, despite repeated orders, was late, but Sergeant Thomas Jeffrey wrote that the battery remained in camp an hour waiting instructions. Once they were on the scene, a dispute arose over the proper disposition. Myers was ordered a hundred yards off the road, into the timber to the right of the cotton field, facing west. The thirty-three-year-old captain demurred and requested to be placed in the field, but the order was peremptory. Although Hurlbut intended for the gunners to unlimber on the reverse slope of a slight crest, the pieces were brought too far forward, thus losing the advantage.[93]

As the Ohio cannoneers complied, they came under a sharp artillery fire. The horses balked and became entangled with the trees and dead logs. Just as the guns came into position, and before a single shot had been fired, a caisson received a direct hit, resulting in a huge explosion that killed one man, wounded eight, and left three horses dead. The teams hauling one gun got spooked and ran out of control through Lauman's infantry—the only piece that was salvaged, as it turned out. With one impulse, the officers and men quit their cannon and fled the field. From the perspective of George LeValley, writing to his parents

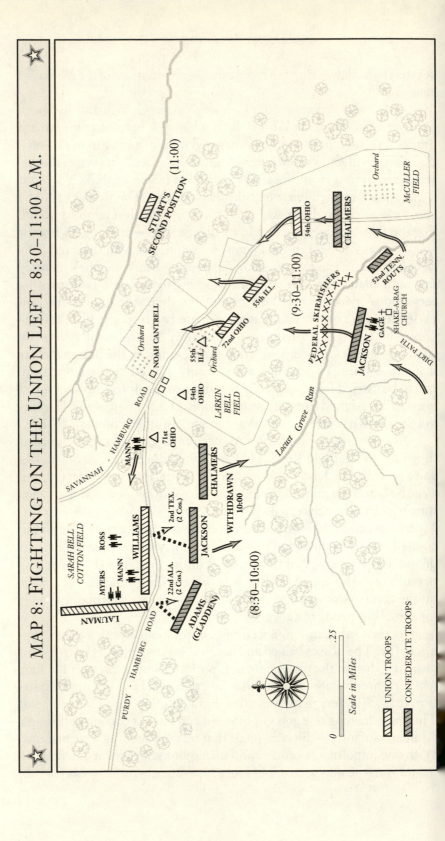

MAP 8: FIGHTING ON THE UNION LEFT 8:30–11:00 A.M.

on April 12, "It was a narrow escape for my horse was killed and my cap was shot off my head." Volunteers from Mann's and Ross's batteries later spiked the abandoned guns and freed the tangled horses.[94]

After the battle, a fuming Hurlbut ordered the battery disbanded, the men transferred to other units, and Myers cashiered. An investigation by the Ohio Adjutant General's Office exonerated Myers, and angry letters were exchanged between Hurlbut and Ohio Lieutenant Governor Benjamin Thomas. The cannoneers received an unlikely ally in postwar years. Captain Felix Robertson, commanding the Florida battery that fired the fateful shot, denounced Hurlbut and implied that the division commander's rage was nothing more than a diversion to cover his own sluggishness in supporting Prentiss.[95]

In Lauman's brigade, the 17th Kentucky fired obliquely at "two small regiments," causing them to veer off "with tremendous loss." The Kentuckians had actually engaged two companies of the 22nd Alabama, which were reconnoitering the Yankee line. The Rebels mostly stayed out of range, causing Lauman's men to expend ammunition needlessly. At forty-nine, Lauman was one of the ablest of Grant's brigadiers, despite his lack of formal military training. He was a veteran of both Belmont and Fort Donelson, wounded at the former and distinguished at both.[96]

The Confederates confronting Hurlbut's troops were those of Jones Withers's division. Following the capture of Miller's camps, the brigades of John Adams (formerly Gladden's), Jackson, and Chalmers converged northwest by an extended left wheel toward the Daniel Davis Wheat Field and Sarah Bell's cotton field. Observing the Federal division blocking their path, they wrongly concluded that the enemy had been reinforced and was forming for an attack. Adams even formed his regiments into squares, an old British defensive maneuver. Meanwhile, Robertson's battery began successfully lobbing shells. About 10:00, Lieutenant George Baylor, a Johnston staff officer, came up with orders to recall Chalmers's and Jackson's brigades. Believing that the Southerners were retreating, the Yankees opened fire, whereupon Chalmers's men faced about and gave a parting volley.[97]

Headquarters, Army of the Mississippi

THROUGHOUT MIDMORNING, Johnston needlessly flitted about while Beauregard established what amounted to command headquarters in the northern portion of Fraley Field. Johnston now faced the decision of where to commit Breckinridge's reserve division. At 7:30, he prematurely sent Colonel Jacob Thompson to Beauregard with orders to send heavy reinforcements to the left. Breckinridge's three brigades were thus set in motion toward the Shiloh Church sector. A later courier from Johnston indicated that he had been mistaken about the Yankee strength on the Confederate left. At 8:30, Colonel Numa Augustin, who had been scouting on the far right, reported that a mile-wide gap still existed toward Lick Creek. The main line had to be extended to avoid being outflanked. The Creole thus countermanded Johnston's order and sent only one of Breckinridge's brigades (Trabue's) to the left, and two brigades to the right.[98]

About 9:00, in company with his staff and escort, Johnston rode into Miller's abandoned camp. Lieutenant George Baylor noticed a neatly ordered row of knapsacks and coats, obviously arranged for morning inspection. Colonel Preston learned from a wounded Federal that they were in the camp of the 18th Wisconsin; the regimental banner was found in the colonel's tent. An officer came up to Johnston and gleefully called attention to his armful of trophies. "None of that, sir; we are not here for plunder!" Johnston sternly replied. Regretting the sharpness of his rebuke, he picked up a tin cup and said: "Let this be my share of the spoils today."[99]

About 9:30, Johnston received the first of several messages from Captain Samuel Lockett. Throughout the early morning, Lockett, along with a squad of cavalry, had been reconnoitering the right. In the twilight hours he spotted Colonel David Stuart's brigade in Larkin Bell's field. There was little activity, and only smoldering fires from the previous night's supper. Eventually the cooks began stirring about, and the men prepared for inspection. Although the Federals had obviously been caught unaware, Lockett remained concerned about what he perceived to be an entire division that far overlapped Johnston's right flank. He deployed his few cavalrymen in a skirmish line, and sent back an urgent message that the right should be immediately reinforced.[100]

Upon receiving the message, Johnston dispatched Colonel Thompson to Beauregard with instructions to move Breckinridge's division to the right, obviously unaware that the Louisiana general had already initiated just such a move. Thompson was also to inform Beauregard that he should rely upon his own information in making final decisions, a virtual admission that the Creole controlled overall tactics. Meanwhile, Lieutenant Baylor was sent to Chalmers's and Jackson's brigades with orders that they should swing to the right.[101]

Johnston and his staff proceeded northeast, toward the river. The cluster of officers made a tempting target for a Federal battery about eight hundred yards distant. A shell burst overhead, startling the staff, although Johnston sat "straight as an Indian." A young member of the escort company recalled that only once during the morning did he see Johnston exhibit any gleam of enthusiasm. Chalmers's brigade was the first to arrive, on the right. As it advanced over the ridge and out of sight, Johnston turned to Munford and exclaimed: "That checkmates them."[102]

Johnston had perhaps overreacted. Although the Yankee "division" on the right was nothing more than an isolated and badly frightened brigade, Johnston had to act upon the premise that an entire division imminently threatened his flank. To meet the threat, however, Johnston committed not only his reserve division, but also Chalmers's and Jackson's brigades. This left only Adams's casualty-ridden brigade, perhaps 1,500 men, in the center, to confront Hurlbut's 4,000 men. Fortunately, the Federals were not of a mind to counterattack, as they had on the Confederate left. It would have been more prudent on Johnston's part to dispatch only Chalmers's brigade to plug the breach, until additional information was forthcoming. On the other hand, by committing so heavily to the right wing, Johnston had inadvertently returned to the original battle plan of a right-flank sweep toward the river. The bulk of Withers's division thus marched toward Stuart's lone brigade. If it was quickly brushed aside, perhaps the Confederates could be in Pittsburg Landing by noon![103]

Hamburg-Savannah Road

DAVID STUART WAS A MAN desperately seeking to remake his tarnished reputation. A former Michigan congressman and wealthy Chicago attorney, he had incurred public disfavor when it was suggested in a divorce case that he had been involved in a notorious affair. When Stuart requested permission to raise a regiment, such was the public outcry that the governor denied him. He subsequently received permission through the War Department. The war would thus become the channel by which he would redeem himself. His opportunity came on the morning of April 6, 1862.[104]

The brigade faced south, with the 54th Ohio (a Zouave regiment) and 55th Illinois camped in Larkin Bell's field and the 71st Ohio about three hundred yards distant, just south of the Purdy-Hamburg Road. Captain George Stone's Missouri Battery had been removed from the division on April 5—part of the inopportune reorganization that took place on that day. Stuart made his headquarters in the white-frame Noah Cantrell house. The three regiments, actually a part of Sherman's 5th Division, represented the extreme left of the Union Army. As such they had been charged with keeping a watchful eye on the Hamburg-Savannah Road ford over Lick Creek. Stuart, Sherman, and Colonel McPherson had scouted the area on April 5 and found the water rapidly receding. Six infantry companies and a squadron of cavalry crossed over and scouted as far as Hamburg. By the morning of April 6, Lick Creek was barely three feet deep and eighty to a hundred yards wide.[105]

On that Sunday morning, Stuart had given his men permission to clear their weapons by firing at the bluff across Locust Grove Run. When Prentiss's division was subsequently attacked, the sound of musketry was ignored. The officers of the 71st Ohio routinely reported to Colonel Rodney Mason to recite tactics lessons. The sudden discharge of artillery alarmed the adjutant of the 54th Ohio, who aroused Colonel T. Kilby Smith. The former United States marshal stumbled from his tent, listened intently for a moment, and shouted: "They are fighting." The long roll was sounded, and the brigade scrambled into line. Even so, confessed Private John P. Wheeler of the 54th, most of the men believed it to be nothing more than preparation for a morning drill.[106]

Stuart, who received a message from Prentiss that he was under attack, deployed his line in the shape of an obtuse angle, with the right of the 71st Ohio in Bell Field, the 55th Illinois on the right, and the 54th Ohio facing south and straddling the Hamburg-Savannah Road. One company remained at the ford, and four others were advanced as skirmishers toward the rugged ravine east of Locust Grove Run.[107]

A few of the skirmishers, Lieutenant Elijah Lawrence among them, crossed the creek and stumbled up the bluff on the opposite bank. There, according to Lawrence, "in an open field, in full view, stood the Confederate host [Jackson's brigade]. Not a hundred yards away and a little to the right, rested the long line of infantry, at right angle with our line." Rebel officers rode up and down the line, encouraging their men. Still nearer and a little to the left, a battery (Girardey's Georgia) unlimbered. The Confederates began a wheel-left in quickstep and perfect alignment. Not fifty feet from where Lawrence and several of his comrades stood was a Confederate officer, who peered at

Stuart's camp through a long glass. One Federal attempted to pick him off, but his musket prematurely discharged as he cocked it. The officer recognized the danger and dashed off.[108]

Jackson's troops had tramped up an old trail leading off the Bark Road. As they approached the terrain of Locust Grove Run, the men came under the peppering fire of Stuart's skirmishers. Jackson halted, advanced his skirmishers, and positioned Girardey's guns on a knoll to the left, at Shake-a-Rag Church. The Augusta cannoneers blasted canister into the creek thickets, successfully chasing off the enemy skirmishers, one of whom noted the time as precisely 9:40. The four guns (there was insufficient room for the third section) now trained on the Federal camps and the 71st Ohio.[109]

Stuart and Mason were in conversation as the Rebel battery redeployed. Mason commented that his men could not hold ten minutes if subjected to artillery fire. Stuart, without giving comment or orders, rode off. The rotund thirty-eight-year-old commander of the 71st Ohio was a former state adjutant general and son of Samuel Mason, a five-term congressman. The Cincinnati press would later condemn him as being nothing more than a political hack of Governor William Dennison. He was detested by many of the officers in the regiment— "They cannot ask him a civil question without getting a cursing for an answer," revealed one.[110]

About 10:00, as the Confederates scurried into the creek embankment, Mason was informed that his left was threatened. "Then we must be getting out of this," he uttered. The Buckeyes, having fired only two or three rounds, fell back in disorder and did not re-form for half a mile. The colonel came under severe censure, some accounts claiming that he had led the way to the rear. Many of the troops defended him in subsequent deposition testimony, claiming that he went in search of Stuart. Corporal Joseph Yount, who was near Mason at the time, emphatically stated that Mason acted calmly in an exposed position—"The bullets were whizzing around us thick." The 71st Ohio did make a subsequent stand on the Hamburg-Savannah Road. The colonel went to Grant after the battle and, with tears in his eyes, claimed extenuating circumstances and pleaded for a second chance. He would receive it. Unfortunately, only four months later, while commanding an outpost in Clarksville, Tennessee, he surrendered half of the 72nd Ohio and some other troops to a band of Rebel partisans. Humiliated and disgraced, he was cashiered from the army.[111]

Jackson's troops rushed the camp of the 55th Illinois, where the Federals fired through the cracks of several log cabins. The 2nd Texas briefly fell back, but re-formed and charged, driving the 55th back in confusion. As the Texans surged through the peach orchard, they encountered fire on their right in the direction of the Larkin Bell cabins. The Yankees eventually pulled back beyond the Hamburg-Savannah Road.[112]

Stuart also had to contend with Chalmers's brigade to the south. The Mississippians and Tennesseans pressed up the Hamburg-Savannah Road, their skirmishers fighting "like Indians, behind trees, logs, and lying down." As the brigade crossed Locust Grove Run, the 52nd Tennessee was ordered to lie down and let the rear rank fire over them. They were then ordered back across the branch to let the artillery fire. In the confusion of orders, the regiment shamefully broke, with only two companies later rallying. In the lower half of McCuller Field was a 350–400-yard-wide orchard, located slightly north of two cabins. The skirmishers of the 54th Ohio concealed themselves behind a fence on the northern edge of the orchard. The ground between Locust Grove Run and the orchard was a gradual ascent, bringing Chalmers's brigade in full view. The grays closed to within forty yards before the Buckeyes fled north through McCuller Field. "I gave it to one old blue belly about where his suspenders crossed, sending him to eternity," boasted a Mississippian.[113]

With two enemy brigades fast closing in, Swedish-born Lieutenant Colonel Oscar Malmborg, formerly an engineer in the Swedish Army, ordered the 55th Illinois to "half wheel left." In executing the complex maneuver under fire, the companies crowded in on one another, spreading panic and causing the troops to break. Stuart, seeing both his brigade and his reputation disintegrate before his eyes, frantically screamed at the top of his voice, "Halt men, halt! Halt you cowards!" Just at that moment, he was struck by a bullet in the shoulder. Everywhere there was frenzy and hysteria. A captain sprinted toward the landing yelling: "Oh! oh! oh! the regiment is all broken to pieces!" About eight hundred men of the brigade (five hundred of the 55th Illinois and three hundred of the 54th Ohio) finally rallied to the east of Bell Field, along a fifty-foot-deep ravine. Malmborg foolishly had them form a square, a drill that had absorbed him prior to the battle. When the Rebels failed to come up, a new line was formed along the southern edge of the ravine.[114]

With the doorway to Pittsburg Landing halfway ajar, the Confederate attack now stalled. Chalmers's men had exhausted their ammunition, and the ordnance wagons were far in the rear. Jackson's famished men milled about in Stuart's camps, feasting on beef and coffee. One pillager even came upon a regimental paymaster's box, filled with hundreds of crisp new greenbacks. He contemptuously gave it a kick, sending bills floating in the air like autumn leaves. As the Southerners rifled the abandoned tents, a squad of a dozen or so Federals boldly marched up under a flag of truce. When only fifty feet away, the sergeant of the squad called at the top of his voice, "Ready, aim, fire!" Several men of the 2nd Texas dropped, two of them dead. The enraged Texans mercilessly annihilated the entire squad.[115]

EIGHT

The Blue Line Stiffens

The Sunken Road

By 11:00, THE CONFEDERATES had succeeded in driving back both Federal flanks. The Yankee defensive line along the Pittsburg-Corinth Road had been smashed, and Stuart's brigade, near Lick Creek, was rapidly breaking apart. To achieve this stunning success, Johnston had committed eight brigades to his left, with a ninth on the way, and two on the right, leaving only one (Adams's) in the center. Two brigades (Stephens's and Gibson's) sat in support positions, and two of Breckinridge's reserve brigades were coming up on the right, but for half an hour (10:00 to 10:30) fighting stalled in the center. The Federals had been given a window of opportunity to stabilize their line and bring up fresh troops.

Although Prentiss's 6th Division had been effectively eliminated as a fighting unit, about six hundred of his men collected in Jacob Barnes's Field. They passed to the right of Hurlbut's line, where one officer described them as acting "like a flock of frightened sheep, ready to start in any direction." Even Prentiss, according to Colonel Hugh Reed of the 44th Indiana, was "clamoring for he knew not what—the line to be pushed forward to his former position, etc. He was as demoralized as his troops."[1]

Prentiss deployed his men between the divisions of Hurlbut and W. H. L. Wallace. The six-hundred-strong 23rd Missouri, which had debarked at the landing only hours earlier, anchored the left of Prentiss's line. The balance of his depleted regiments came into position— from east to west, the 18th Wisconsin, 18th Missouri, 12th Michigan, and 25th Missouri. About sixty men of the 21st Missouri deployed to the left of the 14th Iowa of Wallace's division. The 25th Missouri remnant initially lay in front of the 14th Iowa. When the 14th was also ordered to lie down, the Missourians stampeded over them to the rear. Hickenlooper's remaining four guns unlimbered slightly east of Prentiss's infantry, and Munch's battery had a section on both sides of the Eastern Corinth Road. The 1,200-man command formed a protruding and, as it turned out, crucial salient. Grant visited the spot and ordered Prentiss to "hold at all hazards."[2]

The troops had aligned along an eroded wagon trace (the old Purdy-Hamburg stage road), about two-thirds of a mile in length, that connected the Pittsburg-Corinth Road and the Savannah-Hamburg Road, and crossed the Eastern Corinth Road at right angles. The road had so washed over the years that it now formed a slight embankment of a few inches to upward of one to three feet in depth. In postwar years, the ready-made entrenchment would be labeled the "Sunken Road." The Sarah Bell and Manse George farms fronted the western portion of the road, and the thirty-to-forty-acre Joseph Duncan farm the eastern portion. The center contained small timber and thick undergrowth that had not yet leafed out. A bush-covered rail fence bordered the Duncan field, offering an effective camouflage. It was in this sector, to the right of Prentiss, that W. H. L. Wallace's division was rapidly taking its place in line.[3]

JAMES M. TUTTLE WOULD END his army career in June 1864 amid charges of profiteering, bribery, and collusion so blatant that even veteran politicians were aghast. On the morning of April 6, 1862, however, the slow-speaking colonel, who had no military experience and had held only minor county positions back in Iowa, was at his best.[4]

Tuttle, ill from a Fort Donelson injury, had slept late on Sunday morning. He was awakened by his servant and learned that firing, which could now be clearly heard, had been going on since daybreak. Alarmed by this news, he called his 1st Brigade of the 2nd Division to arms, mounted his horse, and rode from Chambers's Field over to division headquarters, not far from the landing. There he found W. H. L. Wallace dressing to go down to the landing to meet his wife, who, word said, had just arrived. Tuttle was ordered to take his brigade down the Pittsburg-Corinth Road, and Wallace would follow with Colonel Thomas W. Sweeny's 3rd Brigade. Brigadier General John McArthur's 2nd Brigade was divided—two regiments to guard the Snake Creek bridge, one regiment to the intersection of the Pittsburg-Corinth and Purdy-Hamburg Roads, and two regiments to the far left.[5]

The 8,500 men of this mostly veteran division had been taking a leisurely pace that morning. Many were cooking breakfast, while some shaved in preparation for Sunday services. As B. F. Thomas of the 14th Iowa washed dishes, he faintly heard gunshots some two and a half miles away. He jokingly commented to a friend that if the Rebels were going to attack he hoped they would give him sufficient time to complete his work. In the camp of the 52nd Illinois of Sweeny's brigade, the alarm was sounded when an officer rode full-speed into their midst shouting: "Beat the long roll, we're attacked, the enemy are right into us!"[6]

With Tuttle's Iowans in the lead, the two brigades hastened along the Hamburg-Savannah Road and then veered off onto the Pittsburg-Corinth Road. The pace quickened as the sound of musketry increased. "John Gaston gave out after running more than a mile. The last I saw him he was leaning over a stump vomiting," recalled Thomas. Wallace's troops began to encounter fugitives streaming to the rear, "some bare headed—some without guns—some powder begrimed and wounded and some helping off others that were wounded." One horrified straggler cried out: "For God's sake don't go out there; you will all be killed. Come back! Come back!"[7]

Ambling in advance of the division was Captain John Wesley Powell's Battery F, 2nd Illinois Light Artillery. During the reorganization of the artillery, the company had, in a single day, been shifted to three divisions, only to end up in the "unassigned" column by day's end. On the morning of April 6, the outfit sat in the reserve park at the landing. Receiving no orders, and fearing that he had been forgotten in the reorganizational shuffling, Powell struck out with his battery to the front. Arriving near the Duncan cabins, his men strayed into a volley from Shaver's brigade in the Review Field sector. Two gunners and several horses fell wounded. The captain had his two Napoleon guns wheel about and unlimber, but the fire was so intense that several of his men panicked. Powell managed to get five of his cannon out, but left a Napoleon gun and battery wagon by the roadside. The piece would later be recovered.[8]

Tuttle's brigade filed into the Sunken Road, to the right of Prentiss's men. "Our regiment [2nd Iowa] and the 7th [Iowa] rested behind the fence of a cotton field—our right a hundred yards or so from a road running across the field [Pittsburg-Corinth Road], and a couple or three hundred yards from a house [Duncan's cabin] and out-houses deserted by their owner," described Captain Noah Mills.[9]

Sweeny's brigade became fragmented. The 50th Illinois had mis-

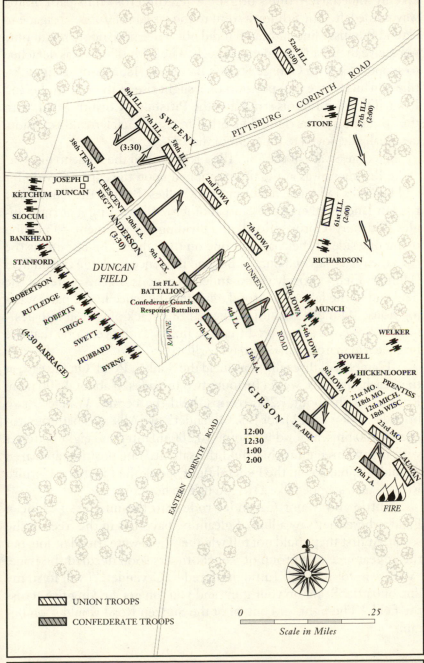

MAP 9: THE HORNET'S NEST

52nd ILL.
(3:30)

8th ILL.

7th ILL.

SWEENY

(3:30)

58th ILL.

38th TENN.

JOSEPH
DUNCAN

KETCHUM

CRESCENT REGT.

SLOCUM

20th LA.
ANDERSON
(3:30)

BANKHEAD

STANFORD

9th TEX.

DUNCAN
FIELD

ROBERTSON

RUTLEDGE

ROBERTS

TRIGG

SWETT

HUBBARD

BYRNE

(4:30 BARRAGE)

1st FLA.
BATTALION
Confederate Guards
Response Battalion

RAVINE

17th LA.

4th LA.

13th LA.

2nd IOWA

7th IOWA

SUNKEN

ROAD

PITTSBURG - CORINTH ROAD

STONE

57th ILL. (2:00)

61st ILL. (2:00)

RICHARDSON

12th IOWA

14th IOWA

MUNCH

WELKER

POWELL

HICKENLOOPER

8th IOWA

21st MO.
18th MO.
12th MICH.
18th WISC.

PRENTISS

23rd MO.

LAUMAN

19th I.A.

FIRE

1st ARK.

12:00
12:30
1:00
2:00

GIBSON

EASTERN CORINTH ROAD

0   .25

Scale in Miles

takenly joined McArthur's brigade when this crossed its path on the way to the left. The 8th Iowa went to the far left of Tuttle's brigade to extend Prentiss's line, although it did not arrive until noon, not in time to receive the first Confederate attack. The 57th Illinois was detached to support Captain George Stone's Battery K, 1st Missouri Light Artillery, which came into position on a slight rise in the rear of the 2nd Iowa. The 58th Illinois straddled the Pittsburg-Corinth Road, with the 7th Illinois on its right. The 8th Illinois, of McClernand's division, eventually deployed to the right of the 7th.[10]

George Swain of the 58th Illinois described the scene to his wife. "The Regiment was at the time stationed upon the edge of a wood—and behind a rail fence flat upon their bodies. Behind the fence was a road or lane [Sunken Road] and another road crossing it at right angles [Pittsburg-Corinth Road] and dividing our regiment—a portion being one side of the road and one on the other. The last one is the road the reg't marched on. . . . Beyond the fence is a large cotton field [Duncan Field] entirely commanded by woods. In the center of the field and to the left of the wood, dividing the fence into 2 parts was a log house [Duncan's cabin] to the left of a stack of cotton in bales." One of Sweeny's men noted that the field was the very one that the brigade had marched in only days earlier.[11]

Elements of three divisions held the Sunken Road. On the east, at the Peach Orchard, were Hurlbut's two brigades of about 4,500 men. Prentiss, with about 1,200 troops, held the center. Wallace's two brigades, along with Major J. S. Cavender's two Missouri batteries, totaled 5,100 present for duty. Some 10,200 infantry and eight batteries with thirty-three guns thus held the salient. The position appeared formidable, but so did the Federal right, along the Pittsburg-Corinth Road, which snapped like a twig in half an hour.[12]

Tuttle and Major Cavender rode into the middle of Duncan Field, where they saw a line of gleaming bayonets in the trees to the south. At first they could not tell whether these were friend or foe, but the appearance of a group of Rebel officers soon decided the issue. "We are in for it now," Tuttle muttered to Cavender. "I will form my line of battle. Bring up your guns and you can get a raking fire across the field." The fight for control of the Sunken Road would soon begin.[13]

The Hornet's Nest

ABOUT 9:20, BEAUREGARD ADVANCED his headquarters from the intersection of the Pittsburg-Corinth and Bark Roads to the northern end of Fraley Field. He became increasingly aware of the dearth of troops in the center and right, where only Withers's division confronted an ever-increasing force. He committed two of Breckinridge's reserve brigades to the right, but they would not arrive before 11:00. Meanwhile, the Creole galloped ahead and spotted Colonel William H. Stephens's brigade of Cheatham's division, which, for half an hour, had been resting near the Pittsburg-Corinth Road, in support of the Shiloh Church sector. Beauregard redirected Stephens to the center of the line.[14]

Cheatham personally led his 2nd Brigade up the Eastern Corinth Road, where he deployed his men in Barnes's Field. The troops then tramped north toward Duncan Field, thus partially filling the large gap that existed to the left of Adams's brigade. At 10:00, the hard-cursing, tobacco-chewing Cheatham glanced across Duncan Field, where he saw the enemy rapidly forming behind a fence along an old, abandoned road. He called up Captain Melancthon Smith's Mississippi Battery to soften up the position. As the battery moved up, and before the guns could even be unlimbered, the artillerymen came under a sharp fire from a Federal rifled battery (Munch's), quickly disabling several horses. The batteries proceeded to pound each other, although Smith's smoothbores were at a distinct disadvantage. Cheatham had his men lie down as shells exploded in the woods edging the field. A few shells burst in the rear of the brigade, causing some consternation in the 1st Mississippi Cavalry, which supported the infantry. A couple of horses were struck before the troopers hastily pulled back to a ravine in the rear.[15]

Captain Noah Mills of the 2nd Iowa was on the receiving end of Smith's salvos. One projectile "knocked the dirt into the faces of several of us," but the shots otherwise "nearly all passed over our heads." The 2nd had at least two casualties, including a soldier who had his foot crushed so badly it had to be amputated, and a captain whose arm was literally ripped from his shoulder. In a state of shock he jumped up shouting, "Here, boys! here!" before dropping into unconsciousness. Erastus Sopher of the 12th Iowa disgustedly concluded that Munch had "a poor battery." "The men unhitched the horses and backed the guns to the brow of a hill, and then all of them wanted to attend the caisson or to hand out the ammunition, but one or two managed to get the guns loaded when some of the boys of Company D & F had to run the guns up the hill for them to discharge them."[16]

About 10:30, Cheatham led Stephens's brigade, about 1,350 infantry, up the Eastern Corinth Road. The right flank of the 6th Tennessee thrashed across the Davis Wheat Field, the 9th Tennessee in the center astride the road, and the 7th Kentucky extending into Duncan Field. Although encountering an immediate fire to the front and left, the brigade remained intact till it reached the center of Duncan Field. What the troops did not know, but would soon discover, was that the Yankees infested a thicket-filled ravine that zigzagged nearly perpendicular from the Sunken Road into the field. Cheatham's men were in essence approaching the apex of a V. "All was silent in front until our ranks were near," wrote 6th Tennessee member R. W. Hurdle. The men suddenly came under a "murderous crossfire."[17]

"We began this charge in good spirits," recorded Captain W. J. Stubblefield of the 7th Kentucky, "but when we got well into the field the enemy infantry as well as artillery turned loose on us with terrible effect and our Colonel commanded us out to the right of the timber. My 3rd scout and 3rd sergeant and Private Mallory got wounded and five or six were killed in companies. The balls jumped me on each side and in great profusion during the charge and after we got into the timber they continued to pass us."[18]

The 6th Tennessee burst from the woods against Colonel William T. Shaw's 14th Iowa. Shaw, a Mexican War veteran, seemed to an observer "to be an old man," who walked with a limp and swore like a sailor. Sensing that his regiment did not hold a favorable angle (the 8th Iowa had not yet come up on his left), the colonel inclined his left wing forward. Holding their fire and hugging the ground until the Tennesseans were within thirty paces, Shaw's 14th suddenly arose and unleashed a terrible volley. "The dead lay in line of battle, as if on dress parade," sadly recalled a member of the 6th Tennessee. A few additional volleys from the Iowans completed the work. Seeing the Rebels in disarray, Shaw boldly ordered a counterattack, in which he was joined by the left wing of the 12th Iowa. Fearing for his flank, however, Shaw soon recalled his men.[19]

Stephens's brigade had been shredded; the 6th Tennessee lost the flower of the regiment within a half-hour span. Among its 250 casualties were fourteen officers and the entire twelve-man color guard. The regimental flag, which fell to the ground six times, was ripped beyond recognition. The other two regiments suffered similarly. Colonel

Stephens, thrown from his wounded horse, attempted to rally his men as they returned to the southern edge of the field, but, having risen from his sickbed in Corinth, fell from exhaustion. His son William, who served on his staff, was seriously wounded. Cheatham had been shot in the ear.[20]

As casualties steadily mounted in the fierce fighting fronting the Sunken Road, the Confederates coined their own name for the place—the "Hornet's Nest."[21] Some historians have suggested that, if initial Southern assaults had been better coordinated, the salient probably could have been crushed before it fully formed.[22] Yet claims of three Rebel assaults prior to 10:30 are most certainly untrue. Cheatham was the first to try his hand at the position. The Federals at that time, though not at peak strength, were fully prepared.[23]

Following the Confederate sweep of Review Field, Shaver's brigade came under fire from Sweeny's sharpshooters at the Duncan farm. A request went out for artillery; Swett's Mississippi Battery promptly responded. Colonel John S. Marmaduke, commanding the 3rd Confederate, exclaimed: "Swett, those fellows are in that piece of woods on our front, let's go for them." "Alright, I'm with you," the captain replied. A few well-placed rounds proved sufficient to chase off Sweeny's men.[24]

Brigadier General Stewart, by Bragg's order, took command of a reinforced brigade, composed of his own 4th Tennessee, Wood's 16th Alabama and 55th Tennessee, and all of Shaver's brigade, and converged from the northwest corner of Review Field toward the Duncan cabin. At noon, additional troops were added: one-half of the 23rd Tennessee and about sixty men from the 6th Mississippi of Cleburne's brigade and the 8th Arkansas of Wood's brigade. This second attempt to break the Sunken Road salient was clearly the most formidable. The Confederate line, perhaps 3,600 strong, stretched from Prentiss's command to the far end of Duncan Field, west of the Pittsburg-Corinth Road. If the Federals, who numbered at least 4,300 troops and nineteen guns in that sector at that time, could have been dislodged, it would have occurred at this time. The blue line held firm.[25]

BY 11:00, THE ALMOST predictable intermingling of Confederate brigades had become so confused that the corps commanders were forced to improvise. "If you take care of the center, I will go to the right," Bragg told Polk. It was assumed that Hardee would supervise the left. Despite the understanding, Bragg became involved in the center and never made it over to the far right. Indeed, the major generals continued to work more or less independently. The task of urging troops to the front fell primarily to staff officers, who became virtual "mini-generals," giving their own orders in the name of various generals. Troops continued to mill about in rear positions, and Jordan wrote that he found batteries and entire regiments halted "for want of orders."[26]

As Bragg moved to his new command sector, he discovered Colonel Randal Gibson's fresh brigade standing idle in Barnes's Field. He apparently believed that the colonel was purposely hanging back, as evidenced by his words to Elise after the battle: "I had not been able to force him [Gibson] into battle up to twelve o'clock." Gibson countered that a Bragg staff officer had earlier instructed him to "move more slowly and to keep at a greater distance from the front line." Bragg promptly ordered Gibson to his "true position."[27]

The suave, Yale-educated, thirty-year-old Colonel Randal Gibson, in wealth, travel, and associations, represented the epitome of Southern aristocracy. He had spent years in Europe and even briefly served as the United States Embassy attaché in Madrid. Only hours earlier, Sidney Johnston had addressed him as "Randal," and told him how much he reminded him of his own son William. His one Arkansas and three Louisiana regiments now headed up the Eastern Corinth Road toward a head-on confrontation with the Yankees along the Sunken Road.[28]

In the van was Colonel Henry Allen's 4th Louisiana. The Harvard-educated attorney and states'-rights advocate had proved to be a scrapper; he had even been wounded in an 1844 duel. His immense land holdings in Louisiana stretched for four miles along the Mississippi River. Shortly before the Civil War, he had journeyed to Cuba, partly for his health. His only previous military duty was a brief stint in the Texas War for Independence.[29]

Allen saw a line of Tennessee troops drawn up along a road—probably some of Stephens's men regrouping south of the Purdy-Hamburg Road. A tall, thin man wearing a white coat and riding a mule (Tennessee Governor Isham G. Harris) spoke to them in an elegant and excited manner. "Come here, Colonel Allen, come here, sir!" he shouted. "Look at this horde of Tennesseans who refuse to go to the front! I have urged them to do their duty, and they do not heed me. See if you can arouse them. Speak to them, sir—Speak to them!" Allen calmly rode over and in a commanding voice shouted: "Attention companies! Right About Face! Forward March!" The troops dutifully obeyed, and Allen galloped off with a smile on his face.[30]

Gibson's brigade, about 2,350 strong, formed line of battle in Barnes's Field, the men "eager for a fight." Aaron V. Vertner, an orderly to Hardee, suddenly rode across the front of the 4th Louisiana in his blue uniform, with a captured Federal flag wrapped around his waist. "Here's your Yankee," someone mistakenly shouted, as dozens of muskets were raised and fired, despite the pleas of officers: "It's only one man, don't shoot." The young lad, a relative of Major General Van Dorn, fell, riddled with bullets.[31]

Many of the stray bullets whizzed through the ranks of the 13th Arkansas of Wood's brigade in Lost Field, killing a captain and wounding one captain, two lieutenants, and a number of privates. Compounding the error, the Arkansans returned fire, as apparently did some of Stephens's men in front of Gibson's line. At least twenty-seven men of the 4th Louisiana dropped wounded to the ground. "This was a terrible blow to the regiment," reported Allen, who conceded that his men became "almost demoralized." The self-destruction might have continued but for a woman in a sunbonnet who appeared out of nowhere and wandered between the lines, causing restraint among the various regiments. It would be a day of oddities.[32]

After regaining their composure, the troops advanced in line of battle—from left to right, the 4th Louisiana, 13th Louisiana, 1st Arkansas, and 19th Louisiana. Colonel B. L. Hodge, commanding the 19th, reported: "Just after crossing the road [Hamburg-Purdy] my regiment entered a small farm, a log cabin [Daniel Davis's] near the center, our line extending across the field." The troops would be clawing through the Hornet's Nest, directly against Prentiss's command and Lauman's brigade of Hurlbut's division. When informed of the assault order, Colonel Allen summoned his servant Hyppolyte and told him: "If I fall, search for me, and take me to the rear if wounded; if dead—bury me decently; and now, God bless you, you have been a faithful servant."[33]

The attack commenced about noon, the troops eagerly plunging into the near-impenetrable thicket. "It was almost impossible for a man to walk through it," Thomas Robertson of the 4th Louisiana wrote his mother. In the dense undergrowth, the men accidentally fired into one another. Colonel James F. Fagan of the 1st Arkansas screamed to a captain in the 4th "for God's sake to cease firing, that we were killing his men and he was killing ours."[34]

Gibson's troops blindly rushed into an ambush. When barely eighty to a hundred yards distant, they were met by "a perfect tornado of rifle fire . . . in our very faces," commented a Louisianian. The color-bearer of the 1st Arkansas fell dead, a bullet through his head. One Razorback recalled that "men fell around us like leaves." The Southerners recoiled in terror. A single artillery projectile killed six Zouaves of the 13th Louisiana, the brains and blood splattering all over Captain Edgar M. Dubroea. The 19th Louisiana lost forty to fifty men of a regiment of fewer than three hundred in this single failed assault. As his men fled back through the thickets, Colonel Allen dashed among them shouting, "Form on this line, men! Form on this line." The woods fronting Lauman's position caught fire, trapping many of the wounded.[35]

One of Breckinridge's reserve batteries, Captain Edward Byrne's seven-gun Mississippi Battery, was on Shaver's left. The captain confronted Bragg and requested permission to move his battery four hundred yards to the left, to play on the enemy's flank. Bragg brusquely asked why he had not sent a lower-grade officer to make such a request. Byrne replied that he could state the case better than a lieutenant. Bragg, incredibly, barked that he should return to his company and that in time Bragg would send an officer to hear his request. A lieutenant eventually arrived and took the request. Bragg granted permission for a change of position, but precious time was lost in the pedantic exchange.[36]

Both Gibson and Hodge requested artillery support from Bragg, but the only response was an order to renew the attack. For a fourth time the piercing Rebel yell filled the Hornet's Nest, although this time Gibson's men were content to keep a greater distance. The Yankees nonetheless "mowed us down at every volley," indicated Private Robertson. The 4th Louisiana stayed only long enough to get off two or three volleys, but the 19th tenaciously, though vainly, held on for half an hour before withdrawing, with the loss of fifteen men.[37]

At the conclusion of Gibson's second assault, Bragg rode up to Colonel Allen and ordered him to move out with the 4th and 13th Louisiana to ambush the enemy, who were believed (incorrectly) to be advancing. "Serve them as they [have] served you," the major general admonished. When Allen again protested that artillery support was needed, Bragg barked: "Colonel Allen, I want no faltering now." The colonel, deeply offended, returned to his troops and pleaded with them to vindicate the reputation of Louisiana.[38]

For a third time Gibson's troops were hurled into the meat grinder. The engagement turned into a long-range, hour-long exchange. The 13th Louisiana was somewhat sheltered in a small ravine, but the other regiments were greatly exposed. Allen suddenly reined in his horse and grabbed his face—a bullet had passed through both cheeks. Colonel Fagan vaulted as his horse dropped dead. Again the troops fell back, this time breaking into unorganized groups; many men expressed reluctance to advance again.[39]

Seeing Gibson's troops recoil across the Davis Wheat Field, Bragg dispatched Captain Lockett to seize the banner of one of the regiments—"The flag must not go back again," he ordered. Lockett rode ahead and grabbed the flag of the 4th Louisiana, just as the color-bearer was shot down. An irritated Colonel Allen came up and inquired: "What are you doing with my colors, sir?" "I am obeying General Bragg's orders, sir, to hold them where they are," Lockett replied. "Let me have them," Allen snarled. "If any man but my color bearer carries these colors, I am the man. Tell General Bragg I will see that these colors are in the right place. But he must attack this position in flank; we can never carry it alone in front."[40]

"Here boys, is as good a place as any on this battlefield to meet death!" Allen proclaimed to his troops. Dismounted and waving his sword, he led the 4th to within fifty feet of the Federal line. For ten minutes, the Louisianians took cover in the underbrush. So much white smoke clouded the air that visibility proved almost nil. Just as the men arose for one last push, a soldier of the 4th Louisiana had half of his head shot off by a cannonball. The troops watched in shock as he continued to walk two or three steps before dropping. The brigade again fell back, under a carnage beyond description.[41]

Gibson's four spasmodic assaults, between noon and 2:00, had left his regiments decimated; casualties totaled one-third. The brigade retired from the field and was not engaged again that day. The feud between Bragg and the brigade officers was still going on a year later. Allen bitterly wrote that the brigade had been sacrificed, and Fagan mentioned the "heaps of killed and wounded." All insisted that the regiments had never been rallied by staff officers, as stated in Bragg's report. The impulsive corps commander, never fully comprehending his role in the slaughter, blamed the failed attacks "entirely for the want of proper handling." Writing to Elise, Bragg unjustifiably denounced Gibson as "an *arrant coward*."[42]

Time remained for yet more blood-letting. At 2:30, Bragg hurled Shaver's brigade, about 1,500 infantry, into the fray. It was the third major engagement for the Arkansans, the first being in front of Peabody's camp and the second in Review Field. With reduced ranks and one detached regiment, Shaver led his men into still another piecemeal assault, the 7th Arkansas on the left against the 14th Iowa and the left of the 12th Iowa, the 2nd Arkansas in the center, and the 3rd Confederate on the right, in front of Prentiss. The Southern troops closed to within sixty yards before being slammed by a wall of fire. Lieutenant Colonel John A. Dean of the 7th Arkansas fell mortally wounded with a bullet through his neck. As the Rebels withdrew, Captain Warren C. Jones of the 14th Iowa ran between the lines and spoke to Dean briefly before he died. Jones respectfully crossed his arms and placed a handkerchief across his face.[43]

About 3:00, two of Sweeny's regiments, the 7th and 58th Illinois, made a sortie to the center of Duncan Field, taking cover in the Duncan cabin and behind a nearby stack of cotton bales. They quickly collided with the Crescent Regiment, 38th Tennessee, and Ketchum's Alabama Battery, marching east along the Pittsburg-Corinth Road. At 2:00, Beauregard had ordered the detachment, on guard duty at the Owl Creek bridge, to proceed toward the center. Ketchum's guns, along with a section of Hubbard's battery, successfully cleared the Duncan farmyard.[44]

The eighth and final thrust occurred about 3:30. Patton Anderson's brigade, reinforced with the Crescent Regiment, marched across Duncan Field, with the 17th Louisiana extending into the underbrush to the east. Anderson, with the 17th, met some retreating Confederates, who warned him that his men could never make it through the thickets. Still he pressed on, only to meet the fate of previous attempts. The 20th Louisiana suffered particularly severe losses.[45]

Probably in the range of 10,000 or so Confederates had been thrown into the Hornet's Nest fight. One historian has placed the casualties at around 2,400, or 24 percent. Postwar and modern writers have castigated Bragg for ordering eleven to fourteen near-suicidal charges. The fact that there were only eight, and some of them were not ordered by Bragg, does little to alter his culpability. Precious time and lives had been lost in attempting to carry the almost impregnable salient with the bayonet. Flanking movements would probably have produced the desired results, but once again the Confederate command relied upon brute strength rather than finesse.[46]

On Line with Breckinridge's Corps

IT IS NOT KNOWN if at Shiloh John C. Breckinridge had started growing the long downward-sloping mustache that would later distinguish him. Johnston highly valued the Kentucky politician, despite his lack of military experience. Back in the fall of 1861, it had been rumored that Breckinridge might land the Cabinet position of secretary of war; instead he came west. Interestingly, as he confided to a friend, the brigadier general believed that the South could not win the war.[47]

Shortly after 7:30 A.M., Breckinridge's division arrived at the intersection of the Pittsburg-Corinth and Bark Roads. The troops impatiently waited as the sounds of battle thundered in the distance. Good reports occasionally filtered back, all of which were greeted with loud cheers. About 9, the order to move out finally came. Breckinridge rode by the Kentucky brigade and gruffly barked: "Fall in if you're going to fight, if you are not give your guns to someone else." One private thought that it was an entirely unnecessary rebuke, for the command to fall in had never been given.[48]

Initially the division marched up the Pittsburg-Corinth Road, but before it had proceeded far, Colonel Jacob Thompson, a Beauregard aide, countermarched two brigades to the right, along the Bark Road. The change came in response to Colonel Numa Augustin's warning of possible trouble on the right. Meanwhile, Johnston had received Captain Lockett's report that the army might be overlapped in the Lick Creek sector. Not realizing that Beauregard had already started Colonel W. S. Statham's and Brigadier General John S. Bowen's brigades in that direction, the army commander dispatched Colonel Preston and Captain Nathaniel Wickliffe to bring up the reserves. At 10:20, the aides encountered the brigades and, on the double-quick, led them up the Eastern Corinth Road through Miller's camp.[49]

Diarist A. H. Mecklin of the 15th Mississippi wrote of halting "in a long level open field [Spain Field] apparently used by them for a drill ground. There had been a hot contest [and] on all sides lay dead & dying. Before us were the rifle pits [earthen debris] dug by the Yankees, behind them lay the camp." While Breckinridge's men rested in Spain Field, Johnston and his staff galloped by, eliciting a thunderous cheer from the men. He appeared surprised, but laughed and, along with his aides, raised his hat.[50]

About noon, Breckinridge's troops marched obliquely to the right, Bowen's brigade in front and Statham's brigade en echelon eight hundred yards in the rear. At 12:30, the 20th Tennessee passed through the camp of the 71st Ohio. The nervous men of the 45th Tennessee, trailing a little to the left and rear, mistakenly thought the 20th to be the enemy and opened fire. Bowen's men also had their problems. As the troops crossed Locust Grove Run, the first battle line, consisting of the 1st Missouri and 2nd Confederate, veered off and became separated from the second line, consisting of the 9th and 10th Arkansas.[51]

Also at 12:30, Statham's Tennesseans and Mississippians deployed under cover of a ridge at the south end of Sarah Bell's cotton field. Pugh's (formerly Williams's) brigade sparred with them at long range. The Southerners took shelter in the abandoned camp of the 71st Ohio, among tents, army wagons, and piles of corn. Private Mecklin saw two men killed in front of him, both shot in the head, and five others wounded. Major Jim Tolbert of the 28th Tennessee was killed in the prolonged exchange.[52]

Only the 20th Tennessee, east of the Savannah-Hamburg Road, held its ground. A fierce and extended exchange ensued with the 9th Illinois of McArthur's brigade, which had fallen back to a deep ravine and lay in ambush. Corporal W. S. Battle, son of Colonel Joel A. Battle, fell dead. At one point the 20th was almost outflanked, but a regiment (probably one of Jackson's) came up and maintained the line. In the midst of the melee, a small herd of goats passed between the lines, only to be slaughtered. When the 45th Tennessee, to the left of the 20th, withdrew, the 32nd Illinois fired obliquely into Battle's men. The 45th could not be urged back up the slope. Squads of men would run up to the fence along the Purdy-Hamburg Road, fire, and hurriedly take cover. The regiment as a unit refused to come together.[53]

Major Dudley Haydon of Johnston's staff complained to the general of being neglected. "You keep all of your staff on the wing; why do you retain me by your side?" "You will have plenty of work to do yet," Johnston replied. Soon a messenger arrived with a report that Breckinridge was sorely pressed and needed help. "Your chance has come," Johnston called to Haydon. "Go as fast as you can and tell Gen. Bowen to move up and prepare for action." Bowen's trans-Mississippians had been held in reserve. Haydon found them in the rear, partly under cover, awaiting orders.[54]

As Bowen's men came up, Johnston personally placed them in line, assuring them, "Only a few more charges and the day is ours." Since Bowen's right lay exposed, Breckinridge rode over to Brigadier General Jackson and requested assistance. Jackson promised to cover the flank as soon as he had cleared out pockets of resistance in Stuart's camp. Jackson's right wing subsequently became involved alongside Chalmers's brigade, leaving only the 17th and 18th Alabama to deploy on Bowen's flank at 1:30.[55]

Johnston positioned himself slightly in Bowen's rear, with Governor Harris at his side. Breckinridge rode to his side and in an excited manner said: "General, I have a regiment of Tennesseans [45th] that refuses to fight. I have been doing my utmost to rally them and get them in." Turning to Harris, Johnston said: "Did you hear that, governor?" Harris responded: "I will see what I can do." Not long after, Breckinridge returned and in an emotional voice exclaimed: "General Johnston, I cannot get my men to make the charge." "Then I will help you," Johnston calmly responded.

Motioning for Bowen's men to clear a path, Johnston rode up and down the line with a tin cup in his hand—his "souvenir," obtained in the camp of the 18th Wisconsin. In a commanding voice he addressed the troops: "Men of Missouri and Arkansas, the enemy is stubborn. I want to show General Beauregard and General Bragg what you can do with your bayonets and tooth picks [Bowie knives]."[56]

After galloping over to Statham's brigade, Johnston spoke briefly to Harris: "Those fellows are making a stubborn stand here. I'll have to put the bayonet to them." Just then a shell from Rutledge's Tennessee Battery exploded over their heads. Colonel Munford was told to go and correct their position, while Harris went, with pistol in hand, to attempt, unsuccessfully, to get the 45th Tennessee back into action. Breckinridge, his seventeen-year-old son, Joseph, by his side, rode to the front of the brigade. Charles Ivey, a young lad who had been a page for Breckinridge during his vice-presidency, rode out in front and attempted to shield him. The boy was ordered to the rear.[57]

By 2:00, a formidable assault force had been collected. Joining Breckinridge's 4,000 troops would be Stephens's fewer than 1,000, who had been bloodily repulsed three hours earlier in the Hornet's Nest. One, possibly two, of Jackson's regiments formed on the far right. To the 28th Tennessee, Breckinridge shouted: "Forward on the double-quick; come on, boys!" As the double line of troops moved ahead with a yell, Major Haydon glanced back and noticed a hundred or so men huddling behind the fence. They happened to be the remains of the 45th Tennessee, the regiment that Harris had earlier been unable to rally. Just then Major T. T. Hawkins, a Breckinridge aide, rode back, blood spewing from his neck. Seeing the Tennessee skulkers, he cried, "Major [Haydon], why don't you shoot the cowards?"[58]

Johnston had made yet another tactical error. He had previously overcommitted strength on the left, although the master plan called for a right-flank swing. He now became obsessed with the destruction of the Peach Orchard sector. At least one of Breckinridge's reserve brigades could have reinforced Withers's division (Jackson's and

Chalmers's brigades) on the far right, where Stuart's lone Federal brigade was ripe for the picking.[59]

The Peach Orchard

"A BRIGADE [STATHAM'S] leaped the fence, line after line, and formed on the opposite side of the [Sarah Bell] field. It was a splendid sight. . . . The field officers were seen waving their hats, a shout arose, and the brigade moved on magnificently." Thus Lieutenant Seymour Thompson of the 3rd Iowa viewed Statham's bayonet charge. J. F. True of the 41st Illinois could distinctly see the "Stars and Bars" waving over them.[60]

Four hours earlier, at 10 A.M., Hurlbut had taken advantage of the lull and withdrawn Pugh's brigade three hundred yards north, toward the six-acre Peach Orchard. The 41st and 28th Illinois deployed west of the Hamburg-Savannah Road in front of the orchard, with Mann's battery in the center, and Ross's Michigan Battery and the 3rd Iowa on the right, behind a fence bordering the Sunken Road.[61]

Canister blasts from Mann's and Ross's batteries created gaping holes in the approaching Confederate line. A member of the 41st Illinois disgustedly noted that Mann's guns were eventually "abandoned by the Dutch gunners." The 32nd Illinois opened fire first. To their right, the 3rd Iowa, in a prone position, withheld fire until the Rebels came to within two hundred yards. They arose with a yell and unleashed a withering fire. "Of the whole Rebel Regiment [fronting the 3rd], I do not believe more than 200 escaped unharmed," observed an Iowan. After the battle, eighteen Rebel corpses were counted in a quarter-acre fronting the 3rd Iowa.[62]

The Southerners angled toward Mann's abandoned guns and the 41st Illinois. Hurlbut pulled the 32nd Illinois out of line (the 3rd Iowa realigned to fill the space) and, marching it behind the brigade, placed the regiment to the right rear of the 41st Illinois. The division commander was perhaps concerned whether or not the 41st would hold; it had reportedly been a bad fighter at Fort Donelson. When the nearly choking smoke dissipated, Hurlbut's midwesterners saw the remains of two enemy brigades racing back across Bell Field.[63]

As the Rebels retreated, the 1st and 2nd Battalions of the 5th Ohio Cavalry, which had just arrived upon the scene, gave a timely charge past Ross's guns. The Ohio troopers chased the Confederate infantry back to the timber south of the Hamburg-Purdy Road, giving Ross's gunners time to change position.[64]

Two o'clock on the afternoon of April 6—the opportune time for Sidney Johnston to have unleashed his 16,000 Fort Donelson troops on his right flank; Federal tenacity could not possibly have resisted such a terrible onslaught. The Fort Donelson troops instead sat confined in Northern prison camps, and the only reinforcements on the way were a meager 1,200 or so infantry and cavalry.

At 11:00, Colonel George Maney, guarding Greer's Ford on Lick Creek, became convinced that Buell would not land at Hamburg. Exerting his discretionary instructions, he took his 1st Tennessee (five companies) and 19th Tennessee and proceeded to the battlefield. Forrest's cavalry regiment remained, but not for long. The scrapping Tennessee cavalryman was not of a temperament to sit while a crucial battle raged only miles away. "Boys, do you hear that musketry and that artillery?" Forrest asked. "It means that our friends are falling by the hundreds at the hands of the enemy, and we are here guarding a DAMNED CREEK! Let's go and help them. What do you say?" In unanimous consent, the troopers rushed to the battlefield.[65]

When near the scene of action, Maney's modest reinforcement was cheered by the wounded. A number of men, having fallen back in sheer exhaustion, joined the ranks of the Tennesseans. Mathias Martin, the wounded colonel of the 23rd Tennessee, bellowed his support: "Give 'em goss, boys. That's right, my brave First Tennessee. Give 'em Hail Columbia." When asked where he was wounded, the rotund colonel answered in his deep bass voice: "In the arm, in the leg, in the head, in the body, and in another place which I have a delicacy in mentioning."[66]

Maney, as senior colonel, took command of Stephens's brigade. At 2:00, Cheatham ordered him to select the units of his choice and attack the battery (Ross's) in his front. Maney located his own 1st Tennessee (battalion) on the left, the 9th Tennessee in the center, and the 19th Tennessee on the right, with the 6th Tennessee and 7th Kentucky in support. The attack began at 2:30, just as the last of Statham's troops filed back toward the Hamburg-Purdy Road. Bearing left, the Tennesseans gained the woods to the west of the Sarah Bell Field. The men came under a crossfire, lay down, and commenced a limited exchange with Lauman's brigade.[67]

Support from Adams's brigade, to the west of Maney, proved limited. Adams had received a bullet in his right eye at 11:30 and was

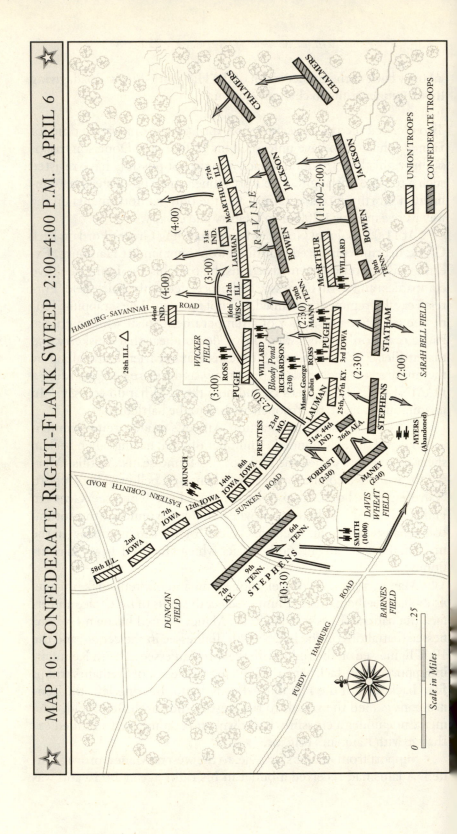

MAP 10: CONFEDERATE RIGHT-FLANK SWEEP 2:00–4:00 P.M. APRIL 6

thrown into a wagon along with other wounded. The driver believed him to be dead and tossed his body along the roadside. He was later found by men of the 10th Mississippi, was taken to Corinth, and recovered. Command of the brigade passed to Colonel Zacariah C. Deas, who had no instructions or mounted aides. He eventually found Breckinridge, who ordered him to support Maney's left flank. Deas sent back for a battery and the 26th Alabama, but the latter never appeared.[68]

By 2:30, Forrest's cavalry regiment had arrived at the Purdy-Hamburg Road and quickly came under artillery fire. When Major General Cheatham demurred in granting permission for a charge, the impatient Forrest snapped: "Then I'll charge under my own orders." Advancing in column of fours, the troopers careened along the eastern edge of the Davis Wheat Field, with a single incoming artillery shell immediately dropping three riders and four horses. Supporting Forrest on his right was the 26th Alabama, which had finally arrived. The gray cavalrymen became entangled in the thickets of the Hornet's Nest and could go no farther. The Alabamians overran the abandoned guns of Myers's Ohio Battery and even gained the Manse George house, but, having only two hundred men, Lieutenant Colonel William Chadick drew his regiment back.[69]

Extending Hurlbut's line east of the Peach Orchard was a portion of Brigadier General John A. McArthur's brigade. The tall and brawny Scottish-born McArthur would develop into one of the ablest Federal generals in the west. His "Highland Brigade" of Illinois troops, veterans of Fort Donelson, all wore Scottish hats. When W. H. L. Wallace moved up his 1st and 3rd Brigades to support Sherman and McClernand, the 2nd Brigade was divided. McArthur took the 9th and 12th Illinois and Willard's Battery A, Chicago Light Artillery, to the left to buttress Stuart. When the troops cut across the line of march of Sweeny's brigade, the 50th Illinois inadvertently (though fortunately, as it turned out) veered into McArthur's line.[70]

The Scottish hats marched in column of fours down the Hamburg-Savannah Road. With flags unfurled, they kept cadence to "The Joy Bird" and other tunes, played by the thirty-member 9th Illinois regimental band. So many fugitives fled past them it proved almost impossible to maintain formation. About fifty of the skulkers heeded their pleas and joined the ranks.[71]

Willard's battery, a Chicago militia company organized in 1854, moved in advance of the infantry and unlimbered in a small field east of the Peach Orchard. The outfit had previously been under the command of Major Ezra Taylor, which was a cause of concern for cannoneer Enoch Colby. He feared that Taylor would "place us in the most dangerous position he can find, for he is down on us for taking the laurels away from his battery at Fort Donelson." The Chicagoans were subjected to artillery fire from Girardey's Georgia Battery, whose shells unhorsed two of the Illinois gunners and blew off the right arm of a third. Willard remained in his first position slightly over an hour, even though they were under a heavy fire that could not be returned. The battery then shifted to a slightly more prominent knoll farther to the east.[72]

McArthur's Illinois Infantry formed a line of battle a quarter-mile south of Hurlbut's headquarters. With drums beating and fifes playing, they marched a half-mile, passing "a large pond," later dubbed "Bloody Pond." The surgeon of the 9th Illinois established a field hospital next to the pool. At 10:30, McArthur's men took cover in a heavily wooded ravine that ran from twenty to forty feet deep, with the 9th Illinois on the right, 12th Illinois in the center, and 50th Illinois on the left. Lieutenant Colonel Augustus L. Chetlain had gotten out of his sickbed that morning and led the 12th into battle. A line of infantry now appeared in his front and, unable to make a positive identity, he hesitated to open fire. A brisk infantry-and-artillery fire suddenly hit his ranks from the ridge above. Chetlain was unhorsed, badly bruising his chest and face, but continued to command feebly on foot. He ordered his men out of the ravine and onto the ridge in the rear.[73]

The 50th Illinois encountered a similar problem: the smoke obscured the identity of the troops across the hollow. When a line of unidentified infantry appeared on the brow of the ridge, a sergeant major cried out: "Don't fire on them; don't you see they are carrying our flag." He rode out to investigate, with Lieutenant Colonel William Swarthout following on foot. Shots rang out, and a riderless horse dashed back into the Federal line. Swarthout, realizing he was in trouble, drew his revolver and attempted to run, but he was shot in the thigh and captured.[74]

For three hours, McArthur's bluecoats held against a lackluster Confederate attempt, primarily of long-range sniping. A soldier in the 9th Illinois had three or four of his ribs blown out by an artillery projectile, which exposed his throbbing heart. He died within minutes, speaking deliriously of a particular woman. His corpse was found three days later, the face now covered with maggots.[75]

At 2:00, the Confederates launched a fierce attack against

McArthur, spearheaded by Bowen's brigade in the center, the 20th Tennessee on the left, and two of Jackson's regiments on the right, perhaps 3,000 troops against 1,500. The 50th Illinois, on McArthur's left, was jolted by the suddenness of the attack. "About 2:00 one of my men . . . could see a flag coming over the brow of the hill," wrote the chaplain of the 50th. "The flag bearer was holding it down around the staff, and I could not tell whether it was the stars and stripes or the stars and bars. The rebels advanced very slow, but at last the flag was above the brow of the hill, and as the breeze caught it gradually unfolded, showing it to be the rebel ensign." An astonished Sergeant C. H. Floyd wrote that the "Rebels came on us before we knew it." The 50th broke, exposing the left flank of the 12th. Chetlain ordered his men back fifty paces, where they again formed. The 9th also fell back in chaos, having lost sixty-one killed and 305 wounded (forty-two mortally) in their first position.[76]

The Southerners surged ahead. On reaching the crest of the hill, the 2nd Confederate received a destructive volley that killed and wounded a dozen men. Colonel A. C. Riley's 1st Missouri (Confederate) slugged it out for half an hour before charging. McArthur's Yankees fell back five hundred yards north, where the wounded brigadier general formed a skeleton line, with Willard's battery in the southeastern corner of Wicker Field and his infantry east of the Hamburg-Savannah Road. The 9th Illinois, having sustained 250 killed and wounded, was ordered by W. H. L. Wallace back to camp to replenish their ammunition. The 12th and 50th Illinois held until reinforcements arrived.[77]

The 57th Illinois, of Sweeny's brigade, which had been in reserve on the right of the Sunken Road sector, came to McArthur's assistance, as did Lauman's entire brigade. Lauman's ranks deployed in open woods east of the Hamburg-Savannah Road, with the 31st Indiana in reserve on the left. At 3:00, the 61st Illinois, also in reserve near the Sunken Road, replaced the 44th Indiana, which had exhausted its ammunition.[78]

Stuart's troops continued to swing to the southern edge of a ravine one hundred feet deep and as wide. About eight hundred blues, the remains of the 55th Illinois and 54th Ohio, stood against Chalmers's Mississippians—at least 1,800 infantry and a battery. Stuart could have been overrun, a fact conceded by his men, but the Confederates contented themselves with skirmishing.[79]

By 2:15, on another part of the field, with ammunition depleted and Stuart wounded, Colonel T. Kilby Smith ordered a withdrawal.

The Federals ran down the imposing ravine and scaled the opposite ridge, as the enemy poured a devastating fire into them. "We were right on top of them. It was like shooting into a flock of sheep," Major F. E. Whitfield of the 9th Mississippi remembered. Kilby Smith's force, reduced to fewer than six hundred, fled north, toward the landing. An urgent message was sent to Hurlbut warning that his flank could soon be turned.[80]

Wicker Field

HURLBUT WORKED FRANTICALLY to shore up the crumbling left flank. An appeal to W. H. L. Wallace had brought two regiments, both of which were committed to McArthur. It would not be enough to stem the advance of Statham's, Bowen's, Jackson's, and Chalmers's brigades. Hurlbut had to abandon either his right or his left flank. Believing that Prentiss could probably hold and extend toward Pugh's brigade, Hurlbut pulled Lauman's 1,000 or so men out of line and sent them to McArthur. A section of twenty-pounder Parrott rifles from Battery H, 1st Missouri Light Artillery, was also drawn from W. H. L. Wallace to back up Pugh's brigade.[81]

Pugh remained in a precarious situation. McArthur's new line was perhaps three hundred yards north of the Peach Orchard, leaving his left exposed. Pugh's 28th and 41st Illinois, low on ammunition, fell back north, toward Wicker Field, the latter almost routing. Colonel John Logan's 32nd Illinois advanced from its support position, but could not hold. By 3:00, Pugh's entire brigade had retired from the Peach Orchard sector and established a new line in southern Wicker Field, backed by Willard's and Ross's batteries and a section of Richardson's.[82]

By 2:30, the situation on the Federal left had temporarily stabilized. Hurlbut's 1st Brigade held Wicker Field, with his 3rd Brigade extending east across the Hamburg-Savannah Road. The remains of McArthur's brigade and the 57th Illinois anchored the far left. The 57th's left flank remained in the air, since Stuart's shattered brigade was essentially out of the fight.

From observations and the sound of skirmishers, Hurlbut knew that the Confederates intended to flank his left. Three Rebel brigades (Bowen's, Jackson's, and Chalmers's) were marching in a wheeling movement east of the Hamburg-Savannah Road, the last far overlapping the 57th Illinois. Colonel Charles Cruft of the 31st Indiana reported seeing large numbers of enemy troops moving up from the large ravine on the left, "moving en echelon, in compact lines, with Confederate flags flying in perfect order, as if on dress parade, and came steadily on our little front." McArthur's men, along with the 31st Indiana, boldly attacked across the ravine in their front, but the position proved impossible to hold. At 3:00, the 44th Indiana, east of the Hamburg-Savannah Road, depleted its ammunition and was replaced with a portion of the 16th Wisconsin.[83]

By 4:00, Hurlbut's line was obviously breaking apart. Efforts at patchwork proved too little, too late. The 44th Indiana spread out across the Hamburg-Savannah Road, performing a rearguard action. As late as 4:30, the 3rd Iowa and a part of Ross's battery remained in southwestern Wicker Field. Hurlbut rode up, expressed shock that the men had not been engulfed, and ordered them to the rear.[84]

Cloud Field

AFTER THE WAR, Cloud Field, because of a defective land title, had no owner and was not plowed under like the other fields. C. A. Kuhl, touring the battlefield twenty-one years to the day later, found the field in a remarkable state of preservation. Tent squares, camp wells, and deserted bake ovens were still plainly visible. A casual stroll across the field turned up camp kettles, cartridge boxes, shoes, bayonets, and even well-preserved clothing fragments.[85]

On the late afternoon of April 6, 1862, Cloud Field was the scene of one of the final delaying actions on the Federal left. Lieutenant Colonel James McPherson placed Richardson's and Welker's batteries in the field, east of the Hamburg-Savannah Road.[86]

Although the Federal left had all but dissolved, the 81st Ohio of McArthur's brigade bungled south toward the enemy tidal wave. The Buckeyes had been guarding the Snake Creek bridge, on the far right, when ordered by Grant to the opposite flank. "We emerged in a clear spot of ground [Cloud Field] when we were suddenly greeted with a discharge from a battery 200 yards away," remembered Major W. H. Chamberlain. The 81st formed line of battle in a prone position across the road, near Hurlbut's old headquarters. Observing heavy enemy forces in his front, and cavalry attempting to gain his rear, Colonel Thomas Morton ordered a retreat.[87]

Headquarters, Army of the Mississippi

IN POSTWAR YEARS, Beauregard derided Johnston's decision to lead from the front rather than the rear. He reduced himself to the "part of a Corps or Division commander," and did little to direct the general movement of the army. Although the Creole never used the term "reckless," as did some others, he did believe that Johnston "uselessly" exposed himself. It is true that at one point the Kentucky general rode forty paces in front of Breckinridge's line. His uniform was torn by Minie balls in several places, and the heel of his boot was cut away. Pointing to his boot, Johnston told Governor Harris: "Governor, they came very near putting me hors de combat in that charge." Harris fearfully asked: "Are you wounded?" The army commander replied negatively and dismissed a mark under his shoulder blade as "only a scratch." Convinced that all was well, Harris left to carry an order to Colonel Statham. In truth, Johnston had been mortally wounded. A bullet had entered his right leg behind the knee, cutting an artery. Although he was bleeding to death, the wound was masked by his high-top boot.[88]

Two staff officers, Captains Lee Wickham and Theodore O'Hara, remained with Johnston. Hearing what he thought to be the thud of a bullet striking Fire-eater, Wickham turned and noticed blood dripping from the heel of Johnston's boot. "General, you are wounded, and we had better go down under the hill, where we will not be exposed to the bullets." The army commander emphatically replied: "No; Hardee's fire is very heavy. We will go where the firing is heaviest." As Johnston turned his horse, O'Hara blurted: "General, your horse is wounded." "Yes, and his master too," came the reply.[89]

Governor Harris returned from his errand and gave a brief report. As he spoke, Johnston began to swirl as though he was about to drop from his saddle. He was caught by Harris and Wickham, the former anxiously inquiring: "General, are you wounded?" "Yes, and I fear seriously," Johnston answered. Harris led Fire-eater to a ravine east of the Hamburg-Savannah Road, about a hundred yards south of Sarah Bell's farm. The army chief was placed on the ground, and Harris frantically ripped his shirt in search of the wound; none was found. A simple tourniquet might have saved Johnston's life, but no one recognized the profuse bleeding in the boot. Dr. D. W. Yandell, the general's personal physician, had been earlier detached (by Johnston) to care for the wounded, including many Federals. Wickham rode hard in search of a surgeon.[90]

As Colonel George Baylor returned to army headquarters, he encountered the anxious Wickham. "[Johnston] is wounded and I fear seriously," he said. "I am now looking for a surgeon, as well as others of the staff." Hoping that a doctor had by now been located, the two officers rode together to the ravine. There they found several staff officers assembled, all bearing a gloomy countenance. A six-to-eight-foot stream of blood ran from Johnston's body, ending in a dark pool. His eyes were open, but his face had turned deathly pale. Brigadier General William Preston, propping his head in his lap, cried: "Johnston, don't you know me?" Major Dudley Haydon poured a few tablespoons of whiskey down his throat, but it merely flowed onto his chin. The major felt for a heartbeat, but got none. In a shrilling tone Preston called out: "My God, my god! Haydon is it so?" Within thirty minutes of being placed in the ravine, Albert Sidney Johnston was dead. The time was 2:30.[91]

There was not a dry eye in the group; Preston wept openly. "Pardon me, gentlemen," he sobbed, "you all know how I loved him." The body was wrapped in a blanket to conceal his death from the troops. When various persons asked who was being taken to the rear, Preston answered: "Colonel Jackson of Texas." A subsequent search of Johnston's body found that he had actually been hit three times, in addition to his mortal wound: once by a spent ball in the middle of the right thigh, once by a shell fragment in the rear of the right hip, and a Minie ball that had cut his left boot sole. Preston, regaining his composure, took out his notebook and penned a message to Beauregard: "Ravine, 2:30 P.M. Gen. Johnston has just fallen, mortally wounded, after a victorious attack on the left of the enemy. It now devolves on you to complete the victory." Governor Harris took the dispatch to Beauregard's headquarters.[92]

Beauregard's Headquarters No. 3

By MIDAFTERNOON, Beauregard and his staff had moved to "Headquarters No. 3," a clump of trees at the intersection of the Pittsburg-Corinth and Purdy-Hamburg Roads—the "crossroads." About 3:00, Governor Harris arrived and informed the Creole of the shocking news of Johnston's death. Beauregard initially said nothing, as if in deep thought, and then replied: "Well, Governor, everything else is progressing well, is it not?" Harris acknowledged as much. Sometime later, Colonel Munford arrived and found the Louisiana general with Captain Wickliffe. Beauregard expressed regret at Johnston's loss, but added that everything else appeared to be going well.[93]

Though postwar rumors that Beauregard was so ill that he commanded from an ambulance were false, he clearly approached exhaustion. That morning, doctors had counted his pulse at a hundred, and urged him to remain in bed, a suggestion that he scoffed. His laryngitis remained so acute that he could barely speak.[94]

Beauregard had an overall grasp of the tactical situation, having been in virtual command of two-thirds of the army (the left and center) since midmorning. It is true that fighting on the Confederate left somewhat diminished in midafternoon, but this had nothing to do with Johnston's death, as his defenders later claimed. The Confederates in that sector faced a serious ammunition shortage. The fighting in the center continued unabated. Indeed, if there was any loss of momentum following Johnston's death, it was on the Confederate right, where the army chief's death had left a command void. About 3:00, Bragg found that Breckinridge's assault had slowed, and Withers's and Cheatham's troops were essentially out of the fight, their men exhausted. The three commands, Bragg reported, did not "have a common head." Beauregard sent messengers to the corps commanders informing them of Johnston's death and the necessity of keeping this information from the troops. They were ordered to push the battle forward.[95]

Duncan Field

IT WAS NOW TIME for the artillery to attempt what the infantry had failed—to break the backbone of the Federal salient along the Sunken Road. Throughout the afternoon, Bragg had ignored several requests for artillery support, insisting that the Yankee stronghold could be carried at the point of the bayonet. Some batteries were eventually brought to bear in piecemeal fashion, including a section of Ketchum's battery, Stanford's battery, and Byrne's battery. At 3:30, a concerted effort was made to gather all available guns.[96]

Exactly who pieced together what would become the largest concentrated use of field artillery on the North American continent up to that time has been disputed. Nearly a year after the battle, Brigadier General Daniel Ruggles claimed the honor, and submitted several affidavits to substantiate his claim. In postwar years, Major Francis Shoup, Hardee's artillery chief, suggested that Ruggles was "merely a spectator," and that *he* had authored the plan. Lieutenant E. C. Williams, an artillery staff officer, wrote immediately after the battle that at 2:00 Brigadier General James Trudeau, the army artillery chief, began collecting guns in response to an order from Beauregard. It would appear that, contrary to Ruggles's supporters, there was no single "controlling genius on that occasion," but that several generals and artillery officers played a part.[97]

Two concentrations appeared to have developed. To the north, near the Pittsburg-Corinth Road and the western end of Duncan Field, a section of Ketchum's battery (two guns) and the Washington Artillery (six guns) were already engaged. To the right of the New Orleans redlegs, Bankhead's Tennessee Battery (six guns), Stanford's Mississippi Battery (six guns), Robertson's Florida Battery (four guns), and Rutledge's Tennessee Battery (six guns) came into position. Captain Smith P. Bankhead, commanding these batteries, was aware of another group of batteries to the south, but "by whom commanded I am unable to state."[98]

The commander of the artillery group to the south, stretching toward the Eastern Corinth Road, was Major Shoup, who had massed his guns near a skirt of light timber. From left to right the batteries included Roberts's Arkansas (four guns), Trigg's Arkansas (four guns), Swett's Mississippi (six guns), Hubbard's Arkansas (four guns), and Byrne's Mississippi (seven guns). These companies advanced and deployed simultaneously. The total number of pieces in both groupings was probably fifty-three, firing at a range of five hundred yards.[99]

The artillery duel that ensued was fierce and not entirely one-sided. Numerous Federal guns along the Sunken Road stubbornly continued to hold their ground and return fire. Robertson's battery came under such a heavy fire from twenty-pounder Parrott rifles that he was forced to retire, leaving two of his Napoleons behind. Ketchum's section also pulled back under a fierce fire. As Swett's battery came into line, Captain Charles Swett "noticed that one of our batteries nearby [Robertson's] was very badly injured." As soon as his men came into sight, someone was heard to shout: "For God's sake hurry!"[100]

Exactly how much damage was inflicted by the Confederate barrage is difficult to determine. "No one who observed the effects of that firing could but be agreeably surprised at its results," gloated one Southern officer. Clearly the concentrated fire proved sufficient to cause the eventual withdrawal of the Union batteries. The overall effects, however, have been exaggerated by some historians. The captain of the Washington Artillery did not even mention the incident in his report, nor, curiously, did the extant letters and diaries of seven artillerymen whose batteries participated. Not until 4:30 did all of the batteries become consecutively engaged, and the barrage at its peak may have lasted only twenty minutes. Major Shoup recalled that "the fire opened beautifully but almost immediately the bluecoats . . . began to break to the rear, and we soon saw white flags." Shoup did not believe that his guns played a significant role in the demise of the Sunken Road position.[101]

The Yankee salient had, in fact, already been breaking apart, even before the barrage began. The 2nd and 7th Iowa had already begun a pullout, and plans were being made to withdraw other units. It was at that moment (4:30) that Colonel Shaw noted that the Confederates opened a "tremendous barrage, the heaviest I ever heard."[102]

The Sunken Road

THROUGHOUT THE AFTERNOON, the defenders of the Sunken Road tenaciously held their ground, despite repeated Rebel assaults: "He failed to move us one inch," boasted 12th Iowa Colonel Joseph J. Woods. A dense pall of smoke obscured the air, and the roadbed became a "carpet of paper" from bitten-off cartridge wrappings. The undergrowth was chopped to pieces, and large trees were so riddled and torn that veterans visiting the battlefield thirty years later still detected the damage.[103]

Eight times the Southerners smashed against the salient, coming so close that "we heard their voices, and we saw them falling," recounted an Iowan. The fighting was the most prolonged in front of the 8th Iowa, where the "maddened demons came up so close as to lay hands upon the guns of the battery [Munch's]," a member of the 8th noted. Two of Munch's six-pounders, firing down "an old road [Eastern Corinth Road]," were actually captured and dragged away, but then retaken by a sortie of the 8th Iowa.[104]

The Southern dead piled in heaps. A 7th Iowa soldier wrote that the ground was covered with Rebel dead. So many were the corpses that it proved possible to walk across them at places without stepping on the ground. "His [Confederate] ranks were mowed down at each fire, but still he pressed forward, and as bravely was received," reported 44th Indiana Colonel Hugh B. Reed. The grays approached to within ten paces of the 31st Indiana. The woods caught fire in front of Lauman's brigade's right, mercilessly consuming many wounded; their screams could be clearly heard. After the battle, 120 charred bodies were counted, including an estimated one hundred wounded who got trapped in the blaze.[105]

Few wavered among Tuttle's Iowans. Despite head-on attacks that sounded "like a hurricane," Leonard B. Houston of the 2nd Iowa noticed birds still chirping in the trees above. A premature shell from one of Richardson's guns burst over the ranks of the 12th Iowa, wounding a man and causing momentary chaos. Eighth Iowa Colonel J. L. Geddes caught a bullet in his knee and also had his horse killed.[106]

Even though Hurlbut's courier to Prentiss had been killed, the sound of battle to the northeast made it increasingly evident that the Union left had been turned. Prentiss swung his command, less than 1,000 men, back north, making a horseshoe-shaped line, with the 8th, 14th, and 12th Iowa in the curved portion. Believing that the Federal right still held firm, and that Lew Wallace's division would yet come up, both W. H. L. Wallace and Prentiss thought the odd-shaped salient would hold.[107]

Shortly after 4:00, Sweeny brought W. H. L. Wallace the stunning news of the imminent breakup of his brigade. The division commander, having placed great confidence in the one-armed colonel, could hardly believe what he was hearing. Even years later, as Tuttle spoke to the survivors of the "Hornet's Nest Brigade," he belittled Sweeny for allowing his brigade to "go to pieces." In truth, McClernand's division had withdrawn a full half-mile from W. H. L. Wallace's right, leaving Sweeny in the air. Lieutenant I. P. Rumsey, a Wallace aide, pleaded with McClernand to advance his left and reconnect with Wallace, but he refused.[108]

Already four of Sweeny's six regiments had been shifted to other parts of the battlefield, leaving only the 7th and 58th Illinois on line. Sweeny had been shot in his one good arm but, despite a loss of blood, remained in command. Seeing that he was about to be flanked, Major Richard Rowlett retired his 7th Illinois up the Pittsburg-Corinth Road. By the time the 58th Illinois attempted to withdraw, however, the Rebels had cut off the retreat to the north. Seventy-three men of the 58th managed to escape, but the majority of the regiment made a stand southwest of the 41st Illinois camp, in an area to become known as "Hell's Hollow."[109]

The Federals, after a six-hour defense along the Sunken Road, had become increasingly isolated. The Rebels approached from both flanks, and the rear was being slowly enveloped. Despite his earlier agreement with Prentiss to hold at all hazards, W. H. L. Wallace now determined to cut his way out. Even as he conferred with Tuttle, a courier galloped up and announced that the woods along the right flank were "full of Rebels."[110]

About 4:15, Tuttle's two left regiments, the 2nd and 7th Iowa, retired up the Pittsburg-Corinth Road under a galling fire. "If we had not left when we did we would all have been taken prisoners," explained 7th member William Richardson. His regiment had, incredibly, sustained only thirty-four killed and wounded throughout the day. Wallace led the column, and Tuttle brought up the rear. Near the intersection of the Pittsburg-Corinth and Eastern Corinth Roads, Lieutenant Cyrus E. Dickey, Wallace's aide and brother-in-law, called the division commander's attention to some enemy activity. Wallace raised himself in the saddle to get a better view; a bullet struck him behind the left ear, exiting the left eye and bringing him crashing to the ground face-first. Dickey and three men carried the body a quarter-mile but, believing him to be dead, tearfully left him beside some ammunition crates so that he might not be trampled. Seeing the enemy in the 3rd Iowa camp in Stacy Field, the 2nd and 7th Iowa formed a line and successfully fought their way past.[111]

Shortly after 4:30, the remaining Federal batteries limbered up. Powell's battery escaped, although Captain John Wesley Powell had his forearm shattered, a wound that required amputation. Hickenlooper moved his battery, minus a disabled gun and an exploded caisson, along a fresh path in his rear, thus eluding the Confederates inching up a ravine on Wallace's line. All four of Munch's guns made it out, although one piece had become disabled when a shot jammed down the bore. Upon reaching a ravine that crossed the Pittsburg-Corinth Road, the Minnesota cannoneers saw a large body of Rebels approaching from the west. They hastily unlimbered and sprayed the area with canister, checking the enemy and buying sufficient time to vacate.[112]

The 12th Iowa next took its turn at extrication. Colonel Joseph Woods ordered his men to about-face and follow the 2nd and 7th Iowa. Marching up the Eastern Corinth Road, the men of the 12th had covered only half the distance to the Pittsburg-Corinth Road when they had to face about and fight a brief action in their rear. At 5:00, the 12th continued its retreat to the right of the 41st Illinois camp. Like the men of the 58th Illinois to the southwest, the Iowans were caught in a trap. Colonel William Lynch of the 58th attempted to organize a force and cut his way out, but his horse fell wounded, badly injuring Lynch's leg in the collapse. No further attempt was made.[113]

By 4:45, the 2nd Division, except four regiments, had effectively retired from the field. The 58th Illinois and 12th Iowa had been cut off in the process and were in a desperate plight. This left Prentiss with about 2,000 men, only 500 of whom were a part of his original division. Prentiss bent his line back along a slight elevation in an open woods, the troops facing east and south. The odd-shaped position vaguely resembled a shepherd's crook, with the 8th and 14th Iowa in the curve. Colonel Madison Miller apprised Prentiss that the new line was untenable, but the brigadier general naïvely insisted that Lew Wallace's division would yet come up and that he would sleep in his own tent that night. Prentiss sent a courier for reinforcements and even contemplated a charge with his entire force, or at least so he wrote seven months later.[114]

In a futile attempt to shore up Prentiss's left, Shaw's 14th Iowa faced about and obliqued to the left, filing behind the 18th Wisconsin. As the Iowans raced ahead, they saw the remains of the 23rd Missouri running in confusion, their colonel having been killed. Shaw rallied the Missourians and formed them on his left. At 4:45, Prentiss arrived, but before orders could be given, he dashed off to another part of the line.[115]

THE CONFEDERATES TIGHTENED the noose. Anderson's and S. A. M. Wood's brigades blocked the Duncan Field sector. By 4:30, Polk and Hardee had moved the left forward, making a sweep around Duncan Field. A mix of regiments converged from the north and west. The 33rd and 38th Tennessee attacked in Stacy Field, the 5th Tennessee to the south of the encampment, and the 22nd Tennessee and Crescent Regiment in the vicinity of the Pittsburg-Corinth and Eastern Corinth Road intersection. "We gave them [12th Iowa] one murderous round of musketry," Joseph Thompson of the 38th Tennessee noted; "then they threw down their arms and surrendered." Trabue's brigade came astride the Pittsburg-Corinth Road to the north, cutting off escape and catching the Yankees in a cul-de-sac.[116]

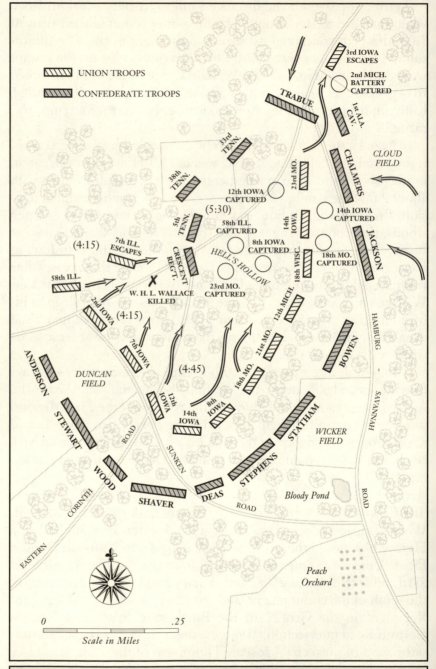

UNION TROOPS

CONFEDERATE TROOPS

3rd IOWA
ESCAPES

2nd MICH.
BATTERY
CAPTURED

1st ALA.
CAV.

TRABUE

CLOUD
FIELD

CHALMERS

33rd
TENN.

23rd MO.

38th
TENN.

12th IOWA
CAPTURED

14th IOWA
CAPTURED

JACKSON

5th
TENN.

58th ILL.
CAPTURED

14th
IOWA

(5:30)

8th IOWA
CAPTURED

18th MO.
CAPTURED

(4:15)

7th ILL.
ESCAPES

CRESCENT
REG'T.

HELL'S HOLLOW

58th ILL.

18th WISC.

X

W. H. L. WALLACE
KILLED

23rd MO.
CAPTURED

2nd IOWA

(4:15)

12th MICH.

BOWEN

7th IOWA

21st MO.

ANDERSON

DUNCAN
FIELD

(4:45)

18th MO.

STEWART

12th
IOWA

8th
IOWA

STATHAM

WICKER
FIELD

ROAD

14th
IOWA

SUNKEN

STEPHENS

WOOD

SHAVER

DEAS

Bloody Pond

ROAD

CORINTH

EASTERN

HAMBURG - SAVANNAH

ROAD

Peach
Orchard

0   .25

Scale in Miles

Two clusters of Federals were bagged east of the Pittsburg-Corinth Road. In the Hell's Hollow sector, the 58th Illinois (223 men) and 8th Iowa (379 troops) surrendered. Nearby, the Crescent Regiment captured the fleeing 23rd Missouri, 410 of whom were eventually counted. Most of the 12th Iowa (429 men) capitulated in the 41st Illinois camp. Confederate cavalrymen joyfully dragged their flag through the mud. Many of the Iowans threw their muskets down the camp well, artifacts that were later retrieved when the national park was established. To the east, near the Hamburg-Savannah Road, Prentiss's dwindling command continued its forlorn stand.[117]

FOLLOWING JOHNSTON'S DEATH, the Confederate advance on the right lost momentum. A foul-tempered Bragg found the divisions of Cheatham, Withers, and Breckinridge "holding back, undecided what to do." Deas's (Adams's former) brigade rested a half-mile in the rear; Bragg promptly "gave them a talk." Many of Statham's exhausted men rushed to drink the water of Bloody Pond. None were deterred by the sight of a dead man at the water's edge; "if the water had been mixed with blood it would have been all the same," noted Private A. H. Mecklin. Bowen had been wounded in the initial attack on Wicker Field, and his troops now rested in the 71st Ohio camp. It was 4:00 before Statham's, Bowen's (now under Colonel John D. Martin), Jackson's, and Chalmers's brigades began their final drive to the northwest.[118]

Chalmers's brigade completed its wide arch and approached parallel to the Hamburg-Savannah Road, the line extending from the 28th Illinois camp north into Cloud Field. Their path was blocked by Prentiss's command, west of the road. Chalmers encountered stiff resistance and went in search of Jackson's brigade. Although he did not locate Jackson, he did find Colonel Joseph Wheeler's 19th Alabama, which he promptly sent forward. Jackson eventually followed with the 17th and 18th Alabama, which moved to the left of the 19th. The 2nd Texas got lost in the woods—"Lord knows where," Colonel John C. Moore recounted—but belatedly aligned with Wheeler's right. The Yankees continued an obstinate stand behind a fence and some outbuildings bordering the Hamburg-Savannah Road.[119]

Heavy casualties mounted in the gruesome struggle; the 19th Alabama lost about twenty killed and 140 wounded within fifty minutes. Chalmers found Jackson and announced that he was turning the fight over to him and retiring his own brigade to rest. When Bragg noticed Chalmers's men pulling back, he sternly ordered them back into action. Even after the 2nd Texas exhausted its ammunition, Jackson ordered it to remain in line and use the bayonet. At 5:00, both brigades sent up a thunderous cheer and pressed across the road, Chalmers in the lead and Jackson in support.[120]

By 5:30, Federal resistance had been smashed. The 9th Mississippi received the arms of the 14th Iowa (236 men) and 18th Missouri (147 troops) in the 32nd Illinois camp. Colonel Shaw collided with the overhanging branch of a tree as he attempted to escape, knocking himself nearly senseless. As he struggled up, he saw Major F. E. Whitfield of the 9th Mississippi, who informed him: "Colonel, I think you will have to surrender, as you are entirely surrounded, and the rest of your troops are already surrendered." Shaw glanced about and saw blue and gray uniforms intermingled. "Well, major, it looks that way," he replied. Shaw took his watch out and noted the time: 5:45. The remains of Peabody's brigade totaled only 236 out of 2,790 men. Only the 3rd Iowa of Hurlbut's division, which had anchored the extreme northern end of Prentiss's line, managed to evade capture, surrendering but thirty men. Prentiss himself made it all the way back to Hell's Hollow before he yielded his sword to Colonel William H. Rankin of the 9th Mississippi, an officer who would fall mortally wounded in the next day's battle. Prentiss urged his men to surrender: "It is useless to fight longer. I must stop this slaughter."[121]

Although organized fighting ceased, pockets of resistance continued. A Confederate officer, shouting to a group of blues to throw their arms down or they would be killed, was himself killed. A Federal colonel came riding up to men of the 2nd Texas and screamed: "Boys, for God's sake stop firing, you are killing your friends." He realized his mistake too late and was shot dead as he attempted to get away. One Union officer was shot as he escaped in a buggy. Some prisoners smashed their weapons against trees rather than surrender them, prompting the Southerners to open fire again. A burly Rebel captain demanded of Captain C. P. Searle: "You damned Yankee, give me your sword." For a fleeting moment Searle contemplated resisting, but discretion prevailed. The 14th Iowa flag was shredded and trampled through the mud.[122]

The number of prisoners has traditionally been placed at 2,200 (Prentiss's figure), which seems nearly accurate. Colonel Shaw later insisted that rations were issued for only 1,558, but this number probably did not include wounded and is too low. A tabulation from after action reports totals 2,201. In postwar years, a Union prisoner claimed that the Southerners got an official count at Monterey: 2,315. The 18th Alabama and Crew's Tennessee Battalion escorted the prisoners back to Corinth. Brigadier General Trabue allowed the 5th and 6th Kentucky to exchange their old muskets immediately for captured Enfield rifles.[123]

Lieutenant Colonel John H. Miller took his battalion of the 1st Mississippi Cavalry toward the river in an attempt to round up stragglers. The battalion had not gone a quarter-mile before an escaping battery was sighted at the intersection of the Pittsburg-Corinth and Hamburg-Savannah Roads. A quick charge captured fifty-six men and all five guns of the 2nd Michigan Battery; not a shot had been fired or a horse disabled. The ordnance was removed to the rear, as if they were on dress parade, with the drivers in their saddles and the gunners in their seats on the caissons grinning over the turn of events. Seeing another battery (Mann's Missouri) madly galloping across a deep ravine in the distance, Colonel A. J. Lindsley took thirty or forty of Miller's men and went in pursuit. The Federals abandoned one caisson, but Lindsley's party was suddenly confronted by a long line of blue infantry poised for action—Grant's Last Line. The troopers looked on in shock as they received a crashing volley. Incredibly, all of the cavalrymen escaped unharmed. Buell, who witnessed the incident, later expressed disbelief that every saddle had not been emptied.[124]

THE PRECISE NUMBER of prisoners captured near the Sunken Road was, of course, supremely irrelevant to the issue of ultimate victory. Colonel Shaw later wrote that Bragg, whom he had known in the Mexican War, snarled about how much time had been consumed in mopping up the Federal stronghold. Neither Johnston nor Beauregard ever questioned the propriety of expending excessive time and manpower in reducing the position.[125]

As for W. H. L. Wallace and Prentiss, neither officer received his full due from Grant. In his memoirs the army chief even censured Prentiss for failing to conduct a timely withdrawal. History would tell a different story. The valiant stand made at the Sunken Road probably saved the army, and clearly turned the tide in Grant's favor.[126]

NINE

Lost Opportunity?

Tilghman Branch

THE DEEP, BROAD RAVINE of Tilghman Branch ran parallel to the Tennessee River and extended from Snake Creek to the Western Corinth Road, where it broke into a number of smaller ravines. Although Sherman's and McClernand's divisions managed to keep the Rebels west of the branch, the bluecoats withdrew to defend the Hamburg-Savannah Road and the Snake Creek bridge, thus securing the approach route for Lew Wallace's belated division. Buckland's brigade, the only intact unit remaining with Sherman, came into line along the northern portion of Perry Field. Although the fences along the road had been torn down, blackberry and sassafras bushes still marked the border of the open field (a cotton field, Sherman later recalled) in their front.[1]

Sherman had dispatched Captain J. H. Hammond to the landing to summon additional artillery. About 3:30, the six guns of Captain Edward Bouton's Battery I, 1st Illinois Light Artillery, rumbled into northern Perry Field. Arriving with the Chicago gunners were 250 men of the 53rd Ohio, about all that remained of Hildebrand's brigade, which was placed in support of the battery. At 5:00, two of Hickenlooper's guns, fresh from their stand in the Sunken Road, unlimbered in Mulberry Field.[2]

Between Perry and Mulberry Fields was a densely wooded ravine that extended two hundred yards. Sherman feared that it might be occupied by enemy snipers in an effort to drive off the artillerymen. He ordered one of his colonels to occupy the area, but the officer failed to grasp the tactic. Colonel Thomas Sweeny, who had gone to the rear to have his wound dressed, happened to be standing nearby and volun-

238

teered. "Sweeny, go at once and occupy that ravine, converting it into a regular bastion," Sherman ordered.[3]

About 4:00, Bouton's battery was shelled from the south end of Perry Field across Tilghman Branch. A lengthy and brutal exchange erupted with Ketchum's Alabama Battery, later reinforced with the Washington Artillery, which the Chicago press labeled the "Great Artillery Duel." Although having one gun and a number of horses disabled, Bouton maintained his position until 5:00.[4]

McClernand's brigades withdrew east through Cavalry Field, camp of the 4th Illinois Cavalry, toward the Purdy-Hamburg Road. Along a ridge between the field and the road, a new line was formed facing west, thus creating an obtuse angle with Sherman's division. McClernand's right probably stretched to the Hamburg-Savannah Road, giving him interlocking fire with Sherman's troops. His command was made up of regiments of his own intermingled with two other divisions. Northeast of a lane that is today known as Cavalry Road, and in front of the 15th Illinois camp, two of Veach's regiments (14th Illinois and 25th Indiana) and one of Raith's (29th Illinois) came into line about 4:00. Straddling the lane was the 52nd Illinois of Sweeny's brigade. Southeast of the road were the disordered fragments of six regiments (three each from Colonel Carroll Marsh's and Raith's brigades), behind which were posted McAllister's three remaining guns. Supporting the cannoneers was the 18th Illinois of Colonel Abraham Hare's brigade. The 13th Iowa (Hare's) came next in line, and on the far left were the 15th and 46th Illinois of Veach's brigade. Another of Sweeny's regiments, the 7th Illinois, served as a reserve. The exhausted Federals braced for yet another shock wave; it was not long in coming.[5]

TWENTY-SEVEN-YEAR-OLD Lieutenant Colonel Samuel Ferguson, aide to Beauregard, had been sent to the Tilghman Branch sector to take command of a Louisiana brigade reportedly without a commander. He reported to Hardee, who ordered him to capture an annoying battery (McAllister's) west of the branch. He was to overlap the enemy's right as far as possible, so as to take the position in reverse. Artillery support would come from Captain William H. Ketchum's and Lieutenant Charles H. Slocomb's batteries, already engaged west of the branch.[6]

Ferguson found his adopted command in the Tilghman Branch ravine, which had previously been cleared of Yankee snipers. The brigade happened to be Pond's, minus its two largest regiments, which had been detached. Contrary to information, however, Colonel Pond had been only temporarily absent on a personal reconnaissance. He now returned, and brushed with Ferguson. Pond balked when told that Hardee desired an immediate assault on the ridge in front. "Go back and tell the General I fear he does not know the great strength of the enemy and the weakness of my command," Pond pleaded. Ferguson rode off to deliver the message, but returned shortly with orders for an immediate attack. "Very well, sir. I will obey the order, but do so under protest," Pond grumbled.[7]

The Louisianians, about 1,000 strong, filed down a hollow and turned east up a ravine that ran between the camps of the 14th and 15th Illinois. When still three hundred yards distant, Ferguson directed Pond to move to the attack. With such an extensive area yet to cover, the plan was virtually doomed from the outset. Pond compounded the error by holding back the 16th Louisiana and Orleans Guard Battalion and ordering Colonel Alfred Mouton to charge solo with his 18th Louisiana. Mouton protested the suicidal order: "You will make me sacrifice all my men to no avail." Realizing the futility of further argument, the colonel stoically led the assault, crying: "Forward, the 18th! Follow me!" His five hundred men scaled the ravine, formed a line in the southwestern corner of Mulberry Field, and advanced southeast on the double-quick.[8]

The 18th never had a chance. The Yankees poured in a storm of bullets from both front and enfilade. "Before we had gone 50 yards the battery [McAllister's] opened upon us," a member of the 18th wrote. "Our company was next to the flag of our regiment, and the bullets rang out about our ears like bees swarming. Once only I looked behind me to see Col. Mouton's horse falling from under him." Mouton's regiment swayed to and fro for a few moments and then gave way. The ground was strewn with the bodies of 207 dead and wounded—41 percent of the outfit. A single round from one of McAllister's twenty-four-pounder howitzers bowled down a file of four men, cutting a sergeant nearly in half.[9]

As the 18th limped back to its starting point, Pond shouted: "Orleans Guard, charge!" Major Leon Querouze's order to "fix bayonets" was greeted with a cheer. The men from New Orleans now scaled the ravine and marched through the survivors of the 18th. "It was truly horrendous, as we ascended the hill [ravine] to see on all sides those unfortunate men of the Eighteenth coming down bathed in their blood; some had been wounded in their face, others, in the body, arm, etc. They fled into our ranks, asking us for water and help," Private Edmond Livaudais of the Orleans Guard jotted in his diary.[10]

One of the first to fall was flag-bearer Gustave Poree. Four men in succession picked up the banner, only to be shot. The standard was finally saved by Captain Alfred Roman, who wrapped it around his body. Stepping over a carpet of their dead and wounded comrades, the Louisianians penetrated to within forty paces, forcing back McAllister's guns. The battalion was eventually checked by the murderous fire and fell back, having lost 90 of about 150 men. Despite their valiant effort, Lieutenant Colonel Ferguson contemptuously wrote: "Those that were unhurt had to tell all about how near they came to being killed. . . . I quit them in despair."[11]

Pond's troops had unwittingly served a useful purpose, although it could have been accomplished at much less cost. His 1,000 men had occupied the remains of two enemy divisions, freeing up several Southern brigades to close in on the Sunken Road. Had McClernand and Sherman known this, which of course they did not, the brigade could have been crushed between them. As it was, Sherman's frazzled men were content to remain in a defensive posture.[12]

Though McClernand's center and right stoutly held, and some Federal regiments even began a cautious advance, the major general was actually in a precarious spot. A 450-yard gap, bisected by Tilghman Branch, existed between his left and the fast-crumbling Sunken Road. The Confederates, more coincidentally than by design, began to exploit the exposed flank.

Simultaneously with Pond's attack, the Confederates launched an assault south of Cavalry Road. Wharton's Texas Rangers trotted through Cavalry Field, where five companies dismounted and advanced as skirmishers. Although the Texans were easily repulsed, the survivors of Cleburne's brigade—the 5th (later 35th), 23rd, and 24th Tennessee—successfully struck McClernand's far left.[13]

The 15th and 46th Illinois were swept back by a flood of fugitives and wagons from the disintegrating Sunken Road sector. As the chaotic flight rippled down McClernand's line, the withdrawal turned into a rout. Lieutenant Colonel Camm attempted to save two of McAllister's pieces. "One gun was unmanned and left, and I ran to help a tall artilleryman hook the other up, but as we stooped over the stock trail the soldier fell dead across it, and one of the horses fell and the driver ran away," Camm wrote. For a moment he stood dazed, but a sergeant grabbed him by the shoulder yelling, "Run colonel, run!"[14]

McClernand's debris fled southeast toward the Hamburg-Savannah Road, where a new line was briefly patched together about 5:00. Roughly speaking, Lieutenant Colonel Enoch Wood's (formerly Raith's) brigade held the right and connected with Sherman's left,

Marsh the center, and Veach the left, at the intersection of the Hamburg-Savannah and Cavalry Roads, although there was much intermingling of units. Colonel Hare had been wounded in the arm and leg during the pandemonium, and most of his brigade fell back to the 14th Iowa camp, east of Chambers Field. At 5:00, three hundred men of the 9th Illinois came into line between Wood and Marsh. The 13th Missouri came alongside the 9th, although Marsh had to threaten its colonel with arrest—he "seemed little inclined to halt short of the river." So reduced was McClernand's command (the 11th Illinois had only a captain and eighty men) that the eight-hundred-yard-long position was simply impracticable.[15]

On the March,
Nelson's Division, Army of the Ohio

FROM HIS UPSTAIRS BEDROOM in the Cherry mansion, a crippled but jovial Major General C. F. Smith laughed at his friend Colonel Ammen for thinking that a battle raged at Pittsburg Landing. The upriver roar he dismissed as a mere "hot picket skirmish." As the sounds grew louder and more distinct, Smith conceded that a part of the army might be engaged. A naval officer visiting with the 2nd Kentucky assured the men that the sounds were nothing more than the gunboats clearing the banks of Rebels to prevent them from planting batteries. Among the troops of Nelson's division, encamped just outside Savannah, wild rumors of a serious defeat circulated. So indifferent did Buell appear to the state of affairs that a captain within forty feet of him railed insults and characterized him as a Rebel. If Buell heard the remarks, he made no response.[16]

The problem was how to get the division the eight miles to Pittsburg Landing. Grant had left orders for Nelson's men to march along the east bank of the river, but the promised guides never arrived. Even though the locals knew of wagon trails winding through the woods and swamps, the recent high water had flooded the bottoms, leaving the impression that the land route was impassable. Buell sent Nelson's escort, Captain J. Miles Kendrick's company of the 3rd Indiana Cavalry, to explore for a trail, though early reports had proved unfavorable. An impatient Buell peered downriver in the hope that Grant would send transports, but none came into view.[17]

At noon, Kendrick's company returned, having literally run several horses to death in the process. The main road was impassable, but a higher trail back from the river, though traversing a marsh, would allow the passage of infantry. Artillery and wagons, however, would never make it through the thick mud. A local man, a self-professed "hater of Rebels," volunteered as guide. A fidgeting Buell could wait no longer. He left orders for Nelson to take the land route if transports did not soon arrive. Meanwhile, he and a few staff members took a smaller steamer at the landing and headed toward the scene of action. At 1:00, Nelson ordered his division forward, prompting a rousing cheer from his men. Ammen's brigade spearheaded the division, with Bruce in the center and Hazen bringing up the rear. Having lost six precious hours, Nelson was finally on the march.[18]

ABOUT 1:00, BUELL ARRIVED at Pittsburg Landing. On the way upriver, he noticed a boat racing toward Savannah. He pulled alongside and was handed a message from Grant. The dispatch stated that the enemy were 100,000 strong, that the attack had been "very spirited," and suggested that the appearance of fresh troops would have a "powerful effect" upon the army. The message failed to convey the urgency of the situation, but Buell was about to get his own firsthand assessment. As his steamer passed the mouth of Snake Creek, Buell saw the first signs of disaster—flooded backwater choked with fugitives attempting to swim across. The scene at the landing proved even more shocking, with some 4,000–5,000 refugees huddled along the riverbank.[19]

About 2:00, Buell, with contained rage, boarded *Tigress* and met Grant at the door of the ladies' cabin. The last time the two had conferred had been in Nashville, where the exchange had been less than cordial. Perhaps Buell now took some perverse pleasure in seeing Grant, the lauded hero of Fort Donelson, in his present nasty predicament. Grant remarked that he had just returned from the front and showed his damaged sword scabbard, which had been struck by a shell fragment. "I did not particularly notice it," Buell contemptuously recorded. The Ohio general believed Grant to be lacking in the "masterly confidence" so frequently attributed to him that day.[20]

The meeting proved brief. The two discussed the progress of the battle, and Buell requested that transports be sent to Savannah for Crittenden's division. According to Rawlins, Buell asked what preparations had been made for a retreat. "I have not yet despaired of whipping them, general," Grant responded. Even though Nelson's division had been delayed, Grant was confident that Lew Wallace's division would arrive shortly. The generals parted company and did not see one another again until later that afternoon.[21]

A foul-tempered Buell toured the landing. He directed a number of wagons down a side road to the landing. When 44th Indiana Colonel Hugh Reed inquired of him where he could obtain ammunition, Buell snapped: "No, sir, nor do I believe you want ammunition, sir." A startled Reed asked his name. "It makes no difference, sir, but I am General Buell." The colonel whirled about and rode off, but a frenzied Buell pursued him, demanding to know his name. "My answer was as fierce and insulting as I could make it in my anger," Reed recounted. Buell later encountered Colonel Tuttle and asked about the battle plan. Came the reply: "By God, sir, I don't know."[22]

THE FIRST THREE MILES of Nelson's march proved uneventful, over undulating ground. The trail then took a sharp turn to the right, leading into a heavily timbered, black-mud bottom. Some of the deeper lagoons were rudely bridged, but essentially no road existed. When a member of the 2nd Kentucky asked the scout about the swamp, he answered: "Wal, stranger, I've been going and coming through that ar swamp fur years and it is nighly hell!" The troops snaked along in column of fours and sometimes only two abreast, as the din of battle increased. Serving as the van of Ammen's brigade was the 36th Indiana, the least experienced of his troops and the most giddy about "seeing the elephant." The 6th Ohio had seen some service, having been in several skirmishes, but had essentially no serious combat experience. The 24th Ohio had been under fire a couple of times and appeared the least anxious about getting into the fight.[23]

Nelson rode ahead and sent back an urgent message to the column: "Hurry up or all will be lost; the enemy is driving our men." Ammen sent his staff officers in advance to intercept any additional messages, so that the men might not get wind of a troubling report. The troops almost childishly asked if the battle would be over by the time they arrived. Ammen played along: "I hope so, if it goes right." Soon a second courier appeared from Nelson with a similar message, then a third; the pace accelerated.[24]

Pittsburg Landing

BY 4:00, THE SITUATION at Pittsburg Landing appeared grim. Peering out the window of a transport, wounded Sergeant Ira Blanchard of the 20th Illinois saw panicked men swimming out and clinging to the rope; some drowned in the attempt. A cavalryman rode his horse straight into the river, desperately hanging on to the animal's tail. From aboard the commissary boat *Continental*, a wounded Iowa sergeant saw officers vainly attempting to rally a mass of stragglers. A cavalry officer rode back and forth across the bluff, elegantly appealing for his comrades to make one more stand. The huddled fugitives sat unmoved, although one commented: "That man talks well, don't he."[25]

The transport *Fort Wayne* arrived in the midst of the turmoil, carrying pontoons from Cincinnati. An officer implored the boat's captain to land, so that the pontoons could be used as boats to get the Army of the Ohio across. Fearful that the mass of skulkers would instead see a convenient escape, Rawlins barked that he would have the boat burned if she did not keep clear of the landing. Shortly thereafter, *Rocket* arrived with two ammunition barges in tow. As the boat docked and the boxes began to be unloaded, a shell exploded nearby, prompting the boat captain to give orders to cast off. Again Rawlins stepped forward and threatened to have every man on board shot if a departure was attempted.[26]

A makeshift perimeter about a mile and a half long formed around the landing as the Federals took their final stand of the day. Sherman continued to hold the right along the Hamburg-Savannah Road, fronting Perry Field. The 14th Missouri and 81st Ohio partially filled the gap between Sherman's right and the Snake Creek bridge, although the latter was reassigned in late afternoon. A mixed regiment, composed primarily of Prentiss's survivors, was placed under the command of Colonel Hildebrand and sent to Sherman's right flank. A company or two of Birge's Sharpshooters (13th Missouri) guarded the Snake Creek bridge.[27]

McClernand's division formed at a right angle to Sherman's, making a backward L along what today is called Grant Road. W. H. L. Wallace's division, now led by Tuttle, was on McClernand's left, at the south end of Chambers's Field. Hurlbut's division extended Tuttle's left. Buell estimated that the whole line did not number 5,000 infantry but an additional 2,000 came into line during the night. Sherman, more realistically, placed the total at 18,000.[28]

Colonel Joseph D. Webster, under orders from Grant, had been frantically collecting artillery for a last-ditch stand. Initially there were only three uncommitted batteries, including the siege guns. As other fragmented units drifted back to the landing toward late afternoon, forty-one pieces were eventually assembled. On the far left, on a ridge near the mouth of Dill Creek, was Captain Louis Margraf's 8th Ohio Battery of six guns and the remaining four pieces of Munch's Minnesota Battery. The batteries were placed so as to enfilade any enemy approach over Dill Creek.

Most of the guns faced south along the Pittsburg-Corinth Road. On the left Webster positioned a section of Powell's battery and four twenty-pounder Parrott rifles, the remaining section of Nispel's battery (protected by the only earthworks thrown up on the battlefield), and Captain Frederick Welker's three pieces.[29]

Grant arrived at the landing about 4:30. He pleaded with the mass of stragglers to redeem themselves and return to the ranks. When his implorings were ignored, he unleashed a squad of cavalry into the mob, driving many of the skulkers to the water's edge. The dispersal was only temporary: by 5:00, the mass had again flocked together along the bank.[30]

Glancing across the Tennessee River, one of the Federal fugitives noticed two men ride up on the opposite bank, one clasping a white flag with red square. "We are gone now," he cried. "There's the Texas cavalry on the other side of the river." It proved to be the advance of Nelson's division, and within fifteen minutes Ammen's brigade emerged from the woods. The time was 5:00.[31]

AMMEN'S MEN STARED in amazement at the panorama of disaster on the opposite bank. By now an estimated 10,000 to 15,000 men jammed the landing below the bluff. "I blush to describe it," a young member of the 6th Ohio wrote. "The entire bank of the river, for a mile up and down, was crowded with cowardly poltroons who were crowding down to be out of harm's way." A little drummer boy was seen furiously beating away, but to what end no one could figure. Two or three transports hugged the shore at the lower end of the landing, while several transports packed with wounded sat motionless in midriver. Frantic signals were sent to hurry over, although a puzzled Colonel Ammen observed that the mob at the landing far outnumbered his own force.[32]

Nelson's pioneers got to work in cutting a road to the bank. No transports were ready to receive them (an issue that should have been resolved in the Grant-Buell meeting), leaving Nelson to compel the

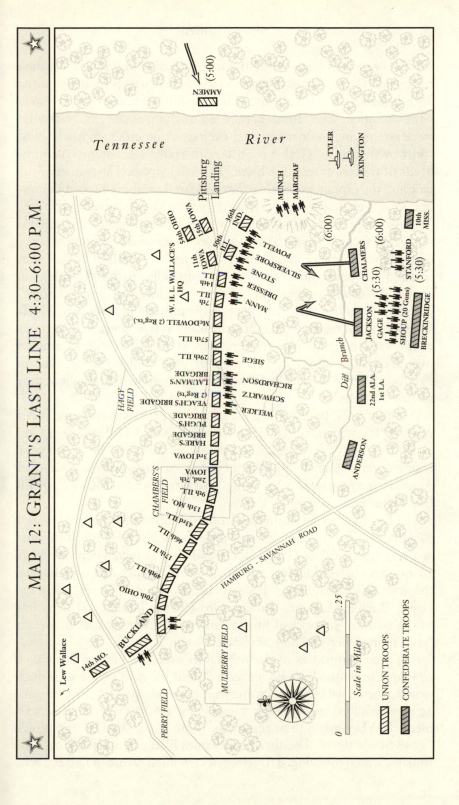

MAP 12: GRANT'S LAST LINE 4:30–6:00 P.M.

Tennessee River

Pittsburg Landing

AMMEN (5:00)

MUNCH
MARGRAF

TYLER

LEXINGTON

54th OHIO
15th IOWA
50th IND.
36th IND.
11th IOWA
11th ILL.
W. H. L. WALLACE'S HQ
14th ILL.
7th ILL.
McDOWELL (2 Reg'ts)
57th ILL.
29th ILL.
LAUMAN'S BRIGADE
YEACH'S BRIGADE (2 Reg'ts)
PUGH'S BRIGADE
HARE'S BRIGADE
3rd IOWA
2nd, 7th IOWA
13th ILL.
9th ILL.
43rd ILL.
46th ILL.
17th ILL.
49th ILL.
70th OHIO
BUCKLAND
14th MO.

SILVERSPORE
POWELL
STONE
DRESSER
MANN
SIEGE
RICHARDSON
SCHWARTZ
WELKER

CHALMERS (5:30)
(6:00)

STANFORD (5:30)
10th MISS.

JACKSON
GAGE
SHOUP (20 Guns)
BRECKINRIDGE

Dill Branch

22nd ALA.
1st LA.

ANDERSON

HAGY FIELD

CHAMBERS'S FIELD

HAMBURG - SAVANNAH ROAD

MULBERRY FIELD

PERRY FIELD

Lew Wallace

(6:00)

Scale in Miles
0   .25

UNION TROOPS
CONFEDERATE TROOPS

captain of a sutler boat to take the first load of men across. Only nine mounted officers and two hundred infantry (three companies of the 36th Indiana) crowded aboard, since the hurricane deck was jammed with wounded. The Hoosiers pleaded to shoot at the runaways who were attempting to float the river on logs. Ammen's men made great sport by shouting, "Grab a root. Grab a root," referring to the hundreds of tree roots near the bank. The boat stopped just short of the landing, the captain explaining that he feared crushing men in the water. Nelson exploded and demanded that the boat steam ahead.[33]

As the prow touched the shore, the first company splashed into the water, securing a beachhead at bayonet point. The mounted party cleared the gangplank and formed two lines, with Nelson in the front. In a commanding voice the division commander roared: "Gentlemen, draw your sabers and trample these ———— into the mud! Charge!" The officers knifed their way through the mass of fugitives, while Nelson violently screamed: "Damn your souls, if you won't fight, get out of the way, and let men come here who will!" The skulkers trampled over each other in terror. As the infantry scrambled ashore, Nelson gave the order to "shout Buell," and he beat time with his saber as they stormed ashore.[34]

As the 36th Indiana filed ashore, a chaplain was running about yelling: "Rally, men, rally, and we may yet be saved. Oh! rally! For God and your country's sake, rally! Rally! Oh! rally around the flag of your country, my countrymen!" The incessant wailing so irritated Colonel Ammen that he snapped: "Shut up, you God damned old fool!, or I'll break your head. Get out of the way."[35]

The Hoosiers formed a line atop the bluff, although demoralized soldiers continued to run through their ranks. Between the 36th Indiana and the log cabin, Grant, Buell, and Nelson held a conference. A six-pounder ball suddenly decapitated one of Grant's aides, splattering the army chief with brains. It was the second close call of the day for Grant. Buell led Colonel William Grose's 36th Indiana to the far left of the road, in support of Stone's and McAllister's guns. Grose sat "cool as an iceberg" as his men braced for an assault.[36]

Three companies of the 6th Ohio were the next to debark. A woman admonished the Buckeyes to "fight for your country, or die," words greeted with a cheer. Some frightened knaves gave less encouraging words: "It's no use," "Last man in my company," and "All cut to pieces." When asked their regiment, some of the skulkers answered: "1448 Skedattlers." The three companies filed to the left of the 36th Indiana, which overlooked the deep, water-filled ravine of Dill Branch.

Ammen had eleven companies, about 550 men, in line when the Rebels launched their attack.[37]

Buell later called the moment "critical," noting that if the 6:00 Confederate attack had come sooner "it would have succeeded beyond all question." He insisted that before the arrival of Ammen's troops there was not an infantryman in line on the Federal left for five hundred yards. There was a genuine belief in Buell's army (and to some extent in Grant's) that only Buell's timely arrival saved the Army of the Tennessee. "If we hadn't have come to his [Grant's] relief when we did his entire army would have been taken prisoners," Samuel Buford, a Nelson aide, wrote.[38]

Grant denied the desperation of the situation, stating that by 6:00 the enemy's momentum had "spent its force." Though such a statement was to be expected, Buell was in error about the number of infantry available on the Federal left. The fragmented remains of Stuart's brigade, reinforced with a number of stragglers who had finally recovered their nerve, deployed to the west of Ammen's men, in support of Captain Axel Silversparre's and Powell's guns. Ammen's and Stuart's infantry together numbered in excess of a thousand. A small detachment of the 15th Iowa and the 50th Illinois of Sweeny's brigade came on line with the 36th Indiana.[39]

Despite this fact, Grant's remarkable optimism, on the face of it, appeared delusional. He had sustained 7,000 killed and wounded and 3,000 captured, and had at least 10,000 others who refused to get back in the ranks. His last line, though formidable, was far from impregnable, and there are several respected modern historians who insist that, given the right circumstances, the line could have been broken.[40]

Yet Grant had a basis for his optimism; time was on his side. He knew that at least two divisions would arrive during the night, bringing 11,000 men, exclusive of the balance of Buell's army. To an Illinois officer he said: "The enemy has done all he can do today. Tomorrow morning, with General Lew Wallace's division and fresh troops of the Army of the Ohio, now crossing the river, we will soon finish him up." A correspondent remembered Grant's words to him: "Oh no, they can't break our lines tonight—it is too late. Tomorrow we shall attack them with fresh troops and drive them, of course."[41]

About dusk, a group of officers were standing around a smoldering fire when McPherson rode up. Grant asked: "Well, Mac, how goes it?" The engineer officer answered that at least a third of the army was out of commission and the balance of it disheartened. He inquired if preparations should be made for a retreat. "Retreat? No! I propose to

attack at daylight and whip them," Grant firmly stated. He expressed
to Sherman that the situation reminded him of the Confederate attack
at Fort Donelson. Both sides appeared defeated, and whoever assumed
the offensive "was sure to win."[42]

Sherman recalled that if anyone appeared nervous that evening it
was Buell. In a conversation with the Ohio general shortly after dusk,
Sherman stood in shock as he got the distinct impression that Buell
would not bring his troops across the river. He "seemed to mistrust
us," and said he "did not like the looks of things." Although never directly denying the comments, Buell brushed them aside. He said that
Sherman's concerns should have been allayed by the fact that at that
very moment his troops were crossing.[43]

Beauregard's Headquarters, Shiloh Church

THROUGHOUT THE EARLY AFTERNOON of April 6, Beauregard anxiously
awaited intelligence on the whereabouts of Buell's army. An aide had
earlier scouted toward Lick Creek and observed steamboats coming
upriver—an ominous sign. What he probably saw were the few boats
that had brought fresh troops to Grant's army that morning. By
midafternoon, a courier who had ridden from Corinth brought glad
news. A telegraph had been received from Colonel Ben Helm in
northern Alabama stating that Buell's army had diverted toward Decatur. Spirits soared! First a surprise attack so successful that Beauregard had been astounded, and now this. The Southerners seemed
fated to win. Their confidence proved unwarranted. Helm's scouts had
detected only Ormsby Mitchel's division marching toward Alabama.
The balance of the army had continued toward Pittsburg Landing,
and advanced units were even then arriving on the battlefield.[44]

Beauregard, reassured by Helm's telegram, had Jordan write a
message to the Confederate adjutant general in Richmond: "We this
morning attacked the enemy in strong position in front of Pittsburg,
and after a severe battle of ten hours, thanks be to the Almighty, gained
a complete victory, driving the enemy from every position."[45]

Shortly before sunset, from his headquarters near Shiloh Church,
Beauregard dispatched staff officers with orders to suspend the fighting. He did so, he later wrote, because he believed insufficient time re-

mained to gather his fatigued and scattered forces for a general assault. He also remained concerned about the arrival of Lew Wallace's division, and desired to get his army in hand before darkness. Because of the fire of the gunboats, further attacks would prove futile. It seems apparent, however, that he principally thought that Grant was whipped and could easily be finished off the next day. When Beauregard later came under severe criticism for the decision, he added that the van of Buell's army had arrived and that Grant had arranged sixty pieces of artillery at the landing—facts he could not have known at the time.[46]

Historians have argued convincingly that Beauregard was out of position to make such a call. He should have consulted with his commanders on the front line, rather than make the decision back at Shiloh Church, two miles from the front lines. From that location all he saw were stragglers, debris, and what appeared to be the wreckage of the army. Doubtless his two-month illness affected his decision not to ride to the front; the man bordered on exhaustion.[47]

Did sufficient time remain for another assault? Reports by Federal officers place the fall of the Hornet's Nest at between 5:30 and 5:45 P.M., with sporadic firing continuing until 6:00. The sun set that day at 6:10. Since some Confederate units were in the process of advancing when the order was received, it is conceivable that additional piecemeal assaults could have been made. Some historians insist that, given the stakes, an attempt should have been made, and that even a rare night assault could have been attempted.[48]

It is possible that the captured Prentiss may have affected Beauregard's decision. Peter W. Alexander, a free-lance correspondent, was at army headquarters when Beauregard and Prentiss met, and he recorded their exchange. "Well, sir, we have felt your power today, and have had to yield," related Prentiss. "You could not expect it otherwise," the Creole replied. "We are fighting for our homes, for our wives and children, and for generations to come after us, and for liberty itself. Why does your government thus war upon us, and seek us upon our own soil?" Prentiss answered that he did not desire to see the breakup of the Union, prompting Beauregard to retort that the Union was already dissolved. When questioned about the size of Grant's army, the Yankee general related with surprising candor that there were six divisions of about 7,000 men each, the total not surpassing 40,000.[49]

Alexander wrote that Beauregard continued the interrogation, but Henry Perry, another journalist present, admitted that the Louisiana general was called away and that a "by-stander" made additional inquiries. When the issue of Buell's army came up, the talkative Prentiss suddenly appeared hesitant. Although Alexander and Perry gave slightly different versions, the gist of Prentiss's response was that the Army of the Ohio was at Columbia or on the road and, even if sent to Pittsburg Landing, it would not arrive for at least forty-eight hours. Alexander detected an effort to evade or deceive.[50]

The *Richmond Dispatch* and *Savannah News* completely discounted Alexander's story. Colonel Jordan did in fact give a different story. Colonels Jordan and Thompson shared quarters with Prentiss that evening, where the Northern division commander openly boasted that Buell's army was on the way. "You gentlemen have had your way today, but it will be very different tomorrow. You'll see! Buell will effect a junction with Grant tonight, and we'll turn the tables on you in the morning." Jordan promptly showed him Helm's dispatch and assured him that he was wrong. At dawn the officers were awakened by the roar of artillery. Prentiss excitedly shouted: "Ah! didn't I tell you so! There is Buell!"[51]

Exactly how much information Prentiss dispensed is not clear. In explaining to Elise why the attack was suspended, Bragg related: "Gen'l Prentiss—a prisoner—had just told Gen'l Beauregard that they were defeated and in route across the river. The General [Beauregard] tho[ugh]t it best no doubt to spare our men, and allow them to go." This statement prompted one historian to suggest that Prentiss may have saved the Union Army twice on April 6—once by his stand in the Hornet's Nest and again when he helped convince Beauregard that Grant was defeated and retreating.[52]

Prentiss apparently believed as much. In a June 1862 interview with Peter Alexander he was quoted as saying: "General Beauregard stopped the pursuit at a quarter to six; had he used the hour still left to him, he could have captured the last man on this side of the river, for Buell did not cross till Sunday night." Prentiss claimed that Beauregard's decision had been based upon faulty information that he had imparted. Colonel Jordan, prompted by Beauregard, fired back an angry letter in August 1862, insisting that the withdrawal order had been well founded. He also believed the journalist to be the "dupe" of a high-ranking officer—probably Jones Withers. Withers submitted his written report concurrently with Alexander's article.[53]

The article, interestingly entitled "A Lost Opportunity at Shiloh," proved to be the opening shot in a war of words that extended well into the postwar years. For decades, proponents of the so-called Lost Opportunity theory, spearheaded by William Preston Johnston, insisted that the Confederate Army was on the verge of a smashing victory when the attack was suspended. Could a final assault have broken the backbone of Grant's Last Line? Had Beauregard ridden to the far right of the Confederate line, he would have seen the true state of affairs.[54]

Dill Creek

DUSK WAS FAST APPROACHING. At 6:00, Bragg hurriedly formed Withers's division and Anderson's brigade of Ruggles's division north of Dill Creek for one final assault. "One more charge, my men, and we shall capture them all," he proclaimed. There were probably not more than 4,000 infantrymen in a line that extended a half-mile. Chalmers's brigade, after replenishing its ammunition, held the far right at the Tennessee River bottoms, Jackson's brigade (minus the 18th Alabama, which was escorting prisoners) formed the center, and 224 troops of Gladden's brigade (remnants of the 22nd Alabama and 1st Louisiana) and Anderson's brigade (except the 20th Louisiana) held the left.[55]

As Bragg moved to the assault, his line was pounded by massed field artillery and the flank fire of the gunboats. Although casualties were taken in all brigades, the number does not appear to be high. Colonel John C. Moore of the 2nd Texas reported that the shells generally went high and did little damage. Gage's Alabama Battery, in support of Chalmers, took several direct hits from naval fire. One shell "killed three [horses] at one pop—all but the driver's horse," according to one of Gage's men. The Mobile gunners lost one wounded and seven horses disabled, and were forced to abandon one piece on the slope of the Dill Branch ravine before retiring.[56]

Blocking the Southern approach on the right was the natural barrier of the Dill Branch ravine. Virtually impassable at its mouth, it was difficult to cross even a half-mile upstream. Chalmers's and Jackson's brigades would have to descend a sixty-foot-deep slope with a shallow backwater at the bottom. At 6:00, the two brigades plunged into the ravine. Chalmers's skirmishers had penetrated to within a hundred yards of Stone's battery when Webster's massed guns erupted. A private in the 50th Illinois witnessed the results: "As soon as they reached the top of the hill in front, the batteries opened upon them, and such cannonading I never heard before. It completely checked the rebels." Jackson's men, many without ammunition, sheltered themselves from the galling fire. Within twenty minutes, the attack had failed. The complete ineffectiveness of the Southern return fire is demonstrated in the fact that Ammen's line lost only one man.[57]

During the assault, the 10th Mississippi veered by the right flank, along a road leading under a hill and around several ponds to the river. Meeting weak resistance, the troops moved toward the river and opened a sniping fire upon a gunboat, causing it to retire across the river. The 10th pushed on a little farther, to a place where the hills came to the river's edge. There they halted till they were ordered back up the bluff, past some Indian mounds on their left, and fell back to Cloud Field.[58]

Near dusk, Captain Thomas Stanford's Mississippi Battery unlimbered on the south bank of Dill Branch. The gunners waited for Chalmers's retreating Mississippians to get out of the way so that they could establish counter-battery fire. Since it was now dark, Stanford decided to withhold his fire, fearing that the gunboat would spot the flash of the guns.[59]

Although the assault had been easily repulsed, Brigadier General Withers was not finished. He rode off in search of support for his division, but to his astonishment he saw the troops to his left withdrawing. He sent aides to arrest the officer who had given the command, and ordered that the troops be returned to the fight. Word was received that the withdrawal order had come from army headquarters.[60]

It was the same in other sectors. At 5:30, Breckinridge's two brigades deployed in support of Withers's right flank. His troops came under gunboat fire; Trabue's brigade lost a dozen men. Meanwhile, the enemy's position was softened up by a barrage of twenty or so guns under the command of Major Shoup. This battery group had been engaged in Ruggles's barrage at the Hornet's Nest and moved as a composite unit along what today is known as Riverside Drive. Shoup's guns blasted away for some time, using a nearby store of captured ammunition. A New Orleans journalist noted that the earth shook and a sulphurous odor filled the air. At 6:00, Shoup sent Breckinridge a dispatch: "If you are going to charge, now is your time." The infantry were marching a few paces beyond the guns when Breckinridge received the withdrawal order.[61]

Bragg was stunned by the turn of events. Years later, Captain S. H. Lockett related that a Beauregard staff officer (Numa Augustin) rode up to Bragg as he observed Chalmers's failed assault. "The General [Beauregard] directs that the pursuit be stopped; the victory is sufficiently complete; it is needless to expose our men to the fire of the gunboats." An astonished Bragg answered: "My God, was a victory ever sufficiently complete?" The corps commander even considered disobeying the order, until he glanced to his left and noticed Polk's troops falling back. "My God, my God, it is too late!" he uttered.[62]

Years later, in correspondence with William Preston Johnston (and after relations with Beauregard had deteriorated), Bragg claimed that his troops were on the verge of a great victory when Beauregard's order called them back. The fire of the gunboats was harmless, and one final assault would have crushed Grant. Some historians have disputed these claims, stating that "memories" improved as years advanced. Thomas Connelly noted that Bragg did not express anger concerning the order in an April 8 letter to Elise, or in his official report on April 30. Dr. J. C. Nott, Bragg's medical director, said that he did not hear the general raise any protest. Two Beauregard staff officers, Colonels Jacob Thompson and Clifton H. Smith, gave postwar testimony contradicting Lockett's account. Another Beauregard aide, Alexander R. Chisolm, recollected that Bragg rode over to Beauregard's headquarters at Shiloh Church and in an excited manner said: "General, we have carried everything before us to the Tennessee River. I have ridden from Owl Creek to Lick Creek, and there is nothing of the enemy to be seen." The Creole calmly answered: "Then, General, do not unnecessarily expose your command to the fire of the gunboats."[63]

Some of the evidence may have been narrowly interpreted. Bragg wrote Elise: "We drove the enemy from every position, captured nearly all of his artillery, and were hotly pursuing him under my command when we were recalled." He noted in his report that a final assault held "every prospect of success." Surgeon Nott did not actually claim that Bragg did not protest; he only indicated that he heard the withdrawal order given. As for the testimony of Thompson and Smith, neither was present when Bragg received the order.[64]

Bragg apparently made no complaint when he later encountered Beauregard at Shiloh Church. He had plenty of opportunity: the two generals shared a tent (Sherman's) that evening. By that time, however, the issue was moot. Corroborating the Bragg version was the testimony of Governor Harris. As Bragg's command withdrew, the governor arrived on the scene. The general related that, had the order been handed him personally, he would have suspended it until Beauregard could have been apprised of the situation. Unfortunately, the order had already been passed down the line.[65]

Whether or not a final assault would have succeeded is a nonhistorical question, but certain facts can be established. Grant's Last Line was far stronger than the Hornet's Nest, which had required six hours to reduce. The suggestion that the Confederates could have permanently breached or pulverized the Federal line in an additional hour or so of piecemeal night assaults simply lacks plausibility.[66]

Whereas Bragg, Polk, Hardee, and Withers all concluded that a final assault could have succeeded, the reports of small-unit commanders tell a different story. Ammunition was low, the troops were exhausted, and some units had begun withdrawing even before the order arrived. Chalmers stated that his men were simply too exhausted to storm the hill. Indeed, thirty-three years later, he wrote that he had never received a withdrawal order and fought until dark. Jackson observed that his troops refused to advance without support. One of Bragg's own staff officers, Colonel David Urquhart, stated that at the time the order arrived "our troops at the front were a thin line of exhausted men who were making no further headway and who were glad to receive orders to fall back." He had previously reported to Bragg that one-third of the army was aimlessly wandering about plundering the Yankee tents.[67]

Headquarters, Third Division, the Shunpike

ON THE MORNING OF APRIL 6, Lew Wallace's division was scattered: Colonel Morgan L. Smith's brigade at Crump's Landing, Colonel John M. Thayer's 2nd Brigade at Stoney Lonesome (two and a half miles from the landing), and Colonel John Whittlesey's 3rd Brigade at Adamsville (five miles from Crump's Landing on the same road). Upon hearing the upriver sounds of battle, and before Grant ever arrived, Wallace made a decision—one entirely justified but also quite wrong, as it turned out. He concentrated his division not at Crump's Landing, but by closing up the 1st and 3rd Brigades on Stoney Lonesome.[68]

The basis for Wallace's decision, strangely ignored by many historians, cannot be understood apart from the events of late March. Fearful that his isolated division might be attacked, the Indianian had to determine the quickest route by which he could be reinforced. Believing that the relief column would come from the front of the army (Sherman's division), rather than the base (W. H. L. Wallace's division), the logical lifeline would be the Shunpike, a "blind and crooked" road that connected the Purdy-Hamburg Road with the Crump's Landing–Adamsville Road. The Shunpike, which struck the former two miles west of Owl Creek and the latter at Stoney Lonesome, was restored, corduroyed, and rebridged for rapid movement. Wallace also banked on a bit of strategy. If his 3rd Brigade was attacked at Adamsville and driven back toward Crump's Landing, reinforcements via the Shunpike would be in a position to assail the Confederate right. During the last week in March, Wallace accompanied Major Charles S. Haynes's battalion of the 5th Ohio Cavalry to inspect the entire route.[69]

By concentrating his division at Stoney Lonesome on the morning of April 6, Wallace was following his original plan only in reverse: rather than having Sherman come to him, he would be going to Sherman. Grant approved the disposition when he conferred with Wallace about 8:30 A.M., initially believing that the Pittsburg Landing fight might be a diversion.[70]

At 11:30, perhaps earlier, a messenger arrived from Pittsburg Landing. Captain A. S. Baxter came to Crump's Landing by boat and then rode to Stoney Lonesome. Wallace was handed an unsigned order from Grant, the precise contents of which are at the heart of the controversy. The original was lost by Captain Frederick Knefler, Wallace's adjutant, who tucked it under his sword belt and later misplaced it. Actually, Grant had only spoken the order to his aide John Rawlins. Rawlins later wrote it down (at Baxter's request) on a tobacco-stained half-sheet of paper. When Wallace asked about the progress of the battle, Baxter replied that the Rebels were being repulsed. Captain Knefler recounted that Baxter brought "cheering intelligence." Although Baxter's evaluation appears strange, it must be remembered that Grant, upon his arrival at Pittsburg Landing, had informed Buell that "all looks well."[71]

As to the content of the order, the accounts disagree. Grant claimed that Wallace was to bring up his division immediately by the River Road. Rawlins stated that the note essentially said to advance "on that road nearest to and parallel with the river, and form in line at right angles with the river," in front of the 2nd Division. Wallace concurred that the order stated to come up and form at right angles with the river, but disagreed that the 2nd Division was mentioned and a specific road designated. In 1868, two of Wallace's staff officers, Colonel James R. Ross and Captain Addison Ware, went a step further, writing that the order stated that Wallace was to come via the Purdy Road and join Sherman's division to form a right angle with the river. It is interesting that even Wallace himself did not make such a claim.[72]

The truth will probably never be known, and historians have lined up on each side. Grant later argued that it really did not matter what the order stated, for common sense dictated that the shortest route must be taken. The River Road, between Crump's Landing and Pittsburg Landing, was only six miles, some six to seven miles shorter than the Shunpike. But, and this is at the crux of the matter, the division was not at Crump's Landing—a fact known to Grant. Indeed, when Baxter arrived at 11:30, the 3rd Brigade, for some unexplained reason, had still not left Adamsville.[73]

Assuming that the River Road was specifically mentioned, Wallace faced a decision. Just past Stoney Lonesome, a small road angled off to the left of the Shunpike to connect with the River Road. It, too, had been repaired, but was not in as good condition as the Shunpike. For days Wallace had only contemplated the Shunpike route, and he was convinced that it was "the nearest and most practicable road to the scene of the battle." By taking the Shunpike, Wallace might very well have concluded that he was following the intent of Grant's order, which was to get to the right of the army in the shortest amount of time.[74]

If such a scenario occurred, it meant that Wallace disobeyed orders. The division commander vehemently denied such, but there are interesting pieces of circumstantial evidence. In ultimately reversing his course and taking the River Road, Wallace wrote, he was carrying out "the spirit of Grant's order [to] join the right of the army." If Wallace admitted to following the spirit rather than the precise letter of Grant's order once, perhaps he did so twice.[75]

In defending his original decision to come via the Shunpike, Wallace later implied that he was attempting to get into the Confederate rear and save the day. Grant hinted that Wallace may have vaingloriously attempted such a ploy. Wallace's assertion has no basis in fact, has been universally rejected by historians, and ultimately damaged his credibility. In presenting such a thought, however, the Indianian may have betrayed himself. If the division commander disobeyed the original order to come by the River Road, perhaps his "save-the-army" prattle was his way of proclaiming that his own idea was better, even if it did not precisely follow orders.[76]

Having decided upon the Shunpike, Wallace now made another decision. He allowed his men a full half-hour to have dinner, and he did not begin the march until noon. In retrospect, it sounded outrageous to squander even a minute, while men were dying by the hundreds only a few miles away. Wallace labored under the delusion that the Rebels were being repulsed, however, and he must be judged in that light. There remained time for yet more errors in judgment.[77]

WALLACE'S TROOPS made good time, albeit on the wrong route. By 1:30, the 1st and 2nd Brigades had cleared Overshot Sawmill and Snake Creek and approached a ridge a half-mile north of Clear Creek. At 1:30, a hatless, blond-haired cavalry lieutenant, with a streak of blood on his forehead, galloped up to Wallace and repeated Grant's request for the column to hurry up. By now some nagging questions were beginning to cross Wallace's mind. If the Rebels were being repulsed, why did the division have to hurry up? The only conclusion he could reach was that his men were needed for a flanking movement or for pursuit. If the enemy were being driven back, however, why did the sounds of battle remain so intense? Wallace figured that the Southerners, although repulsed on the Federal right, continued to press Grant on the left, near the river.[78]

At 2:00, Captain William R. Rowley arrived at division headquarters. Rowley found the 3rd Division resting, with Wallace, surrounded by his staff, at the head of the column. "I've had a devil of a time finding you," the captain stated. He mentioned that a courier had reported to Grant that Wallace would not move without a written order. "[That's a] damned lie!" Wallace blurted, pointing out that he was obviously on the march. Rowley informed him that he was not on the road to Pittsburg Landing, and that he had ridden farther from Crump's Landing to division headquarters than he had from Pittsburg Landing to Crump's Landing. Wallace fired back that it was the only road he knew to reach Sherman's and McClernand's camps. Rowley immediately pulled him over to the side and exclaimed: "My God! Don't you know Sherman has been driven back? Why, the whole army is within a half-mile of the river, and it's a question if we are not all going to be driven into it." Wallace asked if Grant's order was peremptory. "Yes," asserted Rowley, "he wants you at Pittsburg Landing—and he wants you there like hell!"[79]

For the first time, Wallace realized the magnitude of the crisis; he admitted to being "rattled." His cavalry returned shortly and confirmed that if the division continued on its present course it would come up in the enemy's rear. It was at this point, Wallace later claimed, that he momentarily contemplated attacking the Confederates in the flank and rear. If he had such a thought, he never expressed it to Rowley or any of his staff officers.[80]

Would such a plan have worked? In a 1901 visit to the Shiloh field, Wallace, in company with several of his former officers, visited the Owl Creek bridge. He found that the creek was actually a near-impenetrable swamp, except for the narrow half-mile corduroyed road leading up to the bridge. It is, of course, difficult to fathom how he could not have known this fact in 1862. The flooded (in 1862) crossing was guarded by two Confederate regiments and a section of artillery. Faced with such facts, the Indianian reluctantly conceded that his scheme, if indeed the thought ever occurred to him at the time, was not plausible.[81]

Wallace did not know precisely how to get to the River Road from his present location, short of returning to the crossroads just outside Stoney Lonesome. He dispatched his orderlies to bring in a local guide, forcibly if necessary. Meanwhile, the troops began retracing their steps. Rather than simply ordering an about-face, however, Wallace had the 1st Brigade reverse the order of march, thereby doubling back the entire length of the 2nd Brigade. The idea was to put his best regiments in the van. Although not of a comparable magnitude to some other blunders at Shiloh, the quirky decision wasted more precious time.[82]

Wallace's orderlies eventually found a farmer by the name of Dick Pickens who lived across from the Overshot Mill. Pickens led the column to a rugged country lane, not marked on any map, just past the mill. The troops filed off into the woods along the old path, crossing fences and traversing cornfields and pastures. The pace proved intolerably slow.[83]

At 3:30, John Rawlins and James McPherson caught up with Wallace on the Shunpike, near the mill intersection. Wallace blamed his tardiness on a guide who misled him, a fact never mentioned in his memoirs. "For God's sake move forward rapidly!" McPherson pleaded. Wallace assured him that the 3rd Division would arrive "in good season" and that his fresh division would turn the fight into a victory. An orderly was left at the crossroads to show the 3rd Brigade, which had not yet come up from Adamsville, the proper path to take.[84]

Rawlins fumed at the "cool and leisurely" pace of the march. He suggested to Wallace that the batteries be left behind, so as not to encumber the infantry. Wallace rejected the idea, although he did, at Rawlins's urging, send his eleven guns to the rear of the column, a move consuming another half-hour. Rawlins next stated that the regiments should be sent forward as soon as each reached the River Road. The division commander rejected the notion, declaring that Grant "wanted the division, not a part of it." He then coolly sat down on a log. Rawlins privately discussed with McPherson the idea of arresting Wallace (or so the Indianian later wrote) but backed off the idea. Despite Wallace's stubbornness and seeming indifference, the later charge of dilatoriness proved unjustified. Even with all the delays, the division marched fifteen miles in six and a half hours, a speed comparable to Nelson's division.[85]

Near the Snake Creek bridge, the land turned into bog and backwater. The River Road descended into a yellow slick of water, occasionally broken by black mud. The infantry and artillery slogged ahead, the teams staggering from side to side, with an occasional horse's head going underwater, only to rise up frantically. Citizens reported that the bridge was in Rebel hands; Wallace determined to fight his way through. Rawlins and McPherson rode ahead to investigate and found the information incorrect. The 24th Indiana advanced skirmishers to some tents reportedly held by the enemy. The Hoosiers were instead greeted with the cheers of Birge's Sharpshooters. The linkup had at last been completed; the time was 7:15 P.M.[86]

"They say I lost my way from Crump's Landing to the scene of battle," Wallace wrote his wife. "Time will get everything right at last—it did with the Fort Donelson fight." But time did not make amends. Grant and Halleck turned against him, as did most postwar writers. For forty years, Wallace vainly sought to clear his name. He claimed that Grant later exonerated him, but there is no evidence to substantiate this. In his memoirs, Grant resolutely stuck to his guns. He snarled that if Morgan L. Smith, the senior colonel, had been in command the 3rd Division would have arrived by noon.[87]

THE MIGHT-HAVE-BEENS of Shiloh are intriguing to contemplate. Was there a lost opportunity for the Confederates at 6 P.M.? What impact would Lew Wallace's division have had upon the battle if it had arrived in time? Such hypotheticals mask the more obvious truths. Even without Wallace's and Nelson's divisions on the battlefield, Grant's army rebounded and held the line remarkably well. As for the Confederates, if there was a lost opportunity it came at 11:00 A.M. and 2:00 P.M. rather than 6:00—when Johnston overcommitted troops to the left and misused his reserves, and when the Hornet's Nest became an obsession.

TEN

Counterattack

Behind the Confederate Lines

BEAUREGARD SPENT THE EVENING of April 6 in Sherman's tent, where he conferred with each of his corps commanders. All expressed elation over the day's work. Their optimism was affirmed at 9 P.M., when Chief Engineer Jeremy Gilmer reported that the enemy had gone. The various commands would regroup in the morning for a final mop-up action.[1]

Generally speaking, although there was an appalling mixing of units, Bragg's corps bivouacked in the vicinity of Sherman's camps, with the exception of Chalmers's brigade, which withdrew to Stuart's tents. Two of Breckinridge's brigades and Hardee's corps retired to McClernand's camps, although S. A. M. Wood's brigade apparently remained in Hurlbut's tents. Cheatham's division, through some mix-up never quite explained, withdrew three and a half miles to its bivouac of April 5. Several of Cheatham's regiments, the 7th Kentucky, half of the 9th Tennessee, Blythe's Mississippi Regiment, and the 154th Tennessee, became separated and remained at the front. Only Pond's brigade, in Jones Field, stayed on line, in close proximity to the enemy.[2]

A potentially dangerous breakdown of command occurred. Major Shoup waited until 11 P.M. for orders. Receiving none, he mounted his horse and went in search of a general officer. He finally found Pat Cleburne, sitting on a stump and sipping coffee. The Irishman admitted that he did not know anyone's whereabouts; he hardly knew where he was. He had a few of his own men with him, and a good many from other commands. There were no orders or plans for the morning.[3]

Plundering of the Union camps was rampant, although one Louisiana soldier complained that many of the tents had been ransacked a dozen times before night. John Kendall of the 4th Louisiana wrote that, though he personally attempted to sleep, hundreds roamed about with lighted candles in search of plunder. By midnight, a Louisiana surgeon estimated that nearly half the army was on the road to Corinth, "loaded with belts, sashes, swords, officer's uniforms, Yankee letters, daguerreotypes of Yankee sweethearts. . . . [Some were] prostrate with Cincinnati whiskey—some enlivened with Philadelphia claret." In the darkness, A. H. Mecklin heard some of his comrades quarreling over the "carnival feast." Many of the troops, like the high command, believed the battle to be essentially over.[4]

The thundering roar of the gunboats, though causing little damage, proved unnerving and got some of the men to sit behind trees throughout the night for shelter. To one soldier the reverberating sound "was like that of many thunder claps breaking over head at once." Some Confederates feared that the salvos were preparatory to a night assault. In a bizarre scene, four Southerners, playing cards in the supposed safety of a Sibley tent, received a direct hit from one of the big shells. Each was found with three cards in his left hand, and four cards lay on an oilcloth between them.[5]

Adding to the misery was a rainstorm that started at 10 P.M. and turned into torrents at midnight. Lightning flashes, followed by claps of thunder, were numerous. Soldiers of the 22nd Alabama complained that the canvas of their Sibleys had been so shredded by bullets that little rain was kept out.[6]

Even more unsettling were the moans of the wounded. The Rebels had sustained in the neighborhood of 8,000 casualties. One soldier noticed at least two hundred wagons, each filled with eight to twelve wounded, leaving the battlefield between 8 A.M. and 4 P.M. "The groans and piteous shrieks of the wounded were heart-rending in the extreme," recalled an infantryman. A Louisianian declared that throughout part of the night he could hear the moans of the wounded. A Kentuckian, working in a makeshift hospital till midnight, was sick and covered with blood, but conceded that he was "in [a] better fix than many."[7]

Not all the Confederates slumbered that evening. Sometime before midnight, Colonel Nathan Bedford Forrest dispatched a squad of men in Yankee coats to infiltrate the enemy lines near the Tennessee River. They returned and reported that the Federals were receiving heavy reinforcements. Forrest promptly aroused Brigadier General Chalmers and bluntly suggested that the Confederates either attack immediately or quit the field, for "[we] will be whipped like hell before ten o'clock tomorrow." Advised to go to a higher-grade officer, For-rest, at 1 A.M., awakened Hardee with the same message. Hardee in turn sent him to army headquarters, which the colonel was unable to locate in the rain and darkness. Forrest returned to his regiment and at 2 A.M. again sent out scouts. The report was the same—the Yankees were receiving heavy reinforcements. The Tennessee cavalryman again related this information to Hardee, who instructed him merely to maintain a strong picket. This significant intelligence was never mentioned in Hardee's official report.[8]

Over on the Confederate left, the men of Pond's brigade over-heard a commotion from the direction of the landing—the cheering of a large number of men. Thinking that their comrades had achieved success on another part of the field (why, after all, would the Yankees be cheering?), Pond's men joined in the celebration. When all had qui-eted down, another strange sound was heard—a band playing "Hail Columbia."[9]

With the 47th Tennessee, the Ridge Road

ON THE NIGHT OF APRIL 6, the six hundred raw recruits of Colonel Munson R. Hill's 47th Tennessee slogged tirelessly along the Ridge Road in the midst of a downpour. The regiment, poorly armed with shotguns, sporting rifles, and not a half-dozen bayonets, had left their camp of instruction at Trenton, Tennessee, on the morning of April 5, and arrived at Bethel Station at midnight. Awakened at 5 A.M. on the 6th, the troops moved out at 7 A.M., having eaten two crackers per man—their daily fare since April 2. At midnight the exhausted men could go no farther; Hill ordered a four-hour rest in the rain—no tents, no food. Awakened early on April 7, the men arrived on the bat-tlefield about 8 A.M. A staff officer led the regiment to Prentiss's sur-render site, where they were rearmed with a hodgepodge of rifles and percussion muskets and assigned to Preston Smith's brigade. The reg-iment would be the only reinforcements received by the Confederates during the battle.[10]

Aboard U.S.S. Tyler

U.S.S. *TYLER*, a five-year-old wooden sidewheeler fitted up as a gunboat in Cincinnati, periodically shelled the Confederate right flank on the afternoon of April 6. Lieutenant William Gwin, a native of Columbus, Indiana, and an 1846 Annapolis graduate, had received orders from Grant to use his own discretion. *Tyler*'s counterpart, U.S.S. *Lexington*, had earlier gone to Crump's Landing to check the security of that place, but returned to Pittsburg Landing at 4 P.M. Together the boats took up a position three-fourths of a mile above the landing and opened a brief fire at 5:35. At 6:00, *Tyler* again belched forth eight-inch shells in a twenty-five-minute salvo; the results were questionable, but sufficient to help influence Beauregard's decision to halt the Confederate attack. At 8 P.M., *Lexington* again steamed to Crump's Landing. An hour later, Gwin resumed his shelling, firing at intervals of ten minutes. *Lexington* returned at 1 A.M. and continued the shelling at intervals of seventeen minutes, then ceased at 5:30.[11]

Pittsburg Landing

FEDERAL REINFORCEMENTS continued to pour into Pittsburg Landing. By 9 P.M., Bruce's and Hazen's brigades of Nelson's division had crossed the river and, with the use of torches, deployed to the right of Ammen's brigade. Colonel William Hazen watched as a "continuous stream of men, a rod [five and a half yards] or more in breadth," pressed up the bluff. Skirmishers were cautiously advanced across Dill Branch, securing the south ridge. Between 9 and 11 P.M., Thomas Crittenden's division, two brigades of 3,800 men, arrived from Savannah—not overland, as originally planned, but via river transports. So reviled was Crittenden by the sight of the horde of skulkers loitering about the landing that he contemptuously wrote: "I did not wish my troops to come into contact with them." Crittenden's division, which extended Nelson's line westward, brought Buell's total strength to about 8,000. The men settled down in a drenching rain with no tents or blankets.[12]

BUELL PLANNED TO ATTACK in the morning with his own army. He had no consultation with Grant that night—indeed, he saw himself as independent. He later asserted that he "knew nothing of his [Grant's] purpose," although he presumed that "we would be in accord." This was a half-truth. In a meeting with Sherman at sunset, Buell was told of Grant's intention to attack. The understanding was formed that the Army of the Tennessee would be to the right of the Corinth Road and the Army of the Ohio to the left.[13]

THROUGHOUT THE LONG DAY, Grant had remained poised—perhaps his greatest contribution to the battle. It would later be said that if you hit Rawlins in the head you would knock out Grant's brains. In truth, Grant had sent his right-hand man away most of the afternoon. With or without Buell, Grant determined to attack at dawn, although, beyond a general advance, precious few specifics were forthcoming. He was not about to subject himself to Buell's contemptuous stares by consulting with him.[14]

Though Grant attempted to sleep under a tree near the landing, his ankle injury of two days earlier was giving him fits. He hobbled to the cabin on the bluff, but found it being used as a hospital. He found the drenching rain preferable to the screams of the wounded. Why did he not simply sleep aboard *Tigress?* Perhaps one postwar writer was correct: he was thinking that it would provide more fuel for the critics.[15]

Sherman came to see him at midnight. He found the army chief under his tree, hat pulled over his face, collar up, a dimly lit lantern in one hand, and puffing on a cigar. "Well, Grant, we've had the devil's own day, haven't we?" Came the reply: "Yes. Lick'em tomorrow, though."[16]

Headquarters, 3rd Division, Hamburg-Savannah Road

LEW WALLACE frantically interrogated Union stragglers. Having finally crossed Owl Creek, he did not know the location of the Rebel army, or, for that matter, the precise whereabouts of Grant's army. No two fugitives gave the same answer. Searching for reliable intelligence, he cautiously galloped along the Hamburg-Savannah Road through Russian Tenant Field. Just south of the field, he nearly rode over a sergeant of Company I, 4th U.S. Cavalry, in the darkness. The trooper informed him that his division was on the eastern slope of Tilghman

Branch, and the enemy on the opposite slope. "There," he whispered, "see the top line of the trees against the sky? Well, they [Rebels] had a battery here when the sun went down."[17]

The division deployed facing west along the Hamburg-Savannah Road: the 1st Brigade on the left, backed by Thompson's battery, the 2nd Brigade in the center, and the 3rd Brigade, supported by Thurber's battery, on the left. Having positioned his troops, Wallace crouched underneath a tree and covered his face with his cape in a vain attempt to escape the downpour.[18]

To one 3rd Division soldier, Henry Dwight of the 20th Ohio, it was a perfectly miserable night. "To lie on the ground was an impossibility, for the water was flowing in torrents. There were no logs or stones on which to sit, and all that weary night I stood or walked about in the pitiless rain, soaked through and through." The moans of the wounded could be heard in the distance, "but none dared try to help them."[19]

Cloud and Wicker Fields

AT 3 A.M. ON APRIL 7, the rain began to slacken. "Bull" Nelson, wide awake and eager for the coming fray, instructed his officers to advance at dawn. Two hours later, the division quietly moved southwest across the Dill Branch ravine, Ammen's brigade on the left, Bruce's in the center, and Hazen's on the right, the troops frequently having to stop to adjust their alignment. The men had not marched a hundred yards before they grimly viewed corpses from the previous day's fight. Although encountering no opposition for a half-mile, the division warily trekked through the wet underbrush and timber toward Cloud Field. Colonel Ammen rode in advance of his brigade, calmly advising: "Now, boys, keep cool, give 'em the best you've got."[20]

By 8 A.M., Crittenden's division had come up on Nelson's right and formed line of battle in Cloud Field, west of the Hamburg-Savannah Road. The 14th Brigade, under Kentucky slaveholder Brigadier General Jeremiah T. Boyle, was on the right, and Colonel William Sooy Smith's 11th Brigade the left. Attached to the latter were the 730 men of the 14th Wisconsin, one of Grant's regiments that had been stuck in Savannah on April 6. The division used the Pittsburg-Corinth Road as its line of advance.[21]

Nelson's skirmishers uncovered enemy pickets just beyond Hurlbut's old headquarters in Cloud Field. The Rebels fired and ran as "quickly as their legs would carry them," noted a Hoosier. As Hazen's brigade approached Wicker Field, it was suddenly struck by infantry fire backed by artillery. The 9th Indiana was advanced and took position behind a fence on the northern edge of Wicker Field. Fearing that the 9th's left might be turned, Hazen also moved up the 6th Kentucky, although it never became engaged. A sporadic fire continued for an hour and a half.[22]

Meanwhile, Brigadier General Lovell H. Rousseau's 4th Brigade of McCook's division formed in Stacy Field, extending Crittenden's right. The brigade consisted of the 1st Ohio, 5th Kentucky (the "Louisville Legion"), 6th Indiana, and three battalions of United States Regulars. McCook, the former colonel of the 1st Ohio, rode up to the Buckeyes and admonished them that he would "blow his brains out" if anyone in his old regiment ran. As the men filed past the landing, some of the Regulars were warned by Grant's men: "You'll catch regular hell today!" The brigade surged forward on the west side of the Pittsburg-Corinth Road. According to 19th U.S. Regulars Private A. B. Carpenter, "The ground [was] strewn with dead bodies, some wounded, some with their legs shot off, some almost tore to pieces, groaning in the greatest agony."[23]

By the time Nelson's men resumed their advance, the Rebels had been alerted. Bruce's brigade, passing through Wicker Field, was shelled by a hidden battery west of the Manse George cabin. Before the brigade could change front, the 2nd Kentucky was ambushed by the fire of an estimated two regiments, concealed in the underbrush, which also camouflaged the battery. Hazen's brigade, pressing forward to protect Bruce's right flank, was also struck by artillery fire, but with only slight effect. Nelson's right flank began to waver.[24]

Since Nelson had no artillery (he had been forced to leave his guns behind at Savannah), Buell diverted one of Crittenden's batteries to his aid. At 9 A.M., the four pieces of Captain John Mendenhall's Battery H/M, 4th United States Artillery, rumbled into Wicker Field. The rifled section on the left came under sniper fire and was compelled to maneuver 350 yards to the right and forward of the clearing. A spirited half-hour exchange ensued with a Rebel battery, the position of which could only be determined by the smoke of the guns. Skirmishers of the 9th Indiana and two companies of the 1st Kentucky succeeded in driving off the enemy gunners, but before the pieces could be hauled away the supporting Confederate infantry repulsed the bluecoats.[25]

Nelson's division passed beyond Bloody Pond and emerged from the timber, Bruce's brigade fronting the Peach Orchard and Ammen's brigade east of the Hamburg-Savannah Road, along the deep ravine that had served Stuart's brigade so well the day before. Hazen's brigade was on Bruce's right in the thicketed terrain around the Sunken Road, with skirmishers of the 9th Indiana occupying the Manse George cabin. The main Confederate line was sighted in the distance, extending from the Noah Cantrell house on the east to the Eastern Corinth Road on the west. Nelson was temporarily checked.

Davis Wheat Field

ON THE CONFEDERATE RIGHT, Brigadier General Jones Withers began rousing his troops about 4 A.M. Shortly after daylight, he received word that Chalmers's and Forrest's skirmishers had already been engaged— the firefight with Nelson's advance. Every available man was placed on the line, with Chalmers's intact brigade on the right at the Noah Cantrell house. On Chalmers's left was a makeshift brigade under Colonel John C. Moore, consisting of the 19th and 26th Alabama and the 2nd Texas. (Brigadier General Jackson had become separated from his brigade and would lead different regiments throughout the day.)

Extending Moore's left along the Purdy-Hamburg Road were a mix of regiments—the 5th Tennessee and 26th Alabama and, by the southwest corner of the Sarah Bell Field, the 1st (Battalion), 9th, and 15th Tennessee. Martin's (formerly Bowen's) brigade deployed along a ravine south of the Davis Wheat Field, along with the 25th Alabama, which joined the 1st Missouri. Stretching the line toward the Eastern Corinth Road were the 19th Louisiana, Crescent Regiment, 13th Arkansas, and 2nd Tennessee. Artillery supported the thin line: Robertson's battery at the southeast corner of the Sarah Bell Field, McClung's Tennessee Battery between the Bell and Davis Fields, the Washington Artillery at the wheat field, and Harper's Mississippi Battery at the Eastern Corinth Road.[26]

By 9 A.M., Hardee, commanding the Confederate right, had received attack orders from Beauregard. While assembling Martin's brigade, a battery accidentally fired into the rear of the 1st Missouri, which, remarkably, held its formation. Hardee led Martin's trans-Mississippians and a mixed Tennessee-Mississippi regiment known as the 2nd Confederate across the Davis Wheat Field and into the woods

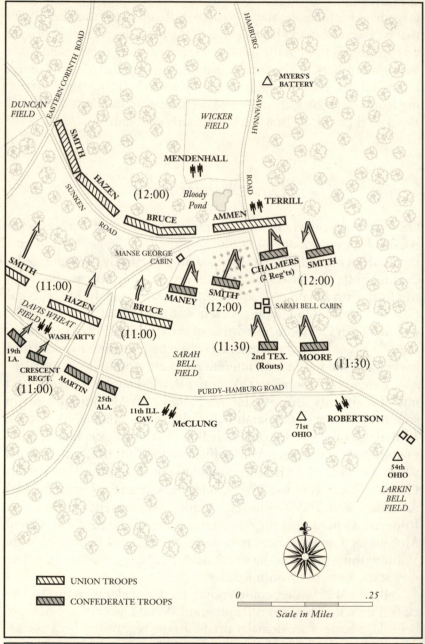

MAP 13: FIGHTING ON THE CONFEDERATE RIGHT

MYERS'S BATTERY

WICKER FIELD

DUNCAN FIELD

EASTERN CORINTH ROAD

HAMBURG

SAVANNAH ROAD

SMITH

HAZEN

SUNKEN ROAD

MENDENHALL

(12:00)

Bloody Pond

BRUCE

AMMEN

TERRILL

MANSE GEORGE CABIN

CHALMERS (2 Reg'ts)

SMITH (12:00)

SMITH

(11:00)

HAZEN

MANEY

SMITH (12:00)

BRUCE (11:00)

SARAH BELL CABIN

DAVIS WHEAT FIELD

WASH. ART'Y

(11:30)

19th LA.

CRESCENT REG'T. (11:00)

MARTIN

25th ALA.

SARAH BELL FIELD

2nd TEX. (Routs)

MOORE (11:30)

PURDY–HAMBURG ROAD

11th ILL. CAV.

McCLUNG

71st OHIO

ROBERTSON

54th OHIO

LARKIN BELL FIELD

⬛⬛ UNION TROOPS

⬛⬛ CONFEDERATE TROOPS

Scale in Miles

0   .25

11:00 A.M.–12:00 Noon   APRIL 7

west of the Manse George cabin. Southern artillerymen cheered them on: "God bless you [1st] Missourians!" A nearby cavalry company, the Memphis Light Dragoons, likewise shouted encouragement: "Well done Missouri, you have saved the guns!" The brigade made slow headway through the thickets, but finally smashed into Hazen's brigade and Mendenhall's guns.[27]

Realizing that Mendenhall's guns might be overrun, Hazen ordered, and personally led, a bayonet charge by the 6th Kentucky. His other regiments, the 9th Indiana and 41st Ohio, moved up in support, although the latter encountered stiff resistance at the Sunken Road. When the Rebels finally broke, the Buckeyes gave chase. "It was a wild pursuit, for a long distance, over rough country. We loaded and fired as we ran," recalled Lieutenant Charles H. Hills.[28]

The Louisiana Washington Artillery, having withdrawn from a more advanced position, was emplaced in the Davis Wheat Field. As Martin's men came streaming back, with Hazen's bluecoats in close pursuit, Captain Irving Hodgson found himself without infantry support and in imminent danger. He attempted to get his guns out, but at 11:00 Hazen's brigade, supported on the right by Sooy Smith's brigade of Crittenden's division, swarmed toward the wheat field.[29]

The New Orleans gunners poured some sixty rounds into the oncoming Yankees, blunting but not checking their attack. Orderly Gordon Bakewell was heard to shout, "We can do nothing more; let's get out of this, or we will all be dead men!" Hodgson finally did give the order to limber up, but according to cannoneer John Pugh, it came five minutes too late. "The balls [bullets] were falling around us like hail, and before we could get ready three horses at my piece and the same at two others were killed, our sergeant was killed and Lieut[.] Slocomb wounded, and we had to run leaving these three pieces on the field."[30]

An artillery officer frantically rode up to the Crescent Regiment and 19th Louisiana, in reserve south of the Purdy-Hamburg Road. "For God's sake, boys, hurry up or our battery is gone!" he screamed. The Louisianians made an impromptu charge that resulted in fierce hand-to-hand fighting. Sixth Kentucky Colonel W. C. Whitaker knifed to death a Southerner. In the confusion, Sooy Smith's men accidentally fired into Hazen's brigade, causing even greater chaos. Hazen himself became separated from his men and did not rejoin them until that afternoon. What remained of the battery was saved, although the Federals had jammed mud down the vents of the guns, rendering them temporarily useless. For the want of animals (twenty horses had been

shot down), the artillerymen were forced to leave behind three caissons, a wagon, and a traveling forge.[31]

The fighting seesawed as the Federals regrouped, counterattacked, and drove the Louisianians past the Purdy-Hamburg Road.
The 1st Missouri, lying under the brow of a hill, fired a volley into the
Federals that sent them reeling. Again the Crescent Regiment
charged, chasing the Federals back through the Davis Wheat Field
and into the underbrush, where they were in turn ambushed by Union
reinforcements and forced to withdraw. Hazen's brigade had been
shattered in the inconclusive fight for the Davis Wheat Field, losing
more than half of the loss suffered by Nelson's division during the entire day. The 41st Ohio alone sustained 140 killed and wounded, of the
371 engaged.[32]

The Sarah Bell Field

WHILE FIGHTING RAGED in the wheat field, Colonel Sanders D. Bruce's
Kentuckians battled to gain control of the Sarah Bell Field. For some
time now, Bruce had been having his own personal battle with Nelson,
which had frequently placed him in and out of arrest. Although surviving the battle unscathed, Bruce would suffer a paralyzing stroke on his
left side within two months. The 2nd Kentucky gained the woods between the Sarah Bell Field and the wheat field and overran one gun,
probably from McClung's Tennessee Battery. The 13th Kentucky lost
one-third of its men in the back-and-forth fighting that ensued.[33]

Bruce's brigade eventually retired, in conjunction with Hazen's
and Smith's brigades to the west. As the Kentuckians withdrew across
the Sarah Bell Field, Ammen's brigade approached from the north,
astride the Hamburg-Savannah Road. In the haze and confusion of
battle, Ammen's men could only see a line of troops approaching them.
Muskets were raised and cocked. Realizing that a tragedy was about to
unfold, Lieutenant Horace C. Fisher rode out toward 2nd Kentucky
Colonel Thomas D. Sedgewick and shook hands, thus averting a
calamity.[34]

HAVING REPULSED THE YANKEES, Hardee—slightly wounded in the
arm, his uniform ripped by several bullets—led a counterattack. He
advanced Colonel David Moore's makeshift brigade north astride the
Hamburg-Savannah Road. The troops were warned that Breckin-

ridge's men (Martin's brigade) were in their front and that under no circumstances should they fire into them. "[We] understood that we were in the second line of battle," 21st Alabama Captain Charles Stewart wrote his wife. They would learn tragically late that the only troops ahead were those of Jacob Ammen's brigade.[35]

The 2nd Texas grimly marched west of the road and into the Sarah Bell Field, placing it in advance of Moore's right wing, which struggled in the underbrush east of the road. "The silence was oppressive," recalled a Texan. "I do not remember that on our way across the open space, a command was given or a word spoken." Some two hundred yards ahead, on the northern edge of the field, a large force was spotted. The Texans were admonished not to fire. As the jagged line pressed ahead, a horrible volley suddenly blasted the Southerners—"Our line seemed actually to wither and curl up." The stunned Texans fled in confusion. As one soldier raised his musket to return fire, an officer threatened to blow his head off, still insisting that the troops were Confederate. So demoralized was the regiment that no amount of threats or persuasion could rally the men. Hardee sent word that he would call the Texans a "pack of cowards"; the men brashly replied that they "did not give a damn."[36]

AT 11 A.M., "OLD JAKEY" AMMEN's brigade, the far left of Buell's army, made headway south along the Hamburg-Savannah Road toward Sarah Bell's cabins. The Federals came under the crossfire of two batteries—Robertson's and probably McClung's; the line halted as skirmishers deployed. The Confederates held a ridge about four hundred yards away, in Stuart's abandoned camp. The 36th Indiana occupied a field east of the Bell cabins, behind a fence mostly now torn down. The 24th Ohio formed across the Hamburg-Savannah Road, and the 6th Ohio in the Peach Orchard.[37]

A section of Captain William R. Terrill's Battery H, 5th United States Artillery, moved up the road in an attempt to establish counterbattery fire. "Captain Tirrell's [sic] relatives are Secessionists," noted an admiring Buckeye. "His father and three brothers hold high positions in the rebel army and he had been disinherited and disowned by them for his loyalty for the Union." Terrill's guns temporarily silenced Robertson's battery and destroyed a caisson.[38]

REALIZING THAT the Confederate right flank was in trouble, Hardee frantically sought reinforcements to shore it up. Withers rushed forward the 5th Tennessee and 26th Alabama, the latter reduced to fewer than 150 men. The regiments were temporarily led by Chalmers, who turned command of his brigade over to Colonel R. A. Smith. Chalmers's ad-hoc demibrigade narrowly averted opening fire on the retreating 19th and 21st Alabama of Moore's brigade. Even so, some sporadic shooting mistakenly killed one and wounded another of the Alabamians.[39]

Chalmers's two regiments charged toward Sarah Bell's cabins, but were soon forced back. Colonel Smith advanced the Mississippi brigade in a desperate attempt to re-form a line. The Mississippians could not hold, were forced back three hundred yards, rallied, counterattacked, but were again driven south.[40]

Withers hastily gathered up portions of two brigades and sent them rushing to plug the hole on the western end of the Purdy-Hamburg Road. The reinforcements were the fragments of Cheatham's division, which had become separated from the parent command during the previous night. Colonel Preston Smith led with his 154th Tennessee, a portion of Blythe's Mississippi Regiment, and a company of the 2nd Tennessee. Colonel George Maney proceeded with the 1st Tennessee (battalion), the 15th Tennessee, and four companies of the 9th Tennessee. The latter had no flag, but picked up a lost Louisianian who carried his regimental banner.[41]

At noon, Smith's and Maney's sparse commands of Tennesseans and Mississippians struck obliquely across the Sarah Bell Field toward Hazen's and Ammen's brigades. Chalmers pleaded with his own men to join in the attack, but the Mississippians would not budge. Only after the brigadier clutched the flag of the 10th Mississippi did the brigade rally to the assault "with a wild shout."[42]

Terrill's battery withdrew from its advanced position at Sarah Bell's cabins to a location east of the Hamburg-Savannah Road and nearly opposite the Bloody Pond. One section supported Hazen's brigade, leaving four pieces to contest the Confederate onslaught. The Southerners closed to within fifty yards before the Regulars limbered up, leaving one caisson behind. At one point a twelve-pounder Napoleon gun was being served by only two men. The Rebels were eventually repulsed, leaving "piles of mangled bodies" fronting Terrill's position.[43]

At the height of the action, Brigadier General Nelson rode up to 6th Ohio Lieutenant Colonel Nicholas Anderson and shouted, "I have conferred upon your regiment the honor of defending the battery [Terrill's], the best in the service. It must not be taken!" The Buckeyes advanced with a yell, supported by the 2nd Iowa of W. H. L. Wallace's brigade, which had been assigned as a reserve to Nelson. Another reserve regiment, the 14th Illinois of Hurlbut's division, filed in on Ammen's left flank. As his troops raced ahead, Lieutenant Colonel Camm noticed "a pond, or sink hole, full of water [Bloody Pond]." It was now noon, and the situation at the Sarah Bell Field, after three hours of vicious fighting, remained stalemated.[44]

The Sunken Road

BY LATE MORNING, the fighting had begun to shift toward the center of the battlefield, along the Sunken Road perimeter. There Crittenden's 4,500-man division held a position on Nelson's right, extending beyond the Eastern Corinth Road. Sooey Smith's brigade occupied the left and Jeremiah Boyle's the right, with the 19th Ohio along the northern border of Duncan Field. Captain Joseph Bartlett's Battery G, 1st Ohio Light Artillery, a Cleveland outfit, unlimbered across the Eastern Corinth Road. At 10:30, Smith's men had participated in the assault on the wheat field, but by noon had been driven back to their original position. Boyd's brigade had been generally passive throughout the morning. Their moment of action was shortly to come.[45]

ROBERT TRABUE's Confederate brigade formed along the Purdy-Hamburg Road early on Monday morning. Intense firing could be heard on the far right, indicating that the battle had been renewed. Bragg ordered Trabue to support Hardee's assaults, which brought the brigade toward the center and Crittenden's Yankee division; it would be Kentuckian against Kentuckian. As Trabue's men hastened into position, 5th Kentucky Sergeant Henry Cowling stuck a hunk of Ohio cheese on the end of his bayonet. Colonel Thomas Hunt saw it and "almost took his head off and made him throw the cheese away."[46]

Trabue's men filed east of the Joseph Duncan cabins, where, unknown to Trabue, Bragg detached the 4th Kentucky and 4th Alabama Battalion to make an attack west of the cabins. The balance of the brigade continued to the Eastern Corinth Road, where it turned north into the Hornet's Nest area. A single volley was fired, but the contest soon focused upon an artillery duel.[47]

Captain Edward Byrne's battery set up on the southwestern edge of Duncan Field, where it quickly became engaged with Bartlett's Ohio battery. The 19th Ohio lost several killed and wounded in the shelling, forcing it back into the timber. Byrne's guns were on a slight ridge, so with each recoil the pieces had to be rolled back into position. The cannoneers soon collapsed from exhaustion, and infantry volunteers kept the guns in action.[48]

Following the artillery duel, Morgan's Kentucky Squadron impetuously charged across Duncan Field—incredibly, coming to within thirty yards of the Federal line before being forced back. As the horsemen retired, a Kentuckian lamented, "Many an empty saddle was seen."[49]

Although several Union reports stated that Sooey Smith's brigade was assaulted, Trabue specifically stated that he did not attack, having only the 5th and 6th Kentucky and a remnant of the 3rd Kentucky. About noon, Crittenden attempted to turn Trabue's left. Bragg personally ordered Byrne's battery eight hundred yards to the right, where the cannoneers virtually emptied their caissons of projectiles, including a homemade canister manufactured in Greenville, Mississippi, and packed with chainlinks and nails.[50]

Crittenden's men slashed through the tangled underbrush of the Hornet's Nest, experiencing the same difficulties as had the Rebels the day before. The 14th Wisconsin of Boyle's brigade broke under heavy fire and ran pell-mell through the ranks of the 13th Kentucky. The 9th Kentucky lost six killed and twenty-one wounded as it hacked its way through the thickets. As the regiment slogged shoe-deep in mud over a small branch, it was suddenly ambushed by Southerners hiding in a hollow barely ten yards away. The Rebels slowly retired to a clearing (probably Barnes's Field) three hundred yards beyond the branch.[51]

Duncan Field

The heart of Brigadier General Lovell H. Rousseau's 4th Brigade of McCook's division comprised three battalions of United States Regulars. Although they were supposedly more experienced than volunteers, such may not have been the case. Edgar R. Kellogg, an officer in the 1st Battalion, 16th United States, revealed that almost all of the men in his outfit were raw recruits, and that he was probably the only man who had ever been in combat.[52]

McCook advanced Rousseau's brigade to the right of Crittenden's division, in the woods north of Duncan Field and west of the Pittsburg-Corinth Road. McCook's 5th Brigade, that of Colonel Edward N. Kirk, had not yet come up from the landing, so Rousseau's right was in the air, guarded only by a section of Terrill's battery. The Rebels brought up a battery under cover of the Duncan cabins and zeroed in, forcing Rousseau to advance his line 150 yards to escape the punishing shelling. Some Federal guns (probably Terrill's) accidentally fired into the 6th Indiana. All the while, the Southern infantry remained concealed in the woods south of Duncan Field.[53]

Although facing a powerful brigade, Bragg, either unaware of Buell's presence on the field or simply reverting to his mostly unsuccessful frontal-assault tactics of the day before, illogically ordered a remnant of Trabue's brigade, the 4th Kentucky and 4th Alabama Battalion, forward, supported by three regiments of Russell's brigade—"a very small force." The Federal skirmish line, consisting of three companies of Regulars, quickly gave way; one company collapsed in panic. Viewing the Confederates approach, one Yankee officer noted: "Soon that dingy gray line had become well defined; three flags floated not three hundred yards distant." Trabue's advance was easily checked.[54]

The inevitable happened; Rousseau counterattacked. "You ought to have seen the Rebels run," related Corporal Alexander Varian of the 1st Ohio. "They were in the woods and we charged across the open field [Duncan] with an awful yell; they only waited to give us a couple of vollies [sic] when they broke and ran for dear life."[55]

In this single action the 4th Kentucky lost a dozen officers killed and wounded, including Major Thomas B. Monroe, the twenty-eight-year-old former mayor of Lexington. His body was buried by his comrades under an oak tree, some eighteen inches in diameter, near Shiloh Church. An inscription carved on the tree read: "T. B. Monroe, C.S.A., Killed April 7, 1862." By 1883, the tree was six inches thicker in diameter, but the inscription was still plainly visible to battlefield visitors. One body left by the Kentuckians was that of Confederate Kentucky Governor George W. Johnson, mortally wounded in the thigh and abdomen. He died aboard a hospital ship two days later.[56]

Beauregard's Headquarters, Near Shiloh Church

NEW ORLEANS JOURNALIST Alexander Walker happened to be near Beauregard's headquarters on the morning of April 7. He noted for his readers that it was a cold morning and murky clouds still spotted the skies. About 5:30, the crack of musketry was heard in an eastwardly direction, prompting the Creole to calmly remark, "The enemy must be near. We will mount, gentlemen, and go to the front." Passing Gibson's brigade, the army commander was heard to shout, "Men, the day is ours, you are fighting a whipped army!"[57]

Despite Beauregard's glee, his army was, to put it bluntly, in an organizational mess. An estimated 8,000 Southerners had become casualties on the first day's battle, and, deducting skulkers and those already on the road back to Corinth, not 20,000 infantry reported on the line. Major W. D. Pickett rode up and, "after a good deal of wrangling," explained the whereabouts of Hardee. During the night, Hardee and Bragg had exchanged wings, although two of Bragg's brigades (Chalmers's and Jackson's) remained on the right. No one knew exactly where Polk was, and Captain B. B. Waddell was sent to bring him up.[58]

Cavalry units and staff officers scoured the rear to round up stragglers and organize them into ad-hoc companies. Engineer officer Captain Samuel Lockett collected bits and pieces of a half-dozen regiments, the 7th and 9th Arkansas having the largest representation, and formed them into the thousand-man "Beauregard Regiment," which was held in reserve.[59]

Jones Field

COLONEL PRESTON POND deployed his brigade in front of a ravine in northern Jones Field, near where it had camped the previous night. Pond did not realize that the army had withdrawn one mile during the night, leaving his lone brigade dangerously exposed. The Orleans Guard Battalion, down to ninety-two men, was coupled with the 18th Louisiana, but together they numbered fewer than a good battalion. The Louisianians were instructed to turn their blue coats inside out and expose the white linings to avoid any more mishaps. The 38th Tennessee had reconnected with the brigade during the evening, adding some strength.[60]

At 6:30 A.M., Yankee skirmishers moved forward and a battery (9th Indiana Artillery) opened fire at four hundred yards. Ketchum's battery was brought up, and a half-hour duel ensued. There were several infantry casualties, including Private John McDonald of the 18th Louisiana. The blast of a shell caused him to make a complete somersault, although, incredibly, he walked away with only a slight injury.

One of Ketchum's officers, Lieutenant Phil Bond, disgustedly related that, "at the third or fourth fire [round], the Infantry on our right ran like sheep. I think they were Tennessee [38th Tennessee] troops."[61]

By 9 A.M., Pond's infantry had been driven back toward the Purdy-Hamburg Road, leaving Ketchum's battery and the Texas Rangers to conduct a rearguard action. Ketchum withdrew to a position southeast of Jones Field and, at 10:30, resumed firing. Pond credited the Mobile gunners with saving the brigade.[62]

AROUND 9 A.M., BRIGADIER GENERAL RUGGLES directed Gibson's brigade to advance toward Jones Field and then oblique to the right. Thomas C. Robertson admitted that the men had not expected to fight and had loaded themselves with plunder. His own share of the spoils included a new blue uniform, an overcoat, a canteen, a new Enfield rifle, and three haversacks filled with coffee, cheese, ambrotypes, stationery, and love letters.[63]

As Gibson's men deployed in the woods southwest of Jones Field, Beauregard ordered up S. A. M. Wood's brigade to their right and two hundred yards in advance, to "conform with their movements." Two regiments and a battalion had been detached to escort Yankee prisoners to Corinth, leaving only the 27th and 44th Tennessee, 8th Arkansas, and 9th Arkansas Battalion—not 650 men. The Tennesseans in the brigade had begun their morning with a stirring speech from Governor Harris. Both brigades had difficulty in crossing an offshoot of Tilghman Branch—a ravine estimated by Gibson to be fifty to sixty feet deep.[64]

As Gibson's men prepared an attack, a soldier in the 4th Louisiana discovered a fife. Remembering his service as a fifer in the Regular Army during the Mexican War, he picked it up and played "Dixie." The shrill notes could be heard for some distance, and a storm of cheers followed. Beauregard passed up and down the line shouting, "The day is ours! One more charge and we have the victory!"[65]

The focus of the Confederate assault would be Lieutenant Charles H. Thurber's Battery I, 1st Missouri Light Artillery, a company recruited in St. Louis. As Captain Noah S. Thompson's battery pulled back to replenish its caissons, Thurber's battery set up in the central portion of Jones Field at 10 A.M. The main infantry assault was preceded by a cavalry dash upon the battery by two companies of the Texas Rangers. The troopers were easily brushed aside by skirmishers of the 8th Missouri. Gibson's subsequent attack was also checked, although the 1st Arkansas succeeded in capturing one gun before being driven back. As the Rebels streamed back, Lew Wallace placed Morgan L. Smith's brigade of one Missouri and two Indiana regiments forward of Thurber's guns. At Gibson's next sortie, an officer of the 4th Louisiana noted that a line of Yankees suddenly arose from the dead cornstalks and stubble and delivered a murderous fire. S. A. M. Wood's brigade fared little better. As two-thirds of his line cleared the skirt of woods and marched into the open field, Thurber's battery delivered an enfilade fire that sent the Southerners running for cover in the woods.[66]

By about 10 A.M., Ruggles had organized a ragtag line of mixed regiments south of Jones Field. The line ran northwest to southeast for a quarter-mile. On the extreme left were the 1st Louisiana and 22nd Alabama, together only three hundred men. The 6th Tennessee and six companies of the 9th Tennessee were to the right, followed by the 33rd Tennessee, three of Russell's regiments, and Wood's brigade, now down to fewer than six hundred troops. The infantry was backed by three batteries—Ketchum's, Smith's, and Girardey's, the latter supported by the 7th Arkansas. There were probably no more than 2,500 men in position, which at that time represented the entire Confederate left flank. In the face of Lew Wallace's 10:30 general advance, Ruggles pulled his line back to the south. S. A. M. Wood reported "large masses of enemy" on his right.[67]

Wharton's Texas Rangers, attempting to get around the Federal right flank, collided with the 23rd Indiana of Thayer's brigade in Sowell Field. The Texans fled in confusion, but soon re-formed and advanced as a dismounted skirmish line. Wharton notified Beauregard that the Yankees were in strength in his front.[68]

EARLY ON APRIL 7, Grant and Lew Wallace passed through a field behind the 1st Brigade, where the army commander studied the terrain for a moment. "Move out that way," he remarked as he pointed west. Wallace acknowledged the order and asked if he was to take any special formation in the attack. "No," said Grant, "I leave that to your discretion." With these few words, Grant launched the attack from the Union right. He did not mention the previous day's battle, Buell's arrival, specifically who would be supporting Wallace, or any order of battle.[69]

The fresh 3rd Division was put in motion. Using the swampy lowland of Owl Creek as protection for his right wing, Wallace guided his three brigades in a half-wheel movement to the southwest, with Morgan L. Smith's 1st Brigade in the lead and the others in echelon.

By 10 A.M., his 7,500 infantry extended from "an oblong field [Sowell's]," through a strip of woods, to a "cleared field, square and very large [Jones]." Here the division was checked by Ruggles's line in the timber to the south.[70]

The remains of Sherman's division came up on Wallace's left, with Buckland's brigade taking position along the ridge mid-field in Jones Field, and Stuart's brigade, with the 13th Missouri attached, in the woods to the east. Three guns each of Mann's and Willard's batteries provided artillery support. Being only a shadow of its former strength, the command extended barely four hundred yards.[71]

At 10:30, a general advance began, just as the troops received word of Buell's landing. Alexander Oliphant, a Hoosier in Wallace's division, described the electric reaction: "Then we advanced yelling like we were wild. . . . And they [Rebels] ran—not retiring in good order, but they ran for their lives."[72]

MCCLERNAND'S AND HURLBUT'S divisions, conforming with the movements of Sherman and Wallace to the right and Rousseau's brigade to the left, trudged through the woods between Jones and Duncan Fields. The one-mile-long Federal line, between Hurlbut's left and Wallace's right, formed roughly a large curve advancing against a convex Confederate line. At 10:30, however, the Rebel left (Russell's, Gibson's, and Wood's brigades) retired south toward the Purdy-Hamburg Road, leaving the blue tidal wave virtually unopposed.[73]

At 10:30, Cleburne's brigade, or at least the eight hundred men who reported on the line, marched obliquely to the southeast of Jones Field, east of a tributary of Tilghman Branch. His closest support to the right was a portion of Trabue's brigade at Duncan Field, a conservative 425 yards distant. Cleburne's left was in the air, and it was precisely from that direction that he saw a blue line "as far as the eye could see." Girardey's Georgia Battery unlimbered in front of Cleburne's men and prepared for action. Two unidentified Federal batteries, one of them possibly Bouton's, opened a deadly fire, which was answered by Girardey's and Byrne's batteries. The latter, on the Pittsburg-Corinth Road, fired obliquely across Cleburne's line of march, knocking down large overhead limbs, which killed some of his men. The exchange broke off after a half-hour, the gray cannoneers having been overmatched.[74]

Cleburne received an order to attack, in conjunction with Trabue's brigade to the right. The Irishman protested the ludicrous order,

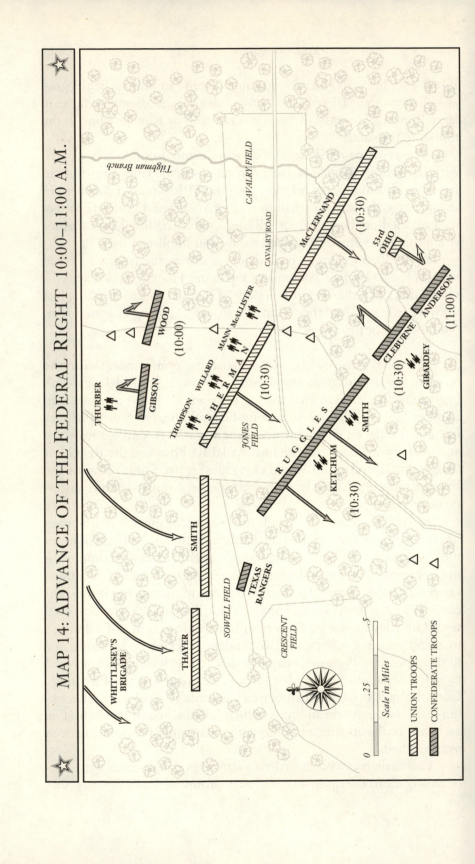

MAP 14: ADVANCE OF THE FEDERAL RIGHT 10:00–11:00 A.M.

Tilghman Branch

CAVALRY FIELD

CAVALRY ROAD

McCLERNAND (10:30)

53rd OHIO

WOOD (10:00)

THURBER

GIBSON

MANN McAllister

THOMPSON

WILLARD

S H E R M A N (10:30)

JONES FIELD

CLEBURNE (10:30)

GIRARDEY

ANDERSON (11:00)

R U G G L E S

SMITH

KETCHUM (10:30)

SMITH

TEXAS RANGERS

SOWELL FIELD

WHITTLESEY'S BRIGADE

THAYER

CRESCENT FIELD

Scale in Miles

0   .25   .5

UNION TROOPS

CONFEDERATE TROOPS

pointing out that his left was completely outflanked. A courier returned with a reply: the order came from Bragg, and Cleburne should attack immediately. Cleburne obeyed, but with predictable results. His isolated brigade was hurled back, with only the 15th Arkansas, down to fifty-eight men, bothering to rally.[75]

Anderson's brigade now went forward to blunt the Federal drive, taking a position behind a breastwork of logs in the camp of the 20th Illinois. Interestingly, the first regiment thrown against them was Jesse Appler's 53rd Ohio—one of Sherman's outfits, but now attached to McClernand. Mirroring their actions of the previous day, the Buckeyes again broke and ran. So disgusted was McClernand at their "disgraceful and cowardly" conduct that he ordered the regiment from the field. With his remaining two brigades he easily drove off Russell's men and reoccupied his camps.[76]

Water Oaks Pond
and Review Field

RESPONDING TO AN IMPERATIVE ORDER, Cheatham's division belatedly came up from the rear. Although delayed by a stampede of fugitives (an indication that something was wrong), Cheatham arrived at a field south of Shiloh Church at 8 A.M. Half of his command had become separated during the night and was already engaged on the Confederate right, leaving him only five regiments—154th Tennessee, 6th Tennessee, 9th Tennessee (six companies), 15th Tennessee (a portion), and 2nd Tennessee (100 men). Breckinridge rode to the church and pleaded for support on his left flank. Cheatham rushed his "division" forward past Shiloh Church, formed line of battle, and advanced at the most opportune moment—just as McClernand and Sherman approached from the north and Lew Wallace from the northwest.

At noon, the Tennessean assaulted east of the "crossroads" and north of Water Oaks Pond. Journalist Walker pronounced the charge "splendid," and a gleeful Beauregard even applauded. Sherman's and McClernand's commands were driven north for three hundred yards, as Cheatham rode up and down the line waving a battle flag and cheering on his men. Sheer force of numbers slowly drove Cheatham back toward Water Oaks Pond, where, along with a conglomerate of reinforcements, a line was formed. In addition to Cheatham's regiments, all or parts of Gibson's, Anderson's, and Wood's brigades came on line. Fearful that his troops would hesitate at the three-foot-deep pond, Wood plunged into the water, his men following with a cheer. For the next hour (until 2 P.M.), some of the fiercest fighting of the day raged along Bragg's patchwork line. When S. A. M. Wood's right was threatened, Rutledge's Tennessee Battery came up and kept the enemy in check for an hour and a half. The regiment next to Wood wavered and then broke, but was rallied and sent back into the fight.[77]

THE CONFEDERATES were being driven back all along the line. By noon, Sooy Smith's brigade pressed Trabue's three regiments down the Eastern Corinth Road. To the east, Boyle's brigade entered Duncan Field. Rousseau's brigade, having crushed Trabue's left wing in northern Duncan Field, advanced on either side of the Pittsburg-Corinth Road.

Russell's small brigade confronted Rousseau's troops along the northern portion of Review Field. Both of his flanks were turned, and a deadly crossfire opened. Within twenty minutes, Russell lost more men than in the rest of the battle. Colonel A. J. Vaughn of the 13th Tennessee was dismounted by a cannon shot. After a forty-minute stand, Russell's men withdrew to avoid annihilation.[78]

Only Stanford's Mississippi Battery, on the eastern edge of Review Field, remained to offer resistance—a plug in a dike that would eventually break. The Mississippi gunners held their fire till Rousseau's and Boyle's troops came within canister range. "Large gaps were made by every gun at each discharge," Stanford noted. "Three regimental flags being in full view, I gave the order to point at them, and soon had the satisfaction of seeing two of them fall to the ground, both being raised again. One was again cut down."[79]

Cannoneer John Magee described the panic: "We stood firm, pouring the canister into them until they got within 75 yards and then the captain gave the order to limber up. Most of the horses were killed, and those living were so badly tangled it was impossible to get them in order under the heavy fire of minie balls coming in around us."[80]

The battery was engulfed and nearly destroyed. Stanford lost twenty men, four guns, and all six caissons. "Lewis Matlock (No. 3 at my gun) was shot in the head and killed instantly," gunner George Jones wrote in his diary. "He died with a smile on his face. . . . [I] called to friend Lacock to come on, but poor fellow—the yankees got him."[81]

BY 1:30, THE BIG FIGHT was shaping up for control of the Water Oaks Pond sector. There the Confederates had put up such fierce resistance that Sherman's and McClernand's lines were on the verge of breaking. At the crucial moment, a relieved Sherman glanced up to see the van of Buell's army. What he in fact saw was Colonel August Willich's 39th Indiana, a crack German regiment in Colonel William Gibson's 6th Brigade, which had passed around the left of Rousseau's brigade and was advancing in column through the thickets north of Review Field. The ridiculous formation drew an enfilade fire that struck the regiment from front to rear, igniting a stampede. Willich later claimed that he was subjected to friendly fire from Rousseau's men in his rear, but a Regular Army officer scoffed at the allegation. He suggested that it was merely an excuse to divert attention from Willich's blunderous formation.[82]

Rousseau's brigade pressed ahead, penetrating as far as Woolf Field, retaking McClernand's headquarters, as well as a couple of Federal guns lost the previous day. The brigade struck the Confederate line east of Water Oaks Pond, forcing it back south after a fierce forty-minute struggle. Having exhausted their ammunition, Rousseau's troops were replaced by McCook's 5th Brigade, under Colonel Edward N. Kirk, which passed to the west of Woolf Field and toward Water Oaks Pond.[83]

LEW WALLACE'S PERFORMANCE on the Union right had proved disappointing. When the Confederates drove Sherman and McClernand back at Water Oaks Pond, Wallace lost his offensive edge and became overly concerned about "an isolation from the rest of the army." Rather than attacking the enemy flank, Wallace went on the defensive, bringing up Thurber's battery, his reserve regiment, and the attached 15th Michigan. Whittlesey's brigade went to the left to support Sherman. Wallace later grumbled about his lack of support and a shortage of ammunition, but, considering his relatively light opposition (his 7,500 men sustained only 296 casualties all day), it is difficult to see how the Confederates could have resisted a determined onslaught.[84]

Only when the Confederate position at Water Oaks Pond was cracked did Wallace resume the offensive. Although one of Whittlesey's regiments remained on the left of the division, the balance of the brigade resumed its place on the right, retaking McDowell's headquarters in Ben Howell Field at 2:00. Thurber's five-gun battery was brought up to knock out a bothersome two-gun section in the camp of the 46th Ohio. The 20th Ohio sustained eleven casualties in the shelling—"muskets and bayonets at all exposed were bent and snapped off," reported Colonel Manning F. Force.[85]

• • •

MAP 15: WATER OAKS POND 10:00 A.M.–2:00 P.M. APRIL 7

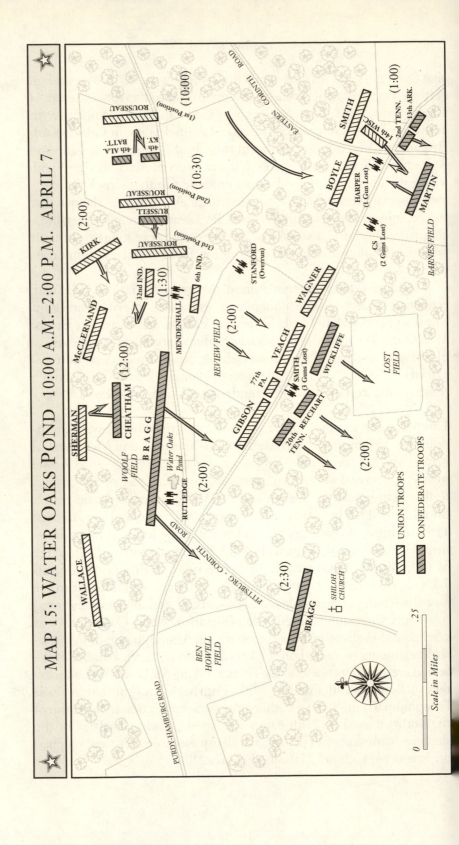

WALLACE

SHERMAN

KIRK (2:00)

ROUSSEAU (1st Position) (10:00)

McCLERNAND

4th ALA. BATT.

4th KY.

ROUSSEAU (2nd Position) (10:30)

RUSSELL

CHEATHAM (12:00)

WOOLF FIELD

BRAGG

32nd IND. (1:30)

ROUSSEAU (3rd Position)

6th IND.

MENDENHALL

Water Oaks Pond

RUTLEDGE (2:00)

STANFORD (Overrun)

REVIEW FIELD

77th PA. (2:00)

VEACH

WAGNER

SMITH (3 Guns Lost)

GIBSON

WICKLIFFE

20th TENN.

REICHART

LOST FIELD

(2:00)

BOYLE

HARPER (1 Gun Lost)

SMITH

2nd WISC.

MARTIN

2nd TENN. (1:00)

13th ARK.

CS (2 Guns Lost)

BARNES FIELD

PURDY-HAMBURG ROAD

BEN HOWELL FIELD

PITTSBURG - CORINTH ROAD

BRAGG (2:30)

SHILOH CHURCH

EASTERN CORINTH ROAD

UNION TROOPS

CONFEDERATE TROOPS

0   .25

Scale in Miles

THE FIGHTING RIPPLED EAST along the Purdy-Hamburg Road, centering on the southern edge of Review Field. Maney rushed reinforcements to that sector—Colonel Joel Battle's 20th Tennessee and Maney's own brigade, under 7th Kentucky Colonel Charles Wickliffe. Beauregard also sent an impromptu brigade under Colonel August Reichard, consisting of the 20th Louisiana, the 5th (later 35th) Tennessee, and a battalion of stragglers under Captain Lockett. The Southerners attacked at noon, in conjunction with Cheatham's assault at Water Oaks Pond, making momentary gains before being driven back with heavy losses. Wickliffe fell mortally wounded with a bullet wound to his head. The 20th Tennessee entered the battle on April 6 with 380 men, and retired the field on the 7th with only 122.[86]

As Rousseau's and Kirk's brigades lunged into the fight at Water Oaks Pond, Rousseau's 6th Indiana turned to support Mendenhall's battery, set up along the Pittsburg-Corinth Road and facing south. The battery fell back, passing through the ranks of the 6th, whereupon the Hoosiers unleashed twenty rapid volleys that sent the Rebels reeling.[87]

The 6th Indiana was replaced by Gibson's brigade, but by the time it came up the Southerners had regrouped and were advancing under cover of the undergrowth and tents. Gibson's infantry surged along the western edge of Review Field, the 15th Ohio on the right, 39th Indiana in the center, and 49th Ohio on the left. The enemy made a desperate attempt to turn his left flank, but was prevented by two guns of Bouton's battery and the 77th Pennsylvania of Kirk's brigade, the latter having rushed to the relief of the 49th Ohio. At 2:00 on April 7, the Pennsylvanians charged across Review Field, capturing two guns (probably from Smith's Mississippi Battery) and Colonel Battle of the 20th Tennessee, and subsequently repelling two cavalry sorties. "At half past 2 o'clock the Rebbels [sic] commenced to flee and the retreat soon became jeneral [sic]," wrote one of Gibson's men.[88]

By 2:30, the Federals had retaken the Purdy-Hamburg Road, from the "crossroads" east beyond Review Field. Veach's brigade of Hurlbut's division, in reserve till noon, moved up to the southern portion of Review Field, securing McCook's left. Colonel George D. Wagner's sizable brigade of Wood's division came up on Veach's left. Together these troops parried sporadic infantry and cavalry sorties and eventually drove the Rebels south.[89]

Intersection of Eastern Corinth and Purdy-Hamburg Roads

HOLDING THE INTERSECTION of the Eastern Corinth and Purdy-Hamburg Roads were Bate's 2nd Tennessee and the 13th Arkansas, supported by Harper's Mississippi Battery and a section of Bankhead's battery. At 1:00, the infantry withdrew south in search of ammunition, leaving Harper's under-strength battery to fare for itself. The Mississippi cannoneers were nearly engulfed by Boyle's brigade (minus the 19th Ohio, sent to support Nelson), but miraculously escaped with the loss of only one gun. Fifty-ninth Ohio Colonel James P. Fyffe reported that his regiment passed "a field to the left [Davis Wheat Field]," and observed on the crest of a ridge "a rebel battery [Harper's] apparently disabled." The artillerymen fled "to a log house [Jacob Barnes's] about 100 yards distant."[90]

Smith's brigade came crashing through the Davis Wheat Field, east of the intersection. Given the courage of some men and the cowardice of others, Smith admitted that his line formation collapsed into a column of attack. The attached 14th Wisconsin raced ahead eighty paces of Harper's captured gun, where it was met by a counterattack by Martin's Confederate brigade and hurled back. Stated 14th Wisconsin member James Newton: "We charged one of their batteries [Harper's] and took it & then they charged in their turn and we couldn't hold it, so we spiked the guns & set fire to cartridges [carriages] so that they couldn't use it on us any more. The next time we charged on that battery we were supported & kept it." At 2:00, Terrill's battery unlimbered on a hill southeast of the intersection and fired directly into Barnes Field, assisting in repelling the Confederate attack.[91]

To the west of the intersection, a mix of Grant's regiments pressed relentlessly forward. The 8th and 18th Illinois (Hare's brigade), supported by the 7th Iowa on the right and 13th Iowa on the left, managed to overrun an annoying two-gun section south of the Purdy-Hamburg Road. The pieces were promptly turned on the retreating foe, creating further disorder in their ranks.[92]

Shiloh Church

By EARLY AFTERNOON, it had become obvious that Buell's army was on the field. The Confederates had been caught off-guard by the sheer magnitude of the Northern assault. Mississippi Private A. H. Mecklin "began to have doubts as to the issue [outcome] of this contest. I knew that the enemy were reinforced and stoutly." By 2:00, the entire Southern line had been driven back south of the Purdy-Hamburg Road.[93]

On the Confederate left, Bragg established a new line north of Shiloh Church and on either side of the Pittsburg-Corinth Road and urgently called for reinforcements. Beauregard committed Preston Pond's brigade—the last of his reserves. Pond had earlier sparred in Jones Field, but Beauregard had pulled the brigade back to a ravine south of the church. The Creole galloped up to the 18th Louisiana and Orleans Guard Battalion (acting as one unit) and seized the colors of the latter. The flagstaff holding the banner was a relic of Fort Sumter, and had been sent by Beauregard to New Orleans earlier in the war. He now personally led the Louisianians to the left of Bragg's line, shouting, "Charge them, charge them my braves!" When a private pleaded with the general not to expose himself to the enemy's fire, Beauregard snapped: "Never mind my good fellow, you do your duty and I will do mine." The private replied that it was his duty to die and not the general's. The army commander smiled and moved to the rear. He then returned to the church and led two Tennessee regiments into position, although he was too weak to carry their large and heavy battle flag.[94]

Beauregard hastily sought other reinforcements. The 5th Kentucky was thrown into line, as well as the 17th Louisiana and a battalion of stragglers. Conrad Chapman, belonging to the latter, wrote: "We were got into line on a hill close by and a Louisiana colonel [Lieutenant Colonel Charles Jones] with his arm in a sling took command of this battalion which was larger than any brigade on the field."[95]

Silas Grisamore of the 18th Louisiana described the fighting along Bragg's line: "At one time Gen. Bragg came up and rode out to the thickets to within 100 yards of the enemy, saw their movements, came back, ordered Ketchum's battery to open on them and, then taking our flag, advanced ahead of us." Colonel Mouton received a facial wound that partially injured his left eye. By 2:30, Bragg's line teetered on collapse.[96]

Colonel Jordan, increasingly concerned for the safety of the army, asked Beauregard if it was not time to disengage. "General, do you not think our troops in the condition of a lump of sugar thoroughly soaked with water, but yet preserving its original shape, though ready to dissolve." The Louisiana general, accepting the inevitable, sadly replied, "I intend to withdraw in a few moments."[97]

Preparations were made for an orderly withdrawal. Colonel Chisolm was sent with a company of cavalry to the rear to repair the road. Jordan was instructed to prepare a final position on the ridge south of Shiloh Church—the swampy morass that had served Sherman so well the day before. A battery was placed at the church and another on the Pittsburg-Corinth Road. Staff officers were sent with orders for a withdrawal. "It was sad beyond measure," Bragg wrote Elise, "but I suppose there was no hope of success against such odds, tho I received the order with surprise and refused to obey until I sent and inquired if it was correct." The retreat commenced at 3 P.M.[98]

Frantic efforts were made to get off as much ordnance as possible. B. B. Waddell, one of Beauregard's aides, was placed in charge of gathering up as many small arms as possible. Because of a shortage of horses, Captain Melancthon Smith decided to leave three of his own guns in lieu of three captured James rifles, and Byrne left some of his caissons behind in order to carry off some of Cobb's guns. The cavalry set fire to the tents, although some were so rain-soaked that they could hardly be burned.[99]

Confederate Last Position, South of Shiloh Branch

By 3:00, THE FINAL CONFEDERATE DEFENSE line had been pieced together. The makeshift line, running northwest to southeast, comprised 1,500 infantry by S. A. M. Wood's estimate. Jordan would later place the number at 2,000 infantry and twelve to fifteen guns. The six regiments, mostly from Wood's and Trabue's brigades and some Louisiana regiments now reduced to companies, were backed by cavalry with instructions to "cut down" any shirkers.[100]

If the Federals had any serious intention of pressing their advantage, which they did not, they were deterred by one final assault. Spearheaded by Colonel R. L. Looney's 38th Tennessee, Beauregard's line made a 4:00 sortie. "We drove the enemy far beyond his camp, my regiment being far in advance of any other troops, when we were ordered to retire," Looney proudly reported. One of his Tennesseans wrote in his diary: "Our regiment was ordered to make a last charge which they did in most gallant style. The enemy's lines were in the woods and we were exposed on the brow of a hill. Their fire was well directed and cut our regiment right and left. We still advanced in the face of their galling fire. They slowly retired. As we advanced, we run over piles of their dead and wounded."[101]

At 5:00, the Southern infantry withdrew. Major Francis Shoup, in charge of the artillery, looked to his rear and was horrified to see no supporting troops within sight. While the guns were being limbered up, Shoup frantically searched for the rear guard. He found no guide at a fork in the road, and so took the most promising path. After riding some distance, he found nothing. "There I was, abandoned by the army at the mercy of the enemy, with all those guns!" he recalled. He doubled back, took the other road, and eventually found the column. His guns were saved![102]

An anemic Yankee advance was undertaken by Veach's brigade and the 1st Ohio of Rousseau's brigade. "We at first saw no enemy in our front," noted Private Levi Wagner, "but we soon discovered that they had left a strong skirmish line behind, who now opened on us, making things lively for a while, as they were behind trees and hard to get at." The chase was at last called off.[103]

Lew Wallace, whose division had been kept at bay by mere pockets of infantry since 2:00, continued his ineffectual performance. Wallace's troops required a protracted time to procure additional ammunition, the ordnance wagons being held back by deep ravines. The division halted at Shiloh Branch at 5:00.[104]

Eastern Corinth Road

BRIGADIER GENERAL JAMES A. GARFIELD would escape injury during the Civil War, only to be assassinated in 1881 as president of the United States. On the afternoon of April 7, 1862, however, the former Ohio Republican senator had his sights only on getting into the Battle of Shiloh. His 20th Brigade of Wood's division left Pittsburg Landing at 1:30 and reached the front via the Eastern Corinth Road at 3:00. Garfield deployed his three regiments to the right of Wagner's brigade. The division had not proceeded far when it was shelled by a Rebel battery off to the right. Buell halted the division so that McCook and Crittenden could come up and Nelson could go south along the Hamburg-Savannah Road. Although they gathered up forty prisoners, Garfield's men never pulled a trigger. One of his Buckeyes noted that the Southerners were "too quick for us for by the time we got *there* they were in full retreat."[105]

Intersection of Bark and Pittsburg-Corinth Roads

BEFORE QUITTING THE FIELD, Bragg ordered Brigadier General Jones Withers to form a rear guard on the crest of a hill near the intersection of Bark and Pittsburg-Corinth Roads. It was a tiered defense, with cavalry thrown out in advance, backed by the 19th Alabama and Crescent Regiment, and in reserve the 1st Missouri, 2nd Texas, and Byrne's battery. As the Louisiana Washington Artillery passed to the rear, twelve volunteers joined Byrne's men to serve the guns. "We expected to remain only three hours," noted Louisiana cannoneer Richard Pugh, "but were kept there all night, standing in the rain, I without either jacket, overcoat or blanket, having lost my jacket in the engagement. . . . As it turned out, there was no necessity of leaving a battery there, for the enemy did not dare move from the place to which we have driven them." The column eventually plodded toward Michie's farm; the Battle of Shiloh was over.[106]

ELEVEN

Retreat

Grant's Headquarters

WITH OVER AN HOUR of sunlight remaining, Grant chose not to pursue the fleeing Rebels. His reasons for doing so were threefold. First, the sheer exhaustion of his men. Even Brigadier General McCook of Buell's army, who came into contact with Grant, appealed to have his wearied division sent no farther. Second, Grant suspected that the enemy were still in his front and might renew the attack. Third, even though Grant was the senior officer on the field, the quasi–command structure constrained him from giving a direct order to Buell. Some historians have added a fourth reason—Halleck's April 7 order to "avoid another battle, if you can."[1]

Grant's explanation bears scrutiny. The troops were unquestionably fatigued, but, as Buell noted, they would have obeyed orders. The Federals were certainly no more jaded than the Confederates, who continued to move. Grant's concern that the enemy remained in his front was legitimate, although, strangely, he never mentioned this fact in his memoirs. A cautious probe was nonetheless in order, if for no other reason than to determine the direction of the enemy. Nor was Halleck's April 7 order a deterring factor: Grant considered himself as having full authority to advance as far as Monterey.[2]

The dual field command was more problematic. After the war, when both Grant and Buell pointed fingers at each other, Buell insisted that Grant was the senior officer and that it was his call to make. Yet he also wrote that he considered himself independent of Grant. It is clear that Buell was hesitant to press ahead. Although he had a fresh division on the field (Wood's), the Ohio general argued that he had no cavalry or knowledge of the terrain. It appears that the relationship between the generals was so strained that neither sought communication with the other.[3]

The final Federal blunder had been committed. What Grant could have done was to send Lew Wallace's division south along the Pittsburg-Corinth Road. Wallace would, of course, have encountered Breckinridge's defense line at the Bark Road. The Confederate rear guard, coupled with a heavy rain that night, probably would have stopped Wallace, but an effort should have been made. In truth, Grant never contemplated a pursuit, only a reconnaissance to determine if the Rebels were still in the area. The Illinois general had had enough and was more than willing to call off the fight. Thus the ultimate irony of the battle: despite appalling casualties on both sides, not an inch of ground had exchanged hands.[4]

With the Retreating Confederate Army

HAD GRANT CHOSEN TO PURSUE the retreating Confederates pitilessly, he would have found an army teetering on disaster. "Our condition is horrible," Bragg notified Beauregard at 7:30 A.M. on April 8. "Troops utterly disorganized and demoralized. Road almost impassable . . . Our artillery is being left all along the road by its officers; indeed, I find but few officers with their men." By 2 P.M., Bragg had dismounted two hundred cavalry to use their horses to bring in the artillery. Fatigue parties were put to work in repairing the muddy road. If the Federals vigorously followed, Bragg admitted, the entire rear of the Confederate Army would have been mauled—"The whole road presents a scene of rout."[5]

Beauregard did all that he could with his limited resources. He notified the Corinth quartermaster to have all unattached animals immediately sent to the rear to bring in wagons and guns, two-thirds of the horses to go by the Monterey Road (by far the worst) and one-third by the Ridge Road. Chalmers, at Monterey, was ordered to send out work parties to obstruct the Hamburg Road. Two guides and a promise of replacements were sent to Breckinridge, who commanded the rear guard at Michie's farm.[6]

The wounded suffered horribly, and many had to be left in homes along the road. "Some of them as they jostled along over the rough road in springless wagons gave most pitiful groans, which made me forget I was hurt," recalled Conrad Chapman. The hospital of the 21st Alabama had to be abandoned, along with seventeen men in the ambulance squad and twenty-five wounded. Eleventh Louisiana surgeon Charles Johnson informed his wife that he had "been on my feet since early morning [April 9] attending to our wounded, who have suffered terribly."[7]

The badly churned roads became nearly impassable. "I am not exaggerating when I inform you that all the way the mud was knee deep, and we were obliged to wade several streams which were waist deep," Private Thomas Robertson noted to his mother. In a letter to his wife, Sergeant R. A. Oliver of the 17th Louisiana wrote that "the trip back to Corinth used me up worse than the battle as we were gone five days and slept about ten hours during the time. We ate nothing almost, traveled very hard, and it rained on us every night." Private R. L. Davis of the 47th Tennessee was of a like mind. "We have been without anything to eat but two crackers per day since Sunday morning & traveled in water & mud waist deep all day."[8]

Lieutenant Phil Bond of Ketchum's battery had doubts whether his outfit would make it back to Corinth. A wrong path was taken in the darkness, and the horses had to be led two miles back to get on the correct road. The guns got mired in mud, and it was 1 A.M. on April 8 before the battery made it to Michie's farm. In the morning the men "looked as if they did not have life enough left in them to move. I was completely saturated with rain, and was standing in the mud ankle deep all night."[9]

The Michie Farm

THE MICHIE FARM, the site of the confusing traffic jam that had delayed the Confederate attack on April 5, again became the focal point of the campaign on the afternoon of April 8. It was here that Breckinridge posted the rear guard of the army. If the Federals undertook a pursuit, it would have to be checked at this place. The Kentucky general had grave concerns about his position. He had only 1,200 infantry, which he feared would not stand after the first volley, and four guns of Byrne's battery. A general hospital with nearly four hundred patients had been established at the farm. A New Orleans journalist witnessed the grotesque sight: "Arms, legs, hands, and feet, just amputated lay scattered about." There were only two days' rations for the men, and no forage for the animals.[10]

After numerous false alarms on the morning of April 8, during the early afternoon Breckinridge received hard intelligence of the approach of the enemy, both on the Monterey Road, to his right, and from the north, along the Ridge Road. Scouts placed the number at five hundred cavalry and several regiments of infantry on the latter. The Kentuckian ordered his cavalry to make a stand, and at 2:30 anxiously notified Beauregard: "We can hear firing in that [northern] direction between them and a part of our cavalry."[11]

Fallen Timbers

THE PERFUNCTORY FEDERAL PURSUIT on the morning of April 8 began belatedly thanks to a blundering episode in John A. McArthur's brigade. Soldiers clearing their weapons ignited a fifteen-minute firefight with an imaginary enemy that brought whole brigades to the front line and sent general officers scrambling. "It was the only time we ever heard Colonel [Charles] Harker swear," remembered a Buckeye in the 65th Ohio.[12]

At 10 A.M., Wood's division finally linked up with Hildebrand's brigade of Sherman's division at the intersection of the Bark and Pittsburg-Corinth Roads. At Sherman's suggestion, Wood's two brigades filed onto the Monterey Road, while Sherman bore to the right on the Ridge Road. "We run them so close that they had to abandon a great many of their wounded and they burned a large amount of provisions," noted one of Wood's men. After only slight harassment from Wirt Adams's Mississippi cavalry regiment, the division returned to camp.[13]

After noon, Dickey's battalion of the 4th Illinois Cavalry sighted the enemy on the Ridge Road, in a muddy cotton field bordered by a clearing of fallen timber several hundred yards wide. Coincidentally, it was the precise location of Hardee's skirmish of April 4. Sherman deployed two companies of the 77th Ohio as skirmishers, supported by the balance of the regiment—in all, only 240 men. The 77th was backed by Dickey's battalion, with carbines at the ready.[14]

Sherman was about to discover just how dangerous Colonel Nathan Bedford Forrest could be. Although a thin line of dismounted cavalry was slowly retiring, the former Memphis slave-trader had actually plotted an ambush. Behind a wooded ridge that ran parallel to the road, Forrest had posted 350 troopers—220 Texas Rangers, forty men of his own regiment, one company of Adams's cavalry, and two companies of Morgan's Kentucky Squadron. Armed with only shotguns and revolvers, the men were instructed to get within twenty paces before opening fire.[15]

Forrest perceived that the bluecoats were having difficulty clearing the fallen timber and a small creek. As he gave the order to charge, his men burst over the ridge in a terrifying scene. Suddenly, remembered 77th Ohio Lieutenant Colonel Wills DeHaas, "a fierce yell filled the air." The skirmishers prematurely discharged their weapons and then stood with fixed bayonets in double line. Forrest's men shotgunned them at short range, sending the infantry fleeing for their lives. The engagement turned into a wild melee, as the entire 77th Ohio and Dickey's battalion broke in panic to the rear. Even Sherman had to admit that he and his staff were forced to flee "through the mud, closely followed by Forrest and his men, with pistols already emptied." With only slight casualties (probably fewer than a score), Forrest killed fifteen, wounded twenty-five, and gathered up fifty-three prisoners.[16]

Sherman sent an aide ahead to form the brigade hurriedly in line of battle. Forrest, either exuberantly or with his horse out of control (depending upon accounts), singly crashed into the line of waiting infantry. Shouts of "Shoot that man!" and "Knock him off his horse" rang out. One Federal fired a musket into the Tennessee cavalryman's side at point-blank range; the ball lodged in his left hip, against the spinal column. Forrest spurred his horse and, according to Sherman, "escaped in the woods to the south." Though painfully wounded, Forrest would see active service again within two months.[17]

Breckinridge pulled his force south of Michie's, leaving the general hospital with 280 Confederate and fifty Union wounded. Sherman paroled the medical staff, buried the dead, and sent for wagons to have the patients removed. The Yankees had nonetheless gotten their noses bloodied and were happy to call it quits.[18]

Pittsburg Landing

As the Federals sifted through the debris of battle, the magnitude of the narrowly averted disaster became evident. "The tents were still standing, though riddled with bullets," recalled Sherman. "At the picket rope in front lay two of my horses, dead. Dead bodies of men in blue and gray lay around thick, side by side." McClernand found his tent perforated with twenty-seven bullet holes. "Within a radius of 200 yards of my headquarters tent the ground was literally covered with dead." Inside his tent, a wounded Rebel had rested his head on the general's desk, and there he died.[19]

The carnage was beyond description. "Where the Morton [Indiana] Battery was captured every horse was stretched on the ground. The stench was intolerable," reported an Indianapolis correspondent. Another journalist counted two hundred Rebel dead in the space of an acre. In one field, probably Rea's, the remains of a Confederate battery were found, with cannon and caissons where they had been left. Thirty bodies and thirty dead horses were discovered in an area fifty feet square.[20]

Evacuating and caring for over 8,400 Federal wounded and 1,000 wounded Southern prisoners proved to be an enormous undertaking. The primary hospital was the small log cabin on the bluff (located approximately where the United States flag stands in the National Cemetery). A Dr. Stephens was placed in charge, with only one steward and two male nurses. On Monday evening, April 7, several additional surgeons arrived, but after applying bandages to two or three of the less seriously wounded, they departed. Stephens had to perform all operations by himself until Tuesday morning, when two more surgeons arrived.[21]

Surgeon Robert Murray, Buell's medical director, arrived midday on April 7. He found nearly 6,000 wounded, with no bedding, no food or cooking utensils, and no table furniture. It proved impossible to obtain tents, and many of the wounded lay exposed to the rain on Sunday and Monday nights. There was hay for bedding aboard some of the transports, but the landing was so clogged that none could be obtained. Many of the regiments in Grant's army had lost all of their medical supplies.[22]

The *City of Memphis*, the only hospital boat with the army, transported two loads of wounded to Savannah, and on the third trip continued on to Mound City, Illinois, with 700 patients. During the battle, 1,800 wounded were transported to Savannah: 1,000 placed in ventilated buildings, 200 in houses, and 600 in tents. Every house, church, and barn was filled to overflowing. Six additional boats were turned over to the medical department on Tuesday, Wednesday, and Thursday. These transports were filled to capacity and sent to St. Louis, Louisville, New Albany, and Cincinnati. Surgeon Murray bitterly complained that the boats sent by the various governors refused to receive wounded from other states or Rebel wounded, "no matter how uncomfortable on shore."[23]

The wounded told stories of excruciating pain. William Swan of the 3rd Iowa was grazed in the head and shot in the arm and shoulder. He was taken aboard the commissary boat *Continental*, where "nearly every spot upon which a man could lie was occupied—on boxes, and under tables; the floor of the cabin was covered." No surgeons attended the wounded, and from Sunday night to Wednesday morning the 1,200 patients had no water—"hundreds begged for water," wrote Swann. Erhard Dittman of the 45th Illinois, shot in the thigh and with a broken leg, was taken aboard the *City of Memphis*. "My suffering was indescribable. My leg burned as if a fire were kindled under it," he wrote his parents.[24]

Numerous boats hurriedly steamed to Pittsburg Landing to evacuate the wounded, but the transports were often understaffed and had few supplies. The *Hiawatha* had five surgeons and thirteen nurses to tend 285 wounded, but no beds, medicines, or stores. The doctors were eventually able to procure eighty cots from the army and blankets and medicine from the Sanitary Commission. The *City of Memphis* was devoid of all stores and sustained forty deaths on the voyage north. The *D.A. January* had 450 wounded aboard, but only two doctors and several "dressers."[25]

The U.S. Sanitary Commission supplemented the work of army surgeons. The Chicago office chartered one boat, Cincinnati two, St. Louis two, Louisville two, and Evansville one. Governor Yates chartered *Black Hawk* and hastened to Pittsburg Landing with over one hundred doctors and nurses, as well as 3,000 Enfield rifles and three six-pounder rifles. At one time forty boats, two and three deep, lined the bank at Pittsburg Landing. Scores of bags of white corn were laid across the muddy bank, creating a kind of wharf.[26]

On April 8, a Confederate officer bearing a dispatch from Beauregard to Grant was stopped four miles from Michie's farm. The Confederate commander requested permission to send details through the lines to bury the Southern dead. In his reply, Grant wrote: "Owing to the warmth of the weather I deemed it advisable to have all the dead of both parties buried immediately. Heavy details were made for this purpose, and it is accomplished."[27]

Burial details were put to work on the grim task of disposing of the dead. Wilbur Crummer was in a party ordered to collect the bodies found in the camp of the 45th Illinois and two hundred yards in advance. The Rebels were buried two deep in a trench sixty feet long and four feet deep. The only monument was a sign carved with Crummer's pocket knife: "125 rebels." The sign over the Union trench read: "35 Union."[28]

"I dread tomorrow," a Hoosier wrote his mother on April 8. "Burying those unfortunate Rebel dead. They are swollen and smell so awful bad and terrible many of them. I do not see how I can stand it." Forty-first Illinois soldier J. F. True explained the process: "We dig holes in the ground, lay them side by side without any coffin, fire a salute over the grave, and then cover their cold bodies with the Tennessee clay. The Secesh we bury with less ceremony, dig a hole, roll them in and cover them."[29]

Though the Southerners officially tallied 1,723 dead, only 1,624 were gathered up on the immediate battlefield and buried. In one of the larger trenches, 147 Confederates were interred, including three lieutenant colonels and four majors. The Rebels were buried, according to one Union soldier, "with as little concern as I would bury a dog." The task (despite Grant's response to Beauregard) was not completed until April 11. The stench from rotting bodies and hundreds of dead horses proved almost unbearable.[30]

The Cherry Mansion

ALTHOUGH BELIEVED TO BE DEAD, the still-breathing body of W. H. L. Wallace was found on April 7. He was eventually taken to a room in the Cherry mansion, where he lingered until Thursday, April 10. Tending his fearful wound was his wife, Ann, who, ironically, had come to Pittsburg Landing on April 6 aboard the *Minnehaha* in a surprise visit. "Will recognized my voice right off and clasped my hand. I noticed it and exclaimed, 'He knows me!' " she wrote. Although he could speak, the brigadier general was encouraged to remain silent. He initially appeared to grow stronger, but fever set in, and he lapsed into a delirious state. Knowing that he was dying, Wallace pressed Ann's head to his breast and uttered his last words: "We meet in Heaven."[31]

On the afternoon of April 25, Major General C. F. Smith died in the downstairs east bedroom of the Cherry mansion, having succumbed to infection and dysentery. It was perhaps ironic that the man who had initially led the campaign had become one of its final victims. His passing, symbolically at least, gave closure to the campaign.[32]

Des Arc, Arkansas

YEARS LATER, BEAUREGARD RECALLED sending a courier to Corinth during the waning hours of the Battle of Shiloh to hurry up Van Dorn's army, which was daily expected. Boldly he told of how he had planned to use these fresh reserves to keep the battle going. Although it made a dramatic story, he must have known that Van Dorn would not arrive in time. The Creole was in telegraphic communication with Memphis, and there had been no dispatches to indicate that the Army of the West was even at that place.[33]

In truth, on April 7 the trans-Mississippi corps was well over 250 miles from the Shiloh battlefield at a place called Des Arc, Arkansas, a village on the west bank of the White River. The van of the army arrived on April 6, but the troops were strung out for miles. Two transports, the *Sharp* and the *Meyors*, awaited the men, with more boats on the way from Memphis. Many of the men were bitter about leaving Arkansas, but there was great joy when one boat brought news of a great victory at Pittsburg Landing. Van Dorn had his field artillery fire a thirteen-gun salute.[34]

On April 8, Arkansan W. C. Porter noted that his regiment, along with another, boarded the *Golden Age*. "We were so thick we could neither sit, stand, nor lie." A Texas artilleryman told of a similar experience. "Our Boat is a fine large packet. We have on board three companies of Artillery with guns, horses, ammunition, etc. and about 600 Infantry." Most of Van Dorn's army did not arrive at Corinth until April 18, and Louis Hébert's brigade, bringing up the rear, trailed in on April 24.[35]

Corinth

ON APRIL 7, THE BLANKET-WRAPPED BODY of Albert Sidney Johnston was taken to the Rose Cottage. Prior to its arrival, Dr. Samuel Choppin had injected the corpse with whiskey as a preservative. The body was cleaned up and prepared for interment by Mrs. Inge, assisted by her neighbor Mrs. Ellen Polk. Two locks of hair were cut, one of which was sent to Johnston's widow. From Corinth the body was taken by train to New Orleans, where it arrived on April 9.[36]

Two dozen physicians and several civilian groups converged on Corinth from New Orleans, Mobile, Natchez, and other places. Reverend B. M. Miller of the Mobile Hospital Aid Society brought twenty-four ladies, and they were joined by a dozen Mississippi women along the way. The Sisters of Charity, consisting of a mother superior and a dozen nuns, arrived to assist.[37]

The wounded were farmed out to hospitals throughout Mississippi—Jackson, Canton, Columbus, Lauderdale, and Holly Springs. About three hundred were sent to Overton and Irving Hospitals in Memphis, and about 125 to the Marine Hospital in Natchez. A train carrying wounded to Memphis derailed outside Grand Junction, causing more serious injury.[38]

The grim sights of death and suffering were everywhere in Corinth. "The Railroad platform is almost covered with coffins and wounded soldiers—every train brings some anxious parent looking after their sons," noted a soldier. A Louisianian passed a church filled with wounded. His eyes were drawn to a grisly sight in the back—a large box "filled with feet and arms & hands. It was so full that 2 horrible & bloody feet protruded out of the top."[39]

A depression swept across the army. "The camp, once so gay, so joyous, now lay under the pall of death. Everywhere prevailed a mournful silence," observed a member of the Orleans Guard. In the camp of the Washington Artillery, wrote cannoneer John Pugh, "everyone was hushed in sadness." Shattered morale and the reality of war led many to agree with the conclusion of 4th Louisiana soldier Josiah Knighton on April 25: "I am afraid the Confederacy is gone forever."[40]

The Confederates began to take stock of their captures. Despite claims of thirty captured cannon, so many pieces exchanged hands on the battlefield that the Southerners came out probably no more than four guns ahead. Thousands of small arms were picked up on the battlefield; the 13th Tennessee was completely rearmed with 429 Springfield rifles. Beauregard reported 3,000 prisoners, some 2,800 of whom arrived in Memphis via rail on April 9.[41]

An interesting event on April 17 captured the attention of the Southern press. Lieutenant Sam S. Harris of the 1st Alabama Cavalry was sent under a flag of truce to General Buell to make inquiries regarding several missing officers. Buell asked how Prentiss was doing and then blurted that he "hoped we would keep him and his brigade." The Northern general also claimed that he had the body of Albert Sidney Johnston. The body in question turned out to be that of Captain Thomas W. Preston, who bore a striking resemblance to Johnston. Before departing, Lieutenant Harris heard Brigadier General Mc-Cook openly state that many of the regiments from Ohio and Iowa were "the greatest cowards in the world."[42]

TWELVE

Ramifications

Washington

THE FIRST RUMORS of a great battle along the Tennessee River came to the Lincoln administration on the night of April 8. The next day, the news was confirmed in a wire received at the Washington bureau of the *New York Herald.* The dispatch was immediately forwarded to the Senate, where Illinois Senator Orville H. Browning suspended business to read it. The "bloodiest battle of modern times" had just concluded at Pittsburg Landing, slaughter had been great on both sides, and the Union remained in possession of the battlefield. A relieved President Lincoln declared a national day of worship and ordered a hundred-gun salute at the National Armory. In the initial report there was no hint that the Union Army had been taken by surprise. *The New York Times* soon followed with its own sensationalized version of the "glorious victory." Grant had once again emerged as a national hero.[1]

Momentary glee quickly evaporated. On April 13, Oregon Senator Benjamin Shanks complained that no official word had been received from Halleck or Grant. Eyewitness correspondents submitted their own accounts of the battle, which were at odds with the *Herald*'s scoop. The extent of the victory and Grant's role came into question. "There was no more preparation by Gen. Grant for an attack than if he had been on a Fourth of July Frolic," decried the *New York Tribune.* Undoubtedly it was the somewhat exaggerated account of Whitelaw Reid of the *Cincinnati Gazette* that sent shockwaves throughout the nation. Written under the pen name AGATE, Reid's 19,500-word story told of the army's being taken by surprise, and that a calamity had narrowly been averted by the timely arrival of Buell's army. The Northern public was horrified to learn (incorrectly) that soldiers had been bayoneted in their tents. Grant had not been present when the battle began, and high-level bungling had prevailed from start to finish. Only Buell emerged a hero; indeed, Sherman charged that Reid had received much of his information from the Ohio general. Although not the first account to suggest that there was little cause for celebration, Reid's article was the most widely circulated. The sheer volume and descriptive quality seemed to lend credence to his version; it would become the account that the nation believed.[2]

Early reports placed Union casualties at 7,000, which was ghastly enough until the true figure of over 13,000 was released. Both the nation and Europe were horrified; the *London Times* spoke of a "fabulous slaughter." The 23,000 combined Union and Confederate casualties were nearly double the killed and wounded at Manassas, Wilson's Creek, Fort Donelson, and Pea Ridge combined. In two days, more men had been made casualties than in all the rest of America's wars added together up to that time! Romantic innocence had vanished; the war had at last turned vicious.[3]

Shiloh had won for the North huge territorial gains, securing both the Tennessee Valley and upper Mississippi Valley. Island No. 10 surrendered to Federal forces the day after Shiloh, Memphis soon fell, and within eleven weeks Union gunboats had made an appearance before Vicksburg, Mississippi. The issue of surprise and the enormity of the casualty list, however, eclipsed much of the political benefits that had been gained. No longer was there popular talk of a near end to the war. Grant later wrote that after Shiloh he gave up the thought of saving the Union except by complete conquest of the South.[4]

As additional details became known, Republican politicians and editors launched brutal attacks. Iowa Senator James Harlan, down on Grant ever since Belmont, saw a consistent pattern of behavior: the Illinois general had been saved by Foote at Belmont, by C. F. Smith at Fort Donelson, and by Buell at Shiloh. Even Ohio Senator John Sherman, the only Republican in the Senate to express support, was embarrassed by Grant's absence on the field when the shooting began. Ohio Governor David Tod stoutly defended the much-maligned 53rd and 57th Ohio Regiments, and denounced the "criminal negligence" of the high command. Lieutenant Governor Benjamin Stanton traveled to Pittsburg Landing and visited Ohio troops in their camps. He reported that most of them felt Grant should be court-martialed or hanged. The *St. Louis Democrat*, which despite its name had Republican leanings, demanded that the administration place responsibility upon Grant. Henry Bentley, the Philadelphia journalist who had been with Colonel Peabody when the battle began, stated that the troops expressed "considerable satisfaction" over a rumor that Grant would be replaced.[5]

The western press, led by the Cincinnati papers, were relentless in their criticism. Even the Democratic-dominated *Chicago Times* railed at the "neglect of one man [Grant]." Congressman Washburne fumed that a slanderous article on Grant had been carried in the *Chicago Tribune*. Joseph Medill of that paper replied that though Washburne's loyalty was admirable it was also misplaced. The general had simply "played out. The soldiers are down on him." A correspondent of the *Indianapolis Journal*, returning from Pittsburg Landing, noted: "Of Grant I heard much, and little to his credit."[6]

Grant was also maligned by some of his own officers, notably Major General McClernand. In a letter to Lincoln, the former Illinois congressman slyly wrote of a "slaughter," exaggerated his own performance, and mentioned the mistake of not pursuing the enemy on Monday night and Tuesday. Confronted with several serious allegations, Lincoln had Secretary of War Stanton write Halleck about possible misconduct on Grant's part.[7]

Halleck noticeably refused to express an opinion on Grant in his response. The severe casualties were the results of inept officers "utterly unfit for their places." In a private letter to his friend General Hitchcock, however, the St. Louis commander sharply criticized Grant. Hitchcock, now living in Washington, replied that Grant was "little more than a common gambler and drunkard," and his mistakes were too grievous for forgiveness. There was "but one opinion here [Washington]. General Grant is absolutely disgraced and dishonored."[8]

Another high-level critic proved to be Buell, who portrayed himself as the savior of the battlefield. Grant maintained that he had not been surprised and that, once Lew Wallace's division arrived, he needed no help from Buell at all. In 1866, Grant, while visiting in Springfield, Massachusetts, was quoted in the *New York Herald* as saying that Buell knew nothing about handling men in an emergency, that he could have gotten to Pittsburg Landing several days earlier, and that "his heart was never in the war from the first." Buell wrote him twice, insisting that he disavow the comments, but Grant only replied that he had been misquoted. For his part, Buell snidely remarked that, had he acted on Grant's dispatch to Brigadier General Nelson, or on

Halleck's authority to halt at Waynesboro, the Pittsburg Landing force would all have been made prisoners.[9]

Obviously stung by the hailstorm of criticism, Grant did himself no credit by covering up information and giving conflicting statements in letters to the *Cincinnati Commercial* and Congressman Washburne. He adamantly denied that a surprise had occurred: "If the enemy had sent us word when and where they were to attack us, we could not have been better prepared." The paper was unaccepting of the lame declaration, and also condemned Grant's "loose, rambling, [and] slovenly" official report. Even fellow Galena officer Colonel J. E. Smith of the 45th Illinois, who staunchly supported the army commander, admitted to Washburne that the army "had not been surprised; it was worse, we were astonished."[10]

The national debate turned mean, as old and false rumors of intoxication surfaced. When a Grant staff officer wrote the secretary of war requesting to see what specific allegations had been filed, Stanton instructed Major A. H. H. Johnson, his confidential secretary, to ignore the request. Privately, Stanton admitted to the major that no charges existed. Captain Rowley eagerly defended Grant, as did Colonel Ammen of Buell's army. Douglas Putman, a volunteer aide who was with Grant throughout Sunday, emphatically denied the rumors. Even Mrs. W. H. Cherry declared that the Illinois general was thoroughly sober on the morning of April 6, when he left the Cherry mansion.[11]

On May 2, Washburne, brushing aside many critical letters to his office, broke his silence and defended his protégé on the floor of the House of Representatives. Clinging to the technicality that the Army of the Tennessee had formed ranks slightly before the main Confederate attack began, he insisted that a surprise had not occurred. He also proclaimed that Grant's proper position on the morning of April 6 was in Savannah, and that he never indulged in liquor. To the charge that Grant had camped on the wrong side of the river and thus invited an attack, the congressman again declared that the correct decision had been made. "To have done otherwise, would have been like keeping the entire Army of the Potomac on this side of the river, instead of crossing it when it could be done." Although his rhetoric strained logic, his defense clearly helped Grant's case.[12]

Twelve days later, Grant responded to Washburne, both thanking him for his efforts and assuring him of his innocence. His 30,000 troops, he claimed, had been attacked by 70,000 Rebels—both figures grossly incorrect. Even if the belief was sincere, it begged the question. If Grant thought himself heavily outnumbered and anticipated danger, why had he not made better defensive preparations? Still in denial, he wrote: "Looking back at the past I cannot see for the life of me any important point that could be corrected." Julia followed with her own letter of appreciation to Washburne.[13]

The British had their own interpretation of affairs, much to the dismay of Foreign Minister Charles Francis Adams. Had Lincoln waited to hear the details before he claimed victory, the *London Times* stated, he would have known that it was "no victory at all. At best it was a drawn battle." Beauregard had struck the Federals a "tremendous blow in the face." The British threat had subsided, however, and their prejudiced acceptance of the Southern version of the battle proved less than troublesome.[14]

The clamor for Grant's removal nonetheless became so intense that Lincoln was harshly criticized for retaining him. There was a near-universal conviction among the president's closest friends and advisers—Ward Lamon and A. K. McClure among them—that the administration would be damaged if Grant was sustained. At 11:00 one evening, McClure called upon the president in the Old Cabinet Room; for two hours he pressed Lincoln to remove the general. The president—his feet propped up on the high marble mantel, exhausted from the day's business—mostly listened. He finally gathered himself up in his chair and in an earnest tone spoke: "I can't spare this man; he fights." It would turn out to be one of the crucial decisions of the war.[15]

Was Lincoln justified in his decision? In the light of the subsequent showdown in Virginia against Robert E. Lee in 1864, it seems clear that he was. Yet the decision cannot be judged in that light. In May 1862, Lee was not the giant killer that he would become. Joseph E. Johnston commanded Confederate forces in Virginia at the time. The decision to keep Grant was thus a gamble, there being absolutely no evidence thus far to suggest that he was destined for greatness. In the midst of serious errors, however, Grant had proved to be a fighter. He seemingly ignored defeats on the second day at Fort Donelson and the first day at Shiloh and went on the offensive. It is true that he received heavy reinforcements at Shiloh, which gave him a significant edge in manpower. McClellan held a similar edge in raw manpower at Antietam in September 1862, yet there was no second day of battle.[16]

Who would have commanded the Army of the Tennessee had Grant been fired is speculation; probably George H. Thomas, who replaced him upon Halleck's arrival at Pittsburg Landing. Though

Thomas was arguably not up to the task of taking on Lee in Virginia, as Grant later did, he might have fared well against the incompetent John C. Pemberton in the Vicksburg Campaign.

Although Lincoln did not sack Grant, he did not offer the whole-hearted endorsement that some have suggested. The president supported Halleck's decision of a de-facto suspension of Grant, by "raising" him to the meaningless position of second-in-command. McClure felt that the move was appropriate and quieted the critics.[17]

Pittsburg Landing

HALLECK DEBARKED AT PITTSBURG LANDING on April 11 and, although he had never commanded more than a platoon in the field, personally assumed command. A week and a half later, John Pope's Army of the Mississippi arrived, fresh from its victory at Island No. 10. Halleck thus led Grant's, Buell's, and Pope's armies, a total of sixteen divisions with 108,500 troops present for duty. Grant's second-in-command position left him, in his own words, "little more than an observer." Since Thomas had assumed Grant's former position, the Illinois general suspected that he had had a hand in the new command structure; their relationship thereafter remained cool.[18]

Throughout May 1862, Grant was virtually ignored; movements and reports were made without his knowledge. He spent much of the time around the campfire, smoking, pacing, and playing cards. "It is generally understood through this army that my position differs but little from that of one under arrest," he complained to Halleck. So embarrassing and ill-suited to his temperament was his present assignment that Grant requested a transfer; his request was denied. His staff jockeyed to have him transferred to the Atlantic Coast, where it was rumored that a position might be open; the effort proved fruitless.[19]

One afternoon, so the story goes, Sherman got wind that Grant was planning to quit the army. He arrived at his headquarters (five tents in a clearing surrounded by a sapling railing) and found the major general on a stool, sorting mail at a camp table. After exchanging the usual greetings, Sherman bluntly asked Grant if he was leaving. "Yes," Grant replied with tears in his eyes. "Sherman, you know [the reason why]. You know that I am in the way here. I have stood it as long as I can, and can endure it no longer." Sherman pleaded with him to remain, using his own example of how, with a single battle, he had risen from the stigma of insanity to "new life" and "high feather." In a dramatic change of mind, Grant decided to remain.[20]

Grant mentioned the incident in his memoirs, although he stated that it was his intention to take a leave of absence, not quit the army. Bruce Catton, who studied the evidence, concluded that Sherman's influence may have been overstated. Grant nonetheless chose to stick it out. Additionally, one of the great partnerships of the war had been cemented. Grant's choice of Sherman to lead the Federal army during the 1864 Atlanta Campaign, rather than George Thomas, cannot be seen apart from post-Shiloh events.[21]

The turning point came six weeks later. Halleck was promoted to chief-of-staff and summoned to Washington. The department was once again divided; Grant received command of an enlarged District of West Tennessee, which included everything between the Mississippi and Tennessee Rivers, north to Cairo, Illinois. It would be an independent command answerable only to Washington. Seeing the position as essentially bureaucratic in nature, Halleck desired the command to go to Colonel Robert Allen, his chief quartermaster. For his part, Grant wrote that he and "Old Brains" had "several little spats but I like and respect him nevertheless." Grant had survived Shiloh.[22]

AN OBVIOUS SCAPEGOAT for Bloody Shiloh would have been 6th Division Commander Sherman. Still under the insanity stigma, he had an ongoing hatred of reporters that made him an obvious target. Surprisingly, he emerged as one of the battle's heroes. His friend Halleck publicly praised him as did many, but not all, newspapers. Although the *Cincinnati Gazette* continued its slurs, the *Cincinnati Commercial*, the very paper that had initiated the insanity charge, and the *Louisville Journal*, a longtime defender, rallied to his side. Unaccustomed to such popularity, Sherman could not refrain from writing Ellen: "They say I accomplished some important results, and General Grant makes special mention of me in his report." When his nomination for major general sailed through the Senate, Sherman took it in stride—"It gives me far less emotion than my old commission as 1st Lieutenant of Artillery."[23]

Sherman continued to lash out at journalists, labeling them as defaming newsmongers. "I am out of all patience that our people should prefer to believe the horrid stories of butchery, ridiculous in themselves, gotten up by cowards to cover their shame, than the plain natural reports of officers," he wrote Senator Sherman. The stories of disaster came from those who had deserted the ranks and now had to "cast about for a legitimate excuse." The senator, perturbed by his brother's continued rancor, advised him to get along.[24]

The advice went unheeded. The Ohio division commander now turned his wrath on Ohio Lieutenant Governor Benjamin Stanton, who had denounced the leadership of Grant and Prentiss. Sherman defended his colleagues in a letter that was characteristically blunt. Stanton responded by adding Sherman to the list of those responsible for the attack. The lieutenant governor challenged him to submit to a court-martial. If he was found innocent, Stanton would accept censure "as the author of a false and calumnious charge." Sherman fired off a letter in response, although he notably ignored the court-martial challenge.

In October and November 1862, Senator Thomas Ewing wrote lengthy defenses of his foster son. His case was strengthened by the fact that several officers denied the quotes that had been attributed to them in Stanton's original document. Stanton refused to back down, declaring that Ewing was more concerned about his family's honor than the nation's. The lieutenant governor had clearly not anticipated such a high-level war of words and, wishing the matter to go away, made no additional responses.[25]

In August 1862, the annoying Colonel Thomas Worthington was court-martialed in Memphis for issues related to Shiloh and thereafter, notably intoxication. The trial, in which Worthington was found innocent on some charges and guilty on others, proved interesting because Sherman was subpoenaed. The division commander denied that certain intelligence had been passed to his headquarters on April 5, and continued to insist that his pickets extended a mile and a half beyond the widow Howell's house, which was simply not true. In postwar years, at Society of the Army of the Tennessee meetings, Sherman persisted in his denial that a surprise had occurred; indeed, it became almost a sacrilege for anyone to suggest such.[26]

ALTHOUGH SHILOH HAD BEEN a tremendous strategic victory for the North, Halleck was so unnerved by the mess he found at Pittsburg Landing that he changed his tactical plans. He commenced a tediously slow march, requiring seven weeks to cover twenty-three miles. The Rebels evacuated the town on the night of May 29. Having attained his personal goal, the capture of the Corinth rail juncture, Halleck was self-satisfied. Actually, the capture of Huntsville on April 10 and the burning of the Big Bear Creek bridge during a Sherman raid on April

12–13, had already effectively neutralized the Memphis & Charleston Railroad.[27]

In his fixation with "strategic points," Halleck had failed to see the true target—the Confederate Army. Grant boasted that he could have taken the town in two days and that the "mere occupation of territory" should never have been the goal. It should be noted that he did not sound such practical advice at the time. The loss of a direct east-west rail link did hamper the Southerners, but they managed simply by shifting to another base.[28]

Halleck's larger blunder was yet to come. Although receiving intelligence (albeit exaggerated) of massive enemy desertions and captures, he continued a weak pursuit south of Corinth. The enemy eventually withdrew fifty-two miles southeast, to Tupelo, Mississippi. Halleck remained passive and advanced only a corps of observation. He decided to break up his host, sending Buell's army to Chattanooga. While the theater commander contemplated all of the problems involved with an overland operation deep into enemy territory, the Rebels again slipped away. The war in the west again became a two-theater war, with Buell pursuing the Army of the Mississippi (later named the Army of the Tennessee), and Grant's forces opposing a new Rebel army in Mississippi under John C. Pemberton and Earl Van Dorn. And thus the war continued.[29]

New Orleans

THE CITY OF NEW ORLEANS, with perhaps 2,000 of her sons in Sidney Johnston's army, awoke to joyous news. The headlines in the *Picayune* heralded a "Glorious Victory" on the banks of the Tennessee River. The men of the Crescent City had "covered themselves with glory." The Southwestern Telegraph Office remained open all night on Sunday, April 6, to provide the latest news. On the morning of April 7, the "news boys gave vent to their feelings by a continual round of cheering."[30]

The celebration soon turned sober as the casualty lists became public. Stunned crowds gathered around newspaper bulletin boards and the telegraph office on St. Charles Street. New Orleans outfits had been particularly hard hit: the Crescent Regiment, 127 casualties; Orleans Guard Battalion, 90 casualties; the Avengo Zouave battalion of the 13th Louisiana, 157 casualties; the Confederate Guards Response

Battalion, 46 casualties (miraculously, all 27 printers in Company D emerged unscathed); the 1st Louisiana Regulars, 232 casualties; the 5th Company Washington Artillery, 26 casualties. The bloody butcher's list totaled 120 killed, 458 wounded, 100 missing—678 men. After Shiloh, attested one New Orleans resident, the South never smiled again.[31]

Richmond

"I HEAR THAT A DISPATCH was rec'd from Corinth, from Gen. A. S. Johnston, last evening, saying that he would attack the enemy today, but we have heard nothing more." Thus noted Thomas Bragg in his diary on April 5. Late on the evening of April 6, Jefferson Davis received a dispatch at the Executive Mansion indicating that the Confederates were "advancing victoriously." The War Department also received a telegram from Corinth: "Our victory complete and glorious." The elated president composed a message to be read before Congress when it convened at noon on April 7.[32]

The next day, Davis was shocked to hear of the death of Johnston. Although he attempted to disclaim first reports, he received confirmation from Beauregard. The president was grief-stricken and wept openly. He added an addendum to his congressional message: "His [Johnston's] last thought was his country, and long and deeply will his country mourn his loss." The message was read and Congress then adjourned out of respect. The bittersweet news spread throughout the capital. "There is no ringing of 'joy-bells,' no standing on head," a journalist noted.[33]

On April 8, Davis appeared before Congress and gave a brief sketch of the battle. The enemy, according to latest accounts, were endeavoring to retreat. Johnston had gained a "complete victory." There was even talk of retaking Tennessee, Kentucky, and possibly Missouri. Wild reports arrived in the capital. Tennessee Representative W. H. Tibbs claimed that the Yankees had suffered 15,000 killed and wounded in the battle, as well as 7,600 captured. The latter figures were tempered by an official estimate of 3,000.[34]

The fickle public, which only weeks earlier had demanded Johnston's removal, now sounded his praises. The politicians who had opposed the general came under attack. "It is thought that he [Johnston] fell a victim to the assaults of the demagogues in and out of Congress. . . . The reaction has already commenced, and the denunciation of Foote and his confederates are now loud and bitter," noted Thomas Bragg.[35]

The State Department moved quickly to use the supposed victory as another appeal for British recognition. Although the British largely accepted the Southern version of the battle, it proved insufficient to reopen the issue of an alliance. Henri Mercier, the French foreign minister in Washington, D.C., happened to believe the Northern version, and used the occasion to embark upon a peacemaking mission to Richmond. Baron Edouard de Stoeckl, the Russian foreign minister, declined an invitation to accompany him, although he supported the mission. Mercier had never hidden his belief that the South was engaged in a war it could not win. Arriving in Richmond on April 16, he met with Judah Benjamin, now in the State Department. Mercier returned to Washington within three days, to report sadly to Lincoln that the South remained defiant.[36]

Slowly the truth of the battle became known. The April 9 entry of Thomas Bragg's diary noted: "The news today from Ten[nessee] is not so favorable. Gen'l Beauregard telegraphs that he had fallen back from the river to his original position at Corinth." Two days later, Edmond Ruffin, circulating throughout the capital, picked up on the news. The loss of Island No. 10 on April 8, with 4,200 prisoners, added to the gloom. The sacrifice of Mackall's division at the Mississippi River fortress would have been given meaning if Shiloh had been a resounding victory. As it was, it simply added to the losses. By month's end, New Orleans had surrendered to the Federal navy. By concentrating Van Dorn's army at Corinth, the Confederates had virtually relinquished most of Arkansas. The Mississippi River forts, now outflanked, quickly toppled, and Memphis fell in June. Such was the sheer magnitude of the geographical loss that by April 29 Davis was writing of the "drooping cause of our country."[37]

ON APRIL 9, BEAUREGARD NOTIFIED the War Department that he had only 35,000 effectives remaining. Van Dorn's army, expected momentarily, would add 15,000 more (actually 21,000 present for duty). The Creole placed Halleck's strength at 85,000; he pleaded for reinforcements lest he be overrun. The dispatch sounded vaguely similar to Johnston's January plea. Interestingly, the Federals broke the telegraph code, and within twelve days Beauregard's dispatch would be plastered in the *New York Herald*. Davis once again moved to reinforce the west. A brigade went from the Atlantic Coast, as well as some scattered units from Mobile and eastern Tennessee, adding a total of nine regiments and three batteries. The number was somewhat offset by the mustering out and transfer of several regiments at Corinth.[38]

On April 16, 1862, only nine days after Shiloh, Davis signed the first conscription bill into law. All white males between the ages of eighteen and forty-five were drafted for three years, and the service of twelve-month troops was extended an additional two years. Although the act proved highly unpopular, it did bring in a flood of new troops, including many who hurriedly volunteered, to avoid the stigma of conscription. By the end of May 1862, over 6,000 troops, mostly from Mississippi and Alabama, had been organized and channeled into a new army forming in Mississippi under Van Dorn.[39]

Davis was in a dilemma. The death of Johnston meant that Beauregard, whom he had no faith in or affection for, was in command. Perhaps speaking the voice of the administration, Thomas Bragg wrote on April 7: "Those who know him [Beauregard] will doubt his capacity. The President, I think, does not entertain a high opinion of him."[40]

Davis considered Corinth of paramount importance; at one time the ridiculous notion of moving the capital there was discussed in a Cabinet meeting. Beauregard, too, thought that the town was the key to the Mississippi Valley. In his May 19 letter to the President, the Louisiana general wrote of his intentions to defend Corinth to "the last extremity"; he also hinted at retreat. By the end of the month the town would be evacuated without a fight.[41]

Although Beauregard found sufficient time to explain his actions in a letter to a Mobile newspaper, by June 12 he had still not filed an official report. When he finally did communicate with Richmond, he immodestly labeled the retreat as "most brilliant and successful." He conveniently neglected to mention the loss of 2,000 convalescents and sixty-two railroad cars. Since Shiloh some 15,000 square miles of territory had been yielded. Beauregard's prestige had been correspondingly reduced. Some rumors even claimed that he had hidden in a tent during the battle.[42]

On June 14, Davis sent Colonel William Preston Johnston, hardly an impartial observer, to Tupelo, Mississippi. He carried with him a series of questions for Beauregard to answer, although Davis had already made up his mind. The day before Johnston left Richmond, Davis had written Varina: "There are those who can only walk a log when it is near to the ground, and I fear [Beauregard] has been placed too high for his mental capacity." William Preston Johnston himself had written: "I fear Beauregard has thrown away the campaign of the West." Not surprisingly, his subsequent report confirmed Davis's preconceived notions.[43]

Beauregard made his removal almost easy for Davis. In mid-June he wired the War Department that he was taking sick leave to go to the spa at Bladon Springs, Alabama, north of Mobile. He would be gone only long enough to restore his "shattered health." He neither asked for permission nor waited for a response. Davis seized the opportunity to have him relieved, ostensibly for leaving his post without proper authorization. A few months later, fifty-nine members of Congress petitioned the president to have Beauregard reinstated; Davis held firm.[44]

Beauregard made his share of mistakes during the campaign: he authored the horrendous battle plan, lost his nerve the night before the attack, and was out of position when he called off the attack late on the afternoon of April 6. Yet, despite his wretched health, he had made his contributions. Without him, it is very possible that the Confederate garrison at Columbus would have been timely evacuated, or that the concentration at Corinth would have come off.[45]

LONG AFTER THE WAR, Davis continued to believe that Johnston's death was the "turning point of our fate" in the west. This assertion is perhaps the most compelling of Shiloh's unanswerables. Had Sidney Johnston lived, would Grant's army have been destroyed? The truth is that, after eight and a half hours of fighting (until his death at 2:30), Johnston was far from destroying Grant's army, despite the tactical surprise, the parity of strength, and the incredible good fortune of not having three fresh Yankee divisions on the field, all of which should have been present by early Sunday afternoon.[46]

It is unlikely that even in the most favorable scenario Grant's force would have been entirely destroyed. At Fort Donelson, the North inflicted a kill/capture ratio of 83 percent. Even applying that unlikely figure to Grant's Pittsburg Landing force means that 7,500 men would have gotten out. This number, added to Lew Wallace's 7,500 and Buell's 35,000, would have meant that 50,000 Federals could have quickly concentrated at Savannah. Reinforcements would have been forthcoming: John Pope's 21,000 troops from Island No. 10, and possibly Ormsby Mitchel's 10,000-man division in northern Alabama, bringing total troop strength to 81,000. This figure would not have included the 18,000-man Federal garrison in middle Tennessee.[47]

Popular thought suggests that, if Grant had been crushed at Shiloh, the psychological effect would have been so great that the

North would have sued for peace. Such an assertion is based upon the rather tenuous notion that the Northern will to win was considerably less than that of the South in the spring of 1862. The Davis administration made no peace overtures when a corps was lost at Fort Donelson, or for that matter an entire army at Vicksburg in 1863.

Yet Shiloh was a must win for the South. Few battles would present such dramatic possibilities. Hopes of recovering the upper Mississippi Valley forever dimmed after Shiloh. There was also another foreboding issue. Within seven weeks, Department No. 2 had lost a staggering 30,000 men. The losses marked the beginning of a war of attrition in the west, a war that the South could not win. In the end, the Confederates failed to achieve what they absolutely had to accomplish at Shiloh—the destruction of Grant's army. The war thus dragged wearily on.

FOR SEVERAL WEEKS, the eyes of the nation were riveted on the west. Both North and South realized that the war had been dangerously escalated. Beyond a devastating body count, something else had died on the fields of Tennessee that April 1862—the innocence of a people. Shiloh would soon be eclipsed by more horrific battles, but at Shiloh the Nation had taken its first gasp.

Appendix A
Order of Battle
Battle of Shiloh, April 6–7, 1862

ARMY OF THE TENNESSEE, MAJ. GEN. U. S. GRANT

First Division: Maj. Gen. John A. McClernand
First Brigade, Col. Abraham C. Hare (W): 8th Ill., 18th Ill., 11th Iowa, 13th Iowa
Second Brigade, Col. C. Carroll Marsh: 11th Ill., 20th Ill., 45th Ill., 48th Ill.
Third Brigade, Col. Julius Raith (MW): 17th Ill., 29th Ill., 43rd Ill., 49th Ill.
Unattached: D, 2nd Ill. Art'y (Dresser's); D, 1st Ill. Art'y (McAllister's); E, 2nd Ill.
    Art'y (Schwartz's); 14th Ohio Battery (Burrow's); 1st Batt'n, 4th Ill. Cav.;
    Carmichael's and Stewart's Cos., Ill. Cav.

Second Division: Brig. Gen. William H. L. Wallace (MW)
First Brigade, Col. James M. Tuttle: 2nd Iowa, 7th Iowa, 12th Iowa, 14th Iowa
Second Brigade, Brig. Gen. John McArthur (W): 9th Ill., 12th Ill., 13th Mo., 14th
    Mo., 81st Ohio
Third Brigade, Col. Thomas L. Sweeny (W): 8th Iowa, 7th Ill., 50th Ill., 52nd Ill.,
    57th Ill., 58th Ill.
Artillery: A, 1st Ill. Art'y (Willard's); Maj. J. S. Cavender's Batt'n: D, 1st Mo. Art'y
    (Richardson's); H, 1st Mo. Art'y (Welker's); K, 1st Mo. Art'y (Stone's)
Cavalry: A and B, 2nd Ill. Cav.; C, 2nd U.S. Cav.; I, 4th U.S. Cav.

Third Division: Maj. Gen. Lew Wallace
First Brigade, Col. Morgan L. Smith: 11th Ind., 24th Ind., 8th Mo.
Second Brigade, Col. John M. Thayer: 23rd Ind., 1st Neb., 58th Ohio, 68th Ohio
Third Brigade, Col. Charles Whittlesey: 20th Ohio, 56th Ohio*, 76th Ohio, 78th Ohio
Artillery: 9th Ind. Battery (Thompson's); I, 1st Mo. Art'y (Buel's Battery)
Cavalry: 3rd Batt'n, 11th Ill. Cav.*; 3rd Batt'n, 5th Ohio Cav.*
*Remained at Crump's Landing and not engaged at Shiloh

Fourth Division: Brig. Gen. Stephen A. Hurlbut
First Brigade, Col. Nelson G. Williams (W): 28th Ill., 32nd Ill., 41st Ill., 3rd Iowa
Second Brigade, Col. James C. Veach: 14th Ill., 15th Ill., 46th Ill., 25th Ind.
Third Brigade, Brig. Gen. Jacob C. Lauman: 31st Ind., 44th Ind., 17th Ky., 25th Ky.
Artillery: B, 1st Mich. Art'y (Ross's); C, 1st Mo. Art'y (Mann's); 13th Ohio Battery
    (Myers's)
Cavalry: 1st and 2nd Batt'ns, 5th Ohio Cav.

319

Fifth Division: Brig. Gen. William T. Sherman (W)
First Brigade, Col. John A. McDowell: 40th Ill., 6th Iowa, 46th Ohio
Second Brigade, Col. David Stuart (W): 55th Ill., 54th Ohio, 71st Ohio
Third Brigade, Col. Jesse Hildebrand: 53rd Ohio, 57th Ohio, 77th Ohio
Fourth Brigade, Col. Ralph P. Buckland: 48th Ohio, 70th Ohio, 72nd Ohio
Artillery, Maj. Ezra Taylor: B, 1st Ill. Art'y (Barrett's); E, 1st Ill. Art'y (Waterhouse's);
    6th Ind. Battery (Behr's)
Cavalry: 2nd and 3rd Batt'ns, 4th Ill. Cav.; Thielemann's two cos. Ill. cavalry

Sixth Division: Brig. Gen. Benjamin M. Prentiss (C)
First Brigade: Col. Everett Peabody: 12th Mich., 21st Mo., 25th Mo., 16th Wis.
Second Brigade, Col. Madison Miller: 61st Ill., 18th Mo., 18th Wis.
Not Brigaded: 15th Iowa, 16th Iowa, 23rd Mo.
Artillery: 5th Ohio Battery (Hickenlooper's); 1st Minn. Battery (Munch's)
Cavalry: 1st and 2nd Batt'ns, 11th Ill. Cav.
Unassigned Troops: 15th Mich., 14th Wis., H, 1st Ill. Art'y (Silversparre's), B, 2nd Ill.
    Art'y (Madison's), 8th Ohio Battery (Margraf's), I, 1st Ill. Art'y (Bouton's)

ARMY OF THE OHIO, MAJ. GEN. DON CARLOS BUELL

Second Division: Brig. Gen. Alexander McD. McCook
Fourth Brigade, Brig. Gen. Lovell H. Rousseau: 6th Ind., 5th Ky., 1st Ohio, 1st Batt'n,
    15th U.S., 1st Batt'n, 16th U.S., 1st Batt'n, 19th U.S.
Fifth Brigade, Col. Edward N. Kirk (W): 34th Ill., 29th Ind., 30th Ind., 77th Penn.
Sixth Brigade, Col. William H. Gibson: 32nd Ind., 39th Ind., 15th Ohio, 49th Ohio
Artillery: H, 5th U.S. Art'y (Terrill's)

Fourth Division: Brig. Gen. William Nelson
Tenth Brigade, Col. Jacob Ammen: 36th Ind., 6th Ohio, 24th Ohio
Nineteenth Brigade, Col. William B. Hazen: 9th Ind., 6th Ky., 41st Ohio
Twenty-Second Brigade, Col. Sanders D. Bruce: 1st Ky., 2nd Ky., 20th Ky.

Fifth Division: Brig. Gen. Thomas L. Crittenden
Eleventh Brigade, Brig. Gen. Jeremiah T. Boyle: 9th Ky., 13th Ky., 19th Ohio, 59th Ohio
Fourteenth Brigade, Col. William Sooy Smith: 11th Ky., 26th Ky., 13th Ohio
Artillery: G, 1st Ohio Art'y (Bartlett's); H/M, 4th U.S. Art'y (Mendenhall's)

Sixth Division, Brig. Gen. Thomas J. Wood
Twentieth Brigade, Brig. Gen. James A. Garfield: 13th Mich., 64th Ohio, 65th Ohio
Twenty-First Brigade, Col. George D. Wagner: 15th Ind., 40th Ind., 57th Ind., 24th Ky.

ARMY OF THE MISSISSIPPI, GEN. ALBERT SIDNEY JOHNSTON (K)
GEN. P. G. T. BEAUREGARD

First Army Corps: Maj. Gen. Leonidas Polk
FIRST DIVISION, Brig. Gen. Charles Clark (W)
First Brigade, Col. Robert M. Russell: 11th La., 12th La., 13th Tenn., 22nd Tenn.,
    Bankhead's Tenn. Battery

Second Brigade, Brig. Gen. Alexander P. Stewart: 13th Ark., 4th Tenn., 5th Tenn., 33rd Tenn., Stanford's Miss. Battery
SECOND DIVISION, Maj. Gen. Benjamin F. Cheatham (W)
First Brigade, Brig. Gen. Bushrod R. Johnson: Blythe's Miss. Reg't, 2nd Tenn., 15th Tenn., 154th Tenn., Polk's Tenn. Battery
Second Brigade, Col. William H. Stephens: 7th Ky., 1st Tenn. (Batt'n), 6th Tenn., 9th Tenn., Stanford's Miss. Battery
Cavalry: 1st Miss. Cav., Brewer's Miss. and Ala. Batt'n Cav.
Unattached: 47th Tenn. (Arrived April 7)

Second Army Corps: Maj. Gen. Braxton Bragg
FIRST DIVISION, Brig. Gen. Daniel Ruggles
First Brigade, Col. Randal L. Gibson: 1st Ark., 4th La., 13th La., 19th La., Vaiden Miss. Battery (at Corinth during battle)
Second Brigade, Brig. Gen. Patton Anderson: 1st Fla. Batt'n, 17th La., 20th La., Confederate Guards Response Batt'n, 9th Tx., La. Washington Artillery (5th Co.)
Third Brigade, Col. Preston Pond: 16th La., 18th La., Crescent Reg't, 38th Tenn., Ketchum's Ala. Battery
Cavalry: Ala. Batt'n
SECOND DIVISION, Brig. Gen. Jones M. Withers
First Brigade, Brig. Gen. Adley H. Gladden (MW): 21st Ala., 22nd Ala., 25th Ala., 26th Ala., 1st La., Robertson's Fla. Battery
Second Brigade, Brig. Gen. James R. Chalmers: 5th Miss., 7th Miss., 9th Miss., 10th Miss., 52nd Tenn., Gage's Ala. Battery
Third Brigade, Brig. Gen. John K. Jackson: 17th Ala., 18th Ala., 19th Ala., 2nd Tx., Girardey's Ga. Battery
Cavalry: Clanton's Ala. Cav. Reg't

Third Army Corps, Maj. Gen. William J. Hardee (W)
First Brigade, Brig. Gen. Thomas C. Hindman (D): 2nd Ark., 6th Ark., 7th Ark., 3rd Confederate, Warren Light Art'y (Swett's)
Second Brigade, Brig. Gen. Patrick R. Cleburne: 15th Ark., 6th Miss., 2nd Tenn., 5th (later 35th) Tenn., 23rd Tenn., 24th Tenn., Shoup's Batt'n: Trigg's, Calvert's, Hubbard's Ark. Batteries
Third Brigade, Brig. Gen. Sterling A.M. Wood (D): 16th Ala., 8th Ark., 9th [14th] Ark. [batt'n], 3rd Miss. Batt'n, 27th Tenn., 44th Tenn., 55th Tenn., Jefferson Miss. Flying Art'y (Harper's), Ga. Dragoons

Reserve Corps, Brig. Gen. John C. Breckinridge
First Brigade, Col. Robert Trabue: 4th Ala. Batt'n, 31st Ala., 3rd Ky., 4th Ky., 5th Ky., 6th Ky., Crew's Tenn. Batt'n, Cobb's Ky. Battery, Byrne's Miss. [Ky.] Battery, Morgan's Ky. Cav. Squadron
Second Brigade, Brig. Gen. John S. Bowen (W): 9th Ark., 10th Ark., 2nd Confederate, 1st Mo., Pettus Miss. Flying Art'y (Hudson's), Watson's La. Flying Art'y, Thompson's Co. Ky. Cav.
Third Brigade, Col. Winfield S. Statham: 15th Miss., 22nd Miss., 19th Tenn., 20th Tenn., 28th Tenn., 45th Tenn., Rutledge's Tenn. Battery
Unattached: Forrest's Tenn. Cav. Reg't, Wharton's Tx. Cav. Reg't, Wirt Adams's Miss. Cav. Reg't, McClung's Tenn. Battery, Roberts's Ark. Battery

K=Killed, W=Wounded, MW=Mortally Wounded, C=Captured, D=Disabled

Appendix B
Strength and Losses

Army of the Tennessee	Present for Duty	Killed	Wounded	Missing	Total
1st Division (McClernand)	6,941	285	1,372	85	1,742
2nd Division (W. H. L. Wallace)	8,408	270	1,173	1,306	2,749
3rd Division (Lew Wallace)	7,564	41	251	4	296
4th Division (Hurlbut)	7,825	317	1,441	111	1,869
5th Division (Sherman)	8,580	325	1,277	299	1,901
6th Division (Prentiss)	7,545	236	928	1,008	2,172
Unassigned	2,031	39	159	17	215
TOTAL	48,894	1,513	6,601	2,830	10,944
Army of the Ohio					
2nd Division (McCook)	7,552	88	823	7	918
4th Division (Nelson)	4,541	93	603	20	716
5th Division (Crittenden)	3,825	60	377	28	465
6th Division (Wood)	2,000	0	4	0	4
TOTAL	17,918	241	1,807	55	2,103
Army of the Mississippi					
1st Corps (Polk)	9,404	385	1,953	19	2,357
2nd Corps (Bragg)	16,279	353	2,441	634	3,628
3rd Corps (Hardee)	6,758	404	1,936	141	2,481
Reserve Corps (Breckinridge)	7,211	386	1,682	165	2,233
47 Tenn.*	731	?	?	?	?
Cavalry	4,316	?	?	?	?
TOTAL	44,699	1,728	8,012	959	10,699

Appendix C

The Confederate Dead

EXACTLY FOUR YEARS to the day after the Battle of Shiloh, *Memphis Argus* editor John P. Pryor toured the battlefield. He noted that most of the Confederates had been buried in shallow graves of twos and threes, up to a dozen. Virtually all of the smaller graves had been uprooted by wild hogs, and everywhere were scattered skulls, leg bones, and vertebrae. The larger burial trenches were deeper and, with one exception, had not been bothered. "Near the Rhea [sic] field about 150 Confederates had been tumbled into a gully and covered with a thin layer of soil," he noted. Hogs and washing rains had exposed many of the bones.[1]

Fifteen years after the battle, in 1877, the state of Tennessee appointed a commission to identify Confederate graves on the battlefield. The task proved depressing, for much deterioration had taken place. "Near Mr. Punt's house, where there are some white posts put up by the Federals, are two large piles and two smaller ones, supposed to contain 300 [bodies] said to be troops from Texas. Many of these ghastly relics are exposed to the light of the sun," reported the committee. A great many single graves were found in gullies and covered by only a few shovelfuls of dirt. "Near Mr. House's farm, two miles from Shiloh church, are many remains, perhaps 250 or 300, all within a quarter of a mile of his house. Most of these are exposed, some washed off by rains others rooted by hogs." The committee concluded that graves could be found for about a thousand men.[2]

About 1880, a few prominent men arranged a mass picnic at Rea Springs. Several thousand people were in attendance, and the idea was to identify Confederate graves. About noon, a terrible storm came up, dispersing the crowd. In getting home, several people, including some children, were killed; the project was never again attempted.[3]

When the federal government established the park in the 1890s, only five trenches could still be identified. Park officials suspect they know of a sixth trench outside the park on private property. In an old National Park handbook by Albert Dillahunty, it was reported that one trench near McClernand's camp contained the bodies of 571 Confederates buried seven deep. I have never been able to validate a source for this statement in years of study, and I long since concluded that it is more legend than fact.[4]

Notes

Abbreviations

ADAH	Alabama Department of Archives and History
CHS	Chicago Historical Society
DU	Duke University
EU	Emory University
FC	Filson Club
GPL	Greenville Public Library
HL	Huntington Library
ILSL	Illinois State Library
INHS	Indiana Historical Society
IOSHD	Iowa State Historical Department
LC	Library of Congress
LHA	Louisiana Historical Association
LSU	Louisiana State University
LU	Lambuth University (Memphis Conference Archives)
MDAH	Mississippi Department of Archives and History
MHC	Michigan Historical Collection
MHS	Missouri Historical Society
NA	National Archives
NEMMA	Northeast Mississippi Museum Association
NPS	National Park Service
OHS	Ohio Historical Society
ONR	Official Naval Records
OR	Official Army Records
PL	Pogue Library Special Collections
SHC	Southern Historical Collection
SHSIO	State Historical Society of Iowa
SNMP	Shiloh National Military Park
TSLA	Tennessee State Library and Archives
TU	Tulane University
UAF	University of Arkansas, Fayetteville
UM	University of Mississippi
UMEM	University of Memphis
US	University of the South
USMHI	United States Military History Institute
WRHS	Western Reserve Historical Society
YU	Yale University

One: The Capitals

1. See "Hermes" column of January 1, 1862, in Charleston *Mercury*, January 4, 1862; James M. McPherson, *Battle Cry of Freedom*, pp. 385–86; Howard Jones, *Union in Peril*, pp. 45, 90.
2. Charleston *Mercury*, January 6, 1862; Hudson Strode, *Jefferson Davis*, vol. 2, p. 189; William C. Davis, *Jefferson Davis*, pp. 263–64, 360, 391–92; Archer Jones, *Civil War Command and Strategy*, pp. 13–15.
3. Belle Becker Sideman and Lillian Friedman, eds., *Europe Looks at the Civil War*, pp. 100–106; Thomas Bragg Diary, January 1, 1862, SHC; Earl Schenck Miers, ed., *A Rebel War Clerk's Diary*, p. 63.
4. William C. Davis, *The Deep Waters of the Proud*, p. 150; McPherson, *Battle Cry of Freedom*, p. 386.
5. *OR*, vol. VI, p. 829; Archer Jones, *Confederate Strategy from Shiloh to Vicksburg*, pp. 16–17, 19–21, 25; Dunbar Rowland, ed., *Jefferson Davis, Constitutionalist*, vol. 5, p. 216; Jones, *Civil War Command and Strategy*, p. 143.
6. Nathaniel C. Hughes, Jr., ed., *Liddell's Record*, p. 41.
7. Charles Roland, *Albert Sidney Johnston*, pp. 12, 170, 259–60; Steven E. Woodworth, *Jefferson Davis and His Generals*, pp. 46–51.
8. These flaws included his "overly gentle nature," his inability to "grasp more than one area of thought at a time," and the fact that he was "easily swayed by subordinates" (Richard McMurry, *Two Great Rebel Armies*, pp. 120–21). Thomas Connelly, James Lee McDonough, and Benjamin Cooling concluded that Johnston's past did not merit his public acclaim. Charles Roland and Steven Woodworth assert that Johnston had peer respect, a good military record, and many honors. (Connelly, *Army of the Heartland*, pp. 60–62; McDonough, *Shiloh*, p. 29; Cooling, *Forts Henry and Donelson*, p. 29; McMurry, *Two Great Rebel Armies*, p. 178; Woodworth, *Davis*, pp. 46, 48–49.)
9. Joseph E. Johnston, for example, had commanded only four companies in combat prior to the war (Craig L. Symonds, *Joseph E. Johnston*, p. 101).
10. Woodworth, *Davis*, pp. 49–50.
11. Linda L. Crist, ed., *The Papers of Jefferson Davis*, vol. 7, p. 351; *OR*, vol. VII, pp. 351, 452–53, 784, 796; W. C. Davis, *Jefferson Davis*, p. 396.
12. McMurry, *Two Great Rebel Armies*, pp. 147–48; *OR*, vol. VII, pp. 792, 796.
13. Roland, *Johnston*, pp. 283–84; *OR*, vol. VII, pp. 792–94, 809. Johnston's estimate of Buell's strength was accurate. On January 23, 1862, Buell reported 72,502 troops and 148 artillery pieces (*OR*, vol. VII, p. 563; *Richmond Examiner*, January 31, 1862).
14. Miers, ed., *Rebel War Clerk's Diary*, p. 65; James D. Richardson, ed., *The Messages and Papers of Jefferson Davis and the Confederacy*, vol. 2, p. 210; Bragg Diary, January 6, 1862, SHC. Connelly and John Deberry deduced that Johnston "badly informed the Richmond authorities" as regards his strength (Connelly, *Army of the Heartland*, p. 93; Deberry, "Confederate Tennessee," Ph.D. dissertation, p. 150).
15. Hughes, ed., *Liddell's Record*, pp. 41–43.
16. Woodworth, *Davis*, p. 70; *OR*, vol. IV, pp. 371, 819; vol. VI, p. 819. Roland concluded: "But Johnston's efforts [at concentration] had been futile because Confederate authorities were unwilling at the time to strip other departments to strengthen Johnston's line. Had his earlier calls been heeded, the present crisis [Fort Donelson] might not have been upon the South." (Roland, *Johnston*, p. 302.)
17. Hughes, ed., *Liddell's Record*, pp. 45–46.
18. Bragg Diary, January 23, 1862, SHC; *OR*, vol. VII, pp. 844–45. The name "Somerset" is used because that is how Confederate officials and the Southern press referred to the battle, but the most commonly used name today is "Mill Springs."

The town of Somerset was actually eight miles from the battlefield.

19. Bragg Diary, January 23, 1862, SHC; *OR*, vol. VII, p. 102. Crittenden's division withdrew to Monticello, Kentucky, and thence to Gainesville, Tennessee.

20. *Richmond Examiner*, January 24, 1862; Roland, *Johnston*, p. 282; R. Gerald Mc-Murty, "Zollicoffer and the Battle of Mill Springs," p. 313. Confederate troops remaining in eastern Tennessee included about 1,500 men at Cumberland Gap and perhaps nine and a half regiments scattered throughout the region (*OR*, vol. VII, pp. 749–50, 786, 800; vol. LII, pt. 2, p. 262).

21. *OR*, vol. VII, pp. 844–45. Two Tennessee regiments experienced a high number of desertions on the retreat, and one cavalry battalion virtually melted away (Connelly, *Army of the Heartland*, p. 99).

22. Charleston *Mercury*, January 28, 1862 (article written January 25); Bragg Diary, January 31, 1862, SHC.

23. Bragg Diary, January 24, 1862, SHC; Charleston *Mercury*, January 30, 1862 (article written January 27); February 1, 1862 (article written January 29); *Nashville Gazette*, January 26, 1862; *Southern Confederacy*, January 29, 1862; *Mobile Advertiser & Register*, February 2, 1862; *OR*, vol. VII, p. 850.

24. *OR*, vol. VII, p. 108. The thesis of numbers versus leadership in the west was proposed by Albert Castel, "The Historian and the General," pp. 54–55. See also Connelly, *Army of the Heartland*, pp. 117, 120–21; William E. Jamborsky, "Confederate Leadership and Defeat in the West," p. 53; Woodworth, *Davis*, pp. 61, 63, 69–70; McMurty, "Zollicoffer," pp. 303, 307; Parks, "Zollicoffer," pp. 346–55. Crittenden claimed that he could not recross his troops to the south bank of the Cumberland River prior to the battle because of swollen rivers and inadequate transportation. Following his defeat, however, the division broke all speed records in recrossing in a single night.

25. Charleston *Mercury* quoted in *Southern Confederacy*, January 29, 1862; *OR*, vol. VII, p. 849. See also *Augusta Constitutionalist*, January 26, 1862.

26. McMurry, *Two Great Rebel Armies*, pp. 121–22; *Mobile Advertiser & Register*, February 8, 1862; Woodworth, *Davis*, pp. 74–76; J. Cutler Andrews, *The South Reports the Civil War*, p. 102.

27. Woodworth, *Davis*, p. 77; Bragg Diary, January 31, 1862, SHC; Larry J. Daniel, " 'The Assaults of the Demagogues in Congress,' " p. 333n; Miers, ed., *Rebel War Clerk's Diary*, p. 65; Alfred Roman, *The Military Operations of General Beauregard*, vol. 1, pp. 210–11; Connelly, *Army of the Heartland*, pp. 128–29; T. Harry Williams, *P. G. T. Beauregard*, p. 114.

28. Williams, *Beauregard*, pp. 114–15; Roman, *Beauregard*, vol. 1, pp. 211–12; Connelly, *Army of the Heartland*, p. 129.

29. *OR*, vol. VII, p. 131.

30. Bragg Diary, February 7, 1862, SHC; Miers, ed., *Rebel War Clerk's Diary*, p. 67; Edward Younger, ed., *Inside the Confederate Government*, p. 24; *OR*, vol. VII, p. 867; *Mobile Advertiser & Register*, February 8, 1862.

31. *OR*, vol. VII, pp. 862–63, 867, 872, 893; vol. VI, pp. 823, 824.

32. Ibid., vol. VII, pp. 861–62, 863–64; Miers, ed., *Rebel War Clerk's Diary*, p. 67.

33. Bragg Diary, February 17, 1862, SHC; *OR*, vol. VII, pp. 255–56.

34. Bragg Diary, February 18, 1862, SHC; *OR*, vol. VII, p. 256.

35. *Richmond Enquirer*, February 18, 1862; Bragg Diary, February 18, 1862, SHC; Scarbrough, ed., *Ruffin*, vol. 2, pp. 237–38; *Richmond Examiner* quoted in Charleston *Mercury*, February 19, 1862.

36. *Richmond Enquirer*, February 18, 1862; *Memphis Appeal*, February 25, 1862; Charleston *Mercury*, February 18, 19, 20, 25, 1862.

37. Bragg Diary, February 19, 20, 1862, SHC; Younger, ed., *Inside the Confederate Government*, p. 25; Miers, ed., *Rebel War Clerk's Diary*, p. 67; Woodworth, *Davis*, pp. 88–89.

38. *New Orleans Picayune*, February 23, 1862; William K. Scarbrough, ed., *The Diary of Edmund Ruffin*, vol. 2, pp. 240–41; Bragg Diary, February 22, 1862, SHC; *Richmond Dispatch*, February 24, 1862.

39. Clement Eaton, *Jefferson Davis*, p. 148; Varina H. Davis, *Jefferson Davis, Ex-President of the Confederate States of America*, vol. 2, pp. 181–82; Edward A. Pollard, *Life of Jefferson Davis*, pp. 196–97; Miers, ed., *Rebel War Clerk's Diary*, pp. 67–68; Irving Werstein, *Abraham Lincoln Versus Jefferson Davis*, p. 186.

40. Strode, *Davis*, p. 199; Thomas C. Schott, *Alexander H. Stephens of Georgia*, p. 350.

41. *OR*, vol. VII, pp. 826–27; Bragg Diary, February 19, 1862, SHC; Grady McWhiney, *Braxton Bragg and Confederate Defeat*, p. 200. Bragg was not the only one counseling concentration. On February 17, 1862, Brigadier General Leroy Walker at Tuscumbia, Alabama, warned the secretary of war: "Better to lose the seaboard than this line. The Memphis & Charleston is the vertebrae of the Confederacy." (*OR*, vol. VII, p. 889.)

42. *OR*, vol. VII, pp. 824, 826.

43. Ibid., vol. VI, p. 828; Woodworth, *Davis*, p. 90.

44. *OR*, vol. IV, p. 166; vol. X, pt. 2, p. 378.

45. *Richmond Inquirer*, March 4, 1862.

46. Jones, *Union in Peril*, pp. 102, 104; *New York Times*, March 12, 13, 15, 1862; Richardson, ed., *Messages and Papers*, vol. 2, pp. 193–94, 197–99, 201, 208; Ephraim D. Adams, *Great Britain and the American Civil War*, vol. 1, pp. 272–73.

47. Miers, ed., *Rebel War Clerk's Diary*, p. 69; Cooling, *Forts Henry and Donelson*, pp. 216, 262. Virtually all of the Fort Donelson outfits were back in service by November 1862, to serve at Vicksburg and Port Hudson, and in the Army of Tennessee.

48. Woodworth, *Davis*, pp. 84–85.

49. Ibid., pp. 30–31, 80, 84–85; McMurry, *Two Great Rebel Armies*, pp. 78–79, 114; Connelly, *Army of the Heartland*, pp. 117, 122–24; *OR*, vol. LII, pt. 2, p. 273; Bragg Diary, February 27, 1862, SHC.

50. Symonds, *Johnston*, p. 91.

51. Bruce Catton, *Grant Moves South*, p. 180; *National Intelligencer*, February 18, 1862; *Chicago Tribune*, February 21, 1862; Fletcher Pratt, *Stanton*, p. 167.

52. *National Intelligencer*, February 17, 1862.

53. Ibid., February 19, 22, 1862; *Chicago Tribune*, February 18, 19, 1862; *New York Tribune*, February 18, 20, 1862; John B. McMasters, *A History of the People of the United States During Lincoln's Administration*, p. 196; J. Cutler Andrews, *The North Reports the Civil War*, p. 168; Louis M. Starr, *Bohemian Brigade*, p. 88; Catton, *Grant Moves South*, p. 180; Albert D. Richardson, *A Personal History of Ulysses S. Grant*, p. 230.

54. *National Intelligencer*, February 19, 1862; James G. Blaine, *Twenty Years of Congress*, p. 358.

55. *Chicago Tribune*, numerous articles between February 20 and March 3, 1862; *Chicago Times*, February 25, 1862; *New York Times*, February 22, 1862.

56. *Chicago Tribune*, February 18, 1862; *New York Tribune*, February 18, 1862; Stephen W. Sears, *George B. McClellan*, p. 154; Blaine, *Twenty Years of Congress*, p. 358; *Indianapolis Journal*, February 18, 1862.

57. McPherson, *Battle Cry of Freedom*, pp. 367–68; Margaret Leech, *Reveille in Washington*, pp. 122–23; Jones, *Union in Peril*, pp. 89, 91, 98; Allen Nevins, *Ordeal of the Union*, vol. 3, pt. 2, p. 4.

58. Carl Sandburg, *Abraham Lincoln*, vol. 1, pp. 456–57.

59. Leech, *Reveille in Washington*, p. 129; Blaine, *Twenty Years in Congress*, p. 358; *National Intelligencer*, February 18, 1862.

60. William B. Hesseltine, *Lincoln and the War Governors*, p. 191; Thomas L. Livermore, *Numbers and Losses in the Civil War in America*, p. 47.

61. *OR*, vol. VII, pp. 511, 529, 544, 616.
62. McClure, *Abraham Lincoln and Men of War-Times*, p. 189; Blaine, *Twenty Years of Congress*, p. 356; Nevins, *Ordeal of the Union*, vol. 3, pt. 2, p. 27.
63. William S. McFeely, *Grant*, pp. 74–75, 83.
64. Patricia L. Faust, ed., *Historical Times Illustrated Encyclopedia of the Civil War*, p. 804; Lloyd Lewis, *Captain Sam Grant*, pp. 396–97; Catton, *Grant Moves South*, p. 16; Gaillard Hunt, *Israel, Elihu and Cadwallader Washburn*, pp. 175–82 (Elihu later added an "e" to his last name); Theodore C. Pease and James G. Randall, eds., *The Diary of Orville Hickman Browning*, vol. 1, pp. 487–88; Maurice G. Baxter, *Orville H. Browning*, p. 162. Grant's nomination was also strongly supported by Illinois Senator Orville H. Browning.
65. Lewis, *Captain Sam Grant*, pp. 56, 338; Catton, *Grant Moves South*, pp. 38, 117.
66. Benjamin P. Thomas, *Abraham Lincoln*, pp. 306–7; Davis, *Deep Waters*, p. 94; W. E. Woodward, *Meet General Grant*, pp. 223–24; McPherson, *Battle Cry of Freedom*, p. 296; *Daily Ohio State Journal*, April 17, 1862.
67. John Y. Simon, ed., *The Papers of Ulysses S. Grant*, vol. 4, p. 284.
68. McFeely, *Grant*, pp. 83–84, 94–95; Catton, *Grant Moves South*, p. 17.
69. Nathaniel C. Hughes, Jr., *The Battle of Belmont*, pp. 194–95, 205–6.
70. Dan Bauer, "The Big Bender," p. 35; Simon, ed., *Grant Papers*, vol. 4, pp. 116–19. Washburne received his information from Benjamin H. Campbell, a Galena resident.
71. *National Intelligencer*, February 17, 18, 1862; *Chicago Tribune*, February 19, 1862; Grant to Washburne, February 21, 1862, Grant-Washburne Papers, ILSL.
72. George B. McClellan, *McClellan's Own Story*, p. 137; Benjamin P. Thomas and Harold M. Hyman, *Stanton*, p. 140.
73. McClellan, *McClellan's Own Story*, p. 137; Thomas and Hyman, *Stanton*, p. 140.
74. H. Engurud, "General Grant, Fort Donelson and 'Old Brains,' " p. 203; McClellan, *McClellan's Own Story*, pp. 136–37; Stephen E. Ambrose, *Halleck*, pp. 27, 29, 32.
75. McClellan, *McClellan's Own Story*, pp. 151–53; George C. Gorham, *Life and Public Service of Edwin M. Stanton*, vol. 1, p. 328; H. J. Eckenrode and Bryan Conrad, *McClellan*, p. 42; Benjamin P. Thomas and Harold M. Hyman, *Stanton*, p. 185. For McClellan's most notorious expression of rudeness, see McPherson, *Battle Cry of Freedom*, pp. 364–65.
76. Charles A. Dana, *Recollections of the Civil War*, pp. 32–33.
77. *Chicago Tribune*, February 19, 21, 1862; *New York Tribune*, February 18, 1862; Cain, *Bates*, p. 173.
78. Tyler Dennett, ed., *Lincoln and the Civil War in the Diaries and Letters of John Hay*, p. 36; Sears, *McClellan*, p. 154; *Chicago Tribune*, February 17, 1862; Thomas and Hyman, *Stanton*, pp. 174–75; Burton J. Hendrick, *Lincoln's War Cabinet*, p. 295.
79. Samuel H. Kamm, *The Civil War Career of Thomas A. Scott*, pp. 108–10, 112.
80. *OR*, vol. VII, pp. 628, 641; Sears, *McClellan*, p. 153; Kamm, *Scott*, p. 111; Stephen Ambrose, "The Union Command System and the Donelson Campaign," p. 66.
81. Thomas and Hyman, *Stanton*, p. 175; *OR*, vol. VII, pp. 648, 652, 655, 660; Kamm, *Scott*, pp. 110, 113; Jones, *Civil War Command and Strategy*, p. 80.
82. *OR*, vol. VII, pp. 678–79; vol. VIII, p. 602. For Halleck's attempt to achieve power by contrivance see Ambrose, *Halleck*, p. 35.
83. Kenneth M. Stampp, *Indiana Politics During the Civil War*, pp. 122–23; Marvin R. Cain, *Lincoln's Attorney General*, p. 173; Nevins, *Ordeal of the Union*, vol. 3, pt. 2, p. 10.
84. James A. Rawley, *The Politics of Union*, pp. 91–92, 121; Frank L. Klement, *The Copperheads in the Middle West*, pp. 1, 3, 6, 10–11, 13–14; A. J. Beitzinger, "The Father of Copperheadism in Wisconsin," p. 18; Hesseltine, *Lincoln and the War Governors*, pp. 194–95, 240; Edward G. Longacre, "Congressman Becomes General," p. 32.

85. *Chicago Tribune*, February 18, 1862; Stampp, *Indiana Politics*, p. 123; Blaine, *Twenty Years of Congress*, p. 356; Catton, *Grant Moves South*, p. 179.

86. *Cincinnati Commercial* quoted in *Indianapolis Sentinel*, April 19, 1862; Blaine, *Twenty Years of Congress*, p. 357.

87. *Chicago Tribune*, February 20, 1862; Hubert H. Wubben, *Civil War Iowa and the Copperhead Movement*, p. 74; McPherson, *Battle Cry of Freedom*, p. 74.

88. Nevins, *Ordeal of the Union*, vol. 3, pt. 2, p. 202; *OR*, vol. VII, p. 616; Simon, ed., *Grant Papers*, vol. 4, p. 284.

Two: A Crisis of Faith

1. James A. Hoobler, *Cities Under the Gun*, pp. 17–18, 29, 41, 45, 48; Thomas L. Connelly, *Civil War Tennessee*, p. 14; Anita S. Goodstein, *Nashville, 1780–1860*, pp. 185, 187; Benjamin F. Cooling, *Forts Henry and Donelson*, pp. 31–32; Walter T. Durham, *Nashville*, pp. 3–6. The thirty-thousand figure represents the metropolitan population.

2. Larry J. Daniel and Riley Gunter, *Confederate Cannon Foundries*, pp. 27–30; *Southern Confederacy*, September 21, 1861; William A. Albaugh and Edward N. Simmons, *Confederate Arms*, pp. 249, 267; *Baton Rouge Daily Advocate*, May 22, 1861; Record of Stores Purchased, Received and Issued, Nashville and Atlanta Arsenal, 1861–1862, chap. IV, vol. 19, record group 109, NA; William Preston Johnston, *The Life of Gen. Albert Sidney Johnston*, pp. 493, 519; Nancy D. Baird, *David Wendall Yandell*, p. 46; *OR*, vol. VII, pp. 818–19; ser. IV, vol. I, p. 1035.

3. Horn, ed., *Tennessee's War 1861–1865*, p. 65; John Miller McKee, *The Great Panic*, pp. 8–11; Durham, *Nashville*, pp. 14–15, 17–18; Sam L. Clark and H. D. Ridley, eds., "Outline of the Organization of the Medical Department of the Confederate Army," p. 59; *Memphis Daily Avalanche*, February 17, 1862; *New Orleans Picayune*, February 20, 1862; Thomas L. Connelly, *Army of the Heartland*, p. 133.

4. *OR*, vol. VII, p. 881; John B. Lindsley, ed., *Military Annals of Tennessee*, pp. 417, 430; Charles Mott, Jr., "War Journal of Confederate Staff Officer Charles R. Mott, Jr.," p. 240; Hobbler, "The Diary of Louisa Brown Pearl," p. 312; Johnston, *Johnston*, p. 515.

5. McKee, *Great Panic*, pp. 18, 19–21, 23–24; Basil W. Duke, *A History of Morgan's Cavalry*, p. 116.

6. Johnston, *Johnston*, p. 496; Broomsfield Ridley, ed., *Battles and Sketches of the Army of Tennessee*, p. 70; Duke, *Morgan's Cavalry*, p. 116; Wyeth, *That Devil Forrest*, p. 73; Thomas Jordan and Roger Pryor, *The Campaigns of Lieut.-Gen. N. B. Forrest*, p. 103; McKee, *Great Panic*, pp. 19, 21, 25; Steven E. Woodworth, *Jefferson Davis and His Generals*, pp. 131–32; Brian Steel Wills, *Battle from the Start*, pp. 26–52.

7. Joseph Boyce, "The Evacuation of Nashville," p. 62; McKee, *Great Panic*, pp. 22–23; *OR*, vol. VII, p. 428; John B. Lindsley Diary, February 20, 1862, TSLA.

8. *OR*, ser. IV, vol. I, p. 1035; Duke, *Morgan's Cavalry*, p. 116; Jordan and Pryor, *Forrest*, p. 73; Charles W. Anderson, "After the Fall of Fort Donelson," pp. 289–90; McKee, *Great Panic*, p. 26; Connelly, *Army of the Heartland*, p. 136.

9. Connelly, *Army of the Heartland*, pp. 135–36; William Stevenson, *Thirteen Months in the Rebel Army*, p. 61; Ridley, ed., *Battles and Sketches*, pp. 72–73; *Cincinnati Commercial*, March 15, 1862; Durham, *Nashville*, pp. 52–53. Despite Forrest's criticism, Floyd had his supporters at the time. See Duke, *Morgan's Cavalry*, pp. 117–18.

10. *New Orleans Picayune*, February 27, 1862; March 7, 1862.

11. Charles Roland, *Albert Sidney Johnston*, pp. 6, 29, 51, 61, 70, 230–32, 236–37, 261; Shelby Foote, *The Civil War*, vol. 1, p. 168; *Nashville Republican Banner*, November 3, 1861; Connelly, *Army of the Heartland*, p. 62; Woodworth, *Davis*, p. 49.

12. Roland, *Johnston*, pp. 30, 31; Jeremy Gilmer to wife, March 6, 1862, Jeremy Gilmer Letters, SHC; Johnston, *Johnston*, pp. 505–6.

13. *OR*, vol. VII, pp. 904–5; Johnston, *Johnston*, p. 504; Nathaniel C. Hughes, Jr., ed., *Liddell's Record*, p. 55.

14. *New Orleans Picayune*, March 6, 1862; Alice Ready Diary, March 3, 7, 13, 1862, TSLA; Liddell to wife, February 28, 1862, St. John Liddell Papers, LSU; Nathaniel C. Hughes, Jr., *General William J. Hardee*, p. 95.

15. Johnston, *Johnston*, pp. 317–18; George W. Baylor, "With Gen. A. S. Johnston at Shiloh," p. 609; Peter J. Sehlinger, " 'At the Moment of Victory, ' " pp. 324–25; William W. Mackall, *A Son's Recollections*, pp. 169–70; Gilmer to wife, March 29, 1862, Gilmer Letters, SHC. Mackall later boasted, "I am a general made by Beauregard."

16. *New Orleans Picayune*, March 6, 1862; *Memphis Appeal*, February 21, 1862; Connelly, *Army of the Heartland*, p. 135; Johnston, *Johnston*, p. 503; P. G. T. Beauregard, "The Shiloh Campaign," p. 5.

17. Roland, *Johnston*, pp. 300–301; Cooling, *Forts Henry and Donelson*, p. 239; Alfred Roman, *The Military Operations of General Beauregard*, vol. 1, p. 223.

18. Connelly, *Army of the Heartland*, p. 138; Cooling, *Forts Henry and Donelson*, p. 238; James L. McDonough, *Shiloh*, p. 67. Woodworth's interpretation suggests that Beauregard's efforts were not toward a bold strategy, but that he desired to pass the responsibility of command (*Davis*, p. 95).

19. Gilmer to wife, February 22, 1862, Gilmer Letters, SHC; Johnston to Hardee, February 22, 1862, Letter Book of the Headquarters of the Western Department, Kuntz Collection, TU; *OR*, vol. VII, p. 905. Lieutenant Colonel S. W. Ferguson arrived in Murfreesboro shortly after Harris. He carried a message from Beauregard requesting that Johnston shift his base from Stevenson to Decatur. (Roman, *Beauregard*, vol. 1, p. 507.)

20. Connelly, *Army of the Heartland*, p. 124; Roland, *Johnston*, p. 306; T. Harry Williams, *P. G. T. Beauregard*, p. 124; Woodworth, *Davis*, p. 86; Roman, *Beauregard*, vol. 1, p. 258.

21. Johnston, *Johnston*, p. 504; Richard E. Beringer et al., *Why the South Lost the Civil War*, p. 242. Just prior to the Battle of Stones River, Joseph E. Johnston inquired of Davis: "Which is more valuable, Tennessee or Mississippi?"

22. *OR*, vol. VII, pp. 277, 862–63, 872; vol. X, pt. 2, pp. 297, 307–9, 320.

23. Connelly, *Army of the Heartland*, pp. 140–42; Johnston, *Johnston*, p. 504; Williams, *Beauregard*, pp. 121–23; Roland, *Johnston*, pp. 302–3. Connelly and Williams have concluded that Johnston was preoccupied with Buell and refused to act as an army commander. Roland rather weakly suggests that Johnston may not have trusted anyone else with the command of the eastern wing.

24. *Mobile Advertiser & Register*, February 4, 1862; Cooling, *Forts Henry and Donelson*, p. 78; Richard McMurry, *Two Great Rebel Armies*, p. 122.

25. Roman, *Beauregard*, vol. 1, pp. 219, 233; Beauregard to Johnston, February 8, 1862, Albert Sidney Johnston and P. G. T. Beauregard Correspondence, LHA; McMurry, *Two Great Rebel Armies*, p. 122; *OR*, vol. VII, p. 193; Connelly, *Army of the Heartland*, pp. 130, 132; Williams, *Beauregard*, p. 121.

26. Connelly, *Army of the Heartland*, pp. 131, 138, 140, 141; Woodworth, *Davis*, p. 95; Roman, *Beauregard*, vol. 1, pp. 233, 244; Beauregard to Johnston, February 22, 26, 1862, Johnston-Beauregard Correspondence, LHA.

27. Joseph H. Parks, *General Leonidas Polk, C.S.A.*, pp. 213–14; Roman, *Beauregard*, vol. 1, pp. 234–35. The facts do not sustain Parks's conclusion that "Polk was too good a soldier not to understand the fate that awaited Columbus." Long after the war, the bishop's biographer-son continued to argue that Columbus should have been held. On Johnston's failure to control Polk, see Connelly, *Army of the Heartland*, pp. 106, 108, 142.

28. *OR*, vol. VII, p. 893.

29. *Richmond Examiner*, February 20, 1862; Paul M. Angle and Earl S. Miers, *Tragic Years 1860–1865*, p. 200; Johnston, *Johnston*, pp. 511–12; *Richmond Whig*, March 8, 1862; *Memphis Appeal*, February 23, 1862; *New Orleans Picayune*, February 19, 1862; J. Cutler Andrews, *The South Reports the Civil War*, p. 134; *Southern Confederacy*, March 20, 1862.

30. *Richmond Whig*, February 21, 1862; Frank E. Vandiver, ed., *The Civil War Diary of General Josiah Gorgas*, p. 3.

31. Tennessee Delegation to Davis, March 8, 1862, Gustavus A. Henry Papers, TSLA; Jefferson Davis, *The Rise and Fall of the Confederate Government*, vol. 2, p. 38; "Proceedings of the First Congress," p. 135.

32. "Proceedings of the First Congress," pp. 132–33.

33. Jon L. Wakelyn, *Biographical Dictionary of the Confederacy*, p. 322; "Proceedings of the First Congress," p. 133; Robert D. Meade, *Judah P. Benjamin*, p. 235; Johnston, *Johnston*, p. 513; John E. Gonzales, "Henry Stuart Foote," p. 386; Hudson Strode, *Jefferson Davis*, p. 206; Thomas Bragg Diary, February 21, 1862, SHC; *Richmond Examiner*, February 21, 1862.

34. Davis exhibited a similar blind loyalty to such friends as Polk, Bragg, Crittenden, and later John Pemberton. It must be pointed out, however, that this loyalty also extended to Robert E. Lee. As for Sidney Johnston, Woodworth extolled Davis for supporting the general "when the fainthearted were clamoring for removal" (*Davis*, p. 308).

35. Johnston, *Johnston*, p. 514; Bragg Diary, March 18, 1862, SHC; Rosser H. Taylor, ed., "Boyce-Hammond Correspondence," pp. 349–50; "Proceedings of the First Congress," pp. 176–77; Strode, *Davis*, p. 222.

36. *Memphis Avalanche*, March 9, 1862; *New Orleans Picayune*, March 21, 1862; *Mobile Adviser & Register*, March 13, 1862.

37. Allen Nevins, *Ordeal of the Union*, vol. 3, pt. 2, pp. 12–13; Kenneth P. Williams, *Lincoln Finds a General*, vol. 3, pp. 104–5; Herman Hattaway and Archer Jones, *How the North Won*, pp. 54–55; J. Cutler Andrews, *The North Reports the Civil War*, pp. 158, 160.

38. William S. McFeely, *Grant*, p. 96; Stephen E. Ambrose, *Halleck*, p. 21; J. F. C. Fuller, *The Generalship of Ulysses S. Grant*, p. 98; Carl Sandburg, *Abraham Lincoln*, vol. 1, p. 467; Cooling, *Forts Henry and Donelson*, p. 249.

39. McFeely, *Grant*, p. 56; Bruce Catton, *Grant Moves South*, pp. 123–24; W. E. Woodward, *Meet General Grant*, pp. 212–13.

40. Andrews, *North Reports the Civil War*, pp. 168, 679–80n.

41. Catton, *Grant Moves South*, pp. 186–87, 506; Charles A. Dana, *The Life of Ulysses S. Grant*, p. 71; McFeely, *Grant*, p. 105; John Y. Simon, ed., *The Papers of Ulysses S. Grant*, vol. 4, p. 306; Benjamin P. Thomas and Harold M. Hyman, *Stanton*, p. 185.

42. McFeely, *Grant*, p. 104; Nevins, *Ordeal of the Union*, vol. 3, pt. 2, pp. 27–28; Woodward, *Meet General Grant*, p. 226. See also Louis A. Coolidge, *Ulysses S. Grant*, p. 77. McFeely deduced, "Once a victor, Grant became a rival." Nevins considered it "difficult to avoid the suspicion that Halleck was jealous of Grant's achievements." Cooling wrote, "The desk-bound Halleck was simply jealous and frustrated" (*Forts Henry and Donelson*, p. 249). Fuller considered Halleck's conduct "obvious—because he was jealous of him" (*Grant*, p. 98n).

43. *OR*, vol. VII, pp. 679, 680.

44. Ibid., pp. 682, 683; William T. Sherman, *Memoirs of General William T. Sherman*, p. 225; Simon, ed., *Grant Papers*, pp. 319, 335. Catton concluded that Halleck "certainly had no intention of driving Grant out of the Army" (*Grant Moves South*, p. 198).

45. McFeely, *Grant*, pp. 105–6; John Brinton, *Personal Memoirs of John H. Brinton*, pp.

148, 150; Woodward, *Meet General Grant*, p. 226; Simon, ed., *Grant Papers*, vol. 4, p. 327.

46. *OR*, vol. X, pt. 2, pp. 2, 5, 13, 15.

47. Ibid., pp. 15, 21, 22.

48. Ezra J. Warner, *Generals in Blue*, pp. 455–56; U. S. Grant, *Personal Memoirs of U. S. Grant*, p. 221; Augustus Chetlain, *Recollections of Seventy Years*, pp. 81–83, 86; *OR*, vol. X, pt. 1, p. 6; Brinton, *Personal Memoirs*, p. 150; Simon, ed., *Grant Papers*, vol. 4, p. 344.

49. Catton, *Grant Moves South*, pp. 212–13; Simon, ed., *Grant Papers*, vol. 4, p. 343.

50. Brinton, *Personal Memoirs*, p. 150; *Chicago Times*, March 17, 1862; Lew Wallace, *An Autobiography*, vol. 1, p. 441.

51. Catton, *Grant Moves South*, pp. 208–9.

52. McFeely, *Grant*, pp. 108–9; Grant, *Memoirs*, p. 221; *OR*, vol. X, pt. 2, p. 36; Simon, ed., *Grant Papers*, vol. 4, p. 338.

53. *Cincinnati Gazette*, March 14, 1862; *Chicago Times*, March 20, 1862.

54. Grant, *Memoirs*, p. 219.

55. J. R. Chumney, Jr., "Don Carlos Buell, Gentleman General," Ph.D. dissertation, pp. 1–5; Warner, *Generals in Blue*, p. 51.

56. *New York Times*, February 23, 1862; Rodney E. Dillon, Jr., "Don Carlos Buell and the Union Leadership," p. 365; Stephen D. Engle, "Don Carlos Buell," p. 94; Durham, *Nashville*, pp. 53–54; Freeman Cleaves, *Rock of Chickamauga*, p. 92.

57. *Cincinnati Commercial*, March 15, 1862; *New York Tribune*, February 26, 1862; Nevins, *Ordeal of the Union*, vol. 3, pt. 2, p. 19. Nevins denounced Buell for his "excessive caution," his "besetting fault of slowness," and engaging in "McClellanesque exaggerations of enemy strength."

58. Rosecrans's army was partially routed at the Battle of Chickamauga in September 1863.

59. *OR*, vol. VII, p. 639.

60. Ibid., pp. 619, 620; *Statement of Major General Buell*, pp. 7–8.

61. *OR*, vol. VII, pp. 648, 649; vol. X, pt. 2, p. 20; *ONR*, vol. XXII, pp. 624, 626. Foote was already embittered that "he [Halleck] and McClellan got the credit for the thing"—the capture of Fort Henry (James M. Hoppin, *Life of Andrew Hull Foote*, p. 260).

62. Grant, *Memoirs*, pp. 215–16; K. P. Williams, *Lincoln Finds a General*, vol. 3, p. 279; *Cincinnati Commercial*, March 1, 1862.

63. Grant, *Memoirs*, pp. 216–17.

64. *OR*, vol. VII, pp. 642, 652, 662, 671; *Statement of Buell*, p. 8; Grant, *Memoirs*, p. 217.

65. Catton, *Grant Moves South*, p. 192; *Chicago Tribune*, March 8, 12, 1862; *New York Times*, March 5, 1862; Durham, *Nashville*, p. 52; *OR*, vol. VII, p. 670. On March 1, Buell wrote that he finally had enough troops in the city "to feel secure" (*OR*, vol. VII, p. 675).

66. McFeely, *Grant*, p. 105; Catton, *Grant Moves South*, p. 192; Simon, ed., *Grant Papers*, vol. 4, p. 344; Grant, *Memoirs*, p. 217. The Federals obtained a February 24, 1862, copy of the *Memphis Avalanche* stating that Johnston's plan was to lure Buell south of the Cumberland River so that his communications might be severed (*Nashville Times*, March 4, 1862).

67. *OR*, vol. VII, pp. 671, 675, 676, 679, 682; vol. X, pt. 2, pp. 10, 11.

68. *Cincinnati Commercial*, March 15, 18, 1862; Durham, *Nashville*, p. 56; *OR*, vol. X, pt. 2, p. 37; William R. Plum, *The Military Telegraph During the Civil War in the United States*, vol. 1, p. 204.

69. Thomas Harrison to wife, March 5, 1862, Thomas Harrison Letters, INHS; James F. Mohr to brother, March 5, 1862, James F. Mohr Letters, FC; James G. Genco, *To the Sound of Musketry and Tap of the Drum*, p. 24.

70. *New York Times*, February 24, 1862; *Chicago Times* quoted in *New York Times*, March 2, 1862; *Statement of Buell*, p. 8; James A. Ramage, *Rebel Raiders*, p. 56.

Three: Golden Opportunities

1. George W. Cable, "New Orleans Before the Capture," pp. 14–19; Charles Dufour, *The Night the War Was Lost*, pp. 25–26; *OR*, vol. VI, pp. 823–24, 825; F. J. Taylor, ed., *The Secret Diary of Robert Patrick, 1861–1865*, p. 37; Patricia L. Faust, ed., *Historical Times Encyclopedia of the Civil War*, p. 647.
2. Arthur W. Bergeron, Jr., ed., *The Civil War Reminiscences of Major Silas T. Grisamore, C.S.A.*, pp. 8, 16–18; William W. Cooper and Donald M. Fowler, eds., " 'Your Affectionate Husband,' " p. 29; *OR*, vol. VI, p. 847; vol. VII, pp. 890, 891, 895.
3. W. H. Stephenson and E. A. Davis, eds., "The Civil War Diary of Willie Micajah Barrow," pp. 718–19; *Memphis Appeal*, March 4, 1862; John A. Cato to wife, February 27, 1862, John A. Cato Letters, MDAH; *OR*, vol. VI, p. 847; Taylor, ed., *Patrick Diary*, p. 34.
4. Alfred Roman, *The Military Operations of General Beauregard*, vol. 1, pp. 240–42; Ephraim C. Dawes, "The Battle of Shiloh," pp. 130–31.
5. *New Orleans Picayune*, March 2, 6, 7, 8, 11, 1862; Joseph Lyman to wife, March 11, 1862, Joseph Lyman Letters, YU; "Memorial to Louisianians at Shiloh," p. 342; Carl Moneyhon and Bobby Roberts, *Portraits of Conflict*, p. 181; Earl C. Woods, ed., *The Shiloh Diary of Edmond Enoul Livaudais*, pp. 15–17. The Orleans Light Horse, with seventy-five men, later came to Memphis on *General Quitman* (Army of Tennessee Papers, TU).
6. Grady McWhiney, *Braxton Bragg and Confederate Defeat*, pp. 191, 202–3.
7. *OR*, vol. VI, pp. 829, 834, 836, 838, 843; Jones to Ruggles, March 5, 1862, Daniel Ruggles Papers, DU; Jones to Bragg, March 8, 1862; Jones to Villepique, March 8, 1862, both in Braxton Bragg Papers, WRHS; *Mobile Advertiser & Register*, March 13, 1862; John K. Folmar, ed., *From That Terrible Field*, p. 45.
8. Hugh C. Bailey, ed., "An Alabamian at Shiloh," p. 146; *Mobile Advertiser & Register*, March 13, 1862; Robert C. Black, *Railroads of the Confederacy*, p. 140; Jones to Bragg, March 9, 1862; Jones to Slaughter, March 15, 1862; Jones to Ruggles, March 15, 16, 1862, all in Bragg Papers, WRHS.
9. *OR*, vol. VI, pp. 828, 868, 875; vol. X, pt. 1, p. 12; Jones to Benjamin, March 15, 1862; Jones to G. G. Flynt, March 18, 1862, both in Bragg Papers, WRHS.
10. McWhiney, *Bragg*, pp. 202–3; *New York Times*, April 5, 1862; Lockwood Tower, ed., *A Carolinian Goes to War*, p. 15. Five of Bragg's regiments were sent to other locations—one to Island No. 10 and four to eastern Tennessee. One of the latter subsequently came to Corinth. (*OR*, vol. X, pt. 2, pp. 308–9, 409.)
11. *New Orleans Picayune*, March 19, 1862; *OR*, vol. VII, p. 912; Beauregard to Johnston, March 17, 1862, Albert Sidney Johnston and P. G. T. Beauregard Correspondence, LHA; Roman, *Beauregard*, vol. 1, p. 513.
12. Roman, *Beauregard*, vol. 1, pp. 245, 507; Thomas Jordan, "Recollections of General Beauregard's Service," p. 404.
13. Bragg to wife, March 20, 1862, Bragg Papers, DU.
14. *OR*, vol. VII, p. 906; vol. X, pt. 2, pp. 300, 306–7; Walker to Ruggles, March 10, 1862; Ruggles to Bragg, March 11, 1862, both in Ruggles Papers, DU.
15. *OR*, vol. VII, pp. 900–901; Roman, *Beauregard*, vol. 1, p. 241; William L. Shea and Earl J. Hess, *Pea Ridge*, p. 23.
16. *OR*, vol. VIII, pp. 539, 591.
17. Ibid., pp. 750–52, 755; Shea and Hess, *Pea Ridge*, pp. 270–71. Although admitting to only 1,300 casualties, Van Dorn had actually suffered at least 2,000, and hundreds deserted on the retreat.

18. Charles Roland, *Albert Sidney Johnston*, p. 311. By the end of March 1862, Halleck had over fifty-eight thousand troops present for duty in Missouri, more than enough to handle Van Dorn's weakened army (*OR*, vol. VIII, pp. 789–90).

19. *OR*, vol. VIII, pp. 103–4, 108, 142, 144–45, 186, 613, 795; McCown to Polk, March 5, 1862, Leonidas Polk Papers, US. Reelfoot Lake, forty miles long, was reported by Chief Engineer Asa Gray to be "very deep and the dead cypress timber scattered about makes it difficult to navigate."

20. Nathaniel C. Hughes, Jr., *The Battle of Belmont*, pp. 37, 201; *OR*, vol. VIII, pp. 765, 766, 770, 771, 772; vol. X, pt. 2, p. 329; Roman, *Beauregard*, vol. 1, pp. 356–57; *New Orleans Picayune*, March 2, 1862.

21. *OR*, vol. VIII, pp. 782, 797; Roman, *Beauregard*, vol. 1, p. 362. The actual number of Confederates at Island No. 2 has long been disputed. A study by the author in preparation for a book on Island No. 10 concludes that probably 5,300 aggregate were present, including 1,300 who were sick. After deducting the heavy artillery, McCown did not have 2,300 present for duty. Pope eventually amassed 21,000 troops, not counting the infantry brigade operating with the fleet. (*OR*, vol. VIII, p. 652.)

22. Roman, *Beauregard*, vol. 1, p. 239.

23. Ibid., p. 248; *OR*, vol. VII, p. 915; Beauregard to Johnston, March 6, 1862, Johnston-Beauregard Correspondence, LHA. The 7,000 figure does not include the 21st Tennessee at Union City or the 35th Tennessee at Trenton (*OR*, vol. X, pt. 2, p. 382).

24. Roman, *Beauregard*, vol. 1, p. 238; *OR*, vol. VII, pp. 910, 915; vol. X, pt. 2, p. 382; Beauregard to Johnston, March 6, 1862, Johnston-Beauregard Correspondence, LHA; Woods, ed., *Livaudais Diary*, p. 19; Charles Johnson to wife, February 23, 1862, Charles Johnson Letters, LSU.

25. Thomas L. Connelly, *Army of the Heartland*, p. 140; Beauregard to Johnston, March 2, 1862, Johnston-Beauregard Correspondence, LHA; Roman, *Beauregard*, vol. 1, p. 249; Gilmer to wife, March 6, 1862, Jeremy Gilmer Letters, SHC; William Polk, *Leonidas Polk*, vol. 2, p. 84; *OR*, vol. X, pt. 2, p. 332; Jordan, "Recollections," p. 408; H. M. Dillard, "Beauregard-Johnston-Shiloh," p. 99.

26. Ernie Rice, "A History of the Corinth, Mississippi Depot," NEMMA. Joseph T. Sanders, "M. A. Miller's Sketch Book of 1860," M.A. thesis, pp. 51–64; *OR*, vol. VII, pp. 890, 894; *Chicago Tribune*, June 6, 1862. M. A. Miller was a civil engineer with the Memphis & Charleston Railroad. In 1860, while staying at Corinth, he sketched every business street and scores of homes, thus capturing the Civil War appearance of the town.

27. Edwin C. Bearss, "A Federal Raid Up the Tennessee River," pp. 261–70.

28. Faust, ed., *Encyclopedia*, p. 797; *OR*, vol. VII, pp. 887–88, 909; vol. X, pt. 2, p. 304.

29. *OR*, vol. X, pt. 1, p. 646; pt. 2, p. 313; Bearss, "Federal Raid," p. 266; Civil War Centennial Commission, *Tennesseans in the Civil War*, vol. 1, pp. 256–57. Chalmers's brigade included the 38th Tennessee, 5th Alabama Battalion, 9th Mississippi, and a section of artillery, and at that time numbered perhaps 1,500.

30. *OR*, vol. VII, pp. 421, 619, 894, 895.

31. Ibid., pp. 895, 909.

32. Faust, ed., *Encyclopedia*, p. 515; *OR*, vol. VII, p. 909; Bergeron, ed., *Grisamore*, pp. 19–20.

33. *New Orleans Picayune*, March 11, 1862; B. G. Brazleton, *A History of Hardin County, Tennessee*, p. 35; *Memphis Commercial Appeal*, May 3, 1952.

34. *Chicago Tribune*, March 7, 8, 1862; *Cincinnati Commercial*, March 4, 5, 1862; *Nashville Times*, March 11, April 9, 1862; *New Orleans Picayune*, March 6, 9, 11, 1862; *Mobile Advertiser & Register*, March 14, 1862; *OR*, vol. X, pt. 2, p. 8; Bergeron, ed., *Grisamore*, pp. 19–22. The gunboats were *Tyler* and *Lexington*. The Federals reported losses of two killed, six wounded, and three missing, but the Southerners found three dead and captured four.

35. *OR*, vol. X, pt. 2, pp. 300, 302–3; Bragg to Ruggles, March 7, 1862, Ruggles Papers, DU.
36. *OR*, vol. X, pt. 1, pp. 16–19; pt. 2, pp. 305–6; *Memphis Appeal*, March 18, 1862.
37. *OR*, vol. X, pt. 2, pp. 316, 317.
38. Roman, *Beauregard*, vol. 1, p. 520; *OR*, vol. X, pt. 2, p. 317; *ONR*, vol. XXII, p. 677; Chalmers to Ruggles, March 12, 1862, Ruggles Papers, DU.
39. *OR*, vol. X, pt. 2, pp. 317, 319.
40. Ibid., pp. 316–17.
41. Ibid., p. 317. Confederate scouts were aware that a detachment of Federal troops had landed at Savannah on March 10 (ibid., pt. 1, p. 15).
42. Ibid., vol. VII, p. 641; Herman Hattaway and Archer Jones, *How the North Won*, pp. 77, 149. Allen Nevins stated: "Beyond question, had he [Halleck] now vigorously pressed a Union advance all along the line, the richest fruits might have been garnered" (*Ordeal of the Union*, vol. 3, pt. 2, pp. 28–29).
43. Nevins, *Ordeal of the Union*, vol. 3, pt. 2, pp. 28–29; Roman, *Beauregard*, vol. 1, p. 233. Nevins deduced that Halleck missed his best opportunity because "he never perceived it."
44. *OR*, vol. X, pt. 2, pp. 8, 10, 12.
45. Nevins, *Ordeal of the Union*, vol. 3, pt. 2, pp. 28–29.
46. *OR*, vol. VII, p. 674; vol. X, pt. 2, p. 7.
47. Nevins condemned the plan as an obscure raid that would strategically isolate Grant's army (*Ordeal of the Union*, vol. 3, pt. 2, p. 28); Archer Jones declared that the Federals gave the Confederates an opportunity to strike when Grant's army operated "far away from Buell's separate army" (*Civil War Command and Strategy*, p. 49).
48. *OR*, vol. X, pt. 2, pp. 10, 11, 16, 18.
49. Ibid., vol. VIII, pp. 582–83, 591, 595, 613; vol. X, pt. 2, p. 7; Richard E. Beringer et al., *Why the South Lost the Civil War*, p. 129. Pope believed that he could take New Madrid if it weren't for the Confederate flotilla (*OR*, vol. VIII, p. 81).
50. *OR*, vol. VIII, p. 682; vol. X, pt. 2, pp. 19, 20.
51. Ibid., p. 677; John Y. Simon, ed., *The Papers of Ulysses S. Grant*, vol. 4, p. 342. The *Cincinnati Commercial* of March 19, 1862, lists by name fifty-seven transports in the expedition, but omitting *Golden State*, *Uncle Sam*, and *Conewaga*; thus the total was actually sixty. Tim Hurst's list ("The Battle of Shiloh," pp. 87–88) apparently includes every vessel that served in the west but is unreliable as regards the Shiloh Campaign. Confederate scouts reported counting sixty-one boats, a figure that may have included one of the gunboats.
52. William T. Sherman, *Memoirs of General William T. Sherman*, pp. 225–26; Dawes, "Battle of Shiloh," p. 109; Thomas Worthington, *Brief History of the 46th Ohio Volunteers*, pp. 10–11.
53. John A. Bering and Thomas Montgomery, *History of the 48th Ohio Volunteer Infantry*, p. 15; Worthington, *46th Ohio*, p. 10.
54. *OR*, vol. X, pt. 2, p. 21; Simon, ed., *Grant Papers*, vol. 4, p. 342.
55. Fritz Haskell, ed., "Diary of Colonel William Camm, 1861–1865," p. 839; Lucius Barber, *Army Memoirs of Lucius W. Barber*, p. 47; Bridgford to wife, March 9, 1862, Oliver A. Bridgford Letters, 45th Illinois File, SNMP; Samuel Stephenson to father, April 4, 1862, Samuel Stephenson Letters, 48th Ohio File, SNMP; Timothy Blaisdell to wife, March 12, 1862, Timothy M. Blaisdell Letters, Civil War Times Collection, USMHI; Edwin C. Bearss, ed., *The Story of the Fifty-Fifth Regiment, Illinois Volunteer Infantry*, p. 63; Thaddeus H. Capron, "War Diary of Thaddeus H. Capron, 1861–1865," p. 341; James R. Zearing, "Letters Written by Dr. James R. Zearing," p. 151; *OR*, vol. X, pt. 1, p. 74.
56. George Mills, ed., "The Sharp Family Civil War Letters," p. 491; Lew Wallace, *An Autobiography*, vol. 1, p. 443; Saul Sylvester Journal, March 11, 1862, IOSHD;

Blaisdell to wife, March 12, 1862, Blaisdell Letters, USMHI; Capron, "War Diary," p. 341; Edwin L. Hobart, *Semi-History of a Boy-Veteran of the Twenty-Eighth Regiment Illinois Volunteers*, p. 7; Leander Stillwell, *The Story of a Common Soldier*, pp. 34–35.

57. Samuel Eels to uncle, March 24, 1862, Samuel Eels Letters, LC; Mildred Throne, ed., *The Civil War Diary of Cyrus F. Boyd*, p. 25; S. Stephenson to W. H. Stephenson, March 7, 1862, S. Stephenson Letters, 48th Ohio File, SNMP; Mildred Throne, ed., "Erastus B. Sopher's History of Company D," p. 175; William H. Warren to wife, March 11, 1862, William H. Warren Letters, SHSIO; Joseph Stibbs to father, March 26, 1862, Joseph Stibbs Letters, TU; Henry Wright, *A History of the Sixth Iowa Infantry*, p. 61; G. A. Stanton Journal, March 6, 1862, UMEM, Mississippi Valley Collection; Franklin Bailey to parents, March 27, 1862, Franklin Bailey Letters, MHC; Sylvester Journal, March 7, 1862 (IOSHD).

58. Edwin Reynolds Diary, March 12, 1862, Civil War Times Collection, USMHI; John Bell, *Tramps and Triumphs of the Second Iowa Infantry*, pp. 14–15; Hobart, *Semi-History*, p. 7; Thomas C. Watkins Diary, March 18, 1862, Civil War Times Collection, USMHI; Thomas Jones, *Complete History of the 46th Regiment, Illinois Volunteer Infantry*, p. 287; Zearing, "Zearing Letters," pp. 151–52; William W. Cluett, *History of the 57th Regiment Illinois Volunteer Infantry*, pp. 15, 16; Adolph Englemann to wife, March 12, 1862, Adolph Englemann Letters, ILSL; Bering and Montgomery, *48th Ohio*, p. 15; S. H. M. Byers, *Iowa in War Times*, p. 497; Jordan and Thomas, "Reminiscences," pp. 309–10; Sylvester Journal, March 7, 1862, IOSHD.

59. Mary Ann Anderson, ed., *The Civil War Diary of Allen Morgan Geer*, p. 21; Haskell, ed., "Camm Diary," p. 840.

60. "Cherry Mansion Report," SNMP; Bruce Catton, *Grant Moves South*, p. 222; Isabel Wallace, *Life and Letters of General W. H. L. Wallace*, p. 175; *Cincinnati Times*, March 21, 1862; April 2, 1862; *Chicago Times*, March 24, 1862; Anderson, ed., *Geer Diary*, p. 22; Throne, ed., "Sopher's History," p. 175; Bering and Montgomery, *48th Ohio*, p. 15; Teuton, *Steamboat Days on the Tennessee River*, p. 7; "Mrs. Annie Irwin Cherry," p. 33. The *Missouri Daily Democrat* of April 29, 1862, stated that as many as five hundred Unionists came into Savannah and 150 enlisted.

61. *OR*, vol. X, pt. 2, pp. 8, 16, 21.

62. Brazleton, *Hardin County*, pp. 29, 56, 67; *Goodspeed's History of Tennessee*, pp. 829–35; Alex McEathron to brother, April 3, 1862, Alexander McEathron Letters, ILSL; William Skinner to brother, March 27, 1862, William Skinner Letters, 71st Ohio File, SNMP.

63. Irving McKee, *"Ben-Hur" Wallace*, pp. 19–23, 45; Ezra J. Warner, *Generals in Blue*, pp. 535–36.

64. L. Wallace, *Autobiography*, vol. 1, pp. 444–45; McKee, *"Ben-Hur" Wallace*, p. 45. In his memoirs, Wallace wrote that Smith, "with a twinkle in his eye," referred to the crossing as Wallace's bridge. Wallace did not actually hear that name until 1901, however, when he visited the battlefield. See Joseph W. Rich, "General Lew Wallace at Shiloh," p. 308.

65. Wallace, *Autobiography*, vol. 1, p. 445; Albert D. Richardson, *A Personal History of Ulysses S. Grant*, p. 234; Warner, *Generals in Blue*, p. 456; Simon, ed., *Grant Papers*, vol. 4, p. 343.

66. L. Wallace, *Autobiography*, vol. 1, p. 447; Marquerites Moore, "A Study of Early Crump, Tennessee," pp. 29, 31; *OR*, vol. X, pt. 1, pp. 13, 15; *Missouri Daily Democrat*, March 24, 1862; James S. Fogle Diary, March 13, 1862, 11th Indiana File, SNMP.

67. *OR*, vol. X, pt. 1, p. 9; *New York Times*, March 30, 1862; Wallace to wife, March 15, 1862, Lewis Wallace Papers, INHS.

68. *OR*, vol. X, pt. 1, pp. 12–13; pt. 2, p. 318.

69. Ibid., pt. 1, pp. 9–10; *Cincinnati Commercial*, March 14, 17, 21, 1862; *New York Times*, March 30, 1862.

70. *OR*, vol. X, pt. 1, pp. 10, 11. The *Memphis Appeal* of March 16, 1862, reported: "The damage done to the [rail]road was slight and was soon repaired."

71. T. Harry Williams, *McClellan, Sherman and Grant*, pp. 48–49.

72. Ibid., p. 49; Joseph T. Glatthaar, *Partners in Command*, p. 137; James M. Merrill, *William Tecumseh Sherman*, pp. 192–93; Richard Wheeler, *We Knew William Tecumseh Sherman*, p. 24; Albert Castel, *Decision in the West*, pp. 39–42.

73. Williams, *McClellan, Sherman and Grant*, pp. 54, 56–57; John F. Marszalek, *Sherman's Other War*, pp. 60–67; John F. Marszalek, *Sherman*, pp. 164–70.

74. Williams, *McClellan, Sherman and Grant*, pp. 52–53; Glatthaar, *Partners in Command*, pp. 135–38.

75. Worthington, *46th Ohio*, pp. 13–14.

76. Sherman, *Memoirs*, p. 227; *OR*, vol. X, pt. 2, p. 22.

77. *OR*, vol. X, pt. 1, pp. 22, 28.

78. Ibid., pp. 30–31; pt. 2, pp. 327–28.

79. Ibid., pt. 1, p. 23; Christian Zook to friends, March 23, 1862, Christian Zook Letters, 46th Ohio File, SNMP; *New Orleans Picayune*, March 8, 1862; Sherman, *Memoirs*, p. 228.

80. *OR*, vol. X, pt. 1, p. 23; Worthington, *46th Ohio*, p. 17; *Missouri Daily Democrat*, March 17, 1862; *National Intelligencer*, March 25, 1862.

81. *OR*, vol. X, pt. 2, p. 612; Benjamin P. Thomas and Harold M. Hyman, *Stanton*, p. 182; Samuel H. Kamm, *The Civil War Career of Thomas A. Scott*, p. 119; John G. Nicolay and John Hay, *Abraham Lincoln*, vol. 5, p. 315.

82. Thomas and Hyman, *Stanton*, p. 182; Kamm, *Scott*, p. 112; *OR*, vol. VIII, p. 596; vol. X, pt. 2, pp. 28–29; George C. Gorham, *Life and Public Service of Edwin M. Stanton*, vol. 1, p. 304. The order also created a Mountain Department under John C. Frémont.

83. Dennet, ed., *Lincoln and the Civil War*, p. 38; *National Intelligencer*, March 12, 1862; McClellan, *McClellan's Own Story*, pp. 218, 224–26; *New York Times*, March 15, 1862; Philippe, Comte de Paris, "McClellan Organizing the Grand Army," p. 122.

84. Richard McMurry, *Two Great Rebel Armies*, pp. 53–55.

Four: The Armies

1. *OR*, vol. VII, p. 915; vol. X, pt. 1, p. 15; pt. 2, pp. 318, 328, 331.

2. John A. Magee Diary, March 14, 1862, *Philadelphia Inquirer*, April 18, 1862; J. G. Law, "Diary of J. G. Law," p. 301.

3. *OR*, vol. X, pt. 1, pp. 11–12, 29; pt. 2, p. 332; Beauregard to Johnston, March 17, 1862, Albert Sidney Johnston and P. G. T. Beauregard Correspondence, LHA.

4. Grady McWhiney, *Braxton Bragg and Confederate Defeat*, pp. 208–10; William T. Sherman, *Memoirs of General William T. Sherman*, p. 228; *National Intelligencer*, March 27, 1862.

5. *OR*, vol. X, pt. 1, p. 25; pt. 2, p. 341; *New York Times*, March 30, 1862; Beauregard to Johnston, March 17, 1862, Johnston-Beauregard Correspondence, LHA.

6. Special Order 39, February 27, 1862, Albert Sidney Johnston Order Book, LHA; William Preston Johnston, *The Life of Gen. Albert Sidney Johnston*, p. 305; Gilmer to W. P. Johnston, January 18, 1878; M. H. Wright to W. P. Johnston, February 2, 1878, both in Albert Sidney Johnston Papers, Barret Collection, TU.

7. Johnston, *Johnston*, p. 509; Charles Roland, *Albert Sidney Johnston*, p. 304; Johnston to Hardee, March 7, 12, 1862; Johnston to Davis, March 7, 1862; Johnston

to Biddle, March 9, 1862, all in Letter Book of the Headquarters of the Western Department, Kuntz Collection, TU; Special Order 39, February 27, 1862, Johnston Order Book, TU; R. R. Hancock, *Hancock's Diary*, pp. 135–36; *New York Times*, March 16, 1862; Dee Alexander Brown, *The Bold Cavaliers*, pp. 37–39; James A. Ramage, *Rebel Raiders*, pp. 56–60; Howell Carter, *A Cavalryman's Reminiscences of the Civil War*, p. 24.

8. A. H. Mecklin Diary, March 2–12, 1862, MDAH; John C. Caldwell Diary, March 12, 1862, Civil War Times Collection, USMHI; Johnston to Benjamin, March 5, 1862, Letter Book of the Western Headquarters, Kuntz Collection, TU; H. Riley Bock, ed., "One Year at War," p. 190; Robert Dunnavant, Jr., *Decatur, Alabama*, p. 45.

9. Mecklin Diary, March 13, 1862, MDAH; William C. Davis, *The Orphan Brigade*, p. 74; Johnston to Tate, March 6, 1862, Letter Book of the Western Headquarters, Kuntz Collection, TU; Johnston to Beauregard, March 11, 1862, Johnston-Beauregard Correspondence, LHA; D. Sullins, *Recollections of an Old Man*, pp. 216–17; Dunnavant, *Decatur*, p. 3.

10. *OR*, ser. IV, vol. I, p. 1035; Johnston to Beauregard, March 5, 1862; Johnston to Davis, March 7, 1862; Johnston to Hardee, March 12, 1862, all in Letter Book of the Western Headquarters, Kuntz Collection, TU.

11. Johnston, *Johnston*, p. 505; Johnston to Davis, March 18, 1862, Johnston Order Book, TU; John Will Dyer, *Reminiscences*, p. 22; *OR*, vol. X, pt. 2, p. 312; *Nashville Times*, March 11, 1862.

12. Thomas L. Connelly, *Army of the Heartland*, p. 149; *OR*, vol. X, pt. 2, p. 338.

13. Johnston to A. J. Hooper, March 14, 1862 (two telegrams); Johnston to Hindman, March 14, 1862, both in Letter Book of the Western Headquarters, Kuntz Collection, TU.

14. Joseph H. Fussell, "Narrative of Interesting Events Just Prior to Battle of Shiloh," p. 62; Johnston to Beauregard, March 17, 1862; Beauregard to Johnston, March 19, 1862, both in Johnston-Beauregard Correspondence, LHA; Johnston to A. J. Hooper, March 14, 1862, Letter Book of the Western Headquarters, Kuntz Collection, TU; Ruggles to Withers, March 4, 1862, Daniel Ruggles Papers, DU; *National Intelligencer*, March 26, 1862.

15. Bowen to Johnston, March 17, 1862, Johnston-Beauregard Correspondence, LHA; *OR*, vol. X, pt. 2, p. 327; Gilmer to wife, March 15, 1862, Jeremy Gilmer Letters, SHC; Johnston, *Johnston*, p. 521.

16. Johnston to wife, March 18, 1862, Johnston Order Book, LHA; Johnston to Helm, March 16, 1862; Johnston to Crittenden, March 20, 1862; Johnston to Wirt Adams, March 20, 1862; Johnston to Biffle, March 20, 1862; Johnston to Beauregard, March 21, 1862, all in Letter Book of the Western Headquarters, Kuntz Collection, TU.

17. Gilmer to wife, March 12, 1862, Gilmer Letters, SHC; McWhiney, *Bragg*, p. 212.

18. Connelly stated that Johnston "dawdled on the march to Corinth" and "moved too slowly" (*Army of the Heartland*, p. 148). Basil Liddell-Hart concluded that Johnston forfeited much of the time the enemy allowed him and did not appreciate the value of concentrating as much as Beauregard did (*Sherman*, p. 122).

19. H. M. Dillard, "Beauregard-Johnston-Shiloh," pp. 99–100; Jordan, "Recollections of General Beauregard's Service," p. 408.

20. Margaret Greene Rogers, "Corinth 1861–1865," p. 6.

21. Alfred Roman, *The Military Operations of General Beauregard*, vol. 1, pp. 258, 265; Johnston, *Johnston*, pp. 539, 543. Beauregard discounted postwar accounts that as early as January 1862 Johnston predicted a battle at Pittsburg Landing. He pointed to Johnston's March 15 telegram as proof.

22. Roman, *Beauregard*, vol. 1, p. 261.

23. Johnston, *Johnston*, p. 520; *Memphis Avalanche*, March 31, 1862; Gilmer to wife, March 24, 1862, Gilmer Letters, SHC.
24. *OR*, vol. X, pt. 1, p. 396; *New York Tribune*, March 31, 1862.
25. *OR*, vol. X, pt. 2, pp. 367–68, 378, 382.
26. Ibid., p. 359; Law, "J. G. Law Diary," p. 302.
27. *OR*, vol. X, pt. 1, pp. 78–79, 443; pt. 2, pp. 367, 375, 378; Law, "J. G. Law Diary," p. 302; Christopher Losson, *Tennessee's Forgotten Warriors*, pp. 38, 55.
28. *New Orleans Picayune*, March 24, 28, 1862; *New Orleans Crescent*, April 1, 1862; *OR*, vol. X, pt. 2, p. 363.
29. Johnson to wife, March 23, 1862, Charles Johnson Letters, LSU; Earl C. Woods, ed., *The Shiloh Diary of Edmond Enoul Livaudais*, p. 19.
30. *New Orleans Crescent*, March 19, 1862; William S. Dillon Diary, March 24, 1862, UM; Woods, ed., *Livaudais Diary*, pp. 19–20. See also John K. Folmar, ed., *From That Terrible Field*, p. 52.
31. Johnston to Davis, March 7, 1862, Letter Book of the Western Headquarters, Kuntz Collection, TU; John Cato to wife, March 20, 27, 1862, John A. Cato Letters, MDAH; A. H. Tarlske to wife, March 23, 1862, A. H. Tarlske Letters, MDAH.
32. *Southern Confederacy*, April 24, 1862; William Stevenson, *Thirteen Months in the Rebel Army*, pp. 36–37; Folmar, ed., *Terrible Field*, p. 88; Ella Lonn, *Foreigners in the Confederacy*, pp. 496–502; John McGrath, "In a Louisiana Regiment," pp. 103–4, 113, 116.
33. Lyman to wife, March 15, 1862, Joseph Lyman Letters, YU; *Cincinnati Commercial*, April 15, 1862; Folmar, ed., *Terrible Field*, p. 59; John C. Moore, "Shiloh Issues Again," pp. 316–17; Barnes F. Lathrop, "A Confederate Artilleryman at Shiloh," p. 378n. Following the battle, a Northern journalist noted that most of the Confederates wore homespun or butternut (*Chicago Times*, April 24, 1862).
34. *New Orleans Crescent*, April 1, 1862; William W. Cooper and Donald M. Fowler, eds., " 'Your Affectionate Husband,' " p. 31; Jobe M. Foxworth Diary, MDAH; *OR*, vol. X, pt. 1, p. 398.
35. *OR*, vol. X, pt. 1, p. 12; Braxton Bragg, "General Albert Sidney Johnston at Shiloh," Johnston Papers, Barret Collection, TU.
36. Bragg, "General Johnston at Shiloh," Johnston Papers, Barret Collection, TU; Roman, *Beauregard*, vol. 1, p. 260; *OR*, vol. IV, pp. 417, 430; vol. LIII, p. 228; vol. X, pt. 1, p. 575; Edward Porter Thompson, *History of the First Kentucky Brigade*, pp. 58, 87; W. J. McMurray, *History of the Twentieth Tennessee Regiment Volunteer Infantry*, pp. 124–26, 204, 212–13, 390; Mecklin Diary, March 13, 1862, MDAH; R. P. Boswell to E. Lee, March 29, 1862, R. P. Boswell Letters, TSLA.
37. Johnston, *Johnston*, p. 332; Larry J. Daniel and Riley Gunter, *Confederate Cannon Foundries*, p. 27; Edward Porter Thompson, *History of the Orphan Brigade*, p. 857; "List of Guns Furnished by Leeds & Company, April 29, 1862," Letters Sent, Ordnance Officer, Army of Tennessee, chap. IV, vol. 141, record group 109, NA; John Clark & Company, Papers Relating to Citizens and Business Firms, record group 109, NA; *Cincinnati Commercial*, May 6, 1862.
38. Michael Madaus and Robert D. Needham, *The Battle Flags of the Confederate Army of Tennessee*, pp. 23–24, 49–50, 101–2.
39. Edward Munford, "Albert Sidney Johnston"; George W. Johnson to Johnston, March 26, 1862, both in Johnston Papers, Barret Collection, TU.
40. Roman, *Beauregard*, vol. 1, p. 266; Munford, "Albert Sidney Johnston," Johnston Papers, Barret Collection, TU.
41. Johnston, *Johnston*, pp. 517, 520, 550. For examples of Beauregard's name coming before Johnston's, see *Memphis Avalanche*, March 11, 1862; *Cincinnati Times*, April 7, 1862; *New York Tribune*, April 3, 5, 1862. See also Steven E. Woodworth, *Jefferson Davis and His Generals*, p. 89. T. Harry Williams concluded that John-

ston may have realized he should have been exercising central command all along and was now attempting to rectify the situation. Or perhaps he still wished to avoid personal responsibility. (*P. G. T. Beauregard*, p. 125.)

42. Connelly, *Army of the Heartland*, pp. 140–41, 142, 146, 151; James L. McDonough, *Shiloh*, p. 60; *OR*, vol. VII, p. 912.

43. Roland believed that Beauregard claimed too much credit for the organization. *Johnston*, 314.

44. Roman, *Beauregard*, vol. 1, pp. 267–68; Roland, *Johnston*, p. 314.

45. Connelly labeled the organization as "impressive," and Williams stated that it was in every way "superior to what had existed before." McWhiney, on the other hand, noted that Williams's conclusion was "hardly praiseworthy, for almost any organization would have been better than the previous hodgepodge." (Thomas L. Connelly, *Civil War Tennessee*, p. 40; Williams, *Beauregard*, p. 125; McWhiney, *Bragg*, p. 217.)

46. William Polk, *Leonidas Polk*, vol. 2, pp. 89–90; McWhiney, *Bragg*, p. 217.

47. Johnson to wife, March 21, April 1, 1862, Johnson Letters, LSU; McWhiney, *Bragg*, p. 218.

48. William W. Mackall, *A Son's Recollection of His Father*, p. 171; Dudley M. Haydon, "Shiloh"; June T. Gow, "Military Administration in the Confederate Army of Tennessee," pp. 184–86.

49. McWhiney, *Bragg*, pp. 213–15.

50. Ibid., p. 216. Bragg was also clearly irked that Polk ranked him (ibid., pp. 207, 212).

51. William C. Davis, *Breckinridge*, pp. 301–2.

52. Lester N. Fitzhugh, ed., *Cannon Smoke*, p. 169.

53. William L. Shea and Earl J. Hess, *Pea Ridge*, pp. 266–68, 287; *OR*, vol. X, pt. 2, p. 354; Roman, *Beauregard*, vol. 1, pp. 259–60.

54. *OR*, vol. X, pt. 1, p. 361; McWhiney, *Bragg*, p. 212; Johnston, *Johnston*, p. 543.

55. *OR*, vol. X, pt. 2, p. 354; Shea and Hess, *Pea Ridge*, pp. 20, 22; *A Soldier's Honor*, p. 71; William C. Davis, *Jefferson Davis*, p. 403; Woodworth, *Davis*, pp. 112–14.

56. *OR*, vol. VIII, p. 796; Fitzhugh, ed., *Cannon Smoke*, p. 174.

57. Nathaniel C. Hughes, Jr., ed., *Liddell's Record*, pp. 57–61.

58. Johnston, *Johnston*, p. 517.

59. Ibid., pp. 518–22. Johnston's letter to Davis was intercepted and deciphered by the Federals and subsequently published in the *Philadelphia Inquirer*, April 16, 1862.

60. Johnston, *Johnston*, pp. 521–22.

61. Sherman, *Memoirs*, p. 228; *OR*, vol. X, pt. 1, pp. 24, 26.

62. *OR*, vol. X, pt. 1, pp. 24–26; Edwin L. Hobart, *The Truth About Shiloh*, p. 102; *Louisville Daily Journal*, April 2, 1862.

63. *OR*, vol. X, pt. 1, pp. 25–26; Hobart, *Truth About Shiloh*, p. 102; Arthur W. Bergeron, ed., *The Civil War Reminiscences of Major Silas T. Grisamore, C.S.A.*, p. 28; Edwin C. Bearss, ed., *The Story of the Fifty-fifth Regiment, Illinois Volunteer Infantry*, pp. 66–67; *Louisville Daily Journal*, April 2, 1862.

64. *OR*, vol. X, pt. 1, p. 25; Henry Wright, *A History of the Sixth Iowa Infantry*, p. 62.

65. *OR*, vol. X, pt. 1, pp. 26–27.

66. Ibid., p. 28; Bearss, ed., *Fifty-Fifth Illinois*, pp. 66–67; *Chicago Times*, March 26, 1862; John S. Wilcox to wife, March 20, 1862, John S. Wilcox Letters, ILSL; Ephraim J. Hart, *History of the Fortieth Illinois Infantry*, p. 80.

67. *OR*, vol. X, pt. 1, p. 27; Don Carlos Buell, "Shiloh Reviewed," p. 495; M. F. Force, *From Fort Henry to Corinth*, pp. 99–100; Ephraim C. Dawes, "Battle of Shiloh," p. 110; B. G. Brazleton, *A History of Hardin County, Tennessee*, pp. 87–88; "Shiloh National Military Park, Office of the Historian," p. 2, SNMP.

68. *OR*, vol. X, pt. 2, p. 32.

69. John Y. Simon, ed., *The Papers of Ulysses S. Grant*, vol. 4, p. 389; Joseph M. Hanson, *The Conquest of Missouri*, pp. 39–40; Bruce Catton, *Grant Moves South*, p. 222; Patricia L. Faust, ed., *Historical Times Illustrated Encyclopedia of the Civil War*, p. 616; Clarence E. Macartney, *Grant and His Generals*, pp. 206–7; James H. Wilson, *Under the Old Flag*, vol. 1, pp. 135–37; W. E. Woodward, *Meet General Grant*, pp. 206–7; Sherman to W. T. Eliot, September 12, 1885, William T. Sherman Papers, LC.

70. James G. Wilson, *Biographical Sketches of Illinois Officers*, p. 47; *OR*, vol. X, pt. 2, pp. 35, 41.

71. *OR*, vol. X, pt. 2, pp. 41, 43; Simon, ed., *Grant Papers*, vol. 4, pp. 386–87. McDonough correctly noted that Sherman "was not recommending, as has often been assumed, that the entire army be placed at Pittsburg Landing": Sherman also advocated placing troops at Hamburg and Tyler's Landing for a concentric move on Corinth. "And certainly the decision was Grant's responsibility," concluded McDonough. (*Shiloh*, p. 46.)

72. *OR*, vol. X, pt. 2, p. 45; Albert D. Richardson, *A Personal History of Ulysses S. Grant*, p. 234; J. F. C. Fuller, *The Generalship of Ulysses S. Grant*, p. 101.

73. *OR*, vol. X, pt. 2, pp. 44, 46, 49, 50–51. Grant apparently intended to use Halleck's instructions "as a springboard to bring on battle. . . . Halleck sensed this from Grant's telegrams and cautioned against it" (Thomas E. Griess, ed., *The American Civil War*, p. 35).

74. Even if Grant had made his raid on Corinth, the prospects for success did not appear bright. By the time his army could have arrived at the town, at least four of Johnston's brigades probably would have been present to bolster the garrison.

75. Lauman to wife, March 19, 1862, Jacob Lauman Letters, CHS; Dawes, "Battle of Shiloh," p. 113; *OR*, vol. X, pt. 2, p. 84.

76. *OR*, vol. X, pt. 2, p. 84. For units not included in the March 31 and April 5 tabulations, see O. E. Cunningham, "Shiloh and the Western Campaign of 1862," Ph.D. dissertation, pp. 171–72; James G. Day, "The Fifteenth Iowa at Shiloh," pp. 178, 180; George W. McBride, "My Recollections at Shiloh," p. 346; Johnston, *Johnston*, pp. 682, 683, 685; *Chicago Times*, April 20, 1862; *OR*, vol. X, pt. 2, pp. 112–13.

77. Ken Baumann, *Arming the Suckers, 1861–1865*, pp. 73–140; Ira Blanchard, *I Marched With Sherman*, p. 23; *New Orleans Crescent*, April 22, 1862; George F. Witham, *Shiloh, Shells and Artillery Units*, pp. 1–35; Olynthus B. Clark, ed., *Downing's Civil War Diary*, p. 38.

78. *Chicago Times*, April 9, 1862; *Medical and Surgical History*, vol. 1, p. 29; *OR*, vol. X, pt. 2, pp. 57, 63, 73; *Cincinnati Times*, April 7, 1862.

79. *OR*, vol. X, pt. 1, pp. 63, 73.

80. Victor Hicken, "From Vandalia to Vicksburg," Ph.D. dissertation, pp. 167–89; Edward G. Longacre, "Congressman Becomes General," p. 34; Englemann to wife, March 31, 1862, Adolph Englemann Letters, ILSL.

81. Ezra J. Warner, *Generals in Blue*, pp. 244–45; Jeffrey N. Lash, "Stephen Augustus Hurlbut," Ph.D. dissertation, pp. 125–26, 140–41; I. C. Pugh to wife, March 22, 1862, Isaac C. Pugh Letters, 41st Indiana File, SNMP; Warren Olney, " 'Shiloh,' " p. 6.

82. Isabel Wallace, *Life and Letters of General W. H. L. Wallace*, pp. 176, 180; T. M. Eddy, *The Patriotism of Illinois*, vol. 1, pp. 261–63.

83. Eddy, *Patriotism of Illinois*, vol. 1, pp. 267–68; Wallace, *Life and Letters*, pp. 20–26; Richardson, *Grant*, p. 184.

84. John F. Marszalek, *Sherman*, p. 173; John F. Marszalek, *Sherman's Other War*, pp. 74–75.

85. Bailey to parents, March 27, 1862, Franklin Bailey Letters, MHC; *Sycamore True Republican & Sentinel*, April 16 [letter written March 31], 1862, 52nd Illinois File,

SNMP; Lauman to wife, April 2, 1862, Jacob Lauman Letters, CHS; Shumway to wife, March 19, 1862, Payton Shumway Letters, ILSL; Wilcox to wife, March 22, 1862, John S. Wilcox Letters, ILSL.

86. Bailey to parents, March 27, 1862, Bailey Letters, MHC; Shanks to mother, March 20, 1862, Edward B. Shanks Letters, 12th Illinois File, SNMP; Wyllie to family, March 31, 1862, William R. Wyllie Letters, 58th Illinois File, SNMP.

87. Hanson, *Conquest*, p. 38; *Chicago Tribune*, February 18, 1862.

88. William L. Burton, *Melting Pot Soldiers*, pp. 77–79; Ella Lonn, *Foreigners in the Union Army*, pp. 668, 669, 670, 671, 674; Nels Hokanson, *Swedish Immigrants in Lincoln's Time*, pp. 114–15; John W. Coons, *Indiana at Shiloh*, p. 77; J. L. Bieler Speech, 11th Indiana File, SNMP; Seymour Thompson, *Recollections with the Third Iowa Regiment*, p. 218; Nathaniel C. Hughes, Jr., *The Battle of Belmont*, p. 23.

89. Fritz Haskell, ed., "Diary of Colonel William Camm, 1861–1865," pp. 840–41; McEathron to brother, March 17, 1862, Alexander McEathron Letters, ILSL; Bridgford to wife, March 25, 1862, Oliver A. Bridgford Letters, 45th Illinois File, SNMP; Gordon C. Jones, ed., *"For My Country,"* p. 37.

90. Colby to father, April 4, 1862, E. Colby, Jr., Letters, A, 1st Illinois Light Artillery File, SNMP; Blaisdell to wife, April 4, 1862, Timothy M. Blaisdell Letters, Civil War Times Collection, USMHI; Bailey to parents, March 27, 1862, Bailey Letters, MHC.

91. St. John to parents, March 26, 1862, Bela T. St. John Letters, LC; McEathron to brother, March 17, 1862, McEathron Letters, ILSL; Jonathan L. LaBrant Diary, March 27, 1862, Civil War Times Collection, USMHI; Thomas C. Watkins Diary, April 1, 1862, Civil War Times Collection, USMHI; Mary Ann Anderson, ed., *The Civil War Diary of Allen Morgan Geer*, pp. 23–24.

92. Colby to father, April 4, 1862, Colby Letters, A, 1st Illinois Artillery File, SNMP; Skinner to brother and sister, March 27, 1862, William Skinner Letters, 71st Ohio File, SNMP; Elijah Shepard quoted in Cunningham, "Shiloh," p. 150; Wallace to wife, March 12, 1862, Lewis Wallace Papers, INHS; Simon, ed., *Grant Papers*, vol. 4, p. 389; Swain to wife, April 1, 1862, George Swain Letters, CHS; Currier to brother, March 26, 1862, Amos Currier Letters, SHSIO.

93. Richardson, *Grant*, p. 234.

94. *OR*, vol. X, pt. 2, pp. 33, 42, 44, 66; *Statement of Buell*, pp. 8–9.

95. *OR*, vol. VIII, pp. 629–31, 649, 652; vol. X, pt. 2, pp. 40, 41, 49, 55, 65.

96. *Statement of Buell*, p. 9; J. R. Chumney, Jr., "Don Carlos Buell, Gentleman General," Ph.D. dissertation, p. 67; *OR*, vol. X, pt. 2, p. 60; *National Intelligencer*, March 31, 1862; *Indianapolis Journal*, March 31, 1862.

97. *Statement of Buell*, p. 9; *National Intelligencer*, March 31, 1862; *New York Tribune*, April 3, 1862; Varian to sister, March 27, 1862, Alexander Varian, Jr., Letters, WRHS; Paul Hubbard and Christine Lewis, eds., " 'Give Yourself No Trouble About Me,' " p. 28; Bloomfield to sister, March 27, 1862, A. S. Bloomfield Letters, LC.

98. W. L. Curry, *Four Years in the Saddle*, p. 30.

99. *New York Tribune*, April 3, 1862; Buell, "Shiloh Reviewed," p. 491; *Statement of Buell*, p. 9; Levi Wagner Memoirs, Civil War Times Collection, USMHI; Edwin Hannaford, *The Story of a Regiment*, p. 227; Kenneth P. Williams, *Lincoln Finds a General*, vol. 3, p. 325.

100. Hannaford, *Story of a Regiment*, p. 228; Edwin Waters Payne, *History of the Thirty-Fourth Regiment of Illinois Volunteer Infantry*, p. 15; Thomas B. Van Horne, *History of the Army of the Cumberland*, p. 100; *OR*, vol. X, pt. 2, p. 48.

101. *OR*, vol. X, pt. 2, pp. 60–61, 82, 86. "Why did not Buell use his twenty days in Nashville to build some pontoons, adopt wagons to carry them, and train an infantry regiment in their use?" questioned Williams (*Lincoln Finds a General*, vol. 3, p. 326).

102. Henry Carman, ed., "Diary of Amos Glover," p. 265; Payne, *Thirty-Fourth Illinois*, p. 15; *OR*, vol. X, pt. 2, pp. 65, 70.

103. *OR*, vol. X, pt. 2, pp. 44, 47, 59; Hannaford, *Story of a Regiment*, p. 231; Chumney, "Buell," pp. 68, 90–91n.

104. Hannaford, *Story of a Regiment*, p. 231; Faust, ed., *Encyclopedia*, p. 523; *National Intelligencer*, April 29, 1862.

105. *OR*, vol. X, pt. 1, pp. 329–30.

106. Ibid.; Henry Stone, "The Battle of Shiloh," p. 49; Bloomfield to sister, March 31, 1862, Bloomfield Letters, LC; Hannaford, *Story of a Regiment*, pp. 232–33.

107. William R. Hartpence, *History of the Fifty-First Indiana Veteran Volunteer Infantry*, pp. 34, 36; F. W. Keil, *Thirty-Fifth Ohio*, p. 61; Frederick D. Williams, ed., *The Wild Life of the Army*, pp. 80–81; Carman, ed., "Diary of Amos Glover," p. 265; *OR*, vol. X, pt. 1, p. 330.

108. Harold Bartlett Diary, April 1, 1862, LC; Jacob H. Smith, "Personal Reminiscences," p. 8; Carman, ed., "Diary of Amos Glover," p. 265; Ralph E. Kiene, Jr., *A Civil War Diary*, p. 83; Hartpence, *Fifty-First Indiana*, p. 36; *OR*, vol. X, pt. 1, p. 330.

109. James G. Genco, *To the Sound of Musketry and Tap of the Drum*, p. 27; Varian to wife, March 28, 1862, Varian Letters, WRHS.

Five: Storm Clouds

1. Edward Munford to James E. Matthews, March 26, 1862, Albert Sidney Johnston Papers, Barret Collection, TU; *New Orleans Picayune*, March 28, 1862; *OR*, vol. X, pt. 1, pp. 395, 552; Stanley Horn, *The Army of Tennessee*, p. 155; Joseph H. Fussell, "Narrative of Interesting Events Just Prior to Battle of Shiloh," p. 64; Samuel H. Lockett, "Surprise and Withdrawal at Shiloh," p. 604.

2. *OR*, vol. X, pt. 2, pp. 375–76; Samuel C. Woods, ed., *The Shiloh Diary of Edmond Enoul Livaudais*, p. 20; Magee Diary, April 1, 1862, *Philadelphia Inquirer*, April 18, 1862; *New Orleans Crescent*, April 7, 1862.

3. *OR*, vol. X, pt. 2, p. 381. There is no indication as to what prompted the April 1 order. The army did not move out on April 2.

4. Ibid., pp. 378, 384, 387; *New Orleans Picayune*, April 2, 3, 4, 1862; R. R. Hancock, *Hancock's Diary*, pp. 138–39; Breckinridge to Bragg, April 1, 1862 (two telegrams), Braxton Bragg Papers, WRHS; John Wyeth, *That Devil Forrest*, pp. 74–75; Thomas Jordan and Roger Pryor, *The Campaigns of Lieut. Gen. N. B. Forrest*, p. 108. For a Federal summary of this tiny expedition, see *OR*, vol. X, pt. 1, pp. 83–84.

5. *OR*, vol. X, pt. 1, p. 79; vol. X, pt. 2, p. 378; George F. McGinnis, "Shiloh," p. 6; Alfred Roman, *The Military Operations of General Beauregard*, vol. 1, p. 270; Christopher Losson, *Tennessee's Forgotten Warriors*, p. 44; *New Orleans Picayune*, April 3, 1862.

6. Lew Wallace, *An Autobiography*, vol. 1, p. 545.

7. P. G. T. Beauregard, "The Campaign of Shiloh," p. 579. Some of the troops apparently believed that the Federals were advancing and the Confederates were going out to meet them. A New Orleans journalist predicted that the battle would be fought at Monterey (*New Orleans Picayune*, April 4, 1862).

8. Thomas Jordan, "Notes of a Confederate Staff Officer at Shiloh," p. 594; Thomas Jordan, "Recollections of General Beauregard's Service," p. 410; William C. Davis, *The Deep Waters of the Proud*, p. 118. Williams never questioned Jordan's version, but Sword, Cunningham, and Roland raised doubts (T. Harry Williams, *P. G. T. Beauregard*, p. 126; Wiley Sword, *Shiloh*, p. 97; O. E. Cunningham, "Shiloh and the Western Campaign of 1862," Ph.D. dissertation,

p. 174; Charles Roland, *Albert Sidney Johnston*, pp. 316–17).

9. Jordan, "Notes," p. 595; Jordan, "Recollections," p. 411.

10. Jordan, "Notes," pp. 595–96. Two years later, the camp table was sent to Charleston, South Carolina, as office furniture. Beauregard noticed that the pencil sketch was still visible. (Roman, *Beauregard*, vol. 1, p. 271; *OR*, vol. X, pt. 2, p. 387.)

11. Williams, *Beauregard*, p. 126; Thomas L. Connelly, *Army of the Heartland*, p. 152; Thomas E. Griess, ed., *The American Civil War*, p. 35; W. C. Davis, *Deep Waters*, p. 118; William E. Jamborsky, "Confederate Leadership and Defeat in the West," p. 62. June I. Gow noted, "It was not Jordan's place to consult Napoleon" ("Military Administration in the Confederate Army of Tennessee," p. 186).

12. *OR*, vol. X, pt. 1, pp. 392–93; Grady McWhiney, *Braxton Bragg and the Confederate Defeat*, p. 221.

13. Herman Hattaway and Archer Jones, *How the North Won*, p. 163; *OR*, vol. X, pt. 1, pp. 385, 397; vol. X, pt. 2, p. 384. Sword called Beauregard's plan "merely a large scale raid" (*Shiloh*, p. 98).

14. Williams, *Beauregard*, p. 129; Roland, *Johnston*, p. 321; McWhiney, *Bragg*, p. 223; Edward Munford, "Albert Sidney Johnston," Johnston Papers, Barret Collection, TU.

15. *OR*, vol. X, pt. 1, p. 387; McWhiney, *Bragg*, p. 221; Roland, *Johnston*, pp. 321–22; William Preston Johnston, "Albert Sidney Johnston at Shiloh," p. 554. Roland writes, "No satisfactory explanation can be given for the disparity between these two plans." He and Williams dismiss the "tampering" charge, but McDonough and Jamborsky give it credence (Williams, *Beauregard*, pp. 128–29; James L. McDonough, *Shiloh*, p. 74; Jamborsky, "Confederate Leadership," p. 62). A New Orleans reporter wrote that the alignment would be Hardee first, supported by Bragg on the right, Polk in the center, and Breckinridge on the left (*Picayune*, April 10, 1862). Shiloh Ranger Stacy Allen has raised an interesting point: because of faulty intelligence on the configuration of Owl and Lick Creeks, Beauregard may have believed that there was insufficient room for additional deployment.

After the war Beauregard vehemently denied William Preston Johnston's charge that Beauregard had tampered with the original order. "He [Johnston] has left no document—not a written line—to prove such a thought [alignment] had even occurred to him." The April 3 telegram was but a synopsis of "the positions of the three Confederate Corps in their line of march to the front. . . . It is clearly no plan at all." (P. G. T. Beauregard, "The Shiloh Campaign," p. 160.)

16. *Memphis Appeal*, April 7, 1887.

17. Steven E. Woodworth, *Jefferson Davis and His Generals*, p. 96; Jamborsky, "Confederate Leadership," p. 62; Williams, *Beauregard*, pp. 128–29; Roland, *Johnston*, p. 323. Williams described Johnston as "an onlooker," whereas Roland stated: "As commander of the army he must bear ultimate responsibility for accepting it [formation]."

18. Johnston to Hunt, March 11, 1862; Johnston to Gorgas, March 12, 15, 1862, both in Letter Book of the Headquarters of the Western Department, Kuntz Collection, TU; E. B. Carruth, "Disagreeable Experiences in War Times," p. 408.

19. *OR*, vol. X, pt. 1, p. 394; Larry J. Daniel, *Cannoneers in Gray*, p. 32. I have been unable to determine which if any of Carroll's regiments remained in Corinth.

20. Munford, "Johnston," Johnston Papers, Barret Collection, TU; Watson to wife, April 5, 1862, C. S. Watson Letters, TU; M. D. L. Stephenson Diary, April 5, 7, 1862, UMEM; Dunbar Rowland, *The Official and Statistical Register of the State of Mississippi*, p. 671.

21. *New Orleans Crescent*, April 19, 1862; Bennie Wall to father, April 3, 1862, Joseph

Embree Papers, LSU; Albert Fielder Diary, April 3, 1862, TSLA; Lyman to wife, April 3, 1862, Joseph Lyman Letters, YU.

22. Jordan, "Notes," pp. 595–96.

23. Ibid., p. 596; Roman, *Beauregard*, vol. 1, pp. 275–76; William Polk, *Leonidas Polk*, vol. 2, pp. 91–93; William M. Polk, "Facts Connected with the Concentration of the Army of the Mississippi," pp. 457–60.

24. Williams, *Beauregard*, p. 129; Nathaniel C. Hughes, Jr., *General William J. Hardee*, p. 102; *OR*, vol. X, pt. 2, pp. 464, 527, 614.

25. Losson, *Tennessee's Forgotten Warriors*, p. 45; Marcus J. Wright Diary, April 5, 1862, TSLA. Cheatham's division entered the Ridge Road at Squire Moore's house, at the present-day community of Needmore.

26. Augusta Inge Reminiscences, NEMMA; Beauregard to Hardee, April 3, 1862, P. G. T. Beauregard Papers, LC; Woods, ed., *Livaudais Diary*, p. 22; Hugh C. Bailey, ed., "An Alabamian at Shiloh," p. 150; James Rosser Diary, April 13, 1862, Gloria Gardner Collection; *OR*, vol. X, pt. 1, p. 607; Johnson to wife, April 4, 1862, Charles Johnson Letters, LSU; Robert Clark, Jr., "The New Orleans German Colony in the Civil War," p. 1002; Fielder Diary, April 3, 1862, TSLA; Lemuel A. Scarbrough Diary, April 3, 1862, EU.

27. Hughes, *Hardee*, p. 102; Roman, *Beauregard*, vol. 1, p. 530; Scarbrough Diary, April 4, 1862, EU; *OR*, vol. X, pt. 1, p. 607.

28. Inge Reminiscences, NEMMA; Munford, "Johnston," Johnston Papers, Barret Collection, TU.

29. *New York Times*, May 15, 1862; Arthur W. Bergeron, Jr., ed., *The Civil War Reminiscences of Major Silas T. Grisamore, C.S.A.*, p. 25. The present day town of Michie, Tennessee, is actually old Monterey. When the town got a post office, there was already a Monterey in the state, so the citizens took the name of Michie. The Monterey Road is present-day Highway 22. The Purdy Road is now called Michie Road and is half paved and half graveled. The Savannah Road, which Bragg's corps took out of Monterey, is present-day Highway 224.

30. *OR*, vol. X, pt. 2, pp. 390, 391; McWhiney, *Bragg*, p. 222; *New Orleans Picayune*, April 10, 1862.

31. Ebin Swift to Reed, November 3, 1905, David W. Reed Papers, SNMP. The road in question is present-day Highway 22, past Michie, Tennessee. The approximate location of the Chamberses' farm is Ivan Fisher's grocery store. My thanks to Stacy Allen for answering Swift's 1905 question.

32. *OR*, vol. X, pt. 2, p. 391; Coleman to father, May 5, 1862, W. E. Coleman Letters, TSLA; Rufus B. Parker Diary, April 5, 1862, TSLA; A. H. Mecklin Diary, April 5, 1862, MDAH; Edward Porter Thompson, *History of the Orphan Brigade*, p. 83; Dudley M. Haydon, "Shiloh." Forrest's cavalry, six hundred strong, arrived at Burnsville on April 1, 1862 (Breckinridge to Bragg, April 1, 1862, Bragg Papers, WRHS).

33. William Preston Diary, April 4, 1862, NA; Haydon, "Shiloh"; Jordan, "Notes," p. 596; Taylor Beatty Diary, April 4, 1862, SHC; Woods, ed., *Livaudais Diary*, pp. 23–24; *New Orleans Crescent*, April 15, 1862; Bergeron, ed., *Grisamore*, p. 32.

34. Haydon, "Shiloh."

35. Preston Diary, April 4, 1862, NA.

36. George W. Baylor, "With Gen. A. S. Johnston at Shiloh," p. 609.

37. *OR*, vol. X, pt. 1, pp. 406, 464, 495, 567; Rosser Diary, April 5, 1862, Gardner Collection; Latta to wife, April 10, 1862, Samuel Latta Letters, TSLA; Beatty Diary, April 5, 1862, SHC. See also Unknown Diarist, April 5, 1862, Historic New Orleans Collection; Magee Diary, April 5, 1862, in *Philadelphia Inquirer*, April 18, 1862; Journal of the Orleans Guard, April 5, 1862, Historic New Orleans Collection.

38. *New Orleans Picayune*, April 10, 1862.

39. F. A. Shoup, "How We Went to Shiloh," pp. 137–38; F. A. Shoup, "The Art of War in '62—Shiloh," pp. 4–5.
40. Polk, "Facts," pp. 460–61; Munford, "Johnston," Johnston Papers, Barret Collection, TU.
41. Munford, "Johnston," Johnston Papers, Barret Collection, TU; *OR*, vol. X, pt. 1, p. 464; Joseph H. Parks, *General Leonidas Polk, C.S.A.*, p. 229; Alexander Walker, "Narrative of the Battle of Shiloh," p. 119.
42. *OR*, vol. X, pt. 1, pp. 464, 532. NPS markers along the Bark Road show the position of Withers's brigades on the evening of April 5.
43. Munford, "Johnston," Johnston Papers, Barret Collection, TU; *OR*, vol. X, pt. 1, pp. 471, 495.
44. Polk, "Facts," pp. 461–62; *OR*, vol. X, pt. 1, pp. 406–7.
45. Roman, *Beauregard*, vol. 1, pp. 277–79; Preston Diary, April 5, 1862, NA; Preston to W. P. Johnston, April 18, 1862, Johnston Papers, Barret Collection, TU; William Preston Johnston, *The Life of Gen. Albert Sidney Johnston*, pp. 566–69; *OR*, vol. X, pt. 1, p. 407; Braxton Bragg, "General Albert Sidney Johnston at Shiloh," Johnston Papers, Barret Collection, TU; Jordan, "Notes," p. 597.
46. Johnston, *Johnston*, pp. 570–71; T. L. Connelly, *Army of the Heartland*, p. 157.
47. *New Orleans Picayune*, April 15, 1862.
48. Bragg, "Johnston at Shiloh," Johnston Papers, Barret Collection, TU; Otto Eisenschiml and Ralph Newman, *The Civil War*, p. 609; Hamilton Basso, *Beauregard*, p. 181. Thomas Jordan and Roger Pryor incorrectly claimed that there was no evening meeting and that Johnston and Beauregard did not meet again "until on their horses as the movement was about to be inaugurated" (*The Campaigns of Lieut.-Gen. N. B. Forrest*, p. 113).
49. Roland, *Johnston*, p. 609; Roman, *Beauregard*, vol. 1, p. 282.
50. Johnston, *Johnston*, p. 567; Journal of the Orleans Guard, April 4, 1862, Historic New Orleans Collection; Woods, ed., *Livaudais Diary*, pp. 23–24; R. L. Davis to John, April 10, 1862, "R. L. Davis Letters," *Sons of the South*, p. 35; J. K. Garrett, ed., *Confederate Diary of Robert D. Smith*, p. 4.
51. Roman, *Beauregard*, vol. 1, p. 282. Roland (*Johnston*, pp. 323–24), McWhiney (*Bragg*, p. 226), Williams (*Beauregard*, p. 132), and Woodworth (*Davis*, p. 97) all criticize Beauregard for his loss of nerve. Only McDonough (*Shiloh*, pp. 81–82) is sympathetic.
52. Roman, *Beauregard*, vol. 1, p. 278. Roland (*Johnston*, p. 323) discounts Beauregard's version as an afterthought to salvage his tarnished reputation. McDonough (*Shiloh*, p. 82) believes that this version may have validity.
53. McDonough, *Shiloh*, pp. 83–84; Parks, *Polk*, p. 230; *OR*, vol. X, pt. 1, p. 403; Sword, *Shiloh*, p. 108; Johnston, *Johnston*, p. 625.
54. R. Clark, "New Orleans German Colony," pp. 1002–3; Scarbrough Diary, April 5, 1862, EU; William C. Davis, *The Orphan Brigade*, p. 82; Rufus Daniel Diary, April 5, 1862, Civil War Misc. Collection, USMHI; George W. Jones Diary, April 5, 1862, GPL; Charles Johnson to wife, April 3, 1862.
55. Roman, *Beauregard*, vol. 1, p. 282; "Caddo Fencibles of Louisiana," p. 499. Shoup recalled that so much sound could be heard from the Federal camps that many Southerners feared that the Yankees were overacting and engaged in a ruse ("The Art of War," p. 7).
56. Johnston, *Johnston*, p. 682; Joseph W. Rich, *The Battle of Shiloh*, p. 57; John F. Marszalek, *Sherman*, p. 174.
57. Loudon to wife, March 23, 1862, DeWitt Clinton Loudon Letters, OHS; Mary E. Stricklin, "Shiloh Church," SNMP; Shiloh United Methodist Church File, Memphis Conference Archives, LU.
58. *OR*, vol. X, pt. 2, p. 50; Rich, *Battle of Shiloh*, p. 58; M. F. Force, *From Fort Henry to Corinth*, p. 102.
59. NPS plaques mark the precise location of McDowell's camps. See also Don Car-

los Buell, "Shiloh Reviewed," p. 511; Henry Wright, *A History of the Sixth Iowa Infantry*, p. 67.

60. Thomas Worthington, *Shiloh*, p. 85. See the Sherman map in Robert C. Johnson and Clarence C. Buel, eds., *Battles and Leaders of the Civil War*, vol. 1, pp. 496–97. The 1901 D. W. Reed map also incorrectly plugged the gap by mislocating the camp of the 4th Illinois Cavalry. The *Cincinnati Commercial* of April 28, 1862, claimed that the gap was a half-mile. See also Wills DeHaas, "The Battle of Shiloh," pp. 679–80.

61. Rachel Sherman Thorndike, ed., *The Sherman Letters*, p. 149; Ezra J. Warner, *Generals in Blue*, p. 50; Addison A. Stuart, *Iowa Colonels and Regiments*, pp. 147–49; John K. Duke, *History of the Fifty-Third Ohio Volunteer Infantry*, p. 40; Ephraim C. Dawes, "The Battle of Shiloh," p. 125.

62. Lloyd Lewis, *Sherman*, p. 213; Testimony of W. T. Sherman, Thomas Worthington Court Martial Proceedings, August 1862, NA; U. S. Grant, *Personal Memoirs of U. S. Grant*, p. 223. McDonough asserted that the haphazard dispositions and lack of entrenchments were more censurable blunders than the decision to locate on the east bank (*Shiloh*, p. 52). For an analysis of Grant's decision on entrenchments, see Edward Hagerman, *The American Civil War and the Origins of Modern Warfare*, pp. 168–70.

63. *OR*, vol. X, pt. 1, pp. 86, 87; vol. X, pt. 2, pp. 82, 90; Sherman Testimony, Sherman, Worthington Court Martial Proceedings, NA.

64. Testimony of Ralph Buckland, Worthington Court Martial Proceedings, NA; *OR*, vol. X, pt. 2, p. 90; T. W. Connelly, *History of the Seventieth Ohio Regiment*, pp. 19–20; Jean Rumsey, ed., *By the Fireside*, p. 6.

65. Robert H. Fleming, "The Battle of Shiloh as a Private Saw It," p. 137; Dawes, "Battle of Shiloh," pp. 115–16.

66. *OR*, vol. X, pt. 1, pp. 89–91; *Society of the Army of the Tennessee*, pp. 75–76; John Geer, *Beyond the Lines*, pp. 26–29; Sherman Testimony, Worthington Court Martial Proceedings, NA.

67. *OR*, vol. X, pt. 1, p. 92; W. D. Pickett, "Biographical Sketch of the Military Career of William J. Hardee," p. 8, ADAH; Powell to unknown, April ?, 1862, John W. Powell Letters, 35th Tennessee File, SNMP; Edwin L. Hobart, *The Truth About Shiloh*, p. 102; Buckland Testimony, Worthington Court Martial, NA. Union infantry casualties were officially placed at eight killed and eleven missing. Ricker made no casualty report, but had at least one killed. (*OR*, vol. X, pt. 1, pp. 90–91.) A Johnston staff officer later claimed that seventeen Yankees were captured (Preston Diary, April 4, 1862, NA). There were probably a score of Southern casualties, including a dozen captured (*OR*, vol. X, pt. 1, p. 90).

68. Worthington, *Shiloh*, p. 101; *Society of the Army of the Tennessee*, p. 76; Michael Beckley, "Buckland's Brigade at Shiloh."

69. Isabel Wallace, *Life and Letters of General W. H. L. Wallace*, p. 181; *Society of the Army of the Tennessee*, pp. 76–77; Pickett, "Hardee," p. 8, ADAH; Sherman quote from Sword, *Shiloh*, p. 124.

70. I. Wallace, *Life and Letters*, p. 181; DeHaas, "Battle of Shiloh," p. 680; Testimony of Sergeant George Gorman, Worthington Court Martial Proceedings, NA; J. K. Duke, *Fifty-Third Ohio*, p. 41; Adam Badeau, *Military History of Ulysses S. Grant*, p. 72.

71. Wright, *Sixth Iowa*, pp. 67–68; Mildred Throne, ed., "Letters from Shiloh," p. 241; Sherman Testimony, Worthington Court Martial Proceedings, NA.

72. Robert W. McCormick, "Challenge of Command," pp. 28–29.

73. William T. Sherman, *Memoirs of General William T. Sherman*, p. 226; Sherman Testimony, Worthington Court Martial Proceedings, NA.

74. Worthington, *Shiloh*, pp. 120–21; Sherman Testimony, Worthington Court Martial Proceedings, NA.

75. Sherman Testimony, Worthington Court Martial Proceedings, NA.

76. Worthington, *Shiloh*, pp. 137, 139, 140.
77. Testimony of Jesse Hildebrand and W. T. Sherman, Worthington Court Martial Proceedings, NA; DeHaas, "Battle of Shiloh," p. 681.
78. Worthington, *Shiloh*, pp. 121, 137, 138, 139.
79. *Official Roster of the Soldiers of the State of Ohio in the War of the Rebellion*, vol. 4, p. 675; Duke, *Fifty-Third Ohio*, p. 41; Dawes, "Battle of Shiloh," p. 125; Remarks of Hon. John Sherman, of Ohio, May 9, 1862, p. 1, OHS.
80. Testimony of W. T. Sherman and David Stuart, Worthington Court Martial Proceedings, NA.
81. I. Wallace, *Life and Letters*, p. 191.
82. *OR*, vol. X, pt. 2, pp. 87–88, 92; Sherman Testimony, Worthington Court Martial Proceedings, NA.
83. Sherman Testimony, Worthington Court Martial Proceedings, NA; Marszalek, *Sherman*, p. 176; McDonough, *Shiloh*, p. 53.
84. DeHaas, "Battle of Shiloh," pp. 681–82.
85. *New Orleans Picayune*, April 11, 1862.
86. Grant, *Memoirs*, p. 224.
87. *OR*, vol. X, pt. 2, pp. 42, 45, 64, 82; Jonathan L. LaBrant Diary, March 30, 1862, Civil War Times Collection, USMHI; Shanks to mother, March 20, 1862, Edward B. Shanks Letters, 12th Illinois File, SNMP; Isaac Pugh to wife, March 22, 1862, Isaac C. Pugh Letters, 41st Illinois File, SNMP; "Shiloh," 52nd Illinois File, SNMP; *New York Tribune*, April 5, 1862; *National Intelligencer*, April 7, 1862; *Chicago Times*, April 8, 1862.
88. Grant, *Memoirs*, pp. 224–25; *OR*, vol. X, pt. 2, pp. 90–91.
89. Grant, *Memoirs*, p. 224; Albert D. Richardson, *A Personal History of Ulysses S. Grant*, p. 235.
90. *OR*, vol. X, pt. 1, p. 89; Edwin Hannaford, *The Story of a Regiment*, p. 236.
91. Hannaford, *Story of Regiment*, pp. 237–38; Horace C. Fisher, *A Staff Officer's Story*, p. 10.
92. *OR*, vol. X, pt. 1, pp. 330–31; Joshua T. Bradford Diary, April 5, 1862, LC.
93. Hannaford, *Story of Regiment*, p. 237; John Y. Simon, ed., *The Papers of Ulysses S. Grant*, vol. 5, p. 348; Ebin Swift to Reed, November 3, 1905, D. W. Reed Papers, SNMP.
94. Hannaford, *Story of Regiment*, p. 239; Fisher, *Staff Officer's Story*, p. 10; *OR*, vol. X, pt. 2, p. 93; Grant, *Memoirs*, p. 225.
95. L. Wallace, *Autobiography*, vol. 1, p. 454; *OR*, vol. X, pt. 2, pp. 93–94. Wallace's dispatch is missing, but Sword believes that it is implied in Sherman's response of April 5 (*Shiloh*, p. 478n).
96. Hannaford, *Story of Regiment*, p. 240; *OR*, vol. X, pt. 2, p. 94; I. Wallace, *Life and Letters*, p. 186.
97. W. A. Neal, *An Illustrated History of the Missouri Engineers and the 25th Infantry Regiment*, p. 130; *OR*, vol. X, pt. 1, p. 282; Charles A. Morton, "A Boy at Shiloh," p. 58; Thomas J. Bryant, *Who Is Responsible for the Advance of the Army of the Tennessee Towards Corinth?*, p. 30.
98. John Robertson, *Michigan in the War*, p. 325.
99. John G. Shea, *The American Nation*, pp. 355–57; *Harvard Memorial Biographies*, vol. 1, pp. 150–63.
100. W. A. Neal, *Illustrated History*, pp. 126–27.
101. *Adjutant General's Report, Illinois*, vol. 1, pp. 551–80; vol. 3, pp. 252–55; vol. 4, pp. 88–90; *Chicago Tribune* quoted in *National Intelligencer*, April 8, 1862.

Six: The Opening Attack

1. *Missouri Daily Democrat*, April 11, 1862; *Chicago Tribune*, April 14, 1862. Seay Field Road is today called Reconnoitering Road.
2. Joseph R. Ruff, "Civil War Experiences of a German Emigrant," pp. 294–95; W. A. Neal, *An Illustrated History of the Missouri Engineers and the 25th Infantry Regiment*, p. 125; *OR*, vol. X, pt. 1, p. 603; "Interview of James Wood," 1934, SNMP; Thomas J. Bryant, *Who Is Responsible for the Advance of the Army of the Tennessee Towards Corinth?*, p. 12.
3. "Interview of James Wood," 1934, SNMP.
4. *OR*, vol. X, pt. 1, p. 603; Alfred Roman, *The Military Operations of General Beauregard*, vol. 1, p. 534; J. S. Carothers, "Forty-Five Mississippi Regiment," p. 175.
5. *OR*, vol. X, pt. 1, pp. 283, 603; Ruff, "Experiences," p. 295. For a summary of the precise starting time of the Battle of Shiloh, see Cunningham, "Shiloh and the Western Campaign of 1862," pp. 210–11n.
6. Ruff, "Experiences," pp. 295–96; Thomas D. Duncan, *Recollections of Thomas D. Duncan*, p. 52.
7. William Preston Johnston, *The Life of Gen. Albert Sidney Johnston*, p. 585; J. B. Ulmer, "A Glimpse of Albert Sidney Johnston," p. 289; Braxton Bragg, "General Albert Sidney Johnston at Shiloh," Albert Sidney Johnston Papers, Barret Collection, TU; William Preston Diary, April 8, 1862, NA; Roman, *Beauregard*, vol. 1, p. 533. Ulmer reported Johnston's words as: "Gentlemen, the 'ball has opened'; no time for argument now."
8. Johnston, *Johnston*, p. 582; "Famous Horses of the Confederate Army," p. 438. Captured Southern prisoners told of what Johnston said about watering their horses in the Tennessee River (Mildred Throne, ed., *The Civil War Diary of Cyrus F. Boyd*, p. 33). Johnston was subsequently misquoted in the Northern press: "Tonight we shall water our horses in the Tennessee River, or in hell" (*Cincinnati Commercial*, May 2, 1862). Northern cartoonists subsequently portrayed a sinister Johnston watering a nag in Hades. For Johnston's hat description, see John P. Broome, "How Gen. A. S. Johnston Died," p. 629.
9. P. G. T. Beauregard, "The Campaign of Shiloh," p. 586; Thomas L. Connelly, *Army of the Heartland*, p. 160; Charles Roland, *Albert Sidney Johnston*, p. 345; Steven E. Woodworth, *Jefferson Davis and His Generals*, p. 99. See also R. Ernest Dupuy and Trevor N. Dupuy, *The Compact History of the Civil War*, p. 80; Clement Eaton, *Jefferson Davis*, p. 151. Johnston's most ardent supporter on this point is Roland; his most vocal critic, Connelly. Woodworth concluded that Johnston's position made no difference, for the faulty alignment left little for the commander to do but feed troops into the fight. I concur with Connelly.
10. *OR*, vol. X, pt. 1, p. 454; A. S. Horsley, "Reminiscences of Shiloh," p. 234; Preston Diary, April 6, 1862, NA; Robert S. Henry, *As They Saw Forrest*, p. 77.
11. *Cincinnati Times*, April 21, 1862; *Philadelphia Inquirer*, April 18, 1862; Leslie Anders, *The Twenty-First Missouri*, p. 65.
12. Lyman Tauty to Reaves, November 13, 1985, SNMP; D. Lloyd Jones, "The Battle of Shiloh," p. 57.
13. *OR*, vol. X, pt. 1, pp. 280, 284; Leslie Anders, *The Twenty-First Missouri*, p. 65; I have found six different quotations attributed to Peabody. I consider the statement of Captain F. C. Nichols, 25th Missouri, the most accurate, for he was within hearing distance (Joseph Rich, *The Battle of Shiloh*, p. 529). For other statements, see Charles A. Morton, "A Boy at Shiloh," p. 60; John G. Shea, *The American Nation*, p. 357; William C. Claxton, "Thirty-Nine Years After Shiloh," MHC; *Harvard Memorial Biographies*, vol. 1, p. 164; Statement of D. B. Baker, 25th Missouri, in Bryant, *Who Is Responsible*, p. 31; Henry Stone, "The Battle of Shiloh," p. 59; "The Shiloh Campaign," *National Tribune*, April 17, 1884. "Spec-

tator" of the 25th Missouri told of the incident in a letter to the *Chicago Tribune*, April 24, 1862, but did not give Peabody's response.

14. Jones, "Battle of Shiloh," p. 56; *OR*, vol. X, pt. 1, p. 285; D. K. Vail, *Company K*, p. 1.

15. Statement of Lieutenant William Hahn, 25th Missouri, in Edwin L. Hobart, *The Truth About Shiloh*, p. 10; W. A. Neal, *Illustrated History*, p. 125; Ruff, "Experiences," p. 296; Anders, *Twenty-First Missouri*, pp. 3, 65.

16. "Federal Veterans at Shiloh," p. 104; *OR*, vol. X, pt. 1, pp. 278, 282, 283; Anders, *Twenty-First Missouri*, pp. 13, 38, 45, 63, 65.

17. *OR*, vol. X, pt. 1, p. 283; "Interview of James Wood," 1934, SNMP; Tony Hays, *No Man's Land*, p. 28. The Thom map incorrectly locates the Seay house on the eastern edge of the field.

18. Jones, "Battle of Shiloh," pp. 56–57; *OR*, vol. X, pt. 1, pp. 283, 285; Statement of William French, 21st Missouri, in Bryant, *Who Is Responsible*, p. 35; W. A. Neal, *Illustrated History*, pp. 125–26; Statement of William J. Hahn, 25th Missouri, in Hobart, *Truth About Shiloh*, p. 12; Anders, *Twenty-First Missouri*, p. 66; T. W. Holman, "The Battle of Shiloh"; T. W. Holman, "The Story of Shiloh." Moore had his leg amputated later in the day.

19. *OR*, vol. X, pt. 1, p. 283; Jones, "Battle of Shiloh," p. 54.

20. *OR*, vol. X, pt. 1, pp. 386, 603. One study maintains that the sun rose at 5:40. See Cunningham, "Shiloh," p. 211n.

21. Thomas Jordan, "The Battle of Shiloh," vol. XXXV, p. 204; Cunningham, "Shiloh," pp. 212–13n; Woodworth, *Davis*, pp. 122, 143; Lockwood Tower, ed., *A Carolinian Goes to War*, p. 78.

22. Patricia L. Faust, ed., *Historical Times Illustrated Encyclopedia of the Civil War*, p. 841; Jordan, "Battle of Shiloh," p. 205; *OR*, vol. X, pt. 1, p. 591; Aide to Wood, June 13, 1862, S. A. M. Wood Papers, ADAH.

23. *OR*, vol. X, pt. 1, pp. 590, 598, 600; "Maj. John H. Kelly," pp. 17–41; Ezra J. Warner, *Generals in Gray*, pp. 168–69.

24. Dorothy Stanley, ed., *Autobiography of Henry Sir Morton Stanley*, p. 169; "Col. M. M. Diffie," p. 87; Faust, ed., *Encyclopedia*, pp. 352–53; Warner, *Generals in Gray*, p. 129.

25. *OR*, vol. X, pt. 1, p. 283; NPS plaques 210, 214.

26. *OR*, vol. X, pt. 1, pp. 280, 590–91; Johnston, *Johnston*, p. 676; Morton, "Boy at Shiloh," pp. 59–60; Charles A. Morton, "Opening of the Battle of Shiloh," pp. 15–17; Statement of William J. Hahn, 25th Missouri, in Hobart, *Truth About Shiloh*, p. 12; Statement of D. B. Baker, 25th Missouri, in Bryant, *Who Is Responsible*, p. 31; Anders, *Twenty-First Missouri*, p. 67; Letter from "Spectator," 25th Missouri, in *Chicago Tribune*, April 24, 1862; W. E. Woodward, *Meet General Grant*, p. 248.

27. *OR*, vol. X, pt. 1, pp. 577, 591; Johnston, *Johnston*, p. 589.

28. Morton, "Opening of Battle of Shiloh," p. 16; Jones, "Battle of Shiloh," p. 57; Letter from "Spectator," 25th Missouri; Morton, "Boy at Shiloh," p. 61; *OR*, vol. X, pt. 1, pp. 283, 285.

29. George A. Grammer Diary, April 6, 1862, MDAH; *OR*, vol. X, pt. 1, p. 574.

30. Morton, "Boy at Shiloh," pp. 61–62; *Missouri Daily Democrat*, April 21, 1862; Shea, *American Nation*, p. 357; *Harvard Biographies*, vol. 1, p. 165; *Springfield Weekly Republican*, May 24, 1862. D. W. Reed states that Peabody's troops fled north through Jacob Barnes Field (*The Battle of Shiloh and the Organizations Engaged*, p. 70).

31. *OR*, vol. X, pt. 1, pp. 285–86; *Chicago Tribune*, April 16, 1862.

32. Samuel Eels to friends, April 13, 1862, Samuel Eels Letters, LC.

33. Leslie Anders, *The Eighteenth Missouri*, pp. 22–23, 30–31, 32–33; Johnston, *Johnston*, p. 683; *Society of the Army of the Tennessee*, p. 63.

34. Leander Stillwell, "In the Ranks at Shiloh," pp. 115–16.

35. F. H. Magdeburg, *Wisconsin at Shiloh*, pp. 53–54; Johnston, *Johnston*, p. 683; *Chicago Tribune*, March 31, 1862.

36. *Society of the Army of the Tennessee*, p. 63; Andrew Hickenlooper, "The Battle of Shiloh," pp. 11–12; Henry S. Hurter, "Narrative of the First Battery of Light Artillery," vol. 1, p. 640; vol. 2, pp. 91–92; *Official Roster of the Soldiers of the State of Ohio in the War of the Rebellion*, vol. 10, p. 479. Although Miller complained about his new position, an examination of the actual site reveals that Prentiss's decision was a good one.

37. Wiley Sword, *Shiloh*, pp. 159–60; James Sligh to wife, April 7, 1862, James Sligh Letters, MHC; *New York Tribune*, April 21, 1862. Colonel John Oliver wisely withdrew his regiment and returned to the landing.

38. Edgar Embly to brother and sister, April 28, 1862, Edgar Embly Letters, Harrisburg Civil War Round Table Collection, USMHI.

39. *OR*, vol. X, pt. 1, pp. 532, 548; T. L. Connelly, *Army of the Heartland*, pp. 162–63.

40. *OR*, vol. X, pt. 1, pp. 532, 536, 545, 548; John K. Folmar, ed., *From That Terrible Field*, p. 55; Hugh C. Bailey, ed., "An Alabamian at Shiloh," p. 152; S. H. Dent to wife, April 9, 1862, quoted in Cunningham, "Shiloh," p. 270.

41. *OR*, vol. X, pt. 1, p. 537; L.D.G. to mother and father, April 8, 1862, Gage's Alabama Battery File, ADAH; *Mobile Advertiser & Register*, April 29, 1862. Munch and Hickenlooper may also have come under an enfilade fire from Swett's and Harper's batteries near the Eastern Corinth Road. See *OR*, vol. X, pt. 1, p. 609; D. W. Reed, *Shiloh*, p. 70.

42. *OR*, vol. X, pt. 1, pp. 536, 538; *The Grayjackets*, p. 276; Alexander Walker, "Narrative of the Battle of Shiloh," pp. 130–31.

43. Faust, ed., *Encyclopedia*, p. 2; *OR*, vol. X, pt. 1, pp. 536–37; *Mobile Advertiser & Register*, April 29, 1862.

44. *OR*, vol. X, pt. 1, p. 548; Taylor Beatty Diary, April 6, 1862, SHC; Walker, "Narrative of Battle of Shiloh," p. 129; "Haratio" to Josie, April 11, 1862, 22nd Alabama File, SNMP.

45. Hickenlooper, "Battle of Shiloh," pp. 13, 35; Folmar, ed., *Terrible Field*, p. 55.

46. Hurter, "Narrative," vol. 1, pp. 640–42; vol. 2, pp. 92, 95. It is commonly, though incorrectly, written that the Confederates captured two of Munch's guns.

47. Stillwell, "In the Ranks," pp. 118–19; *Chicago Tribune*, April 15, 1862; *Society of the Army of the Tennessee*, p. 63.

48. *OR*, vol. X, pt. 1, pp. 537, 545, 548; Bailey, ed., "Alabamian at War," p. 152; *New Orleans Picayune*, April 18, 1862.

49. John P. Howell to Mr. Brewington, September 26, 1990, SNMP. Wills DeHaas stated that Rea Field had been a peach orchard ("The Battle of Shiloh," p. 685). Joanna Rea Howell died in 1895 and is buried in Shiloh Church Cemetery (Extract from Miss Mary Dishmore to J. W. Gilbert, n.d., 2nd Tennessee File, SNMP).

50. Remarks of Hon. John Sherman, p. 1, OHS; *Indianapolis Journal*, April 15, 1862.

51. John K. Duke, *History of the Fifty-Third Ohio Volunteer Infantry*, pp. 1–2, 39, 44; Remarks of Hon. John Sherman, p. 1, OHS.

52. J. K. Duke, *Fifty-Third Ohio*, p. 42; *Cincinnati Commercial*, April 28, 1862. Sherman never commented on the incident in his memoirs.

53. B. D. Fearing, "The 77th Ohio Volunteer Regiment at Shiloh," p. 50; DeHaas, "Battle of Shiloh," p. 684; Robert H. Fleming, "The Battle of Shiloh as a Private Saw It," pp. 138–39; *OR*, vol. X, pt. 1, p. 276; vol. LII, pt. 2, p. 23. Sergeant Ed Bryant of the 57th Ohio wrote: "This firing [Fraley Field] was severe and could plainly be heard by us all the way back to camp" (Bryant, *Who Is Responsible*, p. 13). The area around Shiloh Church today is heavily wooded, and it is difficult to envision Hildebrand's line. Rea Field is also considerably smaller, because of trees

and undergrowth. Prentiss has been criticized for not warning Sherman, but it is clear that messengers were sent.

54. Milton K. Bosworth to father, April 13, 1862, 53rd Ohio File, SNMP; J. K. Duke, *Fifty-Third Ohio*, p. 43; *OR*, vol. X, pt. 1, pp. 264, 581.

55. The traditional account of this scene is given in J. K. Duke, *Fifty-Third Ohio*, p. 44. A slightly different, but because of the date perhaps somewhat more accurate, version is given in *Cincinnati Commercial*, April 28, 1862. See also William T. Sherman, *Memoirs of General William T. Sherman*, p. 230; John T. Taylor, "Reminiscences of Services as an Aide-de-Camp," p. 132; Jesse Bowman Young, *What a Boy Saw in the Army*, p. 105. The 53rd Ohio Monument in Rea Field incorrectly states that the regiment formed at 8 A.M. Other, nearby plaques and monuments place the beginning action at 7 A.M.

56. Charles E. Nash, *Biographical Sketches of Gen. Pat E. Cleburne and Gen. T. C. Hindman*, pp. 7, 10, 11, 15, 16–17, 38–39; Howell Purdue and Elizabeth Purdue, *Pat Cleburne*, pp. 5, 7, 9, 20–21, 23, 31–32; Woodworth, *Davis*, pp. 140–43.

57. *OR*, vol. X, pt. 1, pp. 581, 590; Statement of Edward Jordan, 57th Ohio, in Bryant, *Who Is Responsible*, p. 13; J. K. Duke, *Fifty-Third Ohio*, p. 45. The creek was Shiloh Branch of Owl Creek.

58. Bosworth to father, April 14, 1862, 53rd Ohio, SNMP; Jasper Kelsey, "The Battle of Shiloh," p. 72; *OR*, vol. X, pt. 1, p. 581; Letter from "Your Friend," *Ironton Register*, May 8, 1862; J. A. Wheeler, "Cleburne's Brigade at Shiloh," p. 13.

59. William C. Thompson, "From Shiloh to Port Gibson," p. 21; S. N. Bledsoe, "Fifteen Soldiers in One Family," p. 471; T. B. Cox, "Sixth Mississippi Regiment at Shiloh," p. 509; D. B. Gunn, "Reminiscences of the War," John J. Thornton Papers, MDAH; Bosworth to father, April 14, 1862, 53rd Ohio File, SNMP; *OR*, vol. X, pt. 1, p. 581; H. Grady Howell, Jr., *Going to Meet the Yankees*, pp. 21, 86–87.

60. *OR*, vol. X, pt. 1, p. 262; J. K. Duke, *Fifty-Third Ohio*, pp. 45–46; Bosworth to father, April 14, 1862, 53rd Ohio File, SNMP; Remarks of Hon. John Sherman, p. 2, OHS.

61. *OR*, vol. X, pt. 1, p. 264; Fleming, "As a Private Saw It," pp. 141–42; Statement of Edward Jordan, 57th Ohio, in Bryant, *Who Is Responsible*, pp. 13–14; Sherman to brother, April 22, 1862, in Rachel Sherman Thorndike, ed., *The Sherman Letters*, p. 143; John Ruckman to friends, April 12, 1862, 57th Ohio File, SNMP.

62. *OR*, vol. X, pt. 1, pp. 249–50, 252; Fleming, "As a Private Saw It," pp. 140–42; Robert H. Fleming, "The Boys of Ohio Held Fast at Shiloh." Although this is not stated in official reports, Barrett's battery most certainly dueled with the guns of Shoup's Arkansas Battalion. See NPS plaque 428.

63. S. F. Martin to brother, April 11, 1862, S. F. Martin Letters, MHS; NPS plaque A 72.

64. "Allen Cobb Waterhouse," pp. 46–47; "Samuel Eddy Barrett," pp. 91–93; Walter S. to father, April 9, 1862, in *Chicago Times*, April 16, 1862; J. E. Boos, ed., "Civil War Diary of Patrick White," pp. 652–53; David R. Logsdon, *Eyewitnesses at the Battle of Shiloh*, p. 24.

65. *OR*, vol. X, pt. 1, pp. 273, 591, 596–97, 605; John B. Lindsley, ed., *Military Annals of Tennessee*, p. 419; William Clare Report, June 13, 1862, S. A. M. Wood Papers, ADAH. The colonel of the 16th Alabama reported: "My regiment advanced through a thick patch of briers and then through an open field [Rea's]" (*OR*, vol. X, pt. 1, pp. 596–97).

66. Warner, *Generals in Blue*, p. 50; Remarks of Hon. John Sherman, p. 2, OHS; Walter S. to father, April 9, 1862, in *Chicago Times*, April 16, 1862. Postwar comments that many men expected an attack are borne out in contemporary letters. See statement of M. T. Williamson in *Society of the Army of the Tennessee*, p. 84.

67. *Society of the Army of the Tennessee*, p. 78; *OR*, vol. X, pt. 1, p. 266.

68. John A. Bering and Thomas Montgomery, *History of the 48th Ohio Volunteer Infantry*, pp. 19–20; Mark M. Boatner, *Civil War Dictionary*, p. 818; *Society of the Army of the Tennessee*, pp. 78–79; *OR*, vol. X, pt. 1, pp. 266, 270; Virgil H. Moats, *Shiloh to Vicksburg*, p. 36.

69. *OR*, vol. X, pt. 1, pp. 266, 270; *Society of the Army of the Tennessee*, p. 79.

70. *OR*, vol. X, pt. 1, pp. 266–67, 581; M. F. Force, *From Fort Henry to Corinth*, p. 129; Sword, *Shiloh*, p. 182; Jill K. Garrett, ed., *Confederate Diary of Robert D. Smith*, p. 4.

71. Dennis Kelly, "Back in the Saddle," p. 28; *OR*, vol. X, pt. 1, pp. 267, 581, 585; Unknown to sister, July 21, 1862, 2nd Tennessee File, SNMP; Garrett, ed., *Smith Diary*, p. 4; Johnston, *Johnston*, p. 594; Orville Victor, *Incidents and Anecdotes of the War*, p. 364; *Cincinnati Commercial*, April 18, 1862.

72. *OR*, vol. X, pt. 1, p. 581; George W. Cullum to Mary, April 10, 1862, 24th Tennessee File, SNMP; T. H. Peeples, "From a Participant in Battle of Shiloh," p. 281. The colonel of the 24th Tennessee was under arrest at the time and not present.

73. *OR*, vol. X, pt. 1, pp. 273, 276, 585, 587; Faust, ed., *Encyclopedia*, p. 367; Walter S. to father, April 9, 1862, in *Chicago Times*, April 16, 1862.

74. *OR*, vol. X, pt. 1, p. 589.

75. Ibid., p. 585; Kelly, "Back in the Saddle," pp. 28–29.

76. Thomas E. Griess, *The American Civil War*, p. 36; Archer Jones, *Civil War Command and Strategy*, p. 52; Woodworth, *Davis*, pp. 99–100.

Seven: Confederate High Tide

1. *OR*, vol. X, pt. 1, pp. 465, 471, 480.

2. Ibid., pp. 495–496; Alexander Walker, "Narrative of the Battle of Shiloh," p. 124.

3. Walker, "Narrative of the Battle of Shiloh," p. 124.

4. *OR*, vol. X, pt. 1, pp. 471, 496–97, 513. Hodgson reported that he came into action at 7:10 A.M., but the correct time must have been after 8:00. Wiley Sword places it as 8:10 (*Shiloh*, p. 185).

5. *OR*, vol. X, pt. 1, pp. 496–97, 507; Robert Clark, Jr., "The New Orleans German Colony in the Civil War," p. 1003.

6. *OR*, vol. X, pt. 1, pp. 497, 504–5, 510. The 1901 D. W. Reed Shiloh Battlefield map misplaces Anderson's brigade, but NPS plaque 352 gives the proper alignment.

7. *OR*, vol. X, pt. 1, pp. 414–15; A. Walker, "Narrative of Battle of Shiloh," p. 135.

8. *OR*, vol. X, pt. 1, pp. 415, 420–21; Johnson to wife, April 11, 1862, Charles Johnson Letters, LSU; William Preston Johnston, *The Life of Gen. Albert Sidney Johnston*, p. 596.

9. *OR*, vol. X, pt. 1, pp. 416, 505; "Return of the 1st Brigade, R. M. Russell, March 30, 1862," Yerger Papers, MDAH; T. H. Bell, "Rhea [sic] Field," p. 11.

10. Lemuel A. Scarbrough Diary, April 6, 1862, EU; *OR*, vol. X, pt. 1, pp. 415, 416; Patricia L. Faust, ed., *Historical Times Illustrated Encyclopedia of the Civil War*, p. 142.

11. Bragg to wife, April 6, 1862, quoted in Don Seitz, *Braxton Bragg*, pp. 111–12.

12. *OR*, vol. X, pt. 1, pp. 444, 446.

13. Ibid., pp. 450–51; Shelton Diary, *Commercial Appeal*, April 9, 1962.

14. *OR*, vol. X, pt. 1, pp. 414, 444–45, 446, 447; A. Walker, "Narrative of Battle of Shiloh," p. 140; Larry J. Daniel, *Cannoneers in Gray*, pp. 34–35; William S. Dillon Diary, April 6, 1862, UM.

15. *OR*, vol. X, pt. 1, pp. 440, 445, 447, 451, 505–6, 511, 582; *Chicago Tribune*, April 12, 1862. Cleburne reported that about one-half of the 23rd Tennessee and sixty men of the 6th Mississippi participated in the attack. Vaughn claimed that Wa-

terhouse's battery withdrew to within a hundred yards of Shiloh Church. (D. W. Reed Letter, May 27, 1897, 13th Tennessee File, SNMP; Jack D. Welsh, *Medical Histories of Confederate Generals*, p. 117.)

16. *OR*, vol. X, pt. 1, p. 425; Scarbrough Diary, April 6, 1862, EU; A. J. Vaughn, *Personal Record of the Thirteenth Regiment, Tennessee Infantry*, p. 16; Shelton Diary, *Commercial Appeal*, April 9, 1962; Samuel Hoover, "Waterhouse's Battery at Shiloh"; Latta to wife, April 12, 1862, Samuel Latta Letters, TSLA. Cunningham uncovered evidence that the 22nd Tennessee apparently followed close behind Vaughn's six companies (O. E. Cunningham, "Shiloh and the Western Campaign of 1862," p. 261n). See also D. W. Reed Letter, May 27, 1897, 13th Tennessee File, SNMP; John B. Lindsley, ed., *Military Annals of Tennessee*, p. 316; James D. West, "The Thirteenth Tennessee Regiment," p. 183; "What He Saw at Shiloh," *National Tribune*, March 7, 1912.

17. *OR*, vol. X, pt. 1, p. 267.

18. Robert H. Fleming, "The Battle of Shiloh as a Private Saw It," p. 142; *Chicago Times*, April 16, 1862; J. E. Boos, ed., "Civil War Diary of Patrick White," p. 653; Blaisdell to wife, April 12, 1862, Timothy M. Blaisdell Letters, Civil War Times Collection, USMHI. Barrett became a prosperous businessman in postwar years and lived until 1912 ("Samuel Eddy Barrett," pp. 91–93). For a defense of the 77th Ohio, see Robert H. Fleming, "The Boys of Ohio Held Fast at Shiloh."

19. *OR*, vol. X, pt. 1, pp. 146–47; Ephraim C. Dawes, "The Battle of Shiloh," p. 124.

20. John T. Taylor, "Reminiscences of Services as an Aide-de-Camp," pp. 132–33; Albert D. Richardson, *The Secret Service, the Field, the Dungeon and the Escape*, p. 238; John F. Marszalek, *Sherman*, p. 178; Albert D. Richardson, *A Personal History of Ulysses S. Grant*, p. 242; *OR*, vol. X, pt. 1, p. 270.

21. *OR*, vol. X, pt. 1, p. 255; Dawes, "Battle of Shiloh," p. 148.

22. *OR*, vol. X, pt. 1, p. 256; J. L. Beiler Speech, 11th Indiana File, SNMP; Thomas Worthington, *Report of the Flank March to Join on McClernand's Right*, pp. 4–6; S. H. M. Byers, *Iowa in War Times*, p. 138.

23. Ephraim J. Hart, *History of the Fortieth Illinois Infantry*, p. 86; John T. Hurst, "The Battle of Shiloh," 40th Illinois File, SNMP; Earl C. Woods, ed., *The Shiloh Diary of Edmond Enoul Livaudais*, p. 26.

24. *OR*, vol. X, pt. 1, pp. 255–56; Henry Wright, *A History of the Sixth Iowa Infantry*, pp. 79–80; Mildred Throne, ed., "Letters from Shiloh," p. 242.

25. *OR*, vol. X, pt. 1, pp. 495, 516; Woods, ed., *Livaudais Diary*, pp. 26–27.

26. "H.R." to father, April 11, 1862, Civil War Times Collection, USMHI; *New Orleans Crescent*, April 15, 1862; Thomas W. Knox, *Camp-Fire and Cotton-Field: Southern Adventure in Time of War*, p. 157.

27. Journal of the Orleans Guard, April 6, 1862, Historic New Orleans Collection; "Caddo Fencibles of Louisiana," pp. 498–500; Arthur W. Bergeron, Jr., ed., *The Civil War Reminiscences of Major Silas T. Grisamore, C.S.A.*, pp. 33–34.

28. Bruce Catton, *Grant Moves South*, p. 223; *OR*, vol. X, pt. 1, p. 184; A. D. Richardson, *Grant*, p. 238.

29. Catton, *Grant Moves South*, p. 223; Edward Bouton, *Events of the Civil War*, pp. 15–16; "Hillyer on Grant at Shiloh," p. 298; W. E. Woodward, *Meet General Grant*, p. 238; Annie Cherry, "Gen. Grant at Shiloh," p. 44; *OR*, vol. X, pt. 1, p. 184. Rawlins wrote that breakfast began at 6 A.M., but Hillyer placed the time at 7 A.M. The latter is more nearly correct. See Cunningham, "Shiloh," p. 219n.

30. Joseph M. Hanson, *The Conquest of Missouri*, p. 40; *OR*, vol. LII, pt. 1, p. 232; pt. 2, p. 95; Don Carlos Buell, "Shiloh Reviewed," p. 492. Some sources claim that Grant did know that Buell was in Savannah. See Richardson, *Grant*, pp. 238–39; Woodward, *Meet General Grant*, p. 250. In his note to Buell, Grant wrote that he had anticipated an attack—an obvious reference to Crump's Landing.

31. *OR*, vol. X, pt. 1, pp. 175, 184; Lew Wallace, *An Autobiography*, vol. 1, p. 461;

Hanson, *The Conquest of Missouri*, p. 41; Richardson, *Grant*, p. 239.

32. *OR*, vol. X, pt. 1, p. 178; Hanson, *Conquest of Missouri*, p. 40.

33. Hanson, *Conquest of Missouri*, p. 42; William S. McFeely, *Grant*, p. 112; James G. Day, "The Fifteenth Iowa at Shiloh," p. 179; *OR*, vol. X, pt. 1, p. 185; *Philadelphia Inquirer*, April 18, 1862; *Indianapolis Journal*, April 15, 1862. Rawlins wrote that Grant arrived at 8 A.M., but I agree with Sword (*Shiloh*, p. 217) that the time must have been closer to 9:00. See Edwin Hannaford, *The Story of a Regiment*, pp. 252–53.

34. J. F. C. Fuller, *The Generalship of Ulysses S. Grant*, p. 111; William W. Belknap, *History of the 15th Regiment Iowa*, pp. 289–90; *OR*, vol. X, pt. 1, pp. 278, 286–88; Kenneth P. Williams, *Lincoln Finds a General*, vol. 3, p. 361; *In the Matter of the Controversy*, p. 13; Throne, ed., "Letters from Shiloh," pp. 244, 247.

35. *OR*, vol. X, pt. 1, pp. 178–79, 185; U. S. Grant, *Personal Memoirs of U. S. Grant*, pp. 225–26.

36. Douglas Putnam, Jr., "Reminiscences of the Battle of Shiloh," p. 200. Marszalek (*Sherman*, p. 178) places the time at 10 A.M., and Sword (*Shiloh*, p. 220) at 11 P.M.

37. Grant, *Memoirs*, p. 231; Leander Stillwell, "In the Ranks at Shiloh," pp. 120–21; *OR*, vol. X, pt. 1, p. 278; W. W. Jackson, "The Battle of Shiloh"; Richardson, *Grant*, p. 242; Seymour Thompson, *Recollections with the Third Iowa Regiment*, pp. 215–16; Putnam, "Reminiscences," pp. 200–201.

38. Grant, *Memoirs*, p. 237; Richardson, *Grant*, pp. 242–43; Putnam, "Reminiscences," p. 201. Sword (*Shiloh*, pp. 349–50) speculates that Smith's Mississippi Battery fired the shot. In his memoirs, Grant incorrectly placed the incident on April 7.

39. *OR*, vol. X, pt. 1, p. 115; *Chicago Tribune*, April 14, 1862; Olynthus B. Clark, ed., *Downing's Civil War Diary*, pp. 39–40; Hicken, *Illinois in the Civil War*, p. 58.

40. *OR*, vol. X, pt. 1, pp. 114–15.

41. George Mason, *Illinois at Shiloh*, pp. 24–25; Mary Ann Anderson, ed., *The Civil War Diary of Allen Morgan Geer*, p. 54; *New York Times*, April 20, 1862.

42. Emmet Crozier, *Yankee Reporters*, p. 220; *Iowa City Republican*, May 14, 1862, quoted in Steve Meyer, *Iowa Valor*, p. 102.

43. *OR*, vol. X, pt. 1, pp. 115, 139; Englemann to wife, April 17, 1862, Adolph Englemann Letters, ILSL; James G. Wilson, *Biographical Sketches of Illinois Officers*, p. 43; *Chicago Tribune*, April 24, 1862; John Y. Simon, ed., *The Papers of Ulysses S. Grant*, vol. 4, p. 492.

44. *OR*, vol. X, pt. 1, pp. 141, 143; Louis Arns to parents, April 14, 1862, 49th Illinois File, SNMP; *Chicago Tribune*, April 14, 1862; James G. Smart, ed., *A Radical View*, pp. 133–34.

45. Thomas J. Bryant, *Who Is Responsible for the Advance of the Army of the Tennessee Towards Corinth?*, p. 34; Dawes, "Battle of Shiloh," pp. 144–45; *OR*, vol. X, pt. 1, pp. 139, 141, 143; M. F. Force, *From Fort Henry to Corinth*, p. 129.

46. *OR*, vol. X, pt. 1, p. 112.

47. Throne, ed., "Letters from Shiloh," p. 250; Franc Wilkie, *Pen and Powder*, p. 160; Wilson, *Biographical Sketches*, p. 45; *OR*, vol. X, pt. 1, pp. 114, 123–24, 133; George F. Witham, *Shiloh, Shells and Artillery Units*, pp. 1, 2, 4, 6; Mason, *Illinois at Shiloh*, p. 25; Throne, ed., "Letters from Shiloh," p. 250; *New York Tribune*, April 4, 1862.

48. *OR*, vol. X, pt. 1, pp. 159, 267, 270; Force, *From Fort Henry to Corinth*, p. 130; John K. Duke, *History of the Fifty-Third Ohio Volunteer Infantry*, pp. 49–50; Carrington Diary, April 6, 1862, CHS.

49. D. W. Reed, *The Battle of Shiloh and the Organizations Engaged*, pp. 81–82; *OR*, vol. X, pt. 1, p. 427. The 12th Tennessee also passed through the camp of the 4th Illinois Cavalry. The so-called Lost Field had been owned and cleared by Jacob Barnes, but he died before the war. The field, which no longer exists, was in bad

condition by 1897. (Ed Bearss, "Base Map Book," pp. 59–60, SNMP.)

50. D. W. Reed, *Shiloh*, p. 82; Various D. W. Reed Letters in 4th Tennessee File, SNMP; J. B. Ulmer, "A Glimpse of Albert Sidney Johnston," pp. 290–91; Welsh, *Medical Histories*, p. 102; Thomas Jordan, "The Battle of Shiloh," vol. XXXV, p. 212; Diane Neal and Thomas W. Kremm, *The Lion of the South*, p. 108.

51. *OR*, vol. X, pt. 1, pp. 423, 427, 432; A. J. Meadows, "The Fourth Tennessee Infantry," p. 312; Wilbur Crummer, *With Grant at Fort Donelson*, pp. 57–59; Mason, *Illinois at Shiloh*, p. 26; D. W. Reed, *Shiloh*, p. 82; Bell, "Rhea [sic] Field," p. 13; Various D. W. Reed Letters in 4th Tennessee File, SNMP; NPS plaques 310, 319.

52. *OR*, vol. X, pt. 1, pp. 124, 126, 128, 133, 574, 576, 578; Thomas C. Watkins Diary, April 6, 1862, Civil War Times Collection, USMHI.

53. *OR*, vol. X, pt. 1, pp. 592, 605; Lindsley, ed., *Military Annals*, pp. 419–21. The 3rd Mississippi Battalion of Wood's brigade was not present for the attack.

54. *OR*, vol. X, pt. 1, pp. 123, 133; Lindsley, ed., *Military Annals*, pp. 419–20; Lucius Barber, *Army Memoirs of Lucius W. Barber*, p. 53; *Official Roster of the Soldiers of the State of Ohio in the War of the Rebellion*, vol. X, p. 555.

55. *OR*, vol. X, pt. 1, p. 223; Fritz Haskell, ed., "Diary of Colonel William Camm," p. 845; James Dungan, *History of Hurlbut's Fighting Fourth Division*, p. 101.

56. *OR*, vol. X, pt. 1, p. 226; Barber, *Memoirs*, p. 54; McEathron to brother, April 9, 1862, Alexander McEathron Letters, ILSL.

57. John W. Foster, *War Stories For My Grandchildren*, pp. 62–63; *OR*, vol. X, pt. 1, p. 226; Barber, *Memoirs*, p. 53; McEathron to brother, April 8, 9, 1862, McEathron Letters, ILSL.

58. B. F. Sawyer, "Battle Scenes at Shiloh," pp. 54–55; *OR*, vol. X, pt. 1, p. 447.

59. *OR*, vol. X, pt. 1, pp. 417, 427, 430, 433.

60. NPS plaques 331, 302, 316, 353.

61. Dawes, "Battle of Shiloh," p. 148; *OR*, vol. X, pt. 1, pp. 250, 267, 270; J. L. Bieler Speech, 11th Indiana File, SNMP.

62. *OR*, vol. X, pt. 1, pp. 131, 144; Wilson, *Biographical Sketches*, p. 43.

63. *OR*, vol. X, pt. 1, pp. 116, 141, 144, 146–47; John G. Shea, *The American Nation*, pp. 331–32; D. W. Reed, *Shiloh*, p. 47; Bouton, *Events of the Civil War*, p. 31.

64. Wood to Davis, June 12, 1862, S. A. M. Wood Papers, ADAH; O. B. Clark, ed., *Downing's Diary*, p. 40; Throne, ed., "Letters from Shiloh," p. 253.

65. *OR*, vol. X, pt. 1, p. 130; vol. LII, pt. 1, pp. 22–23; *Missouri Daily Democrat*, April 29, 1862.

66. *OR*, vol. X, pt. 1, pp. 408–9, 435. I place this incident at a different time of day from either Sword ("Shiloh," p. 331) or Cunningham ("Shiloh," p. 313).

67. *OR*, vol. X, pt. 1, p. 116; *Missouri Daily Democrat*, April 16, 1862.

68. *OR*, vol. X, pt. 1, p. 255; D. W. Reed, *Shiloh*, p. 56.

69. Dawes, "Battle of Shiloh," p. 153.

70. *OR*, vol. X, pt. 1, pp. 286, 288–89; Johnston, *Johnston*, pp. 682–83; *In the Matter of the Controversy*, pp. 13, 14, 21, 31; Mildred Throne, ed., *The Civil War Diary of Cyrus F. Boyd*, p. 29; Day, "Fifteenth Iowa at Shiloh," p. 180; *Missouri Daily Democrat*, April 25, 1862; *Cincinnati Commercial*, April 14, 1862; Belknap, *15th Iowa*, p. 107.

71. *OR*, vol. X, pt. 1, pp. 287, 289; Belknap, *15th Iowa*, pp. 107, 179, 191; Throne, ed., *Boyd Diary*, pp. 30–31; Day, "Fifteenth Iowa at Shiloh," pp. 180–81; Throne, ed., "Letters from Shiloh," p. 245; Adolphus G. Studer Letter of May 15, 1862, quoted in Steve Meyer, *Iowa Valor*, p. 92.

72. *OR*, vol. X, pt. 1, pp. 104, 105, 287, 289; *Missouri Daily Democrat*, April 25, 1862; Belknap, *15th Iowa*, pp. 179–81, 189; Harmon to brother, April 11, 1862, Francis M. Harmon Letters, INHS; Day, "Fifteenth Iowa at Shiloh," pp. 182, 184; Throne, ed., "Letters from Shiloh," pp. 245, 248.

73. *OR*, vol. X, pt. 1, pp. 142, 147, 255, 274, 276; Blaisdell to wife, April 12, 1862, Blaisdell Letters, Civil War Times Collection, USMHI; *Chicago Times*, April 16, 1862; Hart, *Fortieth Illinois*, p. 88. NPS plaque 56 states that Nispel used two guns, but he officially reported only one. Sword (*Shiloh*, p. 332) suggests that the Federal gunners engaged the Washington Artillery, but NPS plaques in Jones Field state that the Federal guns withdrew at noon, before the New Orleans gunners came into position.

74. *OR*, vol. X, pt. 1, pp. 138, 144; D. W. Reed, *Shiloh*, pp. 45–47, 54; Force, *From Fort Henry to Shiloh*, p. 137. NPS plaques and monuments document that fourteen regiments participated in the attack, although it is possible that others were also engaged.

75. O. B. Clark, ed., *Downing's Diary*, pp. 40–41.

76. *OR*, vol. X, pt. 1, pp. 137, 138, 144–45; Throne, ed., "Letters from Shiloh," pp. 250, 254; D. W. Reed, *Shiloh*, p. 47.

77. Worthington, *Report of the Flank March*, pp. 6–10.

78. Ibid., p. 10; Hart, *Fortieth Illinois*, p. 88.

79. Hart, *Fortieth Illinois*, pp. 88–89; *OR*, vol. X, pt. 1, pp. 103, 252; D. W. Reed, *Shiloh*, p. 56.

80. William C. Davis, *The Orphan Brigade*, pp. 19, 84–85; *OR*, vol. X, pt. 1, pp. 614–15. Trabue had previously had the 3rd Kentucky, the 4th Alabama Battalion, and Crew's Tennessee Battalion detached.

81. *OR*, vol. X, pt. 1, pp. 513–14; Barnes F. Lathrop, "A Confederate Artilleryman at Shiloh," pp. 377–78. The 12:30 time is based upon NPS plaque 359.

82. *OR*, vol. X, pt. 1, pp. 616–17; vol. XXXII, pt. 3, p. 703; "Cobb's Battery Not Captured at Shiloh," p. 68; A. D. Kirwan, ed., *Johnny Green of the Orphan Brigade*, p. 26; Lathrop, "Confederate Artilleryman," pp. 377–78; D. W. Reed, *Shiloh*, p. 45.

83. Bergeron, ed., *Grisamore*, p. 34; *OR*, vol. X, pt. 1, pp. 517, 521, 616; Journal of the Orleans Guard, April 6, 1862, Historic New Orleans Collection; Woods, ed., *Livaudais Diary*, pp. 27–28. An often repeated story (Basil W. Duke, *A History of Morgan's Cavalry*, pp. 148–49) relates that the Louisianians returned fire. When the major was told that he was firing into friendly troops, he replied: "I know it, but, damn it, we fire on anybody who fires on us." The story is not confirmed in any eyewitness accounts and may be apocryphal.

84. Faust, ed., *Encyclopedia*, pp. 817–18; *OR*, vol. X, pt. 1, pp. 569, 626; J. Blackburn, "Reminiscences of the Terry Texas Rangers," p. 56; Robert Bunting Letter, April 6, 1862, UT. I have accepted Sword's time frame of 2:30 as being approximately correct (*Shiloh*, p. 327).

85. D. W. Reed, *Shiloh*, p. 86; B. W. Duke, *Morgan's Cavalry*, pp. 149–50; Dee Alexander Brown, *The Bold Cavaliers*, p. 50; William E. Metzler, *Morgan and His Dixie Cavaliers*, p. 13.

86. D. W. Reed, *Shiloh*, pp. 69, 77–78, 81, 82, 84; Johnson casualty percentage based upon NPS plaque 332.

87. NPS plaques mark Hurlbut's campsites.

88. Jesse B. Connelly, April 6, 1862, Jesse B. Connelly Diary, INHS; F. Y. Hedley, *Marching Through Georgia*, p. 45; Lieutenant Belzar Grebe Biography, 14th Illinois File, SNMP; Throne, ed., "Letters from Shiloh," p. 258; R. M. McFadden to Editor of *Gazette*, April 18, 1862, 41st Illinois File, SNMP; "W.H.S.," p. 332.

89. *OR*, vol. X, pt. 1, pp. 203, 235; James C. Veach, "The Battle of Shiloh"; Haskell, ed., "Camm Diary," p. 843; Jackson, "Battle of Shiloh."

90. Hedley, *Marching Through Georgia*, p. 46; Unknown to Eason Johnson, April 25, 1862, 41st Illinois File, SNMP; "W.H.S.," p. 332; Stimpson to wife, April 10, 1862, William R. Stimpson Letters, LC; Thompson, *Recollections*, p. 210.

91. *OR*, vol. X, pt. 1, pp. 203, 213, 245, 246; Hedley, *Marching Through Georgia*, p. 46; Edwin L. Hobart, *Semi-History of a Boy-Veteran of the Twenty-Eighth Regiment Illi-*

nois Volunteers, pp. 7–8; Larry R. Houghton, "Captured at Shiloh," p. 37. Manse George married Sarah Bell's daughter Nancy and thus obtained the property for his pig farm (Jane Kemble, "The Manse George Cabin," SNMP).

92. Ezra J. Warner, *Generals in Blue*, p. 561; Addison A. Stuart, *Iowa Colonels and Regiments*, p. 96; *OR*, vol. X, pt. 1, pp. 211, 214, 217, 233, 246; Phillip Shaw Journal, April 6, 1862, 32nd Illinois File, SNMP; *Missouri Daily Democrat*, April 24, 1862; Seymour Thompson, *Recollections with the Third Iowa Infantry*, p. 213. Hedley, *Marching Through Georgia*, pp. 45–46; Pugh to wife, April 25, 1862, Isaac C. Pugh Letters, 41st Illinois File, SNMP; McFadden to Editor, April 18, 1862, R. H. McFadden Letters, 41st Illinois File, SNMP; Force, *From Fort Henry to Corinth*, p. 150; Throne, ed., "Letters from Shiloh," p. 260.

93. *Official Roster of the Soldiers of the State of Ohio*, vol. X, p. 549; *OR*, vol. X, pt. 1, p. 209; John M. Powers, "That Terrible First Day," p. 40.

94. *OR*, vol. X, pt. 1, p. 103; L. C. Teel to friend, n.d., B, 2nd Michigan Battery File, SNMP; Powers, "That Terrible First Day," p. 40; *Missouri Daily Democrat*, April 24, 1862; J. R. Palmer, "No Surprise at Shiloh."

95. *OR*, vol. X, pt. 1, pp. 210–11; Powers, "That Terrible First Day," pp. 41–42; Felix Robertson to Reed, August 1, 1909, 13th Ohio Battery File, SNMP.

96. *OR*, vol. X, pt. 1, pp. 217, 241; Isaac Yantis, "The 41st Illinois at Shiloh"; Throne, ed., "Letters from Shiloh," p. 260.

97. *OR*, vol. X, pt. 1, pp. 537, 548, 554; George W. Baylor, "With Gen. A. S. Johnston at Shiloh," p. 611.

98. Thomas L. Connelly, *Army of the Heartland*, p. 164; Alfred Roman, *The Military Operations of General Beauregard*, vol. 1, pp. 286–89, 529.

99. Baylor, "With Johnston at Shiloh," p. 610; *OR*, vol. X, pt. 1, p. 404; Johnston, *Johnston*, p. 612.

100. Samuel H. Lockett, "Surprise and Withdrawal at Shiloh," p. 604; "The Last Roll," p. 181; William Preston Diary, April 6, 1862, NA; F. A. Shoup, "How We Went to Shiloh," p. 139.

101. Johnston, *Johnston*, p. 598; Baylor, "With Johnston at Shiloh," p. 610.

102. Baylor, "With Johnston at Shiloh," pp. 610–11; *OR*, vol. X, pt. 1, p. 404; Ulmer, "Glimpse of Johnston," p. 291; Edward Munford, "Albert Sidney Johnston," Albert Sidney Johnston Papers, Barret Collection, TU.

103. Sword criticized Johnston for removing Chalmers and Jackson at the wrong time and sending them on a time-consuming march (*Shiloh*, p. 240). I contend that only one brigade should have been sent.

104. Otto Eisenschiml, "The 55th Illinois at Shiloh," pp. 194–95; Warner, *Generals in Blue*, pp. 484–85.

105. David Stuart Testimony, Worthington Court Martial Proceedings, NA; Elijah C. Lawrence, "Stuart's Brigade at Shiloh," pp. 489–90; Edwin C. Bearss, ed., *The Story of the Fifty-Fifth Regiment, Illinois Volunteer Infantry*, pp. 68–69.

106. *Canton Weekly Register*, May 6, 1862; Statement of John P. Wheeler, 55th Illinois, in Bryant, *Who Is Responsible*, p. 11; Thaddeus H. Capron, "War Diary of Thaddeus H. Capron, 1861–1865," pp. 343–44; Lawrence, "Stuart's Brigade," p. 490; Warner, *Generals in Blue*, pp. 461–62; Dawes, "Battle of Shiloh," p. 158.

107. *OR*, vol. X, pt. 1, pp. 257–58; Dawes, "Battle of Shiloh," p. 158.

108. Lawrence, "Stuart's Brigade," pp. 491–92.

109. *OR*, vol. X, pt. 1, pp. 554, 565; Pennsylvania Battlefield Commission, *The Seventy-Seventh Pennsylvania at Shiloh*, p. 328.

110. *Cincinnati Commercial*, April 29, 1862; Ronald E. Toops, *The McConnell Letters*, pp. 11, 14; Noah A. Trudeau, "Fields Without Honor," p. 44; *Official Roster of the Soldiers of the State of Ohio*, vol. VI, p. 43.

111. Trudeau, "Fields Without Honor," pp. 44–49, 57; W. H. McClure, "The 71st Ohio at Shiloh"; Lawrence, "Stuart's Brigade," p. 492; Bearss, ed., *Fifty-Fifth Illi-*

nois, pp. 85–86; Statement of Lieutenant Jacob Fink, 55th Illinois, in Bryant, *Who Is Responsible*, p. 9; *Cincinnati Commercial*, April 25, 28, May 8, 1862; *Selina, Mercer County, Ohio*, April 17, May 1, 8, 15, 1862; "Testimony Submitted to the President of the United States by Rodney Mason," pp. 4–5, OHS.

112. *OR*, vol. X, pt. 1, p. 561; *Tri-Weekly Telegraph* (Houston), July 10, 16, 1862; Eleanor D. Pace, ed., "The Diary and Letters of William P. Rogers, 1846–1862," pp. 286–87.

113. *OR*, vol. X, pt. 1, p. 549; William Moiser to Reed, December 11, 1912, 52nd Tennessee File, SNMP; Wilkinson to brother, April 16, 1862, Micajah Wilkinson Letters, LSU.

114. Dawes, "Battle of Shiloh," p. 158; Eisenschiml, "Fifty-Fifth Illinois," pp. 196–97.

115. Sam Houston, Jr., "Shiloh Shadows," pp. 330–31.

Eight: The Blue Line Stiffens

1. *OR*, vol. X, pt. 1, pp. 204, 279; Charles Morton to D. W. Reed, April 20, 1909, 25th Missouri, SNMP; *Society of the Army of the Tennessee*, p. 64; John H. Rerick, *The 44th Indiana Volunteer Infantry*, pp. 132, 231.

2. *OR*, vol. X, pt. 1, pp. 279, 290–91; William Preston Johnston, *The Life of Gen. Albert Sidney Johnston*, p. 683; *Society of the Army of the Tennessee*, p. 64; Henry S. Hurter, "Narrative of the First Battery of Light Artillery," vol. 1, p. 643; Andrew Hickenlooper, "The Battle of Shiloh," p. 17.

3. D. W. Reed, *Campaigns and Battles of the Twelfth Regiment Iowa*, pp. 43–44; Swain to wife, April 9, 1862, George Swain Letters, CHS; Mildred Throne, ed., "Erastus B. Sopher's History of Company D," p. 178; "First Reunion of Iowa's Hornet's Nest Brigade," p. 12; Charles A. Morton, "A Boy at Shiloh," pp. 63–64; John Thomas Smith, *A History of the Thirty-First Regiment of Indiana Volunteer Infantry*, pp. 28–29. A Louisiana soldier referred to "an old washed out road . . . three feet deep" (Robertson to mother, April 9, 1862, 4th Louisiana File, LSU). As late as 1887, Union veterans still referred to "an old abandoned road" and "an old road" (*Society of the Army of the Tennessee*, p. 64; "First Reunion," pp. 13, 17, 21; S. H. M. Byers, *Iowa in War Times*, p. 129). In the 1912 reunion of Tuttle's brigade, the term "the old sunken road" was used ("Ninth Reunion of Iowa's Hornet's Nest Brigade," p. 18). The formal name of the "Sunken Road" appears to be an invention of the NPS.

4. Patricia L. Faust, ed., *Historical Times Illustrated Encyclopedia of the Civil War*, pp. 766–767; Addison A. Stuart, *Iowa Colonels and Regiments*, pp. 51–52.

5. Byers, *Iowa in War Times*, pp. 128–29; *OR*, vol. X, pt. 1, pp. 163, 164.

6. Mildred Throne, ed., "Letters from Shiloh," pp. 272–73; B. F. Thomas, *Soldier Life*, p. 41; "Shiloh," 52nd Illinois File, SNMP. See also Wyllie to family, April 6, 1862, William R. Wyllie Letter, 58th Illinois File, SNMP.

7. B. F. Thomas, *Soldier Life*, p. 41; Throne, ed., "Sopher's History," p. 178; Throne, ed., "Letters from Shiloh," p. 273; John Bell, *Tramps and Triumphs*, p. 15.

8. *OR*, vol. X, pt. 1, pp. 164, 574; J. W. Powell to Cornelius Cadle, May 15, 1896, F, 2nd Illinois Artillery File, SNMP.

9. Throne, ed., "Letters from Shiloh," p. 268.

10. Ibid.; *Quincy Daily Herald*, April 15, 1862; Donald F. Dosch, "The Hornet's Nest at Shiloh," p. 176; William W. Cluett, *History of the 57th Regiment*, p. 19; *OR*, vol. X, pt. 1, pp. 150, 151, 153, 164, 165.

11. Swain to wife, April 9, 1862, Swain Letters, CHS; William Harvey Diary, April 6, 1862, 57th Illinois File, SNMP.

12. Johnston, *Johnston*, p. 679; George F. Witham, *Shiloh, Shells and Artillery*, p. 88. The battery count includes Powell (five guns), Hickenlooper (four guns), Munch

(four guns), Richardson (four guns), Stone (four guns), Mann (four guns), Ross (four guns), Welker (four guns). Wiley Sword puts the number in the Hornet's Nest at "more than 11,000," backed by seven batteries of thirty-eight guns. Dosch, who counts only Prentiss's command and seven regiments of W. H. L. Wallace's division, states that probably no more than 4,300 effective infantry were in the Sunken Road, where the brunt of the attacks occurred ("Hornet's Nest," pp. 176–78). There were also, of course, twenty-five guns in that limited sector.

13. Byers, *Iowa in War Times*, p. 129.
14. Alfred Roman, *The Military Operations of General Beauregard*, vol. 1, pp. 286–87, 289, 291, 527, 529; *OR*, vol. X, pt. 1, p. 438. Beauregard's Headquarters No. 2, according to NPS plaque "W," was located in the northern portion of Fraley Field.
15. *OR*, vol. X, pt. 1, p. 438; D. W. Reed, *The Battle of Shiloh and the Organizations Engaged*, p. 85; Throne, ed., "Letters from Shiloh," p. 268; J. G. Deupree, "Reminiscences of Service with the First Mississippi Cavalry," pp. 89–90.
16. Throne, ed., "Letters from Shiloh," p. 268; Bell, *Tramps and Triumphs*, pp. 15–16; Throne, ed., "Sopher's History," p. 182.
17. *OR*, vol. X, pt. 1, pp. 439, 453; John B. Lindsley, ed., *Military Annals of Tennessee*, p. 211; Henry George, *History of the 3d, 7th, 8th, and 12th Kentucky, C.S.A.*, pp. 29–30; Stacy Allen, "Confederate Assaults on the Hornet's Nest, Shiloh," pp. 2–3, SNMP. The troop strength is an estimate based upon Cheatham's division strength of 3,801 effectives (*OR*, vol. X, pt. 1, p. 443).
18. W. J. Stubblefield Diary, April 6, 1862, PL.
19. *OR*, vol. X, pt. 1, p. 153; Benjamin F. Thomas, "Off to War," p. 173; F. F. Kiner, *One Year's Soldiering*, p. 55; D. W. Reed, *Twelfth Iowa*, p. 44; Lindsley, ed., *Military Annals*, p. 211.
20. *OR*, vol. X, pt. 1, p. 153; Lindsley, ed., *Military Annals*, p. 211; George, *History of the 3d*, pp. 29–30.
21. The name "Hornet's Nest" far predates that of "Sunken Road." Although I have yet to find any contemporary use of that name, Confederate officers confirmed the sobriquet in the fall of 1884, as the Shiloh cyclorama painting was being prepared. ("First Reunion," p. 12.) The thicketed section of the road was the actual Hornet's Nest, although the term today is loosely applied to the entire area fronting the Sunken Road. See Don Carlos Buell, "Shiloh Reviewed," p. 505.
22. Dosch, "Hornet's Nest," p. 180; James L. McDonough, *Shiloh*, p. 143.
23. Both D. W. Reed (*Shiloh*, p. 70) and Dosch ("Hornet's Nest," pp. 178–79) claim that the first Rebel attack on the Hornet's Nest came at 9 A.M. by the 3rd Confederate. The evidence (*OR*, vol. X, pt. 1, pp. 281, 574) appears tenuous. It seems highly unlikely that the regiment, in less than an hour, could have pursued Prentiss's survivors for three-quarters of a mile and then formed for a solo attack. Indeed, such a claim is never made in the report. One of Prentiss's officers stated that his men were in position in the Sunken Road and received the first assault at 9 A.M. Yet Prentiss himself (*OR*, vol. X, pt. 1, p. 278) wrote that the first attack came at 10 A.M. By that time, Shaver's entire brigade, 3rd Confederate included, was engaged at Review Field.

Dosch ("Hornet's Nest," p. 179) bases the "second assault" by the 3rd Confederate and 6th Arkansas upon James Tuttle's postwar speech ("First Reunion," p. 13). It was twenty-four years after the fact, and Tuttle's memory obviously failed him. He recalled being attacked shortly after 8:30 A.M. by Ruggles's division—clearly an impossibility. Even Iowa Governor Samuel Kirkwood, speaking at the same reunion ("First Reunion," p. 21), remarked that it was as late as 9 A.M. before Tuttle's brigade moved out of camp, a fact confirmed in Colonel James C. Parrott's report (*OR*, vol. X, pt. 1, p. 150).

The so-called third attack (Dosch, "Hornet's Nest," pp. 179–80), based upon Adams's own report (*OR*, vol. X, pt. 1, p. 537), did not occur. Dosch's evidence (*OR*, vol. X, pt. 1, p. 153; *National Tribune*, April 11, 1935) actually describes Cheatham's attack.

Charles B. Clark and Roger B. Bowen (*University Recruits*, pp. 101, 103) also catalogued two somewhat different assaults prior to 11 A.M. The sources used for the first assault are a description of Cheatham's 11:00 attack. I concur with Sword (*Shiloh*, p. 247) that Cheatham's attack was the first to be made upon the Sunken Road.

24. *OR*, vol. X, pt. 1, p. 574; Charles Swett, Memoirs, Swett's Mississippi Battery File, SNMP.
25. *OR*, vol. X, pt. 1, pp. 428, 597; D. W. Reed, *Shiloh*, pp. 70, 71; Dosch, "Hornet's Nest," pp. 182–83. The fighting in Duncan Field appears to have been a long-range exchange of musketry; to the right, in the thickets, there was a direct assault.
26. *OR*, vol. X, pt. 1, p. 408; T. Harry Williams, *P. G. T. Beauregard*, p. 135; Thomas Jordan, "Notes of a Confederate Staff Officer at Shiloh," pp. 599–601; Thomas L. Connelly, *Army of the Heartland*, pp. 160, 166; Connelly asserted that staff officers became mini-generals, who employed a "make yourself useful" policy.
27. *OR*, vol. X, pt. 1, pp. 466, 483; Don Seitz, *Braxton Bragg*, p. 112.
28. Faust, ed., *Encyclopedia*, p. 309; John McGrath, "In a Louisiana Regiment," pp. 118–19; Johnston, *Johnston*, p. 583.
29. Vincent Cassidy and Simpson, *Henry Watkins Allen of Louisiana*, pp. 17, 18–20, 63–64.
30. John Smith Kendall, "Recollections of a Confederate Staff Officer," p. 1063.
31. D. W. Reed, *Shiloh*, p. 77; Robertson to mother, April 9, 1862, Robertson Letter, LSU; Frank L. Richardson, "War As I Saw It," p. 99; Kendall, "Recollections," p. 1061; Dosch, "Hornet's Nest," p. 185.
32. *OR*, vol. X, pt. 1, pp. 430, 489; Robertson to mother, April 9, 1862, Robertson Letter, LSU; Kendall, "Recollections," p. 1062. The 4th Louisiana was probably in the northwestern corner of Barnes Field at the time.
33. *OR*, vol. X, pt. 1, pp. 480, 492–93; Dosch, "Hornet's Nest," p. 184; Cassidy and Simpson, *Allen*, p. 76.
34. *OR*, vol. X, pt. 1, pp. 480, 488; Robertson to mother, April 9, 1862, Robertson Letter, LSU.
35. Kendall, "Recollections," p. 1065; W. E. Bevins, *Reminiscences of a Private*, p. 24; Robertson to mother, April 9, 1862, Robertson Letter, LSU; *OR*, vol. X, pt. 1, pp. 480, 493; D. W. Reed, *Shiloh*, p. 55.
36. "Byrne's Battery," John Joyes, Jr., Papers, FC.
37. *OR*, vol. X, pt. 1, pp. 483, 493; Robertson to mother, April 9, 1862, Robertson Letter, LSU; Kendall, "Recollections," p. 1064.
38. *OR*, vol. X, pt. 1, p. 486; Kendall, "Recollections," p. 1064; Richardson, "War As I Saw It," p. 100.
39. *OR*, vol. X, pt. 1, pp. 491, 493; Kendall, "Recollections," pp. 1064-65; Jack D. Welsh, *Medical Histories of Confederate Officers*, p. 4.
40. Samuel H. Lockett, "Surprise and Withdrawal at Shiloh," p. 605.
41. Kendall, "Recollections," pp. 1065–66. Gibson mentioned four assaults, but Bragg and Colonel Allen specify three (*OR*, vol. X, pt. 1, pp. 466, 480, 486). O. E. Cunningham ("Shiloh and the Western Campaign of 1862," p. 358n) specifies that only three assaults can be documented, but Kendall ("Recollections," pp. 1064–66) relates four.
42. *OR*, vol. X, pt. 1, pp. 466, 483, 485, 486, 488; Seitz, *Bragg*, p. 112.
43. *OR*, vol. X, pt. 1, pp. 466, 574, 578; Dosch, "Hornet's Nest," p. 185; D. W. Reed, *Twelfth Iowa*, p. 82; William Shaw to Reed, April 16, 1896, David W. Reed Papers, Misc. Files, SNMP; Allen, "C.S.A. Hornet's Nest Assaults Update," p. 1, SNMP.

44. *OR*, vol. X, pt. 1, pp. 472, 498, 523, 526; John G. Biel, ed., "The Battle of Shiloh," pp. 264, 265n; *New Orleans Picayune*, April 15, 1862.

45. *OR*, vol. X, pt. 1, p. 498; Dosch, "Hornet's Nest," p. 186. James L. McDonough ("Bayonets and Blunders," p. 11) states that 18,000 Confederates were used to attack 4,300 Federals, although the Confederates never attacked with more than 3,700 at any one time. Although there were actually only 10,000 or so Southern infantry involved, the question still remains: could the troops have been launched as a massive juggernaut against one section of the Sunken Road? Such an assault would have involved in-depth stacking of five brigades, which would have limited firepower. If the brigades were spread over a wide front, then more than 4,300 Federals would, of course, have been engaged.

46. Allen, "Hornet's Nest Assaults Update," SNMP; Dosch, "Hornet's Nest," p. 187. Grady McWhiney concluded that criticism of Bragg "certainly was justified" (*Braxton Bragg and Confederate Defeat*, p. 240).

  In 1887, Tuttle wrote: "According to Rebel reports, they were beaten away from this position seven times. I reported it as five times. It was hard to tell when one charge ended and another began." (D. W. Reed, *Twelfth Iowa*, p. 79.) Stacy Allen's research indicates seven assaults ("Brief Analysis of Donald F. Dosch's 'The Hornet's Nest,'" pp. 1–7, SNMP). I credit Gibson with four attacks, thus making a total of eight.

47. William C. Davis, *Breckinridge*, pp. 302, 305; Faust, ed., *Encyclopedia*, p. 78.

48. Roman, *Beauregard*, vol. 1, p. 527; Edward Porter Thompson, *History of the Orphan Brigade*, p. 99; A. H. Mecklin Diary, April 6, 1862, MDAH; John C. Caldwell Diary, April 6, 1862, Civil War Times Collection, USMHI. See also A. D. Kirwan, ed., *Johnny Green of the Orphan Brigade*, p. 25.

49. Roman, *Beauregard*, vol. 1, pp. 527, 529, 534; *OR*, vol. X, pt. 1, pp. 404, 621; William Preston Diary, April 6, 1862, NA.

50. Mecklin Diary, April 6, 1862, MDAH; Joseph Boyce, "The Second Day at Shiloh." Both accounts misidentify the officer as Beauregard.

51. W. J. McMurray, *History of the Twentieth Tennessee Regiment Volunteer Infantry*, pp. 208–9; *OR*, vol. X, pt. 1, p. 620; Johnston, *Johnston*, p. 610; H. Riley Bock, "Confederate Col. A. C. Riley," p. 177. I have accepted Sword's location of the 20th Tennessee incident as probable, although there is no definite information (*Shiloh*, pp. 259, 262). McMurray mentions a three-to-four-acre mule lot west of the 71st Ohio camp, but that would appear to be too far from the 20th Tennessee. Only one veteran from Statham's brigade came back to the battlefield park, so plaques for that unit are few. (W. B. Pippen, "Concerning Battle of Shiloh," p. 344.)

52. M. F. Force, *From Fort Henry to Corinth*, p. 152; Mecklin Diary, April 6, 1862, MDAH.

53. McMurray, *Twentieth Tennessee*, pp. 208–9, 261; Force, *From Fort Henry to Corinth*, p. 152.

54. Dudley M. Haydon, "Shiloh."

55. *OR*, vol. X, pt. 1, pp. 554, 621; Pennsylvania Battlefield Commission, *The Seventy-Seventh Pennsylvania at Shiloh*, p. 329.

56. Haydon, "Shiloh." For a slightly different version, see Johnston, *Johnston*, p. 612.

57. Edward Munford, "Albert Sidney Johnston," Albert Sidney Johnston Papers, Barret Collection, TU; Davis, *Breckinridge*, p. 307; Pippen, "Concerning Battle of Shiloh," p. 344; Haydon, "Shiloh."

58. *OR*, vol. X, pt. 1, pp. 438–39, 454; Pippen, "Concerning Battle of Shiloh," p. 344; Haydon, "Shiloh."

59. T. L. Connelly, *Army of the Heartland*, p. 166.

60. Seymour Thompson, *Recollections with the Third Iowa Regiment*, p. 216; J. F. True to sister, April 10, 1862, 41st Illinois File, SNMP.

61. *OR*, vol. X, pt. 1, p. 213; Thompson, *Recollections*, pp. 214–15; Edwin L. Hobart,

The Truth About Shiloh, pp. 65, 67, 104; F. Y. Hedley, *Marching Through Georgia*, p. 47; Edwin L. Hobart, *Semi-History of a Boy-Veteran of the Twenty-Eighth Regiment Illinois Volunteers*, pp. 7–8; Throne, ed., "Letters from Shiloh," p. 260.

62. Thompson, *Recollections*, pp. 218, 220; Unknown to Eason Johnson, April 25, 1862, 41st Illinois File, SNMP; Throne, ed., "Letters from Shiloh," p. 260; *Missouri Daily Democrat*, April 24, 1862.

63. *OR*, vol. X, pt. 1, pp. 212, 213, 215; *Chicago Tribune*, April 18, 1862; Hobart, *Truth About Shiloh*, pp. 67, 104.

64. Jay A. Jorgenson, "Scouting for Ulysses S. Grant," p. 74. The 5th Ohio Cavalry lost only one man in this rare cavalry action.

65. *OR*, vol. X, pt. 1, pp. 439, 454; Brian Steel Wills, *A Battle from the Start*, p. 68.

66. *OR*, vol. X, pt. 1, p. 454; Sam Watkins, *"Co. Aytch,"* p. 41.

67. *OR*, vol. X, pt. 1, pp. 438–39, 455.

68. Ibid., pp. 538, 542; Welsh, *Medical Histories*, p. 1.

69. D. W. Reed, *Shiloh*, p. 88; Robert S. Henry, *As They Saw Forrest*, p. 76; Thomas Jordan and Roger Pryor, *The Campaigns of Lieut.-Gen. N. B. Forrest*, p. 127; *OR*, vol. X, pt. 1, p. 546.

70. Ezra J. Warner, *Generals in Blue*, p. 288; John A. Cockerill, "A Boy at Shiloh," p. 365; *OR*, vol. X, pt. 1, pp. 155, 156; *Quincy Daily Herald*, April 15, 1862.

71. James Oates, "A Gallant Regiment," ILSL; Marion Morrison, *A History of the Ninth Regiment Illinois Volunteer Infantry*, pp. 29–30; W. Y. Jenkins, "The Ninth Illinois Volunteer Infantry at Shiloh," 9th Illinois File, SNMP; *Quincy Daily Herald*, April 15, 1862.

72. Charles Bell Kimball, *History of Battery "A,"* pp. 10, 40–41; Colby to wife, April 14, 1862, E. Colby, Jr., Letters, A, 1st Illinois Light Artillery File, SNMP; *OR*, vol. X, pt. 1, p. 565; vol. LII, pt. 1, p. 24; *Chicago Tribune*, April 18, 1862; *Chicago Times*, April 17, 1862. Oates ("Gallant Regiment," ILSL) wrote that Willard's battery was in the road.

73. *OR*, vol. X, pt. 1, pp. 155, 156–57; Oates, "Gallant Regiment," ILSL; Hubert, *Fifteenth Regiment*, pp. 101–102; *Quincy Daily Herald*, April 15, 1862.

74. Charles F. Hubert, *History of the Fifteenth Regiment*, pp. 95–96, 102; *Quincy Daily Herald*, April 15, 1862.

75. Jenkins, "Ninth Illinois," 9th Illinois File, SNMP; D. W. Reed, *Shiloh*, p. 50.

76. *OR*, vol. X, pt. 1, pp. 155, 157; *Quincy Daily Herald*, April 15, 1862; C. H. Floyd to ?, C. H. Floyd Letters, ILSL; Jenkins, "Ninth Illinois," 9th Illinois File, SNMP.

77. *OR*, vol. X, pt. 1, pp. 155, 235, 622; Bock, "Confederate Col. Riley," pp. 177–78; George Mason, "Shiloh," p. 99; Force, *From Fort Henry to Shiloh*, pp. 149–50; D. W. Reed, *Shiloh*, p. 50.

78. *OR*, vol. X, pt. 1, pp. 204, 235; Leander Stillwell, "In the Ranks at Shiloh," pp. 120–21.

79. Lucian B. Crooker, "A Section of Battle," pp. 6–9. Crooker incorrectly claimed that Jackson's brigade was also involved in the assault, and that Stuart's eight hundred men thus stopped over 4,200 troops.

80. *OR*, vol. X, pt. 1, pp. 258–59; Elijah C. Lawrence, "Stuart's Brigade at Shiloh," pp. 494–95; *Canton Weekly Register*, May 6, 1862; Edwin C. Bearss, ed., *The Story of the Fifty-Fifth Regiment, Illinois Volunteer Infantry*, pp. 109–10; Thomas J. Bryant, *Who Is Responsible for the Advance of the Army of the Tennessee Towards Corinth?*, pp. 8–10; Smith to parents, April 27, 1862, T. Kilby Smith Letters, HL; Crooker, "Section of Battle," p. 7.

81. *OR*, vol. X, pt. 1, pp. 168, 204, 235.

82. Ibid., pp. 215, 216–17, 218, 246. The 32nd Illinois of Pugh's brigade formed east of the Hamburg-Savannah Road. See Hobart, *Truth About Shiloh*, p. 65.

83. *OR*, vol. X, pt. 1, pp. 204, 235, 238–39; D. Lloyd Jones, "The Battle of Shiloh," pp. 58–59; Rerick, *44th Indiana*, p. 53.

84. *OR*, vol. X, pt. 1, p. 239; Rerick, *44th Indiana*, p. 241; Thompson, *Recollections*, p. 224.

85. C. A. Kuhl, "Pittsburg Landing."

86. NPS plaques 109, 171.

87. *OR*, vol. X, pt. 1, pp. 161–62; W. H. Chamberlain, *History of the Eighty-First Regiment, Ohio Infantry Volunteers*, p. 17; E. R. Curtis Memoirs, OHS; W. H. Chamberlain, "The 81st Ohio at Shiloh," 81st Ohio File, SNMP.

88. P. G. T. Beauregard, "The Shiloh Campaign," p. 172; Johnston, *Johnston*, p. 613; George W. Baylor, "With Gen. A. S. Johnston at Shiloh," p. 612; John P. Broome, "How Gen. A. S. Johnston Died," p. 629.

89. Lee Wickham, "Statement As to Gen. Johnston's Death," Albert Sidney Johnston Papers, Barret Collection, TU; Lee Wickham, "Maj. Wickham's Account of It," p. 314.

90. Johnston, *Johnston*, pp. 614–15; *OR*, vol. X, pt. 1, p. 404. John P. Broome, a courier, claimed to be present at the time and cited Johnston's words as: "Yes, fatally, I believe." He further stated that Johnston appeared to be dead within two minutes of being removed from his saddle. ("How Gen. Johnston Died," p. 629.)

91. Lee Wickham, "Statement As to Gen. Johnston's Death," Albert Sidney Johnston Papers, Barret Collection, TU; Haydon, "Shiloh"; Baylor, "With Gen. Johnston," p. 611; *OR*, vol. X, pt. 1, p. 404.

92. Baylor, "With Gen. Johnston," p. 611; Johnston, *Johnston*, pp. 614–15; Haydon, "Shiloh"; Preston Diary, April 6, 1862 (2:30 entry), NA.

93. Roman, *Beauregard*, vol. 1, p. 537; Munford, "Albert Sidney Johnston," Johnston Papers, Barret Collection, TU.

94. Alexander R. Chisolm, "Gen. Beauregard at Shiloh," p. 212; Hamilton Basso, *Beauregard*, p. 102; *OR*, vol. X, pt. 1, p. 387; P. G. T. Beauregard, "Notes on E. A. Pollard's 'Lost Cause,' " p. 61.

95. *OR*, vol. X, pt. 1, p. 466; Chisolm, "Gen. Beauregard at Shiloh," p. 213; Beauregard, "Shiloh Campaign," p. 171; Williams, *Beauregard*, p. 140. Roland (*Johnston*, p. 341) believed that at Johnston's death the fighting continued but the momentum waned. Some historians reject such a notion. See McDonough, *Shiloh*, p. 154; Cunningham, "Shiloh," pp. 380–81; Williams, *Beauregard*, p. 140; T. L. Connelly, *Army of the Heartland*, pp. 166–67. I agree with Connelly that any delays that occurred were due to exhaustion and lack of ammunition more than to the leaking of the word of Johnston's death.

96. Larry J. Daniel, *Cannoneers in Gray*, p. 37.

97. *OR*, vol. X, pt. 1, pp. 472–79; F. A. Shoup, "How We Went to Shiloh," p. 139; *New Orleans Picayune*, April 10, 1862.

98. *OR*, vol. X, pt. 1, pp. 472, 475.

99. Ibid., p. 472; Shoup, "How We Went to Shiloh," p. 139. The *New Orleans Picayune* of April 10, 1862, mentioned six batteries involved: two of Brown's (a name unidentified), one of Smith's, one of Arkansas, one of Alabama, and the Washington Artillery.

100. S. H. Dent to wife, April 9, 1862, as quoted in Cunningham, "Shiloh," pp. 398–99; James G. Terry, ed., "Record of the Alabama State Artillery," pp. 316–17; Swett, Memoirs, Swett's Mississippi Battery File, SNMP.

101. *OR*, vol. X, pt. 1, pp. 476, 477, 478; McDonough, *Shiloh*, p. 164; Shoup, "How We Went to Shiloh," p. 139. The letters and diaries of artillerymen S. H. Dent, Phillip Bond, Richard Pugh, John Magee, George Jones, and William Vaught never mention the barrage. A 1956 NPS metal-detector search of the Sunken Road sector failed to find significant artifacts to suggest a prolonged barrage. (Dosch, "Hornet's Nest," p. 189n.)

102. Byers, *Iowa in War Times*, pp. 132–33.

103. Frederick H. Magdeburg, *Wisconsin at Shiloh*, p. 62; Morton, "A Boy at Shiloh,"

p. 64; Throne, ed., "Sopher's History," p. 179; Throne, ed., "Letters from Shiloh," p. 273; *OR*, vol. X, pt. 1, p. 151. Much of the growth of the Hornet's Nest was cleared away by the government in the 1880s. See Ray H. Mattison, "Hornet's Nest Area," pp. 19, 20, 22, SNMP; "Third Reunion Iowa Brigade," p. 33.

104. Byers, *Iowa in War Times*, p. 132; Kiner, *One Year's Soldiering*, p. 56; "First Reunion," pp. 17, 18, 22; *OR*, vol. X, pt. 1, p. 166; Charles V. Searle, "Personal Reminiscences of Shiloh," pp. 331–32.

105. *OR*, vol. X, pt. 1, pp. 233, 235, 238; Smith, *Thirty-First Indiana*, pp. 28, 29; Rerick, *44th Indiana*, pp. 52–53; Throne, ed., "Letters from Shiloh," p. 273; D. W. Reed, *Twelfth Iowa*, p. 52; Hickenlooper, "Battle of Shiloh," p. 434; Searle, "Reminiscences," p. 336; Lauman to wife, April 13, 1862, Jacob Lauman Letters, CHS; D. W. Reed, *Shiloh*, p. 53.

106. "Ninth Reunion," p. 12; Clark and Brown, *University Recruits*, p. 42; Throne, ed., "Sopher's History," p. 179; Throne, ed., "Letters from Shiloh," p. 265; *OR*, vol. X, pt. 1, p. 166; David Palmer, "Recollections of War Times," p. 135.

107. *OR*, vol. X, pt. 1, pp. 154, 279; *Society of the Army of the Tennessee*, p. 64; Albert D. Richardson, *The Secret Service*, p. 237; Throne, ed., "Letters from Shiloh," p. 277.

108. Isabel Wallace, *Life and Letters of General W. H. L. Wallace*, p. 193; "First Reunion," p. 14.

109. Byers, *Iowa in War Times*, pp. 132–33; *OR*, vol. X, pt. 1, pp. 101, 163, 164; *Chicago Tribune*, April 15, 1862. In McArthur's brigade, the 50th Illinois went to the left, the 57th Illinois to reinforce Hurlbut at 2:00, the 8th Iowa to the Hornet's Nest, and the 52nd Illinois to the right at 3:30.

110. Force, *From Fort Henry to Corinth*, p. 146; "First Reunion," p. 14.

111. *OR*, vol. X, pt. 1, p. 150; William Richardson to Dr. Nugent, April 11, 1862, William Richardson Letters, SHSIO; John Mahon, ed., "The Civil War Letters of Samuel Mahon," p. 238; Wallace, *Life and Letters*, p. 198; Lyle Dickey to Aunt Ann, May 17, 1862, 4th Illinois Cavalry File, SNMP; Byers, *Iowa in War Times*, p. 135; "First Reunion," p. 15.

112. *OR*, vol. X, pt. 1, p. 166; *Powell of the Colorado*, F, 2nd Illinois Artillery File, pp. 57, 59, SNMP; J. W. Powell to Cornelius Cadle, May 15, 1896, F, 2nd Illinois Artillery File, SNMP; Hickenlooper, "Battle of Shiloh," p. 421; Ephraim C. Dawes, "The Battle of Shiloh," p. 162; J. W. Cotes, "The Iowa Brigade on Shiloh's Field"; Hurter, "Narrative," vol. 1, pp. 641–43. Powell later became a respected western explorer.

113. *OR*, vol. X, pt. 1, pp. 151–52; *Society of the Army of the Tennessee*, p. 68; "Ninth Reunion," pp. 12–13.

114. *OR*, vol. X, pt. 1, p. 279; *Society of the Army of the Tennessee*, pp. 64–65.

115. *OR*, vol. X, pt. 1, p. 154; *Society of the Army of the Tennessee*, p. 68.

116. *OR*, vol. X, pt. 1, pp. 152, 475, 498; D. W. Reed, *Shiloh*, pp. 69, 78–79, 86; Biel, ed., "Battle of Shiloh," p. 265; NPS plaques 372, 304, 370, 449.

117. *OR*, vol. X, pt. 1, pp. 101, 105, 164; "Ninth Reunion," p. 13; "Federal Veterans at Shiloh," p. 104; "Memorial to Louisianians at Shiloh," p. 342; Y. R. Le Monnier, *General Beauregard at Shiloh*, p. 3; NPS plaques 102, 89, 233.

118. Seitz, *Bragg*, p. 112; Bock, ed., "Confederate Col. Riley," p. 179; Mecklin Diary, April 6, 1862, MDAH; *OR*, vol. X, pt. 1, p. 622; D. W. Reed, *Shiloh*, p. 87. The Bowen, Jackson, and Chalmers NPS plaques (nos. 457, 405, 396) place the attack time at 4 P.M.

119. *OR*, vol. X, pt. 1, pp. 550, 555; John C. Moore, "Shiloh Issues Again," p. 317; Joseph Wheeler, "The Battle of Shiloh," pp. 122–23. Sword reasoned that Chalmers's brigade should have gone northeast, toward the landing, where he would have experienced little opposition (*Shiloh*, pp. 279–80). Such a move was possible, but it seems unlikely that this isolated brigade would have made any

more progress than it did two hours later in consort with other brigades. With time running out, however, Bragg should have at least attempted such a move with Chalmers's and Jackson's brigades, using Statham's and Bowen's brigades to contain Prentiss's command along the Hamburg-Savannah Road.

120. *OR*, vol. X, pt. 1, p. 555; J. Wheeler, "Battle of Shiloh," pp. 122–23; NPS plaques 397, 406.

121. *OR*, vol. X, pt. 1, pp. 101, 550; *Society of the Army of the Tennessee*, pp. 69, 154; Alonzo Abernathy, *Dedication of Monuments Erected by the State of Iowa*, pp. 229–30, 239; Thompson, *Recollections*, p. 228.

122. Mandeville to Josephine Rozert, April 9, 1862, Theodore Mandeville Letters, LSU; Throne, ed., "Letters from Shiloh," p. 276; B. F. Thomas, *Soldier Life*, p. 43; Searle, "Reminiscences," p. 334; Miller Diary, April 6, 1862, MHS.

123. William T. Shaw, "The Battle of Shiloh," p. 203; *OR*, vol. X, pt. 1, pp. 101, 103, 105, 279; Cotes, "Iowa Brigade on Shiloh's Field"; Stacy Allen ("Confederate Assault on the Hornet's Nest," p. 7, SNMP) tabulates 2,254 prisoners; Sword (*Shiloh*, p. 306) 2,320.

124. *OR*, vol. X, pt. 1, pp. 103, 247, 459–60; John Robertson, *Michigan in the War*, p. 348; D. W. Reed, *Shiloh*, p. 79; Jordan, "Notes," pp. 601–2; Deupree, "Reminiscences," pp. 91–92; Larry R. Houghton, "Captured at Shiloh," p. 39; L. C. Teel to friend, n.d., B, 2nd Michigan Battery File, SNMP.

125. Abernathy, *Dedication of Monuments*, p. 229. The Hornet's Nest did not have to be reduced, only contained. The initial troops committed to the Confederate right (Stephens's brigade and Withers's division, about 8,500 men) should have been sufficient to pin down, through long-range skirmishing and limited sorties, the remnant of Prentiss's division, Hurlbut's two brigades, and McArthur's brigade, no more than 7,000 men. Breckinridge's reserve division could then have been hurled upon Stuart's lone brigade.

Under such a plan, Polk's, Ruggles's, and Hardee's commands (nine brigades) would have remained to confront W. H. L. Wallace's, McClernand's, and Sherman's divisions, and Veach's brigade of Hurlbut's division (nine brigades). Concluded Kenneth P. Williams: "It would have been better for the Confederates to contain Prentiss as economically as possible, and move to attack the new Federal lines" (*Lincoln Finds a General*, vol. 3, p. 372).

126. U. S. Grant, *Personal Memoirs of U. S. Grant*, p. 228; Adam Badeau, *Military History of Ulysses S. Grant*, p. 83; William S. McFeely, *Grant*, p. 113.

Nine: Lost Opportunity?

1. *OR*, vol. X, pt. 1, p. 250; Ephraim C. Dawes, "The Battle of Shiloh," pp. 150–51; *Society of the Army of the Tennessee*, p. 55. Although Sherman reported that his right covered the Snake Creek bridge, Don Carlos Buell correctly pointed out that the bridge was one and a quarter miles from his right. "Shiloh Reviewed," pp. 516, 519.

2. *OR*, vol. X, pt. 1, p. 250; Andrew Hickenlooper, "The Battle of Shiloh," p. 22; Dawes, "Battle of Shiloh," p. 151; NPS monument 39; NPS plaque 238.

3. *Society of the Army of the Tennessee*, p. 55.

4. *OR*, vol. X, pt. 1, pp. 265, 274, 514; vol. LII, pt. 1, pp. 25–26; Edward Bouton, *Events of the Civil War*, pp. 21–24; Buell, "Shiloh Reviewed," pp. 517–18; NPS monument 39.

5. *OR*, vol. X, pt. 1, p. 118. D. W. Reed's 1901 map is incomplete in detailing all of the units in McClernand's line. I have relied heavily upon NPS plaques 147, 34, 58, 8, and 14, and NPS monument 68, in reconstructing the line. The Buell map ("Shiloh Reviewed," p. 503) shows McClernand's position marked "W" and "H,"

but places it too close to Cavalry Field, as does Wiley Sword (*Shiloh*, p. 326). Marsh's statement that his troops "faced an open field" (Cavalry Field) has been misinterpreted to indicate that the line bordered the field.

6. Alfred Roman, *The Military Operations of General Beauregard*, vol. 1, p. 528; Patricia L. Faust, ed., *Historical Times Illustrated Encyclopedia of the Civil War*, p. 256; Samuel Ferguson Memoir, Army of the Mississippi File, SNMP; *New Orleans Picayune*, March 17, 1909.

7. *OR*, vol. X, pt. 1, p. 517; *New Orleans Picayune*, March 17, 1909; Samuel Ferguson, Memoir. Army of the Mississippi File (SNMP). In ordering a frontal assault, Hardee was merely doing what the Confederate command had attempted all day—brute force rather than maneuver. In hindsight, Pond's brigade should have gotten between Sherman's right and the Snake Creek bridge in order to block Lew Wallace's division.

8. Arthur W. Bergeron, Jr., ed., *The Civil War Reminiscences of Major Silas T. Grisamore, C.S.A.*, pp. 34–35; *OR*, vol. X, pt. 1, pp. 517, 521; Journal of the Orleans Guard, April 6, 1862, Historic New Orleans Collection. NPS plaque 367 states that Pond attacked en echelon, but extant evidence disputes this.

9. Bergeron, ed., *Grisamore*, pp. 34–35; *OR*, vol. X, pt. 1, pp. 118, 518, 521–22; Earl C. Woods, ed., *The Civil War Diary of Edmond Enoul Livaudais*, pp. 30–31; William Arceneaux, *Acadian General*, pp. 48–50; Fritz Haskell, ed., "Diary of Colonel William Camm, 1861–1865," p. 849.

10. Journal of the Orleans Guard, April 6, 1862, Historic New Orleans Collection; Woods, ed., *Livaudais Diary*, p. 30.

11. Journal of the Orleans Guard, April 6, 1862, Historic New Orleans Collection; Woods, ed., *Livaudais Diary*, p. 31; Ferguson Memoir, Army of the Mississippi File, SNMP.

12. *OR*, vol. X, pt. 1, pp. 127, 224, 231.

13. D. W. Reed, *The Battle of Shiloh and the Organizations Engaged*, pp. 71, 88; Robert Bunting Diary, April 6, 1862, UT; J. Blackburn, "Reminiscences of the Terry Texas Rangers," pp. 58–59; *OR*, vol. X, pt. 1, pp. 582, 587–88, 626; NPS plaques 465, 470.

14. *OR*, vol. X, pt. 1, pp. 118, 125, 127, 132, 231; Haskell, ed., "Camm Diary," pp. 850–51.

15. *OR*, vol. X, pt. 1, pp. 119, 124, 134, 155; D. W. Reed, *Shiloh*, p. 47; NPS plaque 73. For details of this new position, see the 1901 D. W. Reed map.

16. *OR*, vol. X, pt. 1, p. 331; James E. Stewart, "Fighting Them Over"; William R. Hartpence, *History of the Fifty-First Indiana Veteran Volunteer Infantry*, p. 36.

17. *OR*, vol. X, pt. 1, p. 332; Edwin Hannaford, *The Story of a Regiment*, pp. 246, 248–49; Horace C. Fisher, *A Staff Officer's Story*, pp. 10–11.

18. *OR*, vol. X, pt. 1, p. 332; Hannaford, *Story of a Regiment*, p. 249; William Grose, *The Story of the Marches, Battles, and Incidents of the 36th Indiana Volunteer Infantry*, p. 102.

19. Buell, "Shiloh Reviewed," pp. 492–93.

20. Ibid.

21. Ibid., pp. 493–94; *OR*, vol. X, pt. 1, p. 186. A story was told in numerous postwar works that Buell noticed there were sufficient transports for only 10,000 men. "If I have to retreat, ten thousand will be as many as I need transports for," Grant supposedly retorted. Buell dismissed the story as ridiculous and insisted that a retreat was never discussed.

22. Buell, "Shiloh Reviewed," pp. 494–95; John H. Rerick, *The 44th Indiana Volunteer Infantry*, p. 241; Mildred Throne, ed., "Letters from Shiloh," p. 266.

23. Grose, *Marches of the 36th Indiana*, p. 102; *OR*, vol. X, pt. 1, p. 332; Fisher, *Staff Officer's Story*, p. 11; Hannaford, *Story of a Regiment*, p. 251; *The Medical and Surgical History of the War of the Rebellion*, vol. 2, p. 37.

24. *OR*, vol. X, pt. 1, pp. 332–33. The division averaged two miles per hour.

25. Ira Blanchard, *I Marched with Sherman*, pp. 56–57; Victor Hicken, *Illinois in the Civil War*, p. 65; Throne, ed., "Letters from Shiloh," p. 263; Douglas Putnam, Jr., "Reminiscences of the Battle of Shiloh," pp. 201–2. See also Mildred Throne, ed., *The Civil War Diary of Cyrus F. Boyd*, pp. 34–35; Joseph M. Hanson, *The Conquest of Missouri*, pp. 43–44.

26. Hanson, *Conquest of Missouri*, pp. 43–44.

27. *OR*, vol. X, pt. 1, p. 250; *Society of the Army of the Tennessee*, p. 82; W. H. Chamberlain, *History of the Eighty-First Regiment, Ohio Infantry Volunteers*, pp. 17–18; E. R. Curtis Memoirs, April 6, 1862, 81st Ohio File, OHS; Buell, "Shiloh Reviewed," pp. 516–18, 520.

28. M. F. Force, *From Fort Henry to Corinth*, p. 139; Dawes, "Battle of Shiloh," pp. 164–65; Buell, "Shiloh Reviewed," p. 522. Buell estimated that Grant had sustained 10,000 casualties, 7,000 remained on the line, and 15,000 were absent from the ranks. This leaves 8,000 troops unaccounted for. Dawes estimated that 16,000 were at the landing, of which 5,000 were stragglers and 11,000 noncombatants.

29. Nels Hokanson, *Swedish Immigrants in Lincoln's Time*, pp. 72, 113, 114; Bouton, *Events of the Civil War*, p. 27; *OR*, vol. X, pt. 1, p. 274. Kenneth P. Williams (*Lincoln Finds a General*, vol. 3, p. 375) figured the number of guns in Grant's Last Line at forty-three, but overestimated on Munch and Madison. Grady McWhiney concluded that, regardless of the number of guns, the line may not have been as formidable as suggested: many of the pieces were rifles, which were not effective for close-in work ("General Beauregard's 'Complete Victory' at Shiloh," p. 426). Perhaps so, but the gunboats showed that the sheer morale effect of artillery could often turn the trick.

30. Putnam, "Reminiscences," pp. 201–2.

31. John A. Cockerill, "A Boy at Shiloh," p. 369.

32. Gary L. Ecelbarger, ed., "Shiloh," p. 66; *OR*, vol. X, pt. 1, p. 333; Hannaford, *Story of a Regiment*, pp. 566–77.

33. Hannaford, *Story of a Regiment*, p. 281; Fisher, *Staff Officer's Story*, pp. 12–13; *OR*, vol. X, pt. 1, p. 333; Samuel M. Howard, *The Illustrated Comprehensive History of the Great Battle of Shiloh*, p. 96; Blanchard, *I Marched with Sherman*, p. 57; *Cincinnati Daily Examiner*, April 17, 1862; *Cincinnati Commercial*, April 22, 1862.

34. Fisher, *Staff Officer's Story*, p. 13; Cockerill, "Boy at Shiloh," p. 369.

35. John Beatty, *The Citizen-Soldier*, p. 162.

36. Ecelbarger, ed., "Shiloh," p. 50; *OR*, vol. X, pt. 1, pp. 333–34; Fisher, *Staff Officer's Story*, p. 13; Henry Stone, "The Battle of Shiloh," p. 79; Hannaford, *Story of a Regiment*, pp. 568, 577; Grose, *Marches of the 36th Indiana*, p. 104; Orville Victor, *Incidents and Anecdotes*, p. 359; Albert D. Richardson, *A Personal History of Ulysses S. Grant*, p. 247.

37. Hannaford, *Story of a Regiment*, pp. 568, 569, 577, 587; Ecelbarger, ed., "Shiloh," p. 66; Mildred Throne, ed., "Iowa and the Battle of Shiloh," p. 263; *OR*, vol. X, pt. 1, pp. 334, 337, 339; Paul Hubbard and Christine Lewis, eds., " 'Give Yourself No Trouble About Me,' " p. 31; Grose, *Marches of the 36th Indiana*, p. 104.

38. Buell, "Shiloh Reviewed," pp. 507, 522; Buford to Charlie, April 21, 1862, Samuel Buford Letters, LC.

39. U. S. Grant, *Personal Memoirs of U. S. Grant*, p. 233; *OR*, vol. X, pt. 1, pp. 259, 261; Edwin C. Bearss, ed., *The Story of the Fifty-Fifth Regiment, Illinois Volunteer Infantry*, p. 114; Otto Eisenschiml, "The 55th Illinois at Shiloh," p. 205; Correspondence of Job Vaughn, 55th Illinois, *Canton Weekly Register*, May 6, 1862.

40. William T. Sherman, *Memoirs of General William T. Sherman*, p. 245; Dawes, "Battle of Shiloh," p. 165; Hamilton Basso, *Beauregard*, p. 183.

41. Augustus Chetlain, *Recollections of Seventy Years*, p. 89; *Chicago Tribune*, November 21, 1880; Charles F. Hubert, *History of the 50th Regiment Ill. Volunteer Infantry*, p.

93; William H. Heath, "Hours with Grant"; *OR*, vol. X, pt. 1, p. 339.

42. Putnam, "Reminiscences," p. 205; Sherman, *Memoirs*, p. 245.

43. Sherman, *Memoirs*, p. 246; Buell, "Shiloh Reviewed," p. 520.

44. Roman, *Beauregard*, vol. 1, pp. 531–32; Thomas Jordan, "Notes of a Confederate Staff Officer at Shiloh," p. 602. Jordan wrote that he did not reveal Helm's dispatch to Beauregard until after sunrise. Since the message was received in midafternoon, however, it is hardly conceivable that Beauregard was not informed of its contents for several hours.

45. *OR*, vol. X, pt. 1, p. 384; Jordan, "Notes," p. 602.

46. *OR*, vol. X, pt. 1, pp. 386–87; Roman, *Beauregard*, vol. 1, pp. 304, 532, 535; Thomas Jordan, "The Battle of Shiloh," vol. XXXV, p. 217; P. G. T. Beauregard, "The Campaign of Shiloh," p. 590. Beauregard later wrote that he understood "our victory had been incomplete," yet his telegraph to Richmond told of "a complete victory" (P. G. T. Beauregard, "The Shiloh Campaign," pp. 174–75). Years later, a former Federal raised the issue of the withdrawal order with Beauregard. The Creole answered: "I thought I had Grant where I wanted him and could finish him up in the morning." (Putnam, "Reminiscences," pp. 210–11.)

47. McWhiney, "Beauregard's 'Complete Victory,' " pp. 432–33; Steven E. Woodworth, *Jefferson Davis and His Generals*, p. 102. Nathaniel C. Hughes, Jr. (*General William J. Hardee*, p. 109), and Joseph H. Parks (*General Leonidas Polk, C.S.A.*, p. 235) raised the same issue some years earlier. See also William Preston Johnston, "Albert Sidney Johnston at Shiloh," p. 568. In the summer of 1862, Beauregard candidly wrote Jordan that at Shiloh he was "so unwell" that his memory was "not very distinct" concerning the particulars of the withdrawal order (Beauregard to Jordan, July 17, August 8, 1862, P. G. T. Beauregard Papers, LC).

48. *OR*, vol. X, pt. 1, pp. 154, 279, 291; Y. R. Le Monnier, *General Beauregard at Shiloh*, p. 3; Leslie Anders, *The Eighteenth Missouri*, p. 61; McWhiney, "Beauregard's 'Complete Victory,' " p. 433. Jordan ("Battle of Shiloh," p. 311) wrote that the sun went down no later than 6:25. In May 1995, Michael Parish, who at that time was working on a revisionist biography of Beauregard, spoke in Corinth and essentially concurred with McWhiney's position.

49. J. Cutler Andrews, *The South Reports the Civil War*, pp. 141–42.

50. *New Orleans Picayune*, April 11, 1862.

51. *Atlanta Intelligencer*, April 11, 1862; Jordan, "Notes," pp. 602–3.

52. McWhiney, "Beauregard's 'Complete Victory,' " p. 433.

53. *Georgia Weekly Sun*, June 20, 1862; Andrews, *South Reports Civil War*, p. 147.

54. McWhiney, "Beauregard's 'Complete Victory,' " pp. 422–23.

55. *OR*, vol. X, pt. 1, p. 538; Roman, *Beauregard*, vol. 1, p. 300; Samuel H. Lockett, "Surprise and Withdrawal at Shiloh," p. 605; NPS plaques 356, 385, 398, 407.

56. William Moiser to Reed, December 11, 1919, 52nd Tennessee File, SNMP; *OR*, vol. X, pt. 1, pp. 499, 505, 537, 550–51; *Mobile Advertiser & Register*, April 11, 1862; D. W. Reed, *Shiloh*, pp. 74–75.

57. *OR*, vol. X, pt. 1, pp. 334, 550–51, 559, 562; Force, *From Fort Henry to Shiloh*, pp. 171–72, 175; Buell, "Shiloh Reviewed," p. 506; *Quincy Daily Herald*, April 15, 1862.

58. B. F. Leonard to Reed, March 22, 1904, 10th Mississippi File, SNMP. Some cavalry units actually did water their horses in the Tennessee River, thus technically fulfilling Johnston's prophecy (George W. Baylor, "With Gen. A. S. Johnston at Shiloh," p. 612; J. G. Deupree, "Reminiscences of Service with the First Mississippi Cavalry," p. 92).

59. John Magee Diary, April 6, 1862, DU.

60. *OR*, vol. X, pt. 1, p. 534.

61. D. W. Reed, *Shiloh*, p. 87; *OR*, vol. X, pt. 1, p. 616; F. A. Shoup, "How We Went to Shiloh," p. 139; Alexander Walker, "Narrative of the Battle of Shiloh," pp.

144–46. Walker, of the *New Orleans Delta*, claimed thirty-six guns were involved: Bankhead's, Polk's, Smith's, Jefferson Artillery, Washington Artillery, Robertson's, and Watson's. An article in the *New Orleans Picayune* of April 15, 1862, claimed that Watson's six guns and three of Hudson's engaged Grant's Last Line.

62. Lockett, "Surprise and Withdrawal," p. 605.

63. William Preston Johnston, *The Life of Gen. Albert Sidney Johnston*, p. 633; T. Harry Williams, *P. G. T. Beauregard*, p. 142; James L. McDonough, *Shiloh*, pp. 168–70; Thomas L. Connelly, *Army of the Heartland*, pp. 169–70; Roman, *Beauregard*, vol. 1, pp. 535, 538; Alexander R. Chisolm, "The Shiloh Battle Order and the Withdrawal Sunday Evening," p. 606.

64. Don Seitz, *Braxton Bragg*, p. 112; *OR*, vol. X, pt. 1, pp. 466–67; Roman, *Beauregard*, vol. 1, p. 535.

65. Beauregard, "Campaign of Shiloh," p. 591; Roman, *Beauregard*, vol. 1, p. 305; Jordan, "Notes," p. 602; W. B. Ellis, "Who Lost Shiloh to the Confederacy?," p. 314.

66. Many scholars assert that any additional attacks on Grant's Last Line would have been futile. James M. McPherson (*Battle Cry of Freedom*, p. 410) stated that Grant held the advantage in two crucial elements: time and terrain.

67. *OR*, vol. X, pt. 1, pp. 533, 550, 551, 555; Roman, *Beauregard*, vol. 1, p. 533; James Dinkins, "The Battle of Shiloh," p. 309; Chalmers to Mississippi State Auditor, April 3, 1895, Misc. Files, SNMP. McWhiney writes that Ruggles "could scarcely believe" the order, but I do not draw this conclusion. See *OR*, vol. X, pt. 1, pp. 472–73. See also Grady McWhiney, *Braxton Bragg and Confederate Defeat*. Polk complained in his report that an hour remained for more attacks (Parks, *Polk*, p. 237). In a letter to his wife on April 10, however, the bishop wrote: "We would have done so [destroyed Grant] if we had had an hour more of daylight" (William Polk, *Leonidas Polk*, vol. 2, p. 109).

68. *OR*, vol. X, pt. 1, pp. 170, 175; Charles Whittlesey, *General Lew Wallace's Division*, p. 4. The 56th and 68th Ohio and one gun of Thurber's battery remained at Crump's Landing as a garrison.

   Stoney Lonesome today may be found by taking Highway 64 to Crump, Tennessee. The 2nd Brigade camped by a spring in what is today the home of Mr. R. A. Phillips, 1650 Highway 64. Mr. Phillips graciously showed me the campsite—a pasture just east of the house. Directly behind the house can be seen the roadbed of the old Crump's Landing–Adamsville Road, which was in use till the 1920s. Local tradition says that Union soldiers gave the name "Stoney Lonesome" because of the gravel and sandy soil.

69. Lew Wallace, *An Autobiography*, vol. 1, pp. 451–53; *OR*, vol. X, pt. 1, p. 175; K. P. Williams, *Lincoln Finds a General*, vol. 3, p. 379; Whittlesey, *Wallace's Division*, p. 6; "The March of Lew Wallace's Division to Shiloh," p. 609.

   The Crump's Landing–Adamsville Road and Shunpike intersection may be found by driving to the 1200 block of Highway 64 in Crump, Tennessee. A road to the south called Blanton Road is the beginning of the Shunpike. Highway 64 was, of course, not in existence, so the actual intersection is a hundred yards or so to the south, where the remains of the Crump's Landing–Adamsville Road can be seen. Unfortunately, Blanton Road does not continue the historic Shunpike path. The location of the Overshot Mill is today on private property and difficult to find. Remains of the old mill were still visible in the 1920s.

70. Grant placed the meeting time at 8:00, Wallace at 8:30, and Fred Knefler at 9:00 (Whittlesey, *Wallace's Division*, p. 8; L. Wallace, *Autobiography*, vol. 1, p. 461).

71. L. Wallace, *Autobiography*, vol. 1, pp. 463–64; *OR*, vol. X, pt. 1, pp. 175, 181; Whittlesey, *Wallace's Division*, pp. 7–8; Richard S. Skidmore, "Lew Wallace and the Old Wound of Shiloh," p. 12. James McPherson reported (March 1863) that Baxter delivered the order to Wallace and returned to Pittsburg Landing by

10:30—clearly an impossibility. Rawlins (April 1863) placed Baxter's return at noon.

72. *OR*, vol. X, pt. 1, pp. 179, 181, 185. Whether or not Grant specifically mentioned the River Road in his original oral order to Rawlins is insignificant; Wallace was obliged to follow the written order handed him.

73. Skidmore, "Lew Wallace," p. 12. McDonough concluded that logic dictated that Rawlins's version was more accurate (*Shiloh*, p. 157). Sword (*Shiloh*, p. 218) accepted Wallace's version.

74. L. Wallace, *Autobiography*, vol. 1, p. 452; *OR*, vol. X, pt. 1, p. 170.

75. *OR*, vol. X, pt. 1, p. 176.

76. Irving McKee, *"Ben-Hur" Wallace*, p. 55; L. Wallace, *Autobiography*, vol. 1, p. 467.

77. *OR*, vol. X, pt. 1, p. 175; L. Wallace, *Autobiography*, vol. 1, p. 465; Skidmore, "Lew Wallace," p. 14. As it turned out, the decision proved beneficial. Had the column moved out at 11:30, it would have been a half-hour farther down the wrong road.

78. *OR*, vol. X, pt. 1, pp. 185–86; Skidmore, "Lew Wallace," p. 13. The unnamed officer returned to Pittsburg Landing and reported that Wallace refused to move without a written order. Wallace strongly denied this—"I repeat my absolute denial of this statement," he wrote in 1884 ("March of Lew Wallace's Division," p. 610). In his March 1863 letter to Halleck, however, Wallace did complain that he had been handed an order "in writing *unsigned* by *anybody*" (*OR*, vol. X, pt. 1, p. 175).

Grant charged that Wallace should have known something was wrong when the battle sounds could be heard in his rear as he was advancing (U. S. Grant Letter, June 22, 1885, Lew Wallace Papers, Misc. Files, SNMP).

79. *OR*, vol. X, pt. 1, pp. 170, 175, 179–80; L. Wallace, *Autobiography*, vol. 1, pp. 466–67. Rowley came by the River Road via Crump's Landing to Stoney Lonesome ("Gen. Wallace at Battle of Shiloh," Box 8, Folder 7, Lew Wallace Papers, INHS).

Rowley's report stated that Wallace claimed he did not know of a River Road. The division commander later explained the comment by saying he was referring to "a crossroad to the River Road" ("March of Lew Wallace's Division," p. 610). Wallace had been camped for four weeks near the River Road, his men had helped repair it, and a messenger had reported its condition the night before (Skidmore, "Lew Wallace," p. 13).

80. *OR*, vol. X, pt. 1, p. 180; L. Wallace, *Autobiography*, vol. 1, p. 467.

81. Joseph W. Rich, "General Lew Wallace at Shiloh," p. 308. The Confederates had Wallace's column under close observation. In 1901, Wallace held a lengthy conference with Captain T. A. Johnson, the Southern officer in charge.

82. *OR*, vol. X, pt. 1, p. 170. Harold Wallace ("Lew Wallace's March to Shiloh Revisited," p. 29) agreed with Wallace's decision, but Skidmore ("Lew Wallace," p. 14) and K. P. Williams (*Lincoln Finds a General*, vol. 3, p. 379) are critical.

83. Atwell Thompson to Cornelius Cadle, August 2, 1895, Army of the Tennessee, 3rd Division File, SNMP. Grant sent an entire cavalry company (A, 2nd Illinois Cavalry) to assist Wallace, but it was used only as a rear guard. So strung out was the column that, by the time the troopers got to Overshot Mill, the head of the column was returning. (Samuel H. Fletcher, *The History of Company A*, pp. 50–51.)

84. *OR*, vol. X, pt. 1, pp. 180, 182, 186–87; Whittlesey, *Wallace's Division*, p. 6. When McPherson and Rawlins caught up with Wallace, his men had made about nine miles in three and a half hours, or two and a half miles per hour (Skidmore, "Lew Wallace," p. 13). The 3rd Brigade, for some unknown reason, did not leave Adamsville until 3 P.M. (Albert Castel, ed., "The War Diary of Henry Dwight," p. 34).

85. *OR*, vol. X, pt. 1, pp. 180, 182, 187; Skidmore, "Lew Wallace," p. 13.

86. *OR*, vol. X, pt. 1, pp. 178, 187–88, 191; L. Wallace, *Autobiography*, vol. 1, p. 468; Whittlesey, *Wallace's Division*, pp. 6–8. The head of the column reached Grant's army at 5:00. Skidmore calculates that it required 7.5 hours to march 13 miles, or 1.75 miles per hour. Ammen's brigade, in comparison, marched at the rate of 2.25 miles per hour. ("Lew Wallace," p. 13.)
87. I. McKee, *"Ben-Hur" Wallace*, pp. 54–56; Bouton, *Events of the Civil War*, p. 31.

Ten: Counterattack

1. Thomas Jordan, "Notes of a Confederate Staff Officer at Shiloh," p. 602; *Society of the Army of the Tennessee*, p. 54; Alfred Roman, *The Military Operations of General Beauregard*, vol. 1, p. 305; Preston Smith Diary, April 6, 1862, NA.
2. D. K. Reed, *The Battle of Shiloh and the Organizations Engaged*, pp. 77, 78, 81, 82, 84, 87; *OR*, vol. X, pt. 1, p. 518; Roman, *Beauregard*, vol. 1, p. 313; P. G. T. Beauregard, "The Campaign of Shiloh," p. 591; Christopher Losson, *Tennessee's Forgotten Warriors*, p. 50; Henry George, "The 7th Kentucky at Shiloh," 7th Kentucky File, SNMP.
3. Shoup, "The Art of War in '62—Shiloh," p. 11.
4. *New Orleans Crescent*, April 21, 1862; John Smith Kendall, "Recollections of a Confederate Staff Officer," pp. 1067–68; Johnson to wife, April 11, 1862, Charles Johnson Letters, LSU; A. H. Mecklin Diary, April 6, 1862, MDAH. See also Ben Bassham, " 'Through a Mist of Powder and Excitement,' " p. 133; A. D. Kirwan, ed., *Johnny Green of the Orphan Brigade*, pp. 28–29; James G. Terry, ed., "Record of the Alabama State Artillery," p. 314; Thomas Chinn Robertson to mother, April 9, 1862, 4th Louisiana File, LSU; Latta to wife, April 10, 1862, Samuel Latta Letters, TSLA; James M. Merrill, ed., " 'Nothing to Eat But Raw Bacon,' " p. 144.
5. Mecklin Diary, April 6, 1862, MDAH; John G. Biel, ed., "The Battle of Shiloh," pp. 265–66; William C. Davis, ed., *Diary of a Confederate Soldier*, p. 32; Roman, *Beauregard*, vol. 1, p. 306; Frank L. Richardson, "War As I Saw It," p. 103.
6. Biel, ed., "Battle of Shiloh," pp. 265–66; Mecklin Diary, April 6, 1862, MDAH; O. E. Cunningham, "Shiloh and the Western Campaign of 1862," p. 457.
7. Biel, ed., "Battle of Shiloh," pp. 265–66; Earl C. Woods, ed., *The Shiloh Diary of Edmond Enoul Livaudais*, p. 31; *Indianapolis Sentinel*, April 15, 1862; Davis, ed., *Jackman Diary*, p. 32.
8. Thomas Jordan, "The Battle of Shiloh," vol. XXXV, p. 219; James R. Chalmers, "Forrest and His Campaign," p. 458; John A. Wyeth, "Appearances and Characteristics of Forrest," p. 42; Thomas Jordan and Roger Pryor, *The Campaigns of Lieut.-Gen. N. B. Forrest*, pp. 136–137; Sheppard, *Bedford Forrest*, p. 60; *OR*, vol. X, pt. 1, p. 570.
9. *OR*, vol. X, pt. 1, p. 518. The scene of the band playing is described in George H. Daggett, "Thrilling Moments," p. 450, and *Louisville Daily Journal*, April 18, 1862.
10. "The Only Confederate Re-Enforcements at Shiloh," pp. 22, 34–35; "Forty-Seventh Tennessee Ordnance Return," Yerger Papers, MDAH.
11. Paul H. Silverstone, *Warships of the Civil War Navies*, p. 159; *ONR*, vol. XXIII, pp. 762, 764–65, 786; *Indianapolis Journal*, April 19, 1862; *Cincinnati Commercial*, April 15, 1862.
12. *OR*, vol. X, pt. 1, pp. 324, 334, 354, 355, 359, 372; Alexander S. Johnstone, "Scenes at Shiloh," p. 49; Henry Stone, "The Battle of Shiloh," p. 81; Samuel M. Howard, *The Illustrated Comprehensive History of the Great Battle of Shiloh*, p. 96; W. B. Hazen, *A Narrative of Military Service*, p. 25; Gary L. Ecelbarger, ed., "Shiloh," p. 50.

13. Don Carlos Buell, "Shiloh Reviewed," p. 519; T. M. Eddy, *The Patriotism of Illinois*, p. 258.
14. William S. McFeely, *Grant*, p. 115; *OR*, vol. X, pt. 1, pp. 109, 186; W. E. Woodward, *Meet General Grant*, p. 256; Eddy, *Patriotism of Illinois*, vol. 1, p. 258.
15. U. S. Grant, *Personal Memoirs of U.S. Grant*, pp. 234–35; Woodward, *Grant*, p. 254.
16. Bruce Catton, *Grant Moves South*, p. 242.
17. Lew Wallace, *An Autobiography*, vol. 1, pp. 473–74.
18. D. W. Reed, *Shiloh*, p. 50; NPS plaques 117, 116, 129; L. Wallace, *Autobiography*, vol. 1, p. 474.
19. Albert Castel, ed., "The War Diary of Henry Dwight," p. 34.
20. *OR*, vol. X, pt. 1, pp. 324, 328, 335, 337, 339, 340; Hazen, *Narrative*, p. 25; Edwin Hannaford, *The Story of a Regiment*, pp. 263, 572.
21. Ezra J. Warner, *Generals in Blue*, p. 40; *OR*, vol. X, pt. 1, pp. 241, 342, 343, 357, 372; NPS plaques 278, 281, 275, 255.
22. *OR*, vol. X, pt. 1, pp. 335, 341, 342, 343; Alfred Allen, "The 9th Indiana at Shiloh"; Hazen, *Narrative*, p. 26.
23. *OR*, vol. X, pt. 1, pp. 307–8; Richard B. Harwell, ed., *The Union Reader*, p. 116; Levi Wagner Memoirs, pp. 28–29, Civil War Times Collection, USMHI; A. B. Carpenter to parents, April 13, 1862, A. B. Carpenter Letters, YU.
24. *OR*, vol. X, pt. 1, pp. 350, 351, 514; Hazen, *Narrative*, p. 26; Jacob H. Smith, "Personal Reminiscences," p. 12.
25. *OR*, vol. X, pt. 1, pp. 373, 342, 350; Johnstone, "Scenes at Shiloh," p. 50; NPS plaque 289; M. F. Force, *From Fort Henry to Corinth*, p. 165. I have been unable to identify the Confederate battery in question. Wiley Sword (*Shiloh*, p. 384) says it was probably Robertson's, but O. E. Cunningham ("Shiloh and the Western Campaign of 1862," p. 473) ventures McClung's.
26. *OR*, vol. X, pt. 1, pp. 434, 534, 544, 551, 554; NPS plaques 391, 468, 363, 324. Although Chalmers claimed that the Crescent Regiment fell in line with the 5th Tennessee and 26th Alabama, it is clear that Smith's regiment was at the Wheat Field.
27. *OR*, vol. X, pt. 1, pp. 534, 622; Joseph Boyce, "The Second Day at Shiloh"; H. Riley Bock, "Confederate Col. A. C. Riley," p. 179.
28. *OR*, vol. X, pt. 1, pp. 342, 343, 344–45, 347–48, 373–74; Johnstone, "Scenes at Shiloh," p. 50; Hazen, *Narrative*, pp. 26, 41.
29. D. W. Reed, *Shiloh*, pp. 64–65; Force, *From Fort Henry to Corinth*, p. 169.
30. *OR*, vol. X, pt. 1, p. 515; Barnes F. Lathrop, ed., "A Confederate Artilleryman at Shiloh," p. 380; John Dimitry to William Bullitt, n.d., LSU; Gordon Bakewell, "Orderly That Was of the Fifth Company Washington Artillery," p. 19. Several Federal regiments claimed honors on the guns.
31. *OR*, vol. X, pt. 1, pp. 342, 343, 345, 348, 366, 367, 368–69, 370, 372, 494, 542; "John Dimitry," p. 72; "Memorial to Louisianians at Shiloh," p. 343; *New Orleans Crescent*, April 15, 19, 1862; Alexander Walker, "Narrative of the Battle of Shiloh," p. 153; Hazen, *Narrative*, pp. 28, 29, 37.
32. *OR*, vol. X, pt. 1, pp. 342, 524; Thomas B. Van Horne, *History of the Army of the Cumberland*, p. 112; Force, *From Fort Henry to Corinth*, p. 165.
33. *OR*, vol. X, pt. 1, pp. 349, 350, 351; Smith, "Personal Reminiscences," p. 13; Horace C. Fisher, *A Staff Officer's Story*, pp. 15–16; *Louisville Daily Journal*, April 25, 1862.
34. Fisher, *Staff Officer's Story*, pp. 15–16.
35. *OR*, vol. X, pt. 1, pp. 537, 556, 564; Stewart to wife, April 12, 1862, Charles Stewart Letters, Civil War Times Collection, USMHI; Jack D. Welsh, *Medical Histories of Confederate Generals*, p. 93.
36. *OR*, vol. X, pt. 1, pp. 570, 571–72; Sam Houston Jr., "Shiloh Shadows," p. 333.

37. *OR*, vol. X, pt. 1, p. 339; Hannaford, *Story of a Regiment*, p. 574; Cunningham, "Shiloh," p. 478; Ecelbarger, ed., "Shiloh," p. 68.

38. Ecelbarger, ed., "Shiloh," p. 68; Hannaford, *Story of a Regiment*, p. 574; Cunningham, "Shiloh," p. 478.

39. *OR*, vol. X, pt. 1, pp. 434, 546, 551; Stewart to wife, April 12, 1862, Stewart Letters, Civil War Times Collection, USMHI.

40. *OR*, vol. X, pt. 1, p. 551.

41. Ibid., pp. 441, 449, 456, 551; John Bowan Hays, "An Incident at the Battle of Shiloh," p. 265; Jill K. Garrett, ed., *Confederate Diary of Robert D. Smith*, p. 5; D. W. Reed, *Shiloh*, p. 85.

42. *OR*, vol. X, pt. 1, pp. 551–52.

43. Hannaford, *Story of a Regiment*, p. 574; NPS plaque 265; *OR*, vol. X, pt. 1, pp. 301, 322, 336; Ecelbarger, ed., "Shiloh," p. 68.

44. *OR*, vol. X, pt. 1, pp. 149, 224; Hannaford, *Story of a Regiment*, p. 267; Fritz Haskell, ed., "Diary of Colonel William Camm, 1861–1865," p. 855.

45. *OR*, vol. X, pt. 1, pp. 357, 361; James Barnett, "History of G, Ohio Light Artillery," James Barnett Papers, WRHS; NPS plaques 273, 295, 276, 296; NPS monument 114.

46. *OR*, vol. X, pt. 1, p. 617; Kirwan, ed., *Johnny Green*, p. 30.

47. *OR*, vol. X, pt. 1, pp. 617–18; Kirwan, ed., *Johnny Green*, p. 30.

48. *OR*, vol. X, pt. 1, pp. 358, 375–76; Kirwan, ed., *Johnny Green*, p. 30; "Byrne's Battery," John Joyce, Jr., Papers, FC; Edward Porter Thompson, *History of the Orphan Brigade*, pp. 104–5; Force, *From Fort Henry to Corinth*, p. 168.

49. Kirwan, ed., *Johnny Green*, p. 30.

50. *OR*, vol. X, pt. 1, pp. 357, 366, 376, 618; "Byrne's Battery," Joyce Papers, FC.

51. *OR*, vol. X, pt. 1, pp. 357, 358, 360, 361.

52. Edgar R. Kellogg Recollections, Civil War Misc. Collection, USMHI.

53. Lewis M. Hosea, "The Second Day at Shiloh," p. 202; Force, *From Fort Henry to Corinth*, pp. 170–71. Cunningham ("Shiloh," p. 487) states that Stone's Battery K, 1st Missouri Light Artillery, backed Rousseau, but I have been unable to validate.

54. *OR*, vol. X, pt. 1, pp. 308, 311, 418, 618.

55. W. to King, April 14, 1862, in Harwell, ed., *Union Reader*, p. 119; D. McCook, "The Second Day at Shiloh," p. 831; Force, *From Fort Henry to Corinth*, p. 171. Lieutenant Lewis M. Hosea, adjutant of the 1st Battalion, 16th United States Infantry, objected to D. W. Reed's 1901 map. Although McCook's position at 11:00 is correctly shown, the deployments of McClernand and Sherman abreast of McCook make it appear as though there were an orderly advance. McClernand and Sherman did not actually arrive until noon. Hosea, "Second Day," pp. 215–16.

56. *OR*, vol. X, pt. 1, p. 618; A. Walker, "Narrative," p. 157; C. A. Kuhl, "Pittsburg Landing"; William C. Davis, *The Orphan Brigade*, p. 94; *Louisville Journal*, April 21, 1862.

57. A. Walker, "Narrative," p. 151; Roman, *Beauregard*, vol. 1, p. 308; Robertson to mother, April 9, 1862, 4th Louisiana File, LSU.

58. Roman, *Beauregard*, vol. 1, pp. 308–9, 532; Jordan, "Battle of Shiloh," vol. XXXV, p. 221; F. A. Shoup, "The Art of War in '62," p. 12; Joseph H. Parks, *General Leonidas Polk, C.S.A.*, p. 239; T. Harry Williams, *P. G. T. Beauregard*, p. 144.

59. Roman, *Beauregard*, vol. 1, p. 532; Samuel H. Lockett, "Surprise and Withdrawal at Shiloh," p. 605.

60. Woods, ed., *Livaudais Diary*, p. 32; Journal of the Orleans Guard, April 7, 1862, Historic New Orleans Collection.

61. Arthur W. Bergeron, ed., *The Civil War Reminiscences of Major Silas T. Grisamore, C.S.A.*, p. 38; *OR*, vol. X, pt. 1, pp. 519, 520, 522, 528; Phil Bond to brother, April 23, 1862, in James G. Terry, ed., "Record of the Alabama State Artillery," p. 318; Journal of the Orleans Guard, April 7, 1862, Historic New Orleans Collection;

NPS plaques 375, 376; Biel, ed., "Battle of Shiloh," p. 259.

62. J. D. Barnes, "Incidents of the Great Battle," April 11, 1862, Ketchum's Alabama Battery File, ADAH; D. W. Reed, *Shiloh*, p. 79; *OR*, vol. X, pt. 1, pp. 519, 528; NPS plaque 378.

63. *OR*, vol. X, pt. 1, p. 480; Robertson to mother, April 9, 1862, 4th Louisiana File, LSU.

64. *OR*, vol. X, pt. 1, pp. 480, 593, 594, 599; John B. Lindsley, ed., *Military Annals of Tennessee*, p. 421; Robertson to mother, April 9, 1862, 4th Louisiana File, LSU; D. W. Reed, *Shiloh*, p. 69. Wood later placed his numbers as follows: 44th Tennessee, 140; 27th Tennessee, 160; 8th Arkansas, 160; Kelly's battalion, 60 (Wood to Davis, June 20, 1862, S. A. M. Wood Papers, ADAH).

65. Kendall, "Recollections," pp. 1068–69.

66. *OR*, vol. X, pt. 1, pp. 170–71, 473, 480, 488, 593, 626; Kendall, "Recollections," p. 1069; Robertson to mother, April 9, 1862, Robertson Letter, LSU.

67. *OR*, vol. X, pt. 1, p. 594; NPS plaques 388, 342, 325, 312, 445, 378, 343, 422, 327, 411.

68. *OR*, vol. X, pt. 1, pp. 194, 196, 626–27.

69. L. Wallace, *Autobiography*, vol. 2, pp. 544–45.

70. John W. Coons, *Indiana at Shiloh*, p. 190; D. W. Reed, *Shiloh*, p. 52; *OR*, vol. X, pt. 1, pp. 170–71; NPS plaques 118, 119, 120.

71. D. W. Reed, *Shiloh*, p. 56; Force, *From Fort Henry to Corinth*, pp. 173–74; *OR*, vol. X, pt. 1, pp. 251, 274; *Chicago Tribune*, April 18, 1862; *Chicago Times*, April 17, 1862; Charles Bell Kimball, *History of Battery "A,"* p. 45; NPS plaques 186, 202, 106, 173; George H. Woodruff, *Fifteen Years Ago*, p. 403.

72. Oliphant to mother, April 8, 1862, Alexander Oliphant Letters, 24th Indiana File, SNMP.

73. Force, *From Fort Henry to Corinth*, p. 175; *OR*, vol. X, pt. 1, p. 119; D. W. Reed, *Shiloh*, pp. 46–47, 54–55; D. W. Reed Shiloh Battlefield Map, 1901, SNMP.

74. *OR*, vol. X, pt. 1, pp. 274, 565, 583; NPS plaque 432. Cleburne misidentified the battery as the Washington Artillery.

75. *OR*, vol. X, pt. 1, pp. 583–84.

76. Ibid., pp. 119, 135, 500; *New Orleans Picayune*, April 18, 1862; NPS plaque 361.

77. Roman, *Beauregard*, vol. 1, p. 313; *OR*, vol. X, pt. 1, pp. 441, 500, 508, 594; A. Walker, "Narrative," p. 156; *New Orleans Picayune*, April 18, 1862; NPS plaque 464.

78. *OR*, vol. X, pt. 1, pp. 309, 418, 425; *New Orleans Picayune*, April 18, 1862.

79. *OR*, vol. X, pt. 1, pp. 436–37; *Memphis Appeal*, April 10, 1862. I have used D. W. Reed's map in placing Stanford's battery.

80. John Magee Diary, April 7, 1862, DU.

81. *OR*, vol. X, pt. 1, pp. 412, 437; George W. Jones Diary, April 7, 1862, GPL.

82. *OR*, vol. X, pt. 1, pp. 251, 318; Hosea, "Second Day," pp. 204–5; Edwin Waters Payne, *History of the Thirty-Fourth Regiment of Illinois Volunteer Infantry*, p. 21.

83. *OR*, vol. X, pt. 1, pp. 120, 309; Payne, *Thirty-Fourth Illinois*, pp. 17, 20; NPS monument 59.

84. *OR*, vol. X, pt. 1, pp. 102, 172, 200; L. Wallace, *Autobiography*, vol. 1, pp. 558, 565; D. W. Reed, *Shiloh*, p. 52. Cunningham ("Shiloh," p. 497) nonetheless praised Wallace's conservative actions.

85. D. W. Reed, *Shiloh*, p. 52; *OR*, vol. X, pt. 1, pp. 200, 202; NPS plaques 132, 122, 121.

86. *OR*, vol. X, pt. 1, pp. 442, 457, 458–59; W. J. McMurray, *History of the Twentieth Tennessee Regiment Volunteer Infantry*, pp. 211, 212; Henry George, *History of the 3d, 7th, 8th, and 12th Kentucky, C.S.A.*, p. 30; Stubblefield Diary, April 7, 1862; Roman, *Beauregard*, vol. 2, p. 315.

87. *OR*, vol. X, pt. 1, pp. 311, 374; C. C. Briant, *History of the 6th Regiment Indiana Volunteer Infantry*, p. 108.

88. *OR*, vol. X, pt. 1, pp. 304, 315, 414; NPS monument 130, 147; Pennsylvania Battlefield Commission, *The Seventy-Seventh Pennsylvania at Shiloh*, pp. 81–82; Ralph E. Kiene, Jr., *A Civil War Diary*, p. 6.

89. *OR*, vol. X, pt. 1, pp. 221, 377, 380–81; NPS plaque 157; NPS monuments 91, 80; James Dungan (*History of Hurlbut's Fighting Fourth Division*, pp. 104–5) claimed that the 14th and 15th Illinois of Veach's brigade captured three six-pounders at 2:00. This is probably a reference to the guns of Smith's battery, also claimed by the 77th Pennsylvania.

90. *OR*, vol. X, pt. 1, pp. 429, 431, 611, 360, 362, 365, 358; NPS plaques 277, 433, 326, 447. Although the Federals claimed the capture of a two-gun section, Harper reported the loss of only one gun.

91. *OR*, vol. X, pt. 1, pp. 291, 366, 372–73, 623, 625; Stephen E. Ambrose, ed., *A Wisconsin Boy in Dixie*, p. 15; NPS plaques 274, 291. The 14th Wisconsin claimed the capture of a battery, but I am convinced that this was merely overlapping with Boyle's brigade and that the unit in question was Harper's battery. In 1895, 14th Wisconsin veteran John Hancock visited the exact site of the action. He wrote: "The gun and caisson that our regiment captured, and now held as a trophy by the State at Madison, should be taken back and placed as a tablet." (*The Fourteenth Wisconsin*, p. 38.) This statement appears to conform with Harper's report.

92. *OR*, vol. X, pt. 1, pp. 125, 127, 149; NPS plaques 65, 15, 10. I have been unable to identify the Confederate battery in question.

93. Mecklin Diary, April 7, 1862, MDAH; Beauregard, "The Shiloh Campaign," p. 176.

94. *OR*, vol. X, pt. 1, pp. 522, 402; Roman, *Beauregard*, vol. 2, pp. 316–17; P. G. T. Beauregard, "The Shiloh Campaign," p. 177: Bergeron, ed., *Grisamore*, pp. 39–40; *New Orleans Picayune*, April 18, 1862.

95. Kirwan, ed., *Johnny Green*, pp. 30–31; *OR*, vol. X, pt. 1, pp. 506–7; Bassham, "Through a Mist," p. 133.

96. Bergeron, ed., *Grisamore*, p. 40; *OR*, vol. X, pt. 1, p. 522; Roman, *Beauregard*, vol. 2, p. 318. Sword (*Shiloh*, pp. 411–13) describes how the Confederate line drove the Federals back toward McClernand's camps but was in turn repulsed. Perhaps so, but the sources and times are so confused that I have not attempted to reconstruct events.

97. Jordan, "Notes," p. 603.

98. Roman, *Beauregard*, vol. 2, pp. 320–21; Don Seitz, *Braxton Bragg*, p. 111.

99. *OR*, vol. X, pt. 1, pp. 413–14; Biel, ed., "Battle of Shiloh," p. 260; Lathrop, ed., "Confederate Artilleryman," p. 381; Robertson to mother, April 9, 1862, Robertson Letters, LSU; Roman, *Beauregard*, vol. 2, pp. 532–33; "Byrne's Battery," Joyce, Papers, FC.

100. *OR*, vol. X, pt. 1, pp. 490, 594–95; Jordan, "Notes," p. 603; A. Walker, "Narrative," p. 160.

101. *OR*, vol. X, pt. 1, p. 526; NPS plaque 379; Biel, ed., "Battle of Shiloh," p. 260. Lieutenant Lewis Hosea of the 1st Battalion, 16th United States, stated that the impact of Looney's final charge was exaggerated. He hinted that it was due to Colonel Looney's later prominence on the Shiloh Battlefield Commission. (Hosea, "Second Day," pp. 213–14, 217–18.)

102. F. A. Shoup, "How We Went to Shiloh," p. 140.

103. *OR*, vol. X, pt. 1, pp. 221, 224, 225, 309; Wagner Memoirs, Civil War Times Collection, USMHI.

104. *OR*, vol. X, pt. 1, pp. 173, 194, 198, 199; L. Wallace, *Autobiography*, vol. 1, p. 568.

105. Warner, *Generals in Blue*, pp. 166–67; Frederick D. Williams, *The Wild Life of the Army*, p. 81; Wilbur Hinman, *The Story of the Sherman Brigade*, p. 146; *OR*, vol. X, pt. 1, pp. 377–78, 380; Buell, "Shiloh Reviewed," p. 532; Andrew F. Davis to brother, April 21, 1862, Civil War Times Collection, USMHI.

106. *OR*, vol. X, pt. 1, pp. 524, 535, 536, 559; J. A. Wheeler, "The Battle of Shiloh," pp. 126–27; Lathrop, "Confederate Artilleryman," p. 381.

Eleven: Retreat

1. John Y. Simon, ed., *The Papers of Ulysses S. Grant*, vol. 5, pp. 19, 20–21; *OR*, vol. X, pt. 2, p. 99; Adam Badeau, *Military History of Ulysses S. Grant*, p. 90; U. S. Grant, *Personal Memoirs of U. S. Grant*, pp. 237–38. Grant apologist Charles A. Dana declared: "Nothing more could be done" (*The Life of Ulysses S. Grant*, p. 83).
2. Don Carlos Buell, "Shiloh Reviewed," p. 533. Bruce Catton concluded that Grant's army was "ready to drop in its tracks" and "not up to it [pursuit]" (*Grant Moves South*, pp. 245, 247).
3. Buell, "Shiloh Reviewed," pp. 533–34; *OR*, vol. X, pt. 1, p. 295.
4. Grant's failure to pursue the Confederates has been generally condemned by historians. See, for example, James L. McDonough, *Shiloh*, pp. 208–9; William S. McFeely, *Grant*, p. 115; Allen Nevins, *Ordeal of the Union*, vol. 3, pt. 2, pp. 85–86.
5. *OR*, vol. X, pt. 1, pp. 398, 399, 400.
6. Ibid., pp. 401–2; Beauregard to Breckinridge, April 9, 1862, P. G. T. Beauregard Papers, LC.
7. John G. Biel, ed., "The Battle of Shiloh," p. 270; Bassham, "Through a Mist," p. 136; Report of Killed, Wounded, and Missing, Battle of Shiloh, April 6 and 7, 1862, 2nd Corps, Army of the Mississippi, chap. II, vol. 220½, record group 109, NA; Johnson to wife, April 9, 1862, Charles Johnson Letters, LSU. See also Davis, ed., *Jackman Diary*, p. 33.
8. Robertson to mother, April 9, 1862, Robertson Letter, LSU; Earl C. Woods, ed., *The Shiloh Diary of Edmond Enoul Livaudais*, pp. 34–35; William W. Cooper and Donald M. Fowler, eds., " 'Your Affectionate Husband,' " p. 33; Davis to wife, April 8, 1862, in "R. L. Davis Letters," p. 34. See also John Smith Kendall, "Recollections of a Confederate Staff Officer," pp. 1069–70; J. G. Law, "Diary of J. G. Law," p. 462; William S. Dillon Diary, April 8, 1862, UM; Jill K. Garrett, ed., *Confederate Diary of Robert D. Smith*, pp. 5–6; Arthur W. Bergeron, Jr., ed., *The Civil War Reminiscences of Major Silas T. Grisamore, C.S.A.*, p. 41; Journal of the Orleans Guard, April 8, 1862, Historic New Orleans Collection; George W. Jones Diary, April 8, 1862, GPL; John Magee Diary, April 8, 1862, DU.
9. James G. Terry, ed., "Record of the Alabama State Artillery," p. 319.
10. *OR*, vol. X, pt. 1, pp. 399, 400, 619; *New Orleans Picayune*, April 18, 1862; "Byrne's Battery," John Joyce, Jr., Papers, FC.
11. *OR*, vol. X, pt. 1, p. 399; J. Blackburn, "Reminiscences of the Terry Texas Rangers," p. 60.
12. Wilbur Hinman, *The Story of the Sherman Brigade*, pp. 151–52.
13. *OR*, vol. X, pt. 1, pp. 378, 640, 923; Frederick D. Williams, ed., *The Wild Life of the Army*, p. 81; Andrew F. Davis to brother, April 21, 1862, Civil War Times Collection, USMHI; Hinman, *Sherman Brigade*, p. 154.
14. John Wyeth, *That Devil Forrest*, p. 78; *OR*, vol. X, pt. 1, p. 640; *Society of the Army of the Tennessee*, p. 56; Wills DeHaas, "The Battle of Shiloh," p. 689; Andrew W. McCormick, "Sixteen Months a Prisoner of War," p. 69.
15. *OR*, vol. X, pt. 1, p. 923; Wyeth, *Forrest*, p. 78; Blackburn, "Reminiscences," p. 60.
16. DeHaas, "Battle of Shiloh," p. 690; *OR*, vol. X, pt. 1, pp. 266, 640, 924; McCormick, "Sixteen Months," p. 69; P. O. Avery, *The Fourth Illinois Cavalry Regiment*, p. 63; Peters to brother, April 23, 1862, Henry N. Peters Letters, UAF; *Society of the Army of the Tennessee*, p. 56; *Memphis Appeal*, April 11, 1862.

17. Wyeth, *Forrest*, p. 79; Thomas Jordan and Roger Pryor, *The Campaigns of Lieut.-Gen. N. B. Forrest*, pp. 146–48; Wills, *Battle from the Start*, p. 70; *Society of the Army of the Tennessee*, p. 56.

18. *OR*, vol. X, pt. 1, p. 640.

19. *Society of the Army of the Tennessee*, p. 54; Orville Victor, *Incidents*, p. 359; *OR*, vol. X, pt. 1, p. 117; *Cincinnati Times*, April 24, 1862.

20. *Indianapolis Sentinel*, April 17, 21, 1862; *Cincinnati Commercial*, April 15, 16, 1862.

21. *The Medical and Surgical History of the War of the Rebellion*, vol. 2, pp. 38–39; Edwin Hannaford, *The Story of a Regiment*, pp. 285–86.

22. *Medical and Surgical History*, vol. 2, pp. 38–39.

23. Ibid., p. 38.

24. Steve Meyer, *Iowa Valor*, p. 91; Erhard Dittman to parents, April 15, 1862, 45th Illinois File, SNMP. See also Edwin Reynolds Diary, April 6, 1862, Civil War Times Collection, USMHI.

25. Mark M. Krug, ed., *Mrs. Hill's Journal*, pp. 96–97; *Chicago Tribune*, April 18, 1862; *Missouri Daily Democrat*, April 17, 1862; "Journal of a Trip to Pittsburg Landing to Assist in the Care of Sick and Wounded Soldiers," pp. 17–18.

26. *Chicago Tribune*, April 18, 21, 1862; *Chicago Times*, April 10, 1862; *Missouri Daily Democrat*, May 7, 1862; J. S. Newberry, *The U.S. Sanitary Commission in the Valley of the Mississippi*, pp. 33–43.

27. *OR*, vol. X, pt. 1, p. 111; pt. 2, p. 403.

28. Wilbur Crummer, *With Grant at Fort Donelson, Shiloh, and Vicksburg*, pp. 74–75.

29. Oliphant to mother, April 18, 1862, Alexander Oliphant Letters, 24th Indiana File, SNMP; J. F. True to sister, April 10, 1862, 41st Illinois File, SNMP.

30. *OR*, vol. X, pt. 1, p. 395; *New York Tribune*, May 5, 1862; Albert D. Richardson, *The Secret Service, the Field, the Dungeon and the Escape*, p. 240; Joseph A. Frank and George A. Reaves, "*Seeing the Elephant*," pp. 119, 122, 123. See also Miller to sister, April 13, 1862, Stephen A. Miller Letters, INHS; George H. Woodruff, *Fifteen Years Ago*, p. 106.

31. Isabel Wallace, *Life and Letters of General W. H. L. Wallace*, pp. 186–87, 199–200, 214–15, 217–18.

32. *OR*, vol. X, pt. 1, p. 130; Ezra J. Warner, *Generals in Blue*, p. 456.

33. Alfred Roman, *The Military Operations of General Beauregard*, vol. 1, p. 319.

34. J. V. Frederick, ed., "War Diary of W. C. Porter," p. 290; W. H. Tunnard, *A Southern Record*, p. 163.

35. Frederick, ed., "W. C. Porter Diary," p. 294; Lester N. Fitzhugh, ed., *Cannon Smoke*, p. 179; William L. Shea and Earl J. Hess, *Pea Ridge*, p. 289.

36. Charles Roland, *Albert Sidney Johnston*, p. 352; Otto Eisenschiml, *The Story of Shiloh*, p. 76.

37. Richard B. Harwell, ed., *Kate: The Journal of a Confederate Nurse*, pp. 9–10, 12; William Stevenson, *Thirteen Months in the Rebel Army*, p. 124; *Mobile Advertiser & Register*, April 8, 1862; Larry J. Daniel, *Soldiering in the Army of Tennessee*, p. 66.

38. "Report of Killed, Wounded & Missing, Battle of Shiloh," chap. II, vol. 220½, record group 109, NA.

39. Daniel, *Soldiering*, pp. 66, 69.

40. Woods, ed., *Livaudais Diary*, p. 36; Barnes F. Lathrop, "A Confederate Artilleryman at Shiloh," p. 382; Daniel, *Soldiering*, p. 127.

41. *OR*, vol. X, pt. 2, p. 386; Larry J. Daniel, *Cannoneers in Gray*, p. 44; "Ordnance Return of the 1st Brigade, 1st Division, May 12, 1862," Yerger Papers, MDAH; *Arkansas Gazette*, April 12, 1862.

42. *New Orleans Picayune*, April 25, 1862; *OR*, vol. X, pt. 1, p. 428.

Twelve: Ramifications

1. Howard Beale, *The Diary of Edward Bates*, pp. 247–48; Emmet Crozier, *Yankee Reporters*, p. 215; J. Cutler Andrews, *The North Reports the Civil War*, p. 178; W. E. Woodward, *Meet General Grant*, p. 255; Cunningham, "Shiloh and the Western Campaign of 1862," p. 516; Bruce Catton, *Grant Moves South*, p. 252; *London Times*, May 6, 1862; James G. Blaine, *Twenty Years of Congress*, p. 362; *OR*, vol. X, pt. 1, p. 381; William S. McFeely, *Grant*, p. 115.

2. Allen Nevins, *Ordeal of the Union*, vol. 3, pt. 2, p. 109; Catton, *Grant Moves South*, pp. 252–54, 255–56; John F. Marszalek, *Sherman's Other War*, pp. 76–77; John F. Marszalek, "William T. Sherman and the Verbal Battle of Shiloh," p. 80. Reid's account is transcribed in James G. Smart, ed., *A Radical View*, pp. 119–71.

3. *New York Tribune*, April 11, 1862; Fletcher Pratt, *Stanton*, p. 184; *London Times*, April 23, 1862; James M. McPherson, *Battle Cry of Freedom*, p. 413.

4. Archer Jones, *Civil War Command and Strategy*, pp. 53–54; McPherson, *Battle Cry of Freedom*, p. 414.

5. Nathaniel C. Hughes, Jr., *The Battle of Belmont*, p. 195; Shelby Foote, *The Civil War*, vol. 1, p. 372; Remarks of Hon. John Sherman, of Ohio, May 2, 1862, OHS; Victor Hicken, "From Vandalia to Vicksburg," p. 194; *Philadelphia Inquirer*, April 19, 1862.

6. *Cincinnati Gazette*, April 21, 1862; *Cincinnati Commercial*, April 21, 1862; Catton, *Grant Moves South*, p. 254; Joseph Medill to Washburne, May 24, 1862, Elihu Washburne Papers, LC; Andrews, *North Reports the Civil War*, p. 181; *Indianapolis Journal*, April 29, 1862; *Philadelphia Inquirer*, April 19, 1862. The *New York Tribune* of April 22, 1862, also denounced Grant.

7. *OR*, vol. X, pt. 1, p. 114; McFeely, *Grant*, p. 116.

8. Benjamin P. Thomas and Harold M. Hyman, *Stanton*, pp. 190–91; George C. Gorham, *Life and Public Service of Edwin M. Stanton*, vol. 1, pp. 308–9.

9. J. R. Chumney, "Don Carlos Buell, Gentleman General," pp. 81–82; *New York Herald* report quoted in *Memphis Argus*, April 15, 1862.

10. Catton, *Grant Moves South*, p. 257; *Cincinnati Commercial*, April 25, May 2, 6, 1862; J. E. Smith to Washburne, May 16, 1862, Washburne Papers, LC. Grant's denial of a surprise simply has not stood up to historic scrutiny. Kenneth Williams and Liddell Hart state that the General was surprised both tactically and psychologically (Marszalek, "Verbal Battle of Shiloh," p. 78).

11. Frank A. Flower, *Edwin McMasters Stanton*, pp. 368–69; Pratt, *Stanton*, p. 186; Catton, *Grant Moves South*, p. 259; Tim Hurst, "The Battle of Shiloh," p. 86; *Cincinnati Commercial*, May 6, 1862.

12. Remarks of Hon. E. B. Washburne, of Ill., May 2, 1862, ILSL; Blaine, *Twenty Years of Congress*, p. 363.

13. Catton, *Grant Moves South*, pp. 260–63.

14. Howard Jones, *Union in Peril*, pp. 116–17; *London Times*, May 1, 1862.

15. A. K. McClure, *Abraham Lincoln and Men of War-Times*, pp. 194–96.

16. In a panel debate on Shiloh in Corinth in April 1995, Grady McWhiney, John Simon, and John Marszalek all supported Lincoln's decision to retain Grant.

17. McClure, *Lincoln and Men of War-Times*, p. 197; McFeely, *Grant*, p. 116. McPherson writes that Grant's coolness during the battle "barely redeemed" his mistakes before the battle (*Battle Cry of Freedom*, p. 415).

18. Catton, *Grant Moves South*, p. 267; U. S. Grant, *Personal Memoirs of U. S. Grant*, pp. 248, 250–51; Richard E. Beringer et al., *Why the South Lost the Civil War*, p. 132; *OR*, vol. X, pt. 2, p. 235. Modern writers have frequently misjudged Halleck's numbers. Kenneth P. Williams (*Lincoln Finds a General*, vol. 3, p. 428), Foote (*Civil War*, vol. 1, p. 373), and others place the figure at 120,000, but that number includes a division in northern Alabama and another at Cumberland Gap.

19. Grant, *Memoirs*, p. 251; Albert D. Richardson, *A Personal History of Ulysses S. Grant*, pp. 257–58; Catton, *Grant Moves South*, pp. 272–73.

20. McFeely, *Grant*, p. 119; Woodward, *Meet General Grant*, p. 258.

21. Catton, *Grant Moves South*, pp. 274–75; Joseph T. Glatthaar, *Partners in Command*, p. 142.

22. Catton, *Grant Moves South*, pp. 287–88; Grant, *Memoirs*, pp. 262–63; Grant to Washburne, July 22, 1862, Washburne Papers, LC. Grant did not learn of Halleck's attempts to displace him until after the war.

23. M. A. DeWolfe Howe, ed., *Home Letters of General Sherman*, p. 220; Marszalek, "Verbal Battle of Shiloh," pp. 79–82; *OR*, vol. X, pt. 1, p. 98.

24. Rachel Sherman Thorndike, ed., *The Sherman Letters*, pp. 143–46; Howe, ed., *Home Letters*, p. 224; James M. Merrill, *William Tecumseh Sherman*, p. 202.

25. Marszalek, "Verbal Battle of Shiloh," pp. 82–84; Letter of Thomas Ewing to Lt. Gov. B. Stanton, October 4, 1862, OHS; Letter of the Hon. Thomas Ewing to His Excellency Benj. Stanton, November 1, 1862, OHS; Remarks of Hon. Thomas Ewing to His Excellency Benj. Stanton, in Reply to Hon. Thos. Ewing, November 4, 1862, OHS.

26. Robert W. McCormick, "Challenge of Command: Worthington vs. Sherman," pp. 34–39; W. T. Sherman Testimony, Worthington Court Martial Proceedings, NA; *Society of the Army of the Tennessee*, pp. 60–61, 71.

27. Thomas E. Griess, ed., *The American Civil War*, p. 63; Rowena Reed, *Combined Operations in the Civil War*, p. 206; McPherson, *Battle Cry of Freedom*, p. 415; Stephen E. Ambrose, *Halleck*, p. 46; Thomas L. Connelly, *Army of the Heartland*, p. 178. The capture of Corinth, according to Albert Castel, "clinched the Union gains resulting from Forts Henry and Donelson" ("The War Moves West," pp. 270–71). See also A. Jones, *Civil War Command*, p. 54. Grant thought the fall of Corinth "strategic," but "barren in every other particular" (Beringer et al., *Why South Lost*, p. 133).

28. Frank E. Vandiver, *Blood Brothers*, p. 118. McPherson (*Battle Cry of Freedom*, p. 416) wrote that Halleck concentrated on Corinth rather than waging "a modern war of all-out combat to destroy or cripple an enemy army." See also James L. McDonough, *War in Kentucky*, p. 30.

29. Historians have rightly criticized Halleck's failure either to pursue Beauregard to Tupelo or to move on Vicksburg. See Archer Jones, *Confederate Strategy from Shiloh to Vicksburg*, p. 57; Castel, "The War Moves West," p. 271; Griess, ed., *American Civil War*, p. 64. For a sympathetic view of Halleck's problems, see McDonough, *War in Kentucky*, pp. 33–36.

30. *New Orleans Picayune*, April 6, 8, 11, 13, 1862; J. Cutler Andrews, *The South Reports the Civil War*, p. 143.

31. *New Orleans Picayune*, April 10, 18, 1862; Charles Dufour, *The Night the War Was Lost*, p. 209; James L. McDonough, *Shiloh*, p. 225.

32. Thomas Bragg Diary, April 5, 1862, SHC; Hudson Strode, *Jefferson Davis*, p. 231; I. M. Keats to War Department, April 6, 1862, Telegrams Received, Confederate Secretary of War, NA (microfilm M-618, roll 9).

33. Strode, *Davis*, pp. 231–32; William C. Davis, *Jefferson Davis*, p. 404; *Charleston Mercury*, April 7, 1862.

34. Woodworth, *Jefferson Davis*, p. 103; *OR*, vol. X, pt. 1, p. 546; *Atlanta Intelligencer*, April 18, 1862.

35. Clement Eaton, *Jefferson Davis*, p. 150; Bragg Diary, April 7, 1862, SHC.

36. *London Times*, May 1, 1862; H. Jones, *Union in Peril*, pp. 115–17; James D. Richardson, ed., *The Messages and Papers of Jefferson Davis*, vol. 2, p. 234.

37. Bragg Diary, April 9, 1862, SHC; William K. Scarbrough, *The Diary of Edmund Ruffin*, vol. 1, p. 279; T. L. Connelly, *Army of the Heartland*, p. 179; Strode, *Davis*, p. 231; Paul D. Escott, *After Secession*, p. 173; William L. Shea and Earl J. Hess, *Pea Ridge*, p. 289.

38. *OR*, vol. X, pt. 1, pp. 490–91, 523; pt. 2, p. 440; Arthur W. Bergeron, Jr., ed., *Guide to Louisiana Confederate Military Units*, pp. 99, 132; Larry J. Daniel, *Cannoneers in Gray*, p. 45; Lockwood Tower, ed., *A Carolinian Goes to War*, p. xiii.

39. Irving Werstein, *Abraham Lincoln Versus Jefferson Davis*, pp. 196–97; William C. Davis, *The Deep Waters of the Proud*, pp. 206–7.

40. Richard McMurry, *Two Great Rebel Armies*, p. 123; Bragg Diary, April 7, 1862, SHC.

41. Steven E. Woodworth, *Jefferson Davis and His Generals*, p. 103.

42. Ibid., p. 105; *OR*, vol. X, pt. 1, pp. 764, 867, 872–73; T. L. Connelly, *Army of the Heartland*, pp. 178–79; T. Harry Williams, *P. G. T. Beauregard*, p. 148.

43. Woodworth, *Davis*, p. 105; T. L. Connelly, *Army of the Heartland*, pp. 180–82; W. C. Davis, *Jefferson Davis*, p. 406; A. Jones, *From Shiloh to Vicksburg*, p. 62; T. H. Williams, *Beauregard*, p. 148; William Preston Johnston to wife, June 12, 1862, Albert Sidney Johnston Papers, Barret Collection, TU.

44. Woodworth, *Davis*, p. 106; McMurry, *Two Great Rebel Armies*, p. 123; T. L. Connelly, *Army of the Heartland*, pp. 180–81.

45. Vandiver (*Blood Brothers*, p. 121) writes that Beauregard "goaded" Johnston into action and showed "more energy" than his superior. Thomas L. Connelly and Archer Jones (*The Politics of Command*, p. 98) stated that Johnston's passivity allowed Beauregard to implement the Corinth concentration.

46. William Preston Johnston, *The Life of Gen. Albert Sidney Johnston*, p. 690. Nelson's division should have been at Pittsburg Landing by the night of April 5, with Crittenden's division arriving on Sunday (K. P. Williams, *Lincoln Finds a General*, vol. 3, p. 393). Wallace's division could have been on the field by the early afternoon of April 6. W. C. Davis (*Jefferson Davis*, p. 404) deduced that Johnston simply did not fight a good battle. Charles Roland, on the other hand, stated in an April 1995 panel debate that had Johnston lived he would have led the Southern army "to the banks of the Ohio River."

47. K. P. Williams (*Lincoln Finds a General*, vol. 3, p. 393) correctly wrote that boasts of destroying Grant's army were absurd: "Beauregard could not have destroyed Grant without destroying himself."

Appendix C: **The Confederate Dead**

1. *Memphis Argus*, April 6, 1866.

2. "Shocking Condition of the Confederate Dead at Shiloh," *Reporter & Watchtower* (Talladega, Alabama), January 2, 1878.

3. C. A. Kuhl, "Pittsburg Landing."

4. One of McClernand's soldiers stated that "seven hundred bodies of the rebels were put in one grave" (Olynthus B. Clark, ed., *Downing's Civil War Diary*, p. 43). The statement was probably based on rumor. Such a trench would have had to be twelve to fourteen feet deep, yet I have never been able to document a trench more than four feet deep, even with 150 bodies.

Bibliography

Unpublished Materials

Alabama Department of Archives and History, Montgomery (ADAH)
Barnes, J. D. "Incidents of the Great Battle." Ketchum's Alabama Battery File.
Gage's Alabama Battery File.
Pickett, W. D. "Biographical Sketch of the Military Career of William J. Hardee, Lieutenant-General, C.S.A."
Wood, S. A. M. Papers.

Barker Texas History Library, University of Texas, Austin (UT)
Bunting, Robert. Letters. (Texas Rangers)

Chicago Historical Society, Chicago (CHS)
Carrington, George. Diary.
Lauman, Jacob. Letters.
Swain, George. Letters. (58th Illinois)

Filson Club, Louisville, Kentucky (FC)
"Byrne's Battery." John Joyes, Jr., Papers.
Johnston, Albert Sidney. Papers.
Mohr, James F. Letters. (H, 5th U.S. Artillery)

Gloria Gardner Collection, Jackson, Tennessee
Rosser, James. Diary.

Greenville, Mississippi, Public Library (GPL)
Jones, George W. Diary. (Stanford's Mississippi Battery)

Historic New Orleans Collection, New Orleans
Journal of the Orleans Guard.
Unknown Diarist.
Vaught, William. Letters.

Huntington Library, San Marino, California (HL)
Smith, T. Kilby. Letters. (54th Ohio)

Illinois State Library, Springfield (ILSL)
Englemann, Adolph. Letters. (43rd Illinois)
Floyd, C. H. Letters.
Grant-Washburne. Papers.
Harley, Wayne. Letter. (15th Illinois)
McEathron, Alexander. Letters. (15th Illinois)
Oates, James. "A Gallant Regiment." (9th Illinois)
Remarks of Hon. E. B. Washburne, of Ill., in the House of Representatives, May 2, 1862.

Shumway, Payton. Letters.
Wilcox, John S. Letters. (52nd Illinois)

Indiana Historical Society, Indianapolis (INHS)
Connelly, Jesse B. Diary. (31st Indiana)
"Gen. Wallace at Battle of Shiloh." Lew Wallace Papers.
Harmon, Francis M. Letters.
Harrison, Thomas J. Letters. (6th Indiana)
Miller, Stephen A. Letters.
Wallace, Lew. Papers.

Iowa State Historical Department, Des Moines (IOSHD)
Richardson, William. Letters. (7th Iowa)
Sylvester, Saul. Journal. (3rd Iowa)

Library of Congress, Washington, D.C. (LC)
Bartlett, Harold. Diary.
Beauregard, P. G. T. Papers.
Bloomfield, A. S. Letters.
Bradford, Joshua T. Diary.
Buford, Samuel. Letters.
Eels, Samuel. Letters. (12th Michigan)
Grebe, Belzar. Papers. (14th Illinois)
St. John, Bela T. Letters. (46th Illinois)
Sherman, William T. Papers.
Stimpson, William R. Letters. (3rd Iowa)
Todd, O. M. Diary. (78th Ohio)
Washburne, Elihu. Papers.

Louisiana Historical Association, Tulane University, New Orleans (LHA)
Johnston, Albert Sidney. Order Book.
Johnston, Albert Sidney and P. G. T. Beauregard. Correspondence.

Louisiana State University, Baton Rouge (LSU)
Dimitry, John. Letter to William Bullitt.
Johnson, Charles. Letters. (11th Louisiana)
Liddell, St. John. Papers.
Mandeville, Theodore. Letters.
Robertson, Thomas Chinn. Letter to mother. (4th Louisiana)
Wall, Bennie. Letter to father. Joseph Embree Papers.
Wilkinson, Micajah. Letters.

Memphis Conference Archives, Lambuth University, Jackson, Tennessee (LU)
Shiloh United Methodist Church File.

Michigan Historical Collection, Bentley Historical Library, University of Michigan, Ann Arbor (MHC)
Bailey, Franklin. Letters. (12th Michigan)
Claxton, William C. "Thirty-Nine Years After Shiloh."
Sligh, James. Letters. (15th Michigan)

Mississippi Department Archives and History, Jackson (MDAH)
Cato, John A. Letters. (7th Mississippi)
"Forty-Seventh Tennessee Ordnance Return," Yerger Papers.
Foxworth, Jobe M. Diary. (7th Mississippi)
Grammer, George A. Diary. (Swett's Mississippi Battery)
Gunn, D. B. "Reminiscences of the War." John J. Thornton Papers.
Mecklin, A. H. Diary. (15th Mississippi)

"Ordnance Return of the 1st Brigade, 1st Division, May 12, 1862." Yerger Papers.
"Return of the 1st Brigade, R. M. Russell, March 30, 1862." Yerger Papers.
Tarlske, A. H. Letters.

Mississippi Valley Collection, University of Memphis, Memphis (UMEM)
Stanton, G. A. Journal.
Stephenson, M. D. L. Diary.

Missouri Historical Society, St. Louis (MHS)
Martin, S. F. Letters.
Miller, Madison. Diary.

National Archives, Washington, D.C. (NA)
Letters Sent, Ordnance Officer, Army of Tennessee, chap. IV, vol. 141, record group 109.
Papers Relating to Citizens and Business Firms, record group 109.
Preston, William. Diary.
Record of Stores Purchased, Received and Issued, Nashville and Atlanta Arsenals 1861–1862, chap. IV, vol. 19, record group 109.
Report of Killed, Wounded, and Missing, Battle of Shiloh, April 6 and 7, 1862, 2nd Corps, Army of the Mississippi, chap. II, vol. 220½, record group 109.
Smith, Preston. Diary.
Telegrams Received, Confederate Secretary of War. (Microfilm M-618, roll 9)
Worthington, Thomas. Court Martial Proceedings, August 1862.

Northeast Mississippi Museum Association, Corinth (NEMMA)
Inge, Augusta. Reminiscences.
Rice, Ernie. "A History of the Corinth, Mississippi Depot."

Ohio Historical Society, Columbus (OHS)
Curtis, Erastus R. Memoirs. (81st Ohio)
Letter of Lieut. Gov. Stanton, in Reply to Hon. Thos. Ewing, November 4, 1862.
Letter of Thomas Ewing to Lt. Gov. B. Stanton, in Reply to Hon. Thos. Ewing, November 4, 1862.
Loudon, DeWitt Clinton. Letters. (70th Ohio)
Remarks of Hon. John Sherman, of Ohio, in Senate of the United States, May 9, 1862.
Remarks of Hon. Thomas Ewing to His Excellency Benj. Stanton, in Reply to Hon. Thos. Ewing, November 4, 1862.
Testimony Submitted to the President of the United States by Rodney Mason.

Perkins Library, Duke University, Durham, North Carolina (DU)
Bragg, Braxton. Papers.
Floyd, John. Papers.
Magee, John. Diary. (Stanford's Mississippi Battery)
Ruggles, Daniel. Papers.

Pogue Library Special Collection, Murray State University, Murray, Kentucky (PL)
Stubblefield, W. J. Diary. (7th Kentucky C.S.)

Shiloh National Military Park, Shiloh, Tennessee (SNMP)
Allen, Stacy. "Brief Analysis of Donald F. Dosch's 'The Hornet's Nest.' " Misc. Files.
———. "Confederate Assaults on the Hornet's Nest, Shiloh: April 6, 1862," Misc. Files.
———. "C. S. A. Hornet's Nest Assaults Update." Misc. Files.
———. "Hornet's Nest Federal Line: Troops Engaged." Misc. Files.
Arns, Louis. Letter to parents. 49th Illinois File.
Bearss, Ed. "Base Map Book." Misc. Files.

Bieler, J. L. Speech. 11th Indiana File.

Bosworth, Milton K. Letter to father. 53rd Ohio File.

Bridgford, Oliver A. Letters. 45th Illinois File.

Chalmers, James.Letter to Mississippi State Auditor. Misc. Files.

Chamberlain, W. H. "The 81st Ohio at Shiloh." 81st Ohio File.

"Cherry Mansion Report."

Colby, E., Jr. Letters. A, 1st Illinois Light Artillery File.

Cullum, George W. Letter to Mary. 24th Tennessee File.

"Death of Gen. A. S. Johnston." A. S. Johnston File.

Dickey, Lyle. Letter to Aunt Ann. 4th Illinois Cavalry File.

Dishmore, Mary. Paper. 2nd Tennessee File.

Dittman, Erhard. Letters. 45th Illinois File.

Ebenezor, M. Letter. 16th Wisconsin File.

Ferguson, Samuel. Memoir. Army of the Mississippi File.

Fogle, James S. Diary. 11th Indiana File.

George, Henry. "The 7th Kentucky at Shiloh." 7th Kentucky File.

Govan, D. C. Letter. 2nd Arkansas File.

Grebe, Belzar. Biography. 14th Illinois File.

Gross, Karl. Letter. 52nd Illinois File.

"Haratio." Letter to Josie. 22nd Alabama File.

Harvey, George. Letter. 31st Indiana File.

Harvey, William. Diary and Memoirs. 57th Illinois File.

Howell, John P. Letter to Mr. Brewington. Misc. Files.

Hurst, John T. "The Battle of Shiloh." 40th Illinois File.

"Interview of James Wood, 1934." Misc. Files.

Ironton Register. Letter. 53rd Ohio File.

Jenkins, W. Y. "The Ninth Illinois Volunteer Infantry At Shiloh." 9th Illinois File.

Kay, William. "Sunken Road." Misc. Files.

Kemble, Jane. "The Manse George Cabin." Misc. Files.

Leonard, B. F. Letter to Reed. 10th Mississippi File.

McFadden, R. H. Letters. 41st Illinois File.

Mattison, Ray H. "Hornet's Nest Area." Misc. Files.

Mills, L. W. Letter. B, 2nd Michigan Battery File.

Moiser, William. Letter to Reed. 52nd Tennessee File.

Morton, Charles. Letter. 25th Missouri File.

Oliphant, Alexander. Letters. 24th Indiana File.

Powell, J. W. Letter to Cornelius Cadle. F, 2nd Illinois Light Artillery File.

Powell, John F. Letter. Misc. Files.

Powell, John W. Letters. 35th Tennessee File.

Powell, John W. Letter. F, 2nd Illinois Artillery File.

Powell of the Colorado. Selected Pages. F, 2nd Illinois Light Artillery File.

Pugh, Isaac C. Letters. 41st Illinois File.

Reaves, George W. "A Report to Determine the Size and Condition of the Peach Orchard at the Intersection of the Sunken Road and the Pittsburg Landing Road on April 6, 1862." Misc. Files.

Reed, David W. Papers. Misc. Files.

Reed, D. W. Letters. 4th Tennessee File.

Reed, D. W. Letter. 13th Tennessee File.

Reed, D. W. Shiloh Battlefield Map, 1901.

Robertson, Felix. Letter to Reed. 13th Ohio Battery File.

Ruckman, John. Letters. 57th Ohio File.

Shanks, Edward B. Letters. 12th Illinois.

Shaw, Phillip. Journal. 32nd Illinois File.

Shepard, E. L. Letter. B, 2nd Michigan Battery File.

"Shiloh." 52nd Illinois File.
"Shiloh National Military Park, Office of the Historian." Misc. Files.
Skaptason, Bjorn. Letter. 53rd Ohio File.
Skinner, William. Letters. 71st Ohio File.
Stephenson, Samuel. Letters. 48th Ohio File.
Stephenson, William B. Letter. 53rd Ohio File.
Stricklin, Mary E. "Shiloh Church."
Swett, Charles. Memoirs. Swett's Mississippi Battery File.
Swift, Ebin. Letter. D. W. Reed Papers.
Tauty, Lyman. Letter to Reaves. 16th Wisconsin File.
Teel, L. C. Letter to friend. B, 2nd Michigan Battery File.
Thompson, Atwell. Letter to Cornelius Cadle. Army of the Tennessee, 3rd Division File.
True, J. F. Letter to sister. 41st Illinois File.
Unknown. Diary. 154th Tennessee File.
Unknown. Letter to Eason Johnson. 41st Illinois File.
Unknown. Letter to sister. 2nd Tennessee File.
Various Documents Relating to the Movement of the 4th Tennessee. 4th Tennessee File.
Wallace, Lewis. Papers. Misc. Files.
Wyllie, William R. Letter to family. 58th Illinois File.
Zook, Christian. Letters. 46th Ohio File.

Southern Historical Collection, University of North Carolina, Chapel Hill (SHC)
Beatty, Taylor. Diary.
Bragg, Thomas. Diary.
Gilmer, Jeremy. Letters.

State Historical Society of Iowa, Iowa City (SHSIO)
Currier, Amos. Letters. (8th Iowa)
Richardson, William. Letters. (7th Iowa)
Warren, William H. Letters. (13th Iowa)

Tennessee State Library and Archives, Nashville (TSLA)
Boswell, R. P. Letters. (1st Tennessee)
Coleman, W. E. Letters. (5th Kentucky)
Fielder, Albert. Diary. (12th Tennessee)
Henry, Gustavus A. Papers.
Latta, Samuel. Letters. (13th Tennessee)
Lindsley, John B. Diary.
Parker, Rufus B. Diary. (5th Kentucky)
Ready, Alice. Diary.
Wright, Marcus J. Diary.

Tulane University, New Orleans (TU)
Army of Tennessee Papers.
Bragg, Braxton. "General Albert Sidney Johnston at Shiloh." Albert Sidney Johnston Papers, Barret Collection.
Johnston, Albert Sidney. Order Book. Albert Sidney Johnston Papers, Barret Collection.
Johnston, Albert Sidney. Papers. Barret Collection.
Letter Book of the Headquarters of the Western Department, Kuntz Collection.
Munford, Edward. "Albert Sidney Johnston." Albert Sidney Johnston Papers, Barret Collection.
Stibbs, Joseph. Letters. (12th Iowa)
Watson, C. S. Letters. (25th Louisiana) Clement Stanford Watson Family Papers.

Wickham, Lee. "Statement As to Gen. Johnston's Death." Albert Sidney Johnston Papers, Barret Collection.

United States Military History Institute, Carlisle Barracks, Pennsylvania (USMHI)
Blaisdell, Timothy M. Letters. Civil War Times Collection. (B, 1st Illinois Light Artillery)
Caldwell, John C. Diary. Civil War Times Collection. (9th Kentucky C.S.)
Daniel, Rufus. Diary. Civil War Misc. Collection. (6th Arkansas)
Davis, Andrew F. Letter to brother. Civil War Times Collection. (15th Indiana)
Embly, Edgar. Letters. Harrisburg Civil War Round Table Collection. (61st Illinois)
H. R. Letter. Civil War Times Collection. (Crescent Regiment)
Kellogg, Edgar R. Recollections. Civil War Misc. Collection. (16th United States)
LaBrant, Jonathan L. Diary. Civil War Times Collection. (5th Illinois)
Reynolds, Edwin. Diary. Civil War Times Collection. (46th Illinois)
Stewart, Charles. Letters. Civil War Times Collection. (21st Alabama)
Wagner, Levi. Memoirs. Civil War Times Collection. (1st Ohio)
Watkins, Thomas C. Diary. Civil War Times Collection. (18th Illinois)

University of Arkansas, Fayetteville (UAF)
Peters, Henry N. Letters. (4th Illinois Cavalry)

University of the South, Sewanee, Tennessee (US)
Polk, Leonidas. Papers.

Western Reserve Historical Society, Case Western University, Cleveland (WRHS)
Barnett, James. "History of G, Ohio Light Artillery." James Barnett Papers.
Bragg, Braxton. Papers. William P. Palmer Collection.
Varian, Alexander, Jr. Letters. (1st Ohio)

John Davis Williams Library, University of Mississippi, Oxford (UM)
Dillon, William S. Diary. (4th Tennessee)

Robert W. Woodruff Library, Emory University, Atlanta (EU)
Green, Hildreth, Jr. Letters. (Washington Artillery)
Scarbrough, Lemuel A. Diary. (13th Tennessee)

Yale University Library, New Haven, Connecticut (YU)
Carpenter, A. B. Letters. (19th U.S. Regulars)
Lyman, Joseph. Letters. (Confederate Guards Response Battalion)

NEWSPAPERS

Confederate

Atlanta Intelligencer
Augusta Constitutionalist
Baton Rouge Daily Advocate
Charleston Mercury
Georgia Weekly Sun
Louisville Daily Journal
Memphis Appeal
Memphis Argus
Memphis Daily Avalanche
Mercury (Charleston)
Mobile Advertiser & Register

Nashville Gazette
Nashville Republican Banner
Nashville Times
New Orleans Crescent
New Orleans Delta
New Orleans Picayune
Reporter & Watchtower (Talladega, Alabama)
Richmond Dispatch
Richmond Enquirer
Richmond Examiner
Richmond Inquirer
Richmond Whig
Savannah News
Southern Confederacy (Atlanta)
Tri-Weekly Telegraph (Houston)

Federal

Canton Weekly Register
Chicago Times
Chicago Tribune
Cincinnati Commercial
Cincinnati Daily Examiner
Cincinnati Enquirer
Cincinnati Gazette
Cincinnati Times
Columbus Journal
Daily Ohio State Journal
Indianapolis Journal
Indianapolis Sentinel
Ironton Register
Louisville Daily Journal
Louisville Democrat
Missouri Daily Democrat (St. Louis)
Nashville Dispatch
Nashville Republican Banner
Nashville Times
National Intelligencer (Washington, D.C.)
New York Herald
New York Times
New York Tribune
Philadelphia Inquirer
Quincy Daily Herald
Selina, Mercer County, Ohio
Springfield Weekly Republican
Sycamore True Republican & Sentinel
Washington Star

Other

London Times
Memphis Commercial Appeal
Reporter & Watchtower (Talladega, Ala.)
St. Louis Democrat
St. Louis Republican

OFFICIAL RECORDS

The Medical and Surgical History of the War of the Rebellion, 1861–1865. 5 vols. Washington, D.C., 1870.

The Official Records of the Union and Confederate Navies in the War of the Rebellion. 30 vols. Washington, D.C., 1894–1922. (Abbreviated *ONR.*)

The War of the Rebellion: A Compilation of the Official Records of the Union and Confederate Armies, 1861–1865. 128 vols. Washington, D.C., 1880–1901. (Abbreviated *OR.*)

Dissertations

Chumney, J. R., Jr. "Don Carlos Buell, Gentleman General." Ph.D. dissertation, Rice University, 1964.

Cunningham, O. E. "Shiloh and the Western Campaign of 1862." Ph.D. dissertation, Louisiana State University, 1966.

Deberry, John. "Confederate Tennessee." Ph.D. dissertation, University of Kentucky, 1967.

Hicken, Victor. "From Vandalia to Vicksburg: The Political and Military Career of John A. McClernand." Ph.D. dissertation, University of Illinois at Urbana, 1955.

Lash, Jeffrey N. "Stephen Augustus Hurlbut: A Military and Diplomatic Politician, 1815–1822." Ph.D. dissertation, Kent State University, 1980.

Sanders, Joseph T. "M. A. Miller's Sketch Book of 1860." M.A. thesis, Mississippi State University, 1962.

Articles and Pamphlets

Allen, Alfred. "The 9th Indiana at Shiloh." *National Tribune*, November 2, 1922.

"Allen Cobb Waterhouse." *Military Order of the Loyal Legion of the United States*, Illinois Commandery, vol. 13D (1923), pp. 46–47.

Ambrose, Stephen. "The Union Command System and the Donelson Campaign." In *Military Analysis of the Civil War* (Millwood, N.Y., 1977), pp. 58–66.

Anderson, Charles W. "After the Fall of Fort Donelson." *Confederate Veteran*, vol. 4 (September 1896), pp. 289–90.

Bailey, Hugh C., ed. "An Alabamian at Shiloh: The Diary of Liberty Independence Nixon." *Alabama Review*, vol. 11 (April 1958), pp. 144–55.

Bakewell, Gordon. "Orderly That Was of the Fifth Company Washington Artillery—Shiloh!" *Illinois Central Magazine*, October 1915, pp. 18–20.

Bassham, Ben. " 'Through a Mist of Powder and Excitement': A Southern Artist at Shiloh." *Tennessee Historical Quarterly*, vol. XLVII (Fall 1988), pp. 131–41.

Bauer, Dan. "The Big Bender." *Civil War Times Illustrated*, vol. 27 (December 1988), pp. 34–43.

Baylor, George W. "With Gen. A. S. Johnston at Shiloh." *Confederate Veteran*, vol. 5 (1897), pp. 609–13.

Bearss, Edwin C. "A Federal Raid up the Tennessee River." *Alabama Review*, vol. 17 (October 1964), pp. 261–70.

Beauregard, P. G. T. "The Campaign of Shiloh." In *Battles and Leaders of the Civil War.* Vol. 1. Ed. Robert C. Johnson and Clarence C. Buel (1887–88). New York, 1956. Pp. 569–93.

―――. "Notes on E. A. Pollard's 'Lost Cause.' " *The Southern Magazine*, vol. 10 (January 1872), pp. 55–64.

―――. "The Shiloh Campaign." *North American Review*, vol. 142 (1886), pp. 1–24, 159–84.

Beckley, Michael. "Buckland's Brigade at Shiloh." *National Tribune*, November 30, 1922.

Beitzinger, A. J. "The Father of Copperheadism in Wisconsin." *Wisconsin Magazine of History*, vol. 39 (Autumn 1955), pp. 17–25.

Bell, T. H. "Rhea Field." *Sons of the South*, vol. 3 (April 1986), pp. 8–13.

Biel, John G., ed. "The Battle of Shiloh: From the Letters and Diary of Joseph Dimmit Thompson." *Tennessee Historical Quarterly*, vol. 17 (September 1958), pp. 250–74.

Blackburn, J. "Reminiscences of the Terry Texas Rangers." *Southwestern Historical Quarterly*, vol. 22 (July 1918), pp. 38–77.

Bledsoe, S. N. "Fifteen Soldiers in One Family." *Confederate Veteran*, vol. 3 (October 1910), p. 471.

Bock, H. Riley. "Confederate Col. A. C. Riley, His Reports and Letters." *Missouri Historical Quarterly*, vol. LXXXV (January 1991), pp. 158–81.

———, ed. "One Year at War: Letters of Capt. Geo. W. Dawson, C.S.A." *Missouri Historical Review*, vol. LXXI (January 1979), pp. 165–97.

Boos, J. E., ed. "Civil War Diary of Patrick White." *Journal of the Illinois State Historical Society*, vol. XV (1923), pp. 640–63.

Boyce, Joseph. "The Evacuation of Nashville." *Confederate Veteran*, vol. 28 (February 1920), pp. 60–62.

———. "The Second Day at Shiloh." *St. Louis Republican*, May 3, 1884.

Broome, John P. "How Gen. A. S. Johnston Died." *Confederate Veteran*, vol. 16 (December 1908), p. 629.

Buell, Don Carlos. "Shiloh Reviewed." *Battles and Leaders of the Civil War.* Vol. 1. Ed. Robert C. Johnson and Clarence C. Buel (1887–88). New York, 1956. Pp. 487–536.

Cable, George W. "New Orleans Before the Capture." In *Battles and Leaders of the Civil War.* Vol. 2. Ed. Robert C. Johnson and Clarence C. Buel (1887–88). New York, 1956. Pp. 14–21.

"Caddo Fencibles of Louisiana." *Confederate Veteran*, vol. 9 (August 1901), pp. 498–500.

Capron, Thaddeus H. "War Diary of Thaddeus H. Capron, 1861–1865." *Illinois State Historical Society*, vol. XII (October 1919), pp. 330–406.

Carman, Henry, ed. "Diary of Amos Glover." *The Ohio State Archeological and Historical Quarterly*, vol. XLIV (April 1935), pp. 258–72.

Carothers, J. S. "Forty-Five Mississippi Regiment." *Confederate Veteran*, vol. 6 (April 1898), p. 175.

Carruth, E. B. "Disagreeable Experiences in War Times." *Confederate Veteran*, vol. 16 (August 1908), p. 408.

Castel, Albert. "The Historian and the General: Thomas L. Connelly Versus Robert E. Lee." *Civil War History*, vol. XVI (1970), pp. 50–63.

———, ed. "The War Diary of Henry Dwight." *Civil War Times Illustrated*, vol. XIX (1980), pp. 32–36.

———. "The War Moves West." *Shadows of the Storm.* Garden City, N.Y., 1981, pp. 264–78.

Chalmers, James R. "Forrest and His Campaigns." *Southern Historical Society Papers*, vol. VII (October 1879), pp. 451–58.

Cherry, Annie. "Gen. Grant at Shiloh." *Confederate Veteran*, vol. 1 (February 1893), p. 44.

Chisolm, Alexander R. "Gen. Beauregard at Shiloh." *Confederate Veteran*, vol. 10 (May 1902), pp. 212–13.

———. "The Shiloh Battle Order and the Withdrawal Sunday Evening." In *Battle and Leaders of the Civil War.* Vol. 1. Ed. Robert C. Johnson and Clarence C. Buel (1887–88). New York, 1956. P. 606.

Clark, Robert, Jr. "The New Orleans German Colony in the Civil War." *Louisiana Historical Quarterly*, vol. XX (October 1937), pp. 990–1015.

Clark, Sam L., and H. D. Ridley, eds. "Outline of the Organization of the Medical Department of the Confederate Army and Department of Tennessee by Samuel H. Stout." *Tennessee Historical Quarterly*, vol. XVI (Spring 1957), pp. 55–82.

"Cobb's Battery Not Captured at Shiloh." *Confederate Veteran*, vol. 13 (February 1905), p. 68.

Cockerill, John A. "A Boy at Shiloh." In *Under Both Flags*. Philadelphia, 1896. Pp. 363–76.

"Col. M. M. Duffie." *Confederate Veteran*, vol. 15 (February 1907), p. 87.

Cooper, William W., and Donald M. Fowler, eds. " 'Your Affectionate Husband': Letter From a Catahoula Parish Confederate Soldier, September 1861–May 1862." *North Louisiana Historical Association Journal*, vol. XIV (1983), pp. 21–40.

Cotes, J. W. "The Iowa Brigade on Shiloh's Field." *National Tribune*, December 28, 1893.

Cox, T. B. "Sixth Mississippi Regiment at Shiloh." *Confederate Veteran*, vol. 18 (November 1910), p. 509.

Crooker, Lucian B. "A Section of Battle: Observations upon the Conduct of the 55th Illinois Infantry in the First Day's Battle of Shiloh." By author, 1884.

Daggett, George H. "Thrilling Moments." *Military Order of the Loyal Union of the United States*. Minnesota Commandery, 1903. Pp. 440–80.

Daniel, Larry J. " 'The Assaults of the Demagogues in Congress': General Albert Sidney Johnston and the Politics of Command." *Civil War History*, vol. 37 (1991), pp. 328–35.

Dawes, Ephraim C. "The Battle of Shiloh." In *Campaigns in Kentucky and Tennessee, Including the Battle of Chickamauga, 1862–1864*. Boston, 1908. Pp. 103–71.

Day, James G. "The Fifteenth Iowa at Shiloh." In *War Papers Read Before the Iowa Commandery, Military Order of the Loyal Legion of the United States*. Des Moines, 1898. Pp. 173–87.

DeHaas, Wills. "The Battle of Shiloh." In *The Annals of War*. Dayton, 1988. Pp. 677–93.

Deupree, J. G. "Reminiscences of Service with the First Mississippi Cavalry." *Publication of the Mississippi Historical Society*, vol. 3 (1903), pp. 85–100.

Dillard, H. M. "Beauregard-Johnston-Shiloh." *Confederate Veteran*, vol. 5 (March 1897), pp. 99–100.

Dillon, Rodney E., Jr. "Don Carlos Buell and the Union Leadership." *Lincoln Herald*, vol. 82 (1980), pp. 363–73.

Dinkins, James. "The Battle of Shiloh." *Southern Historical Society Papers*, vol. 31 (1903), pp. 298–320.

Dosch, Donald F. "The Hornet's Nest at Shiloh." *Tennessee Historical Quarterly*, vol. XXXVII (1978), pp. 175–89.

Ecelbarger, Gary L., ed. "Shiloh." *Civil War Times Illustrated*, April 1995, pp. 50, 66–69.

Eisenschiml, Otto. "The 55th Illinois at Shiloh." *Journal of the Illinois State Historical Society*, vol. LVI (1963), pp. 193-211.

Ellis, W. B. "Who Lost Shiloh to the Confederacy?" *Confederate Veteran*, vol. XXII (July 1914), pp. 313–14.

Engle, Stephen D. "Don Carlos Buell: Military Philosophy and Command Problems in the West." *Civil War History*, vol. 41 (1995), pp. 89–115.

Engurud, H. "General Grant, Fort Donelson and 'Old Brains.' " *Filson Club Historical Quarterly*, vol. 39 (July 1965), pp. 201–15.

"Famous Horses of the Confederate Army." *Confederate Veteran*, vol. 33 (November 1925), p. 438.

Fearing, B. D. "The 77th Ohio Volunteer Regiment at Shiloh." *The College Olio*, vol. XIII (1885), pp. 49–52.

"Federal Veterans at Shiloh." *Confederate Veteran*, vol. 3 (April 1895), pp. 104–5.

"First Reunion of Iowa's Hornet's Nest Brigade. Held at Des Moines, Iowa, Wednesday and Thursday, October 12 and 13, 1887."

Fleming, Robert H. "The Battle of Shiloh as a Private Saw It." *Military Order of the Loyal Legion of the United States, Ohio Commandery*, vol. 6 (1908), pp. 132–46.

————. "The Boys of Ohio Held Fast at Shiloh." *National Tribune*, June 6, 1925.

Frederick, J. V. "War Diary of W. C. Porter." *Arkansas Historical Quarterly*, vol. XI (Winter 1952), pp. 286–314.

Fussell, Joseph H. "Narrative of Interesting Events Just Prior to Battle of Shiloh." *Historic Maury*, vol. XVIII (1982), pp. 62–65.

Gonzales, John E. "Henry Stuart Foote: Confederate Congressman in Exile." *Civil War History*, vol. 11 (December 1965), pp. 384–95.

Gow, June I. "Military Administration in the Confederate Army of Tennessee." *Journal of Southern History*, vol. XL (1974), pp. 183–98.

Hadley, Charles W. "The Hornet's Nest." *National Tribune*, April 11, 1935.

Haskell, Fritz, ed. "Diary of Colonel William Camm, 1861–1865." *Journal of the Illinois State Historical Society*, vol. 18 (January 1926), pp. 793–861.

Haydon, Dudley M. "Shiloh." *Memphis Appeal*, April 12, 1885.

Hays, John Bowan. "An Incident at the Battle of Shiloh." *Tennessee Historical Magazine*, vol. IX (October 1925), pp. 264–65.

Heath, William H. "Hours with Grant." *National Tribune*, June 29, 1916.

Hickenlooper, Andrew. "The Battle of Shiloh." Cincinnati, 1903.

"Hillyer on Grant at Shiloh." *Confederate Veteran*, vol. 1 (October 1893), pp. 298–99.

Hobbler, James, ed. "The Diary of Louisa Brown Pearl." *Tennessee Historical Quarterly*, vol. XXXVIII (Fall 1979), pp. 308–21.

Holman, T. W. "The Battle of Shiloh." *National Tribune*, January 31, 1901.

————. "The Story of Shiloh." *National Tribune*, September 14, 1899.

Hoover, Samuel. "Waterhouse's Battery at Shiloh." *National Tribune*, September 10, 1925.

Horsley, A. S. "Reminiscences of Shiloh." *Confederate Veteran*, vol. 2 (August 1894), p. 234.

Hosea, Lewis M. "The Second Day at Shiloh." *Sketches of War History 1861–1865: Papers Prepared For the Commandery of the State of Ohio, Military Order of the Loyal Legion of the United States*, vol. 6 (1908), pp. 195–218.

Houghton, Edgar. "History of Company I, Fourteenth Wisconsin Infantry, from October 15, 1861 to October 9, 1865." *Wisconsin Magazine of History*, vol. XI (September 1927), pp. 26–49.

Houghton, Larry R. "Captured at Shiloh." *Michigan History* (March–April 1993), pp. 34–41.

Houston, Sam Jr. "Shiloh Shadows." *Southwestern Historical Quarterly*, vol. XXXIV (July 1930), pp. 329–33.

Hubbard, Paul, and Christine Lewis, eds. " 'Give Yourself No Trouble About Me': The Shiloh Letters of George W. Lennard." *Indiana Magazine of History*, vol. LXXVI (March 1980), pp. 21–53.

Hurst, Tim. "The Battle of Shiloh." *Tennessee History Magazine*, vol. V (July 1919), pp. 81–96.

Hurter, Henry S. "Narrative of the First Battery of Light Artillery." *Minnesota in the Civil and Indian Wars, 1861–1865*. Vol. 1, pp. 640–44; vol. 2, pp. 91–96.

Jackson, W. W. "The Battle of Shiloh." *National Tribune*, December 24, 1885.

Jamborsky, William E. "Confederate Leadership and Defeat in the West." *Lincoln Herald*, vol. 86 (Summer 1984), pp. 50–76.

"John Dimitry." *Confederate Veteran*, vol. 11 (February 1903), pp. 72–73.

Johnston, William Preston. "Albert Sidney Johnston at Shiloh." In *Battles and Leaders of the Civil War*. Vol. 1. Ed. Robert C. Johnson and Clarence C. Buel (1887–88). New York, 1956. Pp. 540–68.

Johnstone, Alexander S. "Scenes at Shiloh." In *Camp-Fire Sketches and Battle-Field Echoes.* Eds. W. C. King and W. P. Derby. Cleveland, 1888. Pp. 49–51.

Jones, D. Lloyd. "The Battle of Shiloh: Reminiscences by D. Lloyd Jones." *Military Order of the Loyal Legion of the United States, Wisconsin Commandery,* vol. 4, pp. 51–60.

Jordan, Thomas. "The Battle of Shiloh." *Southern Historical Society Papers,* vol. XVI (1888), pp. 297–318; vol. XXXV (1907), pp. 204–30.

———. "Notes of a Confederate Staff Officer at Shiloh." *Battles and Leaders of the Civil War.* Vol. 1. Ed. Robert C. Johnson and Clarence C. Buel (1887–88). New York, 1956. Pp. 594–603.

———. "Recollections of General Beauregard's Service in West Tennessee in the Spring of 1862." *Southern Historical Society Papers,* vol. VIII (1880), pp. 404–17.

Jorgensen, Jay A. "Scouting for Ulysses S. Grant: The 5th Ohio Cavalry in the Shiloh Campaign." *Journal of the American Civil War,* vol. 4 (1995), pp. 44–77.

"Journal of a Trip to Pittsburg Landing to Assist in the Care of Sick and Wounded Soldiers." *The Historiographer of the Episcopal Dioceses of Connecticut,* 1975, no. 21, pp. 17–18.

Kelly, Dennis. "Back in the Saddle." *Civil War Times Illustrated,* vol. 27 (December 1988), pp. 27–31.

Kelsey, Jasper. "The Battle of Shiloh." *Confederate Veteran,* vol. XXV (February 1917), pp. 71–74.

Kendall, John Smith. "Recollections of a Confederate Staff Officer." *Louisiana Historical Quarterly,* vol. XXIX (October 1946), pp. 1041–71.

Kuhl, C. A. "Pittsburg Landing." *National Tribune,* May 3, 1883.

"The Last Roll." *Confederate Veteran,* vol. 6 (April 1898), p. 181.

Lathrop, Barnes F. "A Confederate Artilleryman at Shiloh." *Civil War History,* vol. 8 (December 1962), pp. 373–85.

Law, J. G. "Diary of J. G. Law." *Southern Historical Society Papers,* vol. 10 (April–May 1883), pp. 297–303; vol. 10 (October 1883), pp. 460–65.

Lawrence, Elijah C. "Stuart's Brigade at Shiloh." *Military Order of the Loyal Legion of the United States, Massachusetts Commandery,* vol. 2 (1900), pp. 489–96.

Lockett, Samuel H. "Surprise and Withdrawal at Shiloh." In *Battles and Leaders of the Civil War.* Vol. 1. Ed. Robert C. Johnson and Clarence C. Buel (1887–88). New York, 1956. Pp. 604–606.

Longacre, Edward G. "Congressman Becomes General." *Civil War Times Illustrated,* vol. 21 (November 1982), pp. 30–36.

McBride, George W. "My Recollections at Shiloh." In *Under Both Flags.* Ed. C. R. Graham. Philadelphia, 1896. Pp. 346–50.

McClure, W. H. "The 71st Ohio at Shiloh." *National Tribune,* June 6, 1907.

McCook, D. "The Second Day at Shiloh." *Harper's New Monthly Magazine,* vol. XXVIII (1863–64), pp. 828–33.

McCormick, Andrew W. "Sixteen Months a Prisoner of War." *Military Order of the Loyal Legion of the United States, Ohio Commandery,* vol. 5 (1903), pp. 69–87.

McCormick, Robert W. "Challenge of Command: Worthington vs. Sherman," vol. 8 (1991), pp. 28–39.

McDonough, James L. "Bayonets and Blunders: Confederate Tactics Against the Hornet's Nest." *West Tennessee Historical Society Papers,* vol. XXXII (October 1978), pp. 5–19.

McGinnis, George F. "Shiloh." *War Papers Read Before the Indiana Commandery, Military Order of the Loyal Legion of the United States,* 1898, pp. 1–41.

McGrath, John. "In a Louisiana Regiment." *Southern Historical Society Papers,* vol. XXXI (1903), pp. 103–20.

McMurty, R. Gerald. "Zollicoffer and the Battle of Mill Springs." *Filson Club Historical Quarterly,* vol. 29 (October 1955), pp. 303–19.

McWhiney, Grady. "General Beauregard's 'Complete Victory' at Shiloh: An Interpretation." *Journal of Southern History*, vol. XLIX (August 1983), pp. 421–34.

Magee, John A. Diary. *Philadelphia Inquirer*, April 18, 1862.

Mahon, John, ed. "The Civil War Letters of Samuel Mahon, Seventh Iowa Infantry." *Iowa Journal of History*, vol. LI (July 1953), pp. 233–40.

"Maj. John H. Kelly." *Alabama Historical Quarterly*, vol. IX (1947), pp. 9–114.

"The March of Lew Wallace's Division to Shiloh." In *Battles and Leaders of the Civil War*. Vol. 1. Ed. Robert C. Johnson and Clarence C. Buel (1887–88). New York, 1956. Pp. 607–10.

Marszalek, John F. "William T. Sherman and the Verbal Battle of Shiloh." *Northwest Ohio Quarterly*, vol. 42 (Fall 1970), pp. 78–85.

Mason, George. "Shiloh." *Military Essays and Recollections: Papers Read Before the Commandery of the State of Illinois, Military Order of the Loyal Legion of the United States*. Chicago, vol. 1 (1891), pp. 98–101.

Meadows, A. J. "The Fourth Tennessee Infantry." *Confederate Veteran*, vol. 14 (July 1906), p. 312.

"Memorial to Louisianians at Shiloh." *Confederate Veteran*, vol. 22 (August 1914), pp. 342–43.

Merrill, James M., ed. " 'Nothing to Eat But Raw Bacon': Letters from a War Correspondent, 1862." *Tennessee Historical Quarterly*, vol. XVII (June 1958), pp. 141–55.

Mills, George, ed. "The Sharp Family Civil War Letters." *Annals of Iowa*, vol. XXXIV (January 1959), pp. 481–532.

Moore, John C. "Shiloh Issues Again." *Confederate Veteran*, vol. X (July 1902), pp. 316–17.

Moore, Marquerites. "A Study of Early Crump, Tennessee." *Hardin County Historical Quarterly*, vol. IX (January–June 1992), pp. 28–37.

Morton, Charles A. "A Boy at Shiloh." *Military Order of the Loyal Legion of the United States, New York Commandery*, 1907, pp. 52–69.

———. "Opening of the Battle of Shiloh." *Military Order of the Loyal Legion of the United States, Commandery of the District of Columbia*, 1912, pp. 11–20.

Mott, Charles, Jr. "War Journal of Confederate Staff Officer Charles R. Mott, Jr." *Tennessee Historical Quarterly*, vol. V (September 1946), pp. 234–48.

"Mrs. Annie Irwin Cherry." *Confederate Veteran*, vol. 9 (1901), p. 33.

"Ninth Reunion of Iowa's Hornet's Nest Brigade, Held at Pittsburg Landing, April 6 and 7, 1912." Des Moines, 1912.

Olney, Warren. " 'Shiloh': As Seen by a Private Soldier." *A Paper Read Before California Commandery of the Military Order of the Loyal Legion of the United States*, 1889, pp. 3–26.

"The Only Confederate Re-Enforcements at Shiloh." *Sons of the South*, vol. 3 (April 1986), pp. 22–25.

Otis, Ephraim A. "The Second Day at Shiloh." In *Campaigns in Kentucky and Tennessee, Including the Battle of Chickamauga, 1862–1864*. Boston, 1908. Pp. 177–202.

Pace, Eleanor D., ed. "The Diary and Letters of William P. Rogers, 1846–1862." *Southwestern Historical Quarterly*, vol. 32 (April 1929), pp. 259–99.

Palmer, David. "Recollections of War Times." *Annals of Iowa*, vol. IX (April 1909), pp. 134–41.

Palmer, J. R. "No Surprise at Shiloh." *National Tribune*, June 28, 1894.

Parks, Ed Winfield. "Zollicoffer: Southern Whig." *Tennessee Historical Quarterly*, vol. XI (December 1952), pp. 346–55.

Peeples, T. H. "From a Participant in Battle of Shiloh." *Confederate Veteran*, vol. 16 (June 1908), p. 281.

Philippe, Comte de Paris. "McClellan Organizing the Grand Army." In *Battles and Leaders of the Civil War*. Vol. 2. Ed. Robert C. Johnson and Clarence C. Buel (1887–88). New York, 1956. Pp. 112–22.

Pippen, W. B. "Concerning Battle of Shiloh." *Confederate Veteran*, vol. 16 (July 1908), p. 344.

Polk, William M. "Facts Connected with the Concentration of the Army of the Mississippi Before Shiloh, April, 1862." *Southern Historical Society Papers*, vol. VIII (1880), pp. 457–63.

Powers, John M. "That Terrible First Day." *Military History*, October 1984, pp. 39–43.

"Proceedings of the First Congress." *Southern Historical Society Papers*, vol. 44 (June 1923), pp. 5–205.

Putnam, Douglas, Jr. "Reminiscences of the Battle of Shiloh." *Sketches of War History, 1861–1865: Military Order of the Loyal Legion of the United States, Ohio Commandery*, vol. 3 (1890), pp. 197–211.

Rich, Joseph W. "General Lew Wallace at Shiloh: How He Was Convinced of an Error after 45 Years." *Iowa Journal of History and Politics*, vol. 18 (April 1920), pp. 302–8.

Richardson, Frank L. "War As I Saw It." *Louisiana Historical Quarterly*, vol. 6 (1923), pp. 89–106.

"R. L. Davis Letters." *Sons of the South*, vol. 3 (April 1986), pp. 34–40.

Rogers, Margaret Greene. "Corinth, 1861–1865." In *"Historic Corinth Mississippi"* brochure in NEMMA.

Ruff, Joseph R. "Civil War Experiences of a German Emigrant As Told by the Late Joseph Ruff of Albion." *Michigan History Magazine*, vol. XXVII (1943), pp. 271–301.

"Samuel Eddy Barrett." *Military Order of the Loyal Legion of the United States, Illinois Commandery*, vol. 13D (1923), pp. 91–94.

Sawyer, B. F. "Battle Scenes at Shiloh." *Camp Sketches and Battle-Field Echoes*. Cleveland, 1888. Pp. 52–55.

Searle, Charles V. "Personal Reminiscences of Shiloh." *War Papers Read Before the Iowa Commandery, Military Order of the Loyal Legion of the United States*, vol. 1 (1893), pp. 326–39.

Sehlinger, Peter J. " 'At the Moment of Victory . . . ': The Battle of Shiloh and General A. S. Johnston's Death As Recounted in William Preston's Diary." *Filson Club*, vol. LXI (July 1987), pp. 315–45.

Shaw, William T. "The Battle of Shiloh." *War Papers Read Before the Iowa Commandery, Military Order of the Loyal Legion of the United States*, vol. 1 (1893), pp. 183–207.

Shelton, Samuel R. Diary. *Commercial Appeal*, April 9, 1962.

"The Shiloh Campaign." *National Tribune*, April 17, 1884.

Shoup, F. A. "The Art of War in '62—Shiloh." *The United Service: A Monthly Review of Military and Naval Affairs*, vol. XI (July 1884), pp. 1–13.

———. "How We Went to Shiloh." *Confederate Veteran*, vol. 2 (1894), pp. 137–40.

Skidmore, Richard S. "Lew Wallace and the Old Wound of Shiloh." *North South Trader*, vol. 9 (July–August 1982), pp. 10–14, 34.

Smith, Jacob H. "Personal Reminiscences—Battle of Shiloh." *War Papers, Michigan Commandery, Military Order of the Loyal Legion of the United States*, 1894, pp. 8–15.

Stephenson, W. H., and E. A. Davis, eds. "The Civil War Diary of Willie Micajah Barrow, September 23, 1861–July 13, 1862." *Louisiana Historical Quarterly*, vol. XVII (1934), pp. 436–51, 712–31.

Stewart, James E. "Fighting Them Over." *National Tribune*, February 19, 1885.

Stillwell, Leander. "In the Ranks at Shiloh." *Military Order of the Loyal Legion of the United States, Kansas Commandery*, Kansas City, Mo., 1906, pp. 110–26.

Stone, Henry. "The Battle of Shiloh." In *Campaigns in Kentucky and Tennessee, Including the Battle of Chickamauga, 1862–1864*. Boston, 1908. Pp. 32–99.

Taylor, John T. "Reminiscences of Services as an Aide-de-Camp with General William Tecumseh Sherman." *War Papers, Kansas Commandery, Military Order of the Loyal Legion of the United States*, Kansas City, Mo., 1892, pp. 127–42.

Taylor, Rosser H., ed. "Boyce-Hammond Correspondence." *Journal of Southern History*, vol. III (August 1937), pp. 348–54.

Terry, James G., ed. "Record of the Alabama State Artillery from Its Organization in May 1836 to the Surrender in April 1865." *Alabama Historical Quarterly*, vol. XX (Summer 1958), pp. 141–446.

"Third Reunion Iowa Brigade: Held at Newton, Iowa, Wednesday and Thursday, August 21 and 22, 1895."

Thomas, Benjamin F. "Off to War." *The Palimpsest*, vol. XXII (June 1941), pp. 161–77.

Thompson, William C. "From Shiloh to Port Gibson." *Civil War Times Illustrated*, vol. III (October 1964), pp. 20–25.

Throne, Mildred, ed. "Erastus B. Sopher's History of Company D, 12th Iowa Infantry, 1861–1865." *Iowa Journal of History*, vol. LVI (April 1958), pp. 153–87.

————, ed. "Iowa and the Battle of Shiloh." *Iowa Journal of History*, vol. LV (July 1957), pp. 209–74.

————, ed. "Letters from Shiloh." *Iowa Journal of History*, vol. LII (July 1954), pp. 235–80.

Trudeau, Noah A. "Fields Without Honor: Two Affairs in Tennessee." *Civil War Times Illustrated*, vol. 32 (August 1992), pp. 42–49, 57.

Ulmer, J. B. "A Glimpse of Albert Sidney Johnston Through the Smoke of Shiloh." *The Quarterly of the Texas State Historical Association*, vol. X (April 1907), pp. 285–96.

Veach, James C. "The Battle of Shiloh." *National Tribune*, March 15, 1883.

Walker, Alexander. "Narrative of the Battle of Shiloh." In *Diary of the War for Separation*. Vicksburg, 1905. Pp. 114–60.

Walker, Peter Franklin. "Command Failure: The Fall of Forts Henry and Donelson." *Tennessee Historical Quarterly*, vol. XVI (March–December 1957), pp. 335–60.

Wallace, Harold Lew. "Lew Wallace's March to Shiloh Revisited." *Indiana Magazine of History*, vol. LIX (March 1963), pp. 19–30.

West, James D. "The Thirteenth Tennessee Regiment—Confederate States of America." *Tennessee Historical Magazine*, vol. VII (October 1921), pp. 180–93.

"What He Saw at Shiloh." *National Tribune*, March 7, 1912.

Wheeler, J. A. "Cleburne's Brigade at Shiloh." *Confederate Veteran*, vol. 2 (January 1894), p. 13.

Wheeler, Joseph. "The Battle of Shiloh." *Southern Historical Society Papers*, vol. XXIV (1896), pp. 119–31.

"W.H.S." *Confederate Veteran*, vol. 3 (November 1895), p. 332.

Wickham, Lee. "Maj. Wickham's Account of It." *Confederate Veteran*, vol. 6 (July 1898), p. 314.

Wyeth, John A. "Appearances and Characteristics of Forrest." *Confederate Veteran*, vol. 4 (February 1896), pp. 41–42.

Yantis, Isaac. "The 41st Illinois at Shiloh." *National Tribune*, August 22, 1907.

Zearing, James R. "Letters Written by Dr. James R. Zearing to His Wife Lucinda Helmer Zearing During the Civil War, 1861–1865." *Transactions of the Illinois State Historical Society*, vol. XXVIII (1921), pp. 150–58.

Books

Abernathy, Alonzo. *Dedication of Monuments Erected by the State of Iowa*. Des Moines, 1908.

Abernathy, Bryon R., ed. *Private Elisha Stockwell, Jr. Sees the Civil War*. Norman, Okla., 1958.

Adams, Ephraim D. *Great Britain and the American Civil War*. 2 vols. New York, 1924.

Adjutant General's Report, Illinois. Vols. 1, 3, 4. Springfield, 1901.

Albaugh, William A., and Edward N. Simmons. *Confederate Arms.* Harrisburg, Pa., 1957.

Ambrose, Stephen E. *Halleck: Lincoln's Chief of Staff.* Baton Rouge, 1962.

——, ed. *A Wisconsin Boy in Dixie.* Madison, 1961.

Anders, Leslie. *The Eighteenth Missouri.* Indianapolis, 1968.

——. *The Twenty-First Missouri: From Home Guard to Union Regiment.* Westport, Conn., 1975.

Anderson, Ephraim McD. *Memoirs: Historical and Personal; Including the Campaigns of the First Missouri Confederate Brigade.* St. Louis, 1868.

Anderson, Mary Ann, ed. *The Civil War Diary of Allen Morgan Geer, Twentieth Regiment, Illinois Volunteers.* New York, 1977.

Andrews, J. Cutler. *The North Reports the Civil War.* Pittsburgh, 1985.

——. *The South Reports the Civil War.* Pittsburgh, 1985.

Angle, Paul M., and Earl S. Miers. *Tragic Years 1860–1865: A Documentary History of the American Civil War.* New York, 1992.

Arceneaux, William. *Acadian General: Alfred Mouton and the Civil War.* Lafayette, La., 1981.

Avery, P. O. *The Fourth Illinois Cavalry Regiment.* Humboldt, Neb., 1903.

Badeau, Adam. *Military History of Ulysses S. Grant, from April, 1861 to April, 1865.* New York, 1881.

Baird, Nancy D. *David Wendall Yandell: Physician of Old Louisville.* Lexington, 1978.

Barber, Lucius. *Army Memoirs of Lucius W. Barber, Company D, 15th Illinois Infantry.* Chicago, 1894.

Basso, Hamilton. *Beauregard: The Great Creole.* New York, 1933.

Baumann, Ken. *Arming the Suckers, 1861–1865: A Compilation of Illinois Civil War Weapons.* Dayton, 1989.

Baxter, Maurice G. *Orville H. Browning: Lincoln's Friend and Critic.* Bloomington, 1957.

Beale, Howard, ed. *The Diary of Edward Bates, 1859–1866.* Washington, 1933.

Bearss, Edwin C., ed. *The Story of the Fifty-Fifth Regiment, Illinois Volunteer Infantry, in the Civil War.* Huntington, W. Va., 1993.

Beatty, John. *The Citizen-Soldier; Or, Memoirs of a Volunteer.* Cincinnati, 1879.

Belknap, William W. *History of the 15th Regiment Iowa Veteran Volunteer Infantry from October, 1861, to August, 1885.* Keokuk, 1887.

Bell, John. *Tramps and Triumphs of the Second Iowa Infantry.* Des Moines, 1961.

Bergeron, Arthur W., Jr., ed. *The Civil War Reminiscences of Major Silas T. Grisamore, C.S.A.* Baton Rouge, 1993.

——, ed. *Guide to Louisiana Confederate Military Units.* Baton Rouge, 1989.

Bering, John A., and Thomas Montgomery. *History of the 48th Ohio Volunteer Infantry.* Hillsboro, Ohio, 1880.

Beringer, Richard E., Herman Hattaway, Archer Jones, and William N. Still, Jr. *Why the South Lost the Civil War.* Athens, Ga., 1986.

Bevins, W. E. *Reminiscences of a Private, Company "G" First Arkansas Infantry.* Newport, Ark., 1913.

Black, Robert C. *Railroads of the Confederacy.* Chapel Hill, 1952.

Blaine, James G. *Twenty Years of Congress: From Lincoln to Garfield.* Vol. 1. Norwich, Conn., 1884.

Blanchard, Ira. *I Marched With Sherman: Civil War Memoirs of the 20th Illinois Volunteer Infantry.* San Francisco, 1992.

Boatner, Mark M. *Civil War Dictionary.* New York, 1991.

Bouton, Edward. *Events of the Civil War.* Los Angeles, 1906.

Brazleton, B. G. *A History of Hardin County, Tennessee.* Nashville, 1885.

Briant, C. C. *History of the 67th Regiment Indiana Volunteer Infantry.* Indianapolis, 1891.

Brinton, John. *Personal Memoirs of John H. Brinton.* New York, 1914.

Brown, Dee Alexander. *The Bold Cavaliers: Morgan's 2nd Kentucky Cavalry Raiders.* Philadelphia, 1959.

Bryant, Thomas J. *Who Is Responsible for the Advance of the Army of the Tennessee Towards Corinth?* N.p., 1885.

Buell, Don Carlos. *Statement of Major General Buell in Review of the Evidence Before the Military Commission Appointed by the War Department in November 1862.* Cincinnati, 1863.

Burton, William L. *Melting Pot Soldiers: The Union's Ethnic Regiments.* Ames, Iowa, 1988.

Byers, S. H. M. *Iowa in War Times.* Des Moines, 1888.

Cain, Marvin R. *Lincoln's Attorney General: Edward Bates of Missouri.* Columbia, Mo., 1965.

Carter, Howell. *A Cavalryman's Reminiscences of the Civil War.* New Orleans, 1979.

Cassidy, Vincent. *Henry Watkins Allen of Louisiana.* Baton Rouge, 1964.

Castel, Albert. *Decision in the West: The Atlanta Campaign of 1864.* Lawrence, Kan., 1992.

Catton, Bruce. *Grant Moves South.* Boston, 1960.

Chamberlain, Dick and Judy. *Civil War Letters of an Ohio Soldier: S. O. Chamberlain and the 49th Ohio Volunteer Infantry.* Flournoy, Calif., 1990.

Chamberlain, W. H. *History of the Eighty-First Regiment, Ohio Infantry Volunteers, During the War of the Rebellion.* Cincinnati, 1865.

Chetlain, Augustus. *Recollections of Seventy Years.* Galena, 1899.

Civil War Centennial Commission. *Tennesseans in the Civil War: A Military History of Confederate and Union Units with Available Rosters of Personnel.* Vol. 1. Nashville, 1964.

Clark, Charles B., and Roger B. Bowen. *University Recruits—Company C, 12th Iowa Infantry Regiment, U.S.A., 1861–1866.* Elverson, Pa., 1991.

Clark, Olynthus B., ed. *Downing's Civil War Diary.* Des Moines, 1916.

Cleaves, Freeman. *Rock of Chickamauga—The Life of General George H. Thomas.* Norman, Okla., 1948.

Cluett, William W. *History of the 57th Regiment Illinois Volunteer Infantry.* Princeton, N.J., 1886.

Connelly, Thomas L. *Army of the Heartland: The Army of Tennessee, 1861–1862.* Baton Rouge, 1967.

———. *Civil War Tennessee: Battles and Leaders.* Knoxville, 1979.

——— and Archer Jones. *The Politics of Command: Factions and Ideas in Confederate Strategy.* Baton Rouge, 1973.

Connelly, T. W. *History of the Seventieth Ohio Regiment, from Its Organization to Its Mustering Out.* Cincinnati, 1902.

Coolidge, Louis A. *Ulysses S. Grant.* Boston, 1972.

Cooling, Benjamin F. *Forts Henry and Donelson: The Key to the Confederate Heartland.* Knoxville, 1987.

Coons, John W. *Indiana at Shiloh.* N.p., 1904.

Crist, Linda L., ed. *The Papers of Jefferson Davis.* Vol. 7. Baton Rouge, 1992.

Crozier, Emmet. *Yankee Reporters, 1861–1865.* New York, 1956.

Crummer, Wilbur. *With Grant at Fort Donelson, Shiloh, and Vicksburg.* Oak Park, Ill., 1915.

Curry, W. L. *Four Years in the Saddle: History of the First Regiment Ohio Volunteer Cavalry.* Columbus, 1898.

Dana, Charles A. *The Life of Ulysses S. Grant, General of the Armies of the United States.* Chicago, 1868.

———. *Recollections of the Civil War.* New York, 1963.

Daniel, Larry J. *Cannoneers in Gray: The Field Artillery of the Army of Tennessee.* Tuscaloosa, 1984.

———. *Soldiering in the Army of Tennessee.* Chapel Hill, 1992.

——— and Riley Gunter. *Confederate Cannon Foundries.* Union City, Tenn., 1977.

Davis, Jefferson. *The Rise and Fall of the Confederate Government.* 2 vols. New York, 1881.

Davis, Varina H. *Jefferson Davis, Ex-President of the Confederate States of America: A Memoir by His Wife.* New York, 1890.

Davis, William C. *Breckinridge: Statesman, Soldier, Symbol.* Baton Rouge, 1974.

————, ed. *Diary of a Confederate Soldier: John S. Jackman of the Orphan Brigade.* Columbia, 1990.

————. *The Deep Waters of the Proud.* Garden City, N.Y., 1982.

————. *Jefferson Davis: The Man and His Hour.* New York, 1991.

————. *The Orphan Brigade: The Kentucky Confederates Who Couldn't Go Home.* New York, 1980.

Dennett, Tyler, ed. *Lincoln and the Civil War in the Diaries and Letters of John Hay.* New York, 1988.

Dufour, Charles. *The Night the War Was Lost.* Garden City, N.Y., 1960.

Duke, Basil W. *A History of Morgan's Cavalry.* New York, 1969.

Duke, John K. *History of the Fifty-Third Ohio Volunteer Infantry, During the War of the Rebellion.* Portsmouth, 1900.

Duncan, Thomas D. *Recollections of Thomas D. Duncan: A Confederate Soldier.* Nashville, 1922.

Dungan, James. *History of Hurlbut's Fighting Fourth Division.* Cincinnati, 1863.

Dunnavant, Robert, Jr. *Decatur, Alabama: Yankee Foothold in Dixie 1861–1865.* Athens, Ala., 1995.

Dupuy, R. Ernest, and Trevor N. Dupuy. *The Compact History of the Civil War.* New York, 1993.

Durham, Walter T. *Nashville: The Occupied City.* Nashville, 1985.

Dyer, John Will. *Reminiscences: Or Four Years in the Confederate Army, 1861 to 1865.* Evansville, Ind., 1898.

Eaton, Clement. *Jefferson Davis.* New York, 1977.

Eckenrode, H. J., and Bryan Conrad. *James Longstreet: Lee's War Horse.* Chapel Hill, 1936.

Eddy, T. M. *The Patriotism of Illinois.* 2 vols. Chicago, 1865.

Eisenschiml, Otto, and Ralph Newman. *The Civil War: The American Iliad As Told by Those Who Loved It.* New York, 1991.

Eisenschiml, Otto. *The Story of Shiloh.* Chicago, 1946.

Escott, Paul D. *After Secession: Jefferson Davis and the Failure of Confederate Nationalism.* Baton Rouge, 1978.

Faust, Patricia L., ed. *Historical Times Illustrated Encyclopedia of the Civil War.* New York, 1986.

Fisher, Horace C. *A Staff Officer's Story: The Personal Experiences of Colonel Horace Newton Fisher in the Civil War.* Boston, 1960.

Fitzhugh, Lester N., ed. *Cannon Smoke: The Letters of Captain John J. Good, Good-Douglas Texas Battery, CSA.* Hillsboro, Texas, 1971.

Fletcher, Samuel H. *The History of Company A, Second Illinois Cavalry.* N.p., 1912.

Flower, Frank A. *Edwin McMasters Stanton: The Autocrat of Rebellion, Emancipation, and Reconstruction.* Akron, 1905.

Folmar, John K., ed. *From That Terrible Field: Civil War Letters of James M. Williams, Twenty-First Alabama Volunteers.* Tuscaloosa, 1981.

Foote, Shelby. *The Civil War: A Narrative.* Vol. 1. New York, 1986.

Force, M. F. *From Fort Henry to Corinth.* New York, 1881.

Foster, John W. *War Stories for My Grandchildren.* Washington, D.C., 1918.

Frank, Joseph A., and George A. Reaves. *"Seeing the Elephant": Raw Recruits at the Battle of Shiloh.* Westport, Conn., 1989.

Fuller, J. F. C. *The Generalship of Ulysses S. Grant.* New York, 1958.

Garrett, Jill K., ed. *Confederate Diary of Robert D. Smith.* Columbia, Tenn., 1975.

Geer, John. *Beyond the Lines, or A Yankee Prisoner Loose in Dixie.* Philadelphia, 1863.

Genco, James G. *To the Sound of Musketry and Tap of the Drum.* Detroit, 1990.

George, Henry. *History of the 3d, 7th, 8th, and 12th Kentucky, C.S.A.* Louisville, 1911.

Glatthaar, Joseph T. *Partners in Command: The Relationship Between Leaders in the Civil War.* New York, 1994.

Goodspeed's History of Tennessee. Nashville, 1887.

Goodstein, Anita S. *Nashville, 1780–1860: From Frontier to City.* Gainesville, 1989.

Gorham, George C. *Life and Public Service of Edwin M. Stanton.* Vol. 1. Boston, 1899.

Grant, U. S. *Personal Memoirs of U. S. Grant.* New York, 1990.

The Grayjackets: and How They Lived, Fought and Died, for Dixie. Richmond, 1867.

Griess, Thomas E. *The American Civil War.* Wayne, N.J., 1987.

Grose, William. *The Story of the Marches, Battles, and Incidents of the 36th Indiana Volunteer Infantry.* New Castle, Ind., 1891.

Hagerman, Edward. *The American Civil War and the Origins of Modern Warfare.* Bloomington, 1988.

Hancock, John. *The Fourteenth Wisconsin: Corinth and Shiloh 1862–1895.* Indianapolis, 1895.

Hancock, R. R. *Hancock's Diary, or A History of the Second Tennessee Cavalry with Sketches of the First and Seventh Battalions.* Nashville, 1887.

Hannaford, Edwin. *The Story of a Regiment: A History of the Campaigns, and Associations in the Field, of the Sixth Regiment Ohio Volunteer Infantry.* Cincinnati, 1868.

Hanson, Joseph M. *The Conquest of Missouri.* Chicago, 1909.

Hart, Ephraim J. *History of the Fortieth Illinois Infantry.* Cincinnati, 1864.

Hartpence, William R. *History of the Fifty-First Indiana Veteran Volunteer Infantry.* Cincinnati, 1894.

Harvard Memorial Biographies. Vol. 1. Cambridge, Mass., 1867.

Harwell, Richard B., ed. *Kate: The Journal of a Confederate Nurse.* Baton Rouge, 1959.

———, ed. *The Union Reader.* Secaucus, N.J.

Hattaway, Herman, and Archer Jones. *How the North Won: A Military History of the Civil War.* Urbana, 1983.

Hays, Tony. *No Man's Land: The Civil War and Reconstruction in Hardin County.* Chattanooga, 1986.

Hazen, W. B. *A Narrative of Military Service.* Boston, 1895.

Hedley, F. Y. *Marching Through Georgia.* Chicago, 1890.

Hendrick, Burton J. *Lincoln's War Cabinet.* Gloucester, Mass., 1965.

Henry, Robert S. *As They Saw Forrest.* Jackson, Miss., 1956.

———. *"First with the Most" Forrest.* Indianapolis, 1944.

Hesseltine, William B. *Lincoln and the War Governors.* New York, 1955.

Hicken, Victor. *Illinois in the Civil War.* Urbana, 1966.

Hinman, Wilbur. *The Story of the Sherman Brigade.* By author, 1897.

Hobart, Edwin L. *Semi-History of a Boy-Veteran of the Twenty-Eighth Regiment Illinois Volunteers, in a Black Regiment.* Denver, 1909.

———. *The Truth About Shiloh.* Springfield, Ill., 1909.

Hokanson, Nels. *Swedish Immigrants in Lincoln's Time.* London, 1942.

Hoobler, James A. *Cities Under the Gun: Images of Occupied Nashville and Chattanooga.* Nashville, 1986.

Hoppin, James M. *Life of Andrew Hull Foote, Rear Admiral United States Navy.* New York, 1874.

Horn, Stanley. *The Army of Tennessee: A Military History.* Norman, Okla., 1955.

———, ed. *Tennessee's War, 1861–1865: Described by Participants.* Nashville, 1965.

Howard, Samuel M. *The Illustrated Comprehensive History of the Great Battle of Shiloh.* Kansas City, Mo., 1921.

Howe, M. A. DeWolfe, ed. *Home Letters of General Sherman.* New York, 1909.

Howell, H. Grady, Jr. *Going to Meet the Yankees: A History of the "Bloody Sixth" Mississippi Infantry, C.S.A.* Jackson, Miss., 1981.

Hubert, Charles F. *History of the Fiftieth Regiment Ill. Volunteer Infantry*. Kansas City, 1894.

Hughes, Nathaniel C., Jr. *The Battle of Belmont: Grant Strikes South*. Chapel Hill, 1991.

———. *General William J. Hardee: Old Reliable*. Wilmington, N.C., 1987.

———, ed. *Liddell's Record: St. John Richardson Liddell Brigadier General, CSA Staff Officer and Brigade Commander Army of Tennessee*. Dayton, 1985.

Hunt, Gaillard. *Israel, Elihu and Cadwallader Washburn: A Chapter in American Biography*. New York, 1971.

Indiana Shiloh National Park Commission. *Indiana at Shiloh: Report of the Commission*. N.p., 1904.

In the Matter of the Controversy Between the Shiloh National Military Park Commission and the Iowa Shiloh Commission Relating to Descriptions upon the Regimental Monuments of the 15th and 16th Iowa Volunteer Infantry. N.c., 1903.

Johnson, Robert C., and Clarence C. Buel, eds. *Battles and Leaders of the Civil War*, vol. 1 (1887–88), p. 608. New York, 1956.

Johnston, William Preston. *The Life of Gen. Albert Sidney Johnston, Embracing His Services in the Armies of the United States, the Republic of Texas, and the Confederate States*. New York, 1879.

Jones, Archer. *Civil War Command and Strategy: The Process of Victory and Defeat*. New York, 1992.

———. *Confederate Strategy from Shiloh to Vicksburg*. Baton Rouge, 1961.

Jones, Gordon C., ed. *"For My Country": The Richardson Letters, 1861–1865*. Wendell, N.C., 1984.

Jones, Howard. *Union in Peril: The Crisis Over British Intervention in the Civil War*. Chapel Hill, 1992.

Jones, Thomas. *Complete History of the 46th Regiment, Illinois Volunteer Infantry*. Freeport, Ill., 1907.

Jordan, Thomas, and Roger Pryor. *The Campaigns of Lieut.-Gen. N. B. Forrest, and of Forrest's Cavalry*. New Orleans, 1868.

Kamm, Samuel H. *The Civil War Career of Thomas A. Scott*. Philadelphia, 1940.

Keil, F. W. *Thirty-Fifth Ohio: A Narrative of Service from August, 1861, to 1864*. Fort Wayne, 1894.

Kiene, Ralph E., Jr. *A Civil War Diary: The Journal of Francis A. Kiene, 1861–1864*. N.p., 1974.

Kimball, Charles Bell. *History of Battery "A" First Illinois Light Artillery Volunteers*. Chicago, 1899.

Kiner, F. F. *One Year's Soldiering, Embracing the Battles of Fort Donelson and Shiloh*. Lancaster, Penn., 1863.

Kirwan, A. D., ed. *Johnny Green of the Orphan Brigade*. Lexington, Ky., 1956.

Klement, Frank L. *The Copperheads in the Middle West*. Chicago, 1960.

Knox, Thomas W. *Camp-Fire and Cotton-Field: Southern Adventure in Time of War*. Philadelphia, 1865.

Krug, Mark M., ed. *Mrs. Hill's Journal—Civil War Reminiscences*. Chicago, 1980.

Leech, Margaret. *Reveille in Washington*. New York, 1986.

Le Monnier, Y. R. *General Beauregard at Shiloh, Sunday April 6, 1862*. New Orleans, 1913.

Lewis, Lloyd. *Captain Sam Grant*. Boston, 1950.

———. *Sherman: Fighting Prophet*. New York, 1958.

Liddell-Hart, Basil H. *Sherman, Soldier, Realist, American*. New York, 1929.

Lindsley, John B., ed. *Military Annals of Tennessee: Confederate*. Nashville, 1886.

Livermore, Thomas L. *Numbers and Losses in the Civil War in America: 1861–1865*. Bloomington, 1957.

Logsdon, David R. *Eyewitnesses at the Battle of Shiloh*. Nashville, 1994.

Lonn, Ella. *Foreigners in the Confederacy*. Chapel Hill, 1940.

———. *Foreigners in the Union Army and Navy.* Baton Rouge, 1951.

Losson, Christopher. *Tennessee's Forgotten Warriors: Frank Cheatham and His Confederate Division.* Knoxville, 1989.

Macartney, Clarence E. *Grant and His Generals.* Freeport, 1971.

McClellan, George B. *McClellan's Own Story.* New York, 1887.

McClure, A. K. *Abraham Lincoln and Men of War-Times.* Philadelphia, 1892.

McDonough, James L. *Shiloh: In Hell Before Night.* Knoxville, 1977.

———. *War in Kentucky: From Shiloh to Perryville.* Knoxville, 1994.

McFeely, William S. *Grant: A Biography.* New York, 1981.

Mackall, William W. *A Son's Recollections of His Father.* New York, 1930.

McKee, Irving. *"Ben-Hur" Wallace: The Life of General Lew Wallace.* Berkeley, 1947.

McKee, John Miller. *The Great Panic: Being Incidents Connected with Two Weeks of the War in Tennessee.* Nashville, 1862.

McMasters, John B. *A History of the People of the United States During Lincoln's Administration.* New York, 1927.

McMurray, W. J. *History of the Twentieth Tennessee Regiment Volunteer Infantry.* Nashville, 1904.

McMurry, Richard. *Two Great Rebel Armies: An Essay in Confederate Military History.* Chapel Hill, 1989.

McPherson, James M. *Battle Cry of Freedom: The Civil War Era.* New York, 1988.

McWhiney, Grady. *Braxton Bragg and Confederate Defeat.* Tuscaloosa, 1969.

Madaus, Michael, and Robert D. Needham. *The Battle Flags of the Confederate Army of Tennessee.* Milwaukee, 1976.

Magdeburg, Frederick H. *14th Wis. Vet. Vol. Infantry at the Battle of Shiloh, Tenn., April 7, 1862.* N.p., n.d.

———. *Wisconsin at Shiloh.* N.c., 1909.

Marszalek, John F. *Sherman: A Soldier's Passion for Order.* New York, 1993.

———. *Sherman's Other War: The General and the Civil War Press.* Memphis, 1981.

Mason, George. *Illinois at Shiloh.* Chicago, 1905.

Meade, Robert D. *Judah P. Benjamin: Confederate Statesman.* New York, 1943.

Meek, Samuel. *The Illustrated Comprehensive History of the Great Battle of Shiloh.* Gettysburg, S.D., 1921.

Merrill, James M. *William Tecumseh Sherman.* Chicago, 1971.

Metzler, William E. *Morgan and His Dixie Cavaliers.* N.p., 1976.

Meyer, Steve. *Iowa Valor.* Garrison, Iowa, 1994.

Miers, Earl Schenck, ed. *A Rebel War Clerk's Diary.* New York, 1961.

Moats, Virgil H. *Shiloh to Vicksburg: Dear Eliza.* Pebble Beach, Calif., 1984.

Moneyhon, Carl, and Bobby Roberts. *Portraits of Conflict: A Photographic History of Louisiana in the Civil War.* Fayetteville, 1990.

Morrison, Marion. *A History of the Ninth Regiment Illinois Volunteer Infantry.* Monmouth, Ill., 1864.

Nash, Charles E. *Biographical Sketches of Gen. Pat Cleburne and Gen. T. C. Hindman.* Little Rock, 1898.

Neal, Diane, and Thomas W. Kremm. *The Lion of the South: General Thomas C. Hindman.* Macon, 1993.

Neal, W. A. *An Illustrated History of the Missouri Engineers and the 25th Infantry Regiment.* Chicago, 1889.

Nevins, Allen. *Ordeal of the Union: The Improvised War.* Vol. 3, pt. 2. New York, 1992.

Newberry, J. S. *The U.S. Sanitary Commission in the Valley of the Mississippi, During the War of the Rebellion, 1861–1866.* Cleveland, 1871.

Nicolay, John G., and John Hay. *Abraham Lincoln: A History.* Vol. 5. New York, 1890.

Official Roster of the Soldiers of the State of Ohio in the War of the Rebellion. 8 vols. Cincinnati, 1888.

Parks, Joseph H. *General Leonidas Polk, C.S.A.: Fighting Bishop.* Baton Rouge, 1962.

Payne, Edwin Waters. *History of the Thirty-Fourth Regiment of Illinois Volunteer Infantry.* Clinton, 1903.

Pease, Theodore C., and James G. Randall, eds. *The Diary of Orville Hickman Browning.* Vol. 1. Springfield, Ill., 1925.

Pennsylvania Battlefield Commission. *The Seventy-Seventh Pennsylvania at Shiloh.* Harrisburg, Pa., 1908.

Plum, William R. *The Military Telegraph During the Civil War in the United States.* Vol. 1. Chicago, 1882.

Polk, William. *Leonidas Polk, Bishop and General.* 2 vols. New York, 1915.

Pollard, Edward A. *Life of Jefferson Davis: With a Secret History of the Southern Confederacy.* Philadelphia, 1869.

Pratt, Fletcher. *Stanton: Lincoln's Secretary of War.* New York, 1953.

Purdue, Howell, and Elizabeth Purdue. *Pat Cleburne, Confederate General.* Tuscaloosa, 1977.

Ramage, James A. *Rebel Raiders: The Life of General John Hunt Morgan.* Lexington, 1986.

Rawley, James A. *The Politics of Union: Northern Politics During the Civil War.* Lincoln, Neb., 1974.

Reed, D. W. *The Battle of Shiloh and the Organizations Engaged.* Washington, D.C., 1902.

———. *Campaigns and Battles of the Twelfth Regiment Iowa Veteran Volunteer Infantry.* Evanston, Ill., 1903.

Reed, Rowena. *Combined Operations in the Civil War.* Annapolis, 1978.

Rerick, John H. *The 44th Indiana Volunteer Infantry.* LaGrange, Ind., 1880.

Rich, Joseph. *The Battle of Shiloh.* Iowa City, Iowa, 1911.

Richardson, Albert D. *A Personal History of Ulysses S. Grant.* Cincinnati, 1885.

———. *The Secret Service, the Field, the Dungeon and the Escape.* Hartford, 1865.

Richardson, James D., ed. *The Messages and Papers of Jefferson Davis and the Confederacy, Including Diplomatic Correspondence 1861–1865.* Vol. 2. New York, 1966.

Ridley, Broomsfield, ed. *Battles and Sketches of the Army of Tennessee.* Mexico, Mo., 1906.

Robertson, John. *Michigan in the War.* Lansing, 1862.

Roland, Charles. *Albert Sidney Johnston: Soldier of Three Republics.* Austin, 1964.

Roman, Alfred. *The Military Operations of General Beauregard in the War Between the States, 1861–1865.* 2 vols. New York, 1884.

Rowland, Dunbar. *The Official and Statistical Register of the State of Mississippi.* Nashville, 1908.

———, ed. *Jefferson Davis, Constitutionalist: His Letters, Papers and Speeches.* Vol. 5. Jackson, Miss., 1923.

Rumsey, Jean, ed. *By the Fireside; Being An Autobiography and Civil War Letters of Captain Israel Parsons Rumsey.* N.p., 1981.

Sandburg, Carl. *Abraham Lincoln: The War Years.* Vol. 1. New York, 1939.

Scarbrough, William K., ed. *The Diary of Edmund Ruffin.* Vol. 2. Baton Rouge, 1976.

Schott, Thomas C. *Alexander H. Stephens of Georgia: A Biography.* Baton Rouge, 1988.

Sears, Stephen W. *George B. McClellan: The Young Napoleon.* New York, 1988.

Seitz, Don. *Braxton Bragg: General of the Confederacy.* Columbia, 1924.

Shea, John G. *The American Nation.* New York, 1862.

Shea, William L., and Earl J. Hess. *Pea Ridge: Civil War Campaign in the West.* Chapel Hill, 1992.

Sheppard, Eric. *Bedford Forrest: The Confederacy's Greatest Cavalryman.* New York, 1930.

Sherman, William T. *Memoirs of General William T. Sherman.* New York, 1984.

Sideman, Belle Becker, and Lillian Friedman, eds. *Europe Looks at the Civil War.* New York, 1960.

Silverstone, Paul H. *Warships of the Civil War Navies*. Annapolis, 1989.

Simon, John Y., ed. *The Papers of Ulysses S. Grant*. Vols. 4 and 5. Carbondale, 1973.

Smart, James G., ed. *A Radical View: The "Agate" Dispatches of Whitelaw Reid*. Vol. 1. Memphis, 1976.

Smith, John Thomas. *A History of the Thirty-First Regiment of Indiana Volunteer Infantry in the War of the Rebellion*. Cincinnati, 1900.

Society of the Army of the Tennessee, at the Fourteenth Annual Meeting, Held at Cincinnati. Cincinnati, 1881.

A Soldier's Honor: With Reminiscences of Major-General Earl Van Dorn. New York, 1902.

Stampp, Kenneth M. *Indiana Politics During the Civil War*. Indianapolis, 1949.

Stanley, Dorothy, ed. *Autobiography of Sir Henry Morton Stanley*. Boston, 1906.

Starr, Louis M. *Bohemian Brigade: Civil War Newsmen in Action*. Madison, Wisc., 1987.

Stevenson, William. *Thirteen Months in the Rebel Army*. New York, 1862.

Stillwell, Leander. *The Story of a Common Soldier of Army Life in the Civil War, 1861–1865*. Kansas City, Mo., 1920.

Strode, Hudson. *Jefferson Davis: Confederate President*. New York, 1959.

Stuart, Addison A. *Iowa Colonels and Regiments: Being a History of Iowa Regiments in the War of the Rebellion*. Des Moines, 1865.

Sullins, D. *Recollections of an Old Man*. Bristol, Tenn., 1910.

Sword, Wiley. *Shiloh: Bloody April*. New York, 1974.

Symonds, Craig L. *Joseph E. Johnston: A Civil War Biography*. New York, 1992.

Taylor, F. Jay, ed. *The Secret Diary of Robert Patrick, 1861–1865: The Reluctant Rebel*. Baton Rouge, 1959.

Teuton, Frank L. *Steamboat Days on the Tennessee River*. Washington, D.C., n.d.

Thomas, Benjamin P. *Abraham Lincoln*. New York, 1952.

——— and Harold M. Hyman. *Stanton: The Life and Times of Lincoln's Secretary of War*. New York, 1962.

Thomas, B. F. *Soldier Life: A Narrative of the Civil War*. By author, 1907.

Thompson, Edward Porter. *History of the First Kentucky Brigade*. Cincinnati, 1868.

———. *History of the Orphan Brigade*. Louisville, 1895.

Thompson, Seymour. *Recollections with the Third Iowa Regiment*. Cincinnati, 1864.

Thorndike, Rachel Sherman, ed. *The Sherman Letters*. New York, 1894.

Throne, Mildred, ed. *The Civil War Diary of Cyrus F. Boyd, Fifteenth Iowa Infantry, 1861–1863*. Iowa City, 1953.

Toops, Ronald E. *The McConnell Letters*. N.p., 1975.

Tower, Lockwood, ed. *A Carolinian Goes to War: The Civil War Narrative of Arthur Middleton Manigault Brigadier General, C.S.A.* Columbia, 1983.

Truxall, Aida Craig, ed. *"Respects to All": Letters of Two Pennsylvania Boys in the War of the Rebellion*. Pittsburgh, 1962.

Tunnard, W. H. *A Southern Record: The History of the Third Regiment Louisiana Infantry*. Baton Rouge, 1866.

Vail, D. K. *Company K, of the 16th Wisconsin, at the Battle of Shiloh*. N.p., 1897.

Vandiver, Frank E. *Blood Brothers: A Short History of the Civil War*. College Station, Texas, 1992.

———, ed. *The Civil War Diary of General Josiah Gorgas*. University, Ala., 1947.

Van Horne, Thomas B. *History of the Army of the Cumberland, Its Organization, Campaigns, and Battles*. 2nd ed., Wilmington, N.C., 1988.

Vaughn, A. J. *Personal Record of the Thirteenth Regiment, Tennessee Infantry*. Memphis, 1897.

Victor, Orville. *Incidents and Anecdotes of the War*. New York, 1862.

Wakelyn, Jon L. *Biographical Dictionary of the Confederacy*. Westport, Conn., 1977.

Wallace, Isabel. *Life and Letters of General W. H. L. Wallace*. Chicago, 1909.

Wallace, Lew. *An Autobiography*. 2 vols. New York, 1906.

Warner, Ezra J. *Generals in Blue: Lives of Union Commanders*. Baton Rouge, 1964.

———. *Generals in Gray: Lives of the Confederate Commanders.* Baton Rouge, 1959.

Watkins, Sam. *"Co. Aytch": A Side Show of the Big Show.* New York, 1962.

Welsh, Jack D. *Medical Histories of Confederate Generals.* Kent, Ohio, 1995.

Werstein, Irving. *Abraham Lincoln Versus Jefferson Davis.* New York, 1959.

Wheeler, Richard. *We Knew William Tecumseh Sherman.* New York, 1977.

Whittlesey, Charles. *General Lew Wallace's Division—Battle of Shiloh—Was It Tardy?* N.p., n.d.

Wilkie, Franc. *Pen and Powder.* Boston, 1888.

Williams, Frederick D., ed. *The Wild Life of the Army: Civil War Letters of James A. Garfield.* East Lansing, 1964.

Williams, Kenneth P. *Lincoln Finds a General.* Vol. 3. New York, 1952.

Williams, T. Harry. *McClellan, Sherman and Grant.* New Brunswick, 1962.

———. *P. G. T. Beauregard: Napoleon in Gray.* Baton Rouge, 1959.

Wills, Brian Steel. *A Battle from the Start: The Life of Nathan Bedford Forrest.* New York, 1992.

Wilson, James G. *Biographical Sketches of Illinois Officers.* Chicago, 1862.

Wilson, James H. *Under the Old Flag.* New York, 1912.

Witham, George F. *Shiloh, Shells and Artillery Units.* Memphis, 1980.

Woodruff, George H. *Fifteen Years Ago, Or The Patriotism of Will County.* Joliet, 1876.

Woods, Earl C., ed. *The Shiloh Diary of Edmond Enoul Livaudais.* New Orleans, 1992.

Woodward, W. E. *Meet General Grant.* New York, 1928.

Woodworth, Steven E. *Jefferson Davis and His Generals: The Failure of Confederate Command in the West.* Lawrence, 1990.

Worthington, Thomas. *Brief History of the 46th Ohio Volunteers.* Washington, D.C., 1878.

———. *Report of the Flank March to Join on McClernand's Right, at 9 A.M., etc.* Washington, D.C., 1880.

———. *Shiloh, Or The Tennessee Campaign of 1862.* Washington, D.C., 1872.

Wright, Henry. *A History of the Sixth Iowa Infantry.* Iowa City, 1923.

Wubben, Hubert H. *Civil War Iowa and the Copperhead Movement.* Ames, Iowa, 1980.

Wyeth, John. *That Devil Forrest: Life of General Nathan Bedford Forrest.* New York, 1959.

Young, Jesse Bowman. *What a Boy Saw in the Army.* New York, 1894.

Younger, Edward, ed. *Inside the Confederate Government: The Diary of Robert Garlick Hill Kean.* New York, 1957.

Index